Entrepreneurship

Entrepreneurship
New Venture Creation

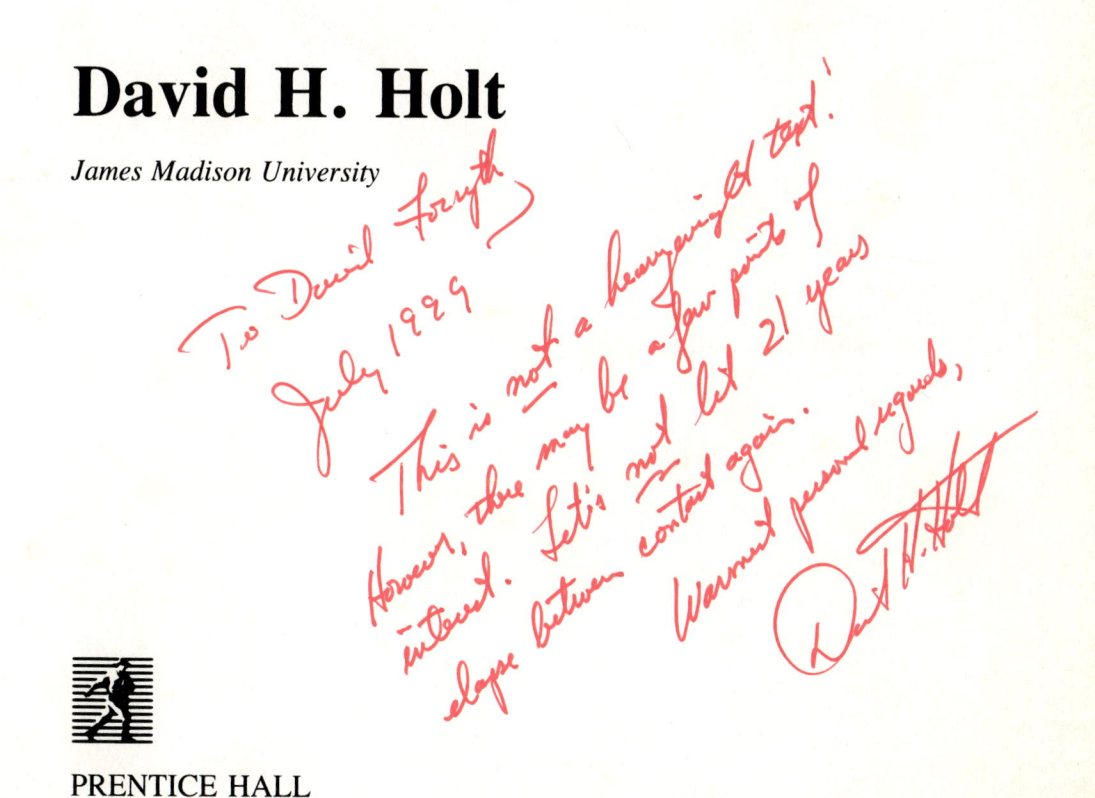

David H. Holt
James Madison University

PRENTICE HALL
Englewood Cliffs, New Jersey 07632

Library of Congress Cataloging-in-Publication Data

Holt, David H.
    Entrepreneurship: new venture creation / David H. Holt.
      p.   cm.
    Includes bibliographical references and index.
    ISBN 0-13-282674-7
    1. Entrepreneurship.   2. Venture capital.   3. New business enterprises.   I. Title.
    HB615.H65   1992
    658.1'141—dc20   91–30503
                                                                                    CIP

Acquisitions editor: Alison Reeves
Copy editor: Peter Reinhart
Editorial/production supervision
  and interior design: Peggy M. Gordon
Cover designer: Ben Santora
Cover art: Merle Krumper
Prepress buyer: Trudy Pisciotti
Manufacturing buyer: Robert Anderson

© 1992 by Prentice-Hall, Inc.
A Simon & Schuster Company
Englewood Cliffs, New Jersey 07632

All rights reserved. No part of this book may be
reproduced, in any form or by any means,
without permission in writing from the publisher.

Printed in the United States of America
10 9 8 7 6 5 4 3 2

ISBN 0-13-282674-7

Prentice-Hall International (UK) Limited, *London*
Prentice-Hall of Australia Pty. Limited, *Sydney*
Prentice-Hall Canada Inc., *Toronto*
Prentice-Hall Hispanoamericana, S.A., *Mexico*
Prentice-Hall of India Private Limited, *New Delhi*
Prentice-Hall of Japan, Inc., *Tokyo*
Simon & Schuster Asia Pte. Ltd., *Singapore*
Editora Prentice-Hall do Brasil, Ltda., *Rio de Janeiro*

*This book is dedicated to my sons
Kevin, Bryan, and Sean,
who have their own way of doing everything*

Contents

Preface xv

PART ONE ENTREPRENEURSHIP AND FREE ENTERPRISE 1

1 Entrepreneurship and New Venture Opportunities 2

An Entrepreneurial Perspective   3
Defining Entrepreneurship   7
   Profile: Henry Ford   8
   Profile: Irving Berlin   10
Perspective on Small Business   12
   Profile: Century 21   15
Corporate Entrepreneurship   16
Entrepreneurship in Practice   17
Focus of the Text   23
Synopsis for Learning   24

Case 1-1: Progress Through Innovation   28
Case 1-2: Luck or Persistence?   29

2 Entrepreneurship and Innovation 31

Creativity as a Prerequisite to Innovation   32
   Profile: Nolan Bushnell   34
Innovation and Entrepreneurship   36

Opportunities Through Change 41
    Profile: William Gates III 44
Windows and Corridors 49
Myths—Fantasies Not Facts 50
Success Factors for Entrepreneurs 54
An Era of Transformation 57
Synopsis for Learning 58
Case 2-1: CareerTrack on a Roll 62
Case 2-2: Stew Leonard—The Great American Milkman 63

3 Small Business and Corporate Entrepreneurship: Contrasting Enterprises 66

The Environment of Small Business 67
    Profile: Dan Bricklin: Small Is Not Bad 68
Risk and Failure 72
    Profile: King Gillette 75
Resolutions for Success 79
Corporate Entrepreneurship—Intrapreneurship 82
    Profile: John D. MacEachron 83
Corporate New Venture Units 87
    Profile: IBM Looks toward Innovation 91
A Concluding Perspective 92
Synopsis for Learning 93
Case 3-1: Her Own Boss 97
Case 3-2: Corporate Adventures, New Units, and Tiger Teams 98

4 A Model for New Ventures: Feasibility Planning 101

The Concept of a Planning Paradigm 101
    Profile: Ready, Aim, Fire, Fire, Fire, Fire 103
The Four-Stage Growth Model 104
    Profile: Jim Strang 111
Fundamentals of a Feasibility Plan 115
The Feasibility Plan 116
    Profile: Wilson Greatbatch 120
Responsibility for Business Planning 131
Synopsis for Learning 132
Case 4-1: "I Can't Believe It's Yogurt!" 136
Case 4-2: The Company as an Environmental Tool 137

Contents   ix

PART TWO   PRODUCT AND SERVICE CONCEPTS FOR NEW VENTURES   139

5   The Product Concept and Commercial Opportunities   140

A Macro View—Manufacturing Matters   141
    Profile: Norman Borlaug—Nobel Peace Prize Laureate   144
    Profile: Who Is Henry Kloss?   146
Products and Technology   148
    Profile: Bush Industries—Filling a Gap   151
Identifying Opportunities   152
The Product Development Process   155
    Profile: Everywhere There's a Phone There's a Fax   162
Beyond Diffusion—A Final Word   164
Synopsis for Learning   165

Case 5-1: Looking at Product Development with New Eyes   168
Case 5-2: A New Industry in Telephones   169

6   Product Protection: Patents, Trademarks, and Copyrights   172

An Introduction to Patents   173
    Profile: Porsche: Engineering Innovations   174
Types of Patents   176
    Profile: Design Patents Protect Ornamental Distinction   177
Disclosures   178
Who May Apply for a Patent   178
The Patent Process   179
Patents in Perspective   184
Trademarks   184
    Profile: Trademarks and Service Marks   185
Copyrights   188
    Profile: Billion-Dollar Industry in New Copyrights   189
    Profile: Bearish Outlook for Software Registration   192
Registering Software as Intellectual Property   192
A Note on Trade Secrets   194
Validating Property Rights   195
Accessing Government Information   195
Implications for Entrepreneurs   196
Synopsis for Learning   197

Case 6-1: Taking an Invention from Drawing Board to Market   201
Case 6-2: Understanding Legal Protection   202

7 Services: The Human Side of Enterprise 204

The Infrastructure of Services 205
Types of Service Ventures 206
    Profile: Redefining Ground Services 207
    Profile: Inventory—Key to Video Success 214
    Profile: Technology Opens Desk-Top Services 216
Success Factors in Service Ventures 218
    Profile: Training: New Game for Sport Pros 223
    Profile: "Be the Best Damn Cheerleader Anybody's Ever Seen." 225
Synopsis for Learning 228
Case 7-1: Services Make Human Resources Productive 231
Case 7-2: Putting Service on the Line 232

PART THREE MARKETING AND NEW VENTURE DEVELOPMENT 235

8 Marketing Research for New Ventures 236

The Marketing Concept 237
    Profile: How to Grow in a Saturated Industry 238
    Profile: Running a Different Kind of Race 241
Perspective on Marketing Research 241
Market Research in the Pre-Start-up Phase 242
    Profile: Coming of the "Green Consumer" 245
    Profile: Niche Marketing in Women's Golf Attire 249
Markets Focused on Organizations 253
    Profile: Austin–San Antonio 255
Sources of Market Intelligence 255
Competitive Analysis: Research after Start-up 258
    Profile: Time—Currency of the Future 263
Implications of Market Research and Competitive Analyses 263
Synopsis for Learning 265
Case 8-1: The Book Nook 269
Case 8-2: Get a "Jolt" out of Life 270

9 Marketing: Functions and Strategies 272

Fundamentals of Marketing 273
Product Concepts 275
    Profile: The Product Is an Experience 276
    Profile: Selling Causes and Cosmetics 277
    Profile: Caterpillar—A Demanding Customer 283

Distribution   284
Promotion   288
    Profile: Marketing Success at Subway Sandwiches   291
Pricing   293
Marketing Strategies   297
    Profile: Top-Flite "Pulls Through" Sales   299
    Profile: Puppy Love   300
The Marketing Plan   302
Synopsis for Learning   303
Case 9-1: Selling in a Nontraditional Market   307
Case 9-2: A Minimum Effort Pays Off   308

10 International Markets: New Venture Opportunities   310

The Changing International Environment   311
    Profile: Manufacturing Opportunities in a Global Environment   317
Exporting   319
Importing   324
Establishing International Ventures   326
    Profile: John Johnson, Ebony *Magazine*   327
The Foreign Environment of Business   333
Getting Help—Sources of Information   338
Synopsis for Learning   341
Case 10-1: Coming Together: The U.S.-Canada Trade Agreement   345
Case 10-2: Going Global with a View toward China   346

PART FOUR   ORGANIZING AND FINANCING THE NEW VENTURE   349

11 The Entrepreneurial Team and Business Formation   350

Matching Human Resource Needs and Skills   351
    Profile: Donald Bonham   352
The Board of Directors   355
Networking—Extending Human Relations   358
Legal Forms of Business in Perspective   361
Sole Proprietorship   363
Partnerships   367
Corporations   371
    Profile: Dave Bing—NBA Star Turns to Steel Business   374
Synopsis for Learning   376
Case 11-1: Defining a Start-up: Who Is in Charge?   380
Case 11-2: Serendipity Enterprises, Inc.   381

12 Business Acquisitions and Franchising 383

Rationale for Acquiring a Business 384
    Profile: "Selling Up" into Success 388
Evaluating Acquisition Opportunities 389
Methods of Valuation 395
Structuring the Acquisition 400
Franchising 403
    Profile: Fred DeLuca, Founder of Subway Sandwiches 404
Synopsis for Learning 411

Case 12-1: Sage Renovations: Buyout Valuation 415
Case 12-2: The Franchise Option 418

13 Financial Resources for New Ventures 419

Asset Management 420
    Profile: Glen Jackson—Minimizing Business Costs 428
Equity Financing 429
    Profile: IPOs—Not for Everyone 434
Venture Capital 435
Debt Financing 439
Government Programs 443
    Profile: The Small Business Credit Program of Eximbank 447
Synopsis for Learning 448

Case 13-1: To Lease or Not: A Cash-Flow Question 452
Case 13-2: Public-Sector Programs Address Seed Capital 453

14 Managing Growth and Transition 455

The Organization Life Cycle 456
    Profile: Debbi Fields 459
    Profile: Domino's Pizza—An Inspired Marketing Strategy 460
Changing Entrepreneurial Roles 463
    Profile: Barry Gibbons—Turnaround at Burger King 469
Perspective on Strategic Management 470
Implications for Entrepreneurial Careers 475
    Profile: Opportunities for Black Entrepreneurs 476
Synopsis for Learning 478

Case 14-1: Forever Young 482
Case 14-2: Is Entrepreneurship Education Useful? 483

Appendix A: Guidelines for a Feasibility Plan (Simplified Business Plan) 486

Appendix B: An Integrated Feasibility Plan for Poly-Chem Associates, Inc. 492

Glossary 528

Index 539

Preface

Entrepreneurs do things that are not generally done in the ordinary course of business. That conclusion is paraphrased from Joseph Schumpeter's 1934 treatise *The Theory of Economic Development,* and although it is incomplete, it captures the essence of entrepreneurial activity. It also helps explain why we are sometimes baffled by entrepreneurs who seem to be out of step with the rest of us. Some are inspired tinkerers, an attribute ascribed to Thomas Edison, and others are gifted dreamers, a phrase once used to describe Steven Jobs. Most entrepreneurs are thought to be, simply, "unusual"; they lead their own parades, hear their own music, and set their own cadence. Consequently, they do unexpected things.

Many entrepreneurs become celebrities through their successes; others become ridiculed for their failed dreams. But there is no doubt that all of them contribute to the spirit of free enterprise. This is the engine of economic endeavor that drives industrial democracy. Although entrepreneurship has enjoyed a resurgent popularity as if we had recently stumbled onto a new concept, it has been the foundation of American economic development. This book is written with that fact firmly in mind.

The purpose of the text is to enrich students with an understanding of the entrepreneurial process. There is no presumption, however, that entrepreneurship can be "taught," because entrepreneurs have their own peculiar way of doing things. Yet it is possible to help them be better prepared for transforming dreams into realities. Consequently, the book is organized to explore the nature of entrepreneurship, provide models for new venture creation, and describe ways to help entrepreneurs succeed.

DISTINGUISHING FEATURES

The book is organized to provide a historical perspective, followed by a systematic presentation of the elements in founding a new venture. Chapters are organized to help students learn about the entrepreneurial process with "checkpoint" questions, examples, and illustrations. Each chapter begins with a set of objectives. These are subsequently addressed at the end of each chapter with a descriptive synopsis for learning that repeats the objectives and briefly summarizes key points. Together with the checkpoint questions within the chapter, the synopsis assures continuity and reinforcement.

Chapter Enhancements

Approximately 50 brief biographies or profiles of successful entrepreneurs are presented throughout the text to illustrate real-world results of new ventures. In addition, there are nearly 40 exhibits and boxed items to amplify presentations and give meaning to complicated concepts. These are further supported by nearly 100 graphic illustrations, and more than 200 examples that are woven into the fabric of presentations.

All biographies, profiles, boxed items, and illustrations reflect actual entrepreneurial events or real people. Some of those people profiled, such as Irving Berlin and Cyrus McCormick, have made significant contributions to society. Others, such as William Gates of Microsoft and Thomas Monaghan of Domino's Pizza, are contemporary entrepreneurs who are still pursuing their extraordinary ideas while contributing to society. Still others are relatively unknown, yet they have given us celebrated innovations; Wilson Greatbatch's Pacemaker, for example, has saved millions of lives. Finally, there are enjoyable stories to relate, such as the trials and tribulations of Teddy Ruxpin, the computerized toy bear that was so unique that its software was copyrighted.

End of Chapter Cases

Each chapter ends with two short cases that can be assigned for research or used in classroom discussions. Every case is real, and most are current. They identify the entrepreneurs by their real names and pose real-world problems that these entrepreneurs face. Discussion questions were written to challenge students to apply concepts presented within the chapters. In most instances at least one question is written as an exercise. The instructor's manual provides an analysis of each case, together with material to enrich classroom discussions.

Appendixes

The two appendixes can be used throughout the course as integrated teaching material. Appendix A is an outline that provides guidelines with summary remarks on how to develop a formal written business plan. The business plan presented here is a simplified model focused on requirements for a pre-start-up feasibility study. Appendix B is an actual business plan with real-world data, presented as the founders wrote it. The only modifications made were to disguise the founders' and original investors' names to protect their privacy. Appendix B is called a feasibility plan because, like the outline in Appendix A, its focus was on pre-start-up activities in preparation for launching a new venture.

ORGANIZATION OF THE TEXT

There are 14 chapters in the text. This number was chosen to provide a sequence of topics that could be presented in a normal semester. There are certainly gaps in coverage, but there was no intention of providing a comprehensive textbook on entrepreneurship. Such a text would require four times the coverage provided here. Nevertheless, the critical elements of planning and starting a new venture are addressed, and the book can be covered comfortably in one term with latitude for supplemental lectures, guest speakers, or case discussion seminars.

Part One includes four chapters that establish a foundation for the course. Chapter 1 emphasizes the historic foundations of entrepreneurship and free enterprise. Chapter 2 introduces the concepts of creativity and innovation and how those processes occur. Chapter 3 contrasts small business and corporate entrepreneurship, differentiating entrepreneurial roles and processes in these environments, as well as for independent new high-growth ventures. Chapter 4 presents the business planning paradigm and the elements of a feasibility model.

The three chapters of Part Two describe product development, legal protection of innovations, and the human side of enterprise in services. Chapter 5 examines new product development, manufacturing, and the way in which innovations are brought to fruition. Chapter 6 addresses legal protection, patents, trademarks, and copyrights. It also examines the controversial nature of protecting intellectual property, such as software programs. Chapter 7 focuses on service industries and opportunities in personal service and professional fields for new ventures.

Part Three concentrates on market research and development. Chapter 8 is a concise presentation of marketing research responsibilities. This chapter discusses marketing research and resources available to help entrepreneurs in this endeavor, but it is not a "how-to" chapter on actually conducting research; such a chapter would require comprehensive treatment beyond the scope of the textbook. Chapter 9 examines marketing functions and strategies peculiar to new ventures, and the focus is on developing a viable marketing plan with a workable program.

Chapter 10 is a unique chapter that addresses international markets and global opportunities for entrepreneurial ventures. This topic is seldom mentioned in other texts, yet global markets represent nearly a quarter of all small business efforts. Consequently, the chapter examines changes taking place in the Soviet Union, Asia, Europe, and North America (with an emphasis on Canada). It treats exporting, importing, and overseas investing in a manner intended to challenge students to think globally. In addition, the chapter addresses government programs aimed at encouraging entrepreneurs to "go global."

Part Four emphasizes the roles of entrepreneurs in their organizations. Chapter 11 explores the personal roles and responsibilities of founders and their entrepreneurial teams. This chapter extends to small business ventures and corporate new venture units, and it addresses the human side of leadership as well as the legal side of creating a viable business entity. Chapter 12 extends the idea of "organization" to include alternative ways to get into business. Acquisitions, buyouts, and franchising are developed as special topics and alternatives to starting new ventures from scratch. Chapter 13 focuses on financial resources. Topics addressed include asset management, obtaining equity, attracting investors, and securing debt funding. In addition, the chapter introduces venture capital, private placement financing, public offerings, and sources of government financial assistance.

Chapter 14 concludes with a view toward the future. Specifically, it addresses new venture growth and the transition roles of entrepreneurs during the organizational life cycle. The final section explores the concept of an entrepreneurial career and challenges students to consider their future options as founders of new ventures, small business owners, or corporate managers.

ANCILLARY MATERIALS

The process of learning is changing, and subsequent editions of this and other current textbooks will surely adopt new applications of information technology. If they do not, some entrepreneur will introduce us to a new way of thinking about education. Meanwhile, we have exceptional learning tools available to enhance the classroom environment.

Instructor's Manual

A comprehensive instructor's manual is available to adopters, and it contains recommended course outlines, chapter summaries, and case analyses. The manual alerts instructors to video programs and exercises that can be used to enhance classroom discussions, and additional teaching tips and information are provided to embellish lectures. The instructor's manual includes transparency masters enlarged from text illustrations.

Supplemental Cases and Exercises

Integrated cases are provided with instruction notes that relate to each of the four major parts of the text. These can be duplicated and assigned for research or used in conjunction with lectures. Experiential exercises are provided as alternatives to case presentations, and these are coordinated with lecture materials in the instructor's manual.

Test Bank and Software

Multiple-choice, true-false, and short-essay questions are provided in published form and contained on floppy diskettes.

Business Plan Software

A comprehensive system of spreadsheets provides detailed pro forma financial statements required for developing a business plan. These spreadsheets are templates created on Lotus 1-2-3.

ACKNOWLEDGMENTS

A tremendous amount of help has been provided by friends, colleagues, and practicing entrepreneurs who have contributed their time and talent to create this instructional package. To thank them all individually would be a pleasant task, but an endeavor that would fall short of its mark even with the best intentions. I would like to acknowledge those who took an active role in preparing materials and making editorial contributions.

A number of reviewers were kind enough to provide invaluable feedback on the early draft and on the final version. Their insights helped mold the text and organize my efforts, and in several instances, they kept me from making inexcusable mistakes. I'm sure mistakes persist, but those are entirely of my own doing, and I am grateful for guidance from the following reviewers: Alan L. Carsrud, Barry L. Van Hook, Tilton L. Willcox, and Louis D. Ponthieu.

I am equally grateful for insights and help from colleagues who personally helped me with cases, experiential exercises, and research. My thanks to the following: Dennis Patzig, James Madison University; Marc Singer, Middle Tennessee State University; Karen Wiggington, James Madison University; Mee Kau Nyaw, Chinese University of Hong Kong; Verne Harnish, University of Maryland; Bruce D. Phillips, Office of Advocacy of the Small Business Administration; Donald L. Sexton, Ohio State University; Carol Ann Meares, Productivity Center of the U.S. Department of Commerce; Andre Mailer, City Polytechnic of East London; Sam Black, vice president, Caterpillar, Inc.; Rick Lundquist, State University of New York, Fredonia; and Robert Kaiser, EximBank.

Many of the examples and comments contained in the text and supplements were provided through interviews and assistance by practicing entrepreneurs. Without their help, this book would have been impossible. They include James B. Strang, president of Spokes Etc.; John D. Hunt and Wayne Hall, cofounders of Foress Systems; Jimmy Calano, cofounder of CareerTrack; Stew Leonard, founder of Stew Leonard's, Inc.; Paul Bush, president, Bush Industries, Inc.; Donald D. Boroian, founder of FranCorp; Charles O. Conrad, president, Poly-Chem Associates, Inc.; Warren Avis, Avis Corporation; Kim Merritt, founder of Kim's Khocolates; Nolan Bushnell, Axlon Corporation; Bill and Melody Conrad, founders of Hickory Knoll Nursery; Robert Lewis Dean III, founder of LimoNet; W. K. Lo, managing director of Computer Products, Ltd.; Dan Wofford, president of Western Polyacrylamide; and John Robertson, founder of Robertson Marketing Group.

Prentice Hall editors have continued to provide excellent support for my projects, and they are dedicated to publishing the highest quality manuscripts. My gratitude, in particular, to Alison Reeves, Executive Editor, who led the editorial team and spearheaded the work on the instructional package.

There are also events and situations that contributed to this text, and it is important to acknowledge them. Through the generous support of the Mary Moody Northen Foundation, my position as the W. L. Moody Professor of Entrepreneurship has allowed me adequate time and funding to pursue research essential to writing this manuscript. Dean Robert E. Holmes supported the academic leave that allowed me to spend a year in Asia, and this was not only a time of intense writing but an experience that opened my eyes to cultures and global involvement by American companies and entrepreneurs. While in Asia, I was also supported in my position as Visiting Scholar at the Chinese University of Hong Kong, and my colleagues there opened doors for research at companies such as Hasbro Toys, Perfectka, Ltd., Inchcape, Ltd., Procter & Gamble (Guangzhou, PRC), American Express, Federal Express (Asia), and a host of private ventures and companies in Hong Kong and the People's Republic of China.

My most sincere gratitude is reserved for my wife, Judith, who has endured my frustration and unorthodox writing schedule that frequently extended until the early morning hours. She has also endured my often distressful behavior and isolation that comes from writing a manuscript. Perhaps I should offer my condolences to my three sons, Kevin, Bryan, and Sean. I have imbued them with the spirit of entrepreneurship, and, consequently, they are constantly at odds with their classmates and conventional teachers who cannot see beyond the pedestrian world of a secure job in a stable environment.

D.H.H.

PART ONE

Entrepreneurship and Free Enterprise

Part One provides an overview of entrepreneurship and the concept of starting new ventures. Chapter 1 is a foundation chapter that defines entrepreneurship and describes entrepreneurial characteristics. The chapter also addresses small business and corporate entrepreneurship, focusing on contemporary issues of new venture development. Chapter 2 introduces the concepts of creativity and innovation, describing how entrepreneurs recognize opportunities and translate ideas into commercial ventures. It also identifies common myths ascribed to entrepreneurs and provides real-world examples of successful entrepreneurs. Chapter 3 addresses small business and corporate entrepreneurship, differentiating between them and the world of high-growth new ventures. The chapter also explores particular considerations for family-owned and personal service businesses, and explains how corporate entrepreneurs reconcile their careers with their entrepreneurial aspirations. Chapter 4 introduces a model for planning a new venture. This model becomes the foundation for the remainder of the text.

Chapter 1

Entrepreneurship and New Venture Opportunities

OBJECTIVES

1. Describe how entrepreneurship evolved from economic theory.
2. Explain entrepreneurship and the characteristics of entrepreneurs.
3. Discuss small business as a dimension of entrepreneurship.
4. Describe the concept of corporate entrepreneurship.
5. Explain how entrepreneurship has influenced economic development and productivity in recent years.

The concept of entrepreneurship has been around for a very long time, but its resurgent popularity implies a "sudden discovery," as if we had stumbled onto a new direction for American enterprise. This is a myth, as we shall see, because the American system of free enterprise has always engendered the spirit of entrepreneurship. America was discovered by entrepreneurs and nourished by entrepreneurs, and the United States became a world economic power through entrepreneurial activity. More important, our future rests squarely on entrepreneurial ventures founded by creative individuals. They are inspired people, often adventurers, who can at once disrupt a society and instigate progress. They are risk takers who seize opportunities to harness and use resources in unusual ways, and entrepreneurs will thrust us into the twenty-first century with a thunderous roar.

Entrepreneurship constitutes the driving force of the American dream. In the chapters that follow, we will study how legendary tycoons created empires from simple ideas, how large corporations evolved from backyard enterprises, and how many new ventures today are poised for growth, perhaps having at their helms the Fords, Rockefellers, and Carnegies of the future.

AN ENTREPRENEURIAL PERSPECTIVE

Entrepreneurship is one of the four mainstream economic factors: land, labor, capital, and entrepreneurship. The word itself, derived from 17th-century French *entreprendre*, refers to individuals who were "undertakers," meaning those who "undertook" the risk of new enterprise. They were "contractors" who bore the risks of profit or loss, and many early entrepreneurs were soldiers of fortune, adventurers, builders, merchants, and, incidentally, funeral directors. How the term "undertaker" became associated with funerals is a mystery, but there is a considerable body of literature on entrepreneurship. Early references to the *entreprendeur* in the 14th century spoke about tax contractors—individuals who paid a fixed sum of money to a government for the license to collect taxes in their region. *Tax entreprendeurs* bore the risk of collecting individual taxes. If they collected more than the sum paid for their licenses, they made profits and kept the excess. If they failed to collect enough to match the cost of their licenses, government officials, who already had their money from license fees, could not care less. Entrepreneurship was a common topic in economic essays for much of the 18th and 19th centuries. Notable early French, British, and Austrian economists wrote enthusiastically about entrepreneurs as the "change agents" of progressive economies.

Economics and Entrepreneurship

Richard Cantillon, a French economist of Irish descent, is credited with giving the concept of entrepreneurship a central role in economics. In his *Essai sur la nature du commerce en général*, published posthumously in 1755, Cantillon described an entrepreneur as a person who pays a certain price for a product to resell it at an uncertain price, thereby making decisions about obtaining and using resources while consequently assuming the risk of enterprise.[1] A critical point in Cantillon's argument was that entrepreneurs *consciously make decisions* about resource allocations. Consequently, astute entrepreneurs would always seek the best opportunities for using resources for their highest commercial yields. Cantillon played out his theory in real life, becoming a wealthy arbitrageur investing in European ventures, dealing in monetary exchange, and controlling commodities, such as farm produce, to auction in high-demand markets. His vision is illustrated for farm produce in Figure 1-1.

Adam Smith spoke of the "enterpriser" in his 1776 *Wealth of Nations*[2] as an individual who undertook the formation of an organization for commercial purposes. He thereby ascribed to the entrepreneur the role of industrialist, but he also viewed the entrepreneur as a person with unusual foresight who could recognize potential demand for goods and services. In Smith's view, entrepreneurs reacted to economic change, thereby becoming the economic agents who transformed demand into supply.

French economist Jean Baptiste Say, in his 1803 *Traité d'économie politique* (translated into English in 1845 as *A Treatise on Political Economy*), described an entrepreneur as one who possessed certain arts and skills of creating new economic enterprises, yet a person who had exceptional insight into society's needs and was able to fulfill them. Say, therefore, combined the "economic risk taker" of Cantillon

```
┌──────────────┐      ┌────────────────┐      ┌──────────────┐
│  Investment  │─────▶│ Transformation │─────▶│ Profit or loss│
└──────────────┘      └────────────────┘      └──────────────┘
┌──────────────────┐  ┌──────────────────┐    ┌──────────────────┐
│Entrepreneur buys │  │Entrepreneur repacks│  │Entrepreneur sells│
│farm produce at   │  │and transports farm │  │food produce in   │
│certain prices    │  │produce to market   │  │city at uncertain │
│                  │  │                    │  │prices            │
└──────────────────┘  └────────────────────┘  └──────────────────┘
```

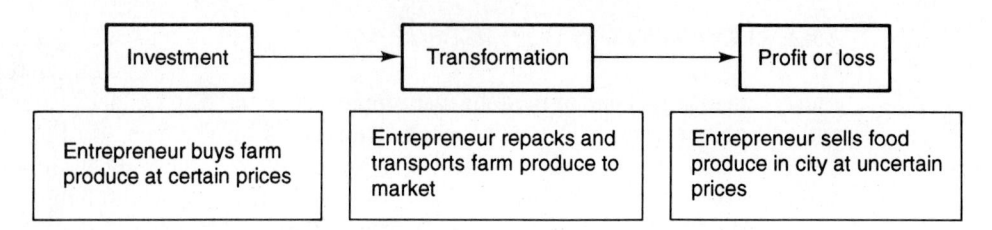

Figure 1-1 **Cantillon's Early View of Entrepreneurial Behavior**

and the "industrial manager" of Smith into an unusual character. Say's entrepreneur *influenced* society by creating new enterprises and at the same time was *influenced by* society to recognize needs and fulfill them through astute management of resources.[3]

In 1848, British economist John Stuart Mill elaborated on the necessity of entrepreneurship in private enterprise. The term *entrepreneur* subsequently became common as a description of business founders, and the "fourth factor" of economic endeavor was entrenched in economic literature as encompassing the ultimate ownership of a commercial enterprise. Mill's work, however, was among the last of the early economic studies in Britain or France that recognized entrepreneurship as central to economic theory. For the greater part of the next hundred years, British and French economists were more concerned with models of macroeconomics, and most of these were reduced to precise mathematical formulae. The human side of enterprise—the role of the adventurer or risk-taking entrepreneur—was left to history.

During that time, however, there was an important movement in Austria that subsequently influenced our 20th-century concept of entrepreneurship. Carl Menger (1840–1921) established the "subjectivist perspective of economics" in his 1871 *Principles of Economics*.[4] In Menger's view, economic change does not arise from circumstances but from an individual's awareness and understanding of those circumstances. The entrepreneur becomes, therefore, the change agent who transforms resources into useful goods and services, often creating the circumstances that lead to industrial growth.

Menger envisioned a causal chain of events whereby resources having no direct use in terms of fulfilling human needs were transformed into highly valued products that directly fulfilled human needs; this is the classic theory of production. However, Menger saw the entrepreneur as an astute individual who could envision this transformation and create the means to implement it. Menger assigned priority numbers to different events (or circumstances) in this chain so that a high-priority event would have a low number (e.g., 1) and would be an ultimate "end use" to satisfy a human need such as providing consumers with baked loaves of bread. At the other extreme, Menger assigned a low-priority event with a high number (e.g., 8), and this might represent raw material needed to create the number 1 event; fields of unharvested wheat would have a low priority. The entrepreneur, in Menger's view, was able to see both extremes and conceive of ways to transform the unharvested wheat into fresh bread. Illustrated in Figure 1-2, Menger's model identified intermediate points of

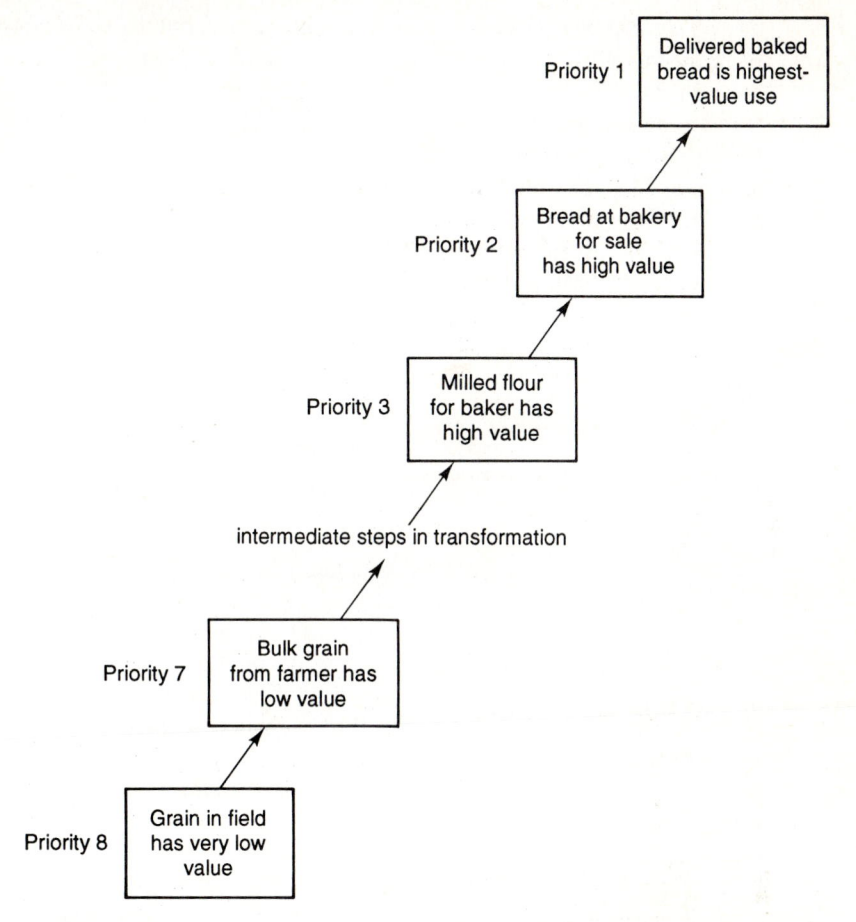

Chapter 1 Entrepreneurship and New Venture Opportunities   5

```
Priority 1 — Delivered baked bread is highest-value use
    ↑
Priority 2 — Bread at bakery for sale has high value
    ↑
Priority 3 — Milled flour for baker has high value
    ↑
        intermediate steps in transformation
    ↑
Priority 7 — Bulk grain from farmer has low value
    ↑
Priority 8 — Grain in field has very low value
```

Figure 1-2   **Menger's Model of Value-Added Transformation of Resources**

transformation—harvesting wheat, grinding grain, making bread, and delivering it—each with opportunities for *adding value to the original resource* in such a way as to eventually satisfy a human need. Critical to Menger's theory was the incentive needed to pursue these transformation activities, and of course that is the profit motive. When value is added to a product, that value is rewarded through profits.

Extending the example, the entrepreneur who invents a way to harvest grain more efficiently or to grind grain into flour more rapidly adds more value to the product because the consumer benefits from more bread at a lower cost. This was precisely what occurred when Cyrus McCormick invented the mechanical reaper in 1831. Farmers had been reaping wheat by hand, just as they had done in ancient times, cutting perhaps an acre or two a day. With the McCormick reaper, farmers could reap a dozen acres a day, and by the 1860s, they were reaping 100 acres a day.[5] The reaper not only revolutionized agriculture, but it also inspired new industries in farm implements, grain processing, and food distribution.

In the 19th century, entrepreneurs were the "captains of industry," the risk takers, the decision makers, the individuals who aspired to wealth (and endured commensurate losses) and who gathered and managed resources to create new enterprises. Menger's model of "subjective enterprise" flourished in the United States, and American adventurers were creating the events that linked the chain between raw resources and useful products. Then an interesting picture began to emerge as huge, often embarrassing, fortunes were made. The connotation of an entrepreneur changed from captain of industry to an elusive character who garnered profits at the expense of others, a flimflam artist on the fringe of legitimate business. The term *entrepreneur* was relegated to obscurity in economic literature for several generations, and management writers focused on factory efficiency and administration.

Entrepreneurship as a Process

Another Austrian economist revived the concept of entrepreneurship when he joined Harvard University and his work was published in the United States in 1934. Joseph Schumpeter (1883–1950) wrote a series of economic articles and treatises between 1911 and 1950 that specifically addressed entrepreneurship. Schumpeter described entrepreneurship as a force of "creative destruction" whereby established ways of doing things are destroyed by the creation of new and better ways to get things done. Entrepreneurship is often a subtle force, challenging the order of society through marginally small changes, but in Schumpeter's view, it can be extraordinarily powerful, like the changes caused by McCormick's reaper or the transformation of crude oil into an energy resource. Schumpeter described entrepreneurship as a *process* and entrepreneurs as *innovators* who use the process to shatter the status quo through new combinations of resources and new methods of commerce.[6]

In retrospect, it is important to recognize that entrepreneurship as an economic concept has suffered a century of obscurity. Most executives will not have heard of Schumpeter, Menger, or Cantillon; most know of Smith, but few will recognize Mill or Say. Today, the resurgence of entrepreneurship in higher education has not come from the discipline of economics but from those who teach small business management or who have instituted new courses in entrepreneurship. During the early 1970s, these were often renegade professors in management, marketing, or engineering. During the 1980s, entrepreneurship education attracted mainstream scholars, and new programs of entrepreneurship began to flourish, led by schools such as Babson College, Wichita State, USC, and Baylor University. As we enter the 1990s, many of the nation's most prestigious business schools are taking a lead to encourage serious entrepreneurship education. Harvard Business School, MIT, Stanford, the Wharton School, and UC Berkeley are among more than 300 colleges and universities with studies in entrepreneurship.[7]

Fortunately, entrepreneurs have ignored theoretical arguments and plunged ahead with tremendous energy to forge new enterprises. This phenomenon has been particularly strong in the United States through several generations of explosive economic activity. It is no accident that every *Fortune* 500 enterprise that exists today was the result of an entrepreneur who took a simple idea and persevered.

▶ **CHECKPOINT**

Compare concepts of entrepreneurship put forward by Cantillon, Say, Smith, Menger, and Schumpeter.

Explain entrepreneurship as a process and the importance of innovation to that process.

DEFINING ENTREPRENEURSHIP

We do not have one indisputable definition of *entrepreneurship* or *entrepreneur*. However, Schumpeter provides us with a framework for understanding both in terms of a process. The **entrepreneur** seeks, in Schumpeter's words,

> to reform or revolutionize the pattern of production by exploiting an invention or, more generally, an untried technological possibility for producing a new commodity or producing an old one in a new way, by opening up a new source of supply of materials or a new outlet for products. . . . Entrepreneurship, as defined, essentially consists in doing things that are not generally done in the ordinary course of business routine.[8]

Schumpeter did not equate entrepreneurs with inventors, suggesting instead that an inventor might only create a new product, whereas an entrepreneur will gather resources, organize talent, and provide leadership to make it a commercial success. This viewpoint was mirrored by Peter Drucker, who described the **entrepreneurial role** as one of gathering and using resources, but he added that "resources, to produce results, must be allocated to opportunities rather than to problems."[9] In Drucker's view, entrepreneurship occurs when resources are redirected to progressive opportunities, not used to ensure administrative efficiency. This redirection of resources distinguishes the entrepreneurial role from that of the traditional management role, a distinction that Henry Ford made in his decisions.

The evolution of the concept has generated many definitions, but perhaps a recent one by writer Robert Ronstadt captures its essence. For our purposes, we shall use Ronstadt's definition of **entrepreneurship:**

> Entrepreneurship is the dynamic process of creating incremental wealth. This wealth is created by individuals who assume the major risks in terms of equity, time, and/or career commitment of providing value for some product or service. The product or service itself may or may not be new or unique but value must somehow be infused by the entrepreneur by securing and allocating the necessary skills and resources.[10]

PROFILE △

Henry Ford

Starting a decade after most automobile manufacturers had been established in the United States, Henry Ford created the manufacturing miracle that launched a modern era in industry. His genuis was in engineering an assembly line process, and his process was an historic innovation. Ford reversed the fundamental way things were manufactured. Rather than have workers go to the product, he brought the product to the workers on highly mobilized assembly lines.

Throughout his life, Ford sought to improve the engineering technology of production. He altered inventory systems to move parts and tools to the workers, structured lines with parts moving along waist high so that workers could perform their tasks comfortably, and grouped tasks logically so that more production could be achieved at lower costs. During his lifetime, Ford instituted more than a thousand innovations, and at one time he had more Ford automobiles on the road than the rest of the world's manufacturers combined.

Source: *The Entrepreneurs: An American Adventure* (Boston: Enterprise Media, 1987), Film No. 2.

Who Is an Entrepreneur?

With a definition in mind, we still have trouble identifying entrepreneurs, finding them, or determining what they do. Is the local gas station owner an entrepreneur? The realtor, the butcher, the franchise computer retailer? Are there entrepreneurs in corporations? In schools? In government? There are no short answers to these questions, and there are no formal guidelines for classifying entrepreneurs. There is no entrepreneurial licensing procedure and no evidence of professional status.

Karl Vesper has researched entrepreneurship and explains that its nature is often a matter of individual perception.[11] Economists, at least those who endorse free enterprise, endorse Schumpeter's viewpoint that entrepreneurs bring resources together in unusual combinations to generate profits. Vesper found that psychologists tend to view entrepreneurs in behavioral terms as achievement-oriented individuals driven to seek challenges and new accomplishments. Marxist philosophers may see entrepreneurs as exploitative adventurers, representative of all that is negative in capitalism. Corporate managers too often view entrepreneurs as small businesspersons lacking the potential needed for corporate management. On a positive note, Vesper suggests that those of us who strongly favor a market economy view entrepreneurs as pillars of industrial strength—the movers and shakers who constructively disrupt the status quo.

Traits versus Characteristics

In an effort to understand entrepreneurs better, researchers have sought to define traits common to a majority of individuals who start and operate new ventures. John Hornaday of Babson College was among the first to use surveys and intense interviews to develop a composite list of entrepreneurial traits.[12] These are summarized in Exhibit 1-1. Although this descriptive list is supported by impressive data, it has the singular restriction of relating only to highly successful entrepreneurs; there is no way of knowing how these traits relate to a majority of entrepreneurs. For example, some people may have the creative talent to generate new ideas but lack the ability to organize resources, and others may have a compelling need to achieve but lack the resourcefulness to create a new venture. Many of these individuals with a limited profile based on traits will start new businesses and succeed. Others with a majority of the traits may start new businesses and fail. Opponents of the trait approach also reverse Hornaday's logic and ask whether those among us who do not choose to be entrepreneurs have similar traits. Put another way, can a "nonentrepreneur" also be achievement oriented, persistent, and creative?

A. David Silver, a successful venture capitalist and author, described the entrepreneur as "energetic, single-minded," and having "a mission and clear vision; he or she intends to create out of this vision a product or service in a field many have determined is important to improve the lives of millions."[13] Silver also suggests that entrepreneurs venture out on their own from a sense of dissatisfaction with their organizations, but they are not necessarily unhappy with their career fields. This point is illustrated by the proliferation of Silicon Valley firms that were established by

---

Exhibit 1-1   **Characteristics of Successful Entrepreneurs**

Self-confident and optimistic	Energetic and diligent
Able to take calculated risk	Creative, need to achieve
Respond positively to challenges	Dynamic leader
Flexible and able to adapt	Responsive to suggestions
Knowledgeable of markets	Take initiatives
Able to get along well with others	Resourceful and persevering
Independent minded	Perceptive with foresight
Versatile knowledge	Responsive to criticism

Source: John A. Hornaday, "Research about Living Entrepreneurs," in Calvin A. Kent, Donald L. Sexton, and Karl H. Vesper, eds., *Encyclopedia of Entrepreneurship* (Englewood Cliffs, NJ: Prentice-Hall, 1982), p. 28. Adapted with permission.

PROFILE △

Irving Berlin

As a child, Irving Berlin sang for pennies on street corners in New York, but when he died in 1989, he left behind an unequaled legacy of music and theater innovations. Born in 1888, Israel Baline came to America as a Russian-Jewish immigrant with his parents, and at the age of five, he was on the streets of New York helping the family earn food money with his singing. His first published song was in 1907 at the age of 19, and his first blockbuster hit came in 1911 with "Alexander's Ragtime Band." During his life, he composed more than a thousand songs, complete scores for 19 Broadway shows, and music for a dozen movies.

Irving Berlin was also an astute businessman who started the Berlin Music Corporation, controlled his own copyrights, opened the Music Box (an innovative New York theater devoted to musical plays), and established foundations for creative artists and musicians. His musical innovations ranged from syncopations of ragtime and jazz to composing "God Bless America"—a song many Americans regard as the unofficial national anthem. Berlin was one of the few to write both his own lyrics and music, and he performed in several of his productions. However, he only played piano in the key of F sharp, and because so many scores had to be written in other keys, he had a special piano developed to transpose his compositions automatically to other keys.

Until a few months before his death, Berlin still called in to his office at Berlin Music Corporation, and he was an active supporter of the American Society of Composers, Authors, and Publishers, an organization he founded to help artists protect their creations.

Source: "One of a Kind," *Sunday Morning Post* (Hong Kong), Spectrum, September 24, 1989, p. 1.

engineers, inventors, scientists, and computer wizards who left established companies to pursue private enterprise, yet did so within the scope of their professions.

Another way to explain entrepreneurship is from a sociocultural standpoint. Albert Shapero made comparative studies between nations, peoples, and ethnic groups, accumulated information from historical trends, and conducted many firsthand interviews with entrepreneurs. He concluded that individuals often become entrepreneurs by being thrown into situations that force them to fashion their own means of economic livelihood.[14] Immigrants fit this model well. As in the past, immigrants come to the United States to avoid war or political oppression. Many leave their home countries because of lack of opportunities and poor economic conditions. When they arrive in the United States, most lack language skills necessary to find decent jobs. Others, stereotyped by their ethnic group or religion, may be barred from employment. Circumstances afford few options for these "displaced persons," who frequently establish independent ventures. Irving Berlin was one of the many immigrants who overcame these barriers to succeed, and in so doing, enriched our culture.

Shapero also found a high correlation between increases in new ventures and rising unemployment. Many individuals become "economically displaced" (unemployed) or find themselves disillusioned with faltering careers. For these individuals, starting a new venture can be exhilarating, a breath of fresh air into an otherwise stale life-style. Individuals who retire, particularly those who retire early, are seldom ready to quit working, and for many, starting a business is an exciting opportunity.

Entrepreneurship, Small Business, and Corporate Ventures

The term *entrepreneur* may be properly applied to those who incubate new ideas, start enterprises based on those ideas, and provide added value to society based on their independent initiative. However, individuals who simply *substitute income* by leaving jobs to operate local stores or independent service businesses are described as **small businesspersons.** The distinction is subtle but important. The person who establishes a fast-food franchise chain is called an entrepreneur, but the local restaurant owner is called a small businessperson. Distinguishing factors are that entrepreneurs have *vision for growth*, *commitment to constructive change*, *persistence* to gather necessary resources, and *energy* to achieve unusual results. The small businessperson may exhibit these characteristics, but only coincidentally, not as a prerequisite to establishing an enterprise.

These are controversial issues because many "small businesspersons" reflect the essentials of entrepreneurship. They incubate ideas, gather resources, take individual risks, and persist in seeing their ventures succeed. They do not, however, pursue growth through constructive change in the same way Schumpeter explained entrepreneurship or in the manner of Drucker's description of the entrepreneurial process. Still, what has *not* been accomplished by research is to clearly differentiate small business from entrepreneurship. If we add a third dimension of corporate entrepreneurship, we have a rather complex controversy.

Corporate entrepreneurship, sometimes referred to as **intrapreneurship,** is concerned with innovation that leads to new corporate divisions or subsidiary ventures in established, larger firms.[15] The concept of entrepreneurship does not exclude managers in large organizations from being entrepreneurs if they combine resources in unusual ways to create innovative new products or services. However, because entrepreneurs take personal investment risks and corporate managers very rarely do, there are grounds for arguing that corporate entrepreneurship is a play on words. Corporate managers may commit time and energy, and perhaps also risk their careers, but there is little evidence of corporate managers risking personal investment capital to champion a corporate innovation. This is an interesting topic that will be explored further in Chapter 3, but for now, let's draw some fundamental distinctions between *small business*, *intrapreneurship*, and *entrepreneurship*.

> **CHECKPOINT**
>
> Describe the critical points in our definition of entrepreneurship.
>
> Identify and discuss the characteristics of entrepreneurs, and discuss how they might differ from those of people not interested in new ventures.
>
> Explain how the definitions of entrepreneurship, small business, and corporate entrepreneurship differ.

PERSPECTIVE ON SMALL BUSINESS

During the 1970s small businesses created more than 6 million new jobs for Americans. At the same time, *Fortune* 500 firms cut employment by nearly 10 percent, for a net loss of more than a million jobs. During the first half of the 1980s, new jobs from small business enterprises eclipsed the gains of the 1970s, and today, more than 16 million small businesses account for approximately 97 percent of all nonfarm businesses. Between 1980 and 1987, 66 percent of all new jobs in the United States were in firms with fewer than 1,000 employees generating less than $10 million in annual sales.[16] Figure 1-3 illustrates these relative changes.

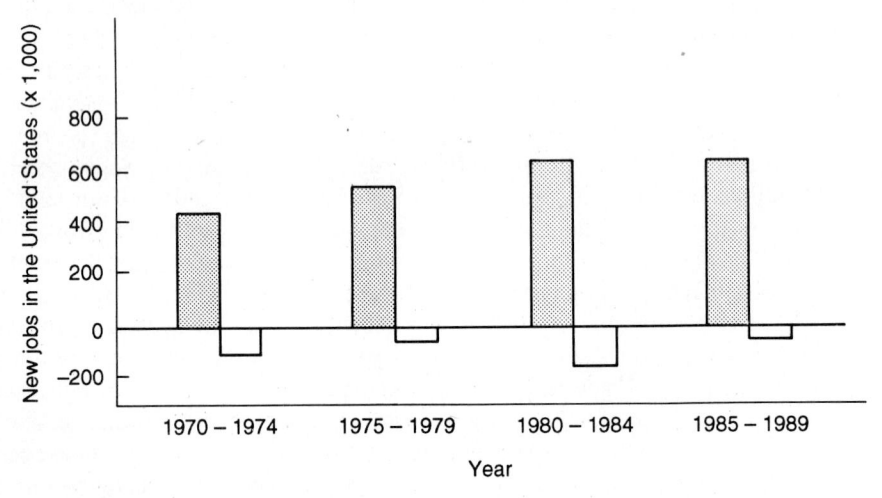

Figure 1-3 **Employment Change in NonFarm Businesses, 1970–1989.** (*Source*: U.S. Department of Labor, Bureau of Labor Statistics, *Handbook of Labor Statistics* (Washington, DC: U.S. Government Printing Office, 1985); annual BLS statistics for 1974, 1979, 1984, 1989 (est.).)

Although these statistics are impressive, the Small Business Administration and U.S. Census of Business taken each year suggest that about 55 percent of all new small businesses fail. The popular idea is that owning or managing a small business is like riding a tiger—survival is not a probable conclusion. This view is inaccurate for a number of reasons. A firm that changes its name is listed as "out of business." A firm that changes from a proprietorship to an incorporation is counted as one "quit" and one "new start." Also, when a firm successfully merges with another, takes on a new partner, or is enfranchised, it can mistakenly be counted as a business failure. In addition, a business may be successfully operated by its owner, then sold, and the assumption of failure is erroneous. For these reasons, research has not accurately established small business failure rates. Recent inquiries suggest that perhaps fewer than one in ten actually dissolves or enters into bankruptcy. Most new ventures and small firms simply go through many changes that disguise their existence.[17]

These points are important because many students will be entering the world of small business; perhaps most will find themselves in small organizations shouldering tremendous responsibilities early in their careers. If employment statistics are accurate, nearly half of all graduates will actually be working in firms with fewer than 1,000 employees, and many more will become independent small businesspersons.

Defining Small Business

According to the Small Business Administration, a **small business** is one that does not dominate its industry, has less than $10 million in annual sales, and has fewer than 1,000 employees.[18] Exceptions to these criteria abound, but the SBA uses these benchmarks for evaluating loans and providing business assistance. "Small" defies clear definition. For instance, in today's markets, firms with fewer than 100 workers but with high-speed production lines can generate $50 million or more in sales. Fast-food franchises, such as McDonald's, generate millions in sales with only a few employees. On the other hand, firms with several thousand workers may have low sales volume. In general, small businesses seldom dominate their industries and rely on filling a "niche" in local or regional markets. Exhibit 1-2 lists three types of small businesses. Their relative advantages and disadvantages are discussed in the following paragraphs.

Family enterprises are locally owned and operated, often by one person called a sole proprietor. Proprietors may have started their businesses in an effort to supplement or replace family income. Many are service-based firms that rely on an owner's skills. Types of businesses that are family owned vary widely and can include retail stores, contracting businesses, small manufacturing firms, and restaurants, among others. The myth of high rates of business failure is particularly irritating to family business owners who often have no (interested) successors. In the absence of a successor, the life of a venture is limited to the working life of its founder. A florist, for example, may operate successfully until the founder retires, but if no one exists to succeed the owner, the business is sold or closed. Succession is a serious problem, and successful business owners often must resign themselves to dissolving their firms.

Personal service firms rely crucially on unique skills of their founders or key

Exhibit 1-2 **Types of Small Business: Advantages and Disadvantages**

Type	Advantages	Disadvantages
Family enterprise	Offers economic independence; promotes family unity	Family liability for the business; unsure succession
Personal service firm (PSF)	Offers personal freedom and use of talents and skills for personal growth	Personal liability and lack of secure income without clear succession
Franchise	Franchisor provides most business start-up needs with relative income security	Less freedom and adventure than others; contracted to franchisor for services and royalty lease payments

employees. In most instances, the business *is* the person, and succession is unlikely unless a son or daughter develops comparable skills. Incidentally, the "personal service firm" (PSF) is a formal category of business according to the Internal Revenue Service, and special tax regulations govern income reporting, deductions, and asset management. Such diverse occupations as golf professionals, interior designers, and freelance writers are considered to be PSFs. Since the early 1980s, the premiere personal service firm has been the computer services enterprise that provides software development, business consulting, office system networking, and similar assistance to other firms. Many of these enterprises become quite large and are distinguished from smaller personal service firms by their growth characteristics. Those with highly personalized services that limit sales to local customers are usually considered "small businesses." Those with broader interests that resell hardware systems, develop software for licensing, and create a high volume of billing income are difficult to label as "small" businesses.

Franchises represent an extraordinary growth sector of the American economy that is spreading overseas at an accelerated pace. A later chapter will explore franchising thoroughly, but it is important to recognize how franchises differ from other small businesses. The individual who buys a franchise store or contracts to franchise services typically is a small businessperson seeking a protected local market with an established business line. Those individuals buying into a franchise are called *franchisees*, and those who sell franchises, the patron corporations, are called *franchisors*.

Franchises are created by contract. An individual receives specific help and advantages in exchange for a franchise fee and, usually, a percentage of sales. The franchisor develops a network of income-producing enterprises that share a common name, use common materials, and sell similar products or services. The franchisee may receive financial help, training, guaranteed supplies, a protected market, and technical assistance with matters such as site selection, purchasing, accounting, and operations management.

PROFILE △

Century 21

Based in Irvine, California, Century 21 is the world's largest real estate sales organization. With more than 6,700 franchised offices in the United States, Canada, Japan, and Great Britian, the company generates $50 billion annually in world revenue. Century 21 plans to open an additional 500 units in England, Scotland, Wales, and Northern Ireland, and 800 units in France, Belgium, Luxembourg, Switzerland, and the Netherlands during the early 1990s. By awarding "subfranchises"—territories or major regions—to one substantial franchisee, Century 21 has created a global network of expanding enterprises, each capable of opening new locations and managing growth.

Source: John F. Persinos, "New Worlds to Franchise," *Venture*, November 1987, pp. 50–51.

We have grown accustomed to franchises, such as Wendy's and McDonald's, but franchises exist in a great many areas. Most stores in shopping malls are franchises, including stores that sell clothing, books, toys, photographic supplies, records, shoes, and computer services. Printers, furniture stores, auto rental outlets, convenience stores, snack shops, and hundreds more comprise a growing list of independent franchises. In franchising, independent owners invest their personal capital, usually operate their businesses, and are limited to one store or one area. These are seldom "mom and pop" enterprises (the familiar connotation of family enterprises), but they are still small businesses as distinguished from corporate endeavors. They do not constitute entrepreneurship in the sense of creating new products or services, but according to U.S. Department of Commerce statistics, franchising is a $40 billion a year business sector and also the fastest growing sector in the United States.[19]

> ▶ **CHECKPOINT**
>
> Discuss why many new ventures start small and remain small.
>
> Define "personal service firm," and describe three that you frequent.
>
> Distinguish between a franchisor and a franchisee.

CORPORATE ENTREPRENEURSHIP

As noted earlier, the popular term for corporate entrepreneurship is *intrapreneurship*. This has a catchy sound to it, but many people avoid the term; it seems too cute to explain a complex concept. To review our introductory comments, corporate managers certainly can be as innovative as anyone else, but when employees create something new within the context of their jobs, there is no requirement that an individual take a personal stake in making it a commercial success. There is no assumption of risk, no assumption of profit, and no assumption of loss. However, many managers are given the opportunity to pursue innovations, and, as we shall see later, many are in farsighted corporations that encourage entrepreneurial activity.

Clearly, larger corporations create remarkable new products and spearhead new technologies. Established corporations have enormous resources to pursue research and development. They can underwrite prodigious innovations, and they have the marketing muscle to commercialize them. Although many corporations back managers with venturesome ideas, corporations reap the lion's share of rewards. Managers generally risk embarrassment, and in some instances their careers, but rewards are usually limited to bonuses and promotions. Corporate entrepreneurship can occur, therefore, with the reservation that risks and rewards are curtailed.

Eminent researcher Hans Schollhammer refers to corporate entrepreneurship as "intra-corporate" entrepreneurship.[20] In his view, an entrepreneurial event does *not* take place when the formal organization is involved in traditional research and development unless individuals can work independently to create a *new venture* while sharing both risks and rewards. Corporate entrepreneurship *does* take place when new products or services are explicitly supported with company resources, and when employees are responsible for championing their innovations. More precisely, these individuals have the opportunity to work independently, are given tremendous latitude, and are expected to generate a new "unit" to extend corporate activities. These new units may take the form of divisions, subsidiaries, or entirely new entities having corporate capital backing.[21]

The concept of corporate entrepreneurship is controversial in part because of rather muddy definitions of entrepreneurship and in part because of ambiguity about the roles of managers within their established organizations. We cannot resolve that controversy, but we can examine the nature of the problem. In part, the problem is one of perception. Recall that entrepreneurship is defined differently by individuals with unique perspectives. For example, many corporate managers view entrepreneurs as individuals incapable of working productively in structured organizations. These managers may even deny that corporate entrepreneurship exists. Depending on one's perspective, then, entrepreneurship takes on different meanings. Consider the second issue: that managerial roles related to innovation can be ambiguous. When does a corporate manager stop being an employee working in a prescribed job and become "entrepreneurial"? How do employees redefine their roles apart from the organization? How are risks and responsibilities identified? What reward exists for the employee? These are only a few of the questions that must be answered to stimulate initiative within larger organizations. As we shall see in Chapter 3, organizations have developed a number of ways to stimulate innovative employees, redefine management roles, and provide rewards commensurate with risks.

> ▶ **CHECKPOINT**
>
> Describe the risks a manager might assume when championing a new corporate innovation.
>
> Discuss the concept of corporate entrepreneurship and whether it can, in reality, take place.

ENTREPRENEURSHIP IN PRACTICE

Entrepreneurship can be explained in part by understanding what motivates individuals to pursue their dreams vigorously. Setting theory aside, students seem to acquire this understanding best by studying examples. Fortunately, the United States is an elegant culture filled with historic precedent and prominent entrepreneurs who have created a national infrastructure of commerce.

Evolution of Contemporary Entrepreneurship

A very long time ago, ancient people invented a hand ax, made the wheel a reality, and discovered new ways to grow crops. Much later, sails mounted on boats made seafaring trade possible. Still later, Robert Fulton's steam engine revolutionized sea and land transportation. These were watershed events in human history, but it was 19th-century entrepreneurs who dramatically thrust the world into industrialism.

Three early pioneers were Samuel Colt, Eli Whitney, and Samuel Morse. Colt's weaponry helped increase the firepower needed to expand westward; Whitney's cotton gin made an extraordinary increase in productivity for exported cotton; and Morse's telegraph revolutionized communications technology. An era of "tycoons" emerged that vaulted America into the 20th century, and during this era the foundations of modern industry were laid. An intrepid adventurer, Andrew Carnegie, founded the American steel industry. Later, Henry Ford pioneered mass assembly of automobiles. Other famous founding names such as Swift (meat packing), Vanderbilt (railroads), and Rockefeller (oil) created empires and fortunes that are legendary. John D. Rockefeller, for example, controlled nearly 2 percent of the entire U.S. gross national product before he was 40 years old, but even more interesting, he was a billionaire and his oil empire was largely in place before he was 30.[22]

Perhaps the contemporary period of entrepreneurship began with innovators such as Cyrus McCormick, who, as noted earlier, constructed a mechanical reaper that revolutionized agriculture, and Alexander Graham Bell, who launched the telecommunications industry with the telephone. Bell's invention of the telephone may have been in great part an accident. Bell had been working for years on a way to improve communications for the deaf and hearing impaired; he really wanted to create a hearing aid, but his mechanical voicebox gave us the telephone. Unlike McCormick and Bell, Henry Ford was *not* an inventor, but he was an astute entrepreneur. When he founded Ford Motor Company, Olds and several other auto companies had been in production for nearly 20 years. Ford, however, created a manufacturing process based on a system of specialization that no one else could match. Some of the early auto inventors that Ford eclipsed combined to become General Motors, but they were pulled together by yet another entrepreneur who was an organizational genius, Alfred Sloan.

Perhaps the most famous individual was Thomas A. Edison, whom we credit with the light bulb. In fact, the light bulb had been around for years, but no one had been able to make one that lasted long, nor one that used alternating current. Edison experimented with more than a thousand models before he was successful, but even then the light bulb was only a gadget. Edison was ridiculed as an "eccentric tinkerer." His light bulb was of little use until it was wired to a source of power, a generating station. Edison was successful only after he made the light bulb *commercially* viable by establishing an electric-generating industry.

These historical underpinnings have one common thread: entrepreneurs were responsible for innovations that significantly improved human productivity. This pattern is repeated time and again. The bicycle mobilized the human race. McAdam (blacktop) gave us the material for commercial highways. Ford gave us the highly productive assembly line. Edison gave us light and a tremendous new use for electric power. And Bell gave us the means to communicate instantaneously.

This productivity pattern is just as clear today. For example, IBM was established through the early efforts of its founder Thomas Watson, Sr., who converted the clumsy mechanical typewriter into an electrically operated office machine. He marketed the electric typewriter aggressively, and then spearheaded the early development of punch card accounting systems. Under the dynamic leadership of Thomas J. Watson, Jr., the founder's son, IBM flourished as a corporate giant in computers.[23] Steven Jobs and Stephen Wozniak made personal computing possible with the Apple.[24] Mitchell D. Kapor, who founded Lotus in 1981, was responsible for the best-selling PC software program ever devised, the Lotus 1-2-3 spreadsheet.[25] In each instance, productivity was improved by extraordinary measures. From a mechanical typewriter to the electronic model, and then to the personal computer with sophisticated word processing, office capabilities have quintupled. Electronic spreadsheets made pencil-and-ledger accounting practices obsolete, and the calculation power of spreadsheets used with high-speed PCs made slide rules museum pieces. These changes are illustrated in Figure 1-4.

Many corporations that we take for granted as industry giants began very modestly as entrepreneurial ventures. Intel Corporation in microelectronics, Data General Corporation and Digital in business and scientific computing, Ashton-Tate in software, Sun Microsystems in electronic workstations, and Wang Laboratories in office systems come to mind as "high-tech" examples in the computer industry.

"High tech" is not limited to information technology, and other firms with

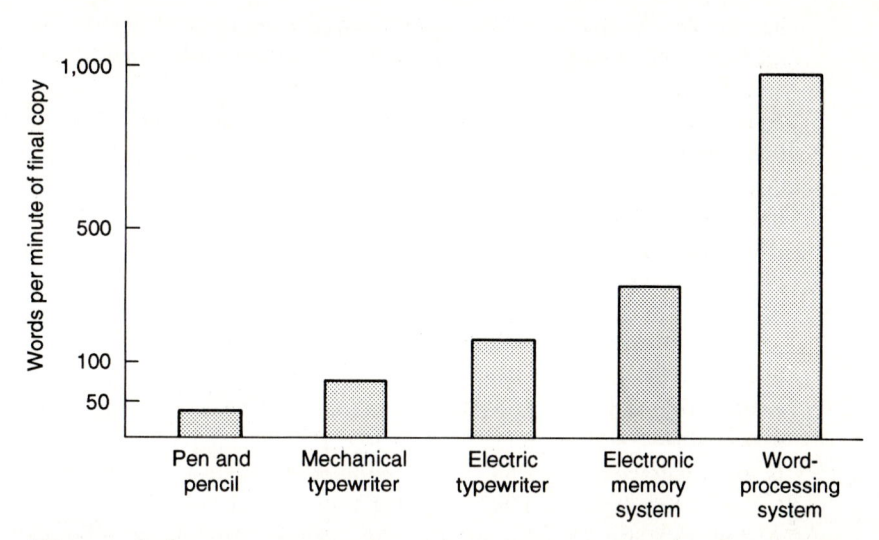

Figure 1-4 Document Preparation Productivity Changes with New Technology

products that seldom become household words have dynamic entrepreneurial foundations. Biopolymers (chemicals secreted naturally from microbes) are being developed for industrial use by a small but rapidly growing firm, Petroferm. These biopolymers allow water and oil to combine, and this ability can in turn help expedite oil extraction. The use of biopolymers could *double* oil field production. The biopolymer process also creates an inexpensive new substitute for fuel oil that alone could free up nearly 2 million barrels of crude oil per day. Genetic engineering is a field only recently making its debut and led by a few entrepreneurial firms that have begun to provide commercially viable medicines and industrial chemicals. These firms have mysterious names such as Genentech and Amgen, and most product names have little meaning by themselves, such as TPA and EPO, but the ramifications of these innovations are awesome. For example, the U.S. Food and Drug Administration recently approved several new genetically engineered products that include therapeutic proteins, human insulin, and human growth hormones. One of these products, interferon, has promising use in cancer treatment. The product known as TPA is now in use in Europe for medical rehabilitation of patients with heart disease, and EPO is being tested for its use in replacing red blood cells for kidney dialysis patients.[26]

There are literally hundreds of examples that have had (or promise to have) extraordinary implications for society. Our methods of communication have changed, our traditional office systems have changed, our medical treatments of serious illnesses have changed, and *many* of our production and manufacturing processes have changed. But that is only a beginning, and it hardly explains the *nature* of entrepreneurship. "High tech" is a buzzword, and productivity is relative. The commercial application of electricity by Edison, the production of steel by Carnegie, the mass assembly of automobiles by Ford, and the systematic packaging of meat products by Swift were all "high tech" in their time; in each instance, productivity improved enormously.

In each example, whether taken from early tycoons or contemporary wizards, there were inspired individuals who went out on very thin limbs to create new ventures that *solved problems* or *created new opportunities*. In the evolution of modern industrial nations, the nature of entrepreneurship is best explained by the profound observation that entrepreneurs "created opportunities." It is completely immaterial whether a venture is high tech or not, or whether it offers a product or a service.

Services offered by entrepreneurs represented nearly 46 percent of all new businesses during the 1980s, and many of these firms were among the most dynamic in terms of increased sales and employment.[27] For example, the tenth-ranked firm on the annual *Inc.* 100 list for 1987 was the Home Shopping Network.[28] This firm created a television "catalog" program for shopping (mainly specialty items of interest to women), and between 1982 and 1987, HSN experienced 17,735 percent growth (annual average rate of 265%). The number of employees expanded from 150 in 1982 to more than 4,200 in 1987. Another firm that recognized an opportunity and capitalized on it was *Inc.*'s highest-ranked firm, Catalyst Energy Development of New York. The energy shortage coupled with deregulation and liberalized laws for cogeneration of electricity led to Catalyst's formation in 1982. Since then, the firm has had a 212,338 percent growth in sales (more than 500% annually), and its employee ranks grew from three individuals to more than 500 in five years.

The *Inc.* 100 represents entrepreneurial firms that are rapidly heading for the "big" list, the *Fortune* 500, but the list comprises more unstable firms because of the high-growth, high-risk nature of most enterprises, and it also reveals a wider assortment of business interests that seldom have "mega" corporation profiles. For instance, Fuddruckers (ranked 85th in 1987 and 62nd in 1989 by *Inc.*) is a chain of unusual and highly successful hamburger restaurants, but not a likely candidate to rival IBM or General Motors. On the other hand, Apple Computers and Lotus Development Corporation began as small companies listed on *Inc.* 100, but both are now major players. The composite *Inc.* list for 1989 shows that 30 percent of the firms were in computers and microelectronics, yet 16 percent of the firms were in health care, and there were several top-rated enterprises in communications, entertainment, food services, genetic engineering, cosmetics, merchandising, and parcel express services.[29]

An interesting example of how entrepreneurs embrace new opportunities is Doskocil, a firm with gross annual sales in excess of a quarter billion dollars. The company's founder, Larry Doskocil, started out in a rented chicken hatchery making sausage in Hutchinson, Kansas. He recognized the growth in the pizza industry during the early 1980s, and began processing wholesale sausage and pepperoni packaged specifically for pizza restaurants. His business has grown to the point of being the pizza-topping king of the United States.[30]

Entrepreneurs such as Larry Doskocil either solved a problem or saw an opportunity, took the risk of a new venture, and succeeded because they gave society something of value. Successful entrepreneurs are also usually close to the problem or opportunity in terms of skill, knowledge, access, or resources. Most entrepreneurs do not dream up radical new ideas or merely brainstorm their way into business. Edison had been working with electricity and various forms of illumination for years. Bell had been working on audio transmission long before he conceived of the telephone. Doskocil had spent years scratching out a living processing sausages in traditional ways before recognizing the market opportunity in pizza toppings. The founders of nearly all genetic engineering firms were research scientists with substantial qualifications. As other examples are presented, it will become apparent that most founders had some knowledge of their markets, some product experience, or a unique skill that guided them toward opportunities. In many instances they have had opportunity thrust on them, but only rarely have new ventures occurred through luck.

Entrepreneurial Characteristics

Earlier in this chapter, characteristics, or "traits," of entrepreneurs were presented as a starting point in our discussion on the nature and meaning of entrepreneurship. Those characteristics were often value-loaded descriptions, even though accurate for successful entrepreneurs. They included such terms as persistent, self-confident, diligent, creative, optimistic, and independent minded. This list is useful, but there are other characteristics to consider.

Several studies have found that entrepreneurs are in unusually good health, are realistic about working hard and driving toward measurable results, tend to have superior conceptual abilities, and are generally emotionally stable.[31] In a 1984 study, Jerome A. Katz found that more than 86 percent of entrepreneurs who start new businesses have bachelor's degrees (more than half of those in liberal arts), and about 71 percent who buy into existing businesses have similar degrees.[32] Katz also found that, although more than 90 percent in both groups had several years of prior experience, only about 18 percent had an "unstable" record (had held ten or more previous jobs). These data, represented in Figure 1-5, suggest that most entrepreneurs are reasonably well educated with solid work experience. They are *not* renegade dropouts, as folklore would have us believe.

86% — Percent of businesses started by entrepreneurs with BA degrees

71% — Percent of businesses bought by entrepreneurs with BA degrees

90% — Percent of new start-ups or businesses purchased by entrepreneurs with more than two years work experience

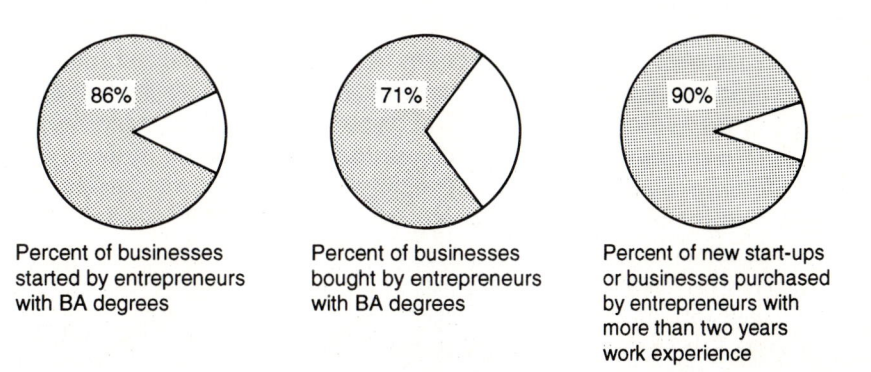

Figure 1-5   Education and Work Experience of Entrepreneurs

Several major research studies also emphasize that many entrepreneurs are coming from the ranks of MBAs, and further, that there is a growing trend by graduates to seek entrepreneurial opportunities rather than corporate careers. For example, at Harvard Business School, nearly half of all MBAs enrolled in entrepreneurship classes during the past several years, and nearly as many have been drawn to new ventures, either as independent business owners or as associates in entrepreneurial enterprises.[33]

Robert Ronstadt explored this phenomenon and correlated start-up ventures with better educated youth who, incidentally, often had entrepreneurial parents. Nearly 76 percent had fathers who were also entrepreneurs, and 13 percent had mothers in entrepreneurial roles. He concluded that the seeds of entrepreneurship were planted early by parental role models. Ronstadt also found that the average age of entrepreneurs at start-up was 32. However, a significant number of entrepreneurs began about the age of 25, many more about the age of 30, and another significant group about the age of 35. There was also a noticeable number of new ventures started by youngsters scarcely out of high school as well as men and women near retirement age.[34]

From Ronstadt's study we can conclude that most new ventures are the result of youthful, reasonably well-educated individuals choosing initially to "go it alone." Further information reveals that more than 60 percent start ventures near their homes, with about 25 percent originating in suburbs, 30 percent in rural towns, and 45 percent in or near urban centers. Slightly more than half of all recently formed ventures are in professional services, but 26 percent are in retailing, and 16 percent are in manufacturing.

Data are only beginning to emerge on minorities in business, and research has not been adequate to support profile characteristics. However, there are accurate data on percentages of different ethnic groups engaged in independent businesses based on Internal Revenue Service records.[35] Only about 3.6 percent of all blacks (male and female) were engaged in independent businesses in 1984. That figure is very low compared with 17.1 percent of white males, 6.3 percent of white females, 7.8 percent of Asians, and 5.3 percent of Hispanics. The number of white females may be somewhat higher, approaching 12 percent, based on estimates of dual career families reporting combined income.

In a milestone 1987 report, characteristics of women entrepreneurs were studied with very good results.[36] Most women entrepreneurs started in business between the ages of 38 and 48, with the mean start-up age being 46. About 56 percent were married, and 42 percent had children, though nearly all children were essentially "out of the house" (over 20 years of age or not residing at home). More than 62 percent of these women had attended college, with 70 percent of those graduating in liberal arts. A third of all women entrepreneurs had graduate degrees. Their parents, like those of most male entrepreneurs, were well educated, and 68 percent of their husbands held college degrees. Only 4 percent of these women entered financial service businesses, another 9 percent were involved in manufacturing, and the remaining 87 percent pursued personal service enterprises or specialty merchandising.

A clear profile of entrepreneurs does not emerge from these studies, yet there is strong evidence that most are well educated and have had successful work experience. Many also have had entrepreneurial parents, are emotionally stable, and have superior conceptual skills. Men tend to launch ventures early in their lives, but women tend to become entrepreneurs after their children are grown. Perhaps the lower percentage of blacks, Asians, and Hispanics implies fewer educational opportunities, less access to resources, or less relevant work experience, but there is little evidence to support these arguments.

> ▶ **CHECKPOINT**
>
> Describe how McCormick, Bell, and Ford solved social problems and created new opportunities through their entrepreneurial efforts.
>
> Explain our contemporary view of an entrepreneurial "profile" and the conclusions we might draw about tomorrow's entrepreneurs.

FOCUS OF THE TEXT

Our introductory comments have emphasized that entrepreneurship can be explained in several ways. The text focuses on new venture creation more than on corporate ventures or small business; however, all three will be addressed. Each has its place in entrepreneurship education, but it is perhaps important here to explain how we distinguish between them.

Most small businesses start small and remain small. They may be constrained by the nature of the enterprise (laundry services, independent restaurants, etc.) or may be limited by their founders' intentions. The new venture orientation of this text emphasizes those small start-ups that *do* grow. The entrepreneurs that the text focuses on are those who *want* to expand, and those who do so through innovative combinations of resources. Because such growth can also occur in large organizations, corporate venturing is important to discuss. Small business is addressed because so often the process of launching new high-growth ventures is similar to that of starting small businesses.

The concept of *business planning* is a vital part of the entrepreneurship process and of this text. The critical elements of a formal business plan are similar for all new ventures, and although the text is not locked into a planning format, planning criteria will be emphasized. Appendixes provide supplemental business plan guidelines and procedures for drafting a feasibility study.

Chapter 2 will enhance the historical perspective of high-growth ventures with a view toward sensitizing students to changes taking place today. Chapter 3 addresses small business and corporate entrepreneurship. Chapter 4 is a pivotal chapter to establish a model of entrepreneurship and to provide a framework for business planning. This will conclude Part One of the text.

Part Two includes three chapters. Chapter 5 introduces product development from a new venture perspective. Chapter 6 is concerned with product protection such as patents, trademarks, copyrights, and other legal considerations, including recent initiatives for protection of intellectual property. Chapter 7 looks more closely at the service industry and new venture opportunities.

Part Three focuses on marketing concepts. Chapter 8 introduces marketing research for new venture planning. Chapter 9 concentrates on marketing strategies and implementing a marketing plan. Chapter 10 extends the concept of new venture creation to international markets, addressing the opportunities for exporting, overseas investments, and importing.

Part Four looks into four aspects of new venture creation. Chapter 11 examines the legal options for business formations and correlates these with the entrepreneurship team, skills, and needs of the proposed business. In Chapter 12, the process of buying an existing business is explored, and a significant part of the chapter is devoted to franchising. Chapter 13 is concerned with venture financing and ways to obtain financial backing. Chapter 14 concludes by addressing entrepreneurial careers and challenges of managing a growing business.

Appendixes provide students with guidelines for creating a business plan. Appendix A outlines the fundamental questions in a realistic business plan, and Appendix B provides an example that can be used in conjunction with chapter material to enhance presentations.

SYNOPSIS FOR LEARNING

1. *Describe how entrepreneurship evolved from economic theory.*

European economists sought to define entrepreneurship based on how entrepreneurs behaved. Richard Cantillon argued that entrepreneurs made conscious decisions about resource allocations, thereby seeking higher yields for their money and materials. Jean Baptiste Say believed that entrepreneurs behaved with exceptional insight to fulfill society's needs through the process of taking risks. He noted that entrepreneurs typically bought goods at known prices and transformed them (or transported them to markets) to sell at unknown prices. Adam Smith described the role of "enterpriser," a person who organized industrial activity, matching demand with supply through commerce. Carl Menger described entrepreneurship as the process of converting resources into goods and services of value to consumers. And Joseph Schumpeter extended the concept to include the importance of innovation. These contributions provide our contemporary foundation for understanding entrepreneurial behavior.

2. *Explain entrepreneurship and the characteristics of entrepreneurs.*

Entrepreneurship is defined as a dynamic process of creating incremental wealth by individuals who assume the risks of equity, time, and careers to infuse resources with value for society. In Drucker's view, the entrepreneur uses resources not merely to solve problems but also to take advantage of opportunities. Combining these concepts with Schumpeter's notion of innovation and his observation that entrepreneurs engage in "creative disruption," we explain entrepreneurship as a process of innovation that reallocates resources to new opportunities, often creating new opportunities through unusual combinations of resources and the skills of risk-taking entrepreneurs.

Research has tried to identify traits or characteristics of entrepreneurs based on explanations of entrepreneurship. They are called risk takers, high achievers, persistent innovators, and inspired, energetic, and single-minded individuals. Few attributes explain entrepreneurs well, and many of these attributes are shared equally by salaried managers and employees. However, entrepreneurs had been described by their activities, and perhaps this approach is more fruitful. They are individuals who start new ventures with a vision for growth, seek constructive change, have the persistence to gather essential resources, and use their energy to achieve unusual results.

3. *Discuss small business as a dimension of entrepreneurship.*

Small business, by definition, includes entrepreneurs because most new ventures start small. However, small business is distinguished by the nature of the enterprise or the intention of its owner. The small businessperson is likely to start a venture that serves a local market with products or services without growth potential (or without the intention of growing). Many businesses are small by their nature. These include "personal service firms" such as beauty salons, medical practices, interior designers, and freelance writers. Others are small by choice, such as "family businesses" in which ownership is retained by family members actively engaged in operating the enterprise. Many restaurants, contractors, small manufacturers, and local service enterprises are family owned and operated. Small businesses may often be created through legal contracts, such as "franchises" that limit the size and scope of commercial activity. These include fast-food outlets, print shops, car dealerships, distributors, retailers, convenience stores, and hundreds more. Small business is a vital sector of the American economy, and a majority of new and existing jobs exist in small businesses.

4. *Describe the concept of corporate entrepreneurship.*

Corporate entrepreneurship, also called intrapreneurship, describes the innovation that occurs inside established companies through efforts of creative employees. It implies more than helping a company to become more productive or to introduce new products or services. Specifically, the corporate entrepreneur is one who helps a company set a "new course" and in the process often generates new divisions, subsidiaries, or new companies that "spin off" from the parent organization. The concept is controversial because no one can accurately explain how a manager assumes the risk of a new venture while remaining employed in a structured organization.

5. *Explain how entrepreneurship has influenced economic development and productivity in recent years.*

In practice, entrepreneurs have historically altered the direction of national economies, industries, or markets. They have invented new products and developed the organizations and means of production to bring them to market. They have introduced quantum leaps in technology, such as the introduction of semiconductor electronics, and they have forced the reallocation of resources away from existing uses to new and more productive uses. Many innovations have altered our pattern of living, and many services have been introduced to alter or create new service industries. These include commercial banking, insurance, credit systems (and credit cards), telecommunications, entertainment, office information systems, medical treatment, food distribution, and many more.

These advances were historically attributed to "inspired tinkerers" like Edison and Bell, but the same can be said about entrepreneurs today. The critical point is that entrepreneurs disrupt the status quo, putting economic development and society on a new course. They create new means of production and new systems of services. Today, these inspired tinkerers are well-educated, experienced, and independent thinkers who can transform society through innovation.

NOTES

1. Richard Cantillon, *Essai sur la nature du commerce en général*, translated by H. Higgs (London: Macmillan, 1931), pp. 47–49, 53, and 151–153.
2. Adam Smith, *Inquiry into the Nature and Causes of the Wealth of Nations*, originally printed in Glasgow, Scotland, 1776, reprinted as *The Wealth of Nations* (New York: Random House, 1937), pp. 48–49, 86, 114.
3. Jean Baptiste Say, *A Treatise on Political Economy*, 4th ed., translated by C. R. Prinsep (Philadelphia: Grigg & Elliot, 1845), pp. 99–100, 127, 330–332.
4. Carl Menger, *Principles of Economics*, translated by J. Dingwall and D. F. Hoselitz (Glencoe, IL: Free Press, 1950), pp. 8–14, 56–57.
5. *The Entrepreneurs: An American Adventure*, Film Series Vol. 2 and Academic Supplement (Boston: Enterprise Media, 1987), pp. 4–6.
6. Joseph A. Schumpeter, *The Theory of Economic Development*, translated by R. Opie (Cambridge, MA: Harvard University Press, 1934), pp.42–46, 78–89. Also see Joseph A. Schumpeter, "Economic Theory and Entrepreneurial History," in Hugh G.J. Aitken, ed., *Explorations in Enterprise* (Cambridge, MA: Harvard University Press, 1965), pp. 45–64.
7. Robert D. Hisrich, "Entrepreneurship: Past, Present, and Future," *Journal of Small Business Management*, Vol. 26, No. 4 (1988), pp. 1–4. Also see Karl H. Vesper, *Entrepreneurship Education* (Wellesley, MA: Center for Entrepreneurial Studies, Babson College, 1985).
8. Schumpeter, *Theory of Economic Development*, p. 74.
9. Peter F. Drucker, *Managing for Results* (New York: Harper & Row, 1964), p. 5. Also see Drucker, *Innovation and Entrepreneurship* (New York: Harper & Row, 1985), p. 143.
10. Robert C. Ronstadt, *Entrepreneurship: Text, Cases and Notes* (Dover, MA: Lord, 1984), p. 28.
11. Karl H. Vesper, *New Venture Strategies* (Englewood Cliffs, NJ: Prentice-Hall, 1980), p. 2.
12. John A. Hornaday, "Research about Living Entrepreneurs," in Calvin A. Kent, Donald L. Sexton, and Karl H. Vesper, eds., *Encyclopedia of Entrepreneurship* (Englewood Cliffs, NJ: Prentice-Hall, 1982), pp. 20–34.
13. A. David Silver, *The Entrepreneurial Life: How to Go for It and Get It* (New York: John Wiley and Sons, 1983), p. 26.
14. Albert Shapero and Lisa Sokol, "The Social Dimensions of Entrepreneurship," in Kent, Sexton, and Vesper, eds., *Encyclopedia of Entrepreneurship*, pp. 72–88. Also see Shapero, "Why Entrepreneurship? A Worldwide Perspective," *Journal of Small Business Management*, Vol. 23, No. 4 (1985), pp. 1–6.

15. Gifford Pinchot III, *Intrapreneuring* (New York: Harper & Row, 1985), pp. 1–4.

16. *The State of Small Business: A Report of the President* (Washington, DC: U.S. Small Business Administration, Office of Advocacy, 1989), pp. ii, 1–3. Also see *Handbook of Small Business Data* (Washington, DC: U.S. Small Business Administration, Office of Advocacy, 1988), pp. 6–9.

17. David L. Birch, "Live Fast, Die Young," *Inc.*, August 1988, pp. 23–24.

18. *The Small Business Data Base: A User's Guide* (Washington, DC: U.S. Small Business Administration, Office of Advocacy, 1988). Also see *Handbook of Small Business Data*, pp. 4, 7–8, 11.

19. Donald D. Boroian and Patrick J. Boroian, *The Franchise Advantage* (Schaumburg, IL: National BestSeller Corporation, 1988), pp. 16–20.

20. Hans Schollhammer, "Internal Corporate Entrepreneurship," in Kent, Sexton, and Vesper, eds., *Encyclopedia of Entrepreneurship*, pp. 209–223.

21. Ibid., pp. 211–212.

22. *The Entrepreneurs: An American Adventure* (Boston: Enterprise Media, 1987), Film No. 2 and Academic Supplement, pp. 4–5.

23. "The Greatest Capitalist in History," *Fortune*, August 31, 1987, pp. 14–25.

24. Brenton R. Schlender, "Apple Era behind Him, Steve Jobs Tries Again, Using a New System," *Wall Street Journal*, October 12, 1988, p. A1.

25. John W. Wilson, *The New Venturers: Inside the High-Stakes World of Venture Capital* (Reading, MA: Addison-Wesley, 1985), pp. 111–113.

26. "Biopolymers Come of Age," *High Technology*, June 1987, pp. 12–13.

27. *State of Small Business*, pp. v–vi, 2–4.

28. "The Inc. 100," *Inc.*, May 1987, pp. 32, 37–38.

29. "The Inc. 100," *Inc.*, May 1989, pp. 49–54, 58.

30. "The Inc. 100: Larry Doskocil, Pizza Toppings," *Inc.*, May 1987, pp. 75–76.

31. John A. Welsh and Jerry F. White, "Converging on Characteristics of Entrepreneurs," *Frontiers of Entrepreneurship Research* (1981), pp. 504–510.

32. Jerome A. Katz, "Entry Strategies of the Self-Employed: Individual Level Characteristics and Organizational Outcomes," *Frontiers of Entrepreneurship Research* (1984), pp. 396–399.

33. John J. Kao, *Entrepreneurship, Creativity, & Organization* (Englewood Cliffs, NJ: Prentice-Hall, 1989), pp. xii–xiii.

34. Ronstadt, *Entrepreneurship*, pp. 95–96. Also see Leonard H. Chusimir, "Entrepreneurship and MBA Degrees: How Well Do They Know Each Other?" *Journal of Small Business Management*, Vol. 26, No. 3 (1988), pp. 71–74.

35. Robert D. Hisrich and Candida G. Brush, "Women and Minority Entrepreneurs: A Comparative Analysis," *Frontiers of Entrepreneurship Research, 1985*, pp. 566–574.

36. Robert D. Hisrich and Candida G. Brush, "Women Entrepreneurs: A Longitudinal Study," *Frontiers of Entrepreneurship Research, 1987*, pp. 187–199.

CASE 1-1

Progress Through Innovation

Throughout history, great innovations have periodically occurred to thrust humankind forward with new technologies, new industries, or new economic systems. These innovations were scarce prior to the 1800s, and those that we recognize had profound effects on society. Portuguese navigational instruments, for example, opened the world to rapid colonization, and Scottish steam engines and power looms vaulted us into the industrial age. American technology during the early 20th century created an industrial society founded on engines of growth such as Ford's assembly-line technology, Bell's telephone, and Edison's electric system. In recent years, major innovations in microelectronics have thrust us into the postindustrial information age.

Many other innovations have occurred, but their significance has been forgotten along with most of their inventors. Nevertheless, efforts by a few inspired entrepreneurs have changed society in extraordinary ways. One of those was inventor and entrepreneur Cyrus McCormick, who created a revolution in agriculture with the first mechanical reaper. He invented the reaper in 1831 and unveiled it in the Shenandoah Valley, cutting 6 acres of wheat in less time than a healthy farmer could cut one acre.

The McCormick Reaper replaced the way farmers had harvested grain for more than 2,000 years, and farm productivity was increased more than tenfold. The invention was not, however, a sudden brainstorm. The idea began with McCormick's father, who was determined to find a way to provide more food for America's growing population. He had witnessed starvation in the cities and undernourished children in townships, and the answer, in his mind, was to create a new method of harvesting food grains. Until that time, farmers would sow only what they could reap, and the amount they could reap was limited to what they could cut with a hand sickle or scythe. McCormick's father died with his dream unfulfilled, but young Cyrus pursued the idea. When the first reaper went into production, it created chaos among farmers because those who had a McCormick suddenly outproduced their neighbors by a substantial amount and could market grain at very low prices. The farmer who worked only with a scythe quickly realized that he had to accept the inevitable change and purchase a reaper or lose his farm.

However, during those early days farmers had little money, so McCormick founded International Harvester Corporation, let farmers use the reapers and pay on credit terms, and soon had sales offices in every state and territory in the country. Later, McCormick refined his credit policies and introduced installment sales with low down payments and periodic payments. This innovation in financing may have been as monumental as the invention of the reaper, and although a credit craze did not materialize, many companies such as Kraft and Wells Fargo quickly adopted credit policies. A commercial finance industry evolved several years later to provide equipment loans to manufacturers.

McCormick was an inventor-turned-entrepreneur who recognized the value of marketing, but he also hired the best people he could find with marketing and engineering talent. He encouraged them to think and act independently, and many unusual innovations were made. Prior to the Civil War, for example, the company introduced four-color advertisements and posters; these were the forerunners of billboards. Later, he created brochures to attract customers, and these evolved into mail-out orders that were among the first efforts at direct marketing.

The heart of McCormick's business, however, was his line of International Harvester machinery. During 20 years spanning the reconstruction period following the Civil War, IH introduced more than 200 models of field planting and harvesting equipment. Each item was based on the simple idea that a standard model using interchangeable parts could be produced in large quantities and sold, repaired, and serviced at very low costs. This system made field repairs easy and allowed farmers to replace worn machinery parts. The idea was adopted by Samuel Colt, who used interchangeable parts in his manufacture of firearms, and the Winchester Company quickly followed. Together, their firearms became legends in western folklore.

CASE QUESTIONS

1. Explain McCormick's experience in entrepreneurial terms based on the concepts of Adam Smith and Carl Menger.
2. Cyrus McCormick was responsible for the first mechanical reaper and the critical idea of interchangeable parts; however, the success of McCormick is often attributed to his ability to organize a company with exceptionally talented engineers and marketers who were responsible for most of the firm's innovations. Evaluate this statement in terms of the classic idea of an entrepreneur and the concept of corporate entrepreneurship.
3. Compare McCormick's contributions that led to a revolution in agriculture with Apple Computer's introduction of the microcomputer that revolutionized how we think about information technology.

Source: *The Entrepreneurs: An American Adventure* (Boston: Enterprise Media, 1987), Film No. 2. Also *International Harvester: A History of Invention* (Chicago: International Harvester Corporation, 1964).

CASE 1-2

Luck or Persistence?

When she was 11 years old, Kim Merritt sampled chocolate at a candy store and thought she could do better. She made her own recipe and began selling small candy bars in her home town of Cumberland, Maryland. The effort was much like that of many youngsters who open lemonade stands to earn a few dollars to spend at the movies; however, people began asking her for more. Using meager profits and her mother's kitchen, Kim began making large batches of candy, then designed her own wrappers and developed a commission system for friends who sold chocolates at several schools.

Business was so good that it became an obsession. Kim worked after school, weekends, and holidays, and aside from a brief period when the health department suspended her operations until she could obtain proper permits to cook candy, she made candy by hand until she graduated from high school. At first, she could meet demand without special equipment or sacrificing other activities, but when she provided candy for a school fund-raising event, demand exceeded capacity, and Kim found herself buying professional equipment, hiring helpers, and purchasing bulk supplies.

Looking back, Kim recalls the obsession, the long hours, and the challenge to learn about business. Always on the initiative, Kim set about placing orders with local stores and developing contracts with dozens of schools and civic organizations. Her business, Kim's Khocolates, soon occupied her entire family and closest friends, and she registered the company and set up a chocolate boutique. During her first month, she had 18,000 orders, and before graduating from high school, Kim was distributing specialty chocolates to retail stores in three states.

In 1989, at age 21, Kim repositioned her company as a major distributor of specialty candies and began planning a chain of upscale chocolate shops for the 1990s. The chain would complement her candy manufacturing and distribution system, but it would also mean major changes in her organization. She paused to think about her plans, realizing that to launch a regional or national chain would mean a corporate endeavor. She and her family could not handle all the responsibilities, and the nature of Kim's Khocolates would change. This was not a pleasant thought, although the idea of pursuing a major business was exciting.

Reflecting on her business, Kim realized that she had had fun and made a great deal of money, but many people considered her success no more than the luck of a personable young lady who made good candies and accidentally stumbled into a few good markets. On the other hand, Kim knew that she had worked extremely hard to attract clients. Most of her customers had not been comfortable buying from a young high school student, and she was seldom taken seriously by customers until they had dealt with her for a long time. Winning over her customers had always been a challenge to Kim, not a roadblock, and creating unusual candies had been a joy, not a job.

Thinking about her plans, she was not anxious to become a corporate manager, and although she had always worked well with others, Kim liked the feeling of independence. Running a company would mean sacrificing her autonomy, yet the idea of a chain of stores selling her specialty candies had been a dream for years. At the same time, expansion would mean financial risk, and Kim had always avoided debt; she dealt in cash and had always carefully calculated her expenses to avoid even the slightest loss. She realized that she was at a major crossroad in her young career, and the choice seemed to be whether to follow her dream and expand or to be content with her existing business.

CASE QUESTIONS

1. Identify the entrepreneurial characteristics of Kim Merritt and how they correspond to characteristics described for successful entrepreneurs.
2. Take a position regarding the decision facing Kim whether to expand into a chain of stores. Explain your position in terms of personal objectives you perceive essential to Kim and in terms of her perceived abilities.
3. Based on what you know about Kim and what you believe her characteristics to be, would you say her success was due to luck or persistence? Explain your position, and how luck plays a role in any new venture.

Source: William Tucker, "Campus Capitalists," *Success!* October 1985, pp. 42–49, and personal interview with Kim Merritt, Association of Collegiate Entrepreneurs convention, March 1990.

Chapter 2

Entrepreneurship and Innovation

OBJECTIVES

1. Explain the process of creativity.
2. Describe how innovation is important as a dimension of entrepreneurship.
3. Identify major changes that create opportunities for entrepreneurs.
4. Explain the concepts of "windows" and "corridors" for new ventures.
5. Discuss popular myths of entrepreneurship and why they are more fantasy than fact.
6. Describe the main factors that lead to success for new ventures.

Chapter 1 provided a general overview of entrepreneurship and included examples of entrepreneurs who exemplify free enterprise. We also introduced a working definition of entrepreneurship in terms of contemporary high-growth new ventures. An essential part of that working definition is that entrepreneurs instigate change thereby shifting economic resources away from established endeavors into areas of greater yield and higher productivity. This is the process of *wealth creation* rather than *wealth accumulation*. A crucial dimension of wealth creation and every new venture is *innovation*.

In Chapter 2, we explore innovation and the creative endeavor that leads to entrepreneurship. We also discuss how entrepreneurs develop new ideas and, from their ideas, establish new enterprises that *add value* to society. Peter Drucker gives us the following framework for study:

> Admittedly, all new small businesses have many factors in common. But to be entrepreneurial, an enterprise has to have special characteristics over and above being new

and small. Indeed, entrepreneurs are a minority among new businesses. They create something new, something different; they change or transmute values.[1]

Building on Drucker's viewpoint, we will explore how entrepreneurs create wealth by creating something new or different and how the opportunities arise. We begin with the topic of innovation. Then we shall see how opportunities arise as "source changes" to inspire new ventures. We will also examine characteristics of new ventures and "myths" about entrepreneurship. We conclude the chapter by describing prerequisites for succeeding in new ventures.

CREATIVITY AS A PREREQUISITE TO INNOVATION

The terms *creativity* and *innovation* are often used to mean the same thing, but each has a unique connotation. **Creativity** is "the ability to bring something new into existence."[2] This definition emphasizes the "ability," not the "activity," of bringing something new into existence. A person may therefore conceive of something new and envision how it will be useful, but not necessarily take the necessary action to make it a reality. **Innovation** is the process of doing new things. This distinction is important. Ideas have little value until they are converted into new products, services, or processes. Innovation, therefore, is the transformation of creative ideas into useful applications, but creativity is a prerequisite to innovation.[3]

The Creative Process

Clearly, action by itself has no meaning; it is of little value to simply "do things" without having inspiration and direction. Entrepreneurs need ideas to pursue, and ideas seldom materialize accidentally. Isaac Newton may have been hit on the head by a falling apple, but he discovered gravity through a lifetime of scientific investigation. Ideas usually evolve through a *creative process* whereby imaginative people germinate ideas, nurture them, and develop them successfully. A model of the creative process is shown in Figure 2-1.

Various labels have been applied to stages in the creative process, but most social scientists agree on five stages that we label as *idea germination*, *preparation*, *incubation*, *illumination*, and *verification*. In each stage, a creative individual behaves differently to move an idea from the seed stage of germination to verification, and as we will discuss, behavior varies greatly among individuals and their ideas.[4]

Idea Germination. The germination stage is a *seeding process*. It is not like planting seed as a farmer does to grow corn, but more like the natural seeding that occurs when pollinated flower seeds, scattered by the wind, find fertile ground to take root. Exactly how an idea is germinated is a mystery; it is not something that can be examined under a microscope. However, most creative ideas can be traced to an individual's *interest in* or *curiosity about* a specific problem or area of study.

For example, Alexander Graham Bell had been fascinated with the physics of

```
┌─────────────────┐     ┌─────────────────┐     ┌─────────────────┐
│      Idea       │     │  Preparation:   │     │   Incubation:   │
│   germination:  │     │    Conscious    │     │   Subconscious  │
│   The seeding   │────▶│    search for   │────▶│   assimilation  │
│     stage of    │     │    knowledge    │     │   of information│
│     a new idea  │     │                 │     │                 │
│   Recognition   │     │ Rationalization │     │   Fantasizing   │
└─────────────────┘     └─────────────────┘     └─────────────────┘
                                                         │
        ┌────────────────────────────────────────────────┘
        │
        ▼
┌─────────────────┐     ┌─────────────────┐
│  Illumination:  │     │  Verification:  │
│  Recognition of │     │  Application or │
│  idea as being  │────▶│  test to prove  │
│     feasible    │     │ idea has value  │
│                 │     │                 │
│   Realization   │     │   Validation    │
└─────────────────┘     └─────────────────┘
```

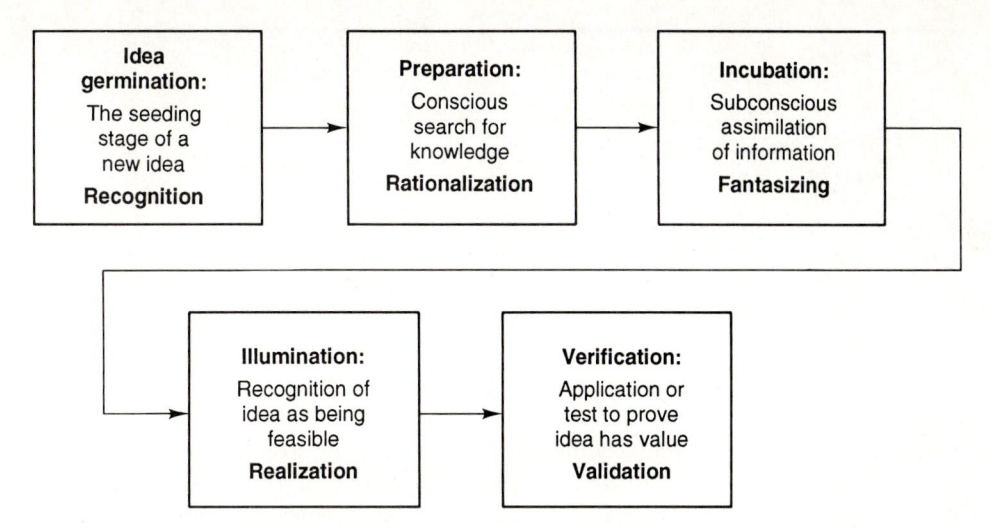

Figure 2-1 **The Creative Process**

sound since childhood. He was influenced to study human hearing systems by his mother, who had a serious hearing problem. As a young adult, Bell taught at a school for the deaf and hearing-impaired, and he set up a laboratory for testing new hearing devices. Many of these devices were awkward mechanical "horns" that amplified sound waves. Bell realized the possibilities of altering sound waves in various types of materials such as steel wire during the 1870s, and he experimented for several years with magnetic devices in an effort to produce a hearing aid. In 1875, his lab assistant, Thomas A. Watson, accidentally clamped a magnetized steel reed too tightly to a magnet, and when he plucked at it, the reed came loose with a "twang" that echoed, sending a signal along a wire to Bell's magnet receiver. Bell heard the twang and recognized that an electrical signal had replicated the vibration caused by Watson's steel reed. At that instant, the harmonic hearing aid became a feasible idea, but exactly when Bell conceived of a harmonic telegraph (telephone) is unknown. It was several years before he turned his attention to commercial communications.[5]

Bell's "idea" for a hearing aid was evidently seeded years before he invented the telephone, and it evolved through his interest in helping others. He had already spent years studying the physics of sound and experimenting with sound-transmitting materials so that his mind was "fertile" and open to the opportunities for harmonic telegraphy. For most entrepreneurs, ideas begin with *interest* in a subject or *curiosity* about finding a solution to a particular problem. More recently, Nolan Bushnell founded Atari and the video game industry by trying to create a way to use microelectronic circuitry to convert home television sets into interactive media.[6]

Preparation. Once a seed of curiosity has taken form as a focused idea, creative people embark on a conscious search for answers. If it is a problem they are trying to solve—such as Bell's determination to help those with impaired hearing—then

PROFILE △

Nolan Bushnell

In 1972, Nolan Bushnell, an electronics engineer with a passion for mind-teasing games, launched a $20 billion industry with Atari Corporation. His first video game was a version of Ping-Pong, but it was Pac Man that institutionalized video games and created a world market for new games, T-shirts, toys, pop songs, and, later, movies based on video war games. By 1982 more than 400,000 Pac Man machines on three continents had generated 7 billion coin-operated plays. The company that Bushnell started using toy parts and scrapped electronics in his daughter's bedroom was sold to Warner Communications in 1976 for $28 million. Although Atari has had a roller-coaster history, Bushnell has gone on to found new enterprises, including Pizza Time Theater, a restaurant chain; Catalyst Technologies, a company designed to help other entrepreneurs start business ventures; and Axlon Corporation, a research company engaged in robotics.

Source: An unpublished profile of Nolan Bushnell at the founding meeting of the Hong Kong Venture Capitalist's Association, 1988.

---

they begin an intellectual journey, seeking information about the problem and how others have tried to resolve it. If it is an idea for a new product or service, the business equivalent is market research. Inventors will set up laboratory experiments, designers will begin engineering new product ideas, and marketers will study consumer buying habits. Any individual with an idea will consequently think about it, concentrating his or her energies on rational extensions of the idea and how it might become a reality. In rare instances, the preparation stage will produce results. More often, conscious deliberation will only overload the mind, but the effort is important in order to gather information and knowledge vital to an eventual solution.

Incubation. Individuals sometimes concentrate intensely on an idea, but, more often, they simply allow ideas time to grow without intentional effort. We all have heard about the brilliant, sudden "flashes" of genius—or more precisely, we have developed fables about them—but few great ideas come from thunderbolts of insight. Most evolve in the minds of creative people while they go about other activities. The idea, once seeded and given substance through preparation, is put on a back burner; the subconscious mind is allowed time to assimilate information.

In Alexander Graham Bell's example, research on harmonic sound transmission occupied a small percentage of his time during a two-decade period. Perhaps the incubation period for the telephone could be expressed as a three-decade, on-again-off-again fascination with human hearing problems. Art Fry, the 3M engineer who invented Post-it Notes, first thought of semi-sticky paper six years earlier when, as a church choir director, he wanted to have page markers for hymn books that would neither damage the books nor slip out easily. He worked on the idea during his spare time at 3M without success, forgot about it for nearly a year, then tried making a new adhesive for the paper, once again forgot about the project for some time, and eventually envisioned a pad of small hymn notes with tear-off edges impregnated with a nonpermanent gum.[7]

Incubation is a stage of "mulling it over" while the subconscious intellect assumes control of the creative process. This is a crucial aspect of creativity because when we consciously focus on a problem, we behave rationally to attempt to find systematic resolutions. When we rely on subconscious processes, our minds are untrammeled by the limitations of human logic. The subconscious mind is allowed to wander and to pursue fantasies, and it is therefore open to unusual information and knowledge that we cannot assimilate in a conscious state. This subconscious process has been called the art of *synectics*, a word coined by W.J.J. Gordon in 1961.[8] **Synectics,** derived from Greek, means a joining together of different and often unrelated ideas. Therefore, when a person has consciously worked to resolve a problem without success, allowing it to incubate in the subconscious will often lead to a resolution.

Illumination. The fourth stage, illumination, occurs when the idea resurfaces as a realistic creation. There will be a moment in time when the individual can say, "Oh, I see!" Bell heard the twang of the steel reed, Fleming watched his penicillin attack infectious bacteria under a microscope, and Art Fry envisioned his gum-lined note pads in use. The fable of the thunderbolt is captured in this moment of illumination—even though the often long and frustrating years of preparation and incubation have been forgotten.

Illumination may be triggered by an opportune incident, as Bell discovered harmonic telegraphy in the accidental twang created by Watson. But there is little doubt that Bell would have had his moment of illumination, triggered perhaps by another incident or simply manifested through hard work. The point, of course, is that he was prepared and the idea was incubated. Bell was ready for an opportune incident and able to recognize its importance when it occurred.

The important point is that most creative people go through many cycles of preparation and incubation, searching for that incident as a catalyst to give their idea full meaning. When a cycle of creative behavior does not result in a catalytic event, the cycle is repeated until the idea blossoms or dies. This stage is critical for entrepreneurs because ideas, by themselves, have little meaning. Reaching the illumination stage separates daydreamers and tinkerers from creative people who find a way to transmute value.

Verification. An idea once illuminated in the mind of an individual still has little meaning until verified as realistic and useful. Bell understood what the twanging steel reed meant, yet he still had years of work ahead to translate this knowledge into a commercial telephone system.

Entrepreneurial effort is essential to translate an illuminated idea into a verified, realistic, and useful application. **Verification** is the development stage of refining knowledge into application. This is often tedious and requires perseverance by an individual committed to finding a way to "harvest" the practical results of his or her creation. During this stage, many ideas fall by the wayside as they prove to be impossible or to have little value. More often, a good idea has already been developed, or the aspiring entrepreneur finds that competitors already exist. Inventors quite often come to this harsh conclusion when they seek to patent their products only to discover similar inventions registered.

▶ **CHECKPOINT**

Define creativity and distinguish it from innovation.

Identify the five stages of creativity and explain why each is important to the creativity process.

INNOVATION AND ENTREPRENEURSHIP

If creativity is the seed that inspires entrepreneurship, innovation is the process of entrepreneurship. This was Schumpeter's conclusion when he wrote about the economic foundations of free enterprise and entrepreneurship, points that we discussed in Chapter 1. Drucker agrees and elaborates: "Innovation . . . is the means by which the entrepreneur either creates new wealth-producing resources or endows existing resources with enhanced potential for creating wealth."[9]

Earlier, we defined innovation as the process of doing new things. It is important to recognize that innovation implies *action*, not just conceiving new ideas. When people have passed through the illumination and verification stages of creativity, they may have become inventors, but they are not yet innovators. The difference between invention and innovation is shown in Figure 2-2.

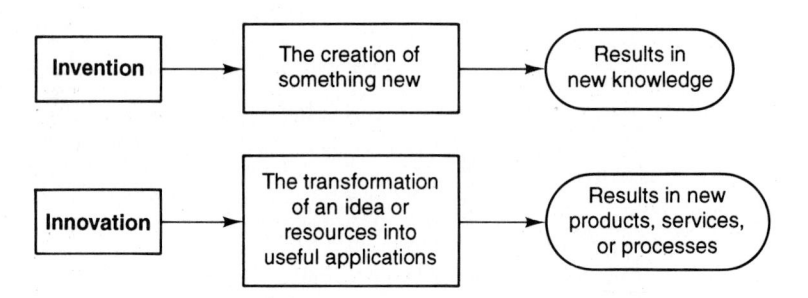

Figure 2-2 **Invention versus Innovation**

Chapter 2 Entrepreneurship and Innovation

```
┌─── Translation of creative idea into a useful application ───┐
↓                                                               ↓
┌──────────┐    ┌──────────┐    ┌──────────────┐    ┌──────────┐
│Analytical│ →  │Organizing│ →  │Implementation│ →  │Commercial│
│ planning │    │resources │    │              │    │application│
└──────────┘    └──────────┘    └──────────────┘    └──────────┘
```

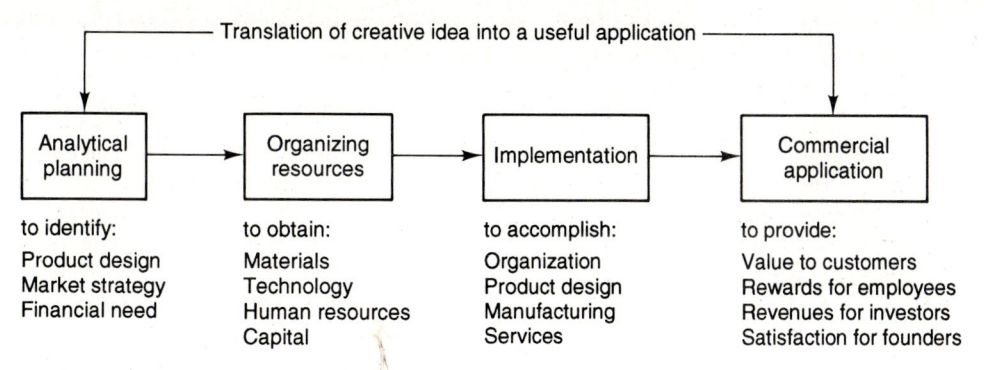

to identify:	to obtain:	to accomplish:	to provide:
Product design	Materials	Organization	Value to customers
Market strategy	Technology	Product design	Rewards for employees
Financial need	Human resources	Manufacturing	Revenues for investors
	Capital	Services	Satisfaction for founders

Figure 2-3 **Elements in the Innovation Process**

Inventors are not limited to those who create new products. They include those who identify new technological processes, new forms of plant life, and new designs. Each of these, incidentally, can lead to new patents, as we shall discuss in a later chapter. Inventors usually are stereotyped as people who deal with "things," such as new products, but most inventions have dealt with new processes or new technical knowledge. Our examples of Bell's harmonic sound transmission and Edison's electric power system illustrate the point, and many new products (and entire industries) were founded on their ideas.

Nevertheless, for an idea to have value, it must be proven useful or be marketable, and to achieve either status, the idea must be developed. Innovation is the development process, as shown in Figure 2-3. It is the translation of an idea into an application. It requires persistence in analytically working out the details of product design or service, to develop marketing, obtain finances, and plan operations. If the entrepreneur is going to manufacture a product, the process includes obtaining materials and technical manufacturing capabilities, staffing operations, and establishing an organization.

Using Left-Brain Skills to Harvest Right-Brain Ideas

Creativity was partially explained as a nonrational process of incubating ideas, allowing the subconscious mind to wander and to pursue fantasies. More precisely, half the subconscious mind is working to wander intuitively through nonrational territory. Substantial research has shown that the human brain has two distinct hemispheres. One, the *right hemisphere*, is the creative side where spatial relationships are developed, intuition prevails, and nonverbal imagining influences one's behavior. The other, the *left hemisphere*, is the analytical side where abstract thoughts and concepts may be formulated, but only through logical and rational processes.[10]

Exhibit 2-1 lists attributes of both hemispheres together with types of managerial activities often associated with skills in each area. Psychologists suggest that most people tend to have a dominant orientation, either to the left side (prone to rational, analytic behavior) or to the right side (prone to creative, intuitive behavior). Indeed,

Exhibit 2-1 Left-Brain, Right-Brain Attributes

Left Hemisphere	Right Hemisphere
Conscious—Aware and focused on specific problem	Unconscious—Unaware and unfocused on specific issues
Rational—Conscious modeling of issues; linearity	Nonrational—Spacial imagining without direction
Analytical—Use of knowledge in descrete applications to evaluate issues	Intuitive—Total experiences and emotions allowed to influence one's ideas
Logical—Deductive reasoning to establish relationships	Synthesizing—Illogical reasoning and fantasizing to create analogies

Source: Jacquelyn Wonder and Priscilla Donovan, *Whole-Brain Thinking* (New York: Morrow, 1984), pp. 60–61. Also Terence Hines, "Left Brain/Right Brain Mythology and Implications for Management and Training," *Academy of Management Review*, Vol. 12, No. 4 (1987), pp. 600–606.

many cultures encourage skills and values that bias human development toward one of these hemispheres. Japan, for example, has been singled out as more left-brain orientated than the United States. The implication is that Japanese youngsters are taught to sharpen their analytical skills and subsequently are rewarded for their technical expertise, but they are not necessarily encouraged to become adept at creative, abstract thinking. In contrast, American youngsters are rewarded for independent thought and abstract, nonrational synthesizing of information. There is, however, no consensus that people can, or should, be taught left- or right-brain skills.[11]

From an entrepreneurial perspective, the right-brain skills are crucial for the vision necessary to be creative, but innovation does not occur until left-brain rationalization takes place. Integrating predispositions from both hemispheres is the critical behavior needed to be a successful innovator, to use left-brain rationality to "harvest" right-brain creativity. Unfortunately, many individuals are only gifted at one or the other. They may be logical and practical, and in the process, be efficient managers, but without some degree of inspired fantasizing, they may be paralyzed by their own analytical behavior. On the other hand, the "inspired tinkerer" may bask in the purity of artistic oblivion without the necessary ability to convert dreams into reality. This dichotomous behavior has been called Janusian thinking. (Janus was a mythological god with two faces looking simultaneously into the future and the past.) To be innovative, the entrepreneur must resolve this dilemma.[12]

Technological Innovation

The battle between rational, left-brain behavior, and creative, right-brain behavior, is a common problem for technological innovation. Because innovation is often explained in technical terms—tangible products or processes that result from technological development—there has been a preoccupation with rational, analytical in-

Chapter 2   Entrepreneurship and Innovation

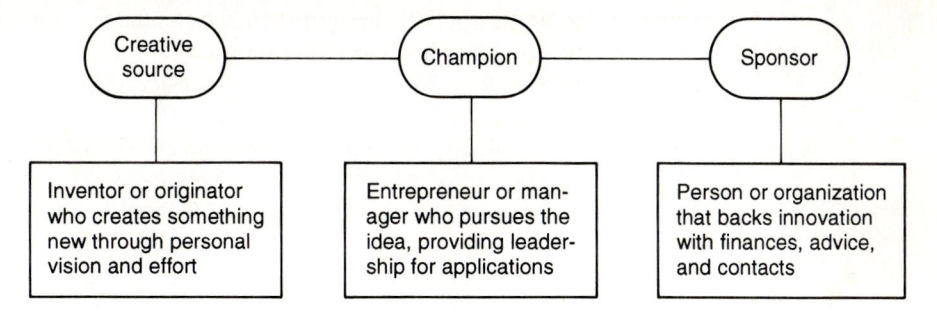

```
          Creative              Champion              Sponsor
          source
             |                     |                     |
  ┌──────────────────┐   ┌──────────────────┐   ┌──────────────────┐
  │ Inventor or      │   │ Entrepreneur or  │   │ Person or        │
  │ originator who   │   │ manager who      │   │ organization     │
  │ creates something│   │ pursues the idea,│   │ that backs       │
  │ new through      │   │ providing leader-│   │ innovation with  │
  │ personal vision  │   │ ship for         │   │ finances, advice,│
  │ and effort       │   │ applications     │   │ and contacts     │
  └──────────────────┘   └──────────────────┘   └──────────────────┘
```

Figure 2-4   **Key People in Technological Innovation**

novation models. A general model of technological innovation is shown in Figure 2-3. However, a number of industrial studies reveal that for a technological innovation to succeed, there are three important people involved and seven important conditions to satisfy. The combination of these people and conditions satisfies the need for creativity and implementation. The three key people are the creative source, the champion, and the sponsor. Their roles are identified in Figure 2-4 and explained as follows:[13]

> *Creative source:* The inventor or originator of the idea that led to the knowledge or vision of something new; the artist of creative endeavor.
> *Champion:* The entrepreneur or manager who pursues the idea, planning its application, acquiring resources, and establishing its markets through persistence, planning, organizing, and leadership.
> *Sponsor:* The person or organization that makes possible the champion's activities and the inventor's dreams through support, including finances, contacts, and advice.

The creative source is an individual; organizations do not create ideas or incubate fantasies. The champion is also an individual—perhaps the creative source, or an entrepreneur who joins with the inventor, or a corporate manager who has the insight to help pursue a creative idea. The sponsor may be an investor (such as a venture capitalist, described in Chapter 13), or an organization, such as 3M, where corporate resources are allocated to innovative projects and their champions.

The seven conditions required for success in technological innovation are related partially to the success of the three key people involved and partially to the environment in which innovation takes place. Although these conditions were derived from corporate studies in research and development, they apply equally to new entrepreneurial ventures, and they include the following:[14]

1. An outstanding person in an executive leadership position to support strategic decisions that encourage creativity and innovation development.
2. An operational leader to carry out the essential tasks of converting knowledge into a commercial application.

3. A clear need for the application by sufficient potential consumers to warrant the commitment of resources to the innovation.
4. The realization of the product, process, or service as a useful innovation providing value to society.
5. Good cooperation among the crucial players and among diversified functions in an organization, all of whom, together, must bring the idea to fruition.
6. Availability of resources and the supporting technology to succeed in the endeavor.
7. Cooperation and support from external sources who can influence the success of an innovation, including government agencies, investors, vendors, suppliers, and creditors.

These seven conditions and the three major players are illustrated in an extraordinary new development in quantum mechanics. Research is being conducted at Spectra Diode Laboratories in California to develop the manufacturing process and applications for a semiconductor laser no larger than a child's thumb.[15] This tiny laser is a thousand times more powerful than anything commercially available in semiconductors. The "creative genius" of quantum physics (the science that made possible innovations in atomic energy and semiconductor electronics) was Albert Einstein.

A number of "champions" in several industries have taken Einstein's creative genius to practical applications, but at Spectra Diode Labs, it is CEO Donald Scifres who is leading the way into semiconductor lasers. The "sponsor" is Xerox Corporation, a joint-venture underwriter of the laser project that provides financial resources and technological knowledge of semiconductor applications markets.

The seven conditions are partially accounted for by the leadership of Scifres, the sponsorship of Xerox, and the collective assimilation of knowledge during the past half century in quantum physics, semiconductor electronics, and computer applications. Still, the tiny laser is no more than a laboratory model because, to date, several conditions for successful innovation remain unsolved. First, the manufacturing technology (process methodology) to produce the lasers does not exist. The lasers require microscopic parts, called quantum wells, that are so small that a million of them would fit onto a pinhead. Second, the lasers must be proved in applications such as replacements for computer chips. In working models, this step has been accomplished—and one laser only $\frac{1}{100}$ the size of a conventional computer chip would quadruple chip performance at one-quarter the power required now. Unfortunately, without cost-effective mass-production technology, the laser is not yet applicable, and consequently, there is no immediate market for it.

Beyond the world of high-tech innovation, entrepreneurs take up the creative challenge of new ideas daily. Many of those innovations we take for granted as we enter the 1990s, but half of all our existing technological applications did not exist two decades ago. This applies equally to products, such as microcomputers; process technologies, such as synthetic fabrics; and services, such as bank credit cards.[16]

In each instance of innovation, there has been an entrepreneurial champion who persisted in developing a creative idea into a marketable application. In each instance,

Chapter 2 Entrepreneurship and Innovation

the entrepreneur has been able to recognize *change*, envision the *opportunities*, and harvest right-brain inspiration through left-brain hard work.

> ▶ **CHECKPOINT**
>
> Explain ''innovation'' and distinguish it from invention.
>
> Describe the concept of right- and left-brain processes.
>
> Identify and describe the three key roles and seven conditions important for technological innovation.

OPPORTUNITIES THROUGH CHANGE

Entrepreneurs tend to be ''strategic thinkers'' who recognize changes and see opportunities where others do not. By creating new ventures based on these strategic changes, entrepreneurs make a contribution and are rewarded in terms of wealth and personal satisfaction. Entrepreneurship is therefore the result of inspired strategy to exploit change, but first ''change'' has to be recognized. In the next few passages, major sources of change are examined together with examples of how entrepreneurs turned these changes into opportunities.

Scientific Knowledge

The history of the Nobel Prize is replete with examples of new scientific knowledge, and our concept of entrepreneurship is stereotyped as a process of commercializing new inventions. Without a doubt, ''scientific knowledge'' has been at the heart of many new enterprises, and we can see how important it is by tracing the development of computers.

Charles Babbage created a mechanical calculating machine more than a century ago; it was the forerunner of mechanized adding machines. Babbage is mentioned historically as contributing to the concept of a computer because he helped revolutionize numerical manipulation. Herman Hollerith used the binary system to create the first punch card in 1890, but this was to be significant only a half century later. Howard Aiken of Harvard University teamed up with IBM and the U.S. War Department in 1944 to create the first ''automatic calculator,'' and although it was only an electromechanical switching system, his work led to an electronic computer developed at the University of Pennsylvania by J. Presper Eckert and John W. Mauchly. It was not until 1951, however, that a commercial electronic computer was sold to the U.S. Census Bureau by Eckert and Mauchly as the *UNIVAC I*.[17] This early progression of events is shown in Figure 2-5.

That brief history of computers is interesting because the only scientists to exploit their inventions were Eckert and Mauchly of Univac. Meanwhile, hundreds

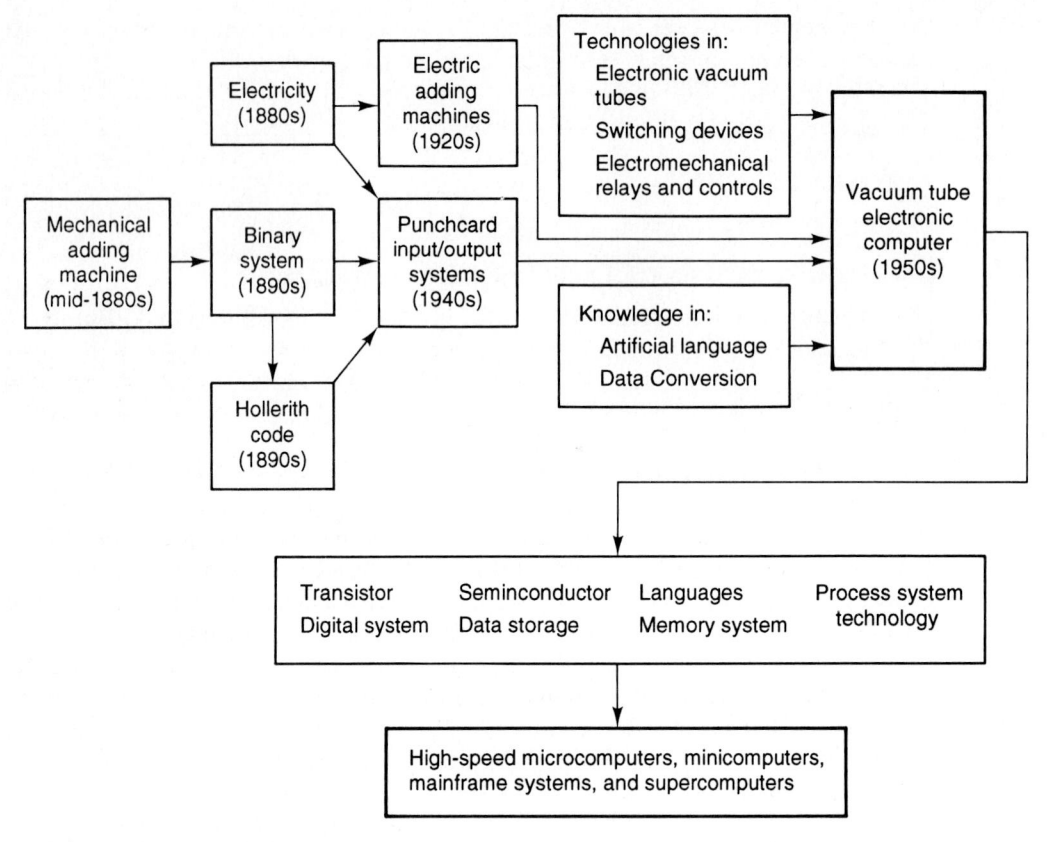

Figure 2-5 **Evolution of the Electronic Computer**

of companies evolved from these pioneer efforts. Burroughs, NCR, and IBM emerged through efforts by their founders, who recognized the commercial value of scientific changes and developed products around early technological advances. The contemporary history of computing includes literally thousands of scientific innovations, each one making computers better, faster, more accurate, easier to use, and less expensive.

William Shockley won his Nobel Prize while at Bell Labs for creating solid-state electronics and the transistor. Shockley left Bell Labs with a group of young engineers to form his own electronics company, but it was Robert N. Noyce, one of those young engineers, who set the pace as the archetypal modern entrepreneur. Noyce left Shockley, cofounded Fairchild Semiconductor, then moved on to found Intel Corporation. Noyce transformed scientific knowledge of the "silicon" technology into an industry and became known as the "Moses of Silicon Valley," where he established Fairchild and Intel, and he is credited with being the father of integrated circuitry. Noyce provided the inspiration to exploit knowledge. He was the change master who gave *strategic* direction to the microelectronics industry.[18]

Process Innovations

Closely associated with new scientific knowledge is the implementation processes, techniques, and methods essential to make knowledge useful. As noted in Chapter 1, Edison's light bulb was only a curiosity until he developed an electric system for supplying power to consumers. Early computers had little value until operating systems and data storage techniques were developed. In fact, computers had only limited value until symbolic languages were created to encode, manipulate, and store data. Because it developed and controlled the *processes* needed to make computers useful, IBM came to dominate a hardware computer industry. During the late 1950s, when virtually every major company making electrical apparatus and communication equipment was also making computer hardware, IBM was relatively unknown, but IBM technicians created symbolic languages in FORTRAN and COBOL, subsequently setting the industry standards.[19]

This pattern of entrepreneurial activity has been repeated often. Steven Jobs and Stephen Wozniak were largely successful establishing Apple Computer because of their proprietary *software processes*. William Gates III founded Microsoft Corporation and set industry standards in MS-DOS operating systems to coincide with the introduction of the IBM PC in 1981. Gates had been out of high school only five years when he and a companion launched their trend-setting venture.

There are literally thousands of examples of entrepreneurs who have recognized opportunities and transformed knowledge into commercial value. For example, typesetting had not changed since Gutenberg's time when, in 1885, Ottmar Mergenthaler developed the linotype machine. The linotype was an inspiration based on growth in publishing and a demand for timely news. The process of typesetting was archaic prior to the linotype, but with its development, there was the technical *method* needed to establish a nationwide industry of daily newspapers.[20] Today, word processors coupled with desk-top publishing systems enable even small businesses to create professional-quality documents. Each of these innovations has precipitated hundreds of new ventures that provide, for example, desk-top software, data storage systems, and publishing supplies.

Industrial Changes

There is little doubt that eventually power sources will be based on solar devices. Safe nuclear systems are also on the horizon. Meanwhile, energy is based on fossil fuels with some alternatives such as hydroelectric and geothermal power, but *someone, someday* will instigate the transition, and the switch will be turned off on fossil fuels. Petroleum replaced whale oil as an important fuel a century ago when Rockefeller built a refining and distribution system capable of making crude oil usable. An energy revolution happened again with Edison's electric generating system. It may happen again with solar power, and many entrepreneurs will be involved. Figure 2-6 illustrates this transition.

Industrial change can occur through natural events, such as the discovery of oil, or as a result of human events. For example, the recent deregulation of the airline

PROFILE △

William Gates III

At 34, William Gates III became the youngest individual billionaire in the world in 1989. He taught himself computer programming at the age of 13, dropped out of Harvard at 19 to start Microsoft Corporation, and at 31 took his company public, cracking the billion-dollar mark for his personal net assets. Microsoft is the power behind MS-DOS computer-operating systems, dozens of software applications, and innovative computer systems technology.

Source: Julianne Slovak, "The Billionaires," *Fortune*, September 11, 1989, p.66; also Microsoft, *Annual Report to Stockholders* (Seattle: Microsoft Computer Systems, 1989).

---

industry forced dozens of major airlines to compete with regional "upstarts" and commuter airlines. Competitors introduced innovations in flights, new fares, travel plans, and new services. People Express, Presidential Airlines, New York Air, USAir, and many others jolted the industry during the 1980s with low-priced fares, no-frills service, and innovations in ticketing, baggage handling, and convenient routing. Some of these have not survived, but others such as Texas International have grown rapidly to be among industry leaders.[21]

A similar pattern of change occurred in postal services that provided unexpected opportunities for UPS, Federal Express, and dozens of regional courier services to

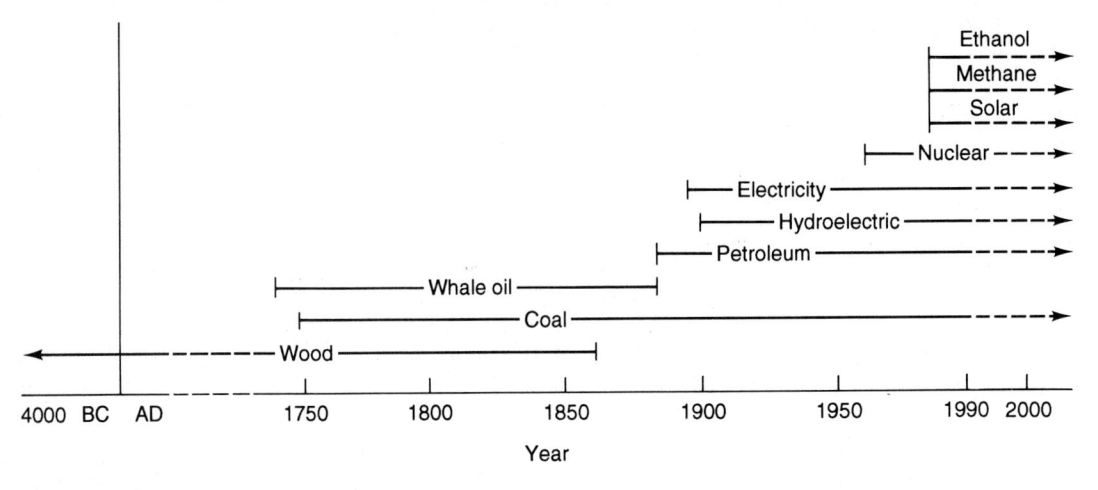

Figure 2-6 **Major Shifts in Industrial Energy**

establish growth ventures in parcel delivery systems. The breakup of AT&T is yet another incident that created opportunities for competition in long-distance telephone services exploited by MCI and US Sprint. New telephone systems have evolved in dozens of regions, and there have been hundreds of new businesses sprouting from the fringes of the AT&T change. New telephone repair services, PBX systems, telecommunications firms, phone leasing companies, and pay phone franchises are among the many examples.

These opportunities occur often because every industry is fragile and subject to sudden change. New laws, the dissolution of old laws, economic influences, social changes, and new technologies are all threats to industrial stability, providing in their wake ample opportunities for entrepreneurs.

Market Changes

Closely associated with industrial changes are those that take place in markets. Historically, we look at the success of Henry Ford when he developed an inexpensive automobile. Until his Model T, most automobiles were luxuries. He recognized the demand and decided that a car built on simple principles would revolutionize the automobile industry. Domino's Pizza was built on the single, important observation that a lot of people ordered pizza to take out. John H. Johnson, the founder of *Ebony* magazine, recognized a neglected segment of American readership, the black American. During World War II, Johnson launched *Negro Digest*, and today he heads a publishing empire with subsidiaries in cosmetics, fashions, perfumes, and entertainment that is the largest black-owned corporation in the United States.

An extraordinary change is taking place now as government services are being *privatized*.[22] The government has long been a major market, particularly for federal programs such as defense, and on state and local levels, government agencies dole out hundreds of millions of dollars to private contractors for everything from cleaning services to construction projects. An important trend emerged during the late 1980s as government agencies began to rapidly endorse privatization. This is the process of turning over to private contractors activities once controlled through government agencies. Government has become a more active consumer and a less active employer. Governmental agencies in Washington are contracting lawn services rather than employing maintenance personnel to do these jobs. Trash collection, rapid transit systems, government document printing, road repair services, security systems, training services, and public utilities are "going private" at an accelerated pace.

Market changes have also had a tremendous effect on education. For the 200-year period prior to World War II, the university system was a market reserved for the upper-class consumer. During a brief but active period just prior to World War II, government sponsored a nationwide movement to expand land-grant colleges. These also served the upper class through a number of limited and specialized programs, but after World War II the American university system became a middle-class market with diversified programs. Metropolitan universities and private institutions grew at a tremendous rate, including such entrants as Pace University, the New York Institute of Technology, Northeastern, and Santa Clara. State systems modified their missions and actively sought the middle-class student. University systems in Wisconsin, New York, and California joined this trend, and with extensive tuition-aid programs, education is now attempting to reach everyone. Entrepreneurs have been an integral part of this change, creating new educational tools, textbook publishing empires, and innovative student services. They have cultivated sporting events and sports-related enterprises, and today entrepreneurs help students compete for limited university spots through programs such as SAT preparation courses, home study courses, and data base search systems that identify scholarship opportunities.

Demographic Changes

Demographic data are concerned with population trends, age, sex, and ethnic characteristics, educational status, and income of a nation's population. As a nation's demographics change, new opportunities to serve human needs arise. By tracking these changes, entrepreneurs can identify opportunities and react to them. Population statistics are well documented by the U.S. Census Bureau, by state and local authorities, and by an enormous number of sociological studies. The composition of human resources is closely tracked to document career behavior, family structures, emigration and immigration, life expectancies, birth rates, and on and on. The data are widely distributed through government publications at all levels, through Chambers of Commerce, and virtually every public library in the United States. An example is illustrated in Figure 2-7.

This information can be exceptionally useful. For example, assume a shrinking family size with, on average, about two children per household born to women with careers who wait several years to bear children. This pattern suggests a trend toward

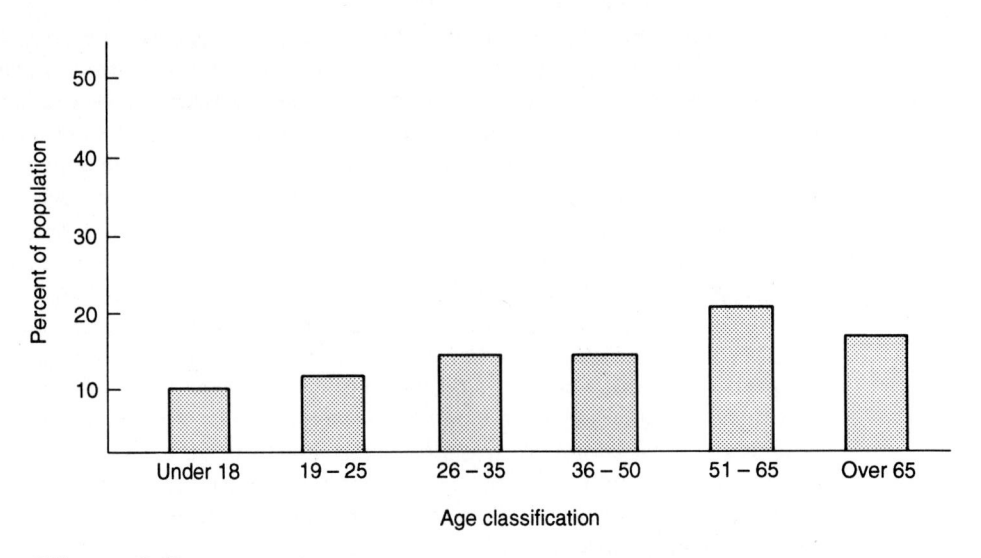

Figure 2-7 **Projected Distribution of U.S. Population in 2000**

smaller housing units, better access to child care for dual-career families, and eating patterns that imply convenience-type foods. Much more can be read into that scenario.

At the other end of the life spectrum, more older people exist and are living longer. They are also retiring earlier, spending more of their improved retirement incomes, demanding more recreational opportunities, and traveling more. We tend to stereotype "the elderly" as retired persons who settle into retirement homes, but this view is fallacious. The retirement years span nearly two decades of life, from the early 60s to the late 70s; lumping the "elderly" together under one umbrella would be like calling all individuals under the age of 21 "children." There are many subtle changes in demand for products and services among more refined stages of retirement. For example, as individuals near retirement, they are at the pinnacle of their careers, and planning for retirement opens opportunities for preretirement counseling, benefit planning, and estate management. Many retirees also seek alternative work, and a question comes to mind: Who provides employment search services for these persons?

Abrupt changes also take place in the composition of populations, such as the periodic thrusts of immigration that have brought significant numbers of Europeans and Asians to the United States. During the 1800s, potato famines brought waves of Irish, and the Chinese arrived in shiploads as the West Coast developed. During the early 1900s, large numbers of Russians and Germans arrived. After World War II, many European Jews came to America. Southeast Asians came in the wake of the Vietnam war. Today, more and more Mexican workers are finding their way into the Southwest. Latin American nations have experienced chronic poverty and periodic revolutions, landing Cubans in Florida, Haitians on the Gulf Coast, and Puerto Ricans in New York. In each instance, sudden bursts of new needs exist for language instruction, specialty foods, bilingual schools, entertainment, exchange banks, housing, and many other services.

The eminent financier J. P. Morgan had a gift of being able to recognize social and cultural shifts, and at the turn of the century he took advantage of these changes to build an extraordinary financial empire.[23] When Morgan was still in his 20s, the House of Rothschild was the dominant banking empire in Europe. The Rothschilds were financiers for the world powers, but it was J. P. Morgan who recognized the transatlantic migration and the tremendous need to provide financial services to these individuals and to underwrite industries that would employ them. Unlike the Rothschilds and most other financiers who served only the wealthy, Morgan served the blue-collar worker who transformed the United States into an industrial nation. He financed Alexander Graham Bell's telephone and helped create the first telephone company in the United States, underwrote Andrew Carnegie (and eventually bought Carnegie's steel mills, renaming the company U.S. Steel), conceived of, and pushed to implement, the Federal Reserve System, financed transcontinental railroads, and set up several immigrant banks.

Aside from these dazzling changes, shifts in population and the structure and composition of that population are continuous and easy to identify. For example, the demand for kindergarten facilities next year (or in four years) is established. The children who will be ready for kindergarten next year were born four years ago; they exist and can be counted accurately. Entering college freshmen candidates for next year are known; they are high school seniors with qualifying grades. We can forecast with accuracy the number of people who will become doctors in the next few years, attain law degrees, start families, retire, and die. We know a lot about a lot of people.

Entrepreneurial opportunities occur whenever a gap exists in services or products for groups of individuals moving into new stages of life cycles, for groups coming into American society, for changes in families, careers, and incomes, and for "systems of needs" that arise from demographic shifts such as those addressed by J. P. Morgan. These opportunities may be on a grand scale, such as new banking systems, or localized, such as new housing construction.

Social and Cultural Changes

Social changes occurred at a snail's pace until the late 18th century. The pace quickened a bit during the 19th century, but as we look back over the 20th century, social changes reached an unprecedented quick pace. There is no evidence of a slowdown as we ready ourselves for the 21st century.

Think of the great historic eras. The Egyptian social order changed little during the 2,000 years preceding the Roman Empire. Rome revolutionized the known world with written language, transportation systems, administration processes, and legal systems. It remained dominant as a military and ruling power for about 500 years. Then the western world entered a thousand-year lull, the medieval era, a time when hundreds of small principalities, city-states, and feudal kingdoms slowly evolved into nations. Very few societies advanced beyond the Roman foundations that preceded them; few innovations occurred in any fashion. The Renaissance was a blossoming of youth, the beginning of modern nations, architecture, mercantilism, education, arts, and the recognition of common "cultures" among peoples with similar ethnic, regional, or religious characteristics.

The industrial revolution stimulated changes in how people lived, worked, spent their money, recreated, and worshiped. Men began working for wages rather than as farmers or in government service. Sailors became merchantmen. Craftsmen moved out of their shops and into factories. Adventurers put aside swords for plows and settled new worlds. These social changes brought new demands that inspired a faster rate of change in innovation. For example, while roads had been made of sand and stone for several thousand years, "industrial city traffic" (although limited to carts, wagons, and buggies) required sturdier materials. Macadam (a material fashioned from coal slag and oil that we know as blacktop) was developed in Scotland. The bicycle, also Scottish in origin, became a useful mode of transportation rather than a curiosity. "Systems" that we take entirely for granted now were major changes made to accommodate growing cities and industrial towns. Sewers, water systems, waste collection, police services, fire brigades, and schools began to evolve during the 19th century. Nevertheless, these thousands of years of innovation are more than matched by innovations that have occurred during the past 20 years. Nearly 70 percent of all scientists and engineers who ever lived were alive in 1980, and about 92 percent of all known technology was discovered or invented during the 20th century; half of that figure and a majority of the living scientists emerged after World War II.[24]

This recent onslaught of innovation could not have happened without commensurate demand for products and services, and this demand has often resulted from social and cultural changes. The demand for timely and accurate information still outraces scientific efforts to provide telecommunications and computer applications. Mass transit systems are at best cumbersome alternatives to fender-bending traffic jams, and we have not yet devised a solution to crowded highways.

In practical terms, many entrepreneurs have found opportunities in such social changes as the increased numbers of dual-career families and working professional women. These changes opened doors for entrepreneurs to create new fashions, to develop educational seminars for career women, and to establish counseling centers for working wives, but entrepreneurs never seem to keep pace with change. Future problems yet unknown will certainly surface to propel the challenge.

▶ **CHECKPOINT**

Describe technological changes that lead to new products and those that lead to new processes.

Explain how economic and legal changes can occur to create new opportunities for industry.

Describe opportunities that arise from social, cultural, and demographic changes.

WINDOWS AND CORRIDORS

A **window** is a time horizon during which opportunities exist before something else happens to eliminate them. A unique opportunity, once shown to produce wealth, will attract competitors, and if the business is easy to enter, the industry will become rapidly saturated. Bicycles did not become viable commercial products until people needed them as transportation. When that need occurred, hundreds of bicycle manufacturers rushed to take advantage of the "window of opportunity." Literally every successful product and service has had an optimal period of time for commercialization. Those introduced too early have usually failed, and those introduced too late suffered from crowded markets.

A brief period of opportunity opened for electronic spreadsheets when microcomputers hit the fast growth curve. Several entrepreneurs entered the market with good spreadsheet products. The first, VisiCalc, was designed for the Apple PC. VisiCalc was quite successful, and later versions for MS-DOS systems were even more successful. But Lotus 1-2-3 and Microsoft's Multiplan and Excel programs forged into industry markets. By 1986, Lotus had set the industry standard, and today a handful of firms offering spreadsheets virtually control the market. Entrepreneurs, therefore, must not only recognize opportunities, but also take advantage of them while windows exist to be successful.

Another aspect of many successful ventures is called the *corridor principle*.[25] The corridor principle suggests that opportunities evolve from entrepreneurs being positioned in similar work or having had experience with related ventures so that when a window opens it is easy for them to move quickly into a new venture. A corollary is that as a venture becomes expert in one activity, related opportunities evolve, and many of them are more rewarding than the initial activity.

William Gates of Microsoft, for example, was first approached by IBM in 1980 to program an operating system for the PC; Gates turned down the offer. He had a fledgling software company and was "hacking" with minor programs he hoped to sell; the idea of a major software effort was inconceivable. However, he and several friends realized the opportunity and began working independently to create the MS-DOS system. His early efforts probably would have kept Gates in an obscure part of the software industry, but the brief opportunity to create the new operating system led to enormous success. Howard Head, the founder of Head Ski, leveraged his "sports manufacturing" experience to create Prince Manufacturing and a revolutionary new line of tennis rackets.

The corridor principle is well known to scientists. For example, Wilson Greatbatch, the inventor of the Pacemaker for heart patients, was an electrical engineer and 41 years of age before the idea evolved from hundreds of other electrical ideas and gadgets concocted in his garage workshop. Probably a thorough résumé of most inventions and the entrepreneurs who commercialized them would reveal a series of closely related experiences that preceded success.

This does not mean that entrepreneurs must first work aimlessly and wait for a twist of fate to create opportunities. It means that entrepreneurs who are active and watching for changes are more likely to recognize opportunities when they occur. Few new ventures arise through "luck," which is one of the popular and inaccurate myths about entrepreneurial success we address next.

▶ **CHECKPOINT**

Discuss why a window of opportunity is critical for success.

Explain how a corridor influences the evolution of an innovation.

MYTHS—FANTASIES NOT FACTS

Folk heroes like Steven Jobs and Mitchell Kapor are beset by myths that they "stumbled into success" and got their ideas by accident. Not so. Several references have been made earlier to each of these popular individuals, but what may not be clear is that they spent several years striving for a foothold in their particular fields. Both men *made* success by creating their own brand of luck. There are other myths to be explored, but let's begin by expanding the notion of "luck."

Luck Is for Gamblers

Clearly, there are individuals who seem to have an uncanny ability to be able to spot and to exploit opportunities, and luck (both good and bad) plays a role in the outcome of many ventures. More often, successful individuals have been nourishing a concept for some time or working on closely related projects when a breakthrough occurs.

As noted earlier, Art Fry of 3M created the Post-it note as a result of trying to make nonslip hymn book markers. He spent several years working on the idea, and he also had to fight an uphill battle convincing 3M executives to manufacture his product. Compressing the story of the Post-it pads into a paragraph makes it seem as if Fry stumbled onto the idea, but the product's development, manufacture, and marketing required extraordinary work and commitment.

For John H. Johnson, the founder of *Ebony* magazine, success was the result of four decades of systematic development from a neighborhood newsletter to the publishing empire that exists today. Along the way, Johnson ran into more bad luck than good as an entrepreneur with little money facing a society not yet ready to endorse black business interests. Persistence and determination played greater roles in Johnson's success than luck.

Make or Break on the First Venture

Another popular myth is that entrepreneurs strike it rich with the first great "flash of genius," or, conversely, they fail miserably with the first venture. Entrepreneurship is not a "boom or bust" process, even though many new firms succeed brilliantly and others do not survive for long. The point is that too much distortion exists on both issues. Bankruptcy statistics suggest that of those who have gone bankrupt, 80 percent were in business for less than five years. That figure sounds terrible, but the qualifying point is that statistics are compiled on those firms who *do* go bankrupt. How many continue in business? How many are sold profitably, merged, or incorporated into larger organizations? How many evolve into new businesses through a corridor of innovation? Bankruptcy represents about 1 percent of the total number of new ventures established, whereas most other outcomes, successes and failures, are only vaguely studied.[26] Statistics can be misleading, and many new ventures evolve and change, generally going unnoticed on the grand scale of economic development. Several of these possibilities are shown in Figure 2-8.

Entrepreneurs Are Mavericks and Misfits

Evidence suggests that many entrepreneurs march to the proverbial different drummer. They are not always among the best students, and they tend to be restless in structured jobs. Consequently, they are likely to be unsettled wanderers. It is true that entrepreneurs prefer independence and can be rather rebellious, and both conditions can affect their performance in school and at work. Most successful entrepreneurs, however, are from the ranks of above average students, and they are relatively unlikely to have drug or alcohol problems or to run afoul of the law.[27] Entrepreneurs are *mavericks* in the sense that they instigate change and challenge the status quo, but they are not "misfits."

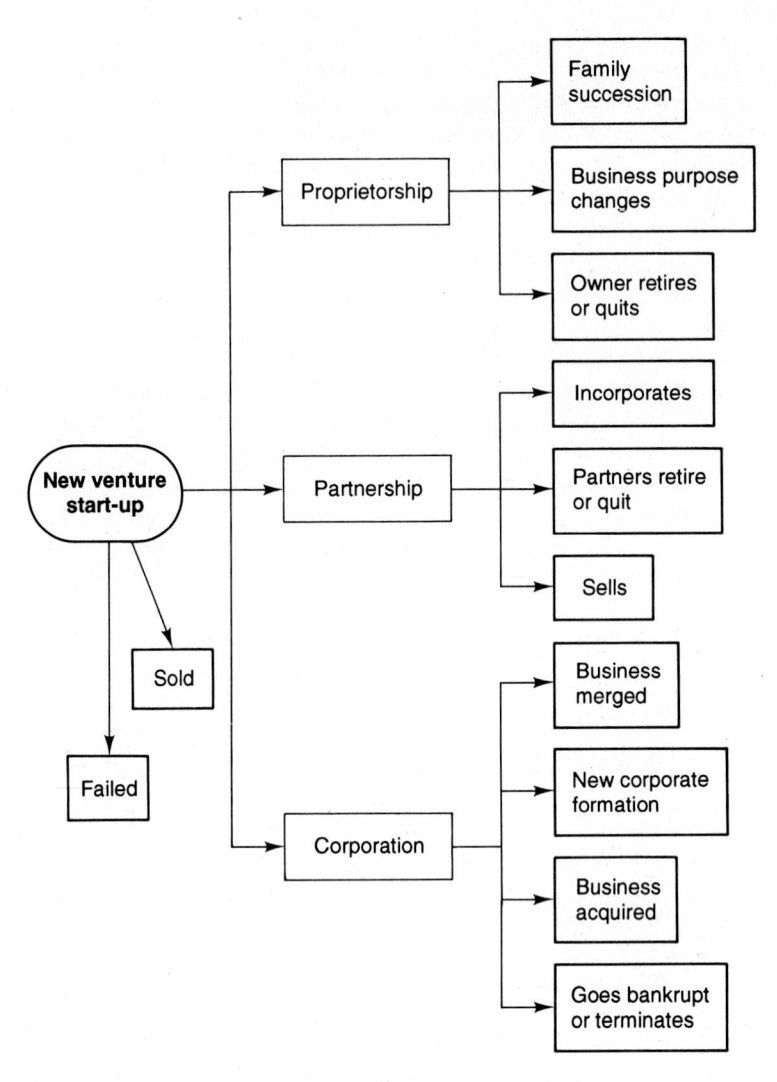

Figure 2-8 **Possible Changes in New Venture Status**

Are Entrepreneurs Born or Made?

A persistent notion is that most entrepreneurs are "born" with innate characteristics that prepare them for the often topsy-turvy life of new venture creation. Clearly, entrepreneurs have personal characteristics that lead to a more venturesome destiny. As noted in Chapter 1, successful entrepreneurs tend to be optimistic, have a keen sense of determination, are energetic, and often have an entrepreneurial parent. However, there is substantial evidence that entrepreneurial characteristics may be environmentally based. Firstborn children, for example, are often expected to take over parental businesses as heirs to established enterprises. One's childhood background often forges an entrepreneurial spirit as individuals from less-fortunate economic conditions have to find routes to success other than through traditional jobs.

Those who believe entrepreneurs are born conclude that entrepreneurship cannot be taught. This corollary myth would suggest that studying how new ventures are formed or how innovation takes place is of little value. If the environmental theme has credence, then learning as much as possible about the entrepreneurial process will better prepare students to succeed in business.

Other Myths and Misconceptions

Historic examples of inventors are used to illustrate success stories, and although these provide valuable insights, inventors are not necessarily entrepreneurs. Recall that we discussed earlier how entrepreneurs are less often inventors than astute businesspersons who can create an organization to bring new ideas to market.

A related misconception is that entrepreneurship must address whatever is called "high tech" at the time. Currently, information technology and biogenetic engineering are high-tech stereotypes. Twenty years ago it was communications, specifically color television and satellite transmission. Twenty years before that, just after World War II, it was the introduction of jet propulsion and new materials such as plastics. A hundred years earlier it was the telephone, petroleum fuel, and electricity. Entrepreneurship has always been associated with technological advances, but low- and no-tech enterprises remain very important.

For example, during the California Gold Rush period (1849 to 1860), everyone's attention was on gold mining; the "rush" to information technology and Silicon Valley has been compared to that era. However, lumber production in Minnesota produced nearly 40 times more revenue than gold did on the West Coast in the 1950s, and more money was made in lumber for homes, buildings, and ships than from the total gold-mining industry. The rush to information systems development today, although vitally important, is still eclipsed by basic food services and the housing industry.[28]

An unfortunate myth that often accompanies failure is "all you need is money" to be successful. Even those with sufficient money to launch an enterprise find that entrepreneurship requires skills in marketing, manufacturing, planning, and managing human resources, to name a few. Money does not assure success, and in some instances it may be a problem because with excess capital entrepreneurs may encumber themselves with unnecessary assets and inefficient organizations.[29] Too little capital is, of course, a more serious problem to overcome.

▶ **CHECKPOINT**

Discuss the arguments for and against *luck*, *boom-or-bust*, and *all-you-need-is-money* perspectives of entrepreneurship.

Contrast the labels *maverick* and *misfit* often ascribed to entrepreneurs.

SUCCESS FACTORS FOR ENTREPRENEURS

Several success factors are apparent from research on innovation and entrepreneurship. We now have fairly solid evidence of what it takes to succeed in a new venture, and although there will always be exceptions, most new ventures succeed because their founders are capable individuals.

The Entrepreneurial Team

At the top of the success factor list is the "entrepreneurial team." The term *team* is used because, more often than not, entrepreneurs do not start businesses by themselves; they have teams, partners, close associates, or extensive networks of advisers. In major studies of entrepreneurs in the United States, Canada, and Europe, between 60 and 70 percent of all technology-based ventures were started by founders with at least one partner or cofounder.[30] Those in nontechnical enterprises (e.g., personal services or merchandising) were less likely to have partners or cofounders, yet they were well networked with associates or expert advisers.

An entrepreneurial team is usually headed by an individual who provides the critical profile of success. This focal entrepreneur typically has an above-average education, with about 35 percent of technical entrepreneurs holding graduate degrees. Most entrepreneurs started their businesses when they were in their 30s, and they had solid job experience. Also, nearly two-thirds of those studied in the United States had attempted a new venture before, and slightly fewer Canadians had made an earlier attempt. Of some interest, far less than half of those from Europe had previously tried to start a business.

Most technical entrepreneurs tend to start businesses closely related to what they did in previous career positions. Those in nontechnical areas often leverage their experience in marketing, merchandising, or a professional service area such as insurance or finance. We can infer that success is closely tied to a solid *knowledge base* and *substantial experience* in related fields of endeavor. They will also have well-developed social and business relationships, and therefore have a strong foundation for building a team or support network. This finding was reinforced in studies of Silicon Valley firms where researchers found entrepreneurs to have good relationships with vendors, potential customers, financiers, bankers, attorneys, and their competitors.[31] Potential network relationships are summarized in Exhibit 2-2.

Venture Products or Services

Nearly all successful ventures start small and grow incrementally; few "gear up" with substantial organizations for a big-bang start. Incremental expansion of products and services also tends to stay within the bounds of positive cash flow. Products tend to have strong profit potential with high initial margins rather than small margins that require a substantial volume of sales to meet profit objectives. Service businesses retain good margins by effective cost controls and well-monitored overheads.[32]

In each instance, products and services tend to display a *distinctive competency*

Exhibit 2-2 Entrepreneurial Network Relationships

Business Relationships

    Formal and informal liaisons with suppliers and wholesalers.

    Contracts or informal relationships with subcontractors.

    Existing contacts with potential customers or clients.

    Potential contacts with clients or customers through networks established in prior employment.

    Collegial relationships related to career specialty or through new membership in professional or trade societies.

Professional Relationships

    Formal or informal relationships with bankers, security analysts, savings and loan managers, and investment fund managers.

    Formal or informal liaisons with insurance companies, venture capitalists, or private investors.

    Existing contacts with attorneys, public accountants, consulting organizations, import/export brokers, and realtors.

Organizational Relationships

    Relationships with previous employers and universities.

    Formal ties with corporations through new venture units.

    Formal or informal ties with government agencies, state agencies, and local political orgnaizations.

Social Relationships

    Membership in local, state, or national professional associations.

    Membership in or attendance at trade and professional conferences.

    Relationships established through local or regional social clubs, community organizations, athletic clubs, and social events.

Other Relationships

    Family relationships and friendship networks through family ties.

    Ethnic, cultural, and religious affiliations.

    Fraternal organizations, trade groups, or union membership.

Source: David H. Holt, "Network Support Systems: How Communities Can Encourage Entrepreneurship," *Frontiers of Entrepreneurship Research*, 1987, pp. 44–56.

in their industries. This is important because very few entrepreneurs start businesses in already competitive situations. This observation relates to an earlier point that we emphasized: Entrepreneurs must assure themselves of a *niche for their services*. A corollary to this rule is that successful entrepreneurs should "stick to their knitting" by concentrating initially on one distinct product or service, making it successful before diversifying.

From an investor's viewpoint, the product or service idea is secondary to the entrepreneur. A popular expression among investors is that they would rather "back a first-rate entrepreneur with a second-rate product than the other way around." This guideline does not mean the business concept can be weak, but it does suggest that investors must have considerable confidence in the entrepreneurial team before buying into the venture.

Markets and Timing

Successful entrepreneurs tend to have a clear vision of both existing and potential customers. A crucial aspect of planning is to have a well-documented forecast of sales based on sensible projections at each stage of incremental growth. A charismatic entrepreneur loaded with talent and a great idea will not convince investors that a venture is viable without valid market research. There are no shortcuts; innovation requires market demand, not simply a good idea.

Markets evolve, and as noted earlier, there are windows of opportunity that can lead to exceptional success. Misjudging those windows can result in dismal failure. Market potential is critically influenced by *timing* of new products or services. Timing pertains to when products or services are introduced, how they are priced, how they are distributed, and how they are promoted. We will pursue these points carefully in Chapters 8 and 9.

Business Ideology

From an entrepreneur's perspective, every venture has an *ideology*, a philosophy or rationale for existing. Although the ideology may be extremely difficult to quantify, it is nevertheless important. A business ideology is defined as a *system of beliefs* about how one conducts an enterprise. These beliefs include a commitment to providing customers with value, the ability to take calculated risks, the determination to grow and to control the fate of the business, the propensity to elicit cooperation among team members, and the perspective of creating wealth realistically. A business ideology may not be entirely defined by these notions, but failure is often blamed on one of them. For example, rarely do we hear that a business failed because the product was flawed, but more often because the firm lost track of its commitment to customers.

▶ **CHECKPOINT**

Describe the four primary factors associated with new venture success, and relate each to an example from the chapter.

AN ERA OF TRANSFORMATION

Given the perspective of how opportunities emerge, it is important to recognize that we are now in an era of transformation. Only a few years ago, *entrepreneurship* was a vague term occasionally used to explain bursts of economic activity. Today, the popular term *entrepreneur* occurs in television commercials, corporate annual reports, and political speeches. This transformation has had serious implications for business education and the way in which success is defined in the minds of young adults.

Before World War II, young people defined success in terms of a decent job with reasonable wages. After the war, they defined success as having corporate careers. During the past few years, more youthful graduates have been intrigued with independent business ventures. The average age of entrepreneurs who start new ventures is dropping, with more people in their 20s taking the entrepreneurial plunge. This trend is strongly evidenced by the extraordinary growth of the Association of Collegiate Entrepreneurs (ACE), founded in 1984 by a group of university students in a Boston pizza parlor. By 1991, ACE had attracted nearly 4,000 college students and more than 600 successful entrepreneurs still in their early 20s. The association has also established an honor roll called the ACE 100, representing millionaire members who, in order to qualify, must have at least $2 million in annual sales and still be under 30 years of age; those at the top, however, have extraordinary sales.[33] Exhibit 2-3 is a recent ACE 100 list.

As we move toward the 21st century, it will be younger people who provide inspiration and innovative leadership. They are the entrepreneurs who will transform

---

Exhibit 2-3 The Top U.S. Young Entrepreneurs under 30 in 1991

1. **Michael S. Dell**, Dell Computer Corporation, age 26. Annual revenue, $531 million.
2. **Neil Balter**, California Closet Company, age 30. Annual revenue, $61 million.
3. **Jeff Bernstein & Brian Hinman**, Picturetel Corporation, ages 29. Annual revenue, $37 million.
4. **Keith McCluskey**, McCluskey Chevrolet, age 30. Annual revenue, $35 million.
5. **Silvano Digenova**, Tangible Investments of America, age 28. Annual revenue, $30 million.
6. **Richard Kirshenbaum**, Kirshenbaum & Bond, age 27. Annual revenue, $25 million.
7. **Teresa McBride**, McBride & Associates, age 29. Annual revenue, $17 million.
8. **Jack Hertzberg**, Hertzberg Rare Coin Investments, age 26. Annual revenue, $17 million.
9. **Jim Moseley**, The Moseley Group/Modern America, age 29. Annual revenue, $16 million.
10. **David Goldman**, MacProducts USA & MacProducts Asia, age 25. Annual revenue, $13 million.

Note: Annual revenue is based on 1990 calendar year.

Source: "The ACE 100 for 1991," Association of Collegiate Entrepreneurs 1991 National Conference and Awards, St. Louis.

society. Just as in centuries past, in the 21st century it will be young entrepreneurs who determine the cadence for change.

> ▶ **CHECKPOINT**
>
> Reflecting on information earlier in the chapter, discuss why this is an era of transformation. Are changes taking place today more than 20 years ago? If so, why? Why are younger entrepreneurs starting new ventures? What opportunities do you see for the future?

▲▲▲▲▲▲ SYNOPSIS FOR LEARNING

1. *Explain the process of creativity.*

Creativity is defined as conceiving of something new. The process of creativity has five stages: idea germination, preparation, incubation, illumination, and verification. Germination is when the seed of an idea is implanted, arising from one's curiosity or interest in a problem or area of study. During preparation, a person embarks on research and a conscious search for bringing the idea to life. Although this search seldom produces results, a creative person becomes "prepared" by gathering information and knowledge related to the problem. During the incubation stage, a person "sleeps on the problem," often for years of periodic subconscious reflection on the idea or the problem to be solved. Illumination occurs when the idea surfaces through incubation, often seeming to have been a sudden flash of genius when, in fact, it was the culmination of conscious preparation and subconscious incubation. Once the idea becomes clear, a person will seek to verify it. Verification is the process of determining whether the idea has merit—whether it is useful and realistic.

2. *Describe how innovation is important as a dimension of entrepreneurship.*

Innovation is defined as the process of doing new things. Therefore, it is often the active translation of a creative idea into a new product, service, or technology. *Innovation* is different from *invention*. Invention is the verified result of a creative idea; innovation is the conversion of something new into useful goods or services. With that distinction in mind, innovation is perhaps the heart of entrepreneurship. Entrepreneurs may also be inventors, but they take the action necessary to redirect resources and convert creations into reality. They build organizations and systems needed to champion ideas and to exploit opportunities.

3. *Identify major changes that create opportunities for entrepreneurs.*

Entrepreneurs are often thought to be "inspired" people, and perhaps they are, but more important, they often recognize changes and opportunities that can result from a dynamic world. Scientific knowledge, one source of change, has been rapidly advancing, and the combination of new knowledge often leads to exciting new innovations. This was the case for computers as a century of periodic changes led to artificial languages, mechanics, electronics, and combinations of technology to fashion new industries in semiconductors, computers, and software. Also important are rapid changes taking place in process innovations. "Processes" are the ways we accomplish tasks, and of course, computers have revolutionized office, manufacturing, and organizational systems, but processes such as the assembly line and petroleum refining resulted in far more pervasive changes in industrialized nations. Industrial changes occur for many reasons, including new knowledge and new processes, but also when there is new legislation or changes in society—for example, when airlines were deregulated or when AT&T was broken up. It occurs daily as new laws are passed to encourage trade, provide loans to businesses, and improve minority hiring. Market changes occur as new competitors enter industries, as social and economic shifts occur, and as cultural norms evolve. Markets also change as the demographic structure of a community or nation changes.

4. *Explain the concepts of "windows" and "corridors" for new ventures.*

A window is a time horizon during which opportunities exist. This can occur, for example, when a new change in technology takes place so that intrepid innovators rush to become early industry leaders. As opportunities for success become known, however, more competitors enter the industry, and the window rapidly closes with market saturation. A corridor is a route or an aisle down which a person travels, often beginning with one idea that leads to revisions and further innovations. It is not uncommon for a person to pursue a weak idea but, in the process, discover some new opportunity or new product that may not have come to light except through fruitless work on the original idea. Corridors also arise from the proximity of a person who is conducting similar work and is therefore positioned to recognize change more rapidly than others.

5. *Discuss popular myths of entrepreneurship and why they are more fantasy than fact.*

Perhaps the most prominent myth is that entrepreneurs are "lucky"; they were just in the right place at the right time. Perhaps in a few cases that assumption is true, but most entrepreneurs make their luck by working hard. They rarely stumble into new million-dollar enterprises but develop the marketing, manufacturing, and organizing skills needed to bring innovations to fruition. A similar myth is that entrepreneurs are "make or break" people; on the contrary, most ventures start slow and make incremental changes. Entrepreneurs are not misfits, as myth suggests, but they do "disrupt" the status quo. They alter the fundamental course of commerce, and in so doing, are clearly out of step with the rest of the parade. More accurately, they are leading the parade in a new direction. Whether entrepreneurs are "born" or "made" is an unresolved issue, but on balance, evidence suggests that most entrepreneurs are influenced to start new ventures through environmental factors and events encompassing their background, education, family, and careers. Finally, the myth that "all you need is money" to succeed has no credibility because few wealthy people have pursued (or have needed to pursue) new ventures, whereas most successful companies have been founded by people with little money and few resources.

6. *Describe the main factors that lead to success for new ventures.*

Perhaps the most important factor is having a good entrepreneurial team. People transform ideas into useful innovations, and few new ventures grow beyond a preliminary start-up stage without a solid team of committed people. Financial backers rarely underwrite an individual but look for a strong team with the diversity of skills and the persistence to succeed. A second success factor is to have a well-planned enterprise that pursues incremental change and growth. It is essential to start with one distinct competency, one product or service, and firmly establish it. To succeed, therefore, a firm must maintain positive cash flow through controlled growth. A third factor is good timing. The most successful firms have timed the introduction of products or services to coincide with windows of opportunity. They did not take shortcuts or enter markets that were already highly competitive. Fourth, successful entrepreneurs have instilled in their companies a sense of purpose. They have created a business ideology to serve their customers, not to exploit them.

NOTES

1. Peter F. Drucker, *Innovation and Entrepreneurship* (New York: Harper & Row, 1985), p. 22.
2. *Webster's Third New International Dictionary* (Springfield, MA: G&C Merriam, 1976).
3. Thomas J. Peters and Robert H. Waterman, Jr., *In Search of Excellence: Lessons from America's Best-Run Companies* (New York: Harper & Row, 1982), p. 206.
4. Frank Baron, "The Psychology of Imagination," *Scientific American*, Vol. 199 (1958), pp. 151–166. Also see John J. Kao, *Entrepreneurship, Creativity, and Organization* (Englewood Cliffs, NJ: Prentice-Hall, 1989), pp. 15–19.
5. "The Mad Idea," in *Communicating and the Telephone*, a biographical monograph by American Telephone and Telegraph Company, July 1979, pp. 4–5.
6. Kao, *Entrepreneurship, Creativity, and Organization*, pp. 55–56.
7. Hollister B. Sykes, "Lessons from a New Venture Program," *Harvard Business Review*, Vol. 86, No. 3 (May-June 1986), pp. 69–74.
8. W.J.J. Gordon, *Synectics* (New York: Harper & Row, 1961), pp.3–4, 47–48.
9. Drucker, *Innovation and Entrepreneurship*, p. 20.
10. Henry Mintzberg, "Planning on the Left Side and Managing on the Right," *Harvard Business Review*, July-August 1976. Also Jacquelyn Wonder and Priscilla Donovan, *Whole-Brain Thinking* (New York: Morrow, 1984), pp.4–6, 24.
11. Wonder and Donovan, *Whole-Brain Thinking*, pp. 60–61. Also see Terence Hines, "Left Brain/Right Brain Mythology and Implications for Management and Training," *Academy of Management Review*, Vol. 12, No. 4 (1987), pp. 600–606.
12. Kao, *Entrepreneurship, Creativity, and Organization*, p. 16.
13. Modesto A. Maidique, "Entrepreneurs, Champions, and Technological Innovation," *Sloan Management Review*, Winter 1980, pp. 59–61.
14. Brian Twiss, *Managing Technological Innovation*, 3rd ed. (New York: Longman, 1986), pp. 15–17.
15. Gene Bylinsky, "A Quantum Leap in Electronics," *Fortune*, January 30, 1989, pp. 113–118.

16. D. Bruce Merrifield, "The Measurement of Productivity and the Use of R&D Limited Partnerships," *U.S. Department of Commerce Papers*, Office of Productivity, Technology, and Innovation, April 1984, pp. 1–2.

17. Steven L. Mandell, *Computers and Data Processing: Concepts and Applications in BASIC*, 2nd ed. (New York: West, 1982), pp. 26–29.

18. John W. Wilson, "Noyce: Silicon Valley's Roving Ambassador," *Business Week*, January 21, 1985, pp. 64–65.

19. "Akers Looks Ahead to IBM's Future Strategies, Principles," *Computer Reseller News*, April 3, 1989, pp. 44–46.

20. Drucker, *Innovation and Entrepreneurship*, p. 70.

21. "Tailspin," *Enterprise II, A Series*, (Boston: WGBH-TV, 1983). Also see Alfie Kohn, *No Contest: The Case against Competition* (Boston: Houghton Mifflin, 1986), pp. 75–78.

22. Jay Finegan, "Star Wars, Inc.," *Inc.*, August 1987, pp. 68–76. Also see John Case, "The Invisible Powerhouse," *Inc.*, September 1989, pp. 25–26.

23. Drucker, *Entrepreneurship and Innovation*, p. 90.

24. D. Bruce Merrifield, "Industrial Survival via Management Technology," *Journal of Business Venturing*, Vol. 3, No. 3 (1988), pp. 171–185.

25. David Kopcso, Robert Ronstadt, and William Rybolt, "The Corridor Principle: Independent Entrepreneurs versus Corporate Entrepreneurs," *Frontiers of Entrepreneurship Research, 1987*, pp. 259–271.

26. Robert C. Ronstadt, *Entrepreneurship: Text, Cases, and Notes* (Dover, MA: Lord, 1984), pp. 36–37. Also see David L. Birch, "Live Fast, Die Young," *Inc.*, August 1988, pp. 23–24.

27. Ronstadt, *Entrepreneurship: Text, Cases, and Notes*, p. 33.

28. *The Entrepreneurs: An American Adventure*, Film Series, Vol. 2 and Academic Supplement (Boston: Enterprise Media, 1987), pp. 4–6.

29. Albert V. Bruno and Joel K. Leidecker, "Causes of New Venture Failure: 1960s vs. 1980s," *Business Horizons*, Vol. 31, No. 6 (1988), pp. 51–56. Also see Dawit Kibre, "Myths of Small Business Failure," *The CPA Journal*, September 1983, pp. 73–74.

30. A. B. Ibrahim and J. R. Goodwin, "Perceived Causes of Success in Small Business," *American Journal of Small Business*, Vol. 11, No. 3 (1986), pp. 41–50. Also see Karl A. Egge, "Expectations vs. Reality Among Founders of Recent Start-ups," *Frontiers of Entrepreneurship Research, 1987*, pp. 322–336.

31. Howard Aldrich and Catherine Zimmer, "Entrepreneurship through Social Networks," in Donald L. Sexton and Raymond W. Smilor, eds., *The Art and Science of Entrepreneurship* (Cambridge, MA: Ballinger, 1986), pp. 3–23.

32. Richard B. Robinson, Jr., Moragla Y. Salem, John E. Logan, and John A. Pearce II, "Planning Activities Related to Independent Retail Firms' Performance," *American Journal of Small Business*, Vol. 11, No. 1 (1986), pp.19–26.

33. "The ACE 100," *ACE Conference News*, February 1991, p. 1.

CASE 2-1

CareerTrack on a Roll

Entrepreneurs seldom march to the same cadence of others, and this "out of step" mindset often ends up costing entrepreneurs their jobs. Jimmy Calano had this experience early in a corporate career that ended at age 24. Together with Jeff Salzman, who left his job at age 28, the partners set up CareerTrack in 1982. Their corporate careers at an end, Calano and Salzman built an organization starting in Calano's bedroom that today has nearly $50 million in sales and is the leading business seminar company in the industry.

CareerTrack offers more than 3,000 seminars annually in nearly 400 cities on three continents, and the numbers are rising. The success of CareerTrack is based on astute marketing and a clear picture of the firm's customers. By pricing seminars as low as $45 rather than several hundred dollars per person, the company captured the market for women in emerging professional careers. "We gave more value at one-fourth the price," says Calano. "A lot of people price seminars according to their costs; we price our programs at what people can afford."

Among CareerTrack themes are "Image and Self-projection," "Getting Things Done," and "How to Get Results with People." More than 500 seminar themes exist in the firm's portfolio, but when the business started, a determined effort was made to identify women in dynamic career positions. Once established, CareerTrack diversified to provide on-site seminars to large corporations, including IBM, AT&T, and General Motors. Reaching $25 million in 1986, the entrepreneurs took aim at government agencies, including the IRS and the CIA. New themes emerged for corporate and governmental clientele, such as productivity improvement, quality performance, creativity, and office system development.

Calano recalls that the company began with a vision of success that had little similarity to what it is today. "You have to understand that I was just out of college and still not entirely sure what my final grades were when Jeff and I decided to do it," Calano explains. "Jeff had been through several jobs in sales, and I had been working for a guy who did the Saturday-morning-you-are-gonna-get-rich seminars. Every Saturday we'd collect a couple of hundred bucks from 20 or 30 people eager to hear how to get ahead in real estate or stocks or something. I realized very quickly that nearly anyone could put on a seminar with a sexy message, and Jeff and I decided to do it right."

CareerTrack's first seminar for working women on "assertiveness training" was held in a Colorado hotel conference room. Calano and Salzman worked for several months researching the topic and putting the seminar together, then they decided on a $40 fee and placed several ads, and the company was born.

"The concept was to provide a valuable seminar worth $40," explains Calano, "and we felt good about what we were offering. The topic seemed obvious because no one seemed to be paying any attention to working women or their career problems. A half-day seminar on how to be more assertive in their jobs just seemed the ticket. But our so-called vision was just that—to offer one seminar to working women on assertiveness and hopefully make enough to buy tacos for a week or two. We had no idea of making lots of money, running courses for IBM, or hiring people like Tom Peters to lead seminars.

"Once we realized how many people

wanted quality seminars," Calano notes, "opportunities seemed to be everywhere. If we had mapped out a business plan then, it would have looked like a spider web with market opportunities in every direction. College students needed—and still need—practical information on writing résumés and getting jobs. Women still need help negotiating for promotions and being assertive about their careers. Men need stress management. And we all need to improve our careers, our self-images, and our knowledge of the world around us. If we had not created CareerTrack, someone would have, and, in fact, a lot of companies are doing the same thing now. All we had to do in 1982 was pick a direction and go. We are still doing that."

Today, Calano and Salzman spend their time on two distinct business activities. The first, and most consuming, is *market research*. The second is the actual development of CareerTrack training programs. Success, in their eyes, comes from first *understanding* the $4 billion seminar and training industry, then *planning* carefully to address a distinct customer within that industry. The firm's products evolve from a marketing base, that, today, includes films, videos, audiotapes, books, and seminars ranging in topics from "How to Survive Your College Days" to "The Masters of Excellence" by Tom Peters.

CASE QUESTIONS

1. Identify and discuss CareerTrack's window of opportunity. What social or economic changes occurred to create this window? Do you think the window is still open today? Explain.
2. Describe the corridor principle and how it seemed to propel CareerTrack from a Saturday morning seminar to a global business.
3. Put yourself in Calano's shoes today. What opportunities exist now and for the immediate future in a similar business?

Source: Interview with Jimmy Calano and staff at CareerTrack. Also Jimmy Calano and Jeff Salzman, *CareerTracking* (New York: Simon and Schuster, 1988), pp. 32–34, 95–96.

CASE 2-2

Stew Leonard—The Great American Milkman

Stew Leonard was a second-generation milkman with a home delivery route until 1968 when state highway construction forced him to relocate. Because of this change coupled with the realization that home milk delivery was going the way of buggy whips, Stew Leonard built a barnlike retail dairy store with glass viewing windows separating his customers and milk cows. The dairy plant provided milk so fresh that the only way to get fresher milk was to own a cow. After 26 additions, the small barn has become an 8-acre complex with more than 600 employees in Norwalk, Connecticut.

In a White House ceremony in 1986, Leonard received the Presidential Award for Entrepreneurial Achievement from President Ronald Reagan, and Leonard was featured in Tom Peters' best-seller *A Passion for Excellence* as one of America's best-run companies. Featured in the television special "In Search of Excellence," Stew Leonard was heralded as one of the nation's most innovative companies alongside Disney, McDonald's, and Apple.

The genius of Stew Leonard is making customers happy through quality service and innovative marketing. His "Rock of Commitment" credo is "Rule 1: The customer is always right. Rule 2: If the customer is ever wrong, reread Rule 1." Leonard says he wants to make customers say "Wow!" and then return—again and again. A trip to Stew Leonard's store is an experience that reinforces his credo and his policies. Disneylike farm characters play music, perform, and mingle with customers. Live farm animals give children up-close encounters with egg-laying chickens, milk-producing cows, friendly rabbits, ducks, geese, and other domestic animals. On any given day, there is likely to be a live band, free gifts, and ice cream for youngsters. Stew Leonard and his family will be there every day, talking with customers, soliciting suggestions, and managing the business with one clear objective: Make customers happy.

His success is dependent on the sincerity of his policies and the attention to planning that result in what Leonard calls "action-based policies." These include "If you wouldn't take it home to your mother, don't put it out for customers"; "Only happy customers come back"; "A customer who complains is our best friend because we get the opportunity to improve"; "When in doubt, throw it out"; "Do it right the first time"; and "If you're training someone to be even better at your job than you are, then you're one of the most valuable people in our company."

Leonard often generates ideas from customers who are involved in his weekly creative brainstorming sessions. About a dozen customers are chosen at random and invited to sit down with Leonard's family and staff to explore ideas for the store. Meetings can last for several hours, and the results are often quite stunning. A complaint about strawberries always being prepackaged so that customers could not see whether they were getting their money's worth led to an open-bin arrangement where customers could pick and choose. The result was that, on average, customers bought more strawberries, and total sales nearly tripled. Another suggestion was that friendly cashiers be openly rewarded. Leonard started a daily program of "stopping the line" to announce and reward the best cashier in a fanfare manner. Customers periodically win free shopping sprees. There are two fish counters—one with prepackaged seafood and another with "morning fresh" seafood on ice. Leonard conducts classes through his employees for customers on cooking, and he periodically hires specialists in nutrition and diet control both to train employees and to guide customer purchases.

In Leonard's view, creativity is "listening" to others and building a business around the total environment rather than just a merchandise line. Consequently, his store sells more than food and more than service, it sells the idea of food preparation as a fun concept. Customers are on his organizational chart as participants in the store and its environment.

Success is reflected in more than 100,000 customers a week and more than $100 million in annual sales, making Stew Leonard's the largest retail dairy in the world. In fact, he sells more of each item that he stocks than any other store in the world, including 10 million quarts of milk, or about 18,000 quarts per hour. Annual sales also include 100 tons of cottage cheese, 800 tons of salad, 1,000 tons of hamburger meat, 1,800 tons of poultry products, a million ice cream cones, nearly 3 million quarts of orange juice, 250 tons of butter, 5.6 million bananas, and 7.8 million ears of corn. These are a few of Stew Leonard's 800 record-setting products epitomizing a record-setting family business.

CASE QUESTIONS

1. Describe how Stew Leonard's methods compare with a prescribed process of innovation.
2. Selling groceries is hardly a new type of business, and it is far from "high tech," so explain how Leonard found "new opportunities" in this business.
3. Identify the main success factors of Leonard's business and tell how they relate to similar factors described in the chapter for successful ventures.

Source: Courtesy of Stew Leonard, June 1988.

Chapter 3

Small Business and Corporate Entrepreneurship: Contrasting Enterprises

OBJECTIVES

1. Describe the environment of small business and how it is changing.
2. Identify the most common causes for small business failure.
3. Explain the important success factors for small business enterprises.
4. Describe corporate entrepreneurship.
5. Discuss the major approaches to corporate entrepreneurship.
6. Describe emerging ways corporations are encouraging entrepreneurship.

Fundamental concepts of entrepreneurship, creativity, and innovation were introduced in the first two chapters. We also provided a framework of definitions on which we can build more thorough discussions. In Chapter 3, we explore in more detail "small business" and "corporate entrepreneurship" as two highly contrasting approaches to new venture creation. Small businesses are as essential to the American economy as successful large corporations are, and both contribute to the high quality of life that we enjoy in the United States.

    Small business will be examined in terms of the many services, local professional practices, and merchandisers that all of us rely on. Without the clothiers, shoe stores, convenience stores, restaurants, laundries, gas stations, and many other small enterprises, we could not function. Without accounting firms, dentists, pharmacies, and attorneys, we would lack important services. Without music stores, florists, photography shops, candy stores, theaters, beauty salons, and bookstores, life would be bland. On the other hand, without larger firms to support economic development, jobs, major product development, and communication systems, utilities, and energy resources, the country would be little more than a wilderness.

In terms of entrepreneurship, small business is a very personal approach to creating new enterprises. Small businesses usually have limited growth opportunities and operate in a community atmosphere. Corporate entrepreneurship encompasses major innovations and organizations that can leverage their massed resources to provide systems of technology, products, and services on national and global scales. This chapter examines how entrepreneurial activities occur in both sectors.

THE ENVIRONMENT OF SMALL BUSINESS

The environment of small business is often defined by the type of business or service rendered, and in most instances the opportunities for small business are defined by the characteristics of a community. To emphasize the role of small business, it is important to recall the introduction in Chapter 1. Small business comprises many local enterprises, service companies, and professional organizations that constitute more than half of all nonfarm employment in the United States. This profile of small business is remarkably similar among most free-market nations. Small businesses include merchandisers to which we turn for a significant amount of our daily purchases. It also includes "practices" and "personal service" enterprises of doctors, accountants, tailors, interior designers, and many others to whom we turn for personal needs.

There is also a substantial number of small manufacturers, wholesalers, distributing companies, and vendors who focus on specialized niches to provide everything from local bakery goods to space telecommunication equipment. Many of these entrepreneurs are small *by choice*. They probably have opportunities to expand into new markets or to develop into larger organizations, but they prefer the autonomy of a small business and subsequently avoid rapid expansion. The entrepreneurial profile on Dan Bricklin is illustrative.

Franchises, owned and operated by independent businesspersons, provide us with local products and services that range from fast foods to microcomputer services. These independent businesses represent an extraordinary range of activity that has given us a high-quality life-style. A short list of these would include quick printing services, auto parts and repair services, gift shops, personnel placement services, fashionable men's or women's clothing shops, gourmet candy stores, video rental outlets, yogurt shops, and travel agencies.

For nearly all phases of domestic construction, we rely on small business enterprises, including prime contractors, plumbers, electricians, and other craftsmen. Community radio stations, newspapers, and cable operators help keep us informed and entertained. Our recreation needs are often met through small business endeavors that include golf courses and pro shops, tennis clubs, boating facilities, ski shops, health clubs, and many more.

Opportunities in Small Business

Business students, as well as most business school curricula, focus on careers in the corporate world, but an exceptional number of career opportunities exist in smaller

PROFILE △

Dan Bricklin: Small Is Not Bad

Dan Bricklin was the pioneer of computer spreadsheets who created the first commercial software company for microcomputer applications. He was also credited with the first business software that propelled Apple Computers to prominence, and his innovations became the models for Lotus Development Corporation software. Bricklin graduated from MIT and Harvard Business School, then teamed up with Bob Franston in 1978 to program the first spreadsheet. The result was VisiCalc, a program that swept to prominence five years before Lotus introduced its first product. Apple Computer, and most other computer manufacturers, rapidly adopted VisiCalc, and Bricklin's company grew to a multimillion-dollar industry leader.

By 1983, Bricklin's VisiCalc had expanded to world markets, his staff had expanded to hundreds of employees, and anxious bidders were offering huge sums to purchase the company. Then IBM set a new standard with its PC, and the MS-DOS operating system came to prominence. Lotus 1–2–3 pushed aside VisiCalc, and the VisiCalc family of products eventually faded from the market. Bricklin did not fade away, however, and in addition to being a consultant to Lotus Development Corporation, he set up another software company and quietly (and profitably) closed down the VisiCalc business.

Instead of rebuilding as a major software developer, Bricklin resolved to keep his new company small. Avoiding corporate growth, marketing hype, and global expansion, Bricklin chose to remain independent. By 1989 he had developed several award-winning programs, sold or licensed proprietary software to several major manufacturers, and made an undisclosed but "enormous" amount of money while remaining almost totally anonymous. Bricklin likes the idea of being "small" and keeping his business "lean as a bone." In his view, building a large organization may give a founder honor and glory, but remaining small satisfies his life objectives to be innovative, successful, and independent. Growing a company can be fun, Bricklin admits, but he has no intention of spending a decade organizing and guiding a high-growth enterprise.

Source: Dan Bricklin, "My Company, My Self." Reprinted with permission, *Inc.* Magazine (July, 1989). Copyright © 1989, by Goldhirsh Group, Inc. 38 Commercial Wharf, Boston, MA 02110.

---

enterprises. Of the nearly 19 million businesses in the United States today, about 97 percent, roughly 18 million, are in the small business sector.[1] Although researchers continue to debate the definition of "small," there is a preponderance of evidence that most new jobs are created through new and smaller enterprises. Nearly 42 percent of all sales and 38 percent of the U.S. gross domestic product are derived through small business activity, and more than four times as many new innovations are

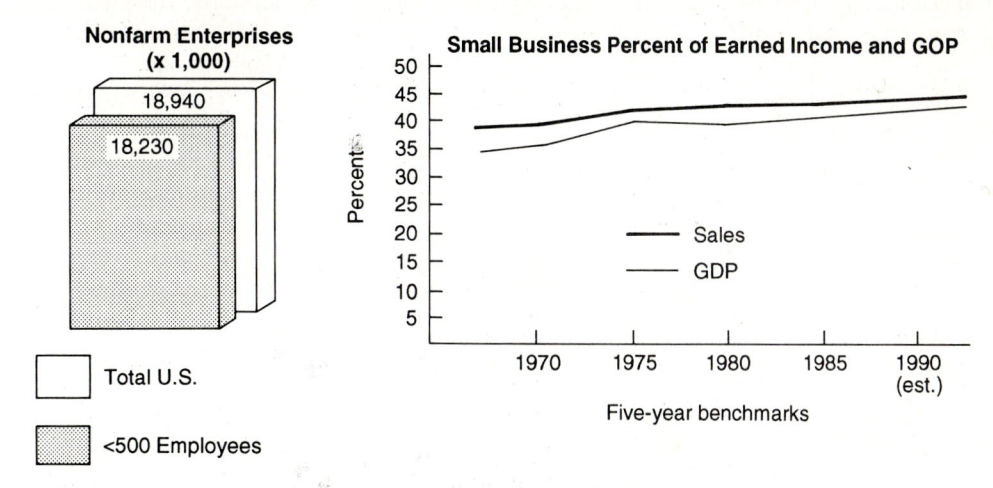

Chapter 3 Small Business and Corporate Entrepreneurship: Contrasting Enterprises   69

Figure 3-1   **Contributions of Small Businesses to the U.S. Economy**

developed through small enterprises as through large corporate endeavors.[2] Several trends are shown in Figure 3-1.

Opportunities in small business are distinct from those of *high-growth* enterprises. Recall from Chapter 1 that we characterized **small businesses** as those started by individuals who seek *income substitution* and who serve a local constituency. Therefore, most small business owners are not concerned with changing the world, finding a cure for the common cold, or setting industry on its heel with some marvelous new invention. To the contrary, they are concerned with filling immediate needs of their customers and clients within the scope of well-defined markets. Opportunities arise from business niches and local shifts in consumer demands, but these often constitute enormous transformations in commercial activity. For example, the city of San Diego, California, grew from a population of barely more than a half million persons in 1960 to approximately 3 million by the late 1980s, creating an eightfold increase in demand for retail merchandisers. In Sun City, Arizona, once an isolated and small retirement community, there are now more than a quarter million residential homes and 50,000 businesses supporting an extensive suburbia near Phoenix.[3] Population increases throughout most of the United States, in particular the southern sunbelt regions, have stimulated an explosion of small business activity.

Opportunities arise from any change that fosters an unfulfilled need. Something as simple as the construction of a new highway off-ramp will create an influx of travelers in search of gasoline and fast food. If the area is scenic, opportunities may be forged by entrepreneurs to provide recreation, lodging, and tourist shopping. As these businesses develop, a network of support businesses is needed to serve them. More houses will be built, groceries and convenience stores will emerge, retailers will become established, schools and churches will appear, and, in turn, these will cause even greater needs to surface. This is not, however, an ever-widening circle of activity. If travel recedes, demand for goods and services may collapse. For example, ''The Colonel'' Harland Sanders was thriving on his unusual chicken recipe and a good restaurant business in Kentucky until the U.S. Interstate Highway System bypassed his town during the 1950s. Sanders was virtually broke within a few months of the highway opening, and he might have quietly retired on social security had he not been determined to find a way to regain his losses. Instead, he conceived of restaurants located in small communities where the new Interstate System would have off-ramps, and when he licensed his chicken recipe to small restaurant owners, Kentucky Fried Chicken was born.[4]

In this age of global communications, small businesses may no longer be severely restricted to local or community endeavors. International trade, export brokerage of products, and instantaneous communications are opening new venues for small businesses. For example, nearly every country in the free world has import and export quotas for products ranging from canned nuts to automobiles. In 1990 the export quota for American eggs to be imported to Hong Kong was set at 26.7 million dozen. The U.S. government noted a shortfall of over 3 million dozen eggs scheduled for export and issued a notice to Americans that a bonus would be paid to fulfill the quota. Individual farmers are unlikely to have the connections to pursue these types of opportunities, but "export brokers" do. Operating out of midwest offices, small companies such as McCall Saunders Marketing monitor government reports, and armed only with a fax machine and telephone, they fill orders from hundreds of independent farmers. McCall reacted to the government report within hours to register export sales of 27,000 dozen eggs.[5] Weekly reports by government agencies throughout the world list thousands of products needed overseas, and a growing number of small businesses are becoming involved in exporting. Perhaps more businesses are involved with importing. The United States is an affluent society, the marketplace of the world, and imported products range from toothpicks to oil tankers.

International business opportunities are growing rapidly, and although we will be attentive to global business throughout this book, small business is most commonly represented by the merchandisers and service firms in a community. Being a small businessperson also shares several characteristics with the role of an independent business owner.

The Small Business Role

The independent businessperson has a role quite different from that of a high-growth entrepreneur or corporate business manager. As a risk-taking owner of an entrepreneurial venture, innovation and growth require the organizational abilities to gather resources and establish new venture teams. Corporate managers become professional specialists, focusing on specific tasks or responsibilities, such as tax accounting, design engineering, or advertising. Small business owners must wear many "professional hats" at once. They may hire a few people, but they behave more as an autonomous owner than as a professional manager. The owner will also assume the risks associated with financing and operating a new business, but those risks are seldom related to innovation development. Some of the many responsibilities of business owners are summarized in Figure 3-2.

Small business owners often keep their own books and do their own taxes, but

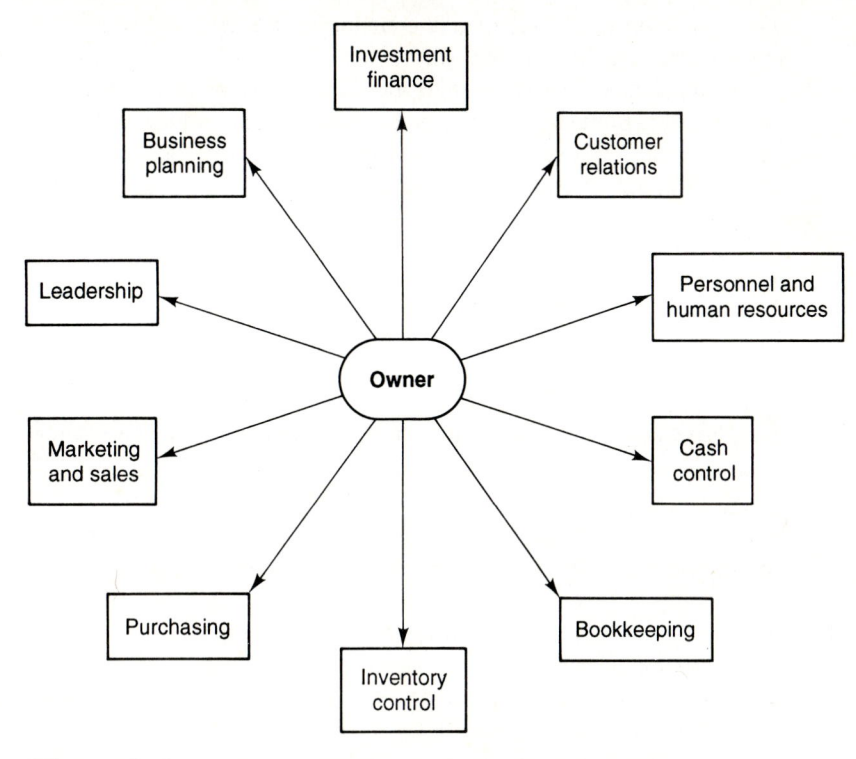

Chapter 3 Small Business and Corporate Entrepreneurship: Contrasting Enterprises

Figure 3-2   **Role Responsibilities of Small Business Owners**

most neither have the time nor the inclination to become expert in tax accounting. They may use personal computers to track inventory and do a bit of word processing, but they rarely care about "knowing computers" or programming. As managers, they must motivate a team of employees, and although this activity is important, weighty theories in leadership will be of little interest to them. They will think strategically but not develop strategic plans, and be concerned about market demand but not engage in market research. In most instances, they do things required to survive tomorrow and to compete next week.

This sense of immediacy coupled with a disregard for management concepts at once helps illustrate the nature of small business and shows why it is important for aspiring small business entrepreneurs to become better educated in business matters. The small business role is complex, encompassing all the activities required to be in business, yet lacks the depth necessary to become specialized in any particular aspect of management. In most instances, the business owner is *technically* competent, perhaps an expert in merchandising, accounting, medicine, engineering, or export brokerage, but often this technical orientation dominates business decision making, further reducing the ability of the owner to deal with management issues such as planning, organizing, leading, and controlling the enterprise. Most business failures are attributed to the incompetency of the owner, and broadly interpreted, this generalization means that independent businesses are often operated in a technically sound manner but managed pathetically.

Management issues will be addressed throughout this book, but not in a "how-to" manner; there are several excellent books and courses specifically designed for that purpose.[6] Understanding why small businesses succeed or fail, however, can forewarn aspiring entrepreneurs about the risks.

> ▶ **CHECKPOINT**
>
> Describe local markets, competition, and types of products or services that constitute the small business environment.
>
> Explain how opportunities arise locally and globally for small business.

RISK AND FAILURE

Failure can be thrust upon an entrepreneur through external conditions or fabricated by the entrepreneur through personal shortcomings. Small business owners are particularly vulnerable to both situations because they are usually preoccupied with the immediate needs of survival. External conditions, such as inflation, threaten us all, and we can be consumed by them. Fabricated failure, unfortunately, can usually be traced to an owner's arrogance or simple lack of management acumen.

External Factors of Failure

Every business is affected by *externalities*: economic business cycles, fluctuating interest rates, interrupted supplies, labor market trends, inflation, government regulations, and unstable financial markets. A general rise in consumer prices will detract from sales. A similar rise in producer prices will inflate costs. However, the smaller enterprise is far more susceptible to these forces than a large firm. For example, IBM has access to capital resources to ride out a recession, but a local contractor may run out of cash quickly and go under. A major toy manufacturer may be able to find alternative financing when interest rates soar, but the local toy store may watch its profits evaporate in precipitous debt obligations.

From a financial standpoint, most small businesses rely on commercial loans tied to premium interest rates. Small changes in economic conditions result in huge changes in profits. Smaller businesses that are relatively debt free still operate in a more intense, price-sensitive environment. Most cannot afford to trim prices, nor can they substantially reduce costs. On the other hand, many smaller firms are isolated from "macro" economic variables. Inflation, for example, rarely affects two communities in exactly the same way. During the early 1980s consumer price levels were very high on a national scale, but there may have been a 10 percent general price

Exhibit 3-1   Pressing Problems for Small Business

- Payroll taxes, contributions to unemployment insurance, disability, and compliance costs often exceed small business margins.
- Estate taxes and a tax program lacking in investment incentives have combined to divert money away from small businesses.
- Changes in institutional credit and investment alternatives have biased lending toward larger companies and publicly traded securities.
- Because small businesses tend to use more debt than larger firms, rising interest rates weigh more heavily on small business than on any other economic sector.
- Government limitations for backing sponsored programs, mainly those administered through the Small Business Administration, have made bank lending less attractive to small start-up enterprises.
- International competition has stiffened, opening opportunities for small businesses in export markets, but the economic power of foreign competitors operating at home and abroad threatens small businesses.

---

increase in New York and only a 3 percent increase in Charleston, South Carolina. Likewise, the extraordinary increase in housing costs in California came when housing costs in Buffalo were falling. In effect, local businesses are often insulated from problems that plague national corporations. In 1988, Houston was in a recession, and there was a general "sell-off" of assets.[7] Bargains abounded in housing, commercial property, cars, computers, and other hard assets. Employment was down and wages dropped drastically, yet this oil-related recession in Houston had little effect on business in Washington, and while Houston was staggering, San Diego was booming with a full-employment economy.

Consequently, smaller enterprises are more susceptible to changes in the external environment, but success or failure is often a result of phenomena peculiar to a community or to a well-defined industry. Small businesses usually operate in an environment composed of local competitors. Still, capital for investment and loans come from institutions that are influenced by national or regional trends. Therein lies the crunch, and too often the small businessperson cannot reconcile these contradictory forces. Even the most astute business owner is preoccupied with the two external issues of financing and taxation. The National Federation of Independent Businesses (NFIB) noted these issues as pressing problems during the 1987 White House Conference on Small Business.[8] Exhibit 3-1 elaborates on these points.

Personal Factors of Failure

Just how many businesses fail because of uncontrollable external factors and how many fail owing to personal factors is debatable. However, Dun and Bradstreet statistics attribute about 52 percent of all business failures to "management issues," and as much as 90 percent of small business failures to incompetent managers. Specifically, D&B cites the inability of small business managers to control purchasing costs (inventory), to control capacity (production or operating costs), to generate customers (lack of marketing expertise), or to manage financial assets (feeble cash control being the primary issue).[9]

Inexperience. Too often, entrepreneurs launch their enterprises without having sufficient experience to succeed. Inexperience can be translated to mean a lack of technical skills or management acumen. Each of these shortcomings can lead to disaster, but they also can be overcome by an individual willing to make the commitment of time and energy to learn about business. Not too long ago, for example, an experienced nurse created a medical newsletter for retirees in north Florida. The idea was sound, there was a good market, and her editorial content was excellent. Six months after her first issue, however, she was bankrupt. Her problems stemmed from lack of experience in publishing (the real nature of her business), not in the medical field. As a result, she had purchased expensive desk-top publishing equipment and produced huge runs of newsletters that stacked up in her garage unsold. At about the same time in 1987, a nurse in Virginia started a similar health newsletter for truckers that focused on safety and stress. She too got into trouble by going to market without solid experience, but she sought advice from small business counselors, took training courses in desk-top publishing, and worked briefly as an intern with a printing firm. She made a second start, and her business is doing well.

Experienced managers often make the mistake of assuming that since they are reasonably successful in a salaried position, they can transfer that knowledge to an independent business. Personnel specialists may feel confident when they strike out on their own to open an executive placement agency, only to find that the "agency" requires marketing expertise, not just knowledge in corporate personnel. Engineers launch their own firms to pursue the manufacture of innovative products only to find that they know practically nothing about production. Each of these individuals may be "experienced," but the kind of expertise they bring to their enterprises has limited value.

In other instances, capable individuals start new enterprises within their respective fields but cannot *manage* their resources or provide *leadership* for their employees. An engineer who starts a consulting firm with excellent credentials, yet who ignores employee needs, risks losing the primary resource essential to succeed. A clothier who is a fashion expert but cannot control inventory costs could easily "buy" into oblivion.

Arrogance. Many small businesspersons—particularly inventors and innovative entrepreneurs with new products—become egocentrically engrossed in their ventures. They become consumed with their own brilliance, convinced beyond reason (often without market research) that their bright idea will change the world—it's *got* to sell! Their arrogance will not allow them to take advice from others. They will shun all innuendo of failure. Such arrogance is often needed to succeed, and there are many fine examples of those who have defied the odds, yet for each success story, there is a legion of failures.

An extraordinary example of success born of this singular-minded arrogance is King Gillette. At the turn of the century, men everywhere had to go through the

PROFILE △

King Gillette

At the turn of the century, shaving was a painful ordeal. Few men really got the hang of using a straight razor, and barbers were expensive. King Gillette was one of those men who were more likely to shave off skin than whiskers, and he set out to solve the problem. His idea for a safety razor was jeered by engineers and barbers who told Gillette his idea was impossible. It took a while to catch on, but during World War I, the safety razor became a standard item in every soldier's field kit, and soon after, the Gillette Safety Razor Company was manufacturing enough replacement blades each year to circle the globe.

Source: The Entrepreneurs: An American Adventure (Boston: Enterprise Media, 1987), Film No. 3.

agony of shaving with a straight razor. This was not an easy task, nor a safe one, and it was expensive to be shaved professionally by a barber. Gillette conceived of the safety razor with replacement blades, but as a merchandising salesman, he wanted expert advice about his invention. King Gillette went to engineers at the Massachusetts Institute of Technology who said it couldn't be done. He talked with experienced manufacturers who laughed at the idea. In the end, Gillette was sure he could create the safety razor and did so. He remarked that he was grateful for not being an "expert" or he too would have realized that the safety razor was impossible to make.[10]

Examples of failure are more subtle. In most instances, the entrepreneur was an independent businessperson who simple focused too intensely on one aspect of the enterprise. This is a case of being tied to an infeasible idea, and then "riding the tiger until consumed."

Mismanagement. Humble entrepreneurs steeped in experience can still go under simply through mismanagement of resources; they simply make bad decisions in critical situations. Given the competitive nature of most small businesses and the volatility of profits, business results are quite sensitive to small errors. Several categories of management mistakes are critical for small businesses to avoid.

Overinvestment in fixed assets is common. When starting or expanding a business, it is tempting to buy facilities and equipment rather than lease or subcontract. For example, we noted earlier that a nurse in Florida had started (and quickly ended) a health newsletter for retirees. One of her mistakes was to purchase $40,000 worth of desk-top publishing equipment. She did so to avoid the high variable cost of paying for commercial printing. She had a good product and could have used her cash and credit to underwrite several years of activity. Perhaps that would have been sufficient time to establish a market. Instead, the $40,000 created a heavy debt burden requiring a huge sales volume to break even. Everyone likes to own assets, but greater investment in fixed assets means less flexibility to adjust to adverse conditions. Of course, there are conspicuous spenders who buy BMWs, join country clubs, and lease Lear Jets before opening day. They are usually doomed to a few wonderful days in fantasy land before the crash.

Poor inventory control threatens the success of nearly all retail enterprises. Inventory is the critical cost factor for most stores. Purchasing too much inventory increases the risk of low turnover and obsolescence. Having too little inventory undermines customer selection and sales. Buying the wrong inventory, or buying at the wrong time, evaporates cash. In each scenario, the business ties up high-powered cash in nonearning assets, and inventory items can rarely be disposed of for more than a fraction of their costs in an emergency. The result is that a business "purchases" itself into insolvency.

Purchasing errors and lack of good inventory management are critical problems for any business. Manufacturers typically have more than 40 percent of their money tied up in raw materials and supplies, and the problem is compounded by those who "build to inventory" (i.e., make products to stock in warehouses), thereby tying up even more capital in finished goods.[11] Many companies build to market (i.e., coordinate production to meet shipping schedules with minimum finished goods). Differences in overhead costs between companies that build to inventory and build to market are shown in Figure 3-3.

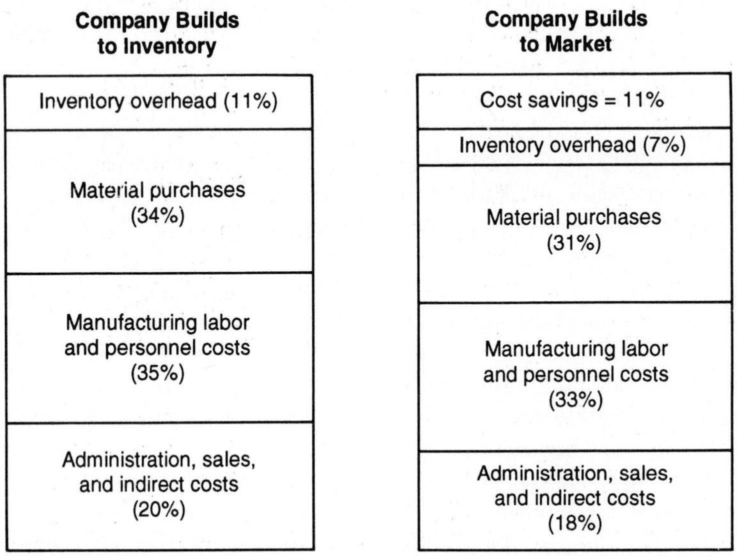

Company Builds to Inventory	Company Builds to Market
Inventory overhead (11%)	Cost savings = 11%
	Inventory overhead (7%)
Material purchases (34%)	Material purchases (31%)
Manufacturing labor and personnel costs (35%)	Manufacturing labor and personnel costs (33%)
Administration, sales, and indirect costs (20%)	Administration, sales, and indirect costs (18%)

Figure 3-3 **Relationships of Inventory Costs to Total Costs.** (*Source:* Adapted from Richard J. Schonberger, *World Class Manufacturing* (New York: Free Press, 1987), Chapter 1; and *Annual Survey of Manufacturers* (Washington, DC: U.S. Department of Commerce, 1989).)

Poor financial control is a fatal flaw for most small businesses. Even for those firms with excellent inventory management, good leadership, solid markets, and a reasonable capital structure, cash-flow problems persist. Many entrepreneurs simply fail to realize that "income" does not mean "cash flow." A record-setting month of perhaps $100,000 in sales is *cash* only to the extent that customers paid in hard money at the point of sale. Most businesses extend substantial credit to customers, and some accounts may remain unpaid for months. The average collection period in retail department stores is 24 days, and it commonly runs to 52 days during slack seasons. In the electronics and computer industry, the average collection period is 40 days, running to 60 days for many hardware firms.[12]

Assuming no "bad credit" and only a few bounced checks or bogus credit cards, small business managers will have to manage credit policies very closely to assure a positive cash flow. Cash problems arise on the "payables" side of the ledger as often as through delayed receipts. Specifically, most inventory purchases require advanced payments (or at least partial payments on receipt). For young enterprises without a track record, inventory purchases may be strictly on a cash-and-carry basis. It follows that cash is needed in advance to underwrite sales; cash from sales may be months away. Meanwhile, loan payments, lease payments, utility costs, telephone bills, and payroll expenses occur with monotonous regularity. Sales do *not* occur regularly. In fact, most sales for most firms in almost every industry have substantial seasonal variations. Income generated from sales during a brief Christmas season may have to underwrite expenses for the next five slow months. Summer sales in recreational sportswear may have to pay bills for a nine-month "off season." And many manufacturers must purchase materials months before they actually create their products, which are in turn sold on credit months before they can expect payment from customers.

Financial problems also arise simply through sloppy bookkeeping. It is not surprising that most small business entrepreneurs see their roles "on the firing line" as marketers, engineers, technicians, or merchandisers and, in the process, forget to attend to "back-shop" books. Others who do attend to the books simply do not know what they are doing. It is rather easy to miss payments to vendors and destroy the company's credit rating (or worse, lose the source of inventory). It is just as easy to overdraw a bank account and nullify loan sources.

Poor Business Philosophy. An unfortunate aspect of many business failures is that too often individual owners' priorities get in the way of sound business practices. In the least obtrusive way, entrepreneurs may not be fully committed to the long hours required to make a venture successful. Working only 40 hours a week is out of the question, particularly for small business retailers. The new venture is a mistress requiring long hours and constant attention, and most retail establishments are expected to remain open 12 to 16 hours a day, seven days a week. The early stages of starting a business require intensity of effort, sacrifices, and the ability to endure at high energy levels without becoming overextended to the point of exhaustion. As the business stabilizes, the challenge is to hire good employees who can manage in the owner's absence.

A more sinister side of business failure is a blatant disregard for customers. The principal success factor of all business is to "create a satisfied customer," and as Peter Drucker explains, "to be of value to society by providing a needed, useful, and safe product or service."[13] This is the essence of the *marketing concept*, and it means that business managers will succeed when they can generate satisfied customers by providing quality goods and services. Too many individuals, however, exploit customers to make a fast buck. Commitment to quality is replaced by a commitment to use the cheapest materials, to pass on marginally safe or defective products, and to serve customers only reluctantly. Cheating and deception exist in small businesses just as they do in large enterprises, but probably to no greater extent than in American society in general. The small business owner, however, will feel the brunt of public reaction much quicker. Customers typically have other options for car repairs, computer services, clothes, professional services, and most other products and services offered by local businesses. If they feel cheated, they will spend their money elsewhere. For that matter, there are usually enough choices that something as simple as a frowning sales clerk will alienate customers.

Lack of Planning. Research shows that less than half of small business owners had formal plans prior to going into business.[14] Many engaged in formal planning soon after starting their businesses, but one-third could not recall ever having a formal business plan. Little research exists to determine the extent of planning in failing businesses. This lack is understandable because few of those who failed are around to be interviewed. However, research supports a strong case for well-developed plans with clear objectives prior to starting any venture. It is nearly impossible to acquire capital, obtain loans, or solidify vendor contracts without documented sales forecasts, financial statements, market analyses, and a clear statement of the business purpose.

Exhibit 3-2 **Planning Considerations for Ventures during Start-up and Early Growth**

Prior to start-up:
- Establish the purpose of the venture and define major objectives.
- Plan the market with attention to a well-defined market niche.
- Forecast sales and translate sales data into resource requirements.
- Document financial requirements and resources.
- Plan with attention to maintain positive cash flow.
- Consciously approach planning as a feasibility study.

During initial business operations:
- Create a clear marketing strategy.
- Position products or services in appropriate growth markets.
- Establish an inventory management plan.
- Plan growth consistent with resources and limitations; rapid growth can create problems in cash flow and financing.
- Adapt plans made prior to start-up; initial assumptions are often found to be flawed.
- Do not allow events to just happen—plan conscientiously to control events and to prevent mistakes.

Plans are guidelines for action, and as businesses evolve, they must be continuously upgraded to reflect changes in the business environment. Too often planning stops after loans and investment capital are acquired. Growth is allowed to occur rather than be managed. New products may be added to a line without clear evaluation of how they fit into the existing business or serve customer needs. Several important planning considerations are noted in Exhibit 3-2.

Many fatal problems emerge from lack of appropriate planning. These include poor business locations, overextended capital requirements, unrealistic sales projections, and nightmarish legal entanglements brought about through poorly conceived partnerships and business naivete. Rather than dwell on the point, understand that a primary objective of this text is to emphasize *conscientious* planning to avoid the mistakes that often lead to failure.

▶ **CHECKPOINT**

Describe external factors that can threaten small businesses.

Identify and discuss the internal factors that threaten small business, and discuss why "immediacy" can affect good business decisions.

RESOLUTIONS FOR SUCCESS

The question of how to dramatically improve the chances for success in small business has a prescriptive answer: *plan well*. This may sound like a hollow platitude, but planning includes careful analysis of the external environment and honest appraisal of the enterprise and its owner's capabilities. As noted earlier, being unprepared for externalities, oblivious to internal business problems, and unaware of personal shortcomings represent a majority of the reasons for failure.

Planning is therefore important, but it is not a panacea for all business ills, and just as important, small business entrepreneurs must protect against overplanning; it is possible to become paralyzed by "preparation," thereby leaving little time for "doing." Because so few businesses plan well, business advisers emphasize planning responsibilities, and perhaps the correct answer rests with a cautionary note to plan well, but to do so with a sense of what is needed in a particular line of business.[15]

Reversing the Factors of Failure

There are several positive steps in addition to planning that business owners can take to improve a firm's chance for success. From the discussion about factors of failure, we can conclude that a proper *attitude* is important to ensure a customer orientation for quality and service; the owner must have a purpose for being in business and want to provide customers with value for their money. We also can conclude that having a variety of basic business skills is important, such as the ability to keep accounting records. During the critical early years of a new business, it is vital to manage cash flow, avoid undercapitalization, and avoid unnecessary acquisitions of fixed assets. If the business relies on performance of good employees, leadership skills will be paramount. As a team leader, a business owner must be capable of influencing others to do quality work, and as an owner-operator, one must be able to set standards for ethical business behavior.

By understanding why businesses fail, as described earlier, entrepreneurs can discover ways to tilt the scales toward success. Better merchandising, for example, requires effective inventory control and purchasing. An aspiring entrepreneur's lack of experience can be overcome by working in a related business before starting a venture. Many business owners update their skills and knowledge through seminars and training programs. Others return to school to take formal courses in such topics as accounting or marketing.

When an owner recognizes a personal shortcoming, it may be necessary to build a business team or join in partnership with someone with complementary skills.[16] Consequently, if a technically competent individual wants to open a computer service center but has no aptitude for marketing, a wise decision would be to bring into the business a capable marketer. In turn, if neither of these people has an aptitude for finance, a third team member might be essential, one who can handle ''back-shop'' numbers. Better control and improved management can be achieved in nearly every instance by ''taking the blinders off.'' This means simply to realize personal limitations and seek help without being too arrogant.

Understanding the Purpose of Being in Business

Business owners should have a clear understanding of the business and the environment in which their firms compete. This *clarity of purpose* is another benefit of planning, and its importance cannot be overstated. If a person intends to produce a health newsletter, the nature of the business and the competitive environment is in publishing, not health counseling. The owner of a computer franchise outlet has to understand that he or she is solving information-related problems for clients, not peddling inanimate hardware.

While the purpose of being in business is never just to make money, the result of knowing why you are in business and then developing a *distinct competency* around that purpose will dramatically improve the likelihood of profits. For example, a computer franchisee committed to solving information-related problems for business clients has *clarity* of purpose beyond the notion of selling computer hardware, but the owner may find even greater rewards by creating a competency distinct from competitors. Such a distinction may be a focus on office networking systems. In a given community, one computer store may emphasize educational systems while another makes a market in business accounting systems. Several options for computer retailing services are shown in Figure 3-4. This reflects classic *niche marketing*, but businesses can differentiate in many ways. For instance, carving out a clear geographic

Chapter 3 Small Business and Corporate Entrepreneurship: Contrasting Enterprises   81

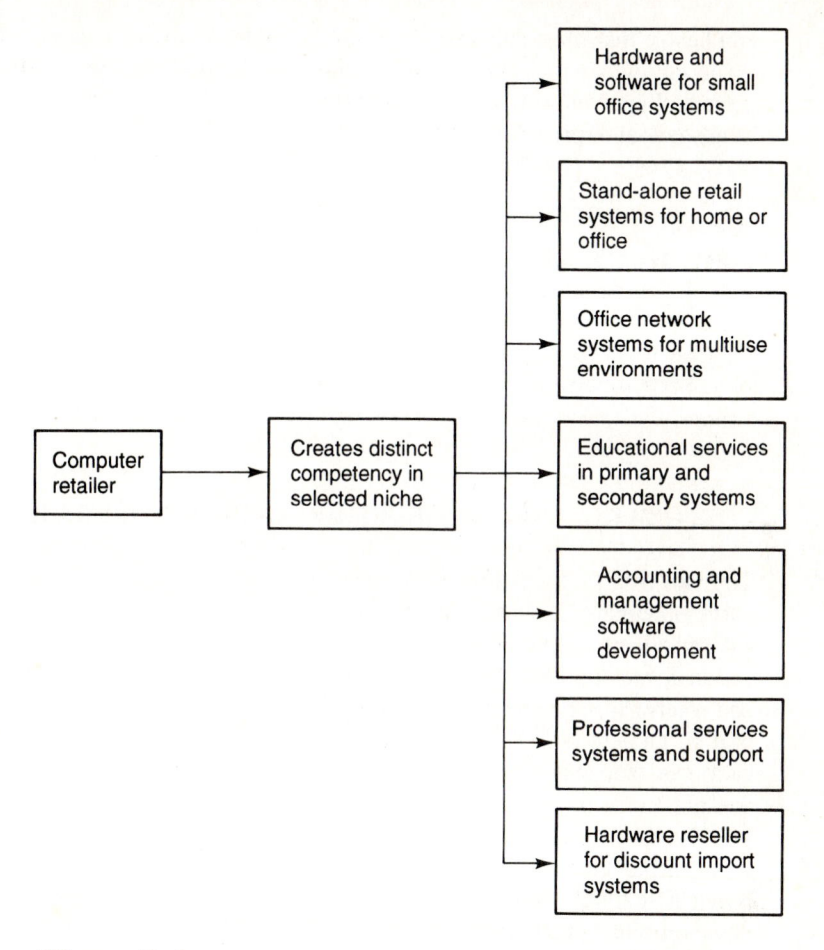

```
                                              ┌─────────────────────┐
                                          ┌──▶│ Hardware and        │
                                          │   │ software for small  │
                                          │   │ office systems      │
                                          │   └─────────────────────┘
                                          │   ┌─────────────────────┐
                                          ├──▶│ Stand-alone retail  │
                                          │   │ systems for home or │
                                          │   │ office              │
                                          │   └─────────────────────┘
                                          │   ┌─────────────────────┐
                                          ├──▶│ Office network      │
                                          │   │ systems for multiuse│
                                          │   │ environments        │
┌──────────┐   ┌──────────────┐           │   └─────────────────────┘
│ Computer │──▶│Creates distinct│──────────┤   ┌─────────────────────┐
│ retailer │   │competency in  │          ├──▶│ Educational services│
└──────────┘   │selected niche │          │   │ in primary and      │
               └──────────────┘           │   │ secondary systems   │
                                          │   └─────────────────────┘
                                          │   ┌─────────────────────┐
                                          │   │ Accounting and      │
                                          ├──▶│ management          │
                                          │   │ software            │
                                          │   │ development         │
                                          │   └─────────────────────┘
                                          │   ┌─────────────────────┐
                                          ├──▶│ Professional services│
                                          │   │ systems and support │
                                          │   └─────────────────────┘
                                          │   ┌─────────────────────┐
                                          └──▶│ Hardware reseller   │
                                              │ for discount import │
                                              │ systems             │
                                              └─────────────────────┘
```

Figure 3-4   **Niche Markets for Computer-Related Retailers**

area for a service such as selling "upmarket" home furnishings in a suburban community will demand an inventory and image different from those of a home furnishings store in a retirement community. Atmospheres can be developed for bookstores emphasizing discount prices or perhaps rare books. The former will have large inventories requiring a rapid turnover in book sales, and the latter may have few books but provide snug reading corners where customers can sip gourmet coffee.

Most business owners intuitively try to distinguish their enterprises, and those who succeed are usually far more successful than those who try to sell everything to everyone. Of course there are huge discount stores and outlet malls that literally do try to sell everything to everyone, but they too have a distinction that attracts customers; they hold out a general perception of numerous bargains with deep no-frill discounts.

Clearly, these few insights cannot hope to encompass all the relevant issues, and as we turn our attention to corporate entrepreneurship, it may be valuable to emphasize that most suggestions for small business owners are equally applicable to corporate enterprises. The small business owner is differentiated by having limited growth objectives, and many are family enterprises, but good business practices apply to all new enterprises.

> ▶ **CHECKPOINT**
>
> Explain the planning role, and tell why it must be a pragmatic process.
>
> Describe why it is important to understand business failures, and discuss several ways to improve the probabilities for success.

CORPORATE ENTREPRENEURSHIP—INTRAPRENEURSHIP

The world is still groping for a single label that captures the nature of "corporate entrepreneurship," and a number of popular terms are being used in books and advertisements. Several already have been introduced. "Intra-corporate venturing" has an academic flare; "intrapreneurship" has achieved a certain degree of popularity; and a term that has recently emerged in the hallways of Washington bureaucracies is ICE, an acronym for intra-corporate entrepreneurs. Whatever the term, the implication is that entrepreneurial activities are explicitly supported within established organizations, provided with organizational resources, and accomplished by company employees.[17]

Just as there is no consensus on a label for corporate entrepreneurship, there is no clear definition for a corporate entrepreneur. There is a sense of understanding, however, that innovative employees *disrupt* the company in *constructive ways* to instigate new products or services. These individuals often work independently, or with some degree of autonomy, and although they are given the latitude to explore new ideas, there is no presumption of business *ownership* apart from the mother organization. As we shall see, recent initiatives by a few corporations *do* provide opportunities for ownership, but this is an exception to prevailing practices. More often than not, entrepreneurial employees find themselves at odds with their companies and leave to pursue their ideas.

Focal Distinctions

Corporate managers who create something new within the context of their jobs seldom have the commensurate responsibility of taking a personal stake in their creations. There is no assumption of personal risk, no assumption of profit, and no assumption of loss. In fact, entrepreneurship is *not taking place* at this point. Hans Schollhammer, an ardent researcher in this area, suggests that employees stop being "employees" and start being "entrepreneurs" when they are charged with the responsibility of

PROFILE △

John D. MacEachron

After 21 years with Xerox Corporation, John D. MacEachron took the entrepreneurial plunge, forming LeaseAd, a company that develops master data files of real-estate lease and rental properties. MacEachron developed his real-estate software system for Xerox as part of his job to solve corporate property management problems. However, he also recognized the value of the software as a commercial product and proposed that Xerox package and market it. His superiors reprimanded him and said it was a pointless idea that did not fit with corporate development plans. As a career "company man" with a record of accomplishments and promotions, he was a successful manager headed for an executive position, but MacEachron was so frustrated by his treatment that he left Xerox and started LeaseAd. Today, his company sells custom software data systems and grosses $10 million in annual sales.

Source: Paul B. Brown, "The Last Company Man," *Inc.*, July 1987, pp. 19–21.

championing their innovations. More precisely, these individuals are expected to create an entrepreneurial team that could evolve into a new operating division or a formal subsidiary.[18] The corporate entrepreneurs often still have no direct investment and bear no financial risk. Consequently, they seldom reap rewards beyond bonuses and promotions, but they do behave as if they are giving birth to new enterprises.

A Matter of Perception

Gifford Pinchot, who wrote the somewhat controversial and best-selling book *Intrapreneuring*, gave us the term "intrapreneurs" and also gave these intrapreneurs a mantle of heroism. In Pinchot's view, intrapreneurs are much like corporate commandos, and he says, "These courageous souls form underground teams and networks that routinely bootleg company resources or 'steal' company time to work on their own missions."[19] In Pinchot's view, they make things happen, creating new commercial successes in spite of stodgy corporate policies and a glacial pace of bureaucratic decision making.

Two important points to emphasize are, first, that entrepreneurs are viewed as disruptive mavericks prone to shatter the status quo and replace "what is" by "what might be," and second, that very few entrepreneurs are motivated by money as much as by the pursuit of a vision to provide something of value. Wealth may come to those who succeed, but the pursuit of wealth is not itself a primary goal; money is simply one way to measure progress. With this in mind, Pinchot describes the corporate entrepreneur as someone who violates policy, ignores the chain of command, defies established procedures, and, perhaps, comes up with a great new product for the company. Successes may garner bonuses for their champions, but failures can end in shattered careers. This perspective assumes that "courageous souls" are at odds with their organizations, so much so that there is no tolerance for failure and only reluctant rewards for success. In many organizations, this view is probably accurate. The challenge of corporate management is to create a supportive environment that attracts, motivates, and retains intrapreneurs—to instill a culture of innovation where renegades are empowered to pursue dreams and to fail without retribution.[20]

If organizations provide these support systems, and also provide the entrepreneur with a safe salary, there should be no reason to start independent ventures; innovative employees would have the best of both worlds—income security and opportunity without risk. Few companies, however, provide all these support systems; they are more likely to discourage independent initiative. Consequently, many new ventures are started by restless employees who have been frustrated by corporate straitjackets. It is not unusual to trace the careers of successful entrepreneurs and find that they left good corporate positions.[21] Sometimes they were fired by inept managers who strangled their creative spirit.

One more important insight can be gained from the corporate scenario that distinguishes *small businesses* from *growth-oriented ventures*. A majority of small businesses are *not* born of controversy and innovation; they are largely focused on providing established products or services in local markets. The primary incentive for opening a small business is the independence gained from personal control over one's life. In contrast, a growth-oriented venture is determined to expand through the commercialization of a new idea. In this sense, the growth-oriented entrepreneur and the intrapreneur are similar, and they are set apart from small business owners by their philosophies of doing business.

Classifications of Corporate Entrepreneurship

Hans Schollhammer provides five classifications of what he calls *intra-corporate entrepreneurship*, each one having an unusual strategy for corporate sponsorship and a distinct role for the innovator. Each classification implies a supportive environment and a cooperate endeavor within an organization that benefits not only the corporation but also the innovative manager.[22]

Administrative Entrepreneurship. Traditional research and development (R&D) is closely approximated in the administrative model. Here, the firm simply moves a step beyond formal R&D projects to encourage greater innovation and commercial development of new inventions. The distinction that makes R&D entrepreneurial is a philosophy of corporate enthusiasm for supporting researchers while systematically providing extensive resources for making new ideas commercial realities. Personnel in R&D will be only partial contributors, implementation relies on contributions from many other departments (marketing, production, and finance, among others), as well as from an entrepreneurial team led by a champion who will set the cadence for team members who are enthusiastic about the innovation. The Sony Walkman resulted from an R&D breakthrough at Sony Corporation, but it was an integrated marketing team that designed the Walkman system, introduced it, and set the industry standard.[23]

Opportunistic Entrepreneurship. Formal structural ties are loosened in this model as champions are given the freedom to pursue opportunities both for the organization and through external markets. For example, commercial banks have begun to give managers profit-and-loss responsibilities for investing funds in unusual high-risk, high-yield opportunities. The investment bankers do not report through existing management hierarchies but enjoy a semiautonomous work environment, report to a highly placed executive, and manage their own budgets. Quad/Graphics, Inc., the company that prints *U.S. News & World Report*, *Inc.*, and *Newsweek*, among others, has taken opportunistic entrepreneurship a step further.[24] When printing technology began to change rapidly with computers, Quad/Graphics challenged its engineers to design state-of-the-art equipment. They did so, but they also convinced management that the technology itself was marketable. Quad/Graphics then created a separate subsidiary, Quad/Tech, and gave its engineers executive control and the autonomy to sell technology openly to anyone. The parent company is still the customer of choice, but Quad/Tech management is not expected to shut out the world. They are compensated according to profit performance, and although isolated from the parent, they have significant support for innovation.

Acquisitive Entrepreneurship. Moving even further from traditional R&D models, the acquisition concept is one of corporate managers in search of external opportunities such as other firms and entrepreneurial start-ups that can enhance the corporate profile through mergers, acquisitions, joint ventures, and licensing agreements. In recent years, this trend has led to almost frantic merger and acquisition activities in virtually every sector of the economy. Rather than develop ideas internally, corporations actively court other firms that have proprietary knowledge or promising products. Major companies such as General Motors, IBM, and General Electric have created joint ventures or new subsidiaries, or have added innovative product lines to their portfolios through acquisitions. Similarly, CitiCorp, Transamerica Corporation, and Sears have extended their services through acquisitive strategies. Kodak and Campbell Soup have infused their companies with innovative marketing through acquisitions.[25] Options for acquisitive strategies are shown in Figure 3-5.

Imitative Entrepreneurship. Sometimes bordering on corporate espionage, imitative entrepreneurship takes advantage of other firms' ideas and simply brings to bear the weight of corporate muscle to control markets. The Japanese have suffered this label for years, perhaps rightly so, as in many instances the Japanese have studied American products, found ways to improve on those products, produced them at lower costs, and exported them to American markets. It can be argued that this is the essence of free enterprise, but others suggest it is espionage. The controversy

```
                              ┌─ Acquire another company that has a product or technology
                              │  Merge with another firm to create a new enterprise
                              │  Enter into a joint venture with another company that has innovation
┌──────────────────┐          │  Purchase an innovative product or technology from others
│ Company seeking  │──────────┤  License an innovation from the innovator
│ innovations can  │          │  Contract with another company to market or act as broker for an
└──────────────────┘          │  innovation
                              │  Create one of several special legal forms of new businesses such
                              └─ as a "limited partnership"
```

Figure 3-5 **Acquisitive Strategies for Portfolio Development**

notwithstanding, the fact remains that if a company (regardless of nationality) provides consumers with valuable products or services, consumers are not really interested in how it all came about. Imitators abound in all cultures; imitation is a way of "shaking out" less efficient producers as more capable firms take the initiative. Society is often the benefactor because many inventors simply cannot get their products off the drawing board, but imitators can often make them commercially viable.

Incubative Entrepreneurship. When new ideas materialize, whether developed in-house, acquired, or imitated, they must be developed to the stage of feasible commercialization. This "incubative" process is necessary for any corporate endeavor, and the pattern for this activity has been to create project teams charged with high-impact implementation programs. These teams are expected to put an innovation through its paces, to enthusiastically subject the idea to torture, to test market prototypes, and then to either kill the project if warranted or push for implementation. Few projects are successful, and project teams are seldom responsible for failure, nor are they rewarded for success.

As a result, the incubative process has rapidly evolved toward a pattern more reflective of risk-oriented entrepreneurship. In this instance, a team is established as a semiautonomous *new venture development unit* that often has seed capital, access to corporate resources, freedom of independent action, and responsibility for implementation from inception to commercialization. This represents a major change in the way corporations approach innovation, and it is important enough to merit more attention.

▶ **CHECKPOINT**

Discuss the often conflicting viewpoints on corporate entrepreneurship.

Identify and discuss the major approaches taken by established companies to encourage corporate entrepreneurship.

CORPORATE NEW VENTURE UNITS

The term **new venture unit** is one of convenience used to capture the notion that teams are formally developed within corporate walls to instigate new ideas, to nourish them through the necessary stages for commercialization, and often to continue as the management cadre in charge of the venture.[26] In many instances, this last criterion becomes the payoff for team members who achieve executive status in autonomous operating divisions. In a few corporations, employees have the opportunity to "buy into" their new ventures through stock plans. These opportunities will become apparent as we describe ways in which new venture units evolve. In general, companies either encourage *spontaneous* team effort or create *formal* venture teams.[27]

The Spontaneous Team. If an organization has no policy for empowering developing venture teams, a "bootlegging" atmosphere may evolve. This leads to informal relationships among a few close associates working on new ideas. Pinchot identified four stages of spontaneous team development. These are illustrated in Figure 3-6 and described as follows:[28]

Stage 1: The first stage is the "solo phase" in which a single innovator cautiously nurtures an idea to the point where he or she has sufficient confidence in the project to confide in one or two close associates. During the solo phase, innovators are likely to be reclusive, slipping into laboratories after hours, working at home on weekends, and very quietly fleshing out their ideas.

Stage 2: The second stage evolves as innovators reach out for advice and support from friends, experts, or sponsors who can find resources to back ideas. This is called the "network phase," and it is a process of gaining allies and sponsors.

Stage 3: The third stage is the "bootleg phase" when an informal team begins to take shape. The innovator is no longer isolated in the endeavor, and team members actually do work of a substantial nature such as helping to develop a prototype, gathering market information, lining up production resources,

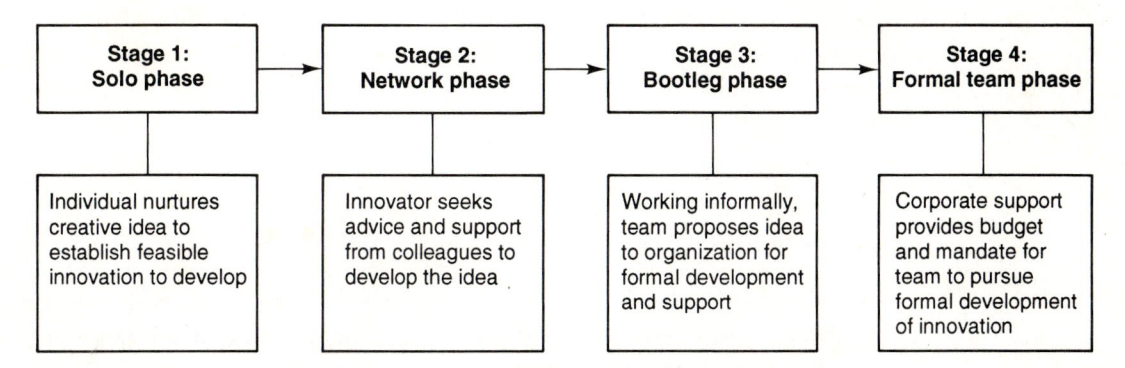

Stage 1: Solo phase	Stage 2: Network phase	Stage 3: Bootleg phase	Stage 4: Formal team phase
Individual nurtures creative idea to establish feasible innovation to develop	Innovator seeks advice and support from colleagues to develop the idea	Working informally, team proposes idea to organization for formal development and support	Corporate support provides budget and mandate for team to pursue formal development of innovation

Figure 3-6   Four Stages of Intrapreneurial Team Development

and gathering essential information needed to *write a proposal*. The proposal is the "business plan" in corporate terminology, and it is almost exactly the same documentation that an independent entrepreneur uses to attract investors. In this instance, the proposal is taken to corporate management to secure support and formal recognition of the project.

Stage 4: When corporate support is given, the final stage is launched. This is the "formal team phase" where team members are given authority to manage the project, budgets are allocated, and resources are lined up for a well-defined commercial development process.

Formal Venture Units. Farsighted organizations have had formal mechanisms in place for years. These allow adventuresome individuals to create legitimate teams at the beginning of an innovation process. The team-building process does not evolve among corporate shadows or with bootlegged resources. In this environment, innovators will still endure a "solo phase" of incubation until they can put enough substance into their ideas to make a *feasibility proposal* to management, but this proposal will *not* resemble a formal business plan. It may be little more than draft sketches and notes, just enough to indicate to management that there is a feasible idea that should be given a reasonable level of support. Obviously, a polished proposal with supported data will enhance the likelihood of a green light and budget support.

Once formal recognition has been achieved, an entrepreneurial team is established to take the idea to a predetermined stage of development. This process may result in prototypes, initial market research, testing, and a cost-and-profit analysis. Organizations usually have review committees that track these efforts or, alternatively, a sponsoring manager to whom the venture team reports. The team will have a first-stage budget called *seed capital*, and the corporate commitment is to allow the team to operate autonomously (within a budget). If the idea fails, the seed money is written off as a necessary investment to encourage creativity. If the idea has merit, recommendations are put forward for various degrees of support. The decision to fund a second stage rests crucially on a rather extensive business plan. This second round of support typically has a *development budget* that allows the team to take a product to limited production and to introduce the product to a select market.

Results are gathered, the team refines its proposal once again, and a corporate-level decision is made either to kill the project or to support its implementation. Every firm will have a method of launching projects, but the following three approaches stand out:

Innovation transfer is accomplished by integrating the new product into existing operations. Integration is spearheaded by the new venture team, which has formal management authority for operational control. This control can extend to research and development, production, marketing, logistics, and most other operational functions. Merck & Company, ranked as America's "Most Admired Firm" by *Fortune*, has recently instigated a program of innovation transfer as a strategic alternative to traditional R&D to encourage corporate entrepreneurship.[29] Merck's efforts are a reflection of top management com-

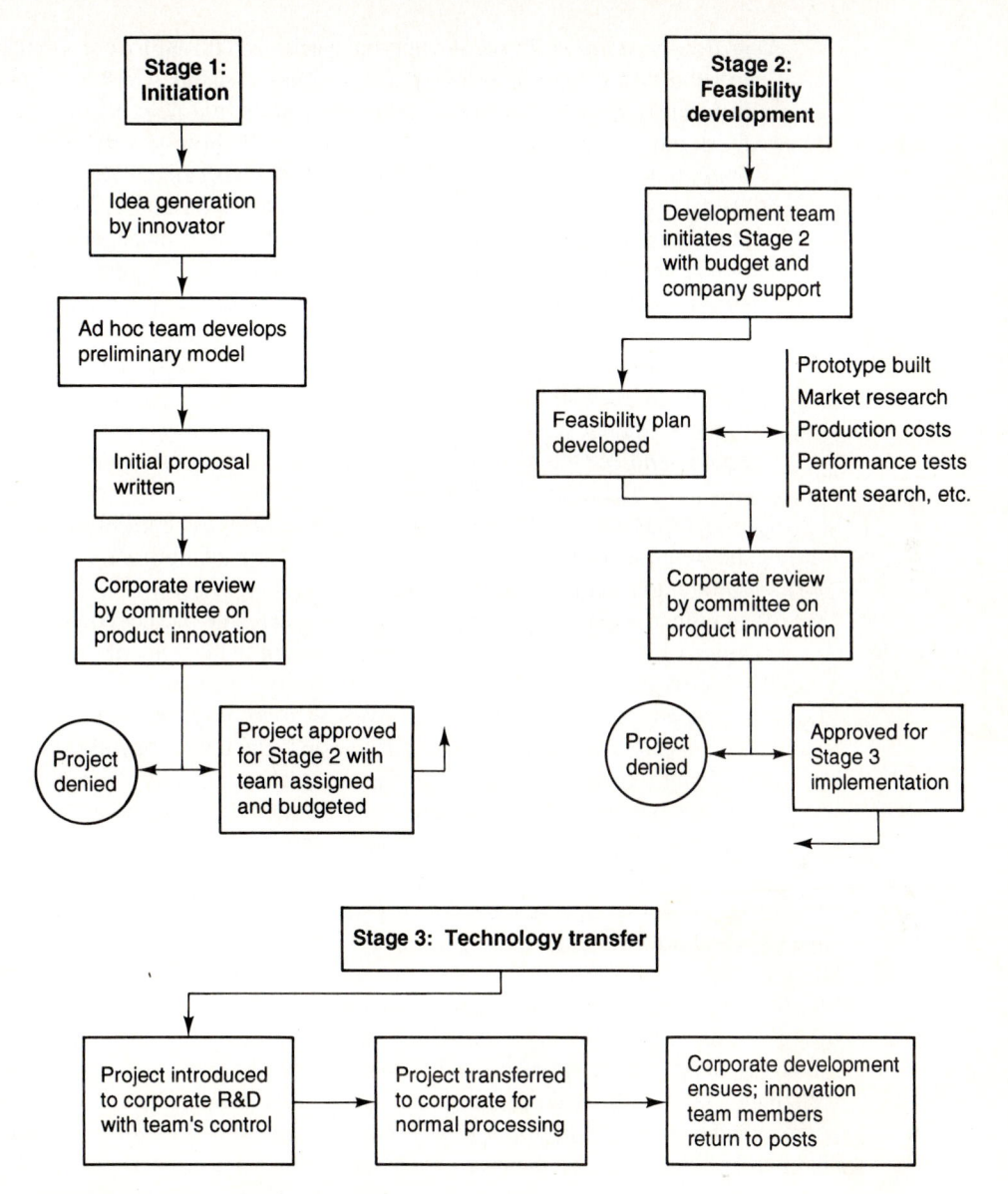

Figure 3-7 Merck's Technology Transfer Process

Stage 1: Initiation
- Idea generation by innovator
- Ad hoc team develops preliminary model
- Initial proposal written
- Corporate review by committee on product innovation
- Project denied ↔ Project approved for Stage 2 with team assigned and budgeted

Stage 2: Feasibility development
- Development team initiates Stage 2 with budget and company support
- Feasibility plan developed (Prototype built, Market research, Production costs, Performance tests, Patent search, etc.)
- Corporate review by committee on product innovation
- Project denied ↔ Approved for Stage 3 implementation

Stage 3: Technology transfer
- Project introduced to corporate R&D with team's control → Project transferred to corporate for normal processing → Corporate development ensues; innovation team members return to posts

mitment, and this was demonstrated in 1987 when the firm granted a young research biochemist a leave of absence to formulate a strategic plan for developing new venture teams. The biochemist, Robert Pengelly, was awarded a corporate grant to pursue his research, and in 1988 he introduced Merck's "innovation transfer" program, which is widely used today. The Merck model is presented in Figure 3-7.

New division status is the second approach achieved through a corporate mandate to solidify a project into a formal operating division. Unlike the innovation transfer approach, this option typically results in a new organization within the parent company, a horizontal extension that allows diversification without disrupting other operations. Companies that are organized through horizontal "stacking" of divisions can implement this decision easily. The new venture team will most likely become the new division's management core, and although ownership resides with the corporation, team members' careers will shift to the new unit. An excellent example is AT&T's American Transtech, a division formed in 1983 to manage the stock transfers resulting from the parent company's forced divestiture of operating divisions. American Transtech grew into a separate operating division that now handles stock transfers, paralegal work, and service development systems for AT&T, Bell South, and NYNEX. The subsidiary has autonomous operations, budgets, research, and compensation systems.[30]

Spin-offs may also be formed. These are new business entities created through the venture team, and they can take the form of corporate subsidiaries or autonomous corporations. Team members often enjoy stock options and significant ownership positions in the spin-off. The mother company typically retains a strong equity position, and although there is no set pattern of equity underwriting, companies such as Tektronix and General Electric have encouraged their venture teams to move toward a complete ownership position.[31] This is called a spin-off for obvious reasons, and it goes beyond the boundaries of being a corporate subsidiary. Team members actually share in success and risk the burden of failure as principal investors. It is the classic free-enterprise scenario of opportunity, rewarding those who bring an idea to fruition.

In new venture units, and specifically in spin-off situations, the parent company appears to relinquish control and give away potential profits, but evidence suggests that the corporation prospers. It does so for several reasons. First, team members are beneficiaries of the parent company's generosity, and that goes a long way in solidifying commercial relationships in which the parent company becomes a prime customer (or supplier), a sponsor, and a strong ally. Second, enlightened managers recognize that fast growth can best be achieved through a lean-and-mean young company. Moreover, if a corporation does not provide a way for team members to take part in developing their ideas, they may leave to set up their own firm or move to a competitor thereby alienating the corporation from its infant offspring.[32]

There also is a certain recognition that corporate mavericks who instigate venture teams are highly motivated by their own achievement orientation; they tend to be zealous about seeing their ideas through from incubation to full commercial development. If a subsidiary is developed with majority interest held by the parent company, the team, in effect, is little more than a subordinated division or "preferred vendor." If the product or service is not proprietary to the parent company, new external markets are likely to emerge; the team, as principal investors, will more tenaciously pursue those markets. The new venture has few limitations, and whatever investment the parent company holds will be enriched by rapid acceleration into new markets.

PROFILE △

IBM Looks toward Innovation

International Business Machines was founded on innovative thinking and the entrepreneurial spirit of Thomas Watson Sr., who built IBM from a struggling small company making mechanical office equipment to the world's largest and most successful computer products corporation. During a "lull" in its innovative history during the 1970s, IBM became more bureaucratic and less adaptive as an organization, allowing the microcomputer industry to develop without IBM's participation. Then, in 1981, IBM's Entry Systems Division, spearheaded by a few employees, created the company's first personal computer, and IBM regained its sense of innovative purpose. Looking to the future, IBM executives are implementing incentive programs, bonus systems, and grants to foster new technologies for the 21st century.

Source: "Akers Looks Ahead to IBM's Future Strategies, Principles," *Computer Reseller News*, April 3, 1989, pp. 44–46.

The Changing Environment for Corporate Entrepreneurship

This chapter has provided a brief glimpse of corporate entrepreneurship, but it should be apparent that there are ample opportunities in most organizations for innovation. A few stale bureaucracies linger in the shadows, but they will disappear unless they instill in managers a spirit of entrepreneurial endeavor. The ultimate challenge for corporations is to attract, nurture, and retain disruptive mavericks who can rejuvenate growth through successful innovations.

Society has extravagant rewards for those who can spearhead new ventures, and although corporate managers often leave their corporate positions to pursue those rewards, many farsighted corporations are helping employees realize their potential through new venture teams. Part of the equation for success is to match rewards with dreams that bear fruit. The entrepreneurial impulse, until recently, has been unleashed only through individual initiative, but amazing success stories have begun to appear as major corporations embrace the entrepreneurial spirit. Far beyond the boundaries of California's Silicon Valley or Boston's Route 128, firms such as AT&T, 3M, Merck & Company, General Electric, and IBM have instigated unusual corporate innovations through new venture teams.

The best known of these efforts may be IBM's Entry Systems Division, and it was an autonomous research group located in Boca Raton, Florida, far from IBM corporate halls, that created the IBM Personal Computer. To encourage development of the PC, IBM acted only as an investor with arms-length mentoring.[33] However, IBM recognized the value of motivating people through company development programs. During the past few years, IBM created research grants, bonuses, and recognition awards through its IBM Fellow Program, and the company has made more than a hundred awards to employees amounting to several million dollars.[34]

The fundamental structure of corporations in the United States may be changing in response to this entrepreneurial surge. Large companies are becoming smaller and more streamlined, and big "rational" bureaucratic organizations are quickly being replaced by decentralized organizations with smaller operating units. The growth of so-called high-tech firms, particularly those in microelectronics, led us into the 1990s with more than half of the emerging *Fortune* 500 firms drawn from "instant successes"—the small entrepreneurial firm turned large through rapid growth and innovation. The new "large" companies, however, are small compared to those of the 1960s. Most have fewer than 5,000 employees, yet they generate sales that match companies four times their size. This trend, called the atomization of America, is partially the result of improved technology and partially the result of a shift in leadership emphasis, away from structured controls toward self-direction for operating units.[35]

There is little doubt that smaller operating units that can respond quickly to market changes and new technologies are reshaping corporations. Rational bureaucracies—corporations with layered functional divisions and narrow specializations—are quickly being replaced by smaller corporations, or by larger ones that have "downsized," streamlining their organizations.[36]

▶ **CHECKPOINT**

Describe the benefits associated with spontaneous and formal new venture units.

Identify and discuss the various approaches taken by established companies to sponsor formal new venture units.

A CONCLUDING PERSPECTIVE

As a conclusion, it is important to reflect briefly on entrepreneurship as it relates to small business and corporate endeavor. The small business sector is growing, not only in the number of new enterprises, but also in the markets they serve. Once thought to be the realm of "shopkeepers" and "mom-and-pop" stores, small business has evolved to include high-profit companies with extensive sales domestically and overseas. Most people who start small businesses will continue to do so because they seek an alternative life-style away from the corporate environment, and they will continue to focus primarily on community endeavors. Nevertheless, they continue to represent nearly half of the U.S. GNP while providing employment for more than half the total nonfarm work force.

From a corporate viewpoint, innovative models of entrepreneurship have only recently begun to surface. Current students of management and entrepreneurship will most likely be the leaders who implement these changes in a pervasive way as the 21st century unfolds. Perhaps the corporate environment will change in such a way that substantial opportunities will emerge for innovative managers. These may be particularly enticing for those who understand challenges such as the creation of new venture units as potential career opportunities.

▲ ▲ ▲ ▲ ▲ ▲ SYNOPSIS FOR LEARNING

1. *Describe the environment of small business and how it is changing.*

Small businesses comprise a large majority of enterprises in the United States, and although they are individually small, they account for a significant portion of GNP and slightly more than half of all nonfarm employees. Small businesses typically provide goods and services to local markets; however, there has been a growing number of small businesses involved in global trade. The environment of small business is described by local or regional conditions. Thus national trends such as unemployment may not have a direct effect on local companies. Small businesses are vulnerable to some national phenomena, such as financial changes, because they often have heavy debt requirements; swings in interest rates rapidly consume a firm's cash flow. Although "macro" factors are important, small business owners are more concerned with "micro" problems. These include short-term cost and price changes, immediate competition, and managing the small business team. Often small business owners are caught up in this sense of "immediacy" and fail to account for threats that arise from externalities.

2. *Identify the most common causes for small business failure.*

A broad and inaccurate statement often heard is that small businesses fail because of "poor management." That begs the question, because businesses are often fragile and particularly susceptible to external influences. These include changes in debt availability, interest rates, local demand for goods and services, regional employment trends, production prices required by larger companies, and government regulations. Slight changes in tax laws, for example, can quickly turn a profitable small business into an unprofitable enterprise. More important, small business owners must wear many hats, and although they are usually technically competent, they may not be adept at marketing, managing employees, controlling cash flow and finances, or strategic planning. One reason for these shortcomings is lack of experience. Another is that many small business owners are arrogant; they simply refuse to acknowledge that they cannot do everything well; consequently, they allow their business to falter. One important "mismanagement" symptom is lack of a clear business philosophy. Many small businesspersons work with blinders on, seeing only the short-term potential for profits without understanding that they must create a lasting organization capable of satisfying customers with quality goods and services.

3. *Explain the important success factors for small business enterprises.*

One of the most important ways to improve the odds for business success is to improve planning. Because so few businesses are planned well before opening, counselors and mentors have been adamant that owners should develop systematic and thorough business plans. Recently, however, advice has been more guarded. Business owners are encouraged to plan pragmatically, giving due diligence to business issues supported by adequate market research and well-developed objectives, yet avoiding paralysis caused by overzealous planning. In addition, probabilities for success can be improved by reversing the factors of failure. Therefore, understanding why and how small businesses fail is crucial to safeguarding against failure. Inexperience and personal shortcomings can be offset by creating a team with skills that complement those of the entrepreneur.

4. *Describe corporate entrepreneurship.*

Corporate entrepreneurship, also called intrapreneurship or intra-corporate entrepreneurship, is the process of encouraging innovation within existing companies through motivated employees who are supported with company resources. An exact definition is lacking, but various perceptions exist. At one end of a spectrum of opinion are those who view corporate entrepreneurship as a contradiction in terms; that is, entrepreneurship does not exist because salaried employees who innovate take little or no personal risk in the process, and they seldom reap rewards for their achievements. At the other end of the spectrum, corporate entrepreneurs are cast in heroic terms as corporate commandos who alter the course of their companies through tenacious innovation. They are called courageous souls who risk their careers for little compensation, championing new ideas as mavericks bent on smashing the status quo. However, they behave this way while they are protected in their jobs and have access to corporate resources.

5. *Discuss the major approaches to corporate entrepreneurship.*

Four approaches to corporate entrepreneurship have been described. First, administrative entrepreneurship describes the traditional R&D process, but with the distinction that researchers who create new ideas become key players in commercializing them. Second, opportunistic entrepreneurship suggests that large companies are positioned to commercialize ideas generated elsewhere. Thus smaller companies and individual inventors may have brilliant innovations but lack the resources or marketing power to develop them. Larger firms with these advantages can prosper by adopting their innovations. Third, imitative entrepreneurship implies industrial espionage (or liberal borrowing of another's ideas). Large companies with relatively more resources and lower costs can take an existing innovation, make it cheaper, finance it at a lower cost, and market it more efficiently than smaller firms. Fourth, incubative entrepreneurship suggests an intensive in-house effort to establish new methods of innovation. New venture units, project teams, and systems of "spinning off" companies based on innovations developed by company employees are among the ways corporations are trying to encourage entrepreneurship.

6. *Describe emerging ways corporations are encouraging entrepreneurship.*

Corporate venture teams, also known as new venture units, have become a popular way to encourage employees to develop new commercial ideas. Some of these teams evolve spontaneously as champions "bootleg" product development on company time and resources, creating feasible new ventures that the parent company can reconfigure into divisions or subsidiaries. Formal venture teams are those sponsored by companies to pursue research and development, and they can take several forms. Some large companies, such as Merck, sponsor programs of innovation transfer in which incubative behavior is supported. Teams are given resources and corporate approval to pursue ideas, systematically evolving toward new internal business ventures. Other companies, such as General Electric, set up new venture units with division status, complete with budgets, resources, and entrepreneurial teams. Team members are often given the opportunity to invest in ventures or to share profits, thereby giving them incentives to succeed. Spin-off ventures can also be created whereby parent companies become major investors in separate companies specifically created to pursue innovations.

NOTES

1. *Handbook of Small Business Data* (Washington, DC: U.S. Small Business Administration, Office of Advocacy, 1989), Chap. 2.

2. North River Associates, *Estimating Value Added to Measure the Contributions of Small Business in the U.S. Economy* (Washington, DC: U.S. Small Business Administration, Office of Advocacy, 1988), pp. 1, 4.

3. U.S. Department of Commerce, Bureau of the Census, *County Business Patterns* (Washington, DC: U.S. Government Printing Office, 1989).

4. *The Entrepreneurs: An American Adventure*, Film No. 3 and Academic Supplement (Boston: Enterprise Media, 1987), pp. 4–5.

5. "Bonus Gets US Farmers Cracking on Egg Quotas," *South China Morning Post*, October 4, 1989, p. 12.

6. Clifford M. Baumback, *How to Organize and Operate a Small Business*, 8th ed. (Englewood Cliffs, NJ: Prentice-Hall, 1988).

7. U.S. Department of Commerce, *County Business Patterns*.

8. "Issue Briefs and Facts," *The White House Conference on Small Business* (Washington, DC: U.S. Small Business Administration,1987), pp. 12–13.

9. Albert V. Bruno and Joel K. Leidecker, "A Comparative Study of New Venture Failure: 1960 vs. 1980," *Frontiers of Entrepreneurship Research, 1987*, pp. 375–388.

10. *The Entrepreneurs: An American Adventure*, Film No. 1 and Academic Supplement (Boston: Enterprise Media, 1987), pp. 1–2.

11. Frank L. Bauer, "Better Purchasing: High Rewards at Low Risk," *McKinsey Quarterly*, Winter 1977, pp. 75–86.

12. Dun and Bradstreet Corporation, *Key Business Ratios* (New York: Dun and Bradstreet, 1988).

13. Peter F. Drucker, *People and Performance: The Best of Peter Drucker on Management* (New York: Harper & Row, 1977), p. 89.

14. Jeffrey C. Schuman and John A. Seeger, "The Theory and Practice of Strategic Management in Smaller Rapid Growth Firms," *American Journal of Small Business*, Vol. 11, No. 1 (1986), pp. 7–18.

15. Robert Ronstadt, "The Educated Entrepreneurs: A New Era of Entrepreneurial Education Is Beginning," *American Journal of Small Business*, Vol. 11, No. 4 (1987), pp. 37–53.

16. Thomas Owens, "Business Teams," *Small Business Reports*, January 1989, pp. 52–58.

17. Rosabeth Moss Kanter, Cynthia Ingols, Erika Morgan, and Tobias K. Seggerman, "Driving Corporate Entrepreneurship," *Management Review*, April 1987, pp. 14–16.

18. Hans Schollhammer, "Internal Corporate Entrepreneurship," in Calvin A. Kent, Donald L. Sexton, and Karl H. Vesper, eds., *Encyclopedia of Entrepreneurship* (Englewood Cliffs, NJ: Prentice-Hall, 1982), pp. 209–223.

19. Gifford Pinchot III, *Intrapreneuring* (New York: Harper & Row, 1985), p. xi.

20. Ibid., p. xvii.

21. Robert J. Scaffhauser, "How a Mature Firm Fosters Intrapreneurs," *Planning Review*, March 1986, pp. 6–41.

22. Schollhammer, "Internal Corporate Entrepreneurship," pp. 212–218.

23. Steven C. Wheelwright and W. Earl Sasser, Jr., "The New Product Development Map," *Harvard Business Review*, Vol. 89, No. 3 (May-June 1989), pp. 112–125.

24. "They Sell Their Secrets," *Intrapreneurial Excellence*, March 1987, p. 5.

25. R. Jeffery Ellis and Natalie T. Taylor, "Specifying Intrapreneurship," *Frontiers of Entrepreneurship Research, 1987*, pp. 527–541. Also see "Why Kodak Is Starting to Click Again," *Business Week*, February 23, 1987, pp. 134–135, 138. Also see "Do Mergers Really Work? Not Very Often—Which Raises Questions about Merger Mania," *Business Week*, June 3, 1985, pp. 88–100. In addition, "Marketing's New Look: Campbell Leads a Revolution in the Way Consumer Products Are Sold," *Business Week*, January 26, 1987, pp. 64–69.

26. Hollister B. Sykes, "Lessons from a New Venture Program," *Harvard Business Review*, Vol. 86, No. 3 (May-June 1986), pp. 69–74.

27. Christopher K. Bart, "New Venture Units: Use Them Wisely to Manage Innovation," *Sloan Management Review*, Vol. 28, No. 3 (1988), pp. 35–43.

28. Pinchot, *Intrapreneuring*, pp. 181–184.

29. Robert J. Pengelly and H. Richard Priesmeyer, *Innovation Transfer: An Entrepreneurial Management Model for Product Development and Commercialization*, reprint of Merck & Company manual on innovation transfer, January 1988.

30. "Innovative Work Design Proves Productive," *Intrapreneurial Excellence*, February 1987, p. 3.

31. Charles R. Carson, "How GE Grows Entrepreneurs," *Management Review*, February 1982, p. 29.

32. Watts S. Humphrey, *Managing for Innovation: Leading Technical People*, (Englewood Cliffs, NJ: Prentice-Hall, 1987), pp. 66–69, 124–125.

33. Pinchot, *Intrapreneuring*, pp. 205–206.

34. Humphrey, *Managing for Innovation*, pp. 129–130.

35. David L. Birch, "The Atomization of America," *Inc.*, March 1987, pp. 21–22.

36. "Downsizing: Preserving Company Strength after a Staff Reduction," *Small Business Reports*, January 1989, pp. 29–39.

CASE 3-1

Her Own Boss

Katherine Magrini is one of many women who own their own businesses, and her experience is not very different from others who must contend with being a mother, spouse, and family cheerleader in addition to owning and operating a business. Magrini is more successful than most women (or men). She turned her first million at age 28, and ten years later she is on a $10 million annual roll.

Katherine Magrini is owner and president of Gardner Spring & Wire Company, a Chicago corporation that markets industrial springs and spring assembly hardware. She bought the company in 1978, hocking everything she had and borrowing more than a million dollars, and although this was her first business, she had worked for Gardner (and had become its president) several years earlier while she was still in her early 20s.

Magrini grew up in Drumright, Oklahoma, with five brothers. With her brothers, she started working for the Oklahoma Spring Company in sales. Her brothers eventually bought that company, expanded, and bought Gardner Spring & Wire Company. Katherine Magrini was sent to Chicago to help out there, and she took the fledgling division with only $50,000 in sales to more than $400,000 in sales by opening accounts with the federal government and chains such as Ace Hardware. She recalls that she was the first woman ever to call on Ace Hardware, and during the 1970s when this growth occurred, most of her clients could not understand that a woman could sell industrial hardware.

The combination of her brothers' manufacturing business in Oklahoma and her fast-paced marketing in Chicago was so successful that the family sold the business for an undisclosed but "nice" sum. With the sale, Katherine felt she had lost part of herself, and subsequently bought back the Gardner company. During her rise to success and while re-creating her independent business, she managed a family, stayed involved with school and community affairs, and after a divorce remarried to pursue a happy life-style. She does not speak much about her family except to say that the television show *Dallas* held no surprises for her.

In Katherine Magrini's mind, there is nothing more exhilarating than owning your own business, and for her, the fun is in the challenge of making the firm grow from a small business struggling for a foothold. Today, more and more women are making this choice rather than pursuing traditional careers. The SBA notes that for the past ten years, the number of women starting new ventures is three times as large as the number of men. There are several good reasons for this trend. Some women find that owning a business is the only way to combine a decent wage with time for their children by having the flexibility to control their schedules. Others see themselves as unlikely corporate managers, and recognizing the gender problem that exists for achieving success, they choose the entrepreneurial route. Still others see entrepreneurship as a way of controlling their lives, pursuing interests that would be impossible in corporate jobs.

There are prices to pay that many men do not have to consider. The dual roles of mother and business owner often conflict, and husbands and wives tend to develop separate career tracks that often cannot be reconciled. In Magrini's case, the price was divorce, and although failed marriages are not uncommon in America, business pressures played a significant role in dividing her loyalties. Women can also find it lonely in a business world, especially if business clients are predominately men; this too was a problem for Magrini. Many women, however, have businesses that fit well with their interests and with women customers. These include services in beauty care, women's clothing, nutrition, education, and entertainment. Nevertheless, being in business often exacts a double price for women, yet for those with determination like Katherine Magrini, the rewards can increase at an exponential rate.

CASE QUESTIONS

1. Describe the nature of small business ownership, and tell how Katherine Magrini fits the profile of an independent entrepreneur.
2. Discuss problems facing small business owners and entrepreneurs in family businesses. Contrast these with the case and discuss possible issues that women entrepreneurs like Katherine Magrini face.
3. Identify and describe opportunities that women might find rewarding as business ventures. Also discuss the advantages and disadvantages of unusual enterprises such as the industrial spring hardware business in the case.

Source: Susan Ochshorn, "I Am My Own Boss," *Venture*, July 1986, pp. 46–47.

CASE 3-2

Corporate Adventures, New Units, and Tiger Teams

Many corporations are turning to a form of "new venture" creation in an effort to revive their organizations. The objective is to emulate the behavior of smaller, lean and mean, entrepreneurial ventures that are innovative and nimble. Many of these efforts are highly successful, but corporate executives find they cannot always change their behavior. Several examples are noteworthy.

Bausch & Lomb, the multinational medical instrumentation and optics company, has created "tiger teams." These are autonomous groups of scientists given resources and freedom of action to develop new products. Each team has a budget and can assemble its own members from any corporate discipline. When their ideas become marketable products, they share in profits and receive bonuses of cash and stock options, but B&L employees stay within their corporate positions working mainly on projects a few hours each week in special meetings and through R&D departments. Over a period of several years, B&L has introduced several innovative products, altered distribution systems, and marketed improved models of Inter-Plak, the home oral hygiene product.

At Texas Instruments, innovations are encouraged by any employee or company group. If an idea has promise, TI backs the idea with resources and allows employees to form an ad hoc division to pursue it. Once developed to the stage of successful test marketing, the product is brought on line through one of TI's primary divisions. A notable success is the Speak & Spell family of products.

Colgate-Palmolive Corporation created a separate company for innovation development. It is called the Colgate Venture Company, and its mission is to help any corporate group identify and start new businesses related to Colgate's consumer products industry. The venture company underwrites individual projects and helps corporate teams create "spin-off" subsidiaries or separate businesses. This policy has resulted in several new business units, including a retail branch with the initial location in Long Island called Clean Street USA. Colgate venture units also launched the Maniac line of teen personal care products.

On the down side, many corporate efforts to emulate entrepreneurial ventures have failed, but few companies make these failures public. Exxon Corporation wasted more than $10 billion several years ago developing its Exxon Office Systems division, which purportedly was to become the leader in office information systems ahead of IBM. Exxon failed, largely because corporate oil executives were expected to lead the venture, spearheading innovations in computer technology and information marketing.

More recently, Weyerhaeuser Company decided it could put its billion-dollar muscle behind a new disposable diaper to compete with Kimberly-Clark and Procter & Gamble. Weyerhaeuser had been marketing a low-priced product under generic labels for several years. The new diaper was developed by a new venture unit and resulted from careful consumer research. Called UltraSofts, Weyerhaeuser's diaper had unique features that included cushy waistbands and patented cuffs to stop leakage. UltraSofts were made with clothlike covers and used superabsorbent pulp material. Initial consumer reaction was very good, and UltraSofts were proclaimed by Weyerhaeuser as the world's best diaper.

The company's executives decided that UltraSofts were so good that rather than market through generic brands and settle for a small market share, the company would go after a national market, competing head-on with Kimberly-Clark and Procter & Gamble. In early 1990, UltraSofts were introduced through an unprecedented campaign. Samples and discounts were mailed to 50,000 shoppers in the launch area of Rochester, New York, and a blitz of television ads, video promotions, magazine features, and newspaper specials were used to announce UltraSofts. Pricing was also set 10 percent below the competition, and the company employed top market research and consumer affairs consultants to tailor presentations for hundreds of retailers. Sales exceeded expectations, and executives of the corporation envisioned sharing the $3.8 billion diaper market equally with its two primary competitors.

Success lasted a few months, but UltraSofts disappeared from the market in less than ten months. Weyerhaeuser executives blame failure on poor planning and uncoordinated operations that drove costs up too high to compete. In addition to the huge corporate marketing budget that was never absorbed by sales, the company's new venture pilot plant experienced breakdowns, fires, labor problems, and snarled production. The plant was not geared up to meet production schedules created by corporate fiat, and although it had operated efficiently as a small production unit, just the weight of activity created a series of disasters. Prior to the big push, the diaper unit had marketed products designed for the private brands of supermarkets, and these were manufactured and distributed in small batches; the system was cost-effective and allowed favorable private brand prices for retailers. Under mass-production and mass-distribution mandates, neither costs nor prices would be maintained.

CASE QUESTIONS

1. Explain each of the examples in terms of different approaches to achieving corporate entrepreneurship.
2. Describe the advantages and disadvantages of the different approaches taken by each

company to encourage innovation or to introduce new products.
3. Examine the problems, real or perceived, of Weyerhaeuser's effort to position its diaper product against major competitors. What do you see as critical mistakes or problems that led to failure?

Sources: Louis Therrien, "Bausch & Lomb Is Correcting Its Vision of Research," *Business Week*, March 30, 1987, p. 9; Barrie M. Spelling, "Colgate Ventures into New Territories," *Marketing Communications*, December 1987, pp. 17–21; and Alecia Swasy, "Diaper's Failure Shows How Poor Plans, Unexpected Woes Can Kill New Products," *Wall Street Journal*, October 9, 1990, pp. B1, B13.

Chapter 4

A Model for New Ventures: Feasibility Planning

OBJECTIVES

1. Discuss the concept of a planning paradigm for new ventures.
2. Describe the four-stage growth model of entrepreneurship.
3. Discuss the fundamentals of a good feasibility plan.
3. Explain the major components in a feasibility plan.
4. Explore planning responsibilities and ways in which entrepreneurs can get assistance.

Just as there are no absolute answers on how to succeed in business, there are no absolute answers on how to develop a successful new venture. There are no undisputed "models" of entrepreneurship, but there are similarities among the leading ones that suggest a *paradigm*, a general pattern of how to progress from an abstract idea to achieving sustained sales. This chapter provides a paradigm in which the sequence of activities starts with the initial idea and ends with an established enterprise positioned for growth.

The model, or paradigm, encompasses a *feasibility plan*. This is a pragmatic business plan reflecting the philosophy that entrepreneurs should do the planning necessary to ensure the feasibility of a venture without becoming overwhelmed in the process. The planning outline presented here is a foundation for more detailed chapters in the remainder of the text.

THE CONCEPT OF A PLANNING PARADIGM

Karl H. Vesper, a leading educator in the field, concludes that there are perhaps a half dozen leading models that describe the entrepreneurship process. He also notes that these models suggest more than a hundred different sequences for creating new ventures, each sequence having variations according to the unique characteristics of individual ventures. As a result, entrepreneurs can follow one paradigm only with the understanding that it provides a framework—not a mandate—for required activities.[1] This point is illustrated by the experiences of two successful entrepreneurs who established their businesses through entirely different sequences of events.

Called the Cowboy Capitalist, H. Ross Perot, founder of Electronic Data Systems Corporation (EDS), may be one of this century's most unpredictable and successful entrepreneurs. Perot started EDS in 1962 with $1,000 and an idea for using computers as integrated systems. He envisioned computer terminals connected through telecommunication systems and information processing that could link operations instantaneously on a global basis. We take these things for granted today, but they were revolutionary in 1962, when critical technology such as integrated circuitry, microcomputers, and telecommunication software were years away from being developed. Nevertheless, Perot had the vision, and he created EDS to accomplish the feat. Planning was incremental, starting with systems designed for office use, expanding to factory controls, then to companywide integration. Perot hired the best designers and planners possible, established a remarkable market research team, and focused EDS always on possibilities five or ten years into the future. Perot relied on instinct but made informed decisions based on astute strategic plans developed by his staff. As a result, EDS was compared to a tank that could be put into low gear and roll over anything. The company was sold to General Motors in 1984, but Perot is doing it all again with Perot Systems, and looking into the next century as a planning horizon.[2]

In contrast to Perot, Michael Dell began as a premed undergraduate student who, at the age of 20, turned a hunch into the quarter-billion-dollar Dell Computer Corporation. The hunch came to him while working part-time selling IBM PCs near his campus. Through his job, he discovered the huge price markups on computers, and he was convinced that the world was ready for a low-cost "clone" of the IBM PC. To test his idea, he assembled his own PC in his apartment from parts purchased by mail order. It worked, and the total cost was well under $1,000, so he made a few more to sell to friends. The hunch turned into a business, and he called his system the PC Limited. Word spread about Dell's computers, and he began taking orders over the phone. Demand was extraordinary, and his apartment-based business soon turned into a direct sales organization. Planning evolved only as sales growth pushed Dell to make decisions, but his success formula was entrenched by circumstances; build a clone computer at the lowest cost possible and market it directly through an army of salespeople with telephones. Planning became essential to establish purchasing systems and a nationwide distribution system, but planning was done reluctantly process. Nevertheless, it was accomplished by dedicated staff, and the corporation expanded to more than $200 million in sales. Although many of his ideas changed as the business evolved, Dell retained the core strategy of direct sales and low-cost clones.[3]

H. Ross Perot and Michael Dell represent two ends of a spectrum of planning activities, and their businesses evolved through entirely different sets of sequential activities. There is no way to say whether either would have been more or less

Chapter 4   A Model for New Ventures: Feasibility Planning

PROFILE △

Ready, Aim, Fire, Fire, Fire, Fire

After selling Electronic Data Systems Corporation (EDS) to General Motors for $2.5 billion, H. Ross Perot is starting all over again. His new company, Perot Systems, is in the building stage, but Perot promises to make it as successful as EDS. Perhaps more important, he has positioned Perot Systems to compete with EDS, the company he founded in 1962 and took to nearly $4.5 billion in annual sales.

Perot served on GM's board as part of the EDS deal, and while there, he became one of GM's most outspoken critics. Convinced that GM was a huge machine buckling under a mired bureaucracy, Perot condemned management practices as lacking imagination, drive, and innovation. Perot left GM and began an ardent attack on American bureaucracy in general. As one of the country's most successful entrepreneurs, he characterized large corporations—and GM in particular—as paralyzed by inactivity. Paraphrasing a military action, Perot said, "The gunner's command at GM . . . was 'Ready, aim, aim, aim, aim.' " In contrast, the EDS approach was characterized as "Ready, aim, fire, fire, fire, fire."

Perot has been described as an extraordinary thinker with finely tuned instincts, yet a leader who inspired strategic action based on exceptional preparation. Not only was EDS well planned and well staffed, but it was also strategically positioned to make revolutionary changes. Perot Systems promises to be no less dynamic, and H. Ross Perot is positioning his company for 21st-century technology.

Sources: Bo Burlingham and Curtis Hartman, "Cowboy Capitalist," *Inc.*, January 1989, pp. 54–62, 66, 68–69. Ross Perot, "How I Would Turn Around GM," *Fortune*, February 15, 1988, pp. 44–46.

---

successful had they behaved differently. Dell could have planned his business in detail and perhaps been paralyzed by it; or perhaps his business would have doubled in size. Perot might have relied entirely on intuition to stumble into systems technology; he also could have failed miserably. In both instances, however, there was a logical pattern of activities that evolved, planned or not, that led them toward success.

This logical pattern is recognized today as the general paradigm for new venture development. It is called the *four-stage growth model*, and it will be the model, or paradigm, that we use throughout the remainder of this book.

> ▶ **CHECKPOINT**
>
> Discuss the concept of using a model for planning new ventures.
>
> Explain why planning is important for a start-up enterprise.

THE FOUR-STAGE GROWTH MODEL

The **four-stage growth model** consists of categories of distinct activities essential for a new venture to progress from an idea to a substantial enterprise. The four are *pre-start-up*, *start-up*, *early growth*, and *later growth* stages. Figure 4-1 summarizes activities related to each stage.[4]

Pre-start-up Stage

During this initial phase, ideas evolve from a creative process to the point of being consciously perceived as commercial endeavors. Entrepreneurs have already begun to believe that their ideas are feasible, and they become fascinated by visions of their enterprises. As noted earlier, many of them will haphazardly plunge into business, following a popular adage that entrepreneurship is simply a manner of "finding a gap and filling it." As we noted in Chapter 2, however, this lack of preparation too often leads to early failure. Having a gap and filling it are important, but seldom sufficient, for success.

More astute entrepreneurs will begin by asking questions about the actual potential of their products or services. They will try to answer questions about production, operations, markets, competitors, costs, financing, and potential profits. And they will try to resolve questions about their own abilities to start businesses. Depending on the complexity of the proposed enterprise, the range of pre-start-up activities can be quite extensive, but there are four activities common to all new ventures. These are shown in Figure 4-2.

Business Concept Identified. Entrepreneurs must first conceptualize their businesses. This conceptualization may occur as a natural extension of the *creativity process* in which new ideas are shaped into visions of useful products or services. It

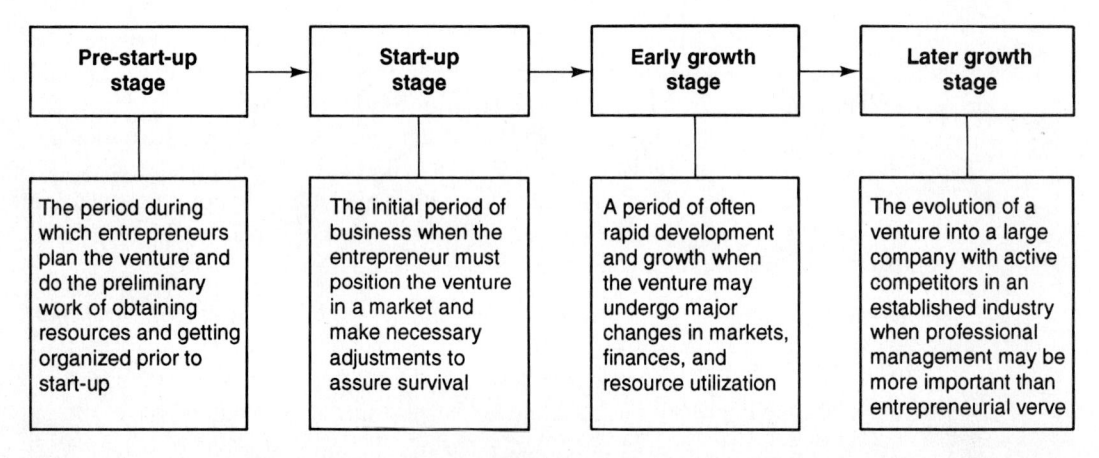

Pre-start-up stage	Start-up stage	Early growth stage	Later growth stage
The period during which entrepreneurs plan the venture and do the preliminary work of obtaining resources and getting organized prior to start-up	The initial period of business when the entrepreneur must position the venture in a market and make necessary adjustments to assure survival	A period of often rapid development and growth when the venture may undergo major changes in markets, finances, and resource utilization	The evolution of a venture into a large company with active competitors in an established industry when professional management may be more important than entrepreneurial verve

Figure 4-1 **The Four-Stage Growth Model**

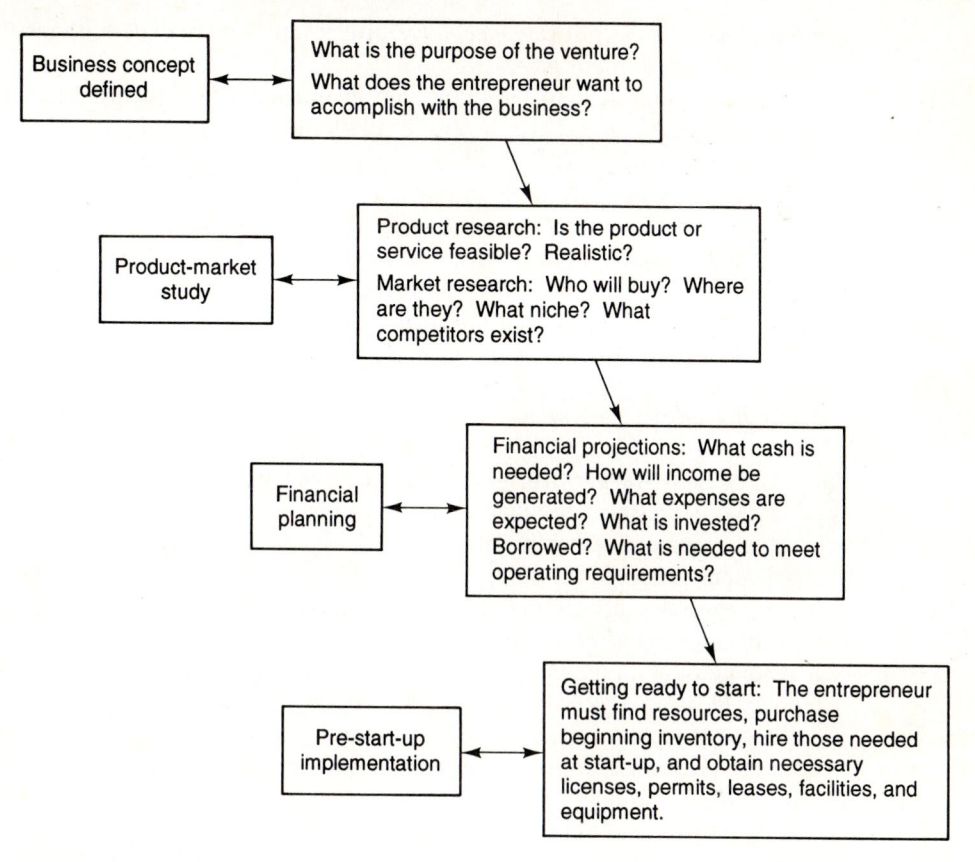

Chapter 4 A Model for New Ventures: Feasibility Planning

```
[Business concept defined] ⟷ [What is the purpose of the venture?
                               What does the entrepreneur want to
                               accomplish with the business?]
                                        │
                                        ▼
[Product-market study] ⟷ [Product research: Is the product or
                          service feasible? Realistic?
                          Market research: Who will buy? Where
                          are they? What niche? What
                          competitors exist?]
                                        │
                                        ▼
[Financial planning] ⟷ [Financial projections: What cash is
                        needed? How will income be
                        generated? What expenses are
                        expected? What is invested?
                        Borrowed? What is needed to meet
                        operating requirements?]
                                        │
                                        ▼
[Pre-start-up implementation] ⟷ [Getting ready to start: The entrepreneur
                                 must find resources, purchase
                                 beginning inventory, hire those needed
                                 at start-up, and obtain necessary
                                 licenses, permits, leases, facilities, and
                                 equipment.]
```

Figure 4-2 **Pre-start-up Activities**

also may occur in a conscientious plan developed around a perceived "gap" that an entrepreneur might "fill." The critical question to be answered is "What do I want to accomplish with this enterprise?"

To illustrate the point, consider how Steve Kirsch developed the concept for his electronic "mouse," a common accessory today for computer systems. Kirsch was an MIT student working in a computer lab where three very expensive machines were all crippled because the mechanical mouse each machine used was broken. He said that it was a sad situation, "like having a Ferrari with only three wheels on it."[5] Kirsch set about designing a reliable electronic mouse, formed his company, Mouse Systems, Inc., in 1982, and now has clients that include most major manufacturers of microcomputers and scientific workstations. He had no preconceived notion of becoming an entrepreneur, but the idea "glared out at him" when he built a reliable mouse for himself. The idea of a business evolved over a period of several months when he realized the market potential. Kirsch's *innovation* was not his business concept; he could have sold or licensed the idea to IBM. Kirsch chose to subcontract production, create a *marketing* company, and position his business to sell mouse accessories. His *business concept* was to design and market high-quality mouse accessories at premium prices.

Many rapid-fire questions jump into an aspiring entrepreneur's head the moment an idea begins to take shape. A few of the important questions are these: Does this thing exist already? If it doesn't, can it be made? Who would buy it? Why would they want it? Where are these customers? Am I the person to make this thing? Am I the one to sell it? Anyway, why would I want to do this?

The business concept may not be fully developed until most of these questions are answered. For instance, Kirsch initially had no intention of establishing his own venture; he wanted to sell the mouse design. When he was turned down, he offered to license his product. Turned down again, he thought of manufacturing, but realizing that he knew very little about production, he decided to focus on designing and marketing mouse accessories.

Product-Market Study. Once an entrepreneur has determined that a product or service is feasible, and that he or she might be capable, the next set of activities involves pragmatic research. This is crucial because entrepreneurs often jump to early conclusions based on intuition that, under close scrutiny, reveal fatal flaws in their plans. Research is necessary in at least two areas: product development and marketing.

Product research should include patent searches to uncover existing products. It is not unusual for dreams to end in the U.S. Patent Office when a half dozen similar product ideas are discovered. Some may be in production, some may be registered but never brought to market, and some may have never worked in the first place. If the search reveals a similar product in production, the proposed new venture usually ends there. If a product was patented but was also a commercial failure, understanding what went wrong could help avoid similar mistakes. It may be necessary to contact the original inventor, talk with the company that made the item, or search for out-of-circulation products in closets. If the product never worked in the first place, its flaw might be discovered, encouraging the entrepreneur to design a successful one.

Product research also requires actual R&D to design the item, investigate development costs, evaluate materials, and explore methods of manufacture. The questions to answer include the following: Can it be done? Can it be done at a cost that could generate profits? How is it to be done? Who will do it? As we shall see later, these questions are addressed in a special section of the feasibility plan, but product research must be *initiated* during the pre-start-up stage.

If the business is concerned with services, such as setting up a travel agency, "product" research in the sense of technical R&D does not exist. However, a travel agency will delineate its range of services, including types of tours offered, destinations, airlines served, travel associations with which to affiliate, and so on. This range of services defines "products" for the travel agency, and the business concept will depend critically on the blend of travel services devised through pre-start-up planning. Similarly, a retail merchandiser must devise an inventory plan. This will define the store's business concept through its product line, cost structure, image, and merchandising strategy.

Market research is the process of answering such questions as these: Who will buy the product or service? What will they be willing to pay? How can I attract them to my business? If this venture is a big success, what will prevent competitors from overwhelming me? Who are my competitors? Can I establish a niche in the market? What are my options for long-term growth? These questions are critical to pursue in concert with product research efforts for several important reasons. First, the product itself is usually modified by feedback from initial market research. Second, how a product is marketed often determines how it is designed, manufactured, and packaged. Third, a product is often commercially viable only when markets can be protected against strong competitors.[6]

The initial stage of marketing research is often rudimentary. Typically, entrepreneurs will confide in close friends or family members to get reactions to their ideas. This feedback is useful but often misleading. Friends and family members seldom want to hurt the feelings of someone close, so feedback is often a cautious nod of approval rather than an objective evaluation. Then too, there is the chance of caustic rejection—again, often without objective evaluation. Ted Turner's father, an entrepreneur himself in the advertising business, seldom found anything worthwhile in his son's ideas. Father-and-son arguments between the Turners were notorious—father wanting son to "do something useful" with his life, and son wanting to "do something different."[7]

Entrepreneurs occasionally seek professional help from market researchers, university centers, and experienced mentors. Unfortunately, most entrepreneurs do not ask enough people enough questions. They seldom ask customers for their opinions, yet when they do, they often gain valuable insights about their ideas. Successful entrepreneurs will try to reach as many people as possible in a systematic manner before making start-up investments. Formal market research, however, can be complicated and expensive, so during the pre-start-up stage, the process is usually *informal*. Specifically, entrepreneurs will personally research industry data, study competitors, and seek advice from people they know and trust.

During pre-start-up planning, informal market research is a minimum requirement. Entrepreneurs must be able to find satisfactory answers about their potential markets and competitors. They also must have some reasonable idea about pricing, promotions, and distribution. Chapter 8 addresses these issues thoroughly.

Financial Planning. The third set of pre-start-up activities relates to money. Although new ventures are usually underwritten by personal savings and cookie-jar money, cash infusions are needed as the business begins to grow. Early cash flow is usually acquired through a combination of short-term loans, home mortgages, and family investments. As the venture evolves further, more cash is needed, and entrepreneurs have to attract capital through sophisticated loans and knowledgeable investors. Attracting capital requires careful planning and documentation about products, services, markets, and the entrepreneur's expectations.

Financial planning during the pre-start-up stage will not necessarily be extensive, but it does have to be based on verifiable information. For example, if an entrepreneur projects a million dollars in sales during the first year, there should be more than intuition behind the forecast. Using product and market information, the entrepreneur should be able to justify cost-price relationships, how sales were estimated, and what will be required in overhead expenses. Using this information, the entrepreneur can forecast profits and cash flow, the two major pieces of information required by bank loan officers and investors.

The type of capital needed will dictate requirements for financial documentation. Most ventures will need seed capital during the pre-start-up and start-up phases. **Seed capital** is the cash needed for product development, market research, and initial operating expenses before sales revenue can begin to offset business expenses.[8] Capital requirements are addressed in Chapter 13, but seed capital can range from a few thousand dollars for a simple barbershop to several million dollars for a complex biotechnology business.

During the pre-start-up stage, entrepreneurs seldom need extensive seed capital, with one exception: When the nature of the business is to create new products through research, the venture may spend years in development without creating anything to sell. As a result, an infusion of substantial capital is needed that far exceeds the concept of seed money. The biotechnology industry exemplifies this phenomenon. Genentech, Inc., a biotech company that manufactures lab testing enzymes and experimental medicines, spent more than three years and $20 million before announcing its first commercial product.[9]

If we stay with a general model of a simple business, financial planning activities are not complicated during the pre-start-up stage, but they require diligence. Investors and lenders want to see financial projections based on reasonable initial research, and they require accurate documentation. They also require financial statements that show how the venture will perform during its first few years of business. Entrepreneurs also will have to clarify their stake in the business, investments by family members or partners, and their personal financial capabilities outside business interests.

Pre-start-up Implementation. If we define the pre-start-up stage as a period that precedes any attempt to generate sales, then it is a stage similar to that of an Olympic sprinter preparing for a race. The sprinter, like the entrepreneur, plans, trains, develops strategies, and gets physically and mentally prepared to run. Just before the race is to begin, the sprinter gets into the starting blocks to await the gun. Like the sprinter, an entrepreneur must commit to action and do certain things before the event.

Entrepreneurs must establish vendor relations with suppliers, establish a business location, hire essential personnel, arrange for initial promotions, and set up administration systems. These activities vary widely with the nature of the business, but they are all essential. If the venture is a new retail store, the premises will have to be leased and renovated (or perhaps a store built). The store will need starting inventory, so advanced purchasing must be accomplished. Sales clerks may be needed on opening day; therefore, they must be hired and trained. Public relations, advertising, and a grand-opening event should be arranged. Finally, administrative systems must be in place, including inventory and cash controls, credit card subscriptions, a merchandise replenishment system, and a payroll system.

If the business is in manufacturing, the pre-start-up stage is much more complex. It will include those activities already noted plus equipment leases (or purchases), performance checks on equipment, engineering, and initial production of starting inventory. In addition, marketing systems must be in place, and the entrepreneur may have to comply with regulations by agencies such as the Food and Drug Administration, Environmental Protection Agency, Equal Employment Opportunity Commission, or Occupational Safety and Health Administration. Service ventures, such as restaurants and realtors, must comply with state and local licensing laws. Attorneys, public accountants, physicians, and other professionals will have to meet criteria established by regulatory agencies and professional licensing associations.

These activities are best accomplished well in advance of opening, not at the eleventh hour; however, some things may be postponed until the last minute. These include signing leases and hiring employees, because they create expenses that cannot be recovered until the firm begins generating revenue. Therefore, the *pre-start-up implementation phase* constitutes a set of well-timed activities that must be accomplished. The entrepreneur is stepping into the sprinter's racing blocks.

Start-up Stage

The **start-up stage** is the initial period of business. For companies with products or services to sell, it is the first foray into revenue-generating activity. The start-up stage has no definite time frame, and there are no models to describe what a business does during this stage; however, there are two benchmark considerations. First, entrepreneurs want to meet operating objectives, such as satisfying revenue and cost targets. Second, they want to position the venture for long-term growth. These objectives are summarized in Exhibit 4-1.

Exhibit 4-1 **Start-up Operating Objectives**

Sales	To attain monthly sales volume as projected at prices projected in feasibility plan.
	To achieve projected sales mix of products and services as summarized in feasibility plan.
Revenue	To achieve cash flow within budget based on sale volume and price projections.
	To meet targets above variable costs with appropriate operating margins.
Growth	To realize incremental growth within seasonal pattern of forecasts.
	To maintain balance of growth with ability to underwrite inventory, materials, and human resources.
Position	To solidify a long-term position in appropriate markets as a result of adaptation during start-up.
	To identify market strategy for niches or opportunities in new products, services, or markets during start-up.

Meeting Operating Objectives. Ideally, the venture will generate projected sales, or do slightly better. If sales are significantly below projections, the venture risks running out of cash and closing. If sales are substantially higher than projections, the firm may find itself equally in distress and unable to either finance growth or replenish inventory. This risk is often overlooked because most people automatically assume that a higher sales volume means higher profits. Unfortunately, the only time this assumption is true is when an entrepreneur sells everything for cash and has an unlimited supply of inventory. Both conditions are rare.

More often, a business has an established inventory that requires time to replace and cash to acquire. If the business sets records on opening day, it may have nothing to sell on day two. One answer to this dilemma is to buy more inventory through rush orders, paying a premium for goods. If the company has large margins, added costs may be easily absorbed, but usually it is the other way around—premium costs absorb cash and profits.

This process is precisely what happened to Osborne Computers.[10] During its first year of operations, Osborne became the fastest-growing corporation in the United States. The company's founders had conceived of the first portable computer in 1980, several years before Compaq and IBM did so, but they had estimated sales at less than a third of the $80 million in orders achieved during the first few months in business. Because most sales were to distributors who had 30-day credit terms, Osborne accumulated huge orders, but without cash receipts. The company acquired debt financing to meet manufacturing costs, shipped computers around the clock, and within a few months was hopelessly in debt. Creditors called in Osborne's debts, and investors quickly liquidated, leaving the company debt ridden but with extraordinary sales orders. Unfortunately, orders could not be filled.

Meeting operating objectives does not necessarily mean making a profit. To the contrary, most new ventures operate at a loss for several years. They "break even" only with carefully monitored controls, but they should be able to structure the business so that *variable costs* are covered and *cash flow* is positive. If either condition cannot be met, the enterprise is not viable. Specifically, when variable costs cannot be met by sales revenue, by definition the company will go deeper into a hole with each sale. In addition, there will be no income to contribute to fixed costs or pre-start-up expenditures.

Maintaining a profitable blend of products and services is also important. For example, a retail bicycle shop may have been planned to generate 60 percent of gross revenue from bicycle sales, 30 percent from accessories, and 10 percent from repairs. It may turn out that 60 percent of total revenue is derived from accessories, 30 percent from bicycles, and 10 percent from repairs. In this situation, the shop owner will have idle inventory in bikes (money tied up in slow-moving inventory) while accessory inventory is depleted. Moreover, unless the cost-price differential is exactly the same for bicycles and accessories, income projections will be seriously distorted. This sequence of events is precisely what happened to Spokes Etc., a bicycle shop located in Alexandria, Virginia.[11] Fortunately the store's owner, Jim Strang, recognized the shift in sales early, quickly adjusted his operations, and avoided catastrophe. Good pre-start-up planning helps reduce these problems.

PROFILE △

Jim Strang

With two locations in northern Virginia, Spokes Etc. is a successful bicycle business founded by Jim Strang, a 1985 college graduate who spent his first two years after earning his business degree in the fast-paced world of corporate sales for Lanier Corporation. Life in the fast lane lost its luster when Strang had to give up biking and his independence; however, he enjoyed the challenge of business and sales. By opening his own bicycle shop, he satisfied his desire to stay close to biking and to pursue a business career. His bicycle stores have the latest equipment, accessories, and clothes, and he has a team of mechanics who share his enthusiasm for biking. Everyone in Spokes Etc. is a competitive rider and eager to share their knowledge with customers. In Strang's view, the business is a "living, personal extension of our philosophy to have fun and help others have fun. If we grow any larger, that could get lost in the shuffle.... I like it the way it is."

Source: Personal interview with Jim Strang, August 1989.

Positioning the Enterprise. Every successful business starts with a preconceived business idea. As noted earlier, this includes a concept of the product or service, markets, and growth potential. Entrepreneurs often find, however, that reality is quite different from what was envisioned. Two considerations are important. First, the business must *survive* in the short run, and second, the business must be *positioned* to achieve long-term objectives.

From a survival viewpoint, the start-up stage is a crucial period when adjustments are made. The entrepreneur who "opens" and smugly waits for sales to occur may not be open for long. Needless to say, some enterprises are so well developed before opening day that customers are lined up with cash in hand. This is not usually the case; more often this stage is a period of acid tests when many things go wrong. The product simply may not work, not sell, be introduced at the wrong time, or be positioned in the wrong market. The entrepreneur may not be capable of running the business. Costs may exceed expectations. Prices may not be low enough to attract customers. Investors may back out. And so on. Consequently, entrepreneurs must make quick adjustments to survive. These may include simple decisions such as adjusting inventory to eliminate slow-moving items, or complex decisions such as restructuring the company's debt when cash flow becomes thin.

From a long-term perspective, the business concept must coincide with realistic prospects for growth. This means that the enterprise must be *positioned* to take advantage of growth markets. Products are positioned by placing them for sale in particular market niches. For example, Michael Dell positioned PC Limited to sell to small businesses and as stand-alone systems through a factory-direct marketing process. He could have positioned his products for home use, education, scientific work, or office networks, each with different distribution systems. Other companies are positioned in these markets. Sun Microsystems, for example, sells mainly to organizations with engineering applications, Hewlett-Packard is strong in scientific research, and Apple Computer is strong in education markets.

Positioning of services is the process of organizing the enterprise to provide expertise to a particular clientele. Hyatt Legal Services, a consortium of independent attorneys, targets family clients with services that include drafting of wills, handling probates, representing clients in divorce suits, and litigating casualty claims. Other attorneys will specialize in criminal law, patents, corporate legal services, or labor relations. Retailers can finely tune their markets for young professionals, married women, single men, children, wealthy clientele, bargain hunters, and so on. Ideally, positioning will be planned during the pre-start-up stage, but even the best plans change soon after the venture opens, and positioning—or *repositioning*—is essential.

Early Growth Stage

Once the venture is positioned, successful enterprises will experience a stage of early growth. This is a period of intense monitoring, and growth can occur at different rates along a long continuum, ranging from slow growth through incrementally higher sales to explosive growth through quantum changes in consumer demand. This continuum is illustrated in Figure 4-3.

At the low end of the continuum, entrepreneurs find that they compete in slow-growth markets. New parcel-delivery systems and mail outlets such as the franchised Mail Boxes Etc. are successful, but they compete in local markets against UPS, Federal Express, and the U.S. Postal Service. As a result, they can achieve immediate success by attracting clients who seek alternative mail services, but annual growth rates are typically less than 5 percent because each store must persuade new customers to change their methods of handling mail.[12] Most highly specialized businesses, particularly those in food and agriculture, will experience slow growth. These include cheese shops, specialty garden farms, dietary consulting, ecology research, organically grown wines and vegetables, and specialty foods like tofu.[13]

At the high end of the continuum, two companies that experienced high-growth sales were Osborne Computers and People Express Airlines. As noted earlier, Osborne

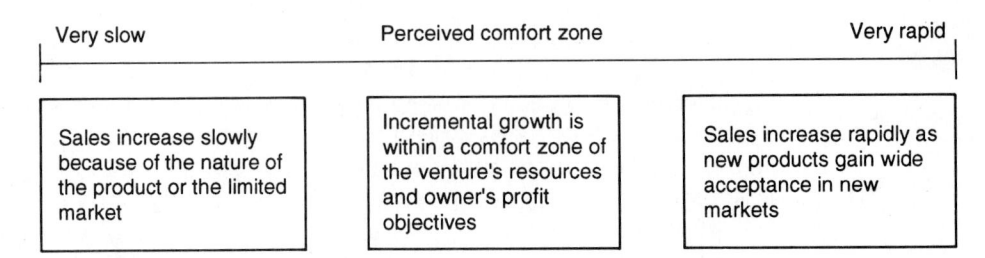

Figure 4-3 **Continuum of Early Growth**

grew so rapidly that it outran its ability to finance expansion. People Express, once listed as the nation's fastest-growing company, also outran its underwriting. Plagued by high expenses and a huge debt burden for aircraft, People Express filed for bankruptcy protection in 1987. However, there is nothing wrong with rapid growth as long as it is managed. For example, Karsten Solheim, a Norwegian immigrant, developed his first Ping putter as a hobby while working for General Electric. He positioned Karsten Manufacturing Corporation to manufacture a full line of golf clubs during the early 1980s when demand for golf equipment was expected to increase exponentially with rapid growth in new courses. Karsten's firm grew at nearly 200 percent annually, and by 1989, Karsten's Ping clubs were leading the market; Ping putters were used by more than half of PGA touring pros. Today, Ping produces 12,000 clubs a day, grossing $100 million annually without being able to meet demand for customer orders.[14]

Between these extremes, a majority of entrepreneurs find a "comfort zone" of expansion. Their ventures may have growth potential, but founders restrain expansion to coincide with personal objectives. Jim Strang, founder of Spokes Etc., quickly succeeded in his first bicycle store, and within a year he opened a second store. Both stores are successful, with annual growth near 20 percent. In 1989, Strang was urged to open a chain of franchises but refused, preferring instead to own and control his own shops. At the same time, Garry Snook founded Performance, Inc., a bicycle business with inventory similar to Strang's. Snook, however, decided to pursue rapid growth. He leveraged the business, created a franchise system, and by 1989 had ten stores in four states and more than $40 million in sales. Snook expects to open 50 stores by 1992.[15] Snook's business is growing more rapidly than Strang's, but not at the frantic pace set by Osborne or People Express. The important point is that both Strang and Snook are meeting their *personal* objectives, staying within their "comfort zones."

Interesting things can happen to a new venture during this stage. If the entrepreneur has a unique product or lucrative patent, the business may be actively courted by larger firms. Such courtships can result in very profitable buyouts or licensing agreements. Mergers are also common, as companies with complementary strengths combine to form a new company positioned for more rapid growth. Many businesses also experience early growth but find that the enterprise has severe limitations. In this case, an entrepreneur may simply recognize that the future holds little growth potential and reposition the venture as a small business.

Later Growth Stage

If the enterprise proves successful in the early growth stage and has momentum, it can find itself in competition with larger companies. This is the **later growth stage,** when the rate of growth may be slower and the industry has attracted competitors. Companies reaching this stage often "go public" with stock offerings. Family fortunes turn into corporate equity positions, private investors convert their holdings into publicly traded securities, and management teams replace the entrepreneurial cadre. In many instances, founders lose the personal identity they had with their firms, and if they are not ready to adapt to corporate management, they leave (or are ousted). Those who do adapt enjoy the benefits of corporate management and the profits of being major stockholders. For example, Jim Jaeger, founder of Cincinnati Microwave, Inc., the company that makes the Escort radar detector, reached a sales plateau in 1984. The market was still strong for radar detectors, but competition required infusions of new products. He developed a complementary product called the Passport, and sales surged. Jaeger found himself heading a $77 million company with hundreds of employees. This growth required a transformation in the company to restructure its equity capital and to establish a professional management team. Jaeger accomplished both, and his company continues to prosper.[16]

A few ventures become large without losing control or going public. Their founders continue to manage their corporations, finance growth through earnings, and avoid the complexities of publicly traded stock. The Du Pont family controlled its chemicals and plastics empire for generations, and today, the Mars family still owns and manages its global company in candy and convenience foods. Perhaps one of the most interesting companies is Mrs. Fields Cookies, a company started in 1978 by Debbi Fields at the age of 22, and now jointly operated by Debbi and Randy Fields. Their business has more than 500 stores spanning five countries and grosses $100 million annually. The business is not franchised; all stores are owned by the company, which is managed by a staff of about 120 people.[17]

Consequently, the later growth stage does not necessarily mean emulating IBM or General Motors, but most ventures outgrow their founders and earlier methods of raising capital. As we shall see in Chapters 13 and 14, there are significant differences between the various stages of development with regard to financing and managing companies.

Understanding the Four-Stage Growth Paradigm

Sequential stages of new venture development represent intervals that focus on different sets of circumstances. During the pre-start-up stage, the focus is on product, service, and market planning. The start-up stage requires entrepreneurs to focus on implementation and early positioning. During the early growth stage, they are concerned with rapid changes in sales and resources. And during the later growth stage, they must make a successful transition from personally managed enterprises to professionally managed companies.

Few companies, however, experience all four stages of growth. As noted earlier, many new ventures simply do not survive long enough to continue past the start-up stage. Others will be started by entrepreneurs who have no intention of expanding beyond a "comfort zone" of operations. Still others will embrace rapid growth, but their founders may not be able to make the transition to professionally managed companies.

The feasibility planning scenario presented in the following pages focuses on the pre-start-up and start-up stages. In the process, we address implications for the early growth stage, but planning for the later growth stage is omitted as a topic more appropriate for management and business policy courses.

> ▶ **CHECKPOINT**
>
> Describe the four stages in the growth model and how they differ.
>
> Explain five sets of activities essential during the pre-start-up stage.
>
> Define the growth continuum and contrast new venture activities at the polar extremes. What is a "comfort zone" in the continuum?

FUNDAMENTALS OF A FEASIBILITY PLAN

In Chapter 1, we defined a *business plan* as a comprehensive set of guidelines for a new venture. We also cautioned that entrepreneurs can become entangled in their plans, and although planning is essential, it must be done in a reasonable manner. Therefore, the term *feasibility planning* is used as a way of moderating the concept of a comprehensive business plan. A **feasibility plan** encompasses the full range of business planning activities, but it seldom requires the depth of research or detail expected for an established enterprise.

Every new business is unique. Each will have something that sets it apart from others, even if it is no more than the personality of an entrepreneur. For that reason, no plan is going to provide an absolute prescription for success. A feasibility plan is an outline of *potential* issues to address and a set of *guidelines* to help an entrepreneur make better decisions.

Developing a Good Plan

Feasibility plans usually are written for investors and lenders, and being aware of this audience often leads to overoptimistic presentations by entrepreneurs who "hard sell" their business concepts. Occasionally this tactic may attract investors and help secure loans, but it will have little value as a management tool for the founder. Writing an *honest* plan with *well-supported* information will benefit everyone.

A well-written plan should be succinct, clearly identifying products, services, markets, and the founders. A feasibility plan does not have to be "slick," but it does have to be prepared *in a quality manner*. The plan should be easy to read, complete, and accurate. There should be no misspellings, improper grammar, or mistakes in data. Effective plans avoid emotion-packed phrases like "This can't miss!" or "Everybody needs this!" They also avoid abstract language. Entrepreneurs who know how to write a good plan will avoid saying they "think" there is a market or they "believe" a product will work. Instead, they will use facts to support their assertions.

Protecting the Business

Since business plans are used to attract investors and lenders, many copies are circulated. Wide circulation can be dangerous if the plan contains sensitive information. Consequently, it is wise to include a strong "nondisclosure statement" on the cover page that states information in the plan is proprietary and cannot be copied, disclosed, shared, or otherwise compromised. Many entrepreneurs also assign an index number on each copy in addition to a signature line for each recipient. This constitutes an agreement on the nondisclosure terms and provides a reference number for documenting circulation. Although this procedure may not always protect entrepreneurs from having their ideas stolen, it can be a strong deterrent.

Making the Plan Readable

A thorough business plan often has more than 50 pages, but many plans based on easily understood business concepts may be less than 20 pages long. Plans for complex enterprises requiring extensive documentation are much longer. If there is a choice, keep it short. Potential investors and lenders receive many proposals, but they rarely read more than the first few pages. If the concept is intriguing, they spend more time probing financial data. It can be quite disturbing to an entrepreneur who has spent months writing a good plan to watch a loan officer spend five minutes reading the front page and skimming projections. Therefore, it is even more important to be convincing in the opening pages.[18]

For those few enterprises that capture an investor's attention (or get past the junior loan officer), there is a more complete study. This means that an entrepreneur must be very careful to capture a reader's attention early, yet provide thorough information for a detailed analysis that occurs later.

> ▶ **CHECKPOINT**
>
> Explain how a feasibility plan is used and why it is important to entrepreneurs.
>
> Describe the elements that go into writing an effective plan.

THE FEASIBILITY PLAN

The composite feasibility plan presented is this section was developed by comparing 26 different published versions. All of the plans included eight common elements that are contained in the feasibility model summarized in Exhibit 4-2. This model is generally adaptable to most types of new ventures.

Executive Summary

The opening section, called the **executive summary**, is a synopsis of the proposed enterprise. It is the "tickler" that either captures an investor's interest or kills all incentive to read further. Usually no longer than three pages, it addresses five subjects noted in Figure 4-4.

Exhibit 4-2 Eight Common Elements in a Feasibility Plan

Executive summary	Venture defined, products or services identified, market characteristics summarized, founders introduced, and financial structure profiled
Business concept	Purpose of the venture and the major objectives of its founders; description of the distinct competency of the firm
Product or service	Function and nature of products and services, proprietary interests, attributes, and technical profile
Market research and analysis	Customer scenario, markets, venture's niche, industry structure, expected competition, and sales forecast
Market plan	Market strategy to compete, pricing, promotion, distribution, service and warranties, and sales leadership
Manufacturing or operations	Facilities, location, inventory and materials needed, human resources, operational processes, technology, security, insurance, and safety
Entrepreneurial team	Profile of founders, key personnel, investors, and management roles
Financial documentation	Financial statements for income and expenses, cash flow, assets and liabilities, break-even projections, and start-up underwriting needed

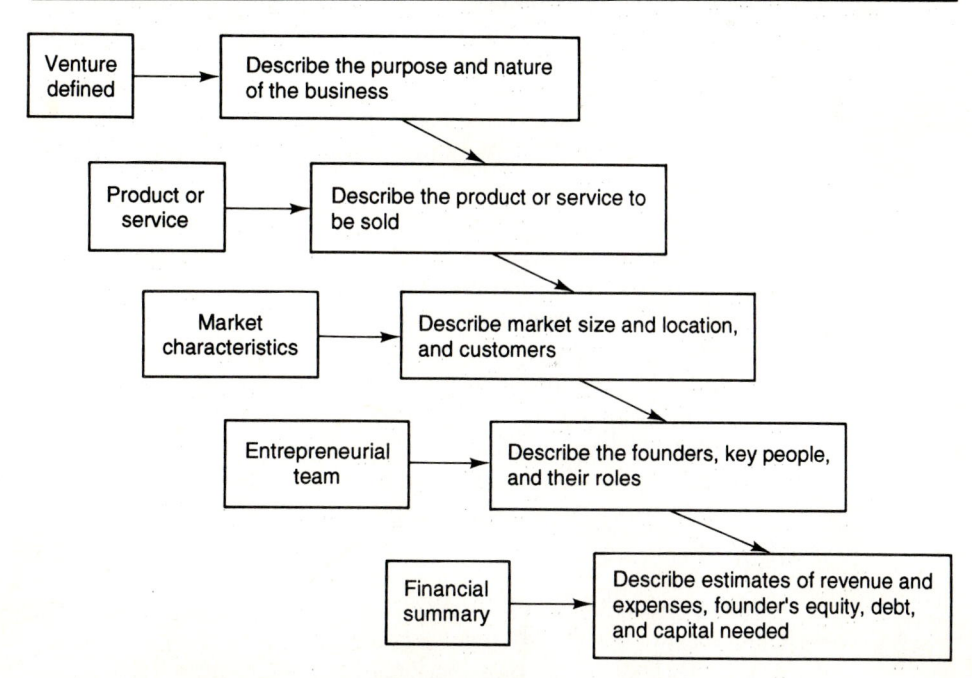

Figure 4-4 Six Key Elements in the Executive Summary

Venture Defined. The company must be identified to include when it was formed, by whom, and for what purpose. The most important requirement is to explain the *purpose* of the new venture. For example, a venture's purpose can be described as manufacturing microelectronics, merchandising women's clothes, or publishing children's books. In each instance, the entrepreneur should briefly extend the definition to explain how the enterprise is unique. Mrs. Fields Cookies, for example, could be described as a chain of confectionery shops, but that description would be superficial. Elaboration is needed to explain the business concept of selling high-quality cookies made from a proprietary recipe. Similarly, a women's clothing store could be described as an upmarket boutique merchandising petite-sized fashions. The definition should also include its legal formation, identifying it as a corporation, partnership, sole proprietorship, or other form of business.

Product or Service. The entrepreneur must describe clearly what will be sold. If there is a proprietary interest (patent, trademark, or copyright), this fact should be stated. The executive summary should briefly describe how far the entrepreneur has gone to develop the product or service. For example, a new product may be in the research stage, design stage, prototype stage, or advanced engineering stage with limited production. Most services are described in terms of customer value. An advertising agency, for instance, might be described as providing mass media promotional programs for professional sports teams.

Products and services should also be described in terms of quality image, pricing, and distinguishing characteristics that might demonstrate a *distinctive competency*. For example, a business formed to provide computer software training is not distinctive, but a business designed to provide "computer-based retail inventory control training" indicates specific services that can be evaluated.

Market Characteristics. Existing and potential markets must be briefly described in terms of size and geographic characteristics. The plan must provide a summary of data to validate projections. If an entrepreneur is going to open a women's clothing boutique with petite sizes, then it will be important to estimate how many women in the market area are likely to need petite-sized clothes. Such an estimate may also require a *brief* description of market demographics, such as changes in local population or data on women in various age groups. Market potential should be estimated over a reasonable period of time (i.e., number of sales or dollar sales for the first three to five years). Summaries of data on growth projections, such as regional trends in specialty merchandising, may be required.

The plan's reader must be convinced that a viable market exists and that the enterprise has a reasonable opportunity to serve this market. However, the executive summary is an overview of market data, not a complicated presentation of detailed market research.

Entrepreneurial Team. An entrepreneurial team may include only the founding entrepreneur, but usually there are other key personnel essential for the firm's success. These individuals must be identified, and their skills and talents must be adequately described. If the business requires individuals with unique qualifications, these should be emphasized. For example, a restaurant may require a chef skilled in preparing French gourmet food, or a health club may require an experienced aerobics instructor.

The executive summary emphasizes strengths of team members and their qualifications, but without "hype." Exaggerations permanently undermine the entrepreneur's credibility, and no matter how exciting the product or service, investors look first to the character and ability of the entrepreneur.[19]

Financial Summary. Critical financial considerations must be summarized to include start-up estimates of revenue, costs, cash-flow requirements, and profits or losses. These should be extended in annual increments for at least three years. A good plan will identify the break-even point in sales volume or sales dollars (i.e., explain when the venture turns profitable). Most important, it will be clear about the financing needed. The plan will establish what is needed and what is being sought from investors and lenders. For instance, a venture may be seeking $400,000 from investors with an established equity base of $100,000 from the founders, or it may be seeking a loan of $200,000 and $200,000 of new investment equity. This summary may be oversimplified, but it indicates to potential investors how much capital is needed, how much the founder has invested, and how much has to be borrowed.

Business Description

Following the executive summary, the plan will provide detailed sections on each major topic. The first section is a thorough description of the business. Essentially the same points covered in the executive summary are covered here, but they are covered in far greater detail. For example, rather than simply naming the business and why it was founded, the entrepreneur should carefully describe evolutionary steps that led to the business formation. It is not unusual to find that a proposed enterprise evolved from an earlier business or from the efforts of an individual who has been working on an innovative product for years.

An interesting example is Wilson Greatbatch, the inventor of the Pacemaker. He had worked alone in his garage for several years engineering the Pacemaker, and, initially, he attempted to do his own marketing.[20] However, he was shunned and ridiculed by doctors until he collaborated with a New York cardiologist who formed a team of specialists to further develop the Pacemaker. The enterprise that evolved was based on the team and its research, not solely on Wilson Greatbatch's invention. Greatbatch established another, separate business that evolved from the Pacemaker research. His venture manufactured an innovative line of batteries required to power Pacemakers. Without having a complete background on the Pacemaker's development, an investor would have only a superficial idea of the importance of Wilson Greatbatch's battery-manufacturing enterprise.

An important area to address is the *nature of market demand*. Is the firm responding to an established demand, or is it trying to establish a new product or service in untested markets? The Pacemaker was developed in response to a critical problem, and today about one of every 500 Americans relies on a Pacemaker to live. However, the first microcomputer marketed by Apple Computer Corporation was a

PROFILE △

Wilson Greatbatch

At the age of 41, Wilson Greatbatch left his job as an engineer to work alone in his garage. He was convinced that he could create a device that regulated the human heart. With a meager savings and an assortment of spare parts and simple tools, Greatbatch invented the Pacemaker. For several years, he traveled in western New York and Pennsylvania showing his "mechanical metronome" to doctors who thought the idea was absurd. Eventually, a cardiologist in Buffalo listened, and the Pacemaker was introduced to medical science. Now applauded for his work and among a select few scientists to be in the Inventor's Hall of Fame, Greatbatch considers his invention a minor one. In his view, the real contribution was power supply technology that he developed with batteries that would operate inside the human body—an environment, he notes, that is far more complex and hostile than the depths of an ocean or outer space.

Source: The Entrepreneurs: An American Adventure (Boston: Enterprise Media 1987), Film No. 3.

---

shot in the dark. Some people saw it as a gimmick, and IBM initially ignored the microcomputer as nothing more than a fascinating toy.[21]

The entrepreneur also needs to explain the *nature of the business* by clearly defining how the firm will operate and what the founders intend to accomplish. For example, MedCon, Inc., has the singular purpose of disposing of infectious waste products from hospitals, clinics, and medical laboratories.[22] MedCon was licensed in 1987 by the state of Texas after rigorous federal tests showed that a patented disposal process would not release potential carcinogens into the air. Larry Dunham, one of the firm's founders, clearly stated the nature of the business as safely disposing of infectious waste products using a patented process. Although there is a potential world market for this service, MedCon has set out clear near-term objectives for plant sites in Texas and New Jersey.

Finally, a firm's *technological profile* should be explained. This may include a description of equipment such as robotic manufacturing. It may require a description of wholesale networks. It may even require an explanation of foreign licensing agreements. For example, toy makers who import inventory manufactured in Taiwan or Singapore should identify import-licensing arrangements that are vital for the business to succeed.

Products or Services

An obvious requirement of every plan is to explain the *product or service concept*. Before we examine this, however, it is important to recognize that planning models do not consistently place this topic immediately after the "business description." A slight majority of business plans treat market issues before providing details of the product or service, but those models require a thorough description of the product or service in both the executive-summary and the business-description sections. For an easily defined concept, such as a specialty clothing store, a brief description early in the plan may suffice. As a general rule, the plan must provide an accurate description of a product or service before attempting to explain how it will be marketed.

Essential information required to describe a product includes distinctive characteristics of the product itself, how it works (or is used), materials, costs, methods of manufacturing, proprietary protection (patents, trademarks, or copyrights), and potential competing (substitute) products. Most new products also will require validated testing, and many will require approval by regulatory agencies. If the product is a new dental instrument, for example, it will have to be approved by the U.S. Food and Drug Administration (FDA). Most services must have licensed owners or employees (cosmetologists, securities brokers, CPAs, real estate brokers, and so on). Restaurants and medical testing laboratories often have to meet state health and safety requirements. Day-care centers, preschools, and counseling centers are required to meet educational credential standards and to comply with state and local regulations.[23]

An important part of this section is to describe how a business is *staged* during the start-up and early growth periods. **Staging** refers to the manner in which products or services will be introduced. It also explains diversification plans and prospects for incremental growth. When Unimation introduced its first commercial robots during the 1960s, they were little more than punch-tape-driven machines, not robots as we know them today. However, Unimation had a *staged development plan* that spanned ten years and three changes in robotics technology. Numerically controlled machines were introduced during start-up, then three years later, bidirectional computer-aided robots were developed, and within ten years, the company planned an integrated robotic system for automated manufacturing. Unimation did not meet the schedule as planned because, after ten years, the microelectronics industry had not yet developed the technology needed for computer-aided manufacturing. Unimation did succeed within 16 years, and Volvo, Chrysler, and Toyota were quick to restructure their auto assembly lines using robotics during the early 1980s. The rest of the automotive industry quickly followed.[24] The critical point is that in 1960, researchers at Unimation envisioned what robotics would be capable of in the 1980s, yet building a plan on that vision would not have attracted investors. Instead, the company presented plans for products that were commercially feasible at that time. These included numerically controlled machines and robots with simple functions.

Market Research and Analysis

The objective of *market research and analysis* is to establish that a market exists for the proposed venture. This may be the most difficult part of the plan, but it also may be the most important. Entrepreneurs must provide a credible summary of potential customers, markets, competitors, and assumptions about pricing, promotion, and

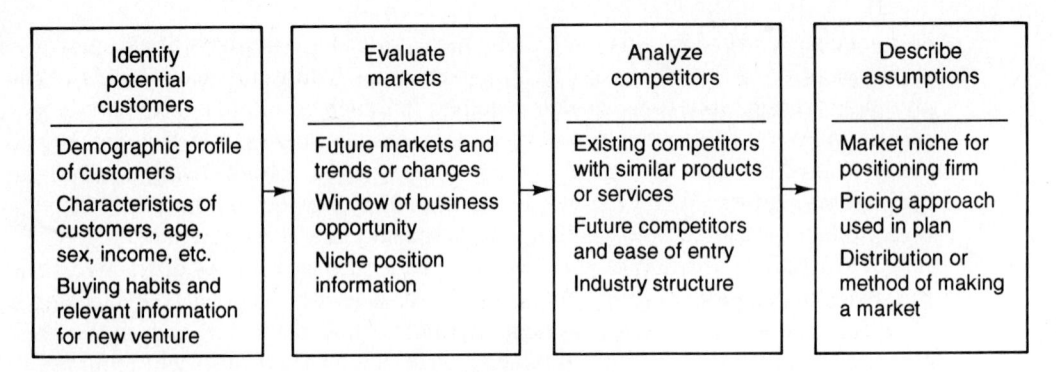

Identify potential customers	Evaluate markets	Analyze competitors	Describe assumptions
Demographic profile of customers Characteristics of customers, age, sex, income, etc. Buying habits and relevant information for new venture	Future markets and trends or changes Window of business opportunity Niche position information	Existing competitors with similar products or services Future competitors and ease of entry Industry structure	Market niche for positioning firm Pricing approach used in plan Distribution or method of making a market

Figure 4-5 **Market Research and Analysis Activities**

distribution. Figure 4-5 summarizes these points. Each must relate to the future period of operations, not merely describe what exists at the pre-start-up stage.

Potential Customers. Research should describe a **customer profile** that includes demographic information such as age, sex, family income, occupation, and location of potential customers. For example, a firm that intends to market microcomputer systems to doctors should provide information on the number of doctors' offices in a marketing area, their ages, gross business income, types of medical services they offer, and how many currently have systems in place. Each bit of information helps to explain the market size and the likelihood of generating sales. To illustrate with just the "age" characteristic, if most physicians in a market area are young, they are probably more likely to consider investments in new technology than older colleagues with established practices.

Customer profiles can include many characteristics, but entrepreneurs should be guided by reason to provide *relevant* information that could affect sales. Consequently, including data about business income for doctors helps to establish their financial ability to invest in new technology, but information about their families and country club memberships would not be relevant to purchasing office computer systems.

Markets. A market exists only when there are qualified buyers, but the entrepreneur must remember that the feasibility plan is a forecast of *future* markets, not merely those that exist. Therefore, *market trends* are important to identify, including, when possible, a window of opportunity for introducing the new business. For a venture positioned to sell computer systems to doctors, the current profile of potential clients is important, but if few new practices are being opened, future prospects for new sales are limited.

Entrepreneurs often find they cannot objectively identify markets because the business has never before been attempted. Apple Computers were introduced in a market void—microcomputers had never been successfully marketed—and when Ultimation introduced industrial robots, people were actually hostile. Ultimation faced an industrial climate in which work was generally accomplished on assembly lines by large numbers of employees. Although Ultimation's robots worked, there were no trained robotic operators or procedures for using robotics. Manufacturers had huge investments in mechanical technology, and employees were suspicious of robots because they could replace large numbers of workers; neither managers nor union leaders were ready to accept this technology. Consequently, Ultimation had difficulty explaining why anyone should buy robots, but when competition between U.S. and Japanese automakers stiffened during the 1970s, it became apparent that the United States would have to retool using advanced technology. A window opened for robotics, and markets could be accurately determined.[25]

Competitors. It is essential to identify *competitors* and to analyze how competition is likely to change when the new venture becomes established. Too often, entrepreneurs skim over these issues and find themselves outgunned in the market. The minimum requirement is to identify existing competitors and to explain their strengths and weaknesses. If a new product is to be introduced in a highly competitive market, just describing competitors may be an overwhelming task. For example, a new software word-processing program not only will have to compete against major products such as Word Perfect, Multimate, and WordStar, but will also compete against more than 200 firms that have specialized market niches in office software systems. The value of marketing research to uncover competitors and to provide an overall assessment of the venture cannot be overstated.[26]

For a new business without known competitors, the challenge is to evaluate the potential for competitors to emerge. In other words, what is the "threat of entry" by other firms. There is also the threat of customers "making" rather than "buying" an entrepreneur's product, and foreign competition is always a threat if the new business proves to be profitable. Successful entrepreneurs know their competition and can demonstrate in their plans how they will compete.

Assumptions about the New Venture. A formal *marketing plan* comprises the next major section of the feasibility plan, yet it is important to describe in the marketing research section assumptions that support market projections for the new venture. Specifically, entrepreneurs must identify the market niche, price system, promotional effort, and distribution method to justify a basis for market research contentions.

Market Niche. A **market niche** is a carefully defined segment of a broader market. It defines the *positioning* of a product or service to create a distinct marketing focus. A brief statement in the plan should explain this focus. Doctors segment their markets by the types of specialized services they offer. Realtors segment services according to commercial, residential, resort, or development properties. Computer retailers may target corporate customers, small business offices, home enthusiasts, or schools. Segments also result from business locations, such as opening a Kwik Kopy franchise near a university; clientele will most likely be faculty members and students.

Pricing Systems. Market research is predicated on a price system that helps describe the venture's market. Describing the price system is essential for developing a customer profile. Luxury prices for name-brand products sold through specialty stores will send a clear signal to customers that quality merchandise and individualized service are offered. Low prices with frequent sales and discounts suggest the opposite. Prices will also be defined by credit policies, location, methods of distribution, and market strategies devised by the founders. These do not have to be elaborate statements, but they must be included.

Methods of Distribution. A **method of distribution** is the manner in which products or services are brought to market. Office supplies, for example, usually are sold through retail stationery stores, but they also can be sold by discount outlets, distributed through catalogs, or sold through direct mail promotions. The choice of a *distribution system* often defines the market niche, influences prices, and delineates promotional activities. For most businesses, one type of distribution system will be customary, but often a creative method of distribution gives a business its distinct competency.

The Sales Forecast. Ultimately, marketing research must conclude with solid data on projected sales. A **sales forecast** is the culmination of research to indicate the quantity of sales and expected gross sales revenue during the planning period. The forecast is the singular most important piece of information in the plan. A good plan will describe projected sales in the executive summary, but present well-documented information here on specific market data and how sales are expected to occur during the first three to five years of business.

A sales forecast includes *quantity* of sales in numerical terms when the products or services can be individually identified. The number of bicycles a shop will sell or the number of vacation plans a travel agency will market can be documented. Merchandisers, on the other hand, have hundreds of products to itemize, and in these instances sales revenues should be summarized.

Most businesses—even retailers—have a few items that constitute a majority of sales. A commercial nursery may receive 60 percent of its revenue from decorative shrubs, and an advertising agency may generate a majority of its revenue from a few corporate clients. For a merchant retailer, one category of products may dominate sales. A bookstore, for example, may earn 70 percent of its revenue from fiction paperbacks. Therefore, the sales forecast should identify the "lead" product or service, describe sales by volume and revenue, and then describe other categories of sales. The point is that success will rest on a pattern of leading sales items that must be accurately identified.

The Market Plan

The **market plan** describes an entrepreneur's intended strategy. It builds on market research and distinct characteristics of the business to explain how the venture will succeed. Some issues addressed in the research section may be reserved for the market

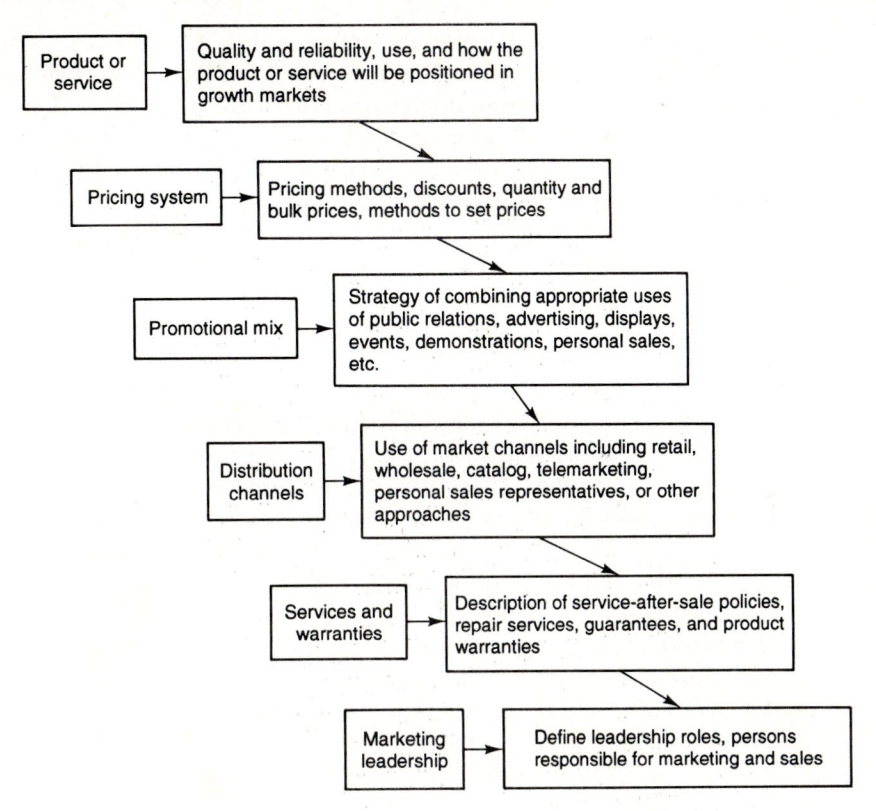

Chapter 4 A Model for New Ventures: Feasibility Planning   125

```
┌──────────┐   ┌─────────────────────────────────┐
│Product or│──▶│Quality and reliability, use, and how the│
│ service  │   │product or service will be positioned in │
└──────────┘   │growth markets                           │
               └─────────────────────────────────────────┘
                                │
                                ▼
         ┌──────────────┐   ┌──────────────────────────────┐
         │Pricing system│──▶│Pricing methods, discounts,   │
         └──────────────┘   │quantity and bulk prices,     │
                            │methods to set prices         │
                            └──────────────────────────────┘
                                          │
                                          ▼
         ┌────────────────┐   ┌──────────────────────────────┐
         │Promotional mix │──▶│Strategy of combining         │
         └────────────────┘   │appropriate uses of public    │
                              │relations, advertising,       │
                              │displays, events,             │
                              │demonstrations, personal      │
                              │sales, etc.                   │
                              └──────────────────────────────┘
                                          │
                                          ▼
         ┌──────────────┐   ┌──────────────────────────────┐
         │Distribution  │──▶│Use of market channels        │
         │channels      │   │including retail, wholesale,  │
         └──────────────┘   │catalog, telemarketing,       │
                            │personal sales representatives,│
                            │or other approaches           │
                            └──────────────────────────────┘
                                          │
                                          ▼
         ┌──────────────┐   ┌──────────────────────────────┐
         │Services and  │──▶│Description of service-after- │
         │warranties    │   │sale policies, repair services,│
         └──────────────┘   │guarantees, and product       │
                            │warranties                    │
                            └──────────────────────────────┘
                                          │
                                          ▼
         ┌──────────────┐   ┌──────────────────────────────┐
         │Marketing     │──▶│Define leadership roles,      │
         │leadership    │   │persons responsible for       │
         └──────────────┘   │marketing and sales           │
                            └──────────────────────────────┘
```

Figure 4-6 **Elements of the Marketing Plan**

plan, such as describing a market niche. This section usually focuses on specific marketing activities. It describes pricing policies, quality image, warranty policies, promotional programs, distribution channels, and other issues such as service-after-sale and marketing responsibility. These are described in the following paragraphs and outlined in Figure 4-6.

Prices. Well-defined prices are obviously necessary to project sales volume and financial performance. As discussed earlier, prices also indicate quality and product image, and depending on the channels of distribution, prices will reflect the nature of the business. Pricing policies relate to bulk, wholesale, retail, and discount methods used to set prices. Such methods as cost-plus pricing or setting prices to match those of competitors indicate how entrepreneurs will make strategic pricing decisions.

Promotions. Advertising and promotional strategies must be consistent with the product or service image. For example, quality office furniture is not apt to be sold through discount newspaper ads. Choosing proper media for advertising is one aspect of the plan, but introductory strategies should relate to the start-up stage. For example, a new software program may be introduced at computer trade shows and be demonstrated at seminars offered to select clientele. Software developers may also sponsor business contests, set up displays in bookstores or computer retail outlets, or provide educational versions of programs to universities. The *promotional mix* is determined by a conscious decision, selecting various promotional tools from advertising, personal selling, public relations, point-of-purchase displays, sampling, and direct-mail solicitation, among others.

Distribution Channels. If distribution channels have not been identified earlier, they must be described here. For example, unusual gift items ranging from greeting cards to imported beef fillets are sold through catalogs, but Hallmark opened chain stores in shopping malls nationwide to market gifts and greeting cards.[27] Liz Claiborne, Inc., reached $3 billion in sales by positioning fashionable women's clothing in department stores through regional distribution centers, but recently the company opened a chain of exclusive stores supplemented with catalog sales.[28]

Service and Warranty Considerations. Most retail stores offer warranties and service-after-sale guarantees in the event a product requires repair or adjustment. Often the distinguishing characteristic of a car dealership is its service and warranty policies. Appliance dealers may also base their strategies on follow-up services and warranties. Telemarketing companies invariably offer money-back guarantees because customers cannot evaluate products before they buy. On the other hand, there are many cash-and-carry discount outlets that sell "seconds" or flawed merchandise, and customers rarely expect warranty service.

Service companies also compete on warranty and service-after-sale policies. Software firms, for example, typically have "hotlines" for answering customer inquiries. Because software programs are updated with new or enhanced versions, an important question to resolve is whether the entrepreneur will provide free updates, discounts on new versions, or trade-in allowances. In estate planning, a recent new service in which consultants help clients plan their investments, service after sale includes periodic reviews of clients' portfolios, investment newsletters, and special reports on tax laws and legislative activities.[29]

Marketing Leadership. The market plan should address the way in which organizational members will be involved in the marketing effort. From a strategic perspective, investors want to know who is going to actually take the lead in making customer sales. If the venture requires a sales force, then issues such as sales training, commission structures, recruitment, and sales management become important.

Investors and lenders are accustomed to seeing two general patterns in poor business proposals that get rejected. First, there are technically competent entrepreneurs who have great ideas but who know very little about marketing. Their plans provide an overkill on product attributes but ignore marketing strategies. Second, there are super salespeople with brilliant ideas who are overenthusiastic about projected sales without providing sufficient supporting evidence to convince investors or lenders that they can achieve the results.

A successful combination would be a team with competent technical people, enthusiastic salespeople, and, between them, someone who can manage the "business" of being in business. Although a later section specifically addresses leadership, sales responsibility must be distinguished because market strategies often reflect prerogatives of the person who will pilot this effort.

Manufacturing or Operations Plan

Depending on the nature of the business, a manufacturing or operations plan may not be required. Many small businesses that offer personal services will have little to say about operations and nothing to say about manufacturing. For ventures that manufacture, design, or sell products, as well as for service firms that require capital equipment, this section is important. Figure 4-7 illustrates elements of the manufacturing or operations plan.

Facilities. Nearly every business requires physical *facilities*. Retailers are usually involved in choosing a location and either securing a lease or purchasing a store. Manufacturers face far more complex issues in leasing or purchasing properties, assuring transportation services, and dealing with legal issues such as EPA requirements and zoning ordinances. Service enterprises will be concerned with having offices easily accessible to clients. Professional businesses require expensive suites in prime locations.

Facilities include fixtures, furniture, equipment, parking space, and renovations necessary to open for business. Simply signing a lease and installing a telephone is rarely sufficient. Equipment lists are usually prepared so that potential investors can evaluate lease-buy decisions and identify collateral. Start-up costs for renovations,

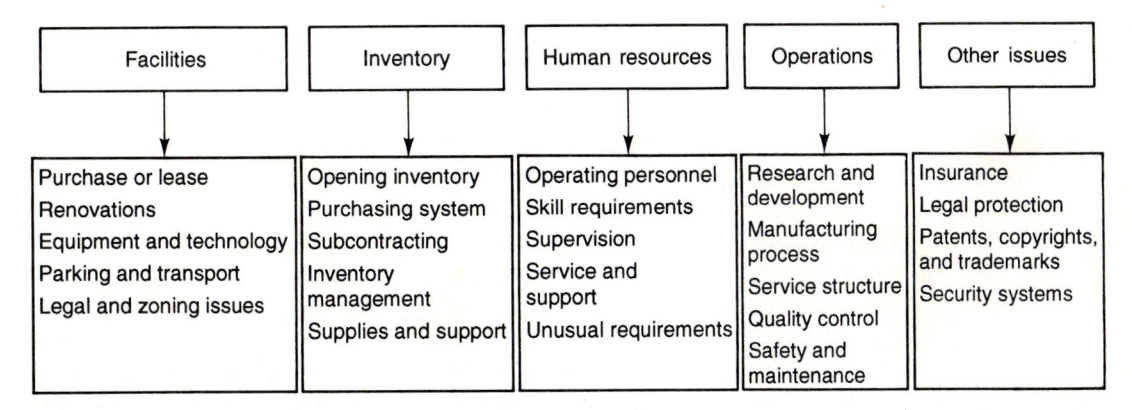

Facilities	Inventory	Human resources	Operations	Other issues
Purchase or lease Renovations Equipment and technology Parking and transport Legal and zoning issues	Opening inventory Purchasing system Subcontracting Inventory management Supplies and support	Operating personnel Skill requirements Supervision Service and support Unusual requirements	Research and development Manufacturing process Service structure Quality control Safety and maintenance	Insurance Legal protection Patents, copyrights, and trademarks Security systems

Figure 4-7 **Manufacturing and Operating Elements**

fixtures, and equipment installation should also be itemized because they represent "sunk costs"—costs that are essential and unrecoverable if the venture fails to open for business.

Inventory Management. Retailers will describe beginning inventory required to open for business and explain how merchandise will be replenished. Manufacturers will describe raw materials and supplies needed in inventory prior to production, and they will also describe projected finished-goods inventory at opening. Many ventures subcontract production; consequently, this section may be simplified to include cost estimates from subcontractors and operational plans for filling inventory. Service-based enterprises may have no inventory to address.

With the exception of personal service firms, entrepreneurs will have to explain their *inventory control* systems, keeping in mind that they are writing a feasibility plan, not a production manual. That is, entrepreneurs should be able to describe briefly how inventory is purchased (or made) and explain the logic behind forecasts for inventory requirements. A sales forecast developed in the marketing research section will anchor inventory requirements, but because inventory must be purchased well in advance of sales, inventory expenses will almost always precede sales revenue. This situation is further complicated by *seasonality*, in which businesses experience peak sales periods and virtual droughts. Poor inventory and purchasing controls can result in "stockouts" during peak periods and excessive inventory stockpiled during sales droughts. Because poor inventory management is one major reason for business failure, investors and lenders are on guard to watch for carefully planned inventory systems.

Human Resource Requirements. From a manufacturing viewpoint, human resource requirements should be summarized with information on the number of personnel and type of skills needed. If the business depends on unusually talented personnel, such as research scientists, then they should be identified. In most instances, specific personnel details can be omitted, but an adequate description is required for management and technical staff.

Similar summaries are required for retail businesses, but services often rely on a few individuals with special qualifications; therefore, human resource requirements may become quite detailed in the plan. An export agent with markets in Japan, for example, may require someone adept at dealing with Japanese business executives (perhaps a Japanese partner).

Operational Rationale. If the firm will engage in R&D, the plan should spell out the extent of this effort. If operations include manufacturing, the plan should describe vendor relations, supply requirements, maintenance expectations, and transport requirements. Manufacturers also will be expected to describe their quality control policies, safety requirements, and other specific operations related to the enterprise. For example, a biotech company producing new enzymes must show how its hazardous waste is disposed of, and a food-processing company must describe how it maintains health and safety standards.

If the company is primarily concerned with marketing, then the market planning section described earlier should be sufficient without further elaboration. However, if success depends on unusual operational procedures (such as product installation and training), then these should be explained.

Legal and Insurance Issues. Most businesses must consider insurance and legal protection to avoid disasters. Specifically, entrepreneurs will need business liability insurance, and when the business relies on a few talented people, the founders may want to purchase personal life and disability insurance on key people. Restaurants will carry substantial fire insurance, and retailers will insure their inventory. Protection through contractual arrangements for markets, supplies, product licensing, and franchise rights may also be essential.

Leadership—The Entrepreneurial Team

Recall an earlier comment that investors put greater emphasis on the entrepreneurial team than on the business concept. This has become an axiom common among venture capitalists who will buy into an "A team with a B product" faster than they will buy into a "B team with an A product." Consequently, entrepreneurs must take care to profile the entrepreneurial team honestly but effectively. They should emphasize team members' strengths, past successes, and positive characteristics, and they should include brief résumés of the principals. Each person's role in the new venture should be described briefly, including board members or investors who may not be involved directly in operations yet be able to influence decisions.

Major Events, Risks, and Progressive Checkpoints

Major events, critical risk factors, and activities that constitute progressive checkpoints are important to delineate in the plan. They provide the entrepreneur with a set of controls for monitoring the new venture. Major events might include a schedule for lining up facilities, testing prototypes, hiring personnel, acquiring inventory, and staging a grand opening. Figure 4-8 shows how a desk-top publishing firm scheduled its start-up events.

After the business is started, a schedule of important events might include periodic performance reviews, meetings with stockholders, and special promotions designed to position the business in new markets. An enterprise may have to leap hurdles during each stage, such as obtaining FDA approval on a new medical instrument or obtaining a patent for a new product.

Critical risk factors should be identified to help prevent unforeseen disasters. For example, if success depends on holding product costs below a certain point, and those costs escalate, then the business may fail. If success depends on entering markets without competition, and competitors appear, the venture is threatened. If an entrepreneur has assumed that certain economic conditions will prevail (such as stable interest rates), and these things change, the business may be at risk. Every business

Progressive Events

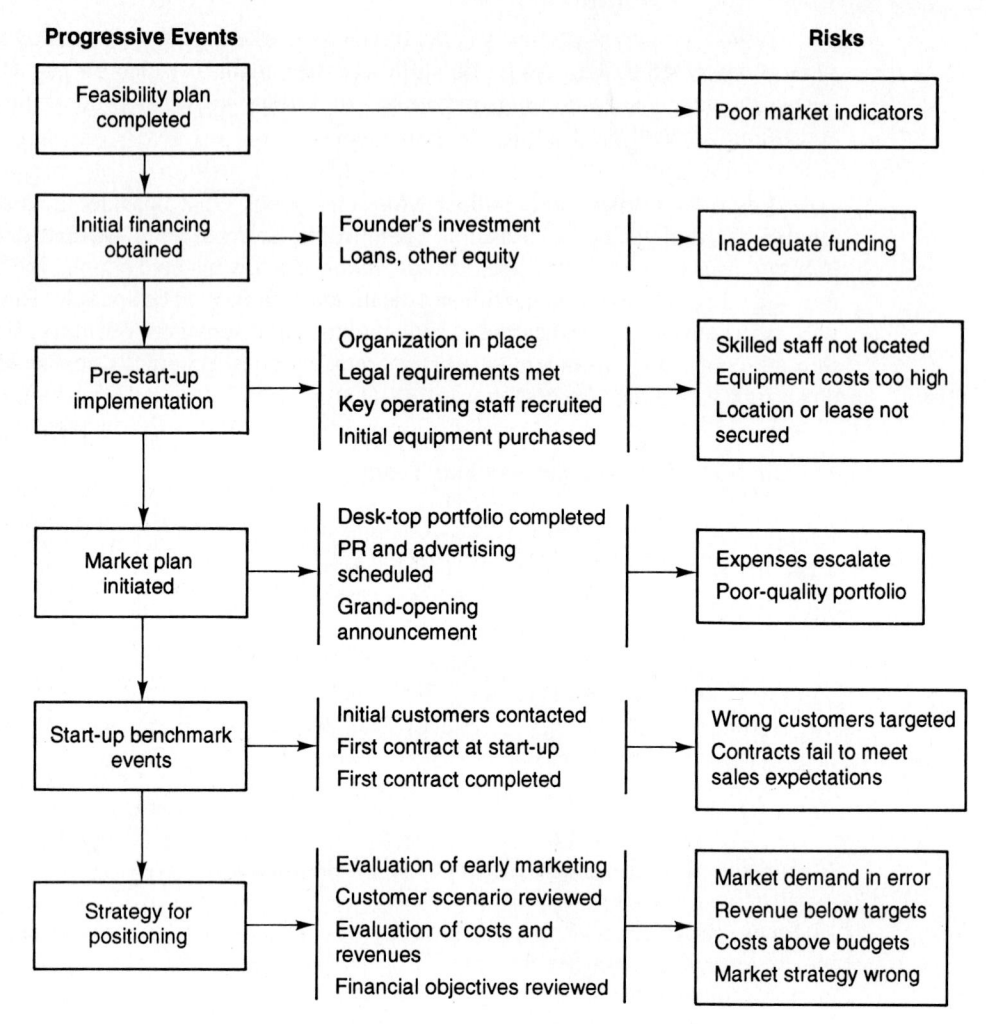

```
┌─────────────────┐
│ Feasibility plan│ ─────────────────────────────────►  ┌──────────────────────┐
│   completed     │                                     │ Poor market indicators│
└────────┬────────┘                                     └──────────────────────┘
         ▼
┌─────────────────┐      Founder's investment          ┌──────────────────────┐
│ Initial financing│ ──► Loans, other equity      ──► │ Inadequate funding   │
│    obtained     │                                    └──────────────────────┘
└────────┬────────┘
         ▼
┌─────────────────┐      Organization in place         ┌──────────────────────┐
│   Pre-start-up  │ ──► Legal requirements met     ──►│ Skilled staff not located│
│  implementation │      Key operating staff recruited │ Equipment costs too high│
└────────┬────────┘      Initial equipment purchased   │ Location or lease not │
         │                                             │ secured              │
         │                                             └──────────────────────┘
         ▼
┌─────────────────┐      Desk-top portfolio completed  ┌──────────────────────┐
│   Market plan   │ ──► PR and advertising         ──►│ Expenses escalate    │
│    initiated    │      scheduled                    │ Poor-quality portfolio│
└────────┬────────┘      Grand-opening                 └──────────────────────┘
         │                announcement
         ▼
┌─────────────────┐      Initial customers contacted   ┌──────────────────────┐
│ Start-up benchmark│ ──► First contract at start-up  ──►│ Wrong customers targeted│
│     events      │      First contract completed     │ Contracts fail to meet│
└────────┬────────┘                                    │ sales expectations   │
         │                                             └──────────────────────┘
         ▼
┌─────────────────┐      Evaluation of early marketing ┌──────────────────────┐
│   Strategy for  │      Customer scenario reviewed    │ Market demand in error│
│   positioning   │ ──► Evaluation of costs and    ──►│ Revenue below targets│
└─────────────────┘      revenues                      │ Costs above budgets  │
                          Financial objectives reviewed │ Market strategy wrong│
                                                       └──────────────────────┘
```

Figure 4-8 **Schedule of Major Events for a Desk-top Publisher**

is predicated on certain assumptions, and when these assumptions are faulty the business is affected.

Financial Documentation

Since money is the objective measure used to gauge a firm's progress, it follows that financial statements come under close scrutiny. Financial statements for a new venture, called *pro formas*, are projections based on previously defined operating and marketing assumptions. If earlier parts of the plan are accurate, the financial pro formas can be completed with little difficulty. However, if marketing research or cost data are vague, these efforts can be painful.

An income statement, or *profit and loss statement*, is required to show revenue, cost of goods sold, operating expenses, and net income. *Cash-flow* budgets reflect information from the profit and loss statement adjusted properly for credit sales (actual cash flow indicated rather than accrual income), non-cash expenses (depreciation), and cash obtained and used outside of operational income (infusions of capital from investors and cash payments on loan principle). A projected *balance sheet* will summarize assets and liabilities, and a *break-even analysis* will reveal when the enterprise begins to turn a profit.

The income and cash-flow statements are typically developed for monthly information during the first year of operations, then quarterly for at least two successive years. Many investors prefer to see five-year plans with footnotes to the statements indicating assumptions about growth or changes in performance. A balance sheet is usually prepared in a "comparative form" with the firm's position at start-up and at year-end for up to five years.

In addition to these documents, a venture in the development stage without income will provide a development budget outlining expenses and overhead. For example, the commercial development of videocassette recorders (VCRs) began in 1965 through research by several small U.S. and Japanese companies. By 1971 these pioneering firms had given up because of a lack of funding, and research migrated to university centers. Funding was still insufficient, and research evolved toward industrial backers. Three Japanese firms—Matsushita, JVC, and Sony—took the lead, and in 1974, after a decade of research by a dozen different organizations, Sony introduced the first commercial VCR. Observers who studied failures found that researchers had inadequate development budgets, thus opening opportunities for others to put resources behind successful VCR projects.[30]

During a development period, people must be paid, research supported, facilities and materials underwritten, and start-up costs funded. Although most small businesses have a brief pre-start-up development period measuring in weeks or months, they require expenditures that must be covered. The plan should spell these out clearly so that proper allowances are made for financial underwriting.

▶ **CHECKPOINT**

Identify each major section of the feasibility plan and describe one key activity in each that an entrepreneur should address.

Explain how a sales forecast influences marketing and financial plans.

RESPONSIBILITY FOR BUSINESS PLANNING

The entrepreneur is the most knowledgeable person about the proposed business, and although there are many ways to get help, the entrepreneur is ultimately responsible for planning. No outsider will have the same vision or motivation, and *vision* and *motivation* are prominent features that emerge from between the lines. Unfortunately, many entrepreneurs do not know how to write a plan, and many others avoid it.

One solution to this problem is to work with a consulting organization that has an established track record in new venture planning. Ernst & Young; Deloitte & Touche; Peat, Marwick, Mitchell & Company; and Price Waterhouse are a few companies with services for new venture planning.[31] A second option is to seek assistance through universities with entrepreneurship centers. A third option is to seek assistance through the Small Business Administration or one of many federal and state agencies established to encourage venture development.

With all the help available, it is curious that so few entrepreneurs want to create a plan. It is the most compelling way to attract investors and to convince lenders of a venture's worth, but it is also a prodigious marketing tool, the entrepreneur's pronouncement to the world that a new and exciting venture is about to be born. Perhaps most important, the plan is an asset to the entrepreneur as his or her personal set of guidelines for creating a successful venture. It is a toolbox of decision-making criteria and a synopsis of expectations, objectives, and essential activities.

Writing the plan can be an extraordinary task, but the entrepreneur is the only person who can articulate the necessary information effectively. However, the plan should not be written in isolation. To the contrary, the more help an entrepreneur can garner the better the final plan will be, but its composition rests squarely with the entrepreneur. As a closing note, we must repeat that a feasibility plan is not carved in granite. It is flexible and should be a pragmatic effort to present an entrepreneur's proposed enterprise logically and succinctly.

▶ CHECKPOINT

Explain why planning benefits an entrepreneur and why the planning process can, by itself, be helpful to an entrepreneur.

Consider how you might realign a plan to fit a hypothetical business.

SYNOPSIS FOR LEARNING

1. *Discuss the concept of a planning paradigm for new ventures.*

A planning paradigm is a model for new ventures, and although there are several models to choose from, there is no fixed set of guidelines or one ideal model. Planning should be pragmatic—a feasibility study that gives information needed to investors and bankers for their decisions but does not entangle the entrepreneur in busywork. A feasibility plan is more important to entrepreneurs to establish decision-making criteria concerning products or services, markets, and finances. A planning paradigm is also important to help entrepreneurs envision the future of a business rather than focusing narrowly on the present.

2. *Describe the four-stage growth model of entrepreneurship.*

The four-stage growth model identifies *pre-start-up*, *start-up*, *early growth*, and *later growth* stages. The pre-start-up stage is concerned with planning the venture and preparing to open the business. During this first stage, the business concept, products and services, customer scenario, markets, operating procedures, and projected financial resources are researched and described. In addition, the entrepreneur must assemble resources and organize the venture for opening. The start-up stage is concerned with initial business operations. This is the critical period of intense development when a venture is given the acid test of operations. It is a stage in which "reality shock" sets in as an entrepreneur positions the business to compete in the real world. The early growth stage assumes the venture has been initially successful and is growing at a healthy rate. It is a stage that requires careful coordination of resources so that an entrepreneur does not outrace his or her ability to underwrite growth, nor grow too slowly to be profitable. The fourth stage represents an evolution into an established enterprise when the venture must be professionally managed.

3. *Discuss the fundamentals of a good feasibility plan.*

A good feasibility plan will identify the essential information needed by investors and bankers to make decisions about equity financing or loans. It will be succinct, yet thorough. It will be clearly written and include essential details with supporting documentation without the tedious attention to detailed research that might characterize a fully developed business plan in a major company. The feasibility plan is meant to be an *initial* effort to show that a business idea can be realized and to give reasons why it will succeed. The plan will describe the entrepreneurial team and the crucial assumptions underpinning projections for success.

4. *Explain the major components in a feasibility plan.*

The first component is the *executive summary*, which is a synopsis of the enterprise. The second is the *business concept*, in which the product or service is described, the entrepreneur's purpose and major objectives are identified, and the concept of how business will be conducted is defined. The third section is usually the *marketing* section, presented here in two parts: *marketing research and analysis* and the *marketing plan*. Marketing research identifies the customer, market niche, and assumptions of price, promotion, and distribution. It is critical here to culminate in a *sales forecast* that clearly establishes the volume and revenue expected from business operations. The marketing plan focuses on strategies employed to make the business succeed, and it defines the pricing, promotional mix, distribution system, and responsibility for marketing. The next component is the *manufacturing and operations* section, which describes how business is conducted. A manufacturer will describe facilities, technology, materials, processes, human resource requirements, and administrative systems. A service firm will identify most of the same elements but will emphasize human resource requirements and skills. An important component is devoted to the *entrepreneurial team*. In this section, principal people are identified and their responsibilities delineated. Finally, a *financial* section will provide financial statements that include at least profit-and-loss, cash-flow, and projected balance sheet summaries for a minimum of three years. In addition, a break-even analysis and, when needed, a development plan will be presented.

5. *Explore planning responsibilities and ways in which entrepreneurs can get assistance.*

The entrepreneur is ultimately responsible for the feasibility plan, but there are many ways to find help. The Small Business Administration has specific programs to assist new ventures. Major consulting firms also have small business divisions. State and local agencies provide assistance, and Chambers of Commerce can direct entrepreneurs toward help. In addition, a number of universities have centers for entrepreneurship specifically developed to help new ventures.

NOTES

1. Karl H. Vesper, *New Venture Strategies* (Englewood Cliffs, NJ: Prentice-Hall, 1980), p. 99.
2. Bo Burlingham and Curtis Hartman, "Cowboy Capitalist," *Inc.*, January 1989, pp. 54–62, 66, 68–69.
3. "US Top 100 Young Entrepreneurs under 30," *Network News*, June 1988, p. 3. Also Michael S. Dell, "Planning for Success," keynote address, Association of Collegiate Entrepreneurs Conference, San Francisco, February 1989.
4. Arnold C. Cooper, "The Entrepreneurship–Small Business Interface," in Calvin A. Kent, Donald L. Sexton, and Karl H. Vesper, eds., *Encyclopedia of Entrepreneurship* (Englewood Cliffs, NJ: Prentice-Hall, 1983), pp. 193–205. Also see Robert Buchele, *Business Policy in Growing Firms* (New York: Harper & Row, 1967), pp. 1–9.
5. Brett Kingstone, *The Dynamos: Who Are They Anyway?* (New York: John Wiley & Sons, 1987), pp. 78–79.
6. Michael E. Porter, *Competitive Strategy: Techniques for Analyzing Industries and Competitors* (New York: Free Press, 1980), Chap. 4. Also see Michael E. Porter, *Competitive Advantage* (New York: Free Press, 1985), Chap. 2.
7. John J. Kao, *Entrepreneurship, Creativity, & Organization: Text, Cases, and Readings* (Englewood Cliffs, NJ: Prentice-Hall, 1989), pp. 121–127.
8. John W. Wilson, *The New Venturers: Inside the High-Stakes World of Venture Capital* (Reading, MA: Addison-Wesley, 1985), pp. 109–113.
9. Kathryn Christensen, "Gene Splicers Develop a Product: New Breed of Scientist-Tycoons," *Wall Street Journal*, November 24, 1980, p. 1. Also see Amal Kumar Naj, "Clouds Gather over the Biotech Industry," *Wall Street Journal*, January 30, 1989, p. B1.
10. Kathleen K. Wiegner, "The Anatomy of a Failure," *Forbes*, November 5, 1984, p. 42.
11. David H. Holt, *Principles of Management* 2nd ed., (Englewood Cliffs, NJ: Prentice-Hall, 1990), p. 226.
12. *Mail Boxes Etc.*, prospectus (San Diego: Mail Boxes Etc., 1989).
13. Gene Logsdon, "Specialty Food Production," *In Business*, March/April 1989, pp. 26–28.
14. Wendy Cole, "Tee Time for Baby Boomers," *Venture*, June/July 1989, pp. 69–73.
15. W. David Gibson, "Look Ma, No Brakes," *Venture*, September 1989, pp. 52–54.
16. Philip D. Olson, "Entrepreneurship and Management," *Journal of Small Business Management*, Vol. 25, No. 3 (1987), pp. 7–13.

17. Tom Richman, "Mrs. Fields' Secret Ingredient," *Inc.*, October 1987, pp. 65–72.

18. Arthur Lipper III, *Guide to Investing in Private Companies* (Homewood, IL: Dow Jones–Irwin, 1984), pp. 57–65.

19. Ibid., p. 116. Also Norman R. Smith and John B. Miner, "Motivational Considerations in the Success of Technologically Innovative Entrepreneurs," *Frontiers of Entrepreneurship Research, 1984*, pp. 488–499.

20. *The Entrepreneurs: An American Adventure*, Film No. 2 and Academic Supplement (Boston: Enterprise Media, 1987), pp. 4–5.

21. "How the PC Project Changed the Way IBM Thinks," *Business Week*, October 3, 1983, p. 86.

22. "Finding Opportunities in Waste," *Venture*, February 1988, p. 15.

23. Rogene A. Bucholz, *Business Environment and Public Policy: Implications for Management* (Englewood Cliffs, NJ: Prentice-Hall, 1982), pp. 8–12. Also see U.S. Equal Employment Opportunity Commission, *Affirmative Action and Equal Employment: A Guidebook for Employers* (Washington, DC: U.S. Government Printing Office, 1974), Sec. D, p. 28.

24. Joseph F. Engelberger, *Robotics in Practice: Management and Applications of Industrial Robots* (New York: John Wiley & Sons, 1980), pp. 8, 44, 116.

25. M. T. Midas, "The Productivity/Quality Connection," in Y. K. Shetty and V. M. Buehler, eds., *Quality and Productivity Improvements: U.S. and Foreign Company Experiences* (Chicago: Manufacturing Productivity Center, 1983), pp. 27–40.

26. Gerald E. Hills, "Marketing Analysis in the Business Plan: Venture Capitalists' Perceptions," *Journal of Small Business Management*, Vol. 23, No. 1 (1985), pp. 38–46.

27. Bill Saporito, "Cutting Costs without Cutting People," *Fortune*, May 25, 1987, pp. 26–32.

28. Kathleen Deveny, "Can Ms. Fashion Bounce Back?" *Business Week*, January 16, 1989, pp. 64–70. Also Jeffrey A. Trachtenberg and Teri Agins, "Can Liz Claiborne Continue to Thrive When She Is Gone?" *Wall Street Journal*, February 28, 1989, pp. A1, A11.

29. David J. Kautter, *Benefit Planning* (Washington, DC: Arthur Young and Company, 1984), pp. 11–12. Also, for example, see *Fidelity's Family of Estate Planning Programs*, a brochure by Fidelity Group Fund Management, 1989.

30. Richard S. Rosenbloom and Michael A. Cusumano, "Technological Pioneering and Competitive Advantage: The Birth of the VCR Industry," *California Management Review*, Vol. 29, No. 4 (1987), pp. 51–76.

31. Ron Christy and Billy M. Jones, *The Complete Information Bank for Entrepreneurs and Small Business Managers* (New York: American Management Association, 1988), Section 7 and pp. 229–236.

CASE 4-1

"I Can't Believe It's Yogurt!"

"I can't believe it's yogurt," an outburst by an obscure customer, became the founding name of one of the nation's most successful new ventures. The company—the I Can't Believe It's Yogurt!—is the result of hard work and solid planning by founders Julie and Bill Brice. In 1979, Julie and Bill were students in Dallas, Texas. Julie had only recently completed her introductory courses in business at Southern Methodist University, and the brother-and-sister team were busy working at a local ice cream shop to help pay college costs. Before the year ended, they had purchased the shop and converted from ice cream to yogurt. The idea came to them as their friends and students became preoccupied with low-calorie foods and health-conscious diets. Yogurt fit the bill.

Julie and Bill worked 70 to 80 hours a week in their store, expanded to a second store, and managed to carry a full load of courses at SMU. Both graduated with honors and soon set about creating Brice Foods, Inc., the parent firm of their current system of franchise operations. During those early years, however, the Brices behaved more as students running a pair of small businesses than entrepreneurs trying to create an integrated company. They admit that they did little planning beyond ways to make ends meet. The venture was little more than a classroom exercise in entrepreneurship, and the Brices only had $10,000 tied up in equipment when they started. The weekly income from sales returned that investment quickly.

After they graduated and began thinking about their careers, the notion of Brice Foods as an expanding franchise business pushed them into systematic planning. For both, planning was the most difficult part of business, and it consumes much of their time today. Nevertheless, planning has paid off.

The first stage of planning focused on creating a small chain of a dozen stores. Franchising was not yet a consideration, but costs were. The cost of buying yogurt mix for a chain was too high to provide good profit margins, and through careful cost analysis, the Brices decided to build their own factory to produce the mix. Within a year after accomplishing this feat, they found themselves trying to manage too many locations and decided to franchise, an effort that meant major expansion and a new corporate format. By 1985 they had made the transition and had opened franchises in nearly 20 states. This expansion also created a distribution problem, so further changes resulted in plans for a fully integrated company.

Today, Brice Foods, Inc., includes a European purchasing network for yogurt ingredients, a large dairy that provides millions of gallons of milk needed for ICBIY stores, yogurt production facilities, and two distribution systems. One is directed at franchises, and the other supplies a wholesale market for the ICBIY products to major grocery chains such as Safeway, Krogers, and Skaggs.

Julie and Bill Brice are innovators who have expanded into cookies and other food lines to complement yogurt. They have a franchise network of nearly 200 stores and expect to triple in size during the 1990s. Ranked among the top ten "under-30 entrepreneurs" in the United States, the Brices point to an extraordinary record of having no franchise failures. Success, they conclude, is due largely to comprehensive business planning and training provided to franchisees.

The Brices have a vision for success, and they are determined to be the best in their field.

They want every customer in every store to be 100 percent satisfied, and they instill this philosophy in their franchisers. Both are also active in community affairs and sponsor a nationwide scholarship contest for "new business plans" through the Association of Collegiate Entrepreneurs. They attribute their success partly to excellent business planning, and although they did not plan their initial venture, planning was paramount to building the company beyond their first two shops near SMU.

CASE QUESTIONS

1. Identify the four stages of growth and how they might be described for ICBIY.

What planning challenges faced the Brices during the start-up stage when they defined the business as more than two local shops selling yogurt?

2. A central planning issue is the "business concept." Describe the business concept for ICBIY, and tell how that concept seemed to change over time.

3. Discuss what you feel to be the key success factors for Brice Foods. Why did the first stores succeed, and what assures success today?

Sources: Roger Thompson, "Business Plans: Myths and Reality," *Nation's Business*, August 1988, pp. 16, 20. Also Julie Brice, "Focus on Youth," keynote address at the Association of Collegiate Entrepreneurs convention, Washington, DC, March 12, 1988.

CASE 4-2

The Company as an Environmental Tool

Patagonia Inc., was the brainchild of Yvon Chouinard, a middle-aged sportsman and weekend rock climber who turned his interests in outdoor sports into a multimillion-dollar enterprise. Patagonia has been one of the premiere distributors of outdoor clothing and unusual sporting accessories for nearly a decade. Specializing in products such as Alpine climbing attire and tropical beach attire for Jet Skis, the company uses mail-order techniques to market to a small segment of the population able to afford extravagant prices for the highest-quality product line of its kind.

Chouinard, however, does not describe himself as an avid businessperson or an astute planner. He explains success as having defined a clear market niche, estimated what people wanted and could afford, then satisfied their interests through exquisite catalogs, advertisements, and public relations. Having accomplished his objectives of serving this market, he was ready to get out of business several years ago. "I didn't need the power of having a bigger business. I had no more reason to stay," he explained. "I'd made a successful company. I'd accomplished what I set out to do."

Chouinard had always been concerned about the environment, and he was on the verge of selling his company in order to pursue his personal interests in environmental protection. "What turned me around was the discovery that I could use the company as a tool," he said. "I'd never equated business with doing anything good. . . . I'd always thought that if you're going to do something good, you do it personally."

Today, Chouinard directs the company's profits entirely to environmental causes, but it is more than giving away money. The company recycles all its paper and more than 70 percent of its waste. It even has a system for recycled waste from employees' homes, and through community programs, Patagonia sponsors environmental speakers and encourages its executives to pursue clean-up efforts. This transformation in purpose has had an interesting effect on the company. Managers and employees not in tune with Chouinard's philosophy have left, but in their place have come more dedicated people and many high-powered executives who are there to pursue the environmental purpose of being in business. Profits have increased beyond expectations because earning more profits provides the financial strength to fund more projects. As the company has grown, its prominence has given management the added strength of political leverage.

In communities in several states where Patagonia has operating facilities, managers and employees can demand environmental action. For example, when Chouinard was contemplating locating facilities in Bozeman, Montana, he lashed out at city officials, literally blackmailing them into environmental action. "I happened to tell them they had an ugly town," he explained. When they asked him about moving there, Chouinard replied, "Well, not until you guys get some controls over your future. I'm leaving California because we trashed the quality of life out there. I don't want to come up there and do the same goddamn thing."

Bozeman put in place campaigns to clear out strip malls, tear down billboards, organize waste recycling, and set up long-term planning for environmental protection. Chouinard has repeated this scenario several times, and the leverage of his company has paid off. His company still sells clothes and sporting accessories, and it has global markets now in two customer niches: those who want his extravagant products, and those who feel good about dealing with a company that is doing something positive about the environment.

CASE QUESTIONS

1. Describe company mission and objectives for Patagonia during its early and recent endeavors. In your opinion, do these conflict, or are they compatible with one another?
2. A critical part of good business planning is knowing why a company is in business and how it will serve its customers. Explain these issues with respect to Chouinard as an entrepreneur and with respect to his company.
3. What would you envision as requirements for Patagonia's market research activities? Financial planning activities?

Sources: Yvon Chouinard, "Coming of Age," *Inc.*, April 1989, p. 54. Also "Patagonia's Commitment," *Yosemite Institute Insights*, Spring 1990, p. 1.

PART TWO

▲▲ Product and Service
▲▲ Concepts for New Ventures
▲▲

Part Two is concerned with developing products, obtaining legal protection for them, and creating new service businesses. The presentation begins with Chapter 5, which discusses product and service concepts. Topics include inventions, technology, new processes, and a model of product innovation. Chapter 6 addresses patent, copyright, and trademark protection. It also describes the problems facing entrepreneurs in protecting their ideas, with suggestions on how to resolve those problems. Chapter 7 focuses on service-related business ventures and the challenging opportunities that exist today for developing new services in an information age.

Chapter **5**

The Product Concept and Commercial Opportunities

OBJECTIVES

1. Explore the opportunities in new products and processes, and explain why manufacturing is important in a free-market economy.
2. Discuss the concepts of high-tech, mid-tech, and low-tech products.
3. Examine how products may be conceived.
4. Describe the model for product development as it relates to the general paradigm for creativity.
5. Explain why "diffusion" is a critical dimension of product development.

Historically, entrepreneurship has been associated with new products and extraordinary inventors. Most students, however, think less about new *products* and more about new *services*, and business education is preoccupied with service careers. Consequently, little attention is given to product concepts or opportunities in manufacturing. This lack of attention is unfortunate because even in our so-called *post-industrial economy*, it is a strong industrial sector that drives the nation forward. In this chapter, we present the argument for manufacturing as the cornerstone for technological innovation and significant entrepreneurial activity.

As we shall see, U.S. manufacturers directly employ slightly more than a quarter of the total work force, and indirectly support an equal number of service jobs dependent on manufacturing. Manufacturing accounts for 52 percent of non-farm annual GNP, without any evidence of decline.[1] But this statistic does not necessarily mean that half of the American economy is embedded in cavernous smoke-filled factories, or that services are any less important to a vibrant economy. The nation has changed, and what has changed is *how* work is performed, along with the technologies used to create a remarkable array of exciting new products. Industrialized nations, and the United States in particular, have experienced a metamorphosis away from "labor-intensive production" to "information-age technology." This transformation was born of creative entrepreneurship, and the future promises tremendous opportunities for even greater entrepreneurial efforts as more new products, new technologies, and new services evolve.

Following our discussion of *macro* trends in product development, we will focus on *micro* issues of product innovation, opportunities for new products, and commercialization of new products. The general model of creativity presented in Chapter 2 and the new venture paradigm presented in Chapter 4 provide our framework for exploring product innovation.

A MACRO VIEW—MANUFACTURING MATTERS

To better understand our current and future opportunities, it is important to recognize how important manufacturing is to a nation's wealth and power. More important, it is essential to recognize that the United States is *not* shifting out of manufacturing into services. The so-called *postindustrial economy* is a myth. Evidence for this conclusion is found in major research studies encompassing economic activity from World War II to the present day, in which contributions to gross national product by manufacturing have remained fairly constant between 47 and 53 percent of total goods and services in the United States.[2]

Unfortunately, many of these studies have been misinterpreted (or ignored), and a popular image has emerged in the United States that manufacturing is in a serious decline. Reports in the popular press indicate that today less than 18 percent of direct employment is in manufacturing and that only 24 percent of GNP is created through goods-producing industries. The same reports compare current trends in manufacturing with agricultural trends 50 years ago, and both are labeled shifts in the economy.

Specifically, agriculture currently employs only 3 percent of the work force, whereas in 1946 the figure was about 14 percent, and in 1920, about 21 percent. Using the same criteria, manufacturing employed 37 percent of the work force in 1953, currently about half that number, and fewer workers will be employed in manufacturing in the future.[3] Figure 5-1 reflects these trends.

The crucial point is that these pessimistic data are correct, but they measure only *direct labor* in manufacturing finished-goods products and *direct value added* in those finished goods. The data do not account for inputs (materials, technology, energy, transportation, and services) required "upstream" by suppliers to final-goods manufacturers or "downstream" by those who distribute and sell manufactured products. A similar argument can be made for agriculture, recognizing that food processing, food products manufacturing, packaging, and distributing are all part of a more comprehensive picture of agriculture. Giant corporations such as General Foods, Kraft, Campbell's, Sara Lee, and Kellogg's are quite obviously linked to agriculture but counted "economically" elsewhere.

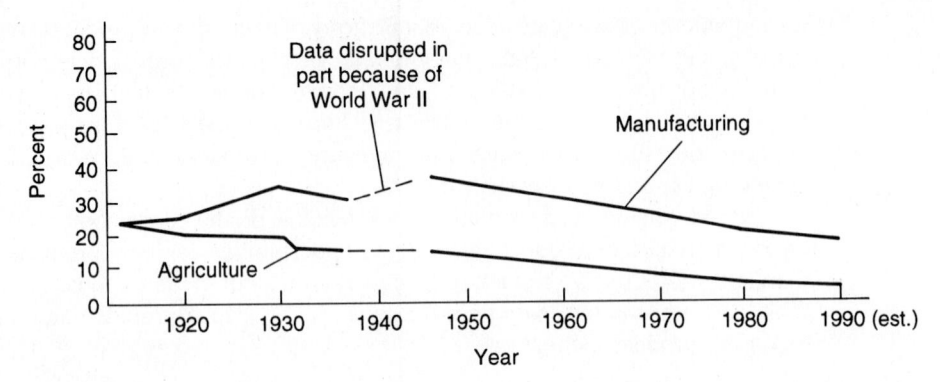

Figure 5-1 **Direct Labor as Percent of U.S. Work Force.** (*Source*: U.S. Bureau of Labor Statistics, *Employment and Earnings*, for selected years and trend series, 1946 to January 1990.)

Clarifying the Role of Manufacturing

Using popular data that report only the value of finished goods added directly by manufacturing, the U.S. manufacturing sector contributes *directly* about 24 percent of GNP annually, and this share has been fairly stable, rising slightly during the past four decades with occasional recessionary periods when steel or automotive industries have suffered setbacks. Add to that the *direct* share of 24 percent of GNP that originates in services that are inputs to manufacturing, and the *direct* share of 4 percent GNP that originates in transportation as an input to manufacturing, and a realistic annual contribution estimated by the manufacturing sector is 52 percent.[4] This point is illustrated in Figure 5-2.

Estimates of the manufacturing sector's contribution could be much higher if energy used in production and finished goods transportation were included. Consequently, we can be easily misled into thinking that the United States is headed toward a service economy. In fact, if that transformation would ever occur, the United States could lose its status as a major economic power. Specifically, if American manufacturing dissolved (or moved "offshore"), those services, energy resources, and transportation systems currently separated as "nonmanufacturing" would also dissolve (or move offshore).

Consider what might happen if General Motors no longer produced cars domestically but instead moved all manufacturing to Taiwan or Korea. Jobs would go overseas, energy used in production would be supplied overseas, most raw materials would be purchased overseas, and a majority of support services would migrate to the production location. Domestic railroads and truck fleets would no longer be needed to transport raw materials, parts, tools, subassemblies, or machinery. Tightly linked "downstream" enterprises such as car dealers and fleet merchandisers would become importers. Loosely linked "upstream" enterprises like advertising agencies would be working for a foreign-located (and possibly foreign-owned) company. Envision how a mass exodus of manufacturing would ripple through the economy. Even the

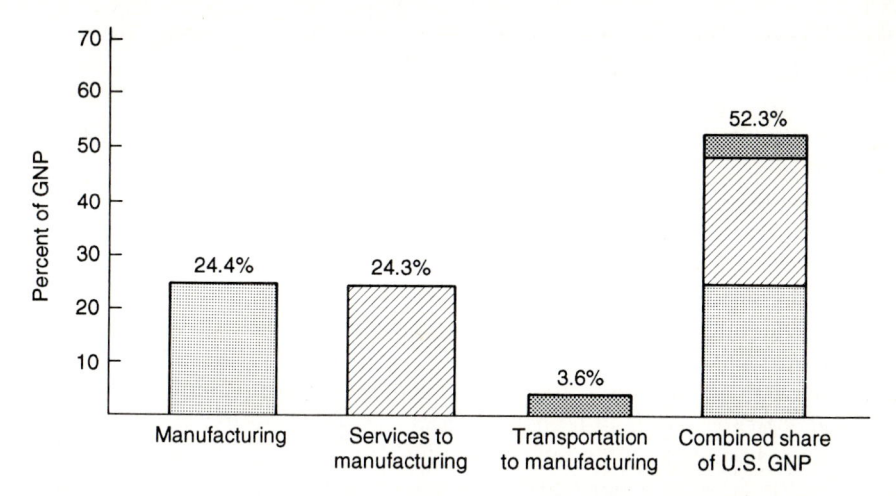

Figure 5-2 Contribution to GNP from Direct Manufacturing, Services to Manufacturing, and Transportation to Manufacturing in the United States. (*Source*: Adapted from Stephen S. Cohen and John Zysman, "Why Manufacturing Matters: The Myth of the Post-Industrial Economy." Copyright 1987 by the Regents of the University of California. Reprinted from the *California Management Review*, Vol. 29, No. 3. By permission of The Regents.)

financing and insurance required for offshore or overseas production would be provided by foreign enterprises, or by other U.S. companies that have moved overseas.

What the continuing importance of manufacturing means for the aspiring entrepreneur is that, first, new products will continue to be the arteries of wealth and, second, that suppliers of parts and services closely linked to new products will be among the best opportunities for high-growth enterprises. On the downside, it also means that suppliers and services closely linked to manufacturers that are moving offshore will suffer, and subcontractors who supply other manufacturers will be at the mercy of global developments by transnational corporations that increase their foreign interests.

The Productivity Shift

As noted earlier, popular themes relate how America "shifted" out of agriculture and into manufacturing and now is "shifting" out of manufacturing and into postindustrial services. In truth, neither shift occurred. In agriculture, a technological revolution made it possible not only to feed a rapidly expanding American population but also to grow surpluses for export with fewer and fewer people directly involved in agricultural jobs. In manufacturing, a technological revolution is taking place with parallel implications.

The Agricultural Perspective. The productivity change in agriculture began when Cyrus McCormick introduced his mechanical reaper in 1831 (see Chapter 1).

PROFILE △

Norman Borlaug—Nobel Peace Prize Laureate

As an Iowa farm boy, Norman Borlaug dreamed of improving the way wheat farmers lived. He recognized that farmers barely made a living, and a harsh one at that, scratching a profitable harvest from the soil each year. The problem was that wheat and grain yields after World War II were low, and although there was a world shortage of food, crops were often devastated by floods or droughts. The answer was to improve productivity through new food products that could withstand nature's challenges and also provide greater profits to farmers as incentives to produce more food.

Borlaug became a trailblazer in agricultural productivity research, and he was instrumental in developing hundreds of vigorous strains of grains that could withstand harsh growing conditions. Borlaug created a green revolution by spreading his findings worldwide, particularly to underdeveloped countries, providing the means for bountiful yields, often in places where food grains had never been successfully planted. For his work, the Swedish Academy awarded Borlaug the Nobel Peace Prize in 1970, citing the continued importance of food production in a global community of nations, many still ravaged by starvation.

Source: "Sixty Years of American Business," *Business Week*, September 25, 1989, p. 24.

A further change occurred when Gustavus Swift introduced systematic meat and food processing in the late 1800s. He also invented the refrigerated railcar that made rapid transportation of meat between Chicago and New York possible.[5] As World War I came to a close, Campbell Soup, Heinz, Kellogg's, Kraft, General Mills, and Pillsbury, among many others, emerged as fast-growing companies with new technologies for harvesting, processing, packaging, and delivering foods.

Many entrepreneurs emerged during the depression of the 1930s and prospered through innovative methods of growing grains and vegetables. Few of these entrepreneurs have gained the same recognition as modern folk heroes, but their contributions have been impressive. For example, J. R. Simplot, a potato farmer at the beginning of the Great Depression is today a billionaire who heads a multifaceted company based largely on farming and food processing. Simplot devised a way to improve potato yields by 250 percent, then developed the technology to process potatoes, reducing costs by 50 percent. By World War II, he had found a way to quick-freeze french fries, and subsequently became the major supplier of prepackaged french fries to both the U.S. Armed Forces and McDonald's Corporation.[6] Another change occurred during the early 1950s, when 40 new strains of grain were developed, and the agronomy research industry emerged to increase food production by nearly 300 percent over the next two decades. This increase was due in no small way to

Norman Borlaug, an Iowa farmer who became a leading researcher in grains. Borlaug developed several of the first strains of high-yield food grains that could withstand extremely harsh conditions, and in 1970 he was awarded the Nobel Peace Prize for introducing these products on a global scale.[7]

The Manufacturing Perspective. One only has to glance around to see how technology has influenced our lives. Televisions, VCRs, CD players, hair dryers, air-conditioning systems, microwave ovens, and automatic coffee makers using materials and technology unavailable several years ago are now commonplace. Microcomputers, fiber-optic telecommunications, surgical lasers, new medicines from biogenetic research, and robotic engineering systems are going through second and third generation changes, yet they are products with nomenclatures that have been in our vocabulary for barely a decade.

Someone, or some team, initially challenged the status quo to develop each of these products, and behind each useful product are hundreds, perhaps thousands, of inventions that provided the technological foundations for new products. As noted in Chapter 2, microcomputers were preceded by integrated circuitry, transistors, vacuum tube technology, artificial language, binary code systems, mechanical calculators, and several other major scientific breakthroughs. In each instance, industrial productivity made quantum leaps through the innovation process of developing these products, and in turn, the products created greater leaps in industrial productivity. More important, these innovative products came about only through extraordinary changes in *process technology*, the means and methods for manufacturing products. Machines were necessary to manufacture a microchip the size of a pencil eraser, and methods for creating the silicon wafer had to be developed. In addition, the development of testing equipment, materials, handling mechanisms, assembly tools, and remarkable design instrumentation had to precede actual manufacturing.

Individuals behind this vast array of modern technology include corporate research and development scientists, college professors, graduate engineering and science students, and an invisible cadre of "tinkerers" working in basements, garages, and home workshops. Corporate efforts, such as development of the transistor at Bell Laboratories, emerged after World War II, and the war itself opened opportunities for innovations. Edwin H. Land, a college professor and physicist, had worked on military optical equipment, then turned his attention to processes for polarized light and launched Polaroid Corporation in 1948. William Hewlett and David Packard started their electronics testing equipment business, Hewlett-Packard, in a garage in 1939. They developed the first cathode-ray tube (known today as the CRT), which led to hundreds of new monitoring and testing devices after the war. Another prewar contributor, Chester F. Carlson, invented xerography in 1938, paving the way for Xerox Corporation to introduce commercial photo-reproduction equipment in 1959.[8]

It is amazing that in 1986 nearly 70 percent of all known inventors, scientists, and researchers responsible for the totality of humankind's technical knowledge were still alive. Most are still alive today, and they are not necessarily old.[9] Recall from earlier chapters that William Gates III (Microsoft Corporation), Mitch Kapor (Lotus Development Corporation), and Steven Jobs and Stephen Wozniak (cofounders of

PROFILE △

Who Is Henry Kloss?

To many people, the name Henry Kloss has no meaning, but his products are used by most of us. Kloss developed the concepts of Dolby sound, chromium dioxide audiocassette tape, and large-screen projection television. His research in acoustics and audiocassette recording has led to commercial equipment that dominated the industry for three decades. Audiophiles know of Kloss as a legendary entrepreneur who not only developed technology but transformed ideas into commercial products. In the 1950s, Kloss sold his innovative hi-fi equipment through Acoustic Research. In the 1960s he marketed stereo sound systems through KLH, his second successful company. Audiocassette technology was introduced through Advent and KLH in the 1970s and early 1980s. Dolby sound and a variety of television projection systems were also introduced through his enterprises.

As the 1990s unfold, Kloss is doing it again. He introduced his prototype speaker system called Ensemble, and he expects a $4 million market during the first 12 months of sales. True to form, Kloss is marketing his innovative speaker systems through Cambridge SoundWorks, Inc., a company he cofounded to manufacture Ensemble.

Source: Edward O. Welles, "What Becomes a Legend," *Inc.*, June 1989, p. 21.

Apple Computer Corporation) are all still in their 30s. Complementing the Americans are cadres of foreign entrepreneurs with similar profiles. Bas Alberts, age 34, developed PIE Medical in the Netherlands through the invention of a scanner that uses sound waves to probe parts of the body X-rays cannot reach. His equipment has led to profound changes in medical diagnosis. Alan Sugar, age 40, heads Amstrad, a consumer electronics manufacturing firm headquartered in Britain, that has revolutionized low-cost VCRs, tape decks, and personal computers. France's Catherine Gassier, at 27, is a rising star heading ChemiProbe, a biotechnology manufacturing firm with medical products positioned in the European hospital market.[10]

Implications of Productivity

What has happened in agriculture and manufacturing is a rapid evolution in techniques of farming and production that have resulted in extraordinary productivity improvements. Fewer people are involved in direct labor in either economic sector today than in the past because fewer people are needed to produce equivalent results. These productivity gains are particularly apparent in developed Western nations where surpluses of food and consumer products exist. It is equally apparent that these gains have not taken place in Communist bloc countries such as those in Eastern Europe,

China, and the Soviet Union, where food and consumer goods must be imported. Following the unprecedented changes in Eastern Europe at the beginning of 1990, it became apparent to new governments in Poland, East Germany, Rumania, and the Soviet Union (under Mikhail Gorbachev's domestic reform initiatives) that their priorities for the 1990s were to center on agricultural reform and manufacturing development.[11]

The implications of an evolution in productivity in free-market economies, as well as the revolution in productivity needed in socialist-based economies, center on entrepreneurial opportunities. Examples cited in the first four chapters of this text and arguments presented earlier in this chapter testify to contributions made by entrepreneurs to technological development. Their efforts transformed our agrarian Western economies into industrial states, and more recently, their efforts have begun to transform the nature of our industrial states from labor-intensive manufacturing to technology-driven economies. Without a doubt, these transformations will occur in Eastern bloc countries that have begun to reassess their priorities, both domestically in terms of productivity and globally in terms of economic trade.

As the 20th century closes, there are extraordinary opportunities for new products, processes, technologies, and services needed in Eastern Europe, Pacific Rim countries, and developing nations in Latin America, Africa, and the Middle East. The opportunities are limited only by one's imagination. For example, with an awakening free press in Rumania, new means of producing and distributing magazines and newspapers are needed, and in East Germany, the unshackling of the media means a proliferation of television programs, stations, television sets, and transmission capabilities. In the Soviet Union, the world's largest McDonald's (a paragon of free enterprise) is setting world sales records in Moscow. What other market-driven enterprises will follow?

Although these are exceptional opportunities born of extraordinary events, there are equally exciting opportunities at home. Agriculture will continue to be a challenge for new products and new technologies in food-growing processes as long as population continues to expand. Productive farmland in the United States is being replaced by cities and highways, requiring new methods of converting arid wastes to agriculture. Water has become a critical resource in America, and there is a pressing need for new farming techniques, water control processes, and urban water technology to serve expanding cities. American consumers are affluent, yet housing systems and technologies are archaic, and a revolution in construction is likely to occur, with new materials and home-building processes emerging. And, of course, information technology is only beginning to find its way into consumer products, homes, and industrial production techniques.

Recall from Chapter 2, as well as from earlier comments in this chapter, that the computer industry is only now emerging from a series of inventions and product innovations that occurred during the past century. The current state of computational technology grew from advances in wiring, vacuum tube development, semiconductors, artificial languages, mechanical adding machines, and discoveries in mathematical processes. There is no reason to believe that we have reached the zenith of information technology knowledge; perhaps we are still only in a stage of infancy. What will evolve in the next few years or decades is beyond imagination. What is certain, however, is that intrepid entrepreneurs will spearhead those changes and, more important, that most changes will evolve through thousands of new products, processes, and technologies with incremental utility and little fanfare. There will be breakthrough sensations such as the transistor, but most will be unheralded innovations (nonetheless important) such as a water-retention agent for semiarid farming or a biodegradable beer can to reduce solid waste. Consequently, the *macro* view of industrialization will continue to focus on revolutionary changes such as the emergence of information technology, but the vast number of opportunities exist at the *micro* level of independent endeavor to "build the better mousetrap."

> ▶ **CHECKPOINT**
>
> Discuss how manufacturing matters, and discuss the opportunities for new products and technologies as America moves toward the 21st century.
>
> Explain how agriculture and manufacturing both continue to be vital economic sectors despite downtrends in direct employment.

PRODUCTS AND TECHNOLOGY

At both the macro and micro levels of innovation, few products require exceptionally sophisticated scientific knowledge. Sensational new products occasionally make headlines, but most are not *high tech* in the sense of having historic significance to humankind, such as Edison's light bulb. Periodically, major inventions or discoveries emerge that are vitally important; the transistor inspired new industries and technological applications impossible with conventional electronics.

A majority of new products, however, will evolve at the other end of the technology spectrum as *low-tech* or *no-tech* innovations. Recent examples include no-glare sunglasses, jogging shoes, automatic coffee makers, and interesting games such as Trivial Pursuit. Between the extremes, there are products that require moderate expertise or special resources but are themselves uncomplicated. We conveniently call these *mid-tech* products. Examples include desk-top publishing software, appealing newspapers such as *USA Today*, ergonomic chairs, exercise machines, and keyboard synthesizers. Exhibit 5-1 provides several examples in each category.

High-Tech Products

A **high-tech** product is more a state of mind than a discernable entity, but calling something high tech is useful for describing products that *currently* reflect state-of-the-art technology. Products we call high tech today might be considered part of our "rust-bucket" technology tomorrow. Edison was certainly engaged in high technology for his era when he fashioned a carbon-filament light bulb, but that was long ago.

Exhibit 5-1 Examples of High-Tech, Mid-Tech, and Low-Tech Products

High-Tech	Mid-Tech	Low-Tech
Semiconductors	Facsimile machines	Office furniture
Digital CD players	Television sets	Plastic toys
Laser instruments	PC mouse controllers	Paper supplies
Computerized cameras	Dot-matrix printers	Printer ribbons
Satellite systems	Cosmetics	Small engines
Guidance systems	Power supplies	Eyeglasses
Aerospace fuels	Desk-top publishing	Candy and cookies
Telecommunications	Fertilizers and nutrients	Building supplies
Holography	VCRs, recorders	Sea van containers
Biogenetic engineering	Machine tool design	Clothing and textiles
Medical instrumentation	Photo reproduction	Printing

More recently, the 1984-vintage microcomputer, revolutionary at the time, has passed into a "mid-tech" stage where it can be reproduced (cloned) in back-alley Asian factories.

The world of high technology promises breathtaking challenges for youthful entrepreneurs willing to pick up the gauntlet. As we go to press, for example, digital audio systems are coming onto the market. Digital technology threatens to make obsolete nondigitalized CDs, which replaced those old cassette tapes, which in turn made LP albums obsolete. At the same time, an enterprising group of entrepreneurs in Sunnyvale, California, has developed a laser stylus using analog signals carried by reflected light to "read" records without friction, The new laser stylus may soon make existing electromechanics used in stereos obsolete.[12] Neither digital systems nor lasers were considered useful in commercial audio systems as the 1980s began; both will probably be replaced by more sophisticated systems before the next decade expires. Someone will develop these products; others will commercialize them; and still others will render them obsolete.

Mid-Tech Products

A majority of familiar products are less sophisticated and more readily understood than high-tech innovations, and we classify them as **mid tech**. An insulated storm window, for instance, is easy to understand. It consists of two or more panes of glass fabricated into a framed unit and manufactured to close specifications to assure reliable insulation. The technology required to fabricate the storm window is much more complex; it requires special machinery, skilled workers, and efficient manufacturing processes. Many existing products have new or unusual (but far from "high-tech") applications. For example, Velcro—that familiar bristles-and-fuzz fastener—has an industrial-strength cousin. The new Velcro fastener is made with small metal hooks rather than bristles. The hooks look like hundreds of very small Js with arrowheads on a metal pad manufactured in much the same way as small integrated circuits. The new product requires a force of more than 100 pounds per square inch to pull apart, and it is strong enough to replace most ordinary metal fasteners (screws, rivets, and bolts).[13] The next generation of clothes washers and dryers may be "stuck together" with strips of metal Velcro, and it will not be long before an enterprising designer creates a "Velcro-separating" tool for repair work.

Mid tech, also a state of mind, assumes new uses of existing resources, or methods of production that result in new products. This category might also include commercialization of existing technology that evolves through proprietary knowledge. Differentiating high-tech from mid-tech products is largely a matter of perception, but unlike high-tech products that presume application of *new* knowledge, mid-tech products can often be fabricated through adaptation of *existing* knowledge. Consequently, entrepreneurs need not be inventive geniuses to pursue mid-tech innovations; they only need to be clever in developing methods to use ideas or resources in beneficial ways.

Low-Tech Products

Perception also plays a role in defining what is meant by **low tech**, but we assume a rather unsophisticated viewpoint. Low-tech products are usually thought to be marginal changes or improvements in existing products. For example, using sheets of plastic and molds, it is not difficult to create boxes to hold floppy disks. With the same materials, most of us could fashion paper trays, desk-top pencil holders, VCR tape racks, and so on. Yet someone had to pull the resources together to manufacture these products. Someone had to design the boxes, trays, and racks, and someone will improve upon them.

Paul Bush, president of Bush Industries, a New York firm that makes computer workstations and a successful line of wooden furniture for electronic products (see the accompanying profile), was nearly bankrupt a few years ago. He took over a second-generation family business in wood and plastic products, began with zero cash and "negative assets" of nearly a million dollars, yet within six years had created a powerhouse company. Success came with the same workers, the same facilities, and the same materials that nearly broke his father's firm. The difference was that Paul Bush introduced new products with innovative designs to provide customers with useful furniture.

During the 1960s, cargo ships were laboriously loaded and unloaded with slow, expensive bulk-loading equipment. A dock worker designed the first prototype cargo container as an experiment to reduce item-by-item loading. This innovation led to improved security and rapid freight packaging. Today "containerized" shipping is the norm. In 1965, Tamon Iwasa, a young Japanese worker tinkering with glass beads, developed the highway reflector so common today. The reflector catches and reflects headlight glare to guide motorists better at night and in foul weather conditions. During the first several years of use in Japan, the Iwasa reflector reduced that nation's accident rate by more than a third. Other low-tech innovations include such common items as disposable razors, butane lighters, felt-tipped pens, and pop-top cans.[14]

Low-tech product development still requires insight by entrepreneurs to see opportunities, and although the resulting products are often short-lived, they represent

PROFILE △

Bush Industries—Filling a Gap

As the 1980s began, Bush Industries, Inc., a Little Valley, New York, manufacturer of plastic bathroom accessories, was on the verge of extinction. The life cycle for cheap "five-and-dime" plastic shelves and makeup trays had run its course. Paul Bush, son of one of the company's founders, had other ideas. He had been fascinated by new microcomputers and the expanding sales of VCRs and microwave ovens, and he envisioned a line of furniture specifically designed for the electronic age.

Starting with a defunct bank account, 73 employees who were owed back pay, and a musty factory, Bush repositioned the company in "electronics" furniture, working with traditional native woods, plastics, and new processes. As Bush Industries entered the 1990s, the firm had five manufacturing locations in the United States and Canada, a product line of more than 200 items ranging from CD player cabinets to executive computer workstations, and a work force of 1,200 employees. The turning point in Paul Bush's mind was the realization that simple skills and materials could be used innovatively to solve everyday problems for consumers.

Source: Personal communications with Paul Bush, President of Bush Industries, Inc.

---

a vast array of most consumer goods. They are short-lived because the lack of skill or technology used in manufacturing makes it easy for new competitors to emerge, or for the existing products to be replaced with slightly improved items. Nevertheless, even in high-tech industries like computer-systems manufacturing, thousands of low-tech products are needed to enhance workstations and to provide computer users with desks, trays, diskette cases, storage bins, printer ribbons, files, and so on.

The low-tech entrepreneur focuses on products that can be made easily, marketed quickly, and terminated with a minimum of effort. The last point is important because low-tech products can seldom be protected by patents, and they can be copied or replicated easy by competitors. A comparison of low- and high-technology product costs during a life cycle is shown in Figure 5-3.

> ▶ **CHECKPOINT**
>
> Describe how high-tech products today will rapidly become mid-tech or low-tech products in only a few years.
>
> Discuss differences between the types of technologies and the implications for entrepreneurs in each category of endeavor.

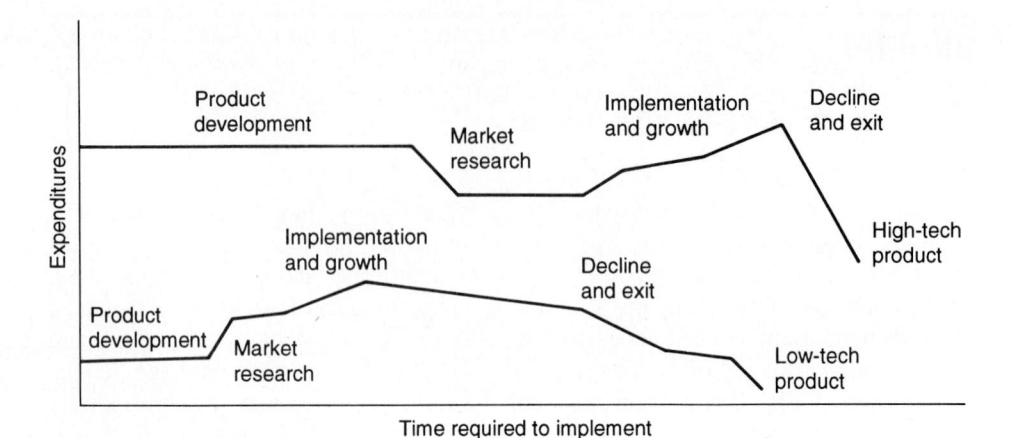

Figure 5-3 Relative Difference in Time and Money for Companies with High-Tech and Low-Tech Products

IDENTIFYING OPPORTUNITIES

In a free-enterprise system, markets arise for new products and services from *wants* and *needs* of consumers. In each of the examples noted previously, the entrepreneurs identified opportunities based on both wants and needs. Paul Bush, for example, recognized that electronic products had to sit on something; home consumers wanted practical television stands, VCR cabinets, and desks designed for microcomputer workstations. However, consumers' *wanting* such products would not have been sufficient to launch a multimillion dollar business; customers also had to *need* them. Bush invested heavily in market research and found that existing products (such as television stands) were often flimsy and ugly. He also found that few companies made computer workstations, and that a large gap existed between functional metal tables (modified typewriter stands) and fashionable office furniture designed specifically for word processors and personal computers. Paul Bush recognized the opportunity and created his product line.

Sea vans and containerized shipping grew from the want of lower-cost global freight and the need for rapid on-shore handling. As Peter Drucker emphatically pointed out, American shipping had almost disintegrated before container systems evolved. Cargo ships were efficient, but the total system of shipping was unprofitable; the high costs of shipping cargo were not incurred in the actual transoceanic transport but in dockside storage and handling. A simple metal container resulted in an integrated system of moving and storing cargo on ships, railcars, and trucks.[15]

Yet another example is the plastic template that can be slipped over a microcomputer keyboard for quick reference to keyboard functions. Templates provide PC users with fingertip information about keys and functions for various software applications. The opportunity gap was one of useful knowledge. Software developers have created exciting applications from word processing to computer-aided design, but learning to use these applications usually means wading through a thick manual written by engineers. Plastic templates help make systems more "friendly," yet they are only printed sheets of plastic costing pennies to make.

Generating Product Ideas

Every person has tremendous experience with a wide array of products and services. We store knowledge far more complex and in quantities that far exceed the capabilities of even the most sophisticated computer system. Yet when students in an entrepreneurship course were asked to brainstorm new product ideas, 35 students representing nearly 735 total years of consumer experience sat numb (and mute) for the first two weeks of the course. With a bit of nudging, however, they formulated a rather impressive list of ideas. They were given an assignment to identify and explain the commercial viability of at least ten new products during the third week of the course. As a result, students identified nearly 800 product ideas—more than one for each year of each student's life.

How did these ideas evolve? For some students, it was a matter of asking critical questions about how to improve things. In one example, a student listed 15 ideas about kitchen improvements while reading a mail-order catalog at her kitchen table. Most of her ideas were unrealistic, but at least she questioned the status quo. Another student listed 18 ideas ranging from new toys to computerized advertisements that could be put on floppy disks. His ideas were triggered by newspaper ads, a shopping trip, watching his younger brother set up a mock war with toys, and trying to jot down a phone number from a television ad. The champion list maker identified 47 ideas, and she turned three of them into money-makers for a student club. Her first success was a colorful wall poster depicting the university. Another was an interactive data base for student housing rentals. The third was an appointment booklet for students, much like the popular Day-Timers except that page formats were printed to coincide with class periods and the university calendar.

These were not earthshaking ideas, but they were money-makers, and although undergraduate business students are more likely to conjure up low-tech ideas than sophisticated technology, they engage the creative process in much the same way as great inventors. The students identified products by observing their surroundings and consciously questioning how to resolve problems familiar to them. The same exercise was assigned to MBA students at the Chinese University of Hong Kong, and because of their proximity to China, 17 of the 19 students proposed products that could be traded in China. As mentioned earlier, there are global opportunities for inspiration, and these are limited only by one's sensitivity to changes taking place. Often it is a matter of simply doing a bit of library research. Government agencies regularly publish ideas that have evolved from publicly funded research. These products are in the "public domain"—open to anyone who has the tenacity to pursue their commercialization. For individuals with some financial resources, many inventors are willing to sell out quickly; lacking either the money or the entrepreneurial drive to pursue their ideas, they may advertise, list their inventions with brokers, or write about them in business or technical publications.[16]

Mapping New Ideas

One way to develop innovative ideas is to **mind-map**. This is a method of brainstorming in which a general idea is refined into components that represent markets, and from those components, product ideas are evaluated for their value to a particular customer. Group decision-making techniques, such as Delphi and the Nominal Group Technique (NGT), have less meaning for entrepreneurs who usually find themselves making individual decisions, yet a mind-mapping process can have interesting results.[17] Figure 5-4 illustrates a mind-mapping exercise.

The first stage of the mind map is to develop likely areas of product or market interests related to an entrepreneur's general business interest. In the illustration, the entrepreneur was an amateur photographer interested in turning a lifelong hobby into a business. From the first stage, she identified "consumer products" as being of more interest to her than other options. From the focus of consumer products, she extended her ideas to specific products or services, including camera bags, developing photography-instruction seminars, designing technical equipment for professional photography, and creating publications on photography. She selected the area of

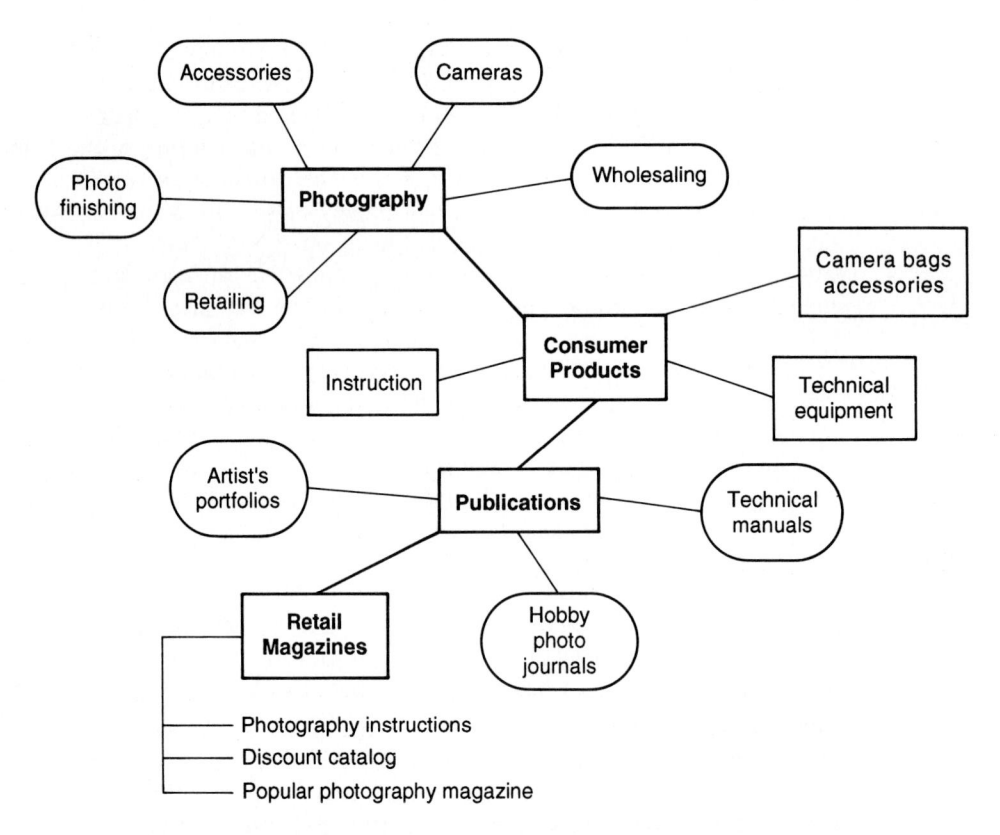

Figure 5-4   **Mind-Mapping for New Product Ideas**

publications to explore, and in the third stage she identified several related business opportunities. Being an avid writer as well as a photographer, she quickly narrowed the field to three types of magazines that would interest her. She researched all three, and eventually decided to create a photography instruction magazine aimed at photography hobbyists and parents.

Although mind-mapping is simply an illustration of how one might go about identifying opportunities, it is more than a gimmick. It reflects the first stage in the creative process described thoroughly in Chapter 2. As part of that discussion, we also described a variety of ways that opportunities arise (such as through demographic changes) and how entrepreneurs allow their ideas to "incubate" into commercially viable innovations. Incubation of ideas reflects the model of innovation described in detail in Chapter 4. We build on these concepts in the next section, specifically expanding the model of a creative process as it relates to bringing a product idea to fruition.

▶ **CHECKPOINT**

Innovators will develop ideas from experiences of their proximity to problems or events. Consider a pressing problem that you face and how you might resolve it with new products or processes.

Try mind-mapping by starting with your favorite activity or hobby and expanding ideas into a focused cluster of business ideas.

THE PRODUCT DEVELOPMENT PROCESS

The product development process is an extension of the general model of innovation introduced in Chapter 2. Recall that there are essentially five stages in the model: *idea germination*, *preparation*, *incubation*, *illumination*, and *verification*. The product development process is more detailed and uses different terms than the general model of innovation. Figure 5-5 illustrates the activities of product development based on an expanded model. A product evolves through this serial process, and product development can be terminated at any point.[18]

The Idea Generation Stage

The idea generation stage is the *conscious* identification of a product idea that logically addresses an opportunity. An opportunity is defined as the identification of a gap in "need" and the likelihood that if a product were developed to fill that need, it would also be "wanted" (i.e., there would be effective consumer demand). This idea may be born of entrepreneurial insight, creative mind-mapping, or accidentally stumbling upon an idea through a corridor of related activity. In Chapter 2, we mentioned the

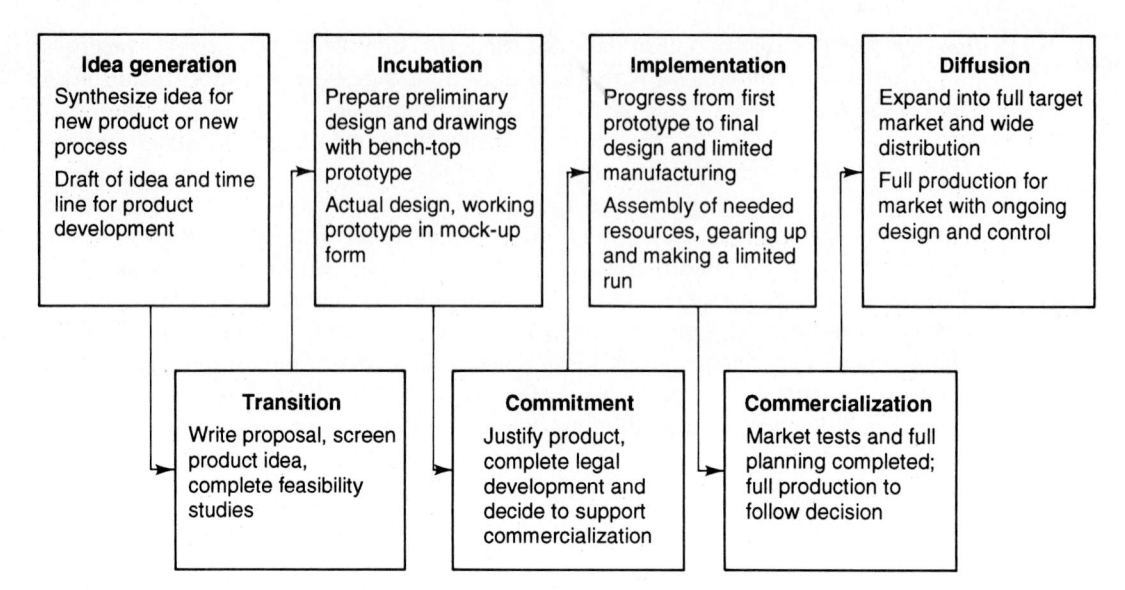

Figure 5-5 Flow of Activities in Product Development

Idea generation	Incubation	Implementation	Diffusion
Synthesize idea for new product or new process	Prepare preliminary design and drawings with bench-top prototype	Progress from first prototype to final design and limited manufacturing	Expand into full target market and wide distribution
Draft of idea and time line for product development	Actual design, working prototype in mock-up form	Assembly of needed resources, gearing up and making a limited run	Full production for market with ongoing design and control

Transition	Commitment	Commercialization
Write proposal, screen product idea, complete feasibility studies	Justify product, complete legal development and decide to support commercialization	Market tests and full planning completed; full production to follow decision

corridor effect. It is one method by which many products are born. For example, when Karstan Solheim first developed his revolutionary Ping golf putter, he had no concept of an entirely new design for golf irons, but the "toe-and-heel weighted" putter worked so well that he experimented with a similar design for all golf clubs. This corridor in golf equipment design led to a new way of manufacturing golf clubs using new lighter weight materials, and today every major golf manufacturer is making so-called game improvement clubs fashioned after Solheim's innovation.

Giving an Idea Form. Once an idea has begun to gel, the entrepreneur must set it down on paper, design it, and if appropriate, make a "bench model." For simple products, a bench model is possible. For example, an early model of an electric toothbrush consisted of four dry-cell batteries linked with yards of wire to a toy motor that had a welded metal toothbrush attached. It looked more like a child's experiment than a product. But the point of the bench model was to identify how the product *could* work. This model gave the designers some form of product on which to build a proposal. Often an idea has no form at this point, and the idea is little more than a concept. For example, a new software program may have no greater degree of development than a rough flowchart of what the software *could* do. It is still important to get it down on paper.

Justifying Further Development. The critical milestone activity at this point is writing the *proposal* to proceed with product research. Working with a bench model, sketches, notes, or flowcharts, the designer-entrepreneur must plan the development process. If this development takes place through corporate R&D, a model

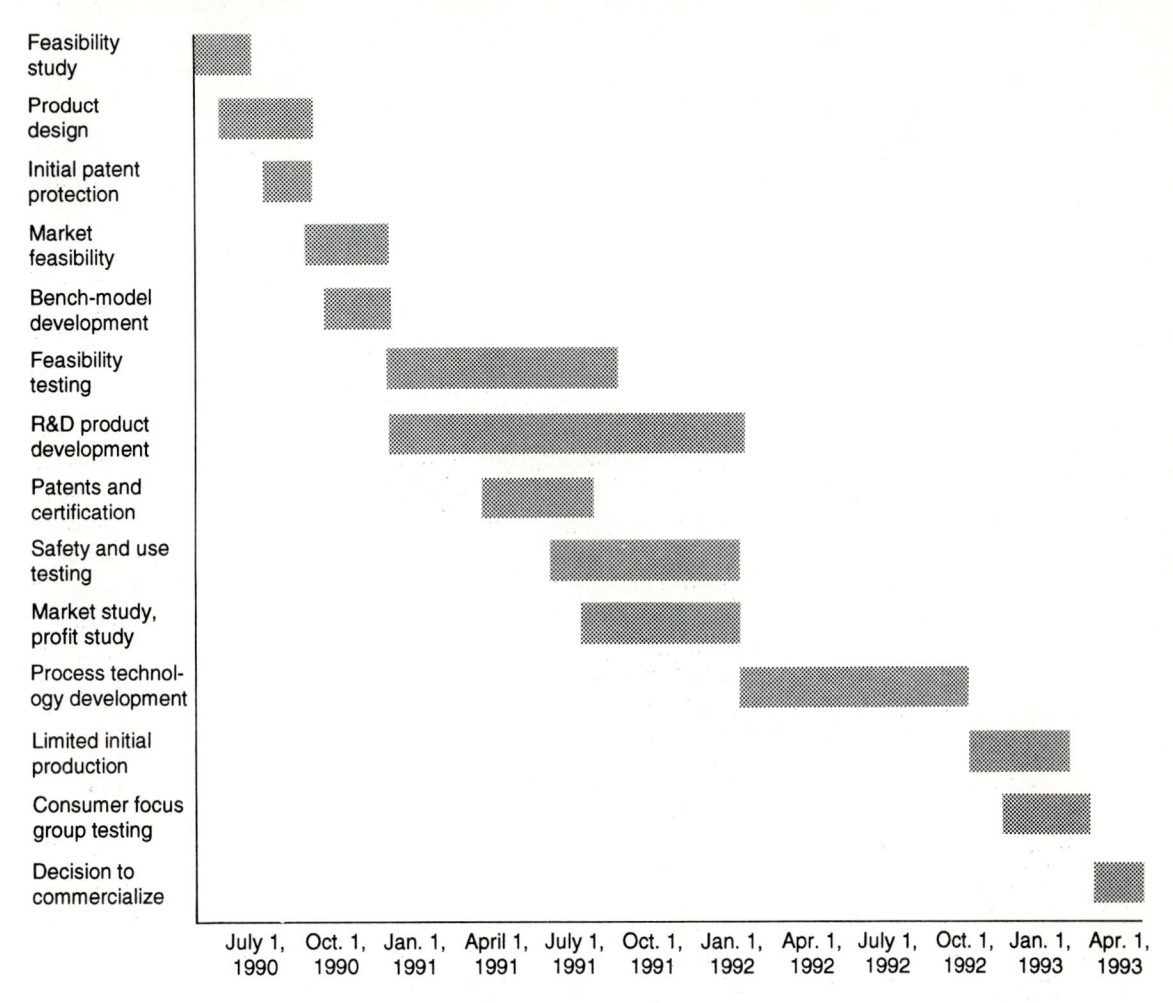

Figure 5-6 Time Line for a Product Proposal

Tasks (top to bottom): Feasibility study; Product design; Initial patent protection; Market feasibility; Bench-model development; Feasibility testing; R&D product development; Patents and certification; Safety and use testing; Market study, profit study; Process technology development; Limited initial production; Consumer focus group testing; Decision to commercialize.

Timeline axis: July 1, 1990; Oct. 1, 1990; Jan. 1, 1991; April 1, 1991; July 1, 1991; Oct. 1, 1991; Jan. 1, 1992; Apr. 1, 1992; July 1, 1992; Oct. 1, 1992; Jan. 1, 1993; Apr. 1, 1993.

of *intrapreneurship* suggests that designers write a program proposal showing how the first-stage model will be systematically built into a working prototype. If an entrepreneur is working solo, he or she may write an initial proposal to attract seed money. In either case, the proposal should include estimates of development costs for materials, labor, engineering assistance, special equipment needed, and so on. The proposal should also have a time line specifying how work will proceed and when the developers will have a testable prototype. This is shown in Figure 5-6.

Transition to the Next Stage. If the proposal is made through corporate R&D, it must be accepted and funded. If management cannot share the same vision of success as the innovator, the product may be terminated without fanfare. If the product seems promising but the proposal is weak, the innovator may be pressed to rewrite the proposal and further justify development plans before approval is given. In the case of a solo entrepreneur, the project may die on a loan officer's desk for lack of funding, or, alternatively, it may die for lack of investment capital.

The risk of losing support and funding can be reduced if entrepreneurs consciously seek advice before presenting their proposals. This intermediate step is called *screening*, a step not often taken seriously by most aspiring entrepreneurs, yet a step that can be of enormous help.

Screening the Product. Screening procedures exist in larger organizations whereby a product is submitted to a formal survey among key managers and engineers. The screening process is a subjective evaluation that relies on expert opinion of a select group to rate the proposal for its commercial feasibility. Several years ago, the National Science Foundation created a formal "innovation evaluation process" (IEP) that is now available through more than a dozen university centers. For a small fee, the university will assemble a panel of experts who rate a product on 31 criteria ranging from physical development feasibility to market potential. The IEP panel also assigns a probability for success and compares several thousand IEP case studies to give an entrepreneur some measure of validity for the panel's recommendations. Investors and lenders who know about the IEP look favorably on an entrepreneur who takes the initiative to have a formal screening evaluation completed.[19]

The Incubation Stage

Having survived a screening process and obtained funding, the innovator must set about implementing the first stage of actual product development. The product must be devised and a prototype developed.

Product Design. Traditional R&D will follow a prescribed path of turning rough sketches into blueprints. These will be expanded into material lists and a plan for making one item—a prototype. The prototype is usually built without the aid of production-level equipment, an expensive process based on custom development of one working product. Ideal materials may not be used, tooling may be a bit rough, and the product may be a bit awkward, but it must closely approximate the end product envisioned by the innovator. This stage of development is often a frustrating period of creating numerous failures. Edison made at least a thousand light bulbs that did *not* work. When questioned about this, Edison said that he had not failed but had discovered a great many ways in which electricity would not work.[20] Success would come only after numerous redesigns, new prototypes, more failures, and finally a feasible product.

Making the Prototype. Assuming the innovator has endured the failures and has a design that finally seems workable, a prototype is built and submitted to testing. This stage of development can be quite lengthy and include having several prototypes field-tested under government supervision (or by approved laboratories) to comply with government regulations. For instance, a new dental instrument may have to be tested by an approved "principal investigator," a qualified dental researcher who runs feasibility tests, rates the instrument's safety, attests to the instrument's usefulness, and writes an opinion for review by the Food and Drug Administration (FDA). The same dental instrument may have to pass certification tests by the National Institutes of Health (NIH) and conform to safety ratings through an approved laboratory.

Market research is usually not pursued at this point. Market tests are reserved for the third stage when a product has undergone some limited manufacturing, gained patent protection, and had other legal groundwork laid such as registration of trademarks or documentation of copyrights. However, during this second stage of incubation, testing is important to establish a product's feasibility and to flesh out specifications so that patents, trademarks, or copyrights can be pursued. An actual sequence of events for developing a dental instrument prototype is shown in Figure 5-7.

Commercialization Decision. The critical milestone activity at this point is to write a formal business plan. The entrepreneur may have written an initial business plan at the proposal stage, but the product has probably undergone substantial changes that will require a revised plan. Corporate managers, or investors and lenders involved with an independent entrepreneur, are unlikely to approve more funding without having a well-developed business plan that spells out product specifications, market projections, and detailed financial requirements. The decision to pursue commercialization rests precariously on the innovator's ability to pass this milestone.

The Implementation Stage

The third stage in product development involves limited manufacturing and is called the *initial implementation stage* (as opposed to the "illumination stage" in the creativity model). This is a preliminary effort to put actual products into the field and to gather market feedback. It is comprised of making a transition from prototype to

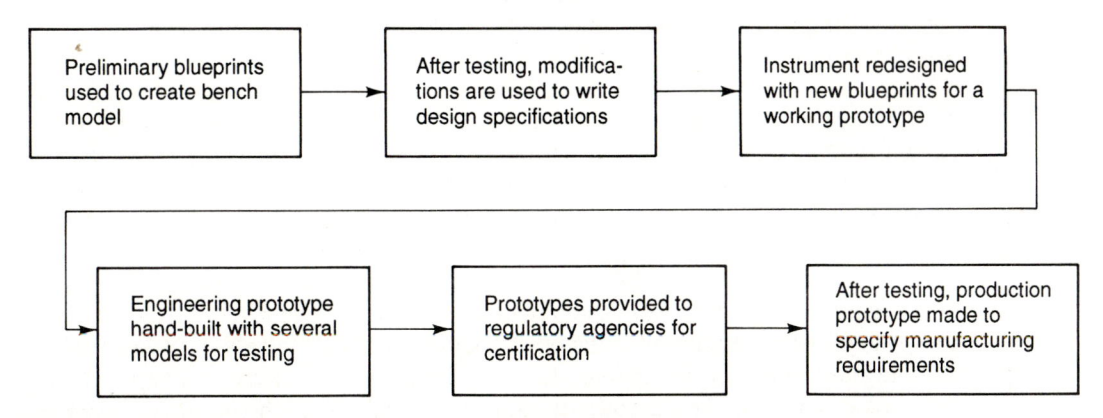

```
┌─────────────────┐     ┌─────────────────┐     ┌─────────────────┐
│ Preliminary     │     │ After testing,  │     │ Instrument      │
│ blueprints used │ ──▶ │ modifications   │ ──▶ │ redesigned with │
│ to create bench │     │ are used to     │     │ new blueprints  │
│ model           │     │ write design    │     │ for a working   │
│                 │     │ specifications  │     │ prototype       │
└─────────────────┘     └─────────────────┘     └─────────────────┘
                                                         │
        ┌────────────────────────────────────────────────┘
        ▼
┌─────────────────┐     ┌─────────────────┐     ┌─────────────────┐
│ Engineering     │     │ Prototypes      │     │ After testing,  │
│ prototype hand- │ ──▶ │ provided to     │ ──▶ │ production      │
│ built with      │     │ regulatory      │     │ prototype made  │
│ several models  │     │ agencies for    │     │ to specify      │
│ for testing     │     │ certification   │     │ manufacturing   │
│                 │     │                 │     │ requirements    │
└─────────────────┘     └─────────────────┘     └─────────────────┘
```

Figure 5-7 **Sequence of Prototype Development Activities for Dental Instrument**

limited manufacturing. This stage does not presume actual market introduction except to "test the waters" and to gather realistic information from selected consumers on product performance under real-world circumstances. It does represent a stage of heavy costs and substantial commitment. The innovator takes his or her greatest risk during this stage of development, which has several incremental activities.

Gearing Up for Manufacturing. The first step, and one with heavy costs for new equipment and production setup, is the initial process of gearing up for manufacturing. Even a simple new plastic toy such as a model car will require expensive dies for casting the model, tooling machines, material purchases, box designs, artwork, packaging, labor allocations, and so on. Initial distribution systems must be arranged, test market criteria established, and, of course, all the legal work completed for introducing the product. For a complicated product like a microcomputer, this step can require an investment of many millions of dollars. For something as simple as a plastic toy, tens of thousands of dollars may be needed.

Limited Production for Testing. The first actual production run of a new product may require several dozen or thousands of items. An expensive dental instrument may have only several dozen items made for selected dentists. A new software program, for instance, will probably be replicated for a hundred users to test. A new laundry soap may have 10,000 items in production to be market-tested in several hundred stores.

Market Testing. Even a simple product will have to be tested with actual consumers. The entrepreneur will be anxious to get feedback from individuals who are most likely to be future consumers. Formal testing can be accomplished through market research teams, and although such testing may be too expensive for small enterprises, it is a standard procedure in larger firms. For example, Pampers was initially test-marketed by Procter & Gamble through 1,200 sample households and field-marketed through more than two dozen chain stores in several cities. It was supported by very expensive advertisements, themselves prototypes of potential marketing techniques, and the product had several test names to evaluate consumer acceptance.

The Market-Test Milestone. Results from market tests constitute another milestone in product development. When the results are in, another critical decision is made whether to pursue *market introduction*. The entrepreneur must decide whether to go into full-scale production or cease and desist. In some instances, a product with potential will be reevaluated, perhaps redesigned, and put back into a testing stage through limited production. Market tests can have all sorts of results, but if the preliminary development was accomplished with due diligence, the likelihood of complete disaster is remote. On the other hand, immediate success is just as remote.

In most cases, market research will reveal a number of unexpected flaws that can require changes. The product is more than a physical object at this point. It constitutes the item itself, the packaging, the name, its image, a price-quality perception, and much more. Most of these points will be addressed when we discuss marketing issues, but it is important to realize that a product has become more than its functional form by this point in development.

If the results indicate a very low probability of success, the project could be shut down. If the results indicate a high probability of success, a green light will be given to implement a full-scale marketing plan. When modifications are required, the decision is less clear. The product development cycle may begin with a late-incubation research effort coupled with new milestone criteria, such as passing certain feasibility tests. In other cases, of course, a product may be pushed back only slightly to iron out minor problems.

Testing an Innovative Process. If the innovation is a *process*, such as a new method of robotic welding, test marketing is not part of the development scenario. However, testing is done in a controlled environment under rigorous conditions. If the new robotic welding process requires safety certification, independent research laboratories may be required to simulate the process on actual products. Consultants may be hired to run in-house tests under predetermined conditions. They will usually rate the process for an extensive list of criteria. For example, a robotic welding process will be validated by testing finished welds for quality and accuracy, for efficiency, for safety, and for cost-effectiveness. Other tests may include stress tests on the new robotic system, performance maintenance checks, efficiency ratings under different line speeds, temperatures, and emergency conditions, and reliability tests of critical parts. Reliability tests typically try to uncover the "weak links" in a new system. If an expensive $100,000 electronic robot welder breaks down when a $2.00 bearing burns out, the process is only as reliable as the $2.00 bearing.

Results from process testing can lead to the same decision criteria as for results from market tests. The process may be reevaluated, modified, or simply halted. Once again, if early development work has been accomplished with due diligence, it is unlikely that the process will be scrapped.

When Projects Are Killed—A Postmortem. Even the best plans go haywire, and it is not unusual for excellent products to fail. There is a classic story of Andrew Carnegie, who, after seeing a multimillion-dollar steel mill open, was stunned to learn of a new process that made his plant obsolete. Carnegie visited his month-old plant and immediately ordered it torn down, stripped to the ground, and then rebuilt using the new process. VisiCorp introduced a new integrated spreadsheet for microcomputers only to find that Lotus Development Corporation would introduce an advanced Lotus 1-2-3 spreadsheet within weeks that was superior.[21] In an era of rapid change, obsolescence is a constant treat, but there are many other reasons why a product may be abandoned.

Several hundred industrial robots sat idle at GM plants during the early 1980s lacking trained operating technicians. A unique burn treatment ointment, tested in the United States in 1987, was later barred because it could not be imported from Yugoslavia. Caterpillar Corporation had to retrench an expensive new off-road earth-moving vehicle after the company found it could not manufacture at a low enough

PROFILE △

Everywhere There's a Phone There's a Fax

In 1980 few people noticed fax (facsimile) machines, and fewer still had any idea of a "go-anywhere portable" microcomputer, but in 1990 these became commonplace. Together with mobile telephones, briefcase fax capability, and computer systems that fit into small handbags, the world has shrunk. Major innovations in telephone transmission, phone connections, and control systems have been coupled with computerized telecommunications technology to create a generation of unusual products. The fax machine, until recently restricted to hard-wired apparatus, has become a common office accessory, and portable fax machines can be carried anywhere, accessing global networks through any common telephone connection.

By the year 2000 these will probably be obsolete—or at least as common as bicycles—and there will be a new generation of entrepreneurs who will open the 21st century with new technology, new applications, and new services. Already, VCR-integrated systems are being used in advanced office designs to complement, if not replace, facsimile transmissions where live communication is more important than hard-copy documentation.

Sources: Frederick H. Katayama, "Who's Fueling the Fax Frenzy," *Fortune*, October 23, 1989, pp. 95-98. "Fast Forward," *Entrepreneur*, November 1989, pp. 132-134, 138-139.

---

price to compete with a Japanese import made by Komatsu. The Ford Pinto was found to be a disaster only after several years in production and a mounting accident record traced to a design flaw. Polaroid introduced instant movies complete with instant processing of 8-mm film only to be caught in the growth cycle of VCRs. In some instances, products are simply introduced at the wrong time. If fax machines had been actively marketed ten years ago, perhaps they would have failed, but as described in the profile on facsimile machines, today the market is vibrant.

The Diffusion Stage

Assuming a product makes it through initial stages to the point of being formally marketed, the process is not complete until the product can prove that it can profitably penetrate the target market. It must be successfully sold through a diffused cross section of the market, showing a pattern of growth in demand. Consequently, although most formal product development has been completed by the time an item is introduced, the new product is much like a child that needs guidance and support during the formative years. Too often, however, little effort is made to nourish the product to ensure success through diffusion; those responsible for product development simply turn to other things.

There are three reasons not to rest on one's laurels. First, the product may rapidly attract competition and therefore require considerable attention to remain viable. Second, test-market data may have given false confidence in results, and once into the market, a product may reveal serious flaws. Third, assumptions made by managers when deciding to go to market may have changed significantly (e.g., demand may be weaker than expected).

Reacting to Competition. When a new software program comes on the market, it attracts immediate attention from competitors. This leads to a "leapfrogging" of product improvements in software—constant updates and revisions, new toots and whistles to leap beyond the other guy, only to find the other guy leaping beyond you. Compare advertising for automobiles, and you will recognize the same phenomenon. There are always new gizmos to enhance a model. This is the pattern of free enterprise, and only in rare instances will a product enjoy unfettered market dominance. Until the breakup several years ago, AT&T enjoyed such a position in telephone services, and utility companies, because of the infrastructure needed to provide gas or electricity, remain dominant in local or regional markets. In most circumstances, however, products will not exist in unchallenged markets.

In most instances, product development remains intense well after the initial introduction. Depending on the life cycle of the product, intense effort can continue until the product has started to decline and the firm can no longer justify further development costs.

Dealing with False Market Tests. Even well-devised market tests may have fatal flaws that render a product vulnerable once it is introduced. Perhaps the product was introduced at an artificially low price during the test, and a higher price in the actual market will be rejected by consumers. Products can also be affected by fateful events. For example, not long ago a headache remedy called Aide was introduced, but as AIDS (the disease) became a highly sensitive public issue, the headache product became a dismal failure and disappeared. There are many causes for market tests to go awry, and management has to remain attuned to market conditions. Slight changes may signal a product's demise or require perplexing redesign efforts. Competition always presents a challenge for forecasting market conditions, and during recent years, the onslaught of Japanese automobiles, electronics, and basic metals such as steel has frustrated even the most astute managers.

Recognizing Management Assumptions. Every new product carries with it a set of assumptions made by management. These include profit forecasts made during development stages, economic forecasts that underpin market demand, scenarios of competition, cost estimates for factors of production, and many more. When one of these assumptions changes, the product may quickly come under scrutiny. For example, a slight change in material costs could render the product a loser, and such a change affected toy manufacturers in dramatic fashion during the 1970s when oil prices soared. Toys made of plastics required petroleum-based resins, and when oil prices tripled, plastic toys became expensive and unprofitable. When something like this happens, management should have contingency plans. Fisher-Price Toys, for example, quickly modified toy designs for wood rather than plastic in response to petroleum costs. Others, such as Tyco, relocated manufacturing to Hong Kong where cheap labor offset higher material costs.

▶ CHECKPOINT

Describe one focal activity that takes place in each of the four stages of product development.

Explain how a bench model, initial prototype, and final prototype are used in the product development process.

Describe why products may fail and how a well-managed ''diffusion'' process can help avoid these disasters.

BEYOND DIFFUSION—A FINAL WORD

While we have identified four stages that take a product from imagination to market introduction, clearly the life-cycle process requires continuous product attention well beyond this early period. If the product is successful, it will enjoy early growth, enter a rapid growth stage, mature as competitors enter the market, and eventually reach saturation in its markets. Beyond that point, new products will be introduced, rendering the existing products obsolete and signaling a period of decline. The later stages may span decades of sales and require organizational changes; these topics are addressed in Chapter 14. Entrepreneurs can, however, recognize the process and be prepared for new generations of products that will emerge.

Reflecting on comments at the beginning of the chapter, product development will continue to be a driving economic force, and manufacturing will continue to be the mainstay of a progressive nation. If products are simply allowed to run their course and decline, they will be replaced through more aggressive efforts by entrepreneurs at home or abroad. Among the most exciting challenges for entrepreneurs as we move toward the 21st century is to recognize the strategic importance of technology, and then to develop products and processes needed in domestic and global markets. These opportunities will create wealth for those with the tenacity to translate them into actions.

In the next chapter we shall enhance the product development process with discussion of patents, trademarks, and copyrights. In addition, we shall introduce the topic of intellectual property protection and describe how services can protect their interests.

Chapter 5 The Product Concept and Commercial Opportunities 165

> ▶ **CHECKPOINT**
>
> Describe why it is important to have a strategic perspective of the product life cycle and opportunities for new products.
>
> Given a global view of business, identify and describe several opportunities for import and export of products or processes.

▲ ▲
▲ ▲ SYNOPSIS FOR LEARNING
▲ ▲

1. *Explore the opportunities in new products and processes, and explain why manufacturing is important in a free-market economy.*

Most opportunities for both products and processes arise from changes that occur in society. Commentary early in the chapter focused on a few strategic considerations, specifically those concerned with a society evolving rapidly into information technology, becoming globally competitive, and becoming affluent. The United States has not become less reliant on manufacturing; to the contrary, new product development coupled with extraordinary new technologies will foster an era of even more rapid infusion of manufacturing. However, the number of people involved in this sector is declining as we quickly leave an age of labor-intensive manufacturing and enter an age in which machines do the work. Perhaps the great challenge of the 21st century is to develop technologically sophisticated systems of work, but to manufacture that technology domestically.

2. *Discuss the concepts of high-tech, mid-tech, and low-tech products.*

All three concepts are perceptual definitions dependent on the current state of technology, education, and diffusion of information. The electric light bulb was high tech a century ago; VCRs were considered high-tech products a decade ago; and high-powered microcomputers are still considered high tech today. All three technologies, however, have become commonplace, easily replicated in factories with production processes that are equally commonplace. Perhaps they have become "mid tech" in the sense that they still require skilled employees to produce them, but they are no longer on the cutting edge of new technology. Low-tech (or no-tech) products are those requiring few skills and common materials or technologies to produce. For example, anyone with simple tools can build television stands or make plastic signs, yet low tech is very much a part of every economy. The fact that a product is simple does not mean it has no value to consumers.

3. *Examine how products may be conceived.*

Aside from the formal methods of R&D, product development, and process research, we introduced in this chapter three ways that entrepreneurs could pursue product ideas. First, because inventors often do not want to organize companies to develop and market their innovations, the rights to these new products can often be purchased. Perhaps an entrepreneur can lease product or process technology, enter joint ventures for commercialization, or license the item from the inventor. Second, the U.S. government underwrites an exceptional number of new products through sponsored research, defense contracts, and social programs. As a result, there are weekly lists of hundreds of product ideas, new processes, and technologies that have become public property. By reading government reports, subscribing to newsletters from the U.S. Patent and Trademark Office, and doing a bit of library research, it is possible to discover an extraordinary number of opportunities waiting to be developed. Third, we introduced the idea of "mind-mapping" as an approach to organized brainstorming. A mind map begins with a person's interest or advocation, expands to include related types of products and market opportunities, then selectively follows a path of investigating each option, further expanding new business ideas.

4. *Describe the model for product development as it relates to the general paradigm for creativity.*

A product development model is generally the same as the creativity model, starting with idea generation, incubation, illumination, and implementation, but each element has more specific meaning, with transition activities between them. Thus idea generation is the way one conceives of a product, but in a formal product development model, it usually means drafting the first design and questioning its feasibility. A transition activity takes place in which decisions are made whether to pursue the idea or not. If it is pursued, an incubation period occurs in which an inventor (or R&D team) is free to explore product ideas, experiment, and try different types of "bench-test" models. Another transition stage occurs as the inventor (or team) puts forward a formal proposal for product development requiring a commitment of time and money. When this is achieved, the illumination stage (more commonly called implementation) occurs, in which the company gears up for test production, completes patent work, develops an engineered prototype, and at the end, actually produces a limited run of new products. These are tested, markets are studied, and various certificates of approval are secured before the company enters the final stage of "diffusion." Diffusion is the process of expanding into full production and into the consumer target markets while continuing to improve the product to meet consumers' expectations.

5. *Explain why "diffusion" is a critical dimension of product development.*

Diffusion is important as part of the development process because design work is not complete until the product has proved effective and profitable. The best products can go sour because of market changes, competition, poor assumptions by management about costs, materials, supplies, distribution, human resources, product reliability, and many other factors. In addition, unforeseen circumstances can arise to require redesign of a product, withdrawal from the market, or repositioning. Too often an entrepreneur (or a major company) simply launches a new product and then turns away to pursue other ideas, and in the wake of this decision, finds that the product is awash in a sea of competition or a failure due to a minor flaw. Development continues through a product's life cycle, or at least into the final period of decline when it is no longer reasonable to pour money into an obsolete product.

NOTES

1. Joseph Duffey, "U.S. Competitiveness: Looking Back and Looking Ahead," in Martin K. Starr, ed., *Global Competitiveness: Getting the U.S. Back on Track* (New York: W. W. Norton, 1988), pp. 72–94.

2. Stephen S. Cohen and John Zysman, "Why Manufacturing Matters: The Myth of the Post-Industrial Economy," *California Management Review*, Vol. 29, No. 3 (1987), pp. 9–26; Council of Economic Advisors, *Economic Report of the President*, February 1984, pp. 254–255; Office of the U.S. Trade Representative, *Annual Report of the President of the United States on the Trade Agreements Program*, 1983, pp. 25–26, and 1988, pp. 23–28; and Bureau of Labor Statistics, *Employment and Earnings*, 1982, 1986, 1988, BLS–790 series.

3. Cohen and Zysman, "Why Manufacturing Matters," pp. 9–26.

4. Office of the U.S. Trade Representative, *Report of the President on the Trade Agreements Program*, 1983, p. 25.

5. *The Entrepreneurs: An American Adventure*, Film No. 2 and Academic Supplement (Boston: Enterprise Media, 1987), pp. 4–5.

6. Alan Farnham, "The Billionaires," *Fortune*, September 11, 1989, pp. 30–34. Also *The Entrepreneurs: An American Adventure*, Film No. 3 (Boston: Enterprise Media, 1987).

7. "Sixty Years of American Business," *Business Week*, September 25, 1989, p. 24.

8. Ibid., pp. 17, 20.

9. D. Bruce Merrifield, "The Measurement of Productivity and the Use of R&D Limited Partnerships," *U.S. Department of Commerce Papers*, Office of Productivity, Technology, and Innovation, April 1984, pp. 1–2.

10. Richard I. Kirkland, Jr., "Europe's New Entrepreneurs," *Fortune International*, May 11, 1987.

11. "Stalinism's Last Strongholds Feel the Strain," *South China Morning Post*, January 6, 1990, pp. 1, 3.

12. Hugh Aldersey-Williams, "Upgrading the Main-Street Cinema," *High Technology*, June 1987, pp. 23–26.

13. "Industrial-Strength Velcro," *High Technology*, March 1987, p. 9.

14. Peter F. Drucker, *Innovation and Entrepreneurship: Principles and Practices* (New York: Harper & Row, 1985), p.73.

15. Ibid., pp. 62–63, 73.

16. Duane Newcomb, *Fortune-Building Secrets of the Rich* (West Nyack, NY: Parker, 1983), pp. 59–61.

17. Lee A. Eckert, J. D. Ryan, and Robert J. Ray, *Small Business: An Entrepreneur's Plan* (New York: Harcourt Brace Jovanovich, 1985), pp. 32–33.

18. Pier A. Abetti and Robert W. Stuart, "Entrepreneurship and Technology Transfer: Key Factors in the Innovation Process," in Donald L. Sexton and Raymond W. Smilor, eds., *The Art and Science of Entrepreneurship* (Cambridge, MA: Ballinger, 1986), pp. 181–210.

19. Gerald G. Udell, ed., *Guideline for Establishing the Preliminary Innovation Evaluation System*, Vol. 2 of the Final Report on the Oregon Innovation Center Experiment, 1973–1980 (Washington, DC: National Science Foundation, 1980). Also see Karl H. Vesper, *New Venture Strategies* (Englewood Cliffs, NJ: Prentice-Hall, 1980), pp. 147–175.

20. "The Entrepreneurs, An American Adventure," Vol. 1, Video and Companion Booklet (Boston: Enterprise Media and Martin Sandler Productions, 1987).

21. William M. Bulkeley, "Software Makers Gird for an Assault against Goliath of Spreadsheets," *Wall Street Journal*, September 25, 1987, p. 29.

CASE 5-1

Looking at Product Development with New Eyes

"An unfortunate problem with business education is that our future managers are being taught that manufacturing is a dirty, smelly, greasy environment with potbellied high school dropouts slugging away at useless, unmotivated jobs." That was one conclusion of Lee Iacocca in a televised response to the *Grace Report* on education. He also concluded: "Fortunately, we know better in business and our best minds—labor and management alike—are skilled, motivated, and interested in their work. We solve problems and make things that people need, and the American worker will take this country into the next century with technological innovations you wouldn't believe."[1]

Iacocca pointed out that business plays a crucial role in solving social problems, not merely in producing items with a "rust-bucket" connotation. New cars, appliances, electronic products, computers, and many consumer goods result from industrial competition and innovations developed for, and often by, the manufacturing community. The notion that businesses help solve problems rather than create them is controversial. Certainly industrial pollution and waste are accelerating problems, yet there is evidence that manufacturers are addressing these issues and, more important, by trying to find solutions, creating new products and new industries.

Consider the related problems of depletion of the ozone layer and the rising greenhouse effect. Both problems are concerned with pollution caused in part by energy consumption that releases pollutants into the air and in part by chemical emissions from various industrial and consumer products. A reduced ozone level, caused primarily by chlorofluorocarbon emissions, leads to increased ultraviolet radiation. If products could be developed to reduce these chemicals, the problem would be eased. If clean energy resources could be developed, air pollution and the greenhouse effect would be moderated.

The refrigeration and air-conditioning industry consumes about half of all industrial chlorofluorocarbons (CFC), most of this being systematically released back into the atmosphere each year by leaks and refrigerant evaporation. Car air conditioners lose refrigerant through leaky seals and hoses at a rate equivalent to all CFC released annually from aerosols. Commercial and home air conditioners, refrigerators, and government buildings match this CFC discharge. To address the problem, more than two dozen manufacturers are creating new products and new processes for controlling CFCs. One recent product, called the vampire, is a pump recovery system that captures coolant, purifies it, and reinjects it into air-conditioning systems. Potential customers include virtually all producers of air-conditioning systems, mass transit companies, airplane manufacturers, government agencies, and the automotive industry. Another product is a new hose assembly developed through NASA projects requiring materials that could be used in space. The hose assembly depends on a material that is leakproof, and once developed fully, it could replace hose technology. Yet another product is a seal coupling that is foolproof. Unfortunately, all these products—and many more under consideration—are currently very expensive to manufacture; consumers are not yet ready to pay $100 for an environmentally safe hose to replace one that now costs $5.[2]

Consumers are buying new products based on safe energy alternatives. Thanks to new developments in heat-absorbing coatings, photovoltaic cells have begun to open the consumer solar products market. Costs for solar products are still high, and uses are limited, but during the last few years coatings have been applied to glass, steel, aluminum, and plastics. Consequently, cheaper solar products have come on line in hundreds of manufacturing businesses. Chronar Corporation of New Jersey, for example, has solar-powered garden lights, night lights, security lamps, and flashlights. These are sold by mail order and through selected outlets, and the company has enjoyed an increase in sales from less than $11 million in 1986 to more than $70 million in 1989. The U.S. Department of Transportation is experimenting with solar-powered highway lighting, and NASA has been using solar-powered cells for low-voltage motors and instrumentation for years. Although solar power is not yet a cost-effective alternative for industrial energy, it has immediate applications for nearly any low-voltage use ranging from swimming pool heaters to external lighting systems.

CASE QUESTIONS

1. Discuss the role of manufacturing in solving future social problems, and in your answer explain the challenge of product innovation.
2. Describe the most likely scenario for developing a new product such as an environmentally safe hose assembly used in automobile air conditioners. What are the steps in the innovation process, and how would they relate to developing a commercial hose assembly?
3. Identify a pressing problem facing us within the next ten years, and using your imagination, explain possible products that might help resolve it.

NOTES

1. "The MacNeil/Lehrer Report," transcript of the panel discussion on the *Grace Report*, January 1988, p. 4.
2. "Research and Opportunity," *In Business*, March/April 1989, p. 35.

CASE 5-2

A New Industry in Telephones

After AT&T was broken up in 1984, the deregulated telecommunications industry became fair game for innovative ideas. Fifty new companies emerged to provide regional services, each competing on various claims of better services, lower costs, new equipment options, or space-age global networks. Giants rose from the shakeout to compete for long-distance markets. More than 20 new ventures appeared to manufacture competing models of mobile, cellular, and cordless phones. And an unexpected new industry rose from the ashes when pay telephones became unwanted orphans of the "Baby Bells."

Pay telephones are an essential part of the nation's telecommunications system, but they are not all profitable. In fact, most pay phone locations under AT&T were more trouble than they were worth. As a regulated company prior to 1984, AT&T had to provide public pay telephones to its service areas regardless of their profitability. Not surprisingly, many inner-city pay telephones were routinely vandalized, maintenance in rural locations was expensive, and money boxes were easy targets everywhere. After the breakup, AT&T felt little remorse about losing control over pay telephone locations, and no one was required by law to provide the service to any particular service area.

Into this breech came the opportunity-seeking entrepreneurs. Within three years of the AT&T breakup, more than 300 adventurers bought rights to nearly 200,000 existing pay phone locations. That number is expected to triple by 1995. Some pay phone owners are individuals—barbers, restaurant proprietors, and 7–11 franchise owners, among others—who bought phones at their businesses. Others organized into companies, owning and servicing perhaps several hundred locations. Today the industry represents more than $16 billion in annual phone calls, and although prime locations such as airports remain owned by telephone companies, a majority of locations are up for grabs.

A standard pay phone in a low-traffic area might gross only $100 a month, and the equipment can cost as little as $800. When a customer makes a call, it is recorded by the telephone company, which bills the pay phone owner monthly at standard rates plus line charges. The cost of a call assures a gross profit of about 40 percent. Profits for a low-traffic location are marginal, and these are poor investments. Consequently, pay phones have disappeared in hard-to-service areas where there is little use or much vandalism. On the other hand, an airport pay phone can bring in $12,000 a month.

The pay phone industry also includes new manufacturers of pay phone systems and a variety of specialized technology. One of these, Intellicall, Inc., designs and manufactures pay telephone units. Intellicall is not involved in collecting coins or owning locations. It makes a line of equipment that, in 1989, approached $40 million in sales. Industry estimates of new phone unit sales approach $700 million for nearly two dozen pay telephone manufacturers.

In addition, there is a submarket of approximately 300 ventures in manufacturing, services, billing systems, maintenance, and publications specific to the pay telephone industry.

New technology is emerging that will give even greater impetus to the industry during the 1990s. For example, one innovation that helped spark the popularity of pay phones was a modification to accept credit cards with the telecommunication linkage for noncoin billing. Today, credit card, third-party, and collect calls represent $6 billion in annual revenues. In turn, new billing technology opened the door for independent companies to compete for customer services such as telemarketing and information bureaus. For example, MoneyCall of New York provides up-to-the-minute financial news for callers. Sports Phone provides game scores and bulletins.

New equipment, switching devices, and data processing equipment have evolved in the wake of deregulation. Much of it is connected with pay telephones, such as half the total billings from MoneyCall and Sports Phones, but much more is the result of incremental innovation that is transforming the entire industry. Facsimile machines have been around for 30 years, but recently they have become available to anyone with a telephone. Photophones that transmit video images are nearing the stage of commercialization. And voice mail systems that are currently feasible for closed-end computer systems will appear soon for any user with a telephone. The interesting aspect of voice mail technology is that it is pay telephone manufacturers who are most likely to make the breakthrough. They have already computerized their pay phones and provided ''portable fax'' hookups; voice mail is merely one more door to open down the corridor.

CASE QUESTIONS

1. Describe high-tech, mid-tech, and low-tech innovations found in the case, and tell how

these evolved from opportunities in telecommunications.
2. Identify critical changes in industry or society that instigated the pay telephone industry and its various corridor ventures.
3. What do you perceive might occur in telecommunications by the year 2000, and what products or new processes might evolve?

Sources: Mark Henricks, "Profiting from the 1990s: Ringing Up Returns," *Venture*, March 1989, pp. 43–46; Cary Lu, "Hello? Hello?" *Inc.*, March 1989, pp. 135–136; and "On Line," *NEC Communications*, July 1990, p. 22.

Chapter **6**

Product Protection: Patents, Trademarks, and Copyrights

OBJECTIVES

1. Describe the requirements for a successful patent grant.
2. Explain the major steps in obtaining a patent.
3. Discuss registration of trademarks and their advantages.
4. Describe a copyright and the concept of fair use.
5. Explain how intellectual property is protected with respect to software programs.
6. Discuss the nature of protection achieved through patents, copyrights, and trademarks in terms of legal recourse.

Most entrepreneurs will not be *inventors*, at least not in the classic sense of following in the footsteps of Thomas Edison, but all entrepreneurs are concerned with protecting their ideas. When those ideas relate to new products, unusual processes, unique designs, or biological innovations such as new plants, understanding *patent law* becomes paramount. When entrepreneurs want to protect unusual brand names or establish ownership of intellectual property, then understanding *trademarks* and *copyrights* is vital.

Federal laws pertaining to patents, trademarks, and copyrights are not complicated. Many entrepreneurs file their own patent claims or prepare the documentation for trademark or copyright protection without professional help from attorneys or patent agents. However, it is always wise to have professional assistance, and although the laws are simple, filing procedures can be complex. In this chapter, we examine patents, trademarks, and copyrights to better prepare individuals for dealing with these issues, but the chapter is not intended to make students legal experts. When help is needed, entrepreneurs will want the best available, and there is a great deal of assistance available from government agencies and patent attorneys.

AN INTRODUCTION TO PATENTS

A **patent** is a grant of a property right by the government to an inventor. It is issued through the U.S. Patent and Trademark Office by the Commissioner of Patents acting under authority of the U.S. Department of Commerce. The most common type of patent is called a *utility patent*, and it is granted for 17 years. Several other types of patents are described later, and each has different requirements for filing with various periods of patent protection. All patents, however, have the distinction of being *assets* with commercial value because they provide exclusive rights of ownership to patent holders, their heirs, and assigns. (An "assign" is anyone who might be assigned ownership or rights through sale or license of a patent.) Congress was empowered to enact patent laws under Article 1, Section 8, of the Constitution, and today, we follow revisions in patent laws enacted July 19, 1952.[1]

Patents are exclusive property rights that can be sold, transferred, willed, licensed, or used as collateral much like other valuable assets. In fact, most independent inventors do not commercialize their inventions or create new products from their ideas. Instead, they sell or license their patents to others who have the resources to develop products and commercial markets.

Patent law stipulates broad categories of what can and cannot be patented, and in the words of the statute, any person who "invents or discovers any new and useful process, machine, manufacture, or composition of matter, or any new and useful improvements thereof, may obtain a patent."[2] There are several crucial words and phrases in the statute that have specific meaning to determine what can be patented and what must be included in a patent application.

Tests of "New" and "Useful"

Anything that is patentable must be *new and useful*. Many applications fail one of these two criteria. Patents are filed and later turned down, for example, because ideas behind them have previously been registered or because they have become public knowledge; they are not *new*. The inventor may have failed to uncover a prior patent or undermined his or her own patent rights by marketing the product before making a patent application. The law specifies that an item cannot be patented if it has been marketed for a period of more than one year prior to application. This provision also extends to advertising or publishing information about the item. Therefore, if an inventor publishes his or her findings and waits a year before filing a patent, the Patent Office will deny the application.

The item must also be *useful*; that is, it must have some demonstrated function. "Contraptions" without some justifiable usefulness other than curiosities fail the criteria. The Patent Office has a pet example of a product routinely turned down for not being useful. It is the perpetual motion machine. Apparently inventors have filed

PROFILE △

Porsche: Engineering Innovations

In 1947, Ferdinand Anton Ernst Porsche was a contract automative design engineer in a stodgy, postwar Europe. Cars were also stodgy, overpowered, and clumsy. Having had a hand in the revolutionary Volkswagon engineering system, Professor Porsche broke from corporate ties and tradition to create a sensation. He introduced his Porsche No. 1, made in Gmund, Austria, in 1948, and has entered the 1990s with newly patented engineering systems and designs. Porsche No. 1 was manufactured with hand-hammered aluminum, a technological breakthrough, and powered by an exceptionally small 35-horsepower engine that rivaled the speed and performance of the best European sports cars. Porsche also created new aerodynamic designs and positioned the engine just ahead of the rear axle, behind the driver.

In order to manufacture the Porsche, hundreds of new patentable products had to be designed, ranging from individual aluminum bolts to transaxle power transfer units. In addition, new tools, new technological processes, and new designs were introduced and registered. Today, the same intensity for new patentable technology drives Porsche, such as the introduction in 1989 of the world's first production car with electronic all-wheel drive. Forty years of design protection on a global scale have assured Porsche of a unique market with unique products, as well as, today, a trademark that is rapidly being commercialized for fashion designer accessories such as rally watches, sunglasses, belts, ties, wallets, jackets, and jewelry.

Source: Prof. Dr. Ing. H.C.F. Porsche, "I Couldn't Find Quite the Car I Dreamed of, so I Decided to Build It Myself," *Porsche Cars North America, Inc.*, 1989.

---

applications on a regular basis for perpetual motion machines when, in point of fact, perpetual motion is a physical impossibility. If the Patent Office is not convinced that an invention will do what it is supposed to do, the patent will be denied.[3]

What Can Be Patented

The terms noted so far do not reveal the nature of patentable inventions. We will describe several categories of inventions momentarily, but first, we discuss what can be patented. These classifications are summarized in Exhibit 6-1.[4]

The word **process** as used in patents refers to new methods of manufacturing or new technological procedures that can be validated as unique. For example, the process of electrical power transmission was unique when patented. A new method of splitting genes was patented. A new process of testing blood samples was patented,

---

Exhibit 6-1 **What Can Be Patented**

Processes	Methods of production, research, testing, analysis, and other technologies with new applications
Machines	Products, instruments, machines, and other physical objects that have proved useful and unique
Manufactures	Combinations of physical matter not found in nature fabricated in unique and useful applications
Compositions of matter	Chemical compounds, medicines, and botanical compositions that do not exist in nature in an uncultivated state, nor those that could evolve in nature, that are new and useful

---

and the process of using radar was patented. In each instance, there was not a specific "product" (no physical object identified by the patent), but each *process* was documented and subsequently demonstrated as being workable, new, and useful.

The word **machine** in patent law means that the patent application is for a specific *physical* item. Most of us think of patents for physical products, and this is the stereotype of all patents. Once again, it has to be new and useful, not merely a work of art or some curiosity. Prior to the 1952 revision in patent law, a prototype of the product had to be developed, and in many instances, the Patent Office inspected the prototype to validate its function and usefulness. Prototypes are unnecessary today, but there are very specific requirements for technical drawings that accompany patent applications.

The word **manufacture** refers to physical items that have been fabricated through new combinations of materials or technical applications. In most instances the application must explain how the product is made, including materials, manufacturing processes, and any additional modifications that the inventor wants to include for protection under the patent grant.

The law also permits patenting **compositions of matter**. This category in patent law relates to chemical compounds such as synthetic materials, medicines, cosmetics, fertilizing agents, and biogenetic catalysts. Simply having a *mixture of ingredients*, however, does not constitute a patentable composition. It follows that a great many medicines and other mixtures of known ingredients do not have patents. The composition must have a new ingredient, often itself patentable, or be a synthetic creation, such as polyacrylamide, one of the synthetically created base materials used in plastics. An important exemption, imposed by the Atomic Energy Act of 1954, excludes the patenting of inventions solely in the utilization of nuclear material or atomic energy for weaponry.[5]

> ▶ **CHECKPOINT**
>
> Describe the essential requirements for obtaining a patent.
>
> Describe what is patentable and what is not patentable.

TYPES OF PATENTS

Patent law provides for three categories of patents: *utility patents*, *design patents*, and *plant patents*. There are no other proper names or categories of patents; however, one often hears an inventor speak of obtaining a "product" patent or a "process" patent. Both of these are normally called utility patents. In some instances they will be design patents, and for botanical creations they are issued as plant patents. These are described in the following paragraphs and in Exhibit 6-2, as an introduction to patent requirements of Title 37, Code of Federal Regulations.[6]

Utility Patents

A **utility patent** is granted for new products, processes, machines, methods of manufacturing, and compositions of matter. This category excludes most botanical creations related to plant and agricultural use. The utility patent is granted for 17 years, and because it is the most common patent sought by inventors, the patent application process described later in the chapter focuses on utility patents in the United States. Similar patents can be filed in more than 80 countries, and there are joint utility patent protection rights that can be obtained for international regions such as the European Economic Community (EEC). A utility patent obtained in the United States extends to all U.S. states, territories, and possessions. These include, for example, the U.S. Virgin Islands and the Marshall Islands in the South Pacific.

Exhibit 6-2 **Types of Patents in the United States**

Utility patents	Granted for new processes, machines, manufactures, and compositions, not including botanical creations, with a protected period of 17 years
Design patents	Granted for any original ornamental design for an article of manufacture with protected periods of $3\frac{1}{2}$, 7, or 14 years
Plant patents	Granted for botanical creations that have been asexually reproduced and do not exist in nature with a protected period of 17 years

PROFILE △

Design Patents Protect Ornamental Distinction

The bicycle was invented in Scotland nearly 200 years ago, and the idea of cycling for exercise and fitness is not patentable; however, with the fitness craze, dozens of manufacturers have introduced hundreds of stationary bicycles that use similar principles of dynamic tension, to equip health salons, homes, and business exercise centers. The models are designed in such a way to appear different and unique, and they have a wide range of prices, attributes, and markets. By obtaining design patents, companies differentiate their products and protect market niches from cloning companies that might replicate successful products—and undercut markets—through cheap labor and materials in foreign factories.

Design Patents

Design patents are granted for any new or original ornamental design for an article of manufacture. A design patent protects the *appearance* of the article, not the article itself. An inventor could easily register both a utility patent and a design patent, but the design patent has a limited life. Design patents can be obtained for $3\frac{1}{2}$, 7, or 14 years. Entrepreneurs can select the period of time for protection in order to commercialize designs and to realize the benefits of their ingenuity. The benefit of a design patent is that the ornamental nature of the patent may be a distinguishing feature that allows an individual to have exclusive use of visual imagery, thus enhancing sales or creating brand identification. For example, a new golf putter will not be granted a utility patent because golf putters have been around for two centuries, yet a new design that changes the physical appearance of the golf club may be granted a design patent.

Plant Patents

In botanical terms, any new variety of plant that has been asexually reproduced can be granted a **plant patent**.[7] The new plant must not exist in nature or in an uncultivated state. Therefore, new plants, mutants, hybrids, and seedlings may be patented, provided the inventor can satisfy the Patent Office that the new plant did not evolve from nature. This is a rather narrow definition, yet hundreds of patents have been granted for unusual hybrid roses, ornamental trees, shrubs, food grains, and an assortment of special-purpose grasses, herbs, and vegetable plants. A plant patent provides the same protection as a utility patent for 17 years.

> **CHECKPOINT**
>
> Describe a utility patent for both products and processes.
>
> Explain a design patent and its value to an entrepreneur.
>
> Explore the nature of plant patents.

DISCLOSURES

An important service provided by the Patent Office is limited protection through the Invention Disclosure Program.[8] As a first step in seeking protection from the Patent Office, most inventors file a *document disclosure* statement. This is simply a statement made by an inventor to register an idea with the U.S. Patent and Trademark Office. It will be retained for two years, then destroyed unless a reference is made to the disclosure in a patent application.

A disclosure is made by writing a letter setting forth the idea. The inventor should explain what the item is, that it is new and useful, how it is to be used, and, generally, how it is expected to be made. The letter should have an accompanying photograph of the item, sketches that illustrate the process, product, or plant, and a declaration by the inventor that it is his or her idea. The drawings need not be formally drafted blueprints. In fact, the Patent Office prefers simple illustrations that can be photocopied and folded to dimensions not to exceed legal-sized paper. The inventor must enclose a self-addressed envelope and a fee of $10. Fees change periodically, but the cost of the disclosure is unimportant. The fact that the inventor has been able to officially register his or her idea *is* important.

The Patent Office takes absolutely no position as to the patentability of an item registered under the disclosure program, but the documents will be stamped with a date and file number. This procedure provides evidence for an inventor to bring to court against a conflicting claim or against a person trying to infringe on the idea. It also provides a legal priority of claim for an invention and allows an inventor some measure of security while the idea is developed well enough for a patent application.

> **CHECKPOINT**
>
> Explain why an entrepreneur would want to file a disclosure.
>
> Describe how a disclosure filing protects a creative idea.

WHO MAY APPLY FOR A PATENT

According to patent law, only an inventor may apply for a patent, but this rule has several refinements.[5] If an inventor dies before making an application, the executor or legal administrator of the estate can file for a patent on behalf of the deceased to protect the interests of heirs. If a person is insane or incapable, a guardian may file for the inventor. When two or more persons have a joint interest, the patent must be filed in all names of parties as joint inventors. There have also been instances when an inventor has refused to file, or has disappeared, and a joint inventor has filed in both names.

Anyone filing for a patent must swear by oath or make a formal declaration that he or she has a proprietary interest in the invention. Merely having an investment in another person's invention is insufficient. Individuals must have been involved in creating the item being patented. No officer or employee of the U.S. Patent and Trademark Office can apply for a patent or acquire an interest in a patent except through bequest or inheritance. In addition, anyone filing for a patent who is not the inventor is subject to criminal penalties.

▶ **CHECKPOINT**

Explain who may apply for a patent as an individual.

THE PATENT PROCESS

When an idea is first reduced to sketches on paper, or when it is mocked up in crude fashion, a *disclosure* should be filed. This is a measure of insurance that precedes actual patent work, and it provides legal recognition for an aspiring inventor. If someone else takes the sketches or steals the idea, at least there is some evidence on record. The filing of the disclosure is ideally done at the earliest stage of the "idea generation" phase. The patent process, shown in Figure 6-1, is typical of a utility patent.

The actual patent process begins with a *patent search*, and when the search reveals no similar item under patent protection, then a *patent application* can be made. An application goes through several stages of development before a patent is issued. There are three stages that represent the status of a patent application. The first is a *patent filed* status, meaning that an inventor has officially made application, but that no action has been taken one way or the other by the Patent Office. The second is a *patent pending* status. This is often referred to as "patent applied for" status. The terms imply that an application has been recorded and the patent examined successfully by the Patent Office. At this stage, a patent has not yet been issued, pending any counterclaims or third-party objections. This status is not something officially granted by the Patent Office. It is simply a means of communication used by the inventor to inform the public that an article being test marketed (or actually sold) is on file in a pending status with the Patent Office. The final stage is *patent issued*. The inventor receives full documentation in what are called "letters patent" of a successful application by the Patent Office.

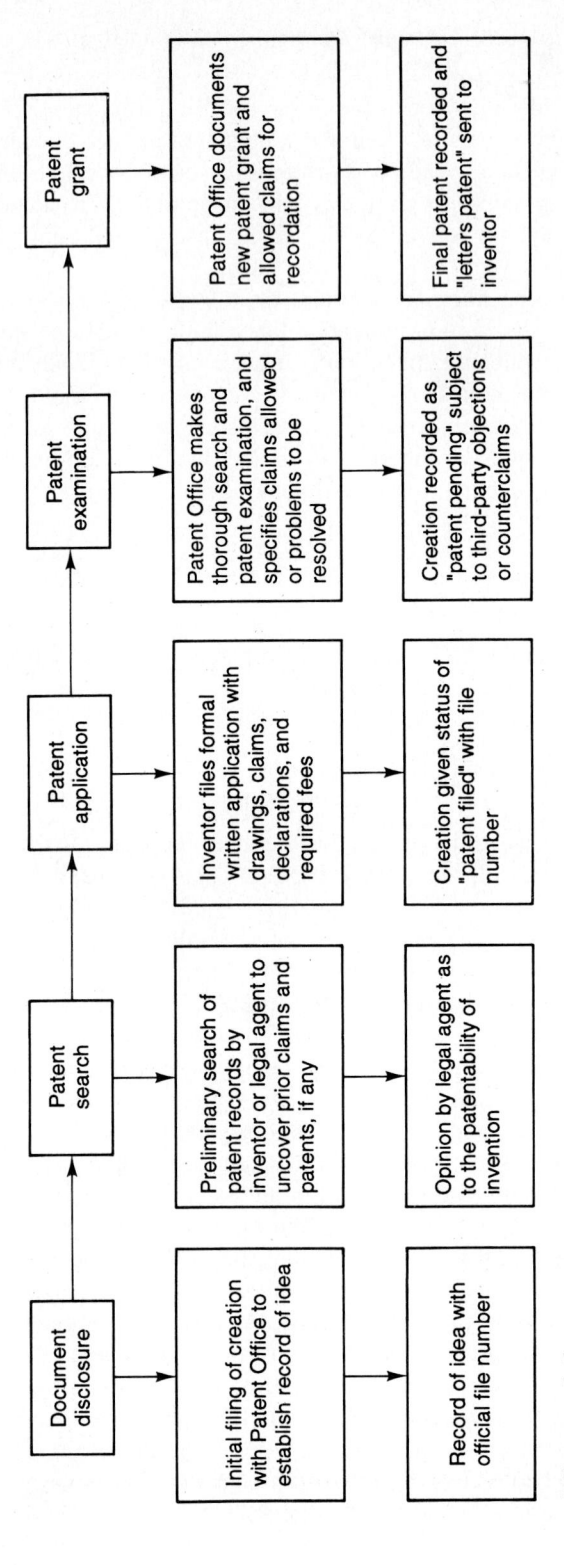

Figure 6-1 The Patent Process

The Patent Search

A **patent search** is required to determine whether an inventor's creation already exists and remains actively protected under the law. Most inventors will retain a patent attorney experienced with the search process. The attorney will do all legal work from search to finalization of the patent. However, the search process is the same whether done by an attorney or by an individual. Someone has to conduct research at the Scientific Library of the U.S. Patent and Trademark Office in Arlington, Virginia, or one of the 56 regional Patent Libraries located throughout the United States. In each location, there is a *Search Room* that contains U.S. patent information; however, the extent of information in each library varies. Some will have all patents issued since 1790, others trace patents to 1836, and still others maintain only recent patent information with cross-reference indexing. These regional libraries are called *Patent Depository Libraries*, and those in major cities will summarize most information maintained in Arlington, where formal records and original documents are maintained.

The Arlington office is just across the Potomac River from downtown Washington, DC, and it has a *Record Room* where the public may inspect records and files of any issued patent. The Patent Office Library in Arlington has more than 120,000 volumes of scientific and technical books in various languages, nearly 90,000 bound volumes of periodicals, official journals from 77 foreign patent organizations, and summary patent information on approximately 12 million foreign patents. All these are supplements to the U.S. register of more than 500 major classes of patents with 200,000 subclassifications.[10] Although this system may sound like a nightmare for the individual inventor, the Patent Office has an excellent classification system with expert staff to help in the search process. A wealth of information can be obtained without too much expense. In addition, there are government services available to search beyond patents for public domain inventions, to access government documents, and to advise on the search process.

Preliminary Search. The first step is to complete a preliminary search that scans patent summaries for prior claims or inventions. Inventors, or their patent attorneys, access patent records, try to be diligent to unearth prior patents (or patents with similarities to the invention), then make a judgment call whether to proceed with an application. A preliminary search may not uncover all prior claims, and a patent may be denied later by an examiner who *does* make a thorough investigation. The preliminary search may also miss something because few individuals actually search the main records. In most instances, the search is done through an on-line computer data bank using key words to sift through classifications. Consequently, an inventor of a new dental instrument may put "dental instrument" into the computer and get several thousand patents to review but miss dental instruments called "probes" that exist in another classification. However, searching on "probe" is likely to get everything from space satellites to acupuncture needles. Some adroitness at word searching is necessary.

Collecting Search Documents. Anyone can obtain hard photocopies of patents or photo facsimiles of summary sheets, drawings, data on microfilm, abstracts, and information maintained in scientific and technical journals. The Patent Office charges a small fee for these services, but the convenience is remarkable. Nearly all major sources of information within the Patent Office system can be accessed through one of the regional depository libraries.

Making the Patent Application

An application is made after the preliminary search, and it is sent to the Commissioner of Patents and Trademarks. There are three main parts to the application. The first is a written document that comprises a description of the invention, its specifications, and "claims." A *claim* is a specific description of the item and how it works. Some inventions have literally hundreds of claims about what they can do or how they can work. When a patent is issued, it may have some of these claims rejected. In any event, the inventor will want to provide complete information about what the invention is to do and how it is to be used. The second part of the application is a set of drawings. When an application is made, these drawings can be rather crude, but they must be accurate, drawn on flexible material (i.e., foldable white paper as opposed to fiberboard or plastic film), and able to be photocopied. The third part of the application is a formal oath or declaration by the inventor. These items are bundled together and accompanied with an application fee. When the Patent Office records the transaction as being a "complete application," a file number is assigned and the inventor notified.

The Written Document. Patent attorneys maintain standard application forms and typically use legal- or standard-size paper for describing the invention. Individuals can write their own applications, but they must conform to Patent Office guidelines. This document will be at least several pages long and contain at least five sections:

- A *formal declaration* that identifies the inventor, what type of patent is being applied for, a summary of prior applications (if any), and a statement that the inventor is claiming that the idea is original.
- A *brief history* that describes how the invention evolved, the background of its development, evidence of testing or certification, and how it was devised.
- An *abstract* that describes what the item is and how it works. An abstract can be very brief, perhaps only several lines or one paragraph.
- A *thorough description* that carefully itemizes the invention's working parts, how they are made, and how the item is used. A description usually refers to associated drawings with extremely detailed information about parts, materials, specifications, and methods of manufacture.
- A *description of claims* that individually lists each modification, use, or alternative material, method of manufacture, or feature that is being claimed for patent protection by the inventor. An inventor must specify at least one claim because a patent will be based on the claims requested, not on a general description. A complicated device, however, may have hundreds of claims in order to protect an inventor who wants the latitude to substitute materials, parts, or processes, and who may find new uses with further development.

The written document may have several other sections. For example, if a patent attorney or patent agent is involved, then the inventor must give the attorney or agent a *power of attorney* to act on behalf of the inventor with the Patent Office. Without a power of attorney, a patent lawyer or agent cannot access the inventor's records or conduct any business with the Patent Office pertaining to the application.

In many instances, a patent application will have an *assignment* whereby the inventor assigns title and rights to a third party. For example, an individual may file an application on an invention made through his or her company. The assignment would be to the company for which the inventor works. Assignments can be made to any legal entity, and the effect of an assignment is to have *letters patent* granted directly to the assignee when a patent is successful.

Drawings. The application need only contain simple, but accurate, hand drawings of the invention. These can be done by the inventor, and there is seldom a need for extensive engineering blueprints. Later in the patenting process, the Patent Office will require formal drawings, and the inventor will most likely have to contract the drafting work to someone who completely understands complex specifications for a final set of illustrations.

Oaths or Declarations. The Patent Office will provide standard forms for oaths and declarations, and while most patent attorneys have their own forms, the law only requires that inventors make an oath or declaration that they believe they are the original and first inventors of the item. The Patent Office has additional rules for oaths and declarations to reveal prior claims, foreign patent applications, and allegations about claims (e.g., what the invention is supposed to do). The inventor must sign the application together with joint inventors, and although standard forms usually have provisions for a notary, the declaration does not have to be notarized to be legal.

Patent Filing Fees

Currently, the basic filing fee for a patent application is $340, but there are additional fees that vary substantially with the complexity and number of patent claims. Realistically, filing fees can approach $800; however there is financial relief for inventors classified as "small entities." A small entity is a sole inventor, a small business, or a nonprofit institution, but to qualify, the applicant must file a verification form that has to be approved by the Commissioner of Patents and Trademarks. If qualified, a small entity pays only half the normal filing fee.

Patent filing fees do not include patent attorney fees or other costs of patent search, patent agency work, preparing drawings, and so on. For a simple invention, the total cost of an application might well exceed $2,000.

> ▶ **CHECKPOINT**
>
> Identify and explain the primary steps in obtaining a patent.
>
> Describe the five major sections of a patent filing document.

PATENTS IN PERSPECTIVE

Applying for a patent can be far less painful than it seems. In fact, the Patent Office can be extremely helpful with document forms, instructions, and personal advice to lead even the least-experienced entrepreneur through the maze. No one at any patent office or facility can recommend patent attorneys or patent agents, but there is a roster of attorneys registered with the Patent Office. Many communities have attorney referral services, but it is important to note that all attorneys and patent agents must be formally recognized by the Patent Office in order to represent an inventor.

An interesting service provided by the Patent Office is assistance in marketing a patent. Since a patent is a valuable asset, inventors can often sell their patents, and the Patent Office provides a published list of new patents for sale in the *Official Gazette*. This is a widely circulated booklet of new inventions, and it costs only $6.00 to have a patent included.

At state and local levels, there are also many government-sponsored agencies anxious to help market inventions. State economic planning agencies, for instance, are always on the lookout for new patents that have commercial potential for local or regional development. Local manufacturers' associations, industrial development groups, and university centers are also excellent sources of help. The U.S. Department of Commerce maintains special staff support agencies for giving inventors assistance, and the Small Business Administration has an extraordinary array of information ranging from how to write a disclosure to samples of technical patent application drawings.

▶ CHECKPOINT

Describe patent legal or filing assistance for an entrepreneur.

Discuss why state and local agencies would assist patent holders.

TRADEMARKS

The registration of trademarks must conform to the Trademark Act of 1946. However, trademarks are protected by *common law* so that an individual does not have to register a trademark formally to establish the validity of ownership. It is important to note that registration with the U.S. Patent and Trademark Office establishes legal documentation that can be used in court. Without registration, the privilege of ownership is subject to contention in a civil action between the parties. It follows that registration is a reasonable course of action.

Defining Trademarks and Service Marks

As defined in Section 45 of the 1946 act, a **trademark** "includes any word, name, symbol, or distinguishing device, or any combination thereof adopted and used by a

Chapter 6 Product Protection: Patents, Trademarks, and Copyrights   185

PROFILE △

Trademarks and Service Marks

The power of words and symbols is recognized as a commercially important asset for establishing brand image and market loyalty among customers. Unique logos, designs, titles, names, insignia, and combinations of words and symbols can be trademarked. Service marks are unique characters or slogans, often quite similar to trademarks, that provide protection for brand images and creative properties that enhance a company's marketability.

Well-known trademarks include the Big Mac and the sign of the golden arch, McDonald's indisputable properties. Adidas, the Workmate by Black & Decker, and Listerine are registered trademarks. The familiar checkerboard of Purina and the running greyhound dog of Greyhound Corporation are registered service marks. The Travelers Insurance Company creates names for insurance products and protects them using service marks that include CommonCents and MasterPac. The Travelers also has the familiar trademark red umbrella logo and the service mark phrase "You're better off under the Umbrella." AT&T is recognized by its unmistakable service mark "Reach out and touch someone."

---

manufacturer or merchant to identify his goods and distinguish them from those manufactured or sold by others."[11] Trademarks can be names used in commerce, such as Coke, clearly trademarked by Coca-Cola Corporation. A trademark can be a symbol, such as Apple Computer Corporation's unusual apple with a bite in the side. Distinguishing devices can be artistic renderings of corporate products, such as the wild mustang horse for the Ford automobile, the intricate shield and eagle design used on beer cans by Anheuser-Busch, Inc., or insignia designed for NFL football teams.

An important qualification for a trademark is that the mark, name, or insignia must be used commercially. Consequently, a logo not actually used in trade may be denied registration, and one that was registered but out of use for an extended period of time may lose registration protection. Also, a company name cannot be registered as a trademark, but it can be registered as a service mark. To be eligible for registration, a distinguishing mark *must be used in commerce* on a continuous basis. For example, the trademarked name "Coke" has been in continuous use since its inception.

A trademark is granted through the U.S. Patent and Trademark office for a period of 20 years. A trademark can also be renewed for an additional 20 years as long as it has not become generic, and as long as it has remained in continuous use. Protecting a trademark can be complicated, and companies such as Coca-Cola Corporation will make sure that whenever their trademarks are used in public communication, readers are clearly informed of the trademark. Those who infringe on trademarks or counterfeit them are guilty of *misappropriation*. Although this is not a felony, offenders can be brought to civil court, enjoined to stop using a trademark, and sued for damages resulting from its misuse. The assumption of misappropriation is that a company's goodwill and reputation can be damaged by infringement, subsequently leading to business losses.

A **service mark** is similar to a trademark and can be registered in the same way with the same protection. A service mark can be a name, wording used in advertising, symbols, or artistic figures that create a distinctive service concept. Therefore, the unique lettering of the abbreviation "IBM" for International Business Machines coupled with a design and a specific blue color cannot be replicated by another firm.

Trademarks and service marks are limited in a number of ways, such as not being permitted to depict flags or insignia of the United States or any state, municipality, or foreign nation. They cannot comprise immoral or deceptive matter, and they cannot disparage others. Qualifying for federal registration is more complicated than indicated here, and it is advisable to make a formal search (similar to searching a patent) before filing a trademark application. This is far less complex than searching a patent, and anyone can access records maintained in the Trademark Search Room in Arlington, Virginia.

Filing to Register a Trademark or Service Mark

There are three major parts to a formal application, but filing is not a difficult procedure. The process is depicted in Figure 6-2. First, a standard form can be obtained from the Patent Office for making a written application. Second, a drawing of the trademark or service mark must be provided. Third, specimens or facsimiles of the mark must be included. With the package complete, a filing fee must be included. The basic application fee is currently $200, but there can be additional fees depending on the complexity of the registration.

Written Application. Using a Patent Office standard form (or simply writing the application on legal-size white paper), an applicant provides conventional information such as name, address, citizenship, identification of partners, and corporate name. Also, the applicant must make a declaration clearly stating the individual or company that claims proprietary ownership. In addition, the applicant must declare that a mark has been adopted and explain how it is being used commercially.

There are several dozen categories of trademarks. These are called *classes* of trademarks, and the applicant must select the appropriate class for filing. For example, a trademark for laundry soap is in Class 3, and a photographic trademark is in Class 9. Coffee is in Class 30, and entertainment marks fall into Class 41. It is not uncommon to have a trademark registered in several classes (but to do so costs additional filing fees). A photographic trademark, for example, might be used in camera manufacturing, television movies, and games. Disney, Inc., has nearly everything the company creates trademarked in multiple classifications (entertainment characters as manufactured toys, clothing, games, candies, glassware, photographs, and so on).

The application must establish a date on which the trademark was first used commercially. This defines the beginning of the term of protection in the event of

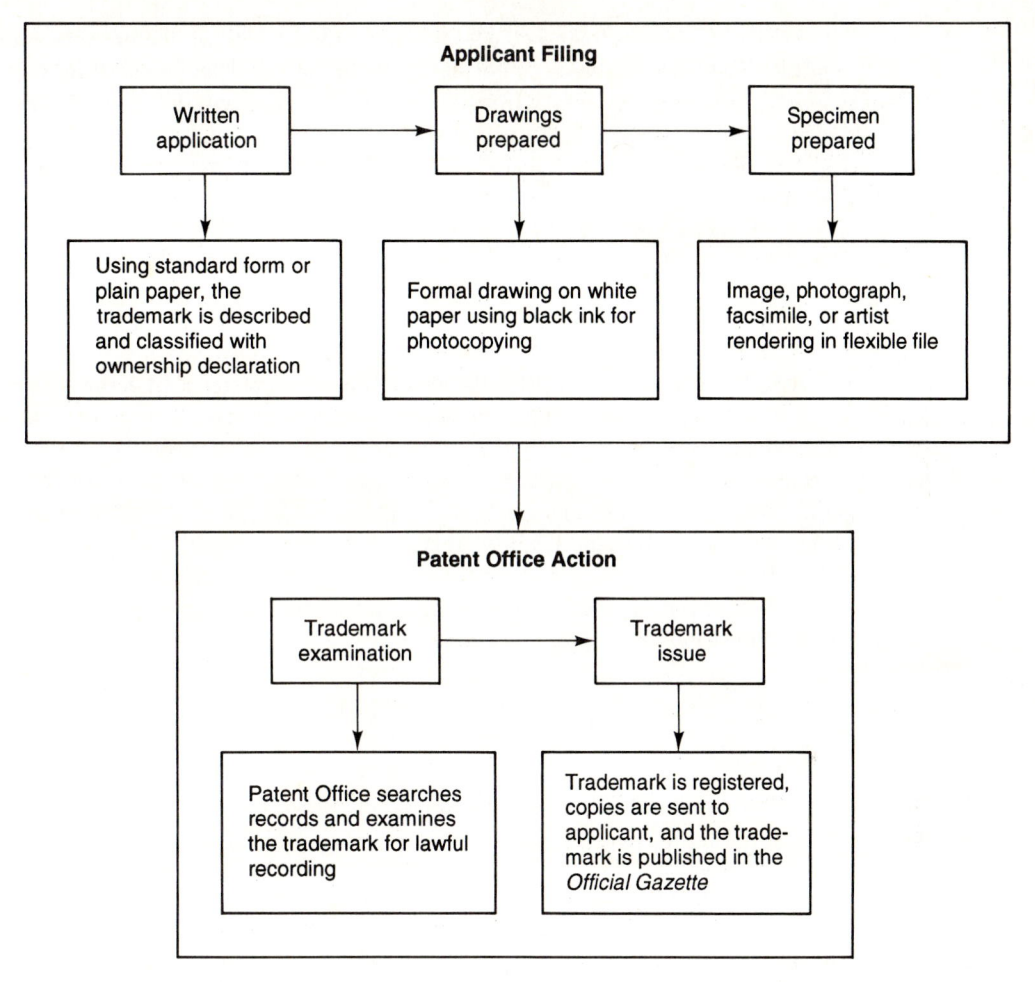

Chapter 6 Product Protection: Patents, Trademarks, and Copyrights 187

```
                        Applicant Filing
   ┌─────────────┐      ┌─────────────┐      ┌─────────────┐
   │  Written    │ ──►  │  Drawings   │ ──►  │  Specimen   │
   │ application │      │  prepared   │      │  prepared   │
   └──────┬──────┘      └──────┬──────┘      └──────┬──────┘
          ▼                    ▼                    ▼
   ┌──────────────┐     ┌──────────────┐     ┌──────────────┐
   │ Using standard│    │ Formal drawing│    │ Image,       │
   │ form or plain │    │ on white paper│    │ photograph,  │
   │ paper, the    │    │ using black   │    │ facsimile, or│
   │ trademark is  │    │ ink for       │    │ artist       │
   │ described and │    │ photocopying  │    │ rendering in │
   │ classified    │    │               │    │ flexible file│
   │ with ownership│    │               │    │              │
   │ declaration   │    │               │    │              │
   └───────────────┘    └───────────────┘    └──────────────┘
                                │
                                ▼
                       Patent Office Action
         ┌─────────────┐           ┌─────────────┐
         │ Trademark   │  ──────►  │ Trademark   │
         │ examination │           │   issue     │
         └──────┬──────┘           └──────┬──────┘
                ▼                         ▼
      ┌──────────────────┐      ┌────────────────────┐
      │ Patent Office    │      │ Trademark is       │
      │ searches records │      │ registered, copies │
      │ and examines the │      │ are sent to        │
      │ trademark for    │      │ applicant, and the │
      │ lawful recording │      │ trademark is       │
      │                  │      │ published in the   │
      │                  │      │ Official Gazette   │
      └──────────────────┘      └────────────────────┘
```

Figure 6-2 **Filing for a Trademark**

any modifications or disputed claims. The applicant must make an oath or formal declaration that he or she (or the organization for which the trademark will be issued) is the originator and therefore has the right to use the trademark in commerce. Then the application is signed by the individual, corporate officers, partners, owners of firms, or association officers, and it is notarized.

Drawings. A formal drawing of each trademark must be submitted on plain white paper (such as a good-quality bond) and permanent black india ink used to pen the lines. The drawing cannot have erasures or ''whiteout'' or multiple colors. Standard-size typing paper is preferred, and there are certain format restrictions for identifying the mark, applicant, and dates of commercial use. This procedure does not require engineering credentials or special skills other than to provide an accurate rendering of the mark one wishes to protect.

Specimens. Five specimens of actual trademarks or *facsimiles* must be submitted with the application, but it is not necessary to submit specimens of all commercial uses or all intended uses. (Imagine what a task that would be for Disney, Inc.) Facsimiles are allowed because actual specimens can seldom be filed in a folder; labels for designer jeans and the Academy Awards Oscar figurine, for example, are registered through validated photographs. Facsimiles can be artistic renderings, reproductions, or photographs. Specimens and facsimiles must be capable of photocopying and fit onto a legal size format.

Obtaining and Verifying Trademarks

Once an application is successful, the Patent Office will register a trademark, send three copies of the registration to the applicant, and date the trademark for tracking the 20-year protection limitation. That's it. The entire process can usually be accomplished inexpensively and rather quickly (a matter of a few months in most cases). The Patent Office *Official Gazette* contains a trademark section that lists trademark registrations on a weekly basis. Clearly, there can be complicated trademark registrations, and the search, application, and verification process can assume enormous proportions, particularly if one is applying for foreign trademark rights or filing for multiple classifications of a single trademark.

▶ **CHECKPOINT**

Define and explain trademarks and service marks.

Describe the trademark filing process and registration requirements.

COPYRIGHTS

Copyrights are similar to patents in establishing ownership and protection for creative endeavor, but they pertain to *intellectual property*. Copyright law in the United States is predicated on English Common Law and the 1710 Statute of Anne that gave special protection rights to writers, artists, and composers. These rights were subsequently written into Article I of the U.S. Constitution to foster creativity and stimulate intellectual endeavor. The description in this text is based on the latest legislation, the Copyright Act of 1976.[12]

The Essence of Copyrights

A **copyright** is distinct from patents and trademarks in that intellectual property is protected for the life of the originator plus 50 years. This protection affords an extraordinary property right and a substantial estate. Copyrights are granted through the Copyright Office, an extension of the Library of Congress, and application is

PROFILE △

Billion-Dollar Industry in New Copyrights

Thorn EMI, the British recording company that holds aging copyrights on nearly 750,000 pieces of music, has found a gold mine in new digital CD and laser media. The company found that it can obtain new copyrights on old material if the result of updating and using new media creates a new form of entertainment distinct from the original. In 1989, EMI released new versions of 1963 Beatles hit songs, obtained new 1989 copyrights, and launched a new industry. Soon EMI and Michael Jackson began negotiating to buy Motown classics, and they were talking with Walt Disney Productions. Also, EMI owns classics, like "Happy Birthday to You" and the *Warsaw Concerto*, but what is the value of "rereleasing" early Mickey Mouse recordings, many created more than 60 years ago? Billions, they say.

Source: Melinda Wittstock, "Mickey Mouse Makes the Fat Cats Lick Their Lips," *The Times*, London, January 6, 1990, Section 3, p. 1.

---

made *after* intellectual property is published but before it is made available to the public. This unusual practice is derived from common law doctrine that requires property to be in final published form before it is copyrighted. Therefore, a printed copyright statement will appear on material before registration occurs.

A copyright extends protection to authors, composers, and artists, and it relates to the *form of expression* rather than the subject matter. This distinction is important because most intellectual property has proprietary information in terms of subject matter, and if that property cannot be patented, the copyright only prevents duplicating or using the original material. This prohibition does not prevent another person from using the "subject matter" and then rewriting the material. For example, the concept of an electronic spreadsheet (subject matter) is not protected; however, the software program devised to create the spreadsheet (form of expressive) is protected by copyright. This subject has become extremely controversial for computer software programs, which are usually copyrighted but not patented. Computer software is a special topic that will be addressed under a separate heading.

Visual materials under copyright protection are photographs, paintings, sculptures, poems, articles, stories, books, music, sound recordings, motion pictures, audiovisual works, periodicals, computer punch cards, microfilm, pantomimes, and choreographic works. These can be accurately differentiated from similar works. Copyright law extends to literary and dramatic efforts, so that performances and recording rights also can be protected. In some instances, new copyrights can be obtained for old material, if the new use represents a new form of expression. This point is illustrated in the accompanying profile of Thorn EMI, the recording company that handled the Beatles.

Material Exempt from Copyright

The first rule of establishing a copyright is that the material must be copyrighted by an unequivocal statement *before* the published material is offered for sale or made public. Consequently, if an author writes a story, publishes it, and offers it for sale, then seeks a copyright, it will be denied. In fact, no one can copyright the story at that point; it has passed into "public domain," and anyone can have access to, use, or copy the story. Material exempt from copyright includes all government documents and anything written by employees of the U.S. government in the normal course of their duties. Also, a "blank form" or an "idea" cannot be copyrighted. As a general rule, anything that lacks creative authorship cannot be copyrighted. Thus slogans, colors, variations on lettering, titles, formulas, measurements, or translations of existing materials have too little creative value to qualify. Mathematical formulas are exempt because they express a "state of nature," not a creative human endeavor.

Fair Use and Limitations of Copyright Protection

Through court interpretations, a concept of **fair use** has been established so that copyright material can be used and copied within limitations.[13] For example, most scientific papers and textbooks build on previously published and copyrighted work. Educational researchers and teachers are expected to make extensive use of previously published materials, either building on prior knowledge to extend their own research or disseminating information to students. As a result, the law allows use of copyrighted information for education within certain stipulated guidelines. If more than 10 percent of a short copyrighted article is quoted or copied, for example, written permission usually is needed from the copyright owner. For longer works such as a textbook, permission may be required for 50-word quotations, and the copyright owners may require payment and attribution for granting that permission. Reproduction of a copyrighted work for criticism, comment, scholarship, research, and classroom teaching is considered fair use, not an infringement of copyright.[14]

The doctrine of fair use was established to encourage dissemination of intellectual property. To that end, scholars are encouraged to draw on published information without undue restrictions. Authors are expected to extend past knowledge into future essays. Teachers are given a great deal of latitude to copy materials for classroom use. These uses are considered essential to "diffuse" knowledge for the benefit of society. When these efforts are not for commercial gain, the doctrine of fair use will be extremely liberal. When a user can realize a commercial gain, the doctrine is interpreted more closely to protect the copyright owner's interests.

Obtaining a Copyright

Once a copyright declaration has been printed on material, a formal filing process will proceed as illustrated in Figure 6-3. However, a copyright does not have to be

Chapter 6 Product Protection: Patents, Trademarks, and Copyrights

Declaration	Application	Issue
Print copyright declaration by the owner on property *Caution:* Owner must declare in published form but not sell or distribute copyright item before it is registered	Make application to the Copyright Office, pay required fees **Deposit** Forward concurrently with application copies of material or excerpts required for deposit with the Library of Congress	Obtain verification of copyright and registration number from Library of Congress

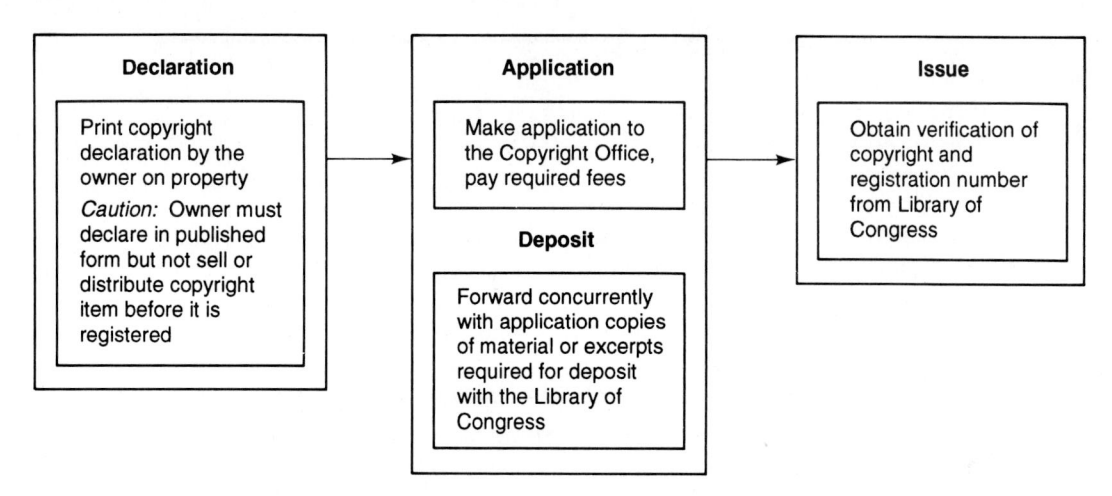

Figure 6-3 **Obtaining a Copyright**

filed to be valid. By printing a copyright statement on material, it is "copyrighted," provided there is no infringement on someone else's material. Merely writing a declaration statement, however, does not constitute a valid claim that can be used in court. Under copyright law, there is a specific requirement that a copyright be registered with the Copyright Office for it to be accepted in court as evidence. To be clear about this matter, courts cannot accept an unregistered claim as evidence, nor can a court act on a copyright infringement when the copyright is unregistered.

To register a copyright, obtain from the Copyright Office a standard form, fill it in, and submit it according to guidelines together with the filing fee. The fee is nominal, less than $20, but varies slightly with the type of filing; until 1978 the filing fee was always $6. In addition, *two copies* of the published work must be deposited with the Library of Congress.

For artistic materials, recordings, audiovisual works, computer programs, and most other copyright deposits, there are more complicated requirements. To register software, for example, a partial reproduction of the first and the last computer program code is needed; exactly how much code must be reproduced and deposited is somewhat arbitrary and varies with the length and complexity of the software program. Requirements for books, articles, periodicals, sheet music, and similar materials are that two copies of the published items be deposited. The deposit can be made concurrently with the copyright filing, and the Copyright Office will document the material, register it, and give the applicant written verification. Registration is simple in most instances, but occasionally it becomes complicated. For example, when the creators of the electronic toy bear, Teddy Ruxpin, tried to register it, they submitted a videotape to establish the unusual toy movements. This was rejected by the Copyright Office, but after several months of legal intervention, Teddy Ruxpin was copyrighted as a "compilation of data."[15] The story is expanded in the adjacent profile.

PROFILE △

Bearish Outlook for Software Registration

Teddy Ruxpin charmed millions of kids several years ago as the first simulated talking teddy bear. In fact, Teddy Ruxpin was much more. The toy was an extraordinary application of computer technology that animated behavior so "bearlike" that it started a revolution in electronic animation. The creators of the electronic toy bear, led by entrepreneur Donald Kingsborough, knew they had made an important breakthrough, and they attempted to protect their creation. After being advised that a patent was impossible, they applied for a copyright, submitting a videotape as evidence of the toy's unusual movements.

The Copyright Office denied the application, stating that Teddy was a system of semiconductor technology. A legal debate ensued over the question of whether the electronic wizardry of a toy bear like Teddy Ruxpin was unique or just an interesting collection of data. The Copyright Office preferred to think of the proprietary software as subject matter to be protected, thus ruling that bearish behavior was incidental. In the final copyright registration, Teddy Ruxpin was described as a "compilation of data . . . resulting in certain bearish behavior." Kingsborough went on to market Teddy Ruxpin though his company, Worlds of Wonder, grossing $93 million during the 1985 Christmas season; in 1986, Teddy contributed a majority of the $327 million in sales for the company.

Sources: "The Wonder Years," *Venture*, May 1989, p. 50. Also Richard H. Stein, "Micro Law: Protecting Hardware against Competition," *IEEE MICRO*, February 1989, pp. 2–5.

▶ CHECKPOINT

Explain the purpose of a copyright and types of properties protected.

Describe the copyright filing procedure for intellectual property.

Discuss the fair-use doctrine and its limitations for education.

REGISTERING SOFTWARE AS INTELLECTUAL PROPERTY

The 1976 Copyright Act spells out several specific criteria for computer programs and registered software. In addition, legislation passed in 1986 affords greater protection for semiconductor manufacturers, and a number of states have passed state laws to help protect software licensing. Most of these laws have yet to be tested in the courts, but software firms have used them aggressively to pursue injunctions against software pirates.[16]

The Semiconductor Chip Protection Act of 1986 established the right of semiconductor manufacturers to obtain a copyright in the architecture of a new integrated circuit. This provides the owner with an exclusive right to sell, import, distribute, or license a new chip for ten years. Several major manufacturers, including Intel, Harris, and Motorola, have registered copyrights for integrated circuits. Unfortunately, critics of legislation related to the computer industry say that it is confusing. For example, Apple Computer Corporation and Microsoft Corporation have been in litigation for several years, both debating uncertain laws and their conflicting copyrights on screen displays and software structure. Lotus Development Corporation was drawn into the fray in 1989 over copyright ownership of software interfaces.[17]

State efforts spearheaded by Illinois and Louisiana have created so-called *shrink-wrap legislation*, an effort to reduce software piracy by binding a software license on anyone who opens a package with a protective seal on mass-marketed software. When an individual breaks the seal (the seal usually being a plastic cover created through a shrink-wrap process), that individual is bound to the license provisions printed on the package. The shrink-wrap issue has been upheld in court, but it is still unclear how a user can be identified as the one who opened the wrapping.[18]

Perhaps the most significant change in rules has been a "special relief" provision for registering software copyrights. The 1976 Copyright Act was amended in 1980 with passage of the Computer Software Protection Act to spell out how a computer software program could be copyrighted and deposited with the Library of Congress. Under the 1976 act, computer software was defined as a "literary work," and to be registered, software had to be deposited in its entirety. Under the 1980 act, software was defined as "statements and instructions" related to computer use to create specific and unique results. Recognizing that many programs have thousands of lines of source code, the formal requirement of submitting two copies of documents was amended. In addition, the Copyright Office recognized that because many computer programs contain source code that could reveal trade secrets or proprietary information, it would be dangerous to require entire computer programs to be deposited. Consequently, a software developer can invoke a special relief option by depositing only a portion of each software program.[19]

Specifically, there are three relief options. The first option is for a deposit of the first and last 25 pages of object code and any 10 pages of source code. The second option is for deposit of the first and last 10 pages of source code in shorter programs where revealing any object code would compromise trade secrets. The third option is to deposit the first and last 25 pages of source code while purposely obscuring any trade secret information, as long as the obscured material does not exceed 50 percent of the deposit.[20]

> ▶ **CHECKPOINT**
>
> Describe the legal definitions for software prior to and after 1980.
>
> Why is there a special deposit requirement for software programs, and how is programming code submitted to the Library of Congress?

A NOTE ON TRADE SECRETS

By definition, **trade secrets** are proprietary information used in the course of business to gain an advantage in manufacture or commercialization of products or services. Trade secrets can be formulas, patterns, lists of customers, data bases, chemical compounds or combinations of ingredients for commercial products, processes of manufacturing, or compiled information that has a specific business application. It does not take much imagination to see how modern information systems with integrated computer programs could contain trade secrets, hence the "special relief" afforded to those in copyright deposits.

There is another dimension to this protection issue. Since many employees have access to their company's trade secrets, employees who leave can easily transfer that information to a competitor. They can also venture out on their own to leverage "inside knowledge" to start a new company. Software copyrights go a long way to discourage misappropriations, and by depositing limited information with the Library of Congress, one can substanstially reduce the risk of having trade secrets compromised. Nevertheless, this is a sensitive problem in high-tech industries where engineers and technicians change employment rather often, and where many create their own ventures in competition with prior employers.[21]

From an entrepreneurial perspective, those employees who leave to launch their own companies usually do not try to misappropriate information, but having worked in one career for some years, a person simply cannot erase his or her memory. To the contrary, their years of experience are valuable intellectual assets, and quite often, they have an idea or invention that is not acceptable to their employers, so that starting a new venture is a plausible alternative.

This is precisely how Steve Wozniak came to leave Hewlett-Packard, teaming with Steve Jobs to start Apple Computers, and there have been several claims and counterclaims between Apple and Hewlett-Packard about the proprietary ownership of trade secrets and software concepts. Herb Boyer and Bob Swanson, cofounders of Genentech, leveraged years of research in other organizations to develop the technology of genetic engineering, and as they incorporated their new company, they actively recruited a scientific team from major pharmaceutical competitors. No one has suggested these entrepreneurs acted improperly, only that a transfer of technological intelligence could have occurred.[22]

▶ **CHECKPOINT**

Explain why trade secrets are difficult to protect.

Discuss how an employee can (and cannot) be held liable for trade secrets and knowledge attained while working in a sensitive position.

VALIDATING PROPERTY RIGHTS

With all the ceremony attached to registering patents, trademarks, and copyrights, one would think that an individual has ironclad protection. That is not the case. In fact, there is no presumption that any form of protection is *valid* until it has been tested in a court of record. A "court of record" is a higher court whose rulings are recorded and open for public reference. The federal court charged with applying patent law is the Court of Appeals for the Federal Circuit. The court can act on criminal infringement cases, render judgments on patent disputes, and hear appeals from lower courts. Most copyright and trademark disputes, however, are resolved through civil court actions (between parties) rather than through criminal proceedings.

This revelation can be quite disturbing to an inventor with patent in hand who thought his or her invention was backed by the federal government. Patent documents, trademark registrations, copyrights, and any other registration is just *evidence*. The Patent Office, Copyright Office, and Department of Commerce have nothing to do with individual cases. They do not resolve disputes or validate property rights, and they cannot help defend a claimant. Nevertheless, registration provides very strong legal documentation for presenting evidence in favor of ownership rights.

When there is a dispute over ownership, the holder of a registered property right (patent, copyright, or trademark) brings suit against an alleged infringer or files criminal charges, and then it is entirely in the court's hands. Patent infringement is a criminal violation; copyright or trademark infringement is *not* "on the surface" a criminal violation. Therefore, a person who violates patent law can be criminally charged and then sued again in a civil court for personal damages. A person who violates a trademark or copyright is typically sued in a civil action and enjoined to stop using the protected materials, and the violator can be held liable for any personal damages suffered by the registered owner. Copyright or trademark violators also can be subject to criminal charges under circumstances that relate to fraud and willful infringement.[23]

> ▶ **CHECKPOINT**
>
> Explain how a patent, copyright, or trademark may be "registered" but not valid.
>
> Describe the responsibility of the Patent or Copyright Office in a lawsuit. What protection is afforded by registration?

ACCESSING GOVERNMENT INFORMATION

There are many ways to obtain information about patents, trademarks, copyrights, and various other forms of government services. First, you can go to a library and find source documents. Second, you can write for information to one of the controlling agencies. Third, you can make a telephone call to the Public Service Center in Washington, DC, and be connected to an automated information system that will direct your call. Simply dial **703-557-4636**, have a pencil and pad handy, and follow instructions. You will be asked to dial an additional two numbers to specifically access a category of information. For example, dialing 11 when instructed results in a summary message on patents. This information includes names of documents the Patent Office can send to you, their costs, and answers to most frequently asked questions about patents. You can also request specific information on trademarks or copyrights, obtain lists of Department of Commerce publications, and get assistance to questions from personnel at the Library of Congress.

You can write directly to the U.S. Department of Commerce, Patent and Trademark Office, Washington, DC 20231. The Patent Office publishes two series of guidelines, *General Information Concerning Patents* and *General Information Concerning Trademarks*. In addition, you can obtain printed copies of existing patents for $1.50, obtain standard forms, and obtain lists of regional agencies. Information concerning copyrights may be obtained from the Register of Copyrights, Library of Congress, Washington, DC 20540.

Rather than printing a directory of other addresses, the best advice is to visit the local Chamber of Commerce, where you can obtain pamphlets, forms, newsletters, published guidelines, and essential addresses. A comprehensive summary of assistance provided through Chambers of Commerce is regularly updated through a strategy handbook, *Helping Small Businesses through Chambers of Commerce*. A copy of this handbook is available through the U.S. Chamber of Commerce, 1615 H Street NW, Washington, DC 20062. Few entrepreneurs really make good use of their Chambers of Commerce, and students are always surprised by the amount of information available. The Small Business Administration supplies Chamber offices with a tremendous number of documents, case analyses, samples of business plans, forms, references, and other matter; and through the SBA and most Chambers, entrepreneurs can get a great deal of personal assistance.

▶ CHECKPOINT

Explain how an entrepreneur can obtain information on registrations.

Identify potential agencies that can help in patent, copyright, and trademark filing procedures.

IMPLICATIONS FOR ENTREPRENEURS

There are several excellent reasons why aspiring entrepreneurs should be well informed on patents, trademarks, and copyrights. Aside from the obvious need to protect one's ideas, the entrepreneur must be careful not to infringe on others. A majority of all infringements are settled out of court or through civil actions to stop misappropriations because a majority of infringements are made unintentionally by naive individuals.[24] It pays to use due diligence when seeking a patent, using copyrighted material, or dealing with trademarks because pleading ignorance does not stop a violator from being sued.

Being familiar with regulations is also important for designing packaging, writing advertisements, and distributing materials. But perhaps most important, obtaining property rights (patents, trademarks, or copyrights) creates valuable assets. Patents can be sold, licensed, assigned, or leveraged as assets of a new enterprise. Trademarks and copyrights can be leveraged in similar ways to provide the entrepreneur with bargaining power or income from royalties.

> ▶ **CHECKPOINT**
>
> As a final exercise, explain why it is important for entrepreneurs to understand patent, copyright, and trademark laws, and how successful registration of intellectual property can be an asset.

▲▲▲▲▲▲ SYNOPSIS FOR LEARNING

1. *Describe the requirements for a successful patent grant.*

Any process, machine, manufacture, or composition of matter that qualifies under the categories of being a *utility*, *design*, or *plant* patent must meet three important criteria. First, the creation must be proved to be that of the person making application. Second, it must be *useful*, meaning that must have a function that can be verified as workable. Third, it must be *new*, meaning that it cannot have existed before or be found in nature. Therefore, an inventor will file an application declaring his or her ownership of the creation, usually after making reasonably certain that a prior patent does not exist and that the item is not a natural phenomenon, then illustrate that it can be made and is useful.

2. *Explain the major steps in obtaining a patent.*

It is a good idea to file a disclosure statement with the U.S. Patent and Trademark Office to establish a recorded date of ownership, but the formal patent process begins with a patent search (either independently or with the help of a registered patent lawyer or agent). This results in an opinion that the invention is patentable. The next step is to make application to the Patent Office, conforming to specific criteria for writing the application, providing drawings, and submitting evidence of workability. The Patent Office then examines the application making a thorough search of records, and if successful, records the patent in a "patent pending" status. This allows a period of time in which third parties can make counterclaims or contest the patent.

Once the pending period elapses, the Patent Office will register the patent and grant "letters patent" to the inventor. At any step in the process, the inventor may have to modify the application, reduce claims, reply to Patent Office inquiries, or, in some instances, have legal intervention to protect a patent application.

3. *Discuss registration of trademarks and their advantages.*

Trademarks or service marks include logos, names, images, designs, artistic renderings, symbols, or combinations of words and symbols that distinguish a product, company, or intellectual property used in commerce. A trademark can be registered for 20 years and renewed if it has been in continuous commerce use. The major advantage is that a brand name or unusual logo (such as IBM's initials, combined with a distinctive blue color and font style) serve to identify a company to customers, communicating a certain image, quality, marketability, or reliability. The trademark is used to establish customer loyalty. In addition, it is used to discourage inappropriate duplication and misrepresentation by competitors.

4. *Describe a copyright and the concept of fair use.*

Copyrights extend protection to authors, composers, and artists, allowing them to register their "intellectual property" as a commercially valuable asset. A registered copyright is admissible in court as evidence of document ownership and priority of claims. Exactly what can be copyrighted is rather vague because new media have been introduced in recent years, such as software programs, screen displays (i.e., unique patterns of pull-down menus and spreadsheets), digital CDs, VCRs, and transmitted facsimiles, which have not been thoroughly tested in court. Court cases do exist with respect to using copyrighted materials, and a "fair use" doctrine has emerged. The fair use doctrine reflects logical use of published information when there is no commercial gain for the user. Thus educators, students, and researchers who are expected to use existing knowledge for teaching, critique, or commentary are allowed rather wide latitude in reproducing copyrighted material. For those who expect to make a commercial gain, the fair use rule is much more restrictive to safeguard interests of authors and artists.

5. *Explain how intellectual property is protected with respect to software programs.*

Typically, software programs are copyrighted, but the significance of a copyright was lost prior to legislation in 1980 and 1986 when software program code was singled out for special treatment by the Library of Congress. Prior to 1980, a software program was treated in the same way as any literary work, and software developers had to submit two full copies of programs for deposit. Because the evidence contained in deposited materials is used to support claims, large and complicated programs are difficult to defend as original. After 1980, specific computer code was allowed to be deposited under "special relief" options, allowing unique compilations of data to be used for defense. Consequently, these parts of a program are deposited while the entire software program is copyrighted.

6. *Discuss the nature of protection achieved through patents, copyrights, and trademarks in terms of legal recourse.*

Entrepreneurs too often believe that "registration" of a patent, trademark, or copyright makes their claims *valid*. Also, they believe that the U.S. government acts to enforce their rights under registration. Neither point is true. Validity is established only through a court of record as a person successfully defends his or her right of ownership. Government agencies do not enforce or defend claims, nor do they bring civil suits to aid individuals. However, any registration becomes extremely powerful evidence in a court of law, and those that hold registered patents, trademarks, or copyrights have the weight of the federal government behind them.

NOTES

1. U.S. Patent and Trademark Office, *General Information Concerning Patents* (Washington, DC: U.S. Department of Commerce, 1989), pp. 1–2.
2. Ibid., p.2.
3. David Burge, *Patent and Trademark Tactics and Practice* (New York: John Wiley & Sons, 1980), pp. 3–4, 112–118.
4. U.S. Patent and Trademark Office, *General Information Concerning Patents and Trademarks*, pp. 3–4.
5. U.S. Department of Commerce, *Q & A about Patents* (Washington, DC: U.S. Government Printing Office, 1976), pp. 3–4.
6. *Code of Federal Regulation, Title 37* (Washington, DC: U.S. Government Printing Office, 1989).
7. U.S. Small Business Administration, Office of Business Development, *Introduction to Patents* (Washington, DC: U.S. Small Business Administration, 1988), p. 4.
8. U.S. Patent and Trademark Office, *General Information Concerning Patents*, p. 4.
9. U.S. Department of Commerce, *Q & A about Patents*, pp. 3–4.
10. U.S. Patent and Trademark Office, *The U.S. Patent and Trademark Office*, bulletin of the Patent Office, Arlington, Virginia, October 1988.
11. U.S. Patent and Trademark Office, *General Information Concerning Trademarks* (Washington, DC: U.S. Department of Commerce, 1988), pp. 1–3.
12. *The Copyright Act of 1976, Public Law 94–553 (90 Stat. 2541)*, revised under Title 17, *United States Code*. Also *General Guide to The Copyright Act of 1976*, United States Copyright Office, Library of Congress, 1977, reprinted September 1987.
13. *The New Copyright Law and Education* (Arlington, VA: Educational Research Service, 1978), pp. 5–7.
14. Kenneth W. Clarkson, Roger Leroy Miller, and Gaylord A. Jentz, *West's Business Law* (St. Paul, MN: West, 1986), pp. 85–86.
15. "The Wonder Years," *Venture*, May 1989, p. 50. Also Richard H. Stein, "Micro Law: Protecting Hardware Against Competition," *IEEE MICRO*, February 1989, pp. 2–5.
16. Richard M. Lucash, "Look and Feel Lawsuits," *High Technology Business*, October 1987, p. 17.
17. Richard H. Stein, "Micro Law: Appropriate and Inappropriate Legal Protection of User Interfaces and Screen Displays," *IEEE MICRO*, August 1989, pp. 7–10.
18. Mary B. Jensen, "The Preemption of Shrink Wrap License in the Wake of *Vault Corp.* v. *Quaid Software Ltd.*," *Computer/Law Journal*, Spring 1988, pp. 157–169.
19. Thomas C. Richards and Ross L. Chan, "Microcomputer Software Piracy and the Law," *Security Audit & Control Review*, Vol. 7, No. 1 (Spring 1989), pp. 37–39.

20. "Intellectual Property," *Newsbrief* (Herndon, VA: Center for Innovative Technology), July 1986, pp. 2–4.

21. John W. Wilson, "Intel and Sequent Kiss and Make Up," *Business Week*, May 25, 1987, p. 120. Also Marian S. Rothenberg, "Bell Labs Spinoffs," *High Technology*, June 1987, pp. 16–22.

22. George McKinney and Marie McKinney, "Forget the Corporate Umbrella—Entrepreneurs Shine in the Rain," *Sloan Management Review*, Vol. 30, No. 4 (1989), pp. 77–82.

23. Robert A. Choate and William H. Francis, *Patent Law: Trade Secrets—Copyrights—Trademarks* (St. Paul, MN: West, 1981), pp. 932–934, 1024–1025, and 1038–1042.

24. Ronald D. Rothchild, "Making Patents Work for Small Companies," *Harvard Business Review*, Vol. 87, No. 4 (July-August 1987), pp. 24–30. For a brief historic summary see Harriet F. Pilpel and Morton David Goldberg, *A Copyright Guide* (New York: R. R. Bowker, 1969), pp. 19–22.

CASE 6-1

Taking an Invention from Drawing Board to Market

In 1975 the United States was mired in an oil crisis, cars burned gas at something like 12 miles per gallon, and the auto industry was frantically searching for ways to improve fuel efficiency. David Hicks, an employee at Digital Equipment Corporation, felt he had one of the answers. He reasoned that car alternators worked continuously, draining power and straining the engine. If they could be switched off when not in use, fuel efficiency could be improved dramatically. Working evenings and weekends on his idea, Hicks developed the Alter Break, an engine load-management system.

The Alter Break was patented in 1981 after six years of designing, building, and testing a prototype. It also required an investment of $73,000, $53,000 coming from a U.S. Department of Energy grant, and another six years to get the product positioned to be manufactured. Hicks retired from DEC before he could make his dream a reality, and reflecting on his invention, he said: "If Edison had to go through what I've gone through . . . we'd still be using kerosene lamps instead of light bulbs. I thought once I had the patent, I had it made, but the work just begins then."

In 1982, Hicks established Nutronics, a company specifically set up to market the Alter Break. The purpose of Nutronics was not to manufacture the product, but to refine it and do the necessary market research, product testing, and planning necessary to license it to a major manufacture. The toughest call every inventor makes is whether to start a business to make the product or to pursue a licensing agreement with an existing firm. Hicks considered the option to manufacture, but that would have meant millions of dollars in production capability. It would have also meant risking everything he had to market the Alter Break. Instead, Nutronics set out to do the business planning essential to license his product.

Dealing with Detroit, Hicks recalls, was fraught with pitfalls. Several shady types tried to lock up Alter Break for themselves and threatened Hicks, and on one occasion, a Detroit car company executive tried to copy the idea after Hicks had made a presentation. In every instance, he was turned away or locked out of talking with the people capable of making a deal. His experience taught Hicks several important lessons. First, everything must be documented from the first rough notes of an invention to the final dot on the *i* of a formal business plan. Second, inventors must write thorough business plans that accurately and completely justify the market opportunities and costs. Third, you have to stick with the idea through the entire cycle of product development—just getting the idea through a patent process is insufficient. And fourth, you have to be tenacious, to pursue the idea with total commitment.

In 1987, Hicks finally signed a licensing agreement with a group of Colorado investors who bought Nutronics and the rights to manufacture the Alter Break. That was 12 years after he inked his original notes, and slightly more than six years after his patent was granted. Along the way, a dozen marketing plans were written, several product feasibility studies were completed, and several thousand hours of testing were done. In the end, Hicks' contract will guarantee him a net of $1.45 million through 1998, including front-end money and royalties. Alter Break has not yet gone into full production, but when it does, it will improve fuel efficiency in today's cars by 20 to 30 percent. In 1975 it could have saved twice as much gas.

CASE QUESTIONS

1. Trace the development of Alter Break and describe the events of gaining a patent that would have taken nearly six years to complete.
2. Discuss the problems Hicks ran into when trying to market his product in Detroit. What protection did he have, and what recourse would he have had if his idea had been copied or stolen?
3. Considering the amount of work that went into market development and research beyond the actual patent, what value was there in the business plan and documentation? How could Hicks have protected this work?

Source: Doug Garr, "The Practical Inventor," *Venture*, October 1988, pp. 35–36.

CASE 6-2

Understanding Legal Protection

Described in the following paragraphs are several innovations that recently appeared for sale or in advertisements. Not all of these are protected by patents, trademarks, or copyrights. Your task is to study each description and answer the assigned questions regarding various types of legal protection available, if any.

1. *Southwestern Bell FF-1700 Cordless Phone*. This cordless telephone has a free-standing dialpad, speakerphone option, ten-channel selection for predial numbers, and intercom with paging. The Bell FF-1700 uses the latest technology to provide clear signals up to 1,500 feet.

2. *The Chef's Choice Knife Sharpener*. This sharpener safely and easily hones the dullest knives in minutes, and it is UL listed. It measures approximately 9 inches by 3 inches by 4 inches and sits nicely on any counter top. Using a unique sharpening method developed by a former Du Pont engineer, the Chef's Choice uses magnets to hold knives at precisely the right angle for clean, sharp bevels.

3. *Brainstorm Turbo-start*. A new program with optional configurations for IBM (and compatible) or Macintosh systems. Turbo-start uses a proprietary coding system to rapidly start your system, run a comprehensive virus check, and provide data-link communications protocol.

4. *The Lifeline Gym*. This is the most space-efficient workout device on the market. Made with latex cable and unbreakable handles, the Lifeline Gym provides stretching, lifting, and resistance exercises. Carried in a briefcase or tucked into a carrybag, it provides a complete workout anywhere you travel.

5. *Rain Man*. The soundtrack release of the hit movie by United Artists is now available, rerecorded on CD and tape through Capitol Records.

6. *The Heat Machine Plus*. This six-inch, five-pound tiny furnace can heat an average room for 24 hours for about $1.00. The unusual ceramic heater is made exclusively for Micromar, and among 12 competing heaters, this is the best. A tip-over switch prevents accidents, and a super fan makes air flow efficient.

7. *The Criss-Cross Posture Chair*. The unique Scandinavian design of this chair allows

a person to sit up straight with little back load. One may rest the knees on the front pad and sit comfortably, making the chair ideal for use at a workstation, desk, or table.

8. *The Coming Soviet Crash.* A new book by Judy Shelton, published by the Free Press, reveals the inside story of economic changes in the Soviet Union. It is a candid look at conditions in the USSR and Gorbachev's desperate bid for Western economic alliances.

9. *The Accounting Package.* A new entry for integrated accounting and word processing software, this package brings together spreadsheet templates and simplified word processing. Designed for stand-alone or network use, the Accounting Package is a versatile new product.

10. *Jockey Club.* Famous name-brand shirts at popular prices for seasonal wear. Dress with the best with Jockey Club men's wear.

CASE QUESTIONS

1. Identify for each item the most probable type of legal protection allowed.
2. Briefly describe the process required to acquire protection of the appropriate type, including the method of filing, general documentation, and agency to which application is made.
3. Explain why protection is needed in each instance, and describe the recourse a person has if infringement occurs.

Chapter 7

Services: The Human Side of Enterprise

OBJECTIVES

1. Explain the nature of professional and personal services.
2. Describe merchandising and the factors that are critical for retailing success.
3. Explain distributive services as an industry.
4. Discuss information services and recent innovations.
5. Describe success factors for service enterprises.

Being in business *is* the business of working with people. Regardless of the nature of a new venture, entrepreneurs cannot lose sight of their customers or their employees, but when the new venture provides a *service*, the human side of enterprise is accentuated. As a result, service entrepreneurs focus on efforts to establish successful relationships between their organizational members and the company's clients.

Good customer relationships are equally important to manufacturing firms and service enterprises, but for entrepreneurs who depend specifically on their human relations skills, success is measured more by satisfied customers than by innovative products. Consequently, most services are closely linked to products, such as fashion merchandising, fast foods, computer retailing, software engineering, and telecommunications. Recall that Chapter 5 described a close relationship between manufactured products and services; both are essential to a vibrant economy, but in this chapter we focus on services.

There are many types of services, ranging from local beauty salons to international consulting groups. Some rely on individual skills of entrepreneurs and grow only to the extent that owners can work longer hours or individually become more productive. An example is a music tutor. Others have service systems, and growth is achieved through organizations that replicate services for many customers in a variety of markets. An example is a chain of hotels.

Service growth is concerned with adding employees, gaining momentum in competitive circumstances, and encouraging others to excel. Encouraging others implies a substantial responsibility for attracting, hiring, training, and motivating employees. These responsibilities in an entrepreneurial service company are quite different from those in a major corporation, and we will discuss these differences. We will also introduce different types of services, how they are positioned to compete in unique markets, and how those with growth potential pursue human resource management as an essential requirement for success.

THE INFRASTRUCTURE OF SERVICES

The one phrase that captures the essence of services is that we are in a *high-touch* era. This means that we value *quality* performance and put a premium on personal attention. When John Naisbitt wrote *Megatrends: Ten New Directions Transforming Our Lives*, the best-selling author and futurist made a crucial distinction between "high tech" and "high touch." High tech was viewed as a buzzword for explaining this generation's preoccupation with extravagant technology. On the other hand, high touch was a way of explaining a social consciousness through which we could embrace so-called high technology yet vivaciously cling to the concept of personal service.[1]

As we crossed the threshold of an information age, we welcomed microcomputers, telecommunications, time-saving microwave ovens, and automatic teller machines. We can now mass-produce letters, fax messages to millions of locations around the world, and instantaneously access information from network data bases. We no longer have to prepare meals; we can microwave prepackaged dinners. We can conduct banking from our automobiles, make deposits through automated tellers, and withdraw cash with a plastic card in most major cities worldwide. But with each innovation there is a threat of isolation in an "overautomated" world. We no longer need to write personal letters or meet with clients or friends (we can communicate or leave messages on electronic bulletin boards). We no longer have to make personal phone calls to relay messages to family or colleagues (we can leave messages on answering phones). Something seems wrong with all this, and Naisbitt recognized the flaw. He suggested that we will value, *even more today and in the future*, the human side of enterprise: the ability to fashion a high-tech age with a high-touch approach to human services.

The infrastructure of service ventures is defined by how a company is organized and managed to personalize our commercial endeavors. For example, IBM holds securely to the concept that excellent service makes the firm successful, not merely the hardware that it sells. Hewlett-Packard views customers as "associates" who are as important to the firm as managers, employees, or technical innovations; HP's associates create new products and serve clients. Forward-thinking bankers are training employees to provide more personalized services rather than expanding the number of mindless ATMs.[2] *Excellence* may be an overused word, and that overuse is unfortunate because the word still captures the essence of good business, yet *excellence* is being translated into human terms by companies that make effective use of new technology without letting technology turn us into robots.

What does this human-resources approach mean in terms of entrepreneurship? It means that there are excellent opportunities for those who can provide the "high touch" of personal services. For example, rather than sell racks of synthetic look-alike clothes in a technological, but sterile, mall store, one can create an atmosphere of friendly service with, perhaps, a bit of old-fashioned fuss. Let clients rummage through the boutique—let them shop; it can be therapeutic—and shoppers may pay a bit extra for both the clothes and the therapy. This idea is the essence of a new wave in airport boutiques that encourage weary travelers to browse without pressure; other airport shops provide efficient no-hassle service for the rushed traveler. Similarly, computer retailers find that it is important to make customers feel comfortable in a nonthreatening environment where salespersons talk "human," not computerese, and novices are given sensible assistance.

For entrepreneurs who unleash their creativity, there can be exceptional opportunities in otherwise mundane businesses. The infrastructure of services is based on quality attention to human needs, and while the ultimate challenge may be to give a virtuoso performance, sometimes just creating a "magical commotion" in a clothing boutique can be the key to success. In the next section we will look at several types of services and see how they are distinguished from one another.

> ▶ **CHECKPOINT**
>
> Describe what is meant by "the ability to develop a high-tech business with a high-touch approach to human resources."
>
> Discuss how entrepreneurs can encourage personal service for customers and why it is important to do so.

TYPES OF SERVICE VENTURES

There are several broad categories of service firms. One category, called *professional services*, relates to enterprises based on the personal skills and knowledge of individuals with well-defined credentials. Physicians, dentists, attorneys, certified public accountants, and architects fall into this group. Another category, *personal services*, includes enterprises that perform specific individual services, but there is not always a requirement that entrepreneurs be credentialed. Examples include quick-print shops, contract custodians, software engineers, interior designers, tailors, and management consultants. As we shall see in a moment, a personal service firm may comprise one individual or a significant organization.

PROFILE △

Redefining Ground Services

With more than a half billion travelers passing through the largest U.S. airports each year, retail services have a highly concentrated market of customers. Most travelers are well educated and have good incomes, and those who have time between flights are looking for a little friendly diversion. Until recently, travelers had few options other than spending money on food, beverages, and souvenirs at the newsstand.

Airport retailing has taken a turn for the "smaller" and "better": smaller in terms of more small businesses and boutiques offering specialty products ranging from ice cream to perfumes; better in terms of offering luxury goods with high price tags on designer fashions, imported soaps and perfumes, and gourmet gifts. Bloomingdale's, Chez Chocolate, Häagen-Dazs, and Crabtree & Evelyn are among big-name retailers bidding for space at metropolitan and international airports. The small-name players are doing well too. Ruth Ann Menutis, cofounder of the Grove, a dried fruit and nut company carved out a rich niche in airports. Starting with modest savings a few years ago, Menutis has an expanding chain of 22 stores in nine airports yielding more than $4 million in sales. Her formula for success is a good display of healthy snacks and young, enthusiastic sales clerks. All customers get full measures of fruit and nuts (plus a bit) on their orders, and her employees throw in smiles and friendly greetings.

Source: Jeannie Ralson, "Airport Retailing Takes Off," *Venture*, May 1988, pp. 37–40.

A third type of service is *merchandising*, and this category covers hundreds of individual services described by their line of business. These include many different retail stores, restaurants, laundries, video rental shops, catalog mail-order companies, and discount clubs. A fourth category, *distributive services*, is concerned with moving products through various marketing channels or linking manufacturers with merchandisers. Examples in this category include wholesalers, contract warehouses, export-import agents, transport firms, and mail or express companies.

Information services, the last broad category, is concerned with processing information, disseminating knowledge, or facilitating transactions. Private schools, for example, disseminate knowledge, and banks facilitate transactions. Newspapers, research labs, and entertainment media process information and disseminate knowledge. Other services, most of which lack specific classifications, include counseling centers, retirement homes, clinics, telemarketing companies, and travel agencies, among many others. Each enterprise may be locally based, such as an independently owned motel, or operate globally, such as the Sheraton Hotel chain. We will not try to pigeonhole these ventures, but it is important to differentiate them.

Professional Services

Distinguished from other forms of business, **professional services** are those that require the principals to hold credentials recognized by professional associations. Most are also licensed to practice by state or national governing bodies. Entrepreneurs can rarely choose to go into a professional service, but many professionals become entrepreneurs. For example, a physician may elect to set up an individual practice rather than work in residence for a large hospital. The same doctor may combine with other doctors to create a medical center. A physician who is more interested in research than in practice may set up a research laboratory, and another colleague may establish educational seminar programs. Still others have established franchise chains of clinics, incorporated joint practices into new hospitals, or built retirement centers.

The point, of course, is that these professionals first had the requisite credentials to choose between organizational careers or private practices. These options and the process of turning to private practice are shown in Figure 7-1. By choosing to engage in professional services, they create dual responsibilities relating to both their professions and to operating successful businesses. Those who became entrepreneurs learn to apply the same fundamental lessons of doing business as their counterparts in manufacturing or retailing. Clearly, success in a professional field depends on quality of service, but good business practices are necessary to succeed. Often professionals have credentials but little knowledge or experience in business.

The profile of a professional physician applies equally well to those in other fields. For example, entrepreneurs can rarely choose to become certified public accountants or attorneys, but CPAs or attorneys can choose to open commercial enterprises based on their credentials. To succeed, they will need business acumen and a commitment to provide quality services.

An interesting observation is that few professionals think of themselves as

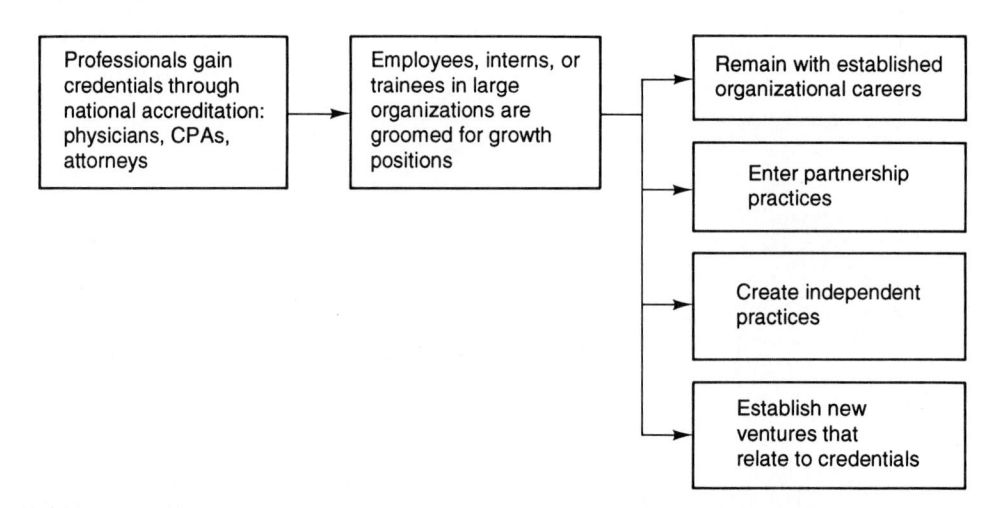

Figure 7-1 **Usual Route to Entrepreneurship for Certified Professionals**

entrepreneurs or businesspersons. Research shows that few physicians take business courses, fewer still want to be associated with entrepreneurship, and only a handful are concerned with marketing concepts or customer services.[3] Accountants are notorious for avoiding entrepreneurship education, and although they are often astute at budgeting and financial procedure, they are rather apathetic about the behavioral side of customer relations.[4] The irony is that most professional enterprises cannot survive without strong customer relations, and today most professional fields are extremely competitive. Success is not guaranteed by having the correct credentials.

Personal Services

The term **personal service** explains the nature of most small businesses that rely on individual skills. Barbers provide one-on-one personal grooming, computer consultants are hired to solve distinct problems for customers, and travel counselors respond to specific requests for travel arrangements. Many entrepreneurs in personal services are credentialed or licensed, but these requirements are substantially different from those for surgeons or attorneys. Also, most of those in personal service enterprises follow a different career path from professionals. This path is shown in Figure 7-2.

Educational levels also differ between those in personal and professional services. Beauticians, for example, seldom attain education levels comparable to physicians. With that said, software consultants working in personal service firms often hold master's or doctoral degrees, although their professional colleagues in public accounting more often hold only bachelor's degrees. Software consultants and certified public accountants may earn comparable fees, have similar clients, and resolve problems of corresponding complexity. The label of "professional" or "personal" service, therefore, is often a matter of perception.

The Internal Revenue Service has further confused the issue by classifying some enterprises as professional services and others as personal services. From an income-tax standpoint, this distinction can be important because the IRS considers computer

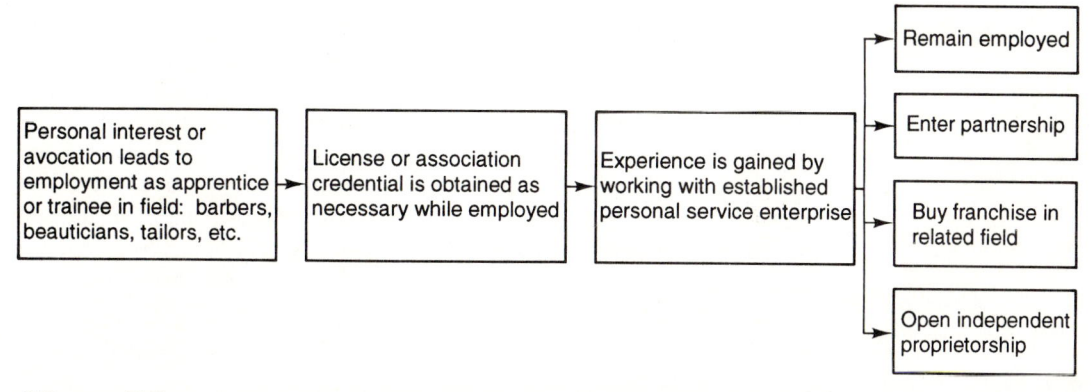

Figure 7-2 **Usual Routes to Entrepreneurship in Personal Services**

software consultants (and many other similar enterprises) as personal services. If those ventures are incorporated, they will fall under the "Personal Service Corporation" (PSC) tax code, which is quite different from other legal forms of incorporation. Generally, a PSC must report income and expenses in a different way from other corporations.[5] Consequently, aspiring entrepreneurs should investigate legal forms of enterprise and recent IRS rulings before establishing their businesses.

We all know, and do business with, those who offer personal services. Aside from barbers and beauticians, there are many local proprietors who make our standard of living what it is. We could not maintain comfortable life-styles without plumbers, carpenters, interior decorators, tailors, photographers, lawn care services, home cleaning services, job placement firms, counselors, and the many others who enrich our lives. Any commercial telephone book will reveal hundreds of examples.

Those who teach entrepreneurship are not entirely comfortable talking about personal services as "entrepreneurial ventures." Recall our opening comments in Chapter 1 and the difficulty we had separating the concepts of small business and entrepreneurship. One characteristic generally separating the two is *growth*. A barber content to provide good haircuts in a cozy shop is not an entrepreneur in the sense that there is no intention to "grow." On the other hand, a beautician who expands into a chain of stores (perhaps a franchised business) is entrepreneurial; an awkward but useful term is to call this type of business owner a growth-oriented entrepreneur.

There are many opportunities for new personal services as the American population continues to expand. The challenge rests with creating new methods of providing services. Three examples of businesses may help decipher the possibilities. Each of the following is engaged in the same line of business and market area near New York City. Ostensibly, they offer the same services.

> *Example 1*. This firm opened for business selling microcomputers and software in 1983. The founders had four employees, grew rapidly to nearly a half million dollars in sales during 1984, expanded into office network systems, hired several more technicians in 1985, and approached a million dollars in sales by 1986. By midyear 1988, the firm had apparently stopped growing even though it had never fully met the demand in a rapidly growing market. In fact, in 1985, four more computer retailers opened in the community, and in 1986, three more firms came into the area. Two of these firms have subsequently failed, and two more joined with a franchise chain, but this first one in the market has appeared to reach a plateau.
>
> *Example 2*. This enterprise also sells microcomputers and related software, and it has developed into a small "community" business that behaves more like a small professional partnership than a high-tech retailer. The firm, opened in 1984 with two partners, still had two partners in 1988. They added a secretary, and the partners work frantically nearly seven days a week (and most nights) to keep up with their accounts. They say they would like to grow, but facts preclude intentions, and what they have fashioned is a business constrained to the physical ability of two individuals to work as many hours as possible.

Example 3. The third firm opened in 1986 with three partners (all recent college graduates), incorporated, and aggressively followed a growth strategy. The firm topped $2.5 million in sales with 14 employees by 1988. The firm offers almost precisely the same categories of services as the other two, yet gross income is triple that of the first firm and nearly ten times that of the second. Moreover, the founders have accomplished this feat quicker than their competitors, and their business continues to grow.

Two critical factors differentiate these ventures: customer service and involved employees. The first firm is loaded with hardware and run by an individual who is enamored with technology. He hires "technicians" who are extremely well qualified to handle computers, make repairs, and write programs, but coming into the store is like visiting a morgue. Personal assistance seems to be an inconvenience.

The second firm is a locked-in partnership, and although the partners have hired people from time to time, employees are expected to do little more than supplement the partners' activities. The two partners are extremely talented, and they offer excellent service, but they are stretched so thin that customers cannot be properly served in an overloaded atmosphere. Both individuals are caught in an activity trap—working more and more to attract business but enjoying it less and less. This phenomenon of personally working to one's limits was appropriate in an era when we ate what we grew (and vice versa), but not in a competitive business environment where profits depend on creating added value.

The third firm offers hardware, network systems, software, and technical maintenance on precisely the same equipment as the first two firms. This company, however, also provides free orientation sessions for their customers, hotline assistance staffed by well-trained assistants, and formal training programs at their clients' offices. The firm does not have "employees"; it has "associates" who are committed individuals having both a monetary and a psychic stake in the venture. Clients enjoy visiting the firm's office where it is *fun* to talk with salespersons and equally enjoyable to experiment with new machines and software.

Customer service and attention to human resources are crucial success factors that will be discussed later, but the lesson should not be lost on small or large personal service firms. Human relations within the organization require a "psyched up" approach to helping others, and human relations outside the organization require a commitment to helping clients.

Merchandising

Merchandising is the primary form of retail trade, typically viewed as a method of distributing products. Successful merchandisers are skillful at selecting inventory that fits a specific market niche for a particular group of customers, but they also recognize that success depends crucially on the *level of service* offered. This rule is particularly true for firms committed to growth. An impeccable store with a prodigious inventory will attract customers, if for no other reason than curiosity, but if there is only a masquerade of personal service, shoppers seldom return unless enticed by unusual bargains.

In each store, well-trained sales clerks who enjoy their jobs, know their merchandise, understand customer needs, and are excited about making others happy about buying something are important resources. They create a cadence of pleasure, and even in a fast-paced discount store, customers will return if they feel that store employees have savoir faire.

The type of merchandising is also important. Customers come to expect certain things from certain stores. If a store is known for discount prices, you can bet that shoppers will have a keen idea of competitors' prices. If a store is "upmarket" and sophisticated, customers will expect higher prices but also a quality environment with quaint appointments and a splendid staff. Excellence in service, however, should not be relative. One does not enjoy being treated any less humanely in a discount store than in a fashionable store.

An example of this commitment to excellence in service is J. B. Robinson Jewelers, a growth-oriented chain based in Cleveland with approximately a hundred stores expanding to a nationwide business. Robinson's built the business from one small store committed to having a superb staff trained in excellent customer service. In fact, the company is almost fanatic about having salespersons who will empathize with customers and be absolutely honest about jewelry purchases. Very few individuals know much about the value of jewelry, and they often make decisions about jewelry purchases based on emotion. Robinson's sales staff is trained in the technical aspects of jewelry, but more important, they have an ongoing program of role playing and in-house training whereby salespersons step into customers' shoes. They are generously rewarded for outstanding customer service, and the entire Robinson system is committed to trustworthy behavior.[6]

Having good customer service and considerate employees are only two parts of a much more complex puzzle for merchandisers. Unlike a consulting firm that can start with little capital, no inventory, and the minimum cost of getting a business license, a retailer has high start-up costs associated with signing leases, making renovations, buying fixtures, and stocking inventory. Most retailers also need employees at start-up to cover store hours. In a mall location, those hours may exceed 12 hours a day for six or seven days a week, year-round. So while the merchandiser and personal service firm have parallel commitments to customer service, they differ significantly in the structure of their enterprises.

Merchandising skills include two important aspects of inventory management. The first is *purchasing*, and the second is *inventory control*. Each topic deserves comprehensive coverage, beyond our capabilities here, but we can alert readers to the nature of these tasks. Figure 7-3 emphasizes that purchasing and inventory issues are critical to merchandising success.

Purchasing. Searching for products, selecting appropriate items, and contracting for inventory constitutes the thrust of **purchasing**. It is vital because correct inventory must be bought at a good price with favorable terms. Correct inventory is that which is in demand by customers and is consistent with the image of the store. Merchandisers do not buy discount items or inferior materials in an upscale location. More important, the items in inventory must "move"—be salable in a reasonable period of time at appropriate prices. Buying slow-moving items ties up hard cash and puts the entire business at risk. Good purchasing requires skill at negotiation, competence in knowing materials, persistence to research suppliers, and the sensitivity to manage budgets.[7]

Buying the *correct* inventory is the essential issue. Buying at a *good* price is important but secondary. Experienced purchasing officers will negotiate rigorously over prices, yet in the end they will pay a premium to establish good vendor relationships that ensure reliable inventory supply. What a company wants from purchasing is not always the lowest price but a vendor that is able to deliver goods on time, in quantities ordered, and at the quality expected. "Quality" is the key word here, and it extends not only to the quality of the physical inventory (no rejects), but quality service, sharp account management, and effective distribution. Buying at a "good" price, therefore, means paying for the quality and performance needed to assure that inventory is provided under the terms and conditions of the purchase agreement.

Getting *favorable* terms is yet another important aspect of merchandising because suppliers who extend favorable terms, such as trade credit, literally underwrite a significant portion of operating expenses for most retailers. It is not unusual for a manufacturer to extend credit for inventory (interest free) for several months, and in these instances, a merchandiser can often sell inventory before paying for it. New ventures without track records are unlikely to enjoy such favorable terms, but whether they do or not depends largely on the nature of the industry. If a manufacturer has finished goods stacked up in warehouses, a merchant may be able to stock inventory with six months of trade credit. If the manufacturer's products are in demand, acquiring inventory may require "cash on the barrelhead."

Distributive Services

Distributive services are engaged in moving products through supply or transport channels. Wholesalers, dealers, import-export agents, and transport companies are examples of companies that distribute products by providing linkage between manufacturers and merchandisers. There are many types of middlemen in every industry, but the most common distributive services are those in trucking, rail transport, and air cargo. Service is defined in these enterprises as "expediting products," which means getting them to their final destinations efficiently. Distributive service companies also move people. These include airlines, rental car agencies, and limousine services that "expedite" travel.

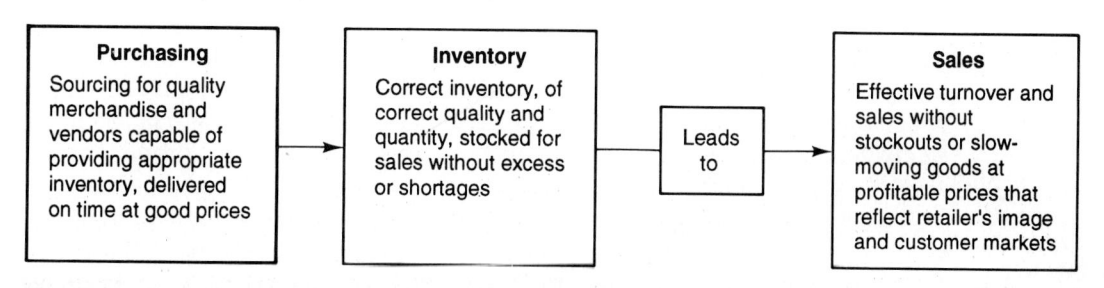

Purchasing	Inventory		Sales
Sourcing for quality merchandise and vendors capable of providing appropriate inventory, delivered on time at good prices	Correct inventory, of correct quality and quantity, stocked for sales without excess or shortages	Leads to	Effective turnover and sales without stockouts or slow-moving goods at profitable prices that reflect retailer's image and customer markets

Figure 7-3 **Merchandising Focus on Purchasing**

PROFILE △

Inventory—Key to Video Success

After the slow introduction of VCRs in the 1970s, the industry roared to success in the early 1980s as video rental stores made millions of tapes available to an eager public. As the 1990s began, there were more than 65 million American homes equipped with VCRs, and retailers rented more than 3.2 billion videocassettes annually. The rental business, once a mom-and-pop industry, "shook out" in the late 1980s as superstores opened, franchises such as 7–Eleven entered the market, and megacorporations such as Wal-Mart stocked tapes. Most independent rental outlets fell victim to these giants, yet some found success in specialized market niches.

For example, Patricia Polinger and Cathy Tauber, founders of Vidiots, enter the 1990s with more than 5,000 members and a fast-growing business. Located in Santa Monica, California, Vidiots stocks nearly 6,000 foreign films, documentaries, avant-garde art tapes, and movies by independent filmmakers. Few of their film titles are available elsewhere, and none are stocked by superstores, which prefer films on the top ten list. Polinger and Tauber are succeeding by sharp purchasing and astute inventory management to focus on a well-defined market niche.

Source: Frances Huffman, "Fast Forward," *Entrepreneur*, November 1989, pp. 132–134, 137, 138–139.

The nature of distributive services is to get something of value from point A to point B in a safe, effective, and timely manner. This process is shown in Figure 7-4. Extraordinary ventures have been built around this single concept, and given the social changes of time-crunching jobs, rapid information exchange, and a growing need for "convenience," distribution firms have enjoyed terrific success. Perhaps the best example of an entrepreneurial success is Federal Express. The idea of an overnight parcel service using airport hubs was conceived by Fred Smith while a student at Yale University. His professors said a new parcel service wasn't needed, and transport experts told him it couldn't be done. In the end, Federal Express became a major company moving millions of dollars of merchandise for thousands of customers every hour throughout the United States.[8]

With an enthusiasm equal to Federal Express, commuter airlines sprouted wings in smaller cities, created networks of travel hubs, and inspired a new growth industry in domestic convenience travel. Several of the fastest growing new ventures in the United States have been air carriers targeting customers outside major metropolitan areas. A global latticework of opportunities has evolved through related activities such as electronic reservation systems, networks of travel agencies, time-share vacation programs, and tour group enterprises. Just as rapidly, new ventures in rental cars, leasing systems, sports equipment rentals, and other similar services have sprung up in the wake of a surging mobile population.

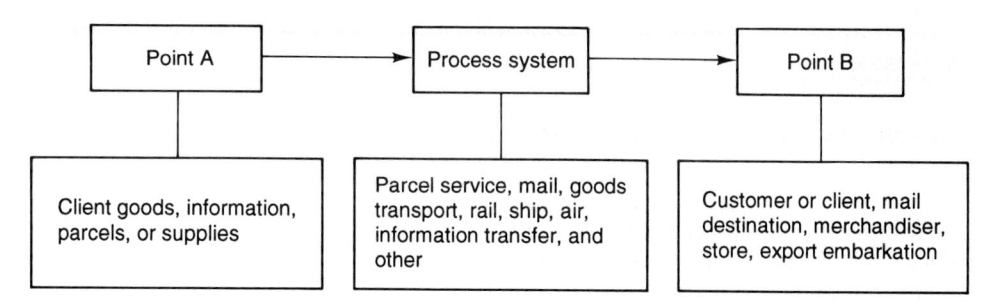

Figure 7-4 **Focus of Distributive Services**

The pervasive element of success in each of these distributive services is *time*. Federal Express and United Parcel Service will deliver overnight to a vast number of locations, and although it seems inexplicable how they accomplish this feat, customers really don't care. The point is that the firms *deliver as promised* at a price that is justified by timely service. We travel on airlines that have convenient flights scheduled to equally convenient locations. The best are those that can deliver on time and through routings that maximize our travel time without delays or cancellations. We want rental cars waiting, and we want to be able to dash through an airport, leap into a decent automobile, and get on the road.

Information Services

The one field that parallels technology changes is **information services**. In just slightly more than one decade, an incredible transformation has taken place in the way we process information. Aside from remarkable computer-based information systems, such as computer-aided design and manufacturing, traditional information systems have been transformed. On-line data bases provide credit reporting, paperless purchasing, and electronic banking. Newspapers are typeset through interactive computer networks, magazines are being developed on home computers, newsletters have proliferated, facsimile machines allow visual images to be transmitted on a global basis, and entire dictionaries can be loaded onto, and accessed from, a floppy disk. Authors write books on word processors and ship manuscripts to publishers on disks (or transport text between offices through modems). In turn, publishers edit text on similar machines (and correct spelling with automated "spell checkers"), then transport materials to printing companies that use even more sophisticated equipment to scan, typeset, and print the final manuscripts.

Opportunities for new information-based enterprises are immense. Ted Leonsis of Redgate Communications Corporation recognized a gap in information when he launched his first computer software magazine, *LIST*, in 1982. He was working in public relations at the time in Florida, and having been intrigued with the new IBM Personal Computer, Leonsis tried to get information on what the new machine would do. He searched through magazines, news stories, and advertisements but could not find reliable information on personal computers or software. Convinced he could publish a magazine that addressed these issues, Leonsis left his job at the age of 26

PROFILE △

Technology Opens Desk-Top Services

Desk-top systems, just one application of information technology, have opened new vistas for service enterprises. Professional reports, newsletters, home business publications, public relations, and data-linked marketing are only a few. Live Maine lobsters are shipped nearly anywhere in the world through an electronic order system run from an apartment. A growing $2 billion annual electronic advertising industry thrives on networked data systems linking 50 nations to cataloged products and services. The travel industry has reduced global reservations to terminal connections that can be accessed in offices, through laptop portable computers at airports, or to subscribers at home.

Interconnected by laser printers, modems, facsimile machines, and rapidly advancing software innovations, commercial banking, securities markets, real estate, industrial purchasing, and law enforcement have entered an age of instantaneous communication complete with hard-copy reports and reproduced graphics transmitted to any destination that has telephone access.

and launched *LIST*. Less than 18 months later, he sold the magazine for $15 million. Before he was 30, he bought the business back and created a series of magazines tailored for major computer firms. Redgate's clients include Apple, Commodore, Compaq, Contel, CCI, Kodak, Harris, Hewlett-Packard, Lotus Development Corporation, Motorola, Texas Instruments, Wang, Warner Communications, and Xerox Information Systems.[9]

Each year, the Association of Collegiate Entrepreneurs (ACE) publishes a list of the top 100 "under 30" entrepreneurs. On the 1989 list, a third of the top 100 were involved in information hardware technology. Another third enjoyed equally profitable businesses outside the information field, such as New York Seltzer (soft-drink manufacturing) and CareerTrack (educational seminars and consulting). The remaining third succeeded in the service side of information-related fields. The names of their companies often reveal the nature of their enterprises. For example, Rob Angel had revenues of $52 million from Pictionary, Inc.; Heidi Wolf grossed $7 million from her firm Ketchum Public Relations; Jeff McGee utilized electronic media to create Zimmerman Partners Advertising, Inc., grossing $4.5 million; and William Cunningham grossed his first million with Dial USA. Incidentally, when the ACE list was published, Cunningham was barely 19 years old. These examples represent new applications of technology, but they also illustrate innovative services in advertising, telecommunications, and pictorial transmission.[10]

In a literate society, there is a growing demand for information delivered in more effective ways, but there have also been changes in how services are performed. For example, the highly successful Home Shopping Network couples television with telemarketing techniques to sell millions of dollars of discount merchandise through an interactive television program. In effect, viewers of HSN call in to buy a televised product and become part of the show.[11]

Professional services also are discovering new ways to use information, and by the time this text is in circulation, our examples will undoubtedly sound hackneyed. Financial analysts can tap into world markets for investments, and global communication systems allow us access to major stock markets somewhere in the world nearly 24 hours a day. Teleconferencing links together hundreds of corporate officers on almost any continent at any time. Doctors collaborate on surgical procedures through electronic media. Homes are virtually becoming offices, and with new portable computers, business can often be conducted from commercial airliners or beach resorts.

New financial planning services also are replacing salespersons armed with rate charts and bulky briefcases. This development should be interesting to business students because the adaptation of financial software programs to portable computers has generated a new degree field called *financial and estate planning*. A financial or estate planner is trained in a variety of investment and retirement benefits, incorporates these into software, and visits with families in the privacy of their homes to simulate different lifetime investment scenarios. The scenarios account for income changes, career changes, projected need for college education funds, disability protection, insurance, and retirement programs, and then evaluate dozens of different methods of investment to meet these needs.[12]

Information services are differentiated from other types of service ventures largely by a *creative use* of information technology. This is apparent in the ventures already noted that rely on telecommunications and computer applications. However, creative delivery systems of traditional information, such as advertising and self-help seminars, have revolutionized the way we think of media. Newspapers, newsletters, brochures, mail order catalogs, magazines, public relations, and many other forms of consumer information are being transformed. Recall that we explained how services and manufacturing technology are complementary. In these examples of new information service, there were preceding changes in technology, yet, like a game of leapfrog, the evolution of new services often prompted inventive entrepreneurs to develop even more sophisticated technology.[13]

▶ CHECKPOINT

Describe and contrast professional and personal service firms.

Explain the nature of merchandising and focal activities that influence success for retailers.

Discuss opportunities in distributive services, and explain how they differ from other types of service enterprises.

Explore the nature of information services and future opportunities.

SUCCESS FACTORS IN SERVICE VENTURES

In each example of service noted in the preceding section, there are critical factors that helped entrepreneurs succeed. The nature of a service venture is different from a product-based company in that services require exceptional human resource skills. Services can usually be initiated with low-entry capital requirements, but having the right people is vital. A good service idea can also be easily copied; therefore, as competitors flock to a growth market, having committed people will often make the difference between success and failure.

Human-resource issues are far-reaching, but we will explore several focal points for new ventures. During the start-up planning phase, for example, an entrepreneur must establish a *vision* that everyone will work to fulfill. This may relate to a distinct competency of quality service in a particular kind of business. At the outset, entrepreneurs must firmly establish sound *policies* for customer service. Service firms rely on capable staff, and this need requires skills at *hiring*, *training*, and *motivating* employees. The *leadership* skills of an entrepreneur are vital to position the service firm for growth. Although we cannot begin to cover each topic in detail, we can describe their importance to new service ventures.

Creating the Vision

A good way to fail quickly in a new business is to start without a clear vision. A **vision** encompasses the value that an entrepreneur will provide for his or her customers, and if that service is achieved, it encompasses the results the entrepreneur will achieve. Without this basic vision, starting a business on a whim is tantamount to shooting dice; you are relying on chance to dictate your fate.

Brett Kingstone, a young entrepreneur who created much of the fiber optic art lighting for Disney's Epcot Center at the age of 22, built his first fiber optic sign in his backyard. However, he envisioned a Disneyland glimmering with radiant colors and miniature lights capturing the fantasy that Disney created. Kingstone *knew* before he started that he could replace conventional lighting with fiber optics, and his vision was one of a fun-filled world of color. Therefore, even as he worked in his backyard, his vision was more pervasive. He was not interested in selling one sign, and he was not concerned about how much money he could pocket from that sale. Instead, he focused his technical and marketing efforts on *adding value* to the Disney experience.[14]

Jimmy Calano, the cofounder of CareerTrack, created a $40 million company in educational seminars before he was 28 years old by starting with a simple but clear vision. He began by addressing career women's needs through cost-effective training symposia that helped them formulate better careers and reconcile problems unique to working women.[15] Fred Smith of Federal Express envisioned hundreds of thousands of customers, frustrated by a behemoth postal system that required standing in post office lines to mail parcels that could take days to be delivered. He knew before he started that personalized service was important and that customers would appreciate a guaranteed rapid-delivery parcel system.[16]

Vision is vital, but it must be orchestrated through effective planning and a

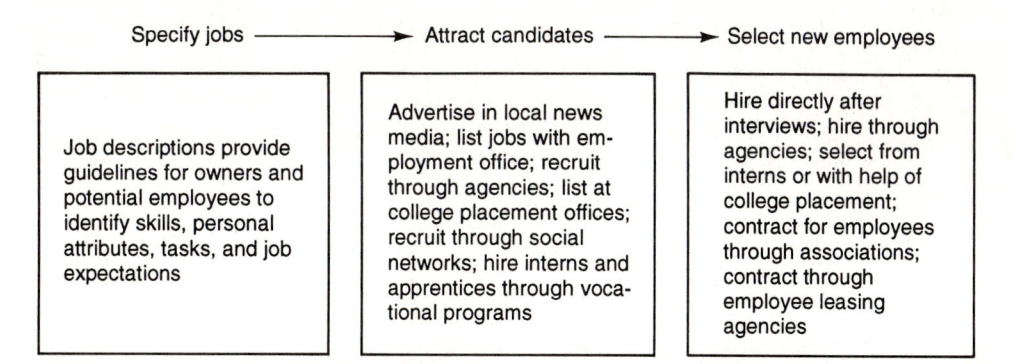

```
Specify jobs  ──▶  Attract candidates  ──▶  Select new employees
```

| Job descriptions provide guidelines for owners and potential employees to identify skills, personal attributes, tasks, and job expectations | Advertise in local news media; list jobs with employment office; recruit through agencies; list at college placement offices; recruit through social networks; hire interns and apprentices through vocational programs | Hire directly after interviews; hire through agencies; select from interns or with help of college placement; contract for employees through associations; contract through employee leasing agencies |

Figure 7-5 **Small-Firm Recruitment**

strong commitment to the image of service one wants to project. The image is a result of conscientious planning to provide value to customers. There has to be a clarity of direction that provides service goals for human endeavor.

Effective Hiring

Three things are generally needed to get a business started. New ventures need a good product or service based on a sound vision, sufficient money to pursue that venture, and people—good people. Research indicates that patterns of employment for most small businesses are relatively fixed at the moment of opening. This generalization is particularly true for personal service enterprises that start and remain small. Consequently, a beauty salon or clothing boutique will open with a few carefully selected employees, and although these employees may be replaced, their numbers and skills will remain fairly constant. Owners are, nevertheless, responsible for staffing the enterprise no matter how small.

The pattern of employment for smaller enterprises is that owners will initially hire one or two full-time persons and supplement busy seasons with part-timers. One of the full-time employees usually will be skilled or experienced in the trade. The rest often will have to be trained. Unfortunately, small business owners rarely follow good personnel practices in hiring, and even less often provide adequate training. Many full-time employees are hired from among friends or family members. This practice provides no assurance of having employees with the required skills or commitment to make a business a success. Part-time employees may come from unemployed walk-ins or students looking for supplemental income.[17] Too many entrepreneurs tend to hire them as a matter of convenience, not as a conscious effort to staff their enterprises. As Figure 7-5 shows, however, there are effective ways to locate and hire good employees.

Perhaps a small firm can survive without systematic hiring and training practices, but entrepreneurs will more often experience high turnover among employees who are poorly prepared to do a good job. Also, there is a fundamental problem with finding highly motivated long-term employees because smaller firms can seldom offer high wages, good benefits, or opportunities for advancement.

There are ways to overcome these problems. Entrepreneurs first must write *job descriptions* that identify the type of employees needed, their skills, past experience, and duties in the new post. These descriptions will help identify qualified job candidates and provide guidelines for advertising for employees, interviewing them, and selecting the best from a field of applicants. Second, entrepreneurs can study the labor market and their competitors to gain a better understanding of comparable wages, expectations by applicants, and patterns of benefits that must accompany job offers. And third, entrepreneurs can train their employees in job-related skills or help them attain off-hours training through local educational programs. For example, most community colleges offer adult education courses and short seminars on retailing, marketing, merchandising, purchasing, and small business management. In addition, Chambers of Commerce and the SBA co-sponsor counseling by the Senior Corps of Retired Executives (SCORE), which is a free service.

When the entrepreneur is not in a position to hire or train employees, and when the business is too small to support an organization, another interesting option is to *lease personnel*. This is a recent innovation in staffing that is, itself, an entrepreneurial service. Unlike temporary service agencies, leasing firms actually hire hundreds of employees, train them, and provide a full range of employee benefits. The leasing company places employees in a client's firm, thereby relieving an owner of hiring, firing, training, and managing a complex system of compensation and benefits.[18] This system overcomes many barriers faced by entrepreneurs, and it is easy to see how a doctor who needs only one or two employees (but wants nothing to do with personnel management) would quickly opt for a leasing program.

For growing companies, increased sales means changes in human resources and a substantial responsibility for attracting, hiring, training, and retaining employees. During the early stage of planning, it is important to clearly understand that there is no way companies can grow if entrepreneurs try to do everything themselves. To resolve this difficulty, the first step is for entrepreneurs to purposely describe their roles and how those roles will change with growth. The second step is to write employee job descriptions for the first stage of business. The third step is to write expanded job descriptions for employees whose jobs will change with growth. These descriptions will help identify how responsibilities will change, and therefore opportunities for career development. They will not only attract better applicants who want a challenge, but also will help clarify how the entrepreneur and the employee will relate to one another over time.[19]

High-growth enterprises are unlikely to follow the recruiting methods of smaller firms, for two reasons. First, professional and personal service firms that remain localized usually will not need highly skilled individuals; they can therefore recruit through local labor markets. Second, small firms that do not intend to grow will not develop management positions for functional specialists in areas such as marketing, operations, or finance.

On the other hand, growing firms will need functional specialists, and in high-tech fields, they will often need research scientists, engineers, and other technical specialists. For these firms, recruiting through newspaper ads in local labor markets is pointless. Professional and managerial talent is found through national searches, professional societies, conferences, university placement services, and networking. The last method, *networking*, is particularly fruitful as entrepreneurs socialize with other entrepreneurs, do business with their counterparts in other firms, and develop contacts with suppliers and customers who may become potential applicants. Networking provides an inside track to key people, but the entrepreneur still has the responsibility to recruit them and help them mold their entrepreneurial careers.

Training

Personal service firms tend to be structured around the skills of the founder. For very small firms, such as independent beauticians or professional photographers, success hinges on the reputation of skilled individuals. When expansion occurs, owners have two options: they can hire comparably skilled individuals or train apprentices. Either option can be extremely difficult to accomplish. For example, if a professional photographer wants to hire someone who can reinforce his or her established reputation, it means getting someone as skilled (or nearly so) as the founder, and hiring such a person translates to a rather high cost. The new employee will demand a substantial income, and the owner initially will have to share clients and income. If a less skilled person is hired, then the owner must train the employee. In either case, initial costs can be high, and there will be inefficiencies until the employee becomes proficient.

These trade-offs exist for most small enterprises in which the owner is an active participant. For service firms that do not require skilled personnel, training is a less sensitive task. For instance, a retailer may require sales clerks who need only know how to use a cash register or to stock shelves. In fast-food restaurants, youthful employees are hired, trained quickly, and replaced easily. They are seldom paid well, and effective personnel practices can be abandoned in favor of getting bodies through the door as cheaply as possible. Training in this environment is a matter of putting employees through a fast-paced, preprogrammed learning session to teach them a few fundamental tasks. One should not conclude, however, that McDonald's or Burger King is a bad place to work, only that employees and their managers are concerned with "jobs" not "careers."

An interesting change has taken place in many areas of the United States for these less skilled positions. The baby boom generation has matured, and in the late 1980s there were nearly a third fewer teenagers than during the late 1970s. During the 1990s there will be 37 percent fewer youth between the ages of 16 and 25 than in the 1970s, thereby shrinking the less skilled labor market on which fast-food chains and retailers rely.[20] This demographic change has already had a tremendous influence on hiring and training practices. In the Atlanta area, for example, fast-food restaurants have hired recruiters, beefed up basic wages, added benefits, improved training programs, and introduced incentive bonus programs to attract and retain employees. In Boston, young employees are bused in from New Hampshire to work at McDonald's, and paid bonuses "up front" just to sign on as employees. Many of these transient employees enjoy wages well in excess of the minimum wage required by law. In fact, the minimum wage has become meaningless in these circumstances.

Unlike fast-food restaurants and discount retailers, computer service firms, telecommunications specialists, antique boutiques, health clinics, and many other enterprises must have competently trained employees. Moreover, *service* and *technical ability* may be comparably important so that, for example, an owner of an antique boutique may require employees who are at once experienced in expensive antiques and able to work with knowledgeable customers.

A computer service firm may require employees who are skilled in technical aspects of hardware, who are capable of working with a substantial range of software, and who also have the human relation skills to "service and sell" to end-users that range from high school students to corporate executives. Finding employees with all these attributes can be extremely difficult. How many skilled computer technicians with sales experience exist? (How many are looking for jobs?) How many experts are there in antiques who also want a job? The same questions apply to hundreds of professionals in equally diverse fields. A safe assumption, therefore, is that "ideal" employees rarely can be found, and it falls to an entrepreneur to find those with potential who can be trained.

Training poses two problems: first, learning how to seek out and hire people with potential, and second, establishing effective methods of employee training. Learning how to seek out and hire good people is not a simple matter that can be addressed here. However, aspiring entrepreneurs can acquire insight by taking formal courses in *personnel administration* or by attending seminars regularly offered by consulting firms, government agencies, and educational institutions. Not least among the options are other new ventures that provide educational services. For example, *Inc.* magazine has announced a subsidiary enterprise called *Real Selling*, the first in a series of video courses for entrepreneurs. Other video courses are available from at least 120 companies with topics that include, for example, how to start your own business, women in business, marketing, hiring and firing, the family business, finding capital, and taxes. People featured in these tapes are star entrepreneurs, including Henry Block of H&R Block, Rosemary Voss of Century 21, Tom Monaghan of Domino's Pizza, and Tom Peters of *In Search of Excellence* fame.[21] As illustrated in the accompanying profile, Fran Tarkenton has launched a series of training seminars featuring other famous sports figures.

The Small Business Administration helps sponsor more than 500 seminars annually, most offered through local Chambers of Commerce in concert with community colleges. In addition, the SBA provides small business management brochures, self-study courses, and pamphlets on more than 80 topics, including recruitment, selection, training, personnel policies, staffing, and employee benefits. Many of the SBA publications focus on specific training needs, such as stock control, selling techniques, advertising, store layout, purchasing, and cash management, among many others.[22]

No complete answer exists to the question of how to recruit good employees, and even successful large corporations grapple with the problem. Business owners

PROFILE △

Training: New Game for Sport Pros

An entrepreneurial enterprise itself, Tarkenton Speakers' Bureau, Inc., focuses on training seminars for other entrepreneurs. Teaming with other sports greats that include Roger Staubach, Rocky Bleier, Pat Riley, and Al McGuire, Fran Tarkenton has launched an enterprise to provide speakers, seminars, and symposia for small business associations and companies. Their focus is on motivation techniques, teamwork, and leadership—qualities that made the speakers outstanding in their pro careers.

Tarkenton's company provides an important service for other entrepreneurs who seek training and counseling for their employees. Besides the obvious "star quality" of the speakers, each has had ownership roles in other businesses, and most have been involved as founders of organizations in diversified fields such as insurance, retailing, sports management, broadcasting, and private charities.

Source: Tarkenton Speakers' Bureau, Inc., adapted with permission.

---

live with this challenge as long as their companies need employees. Exactly the same problem confronts them in training, and as suggested by the sample SBA topics, one way to alleviate the problem is for the entrepreneur to become better trained through courses, seminars, and self-study.

A second, more concrete answer, is to hire training consultants. Consultants can be brought to the company, or employees can be sent to formal training courses, but the entrepreneur must pursue an active program with adequate budgeting. Too often, entrepreneurs are reluctant to spend money on training, although large American corporations spend nearly 7 percent of their operating funds on training each year. For example, IBM spends nearly $900 million annually on corporate training for more than 18,000 employees who benefit from formal programs.[23] Independent business owners rarely commit more than 1 percent of their operating funds to training, and although entrepreneurs spend time training employees, they are usually too preoccupied by the business to do an adequate job.[24]

Effective decisions about training can be made by following a simple process of identifying needs, methods of training available, and resources that an entrepreneur possesses, and then matching needs and methods. This is illustrated in Figure 7-6. For example, if a computer retailer needs a person skilled in accounting software and has employees capable of learning this skill, and if the owner is not skilled in the software but can afford to train employees, then one option is to send them to professional accounting seminars using packaged software systems needed in the business.

```
    Needs              Methods           Resources       Matching needs
                                                          and methods
```

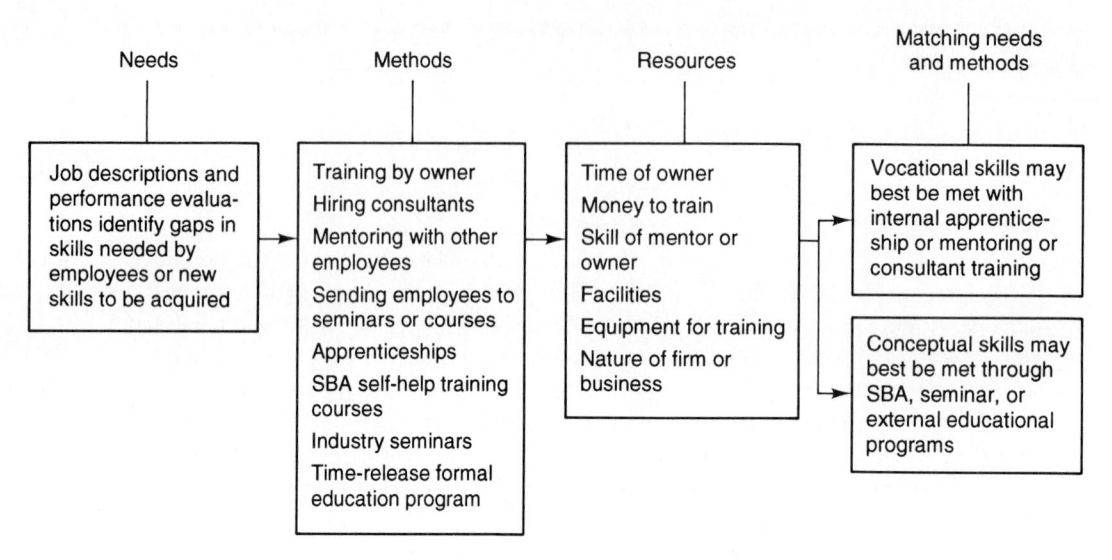

| Job descriptions and performance evaluations identify gaps in skills needed by employees or new skills to be acquired | Training by owner
Hiring consultants
Mentoring with other employees
Sending employees to seminars or courses
Apprenticeships
SBA self-help training courses
Industry seminars
Time-release formal education program | Time of owner
Money to train
Skill of mentor or owner
Facilities
Equipment for training
Nature of firm or business | Vocational skills may best be met with internal apprenticeship or mentoring or consultant training

Conceptual skills may best be met through SBA, seminar, or external educational programs |

Figure 7-6 **Identifying Training Needs and Methods**

Motivating Employees in a Growth Environment

Everything you want to know about motivating employees is *not* in this presentation or in any other collection of works, regardless of scope. There are no fail-safe prescriptions for motivating employees; however, there is a tremendous body of literature about motivation and leadership. Entrepreneurs in service businesses should study everything they can lay their hands on and read about innovations in human resource management made by those who face the challenge on a daily basis. With that said, we can touch on several issues related to growth-oriented new ventures.

Encouraging Creativity. New ventures emerge through creative endeavor, and it has been emphasized from the beginning of this text that creativity drives a firm forward. Although we tend to equate creativity and innovation with new products, most growth-oriented services succeed through similar philosophies. As Jimmy Calano suggested, "Creativity is one quality that separates us from animals."[25] Building on the creativity concept, Pinehurst Hotel and Country Club in North Carolina has been ranked among top American resorts for five decades, and twice in the 1980s it was ranked the number-one resort for service. Pinehurst employees are well trained and encouraged to "create their own jobs" to provide the best service possible for guests. This policy even extends to grounds keepers and maintenance personnel. In 1989, Pinehurst won the top ranking in the United States for the best-kept grounds.[26] Finding ways to help employees become more creative gives them a sense of personal commitment to the venture and helps propel everyone toward success.

Lessons from classic studies apply here. Give employees autonomy, make them feel (and be) important, engage in positive reinforcement, and give them the oppor-

PROFILE △

"Be the Best Damn Cheerleader Anybody's Ever Seen."

Gary Grace built his start-up hair franchise in Northern California as a part-time investment while pursuing his accounting business, but he brought something unusual to his salons: super service achieved by helping his people "care" about the best in customer satisfaction. The business, called Supercuts is all about excitement—among customers who like to go there, stylists who like to work there, and managers who know how to motivate their people.

This philosophy shines through district manager Becky Malie's personal golden rule: "Be the best damn cheerleader anybody's ever seen." Independent shop owners like Flo Curi in Santa Monica throw "Let's Kick Ass Parties" for stylists to compete for all-expense paid bonus vacations, higher commissions, and star recognition that could earn a nod for managing the next Supercut store. Grace's management method, however, is not just faddish parties and incentives. He has created a thorough training program, instilled the concept of extraordinary service for every customer, and insisted on top-notch talent among employees who want to make haircutting fun for their customers and themselves.

Source: Curtis Hartman, "The Best-Managed Franchises in America," *Inc.*, October 1989, pp. 68–72.

---

tunity to grow while doing enjoyable work (i.e., "self-actualize"). A great lesson can be learned from the Disney organization and how it approaches human resource management. When new employees are hired at Disney World, they are hired through a "casting" department, not "personnel." They are trained in "roles," not jobs, and this policy extends from janitorial services to theme characters. They learn that the mission of Disney is to make "guests" (not customers) happy. Then they are provided costumes, paired with "mentors" (other employees in similar character roles or jobs), and sent into the theme park to create the role for which they have been "cast." There are no lock-step jobs but rather general parameters for understanding their roles. There are recognition rewards for being nice to guests, for making guests happy about being at Disney World, and for being innovative while being "in character" while they work.[27]

Disney employees enjoy autonomy and the intrinsic rewards of personal job satisfaction derived from satisfaction they provide for others. This should not be too difficult for a computer service firm to achieve. The keys—based on Disney's model—are giving employees good training, giving them autonomy to be creative in their jobs, and encouraging them to treat customers with respect. A barber can make haircutting fun and the shop atmosphere enjoyable for customers rather than treating customers like sheep to be sheared. Bankers—particularly loan officers—should be able to take the anxiety out of doing business. (How many bankers make you feel like they are doing you a favor by giving you a loan? If you don't borrow, the bank doesn't make money; money in the vault is an idle resource. Who is doing whom a favor?)

Rewarding Quality. Everyone working in a service environment is there to help others, to provide some measure of satisfaction. So in addition to helping employees enjoy providing this satisfaction, and in addition to giving them the autonomy for successful roles, it is also crucial to assure *quality* services. One way to accomplish this goal is to reward quality performance. In personal service firms, employees can be rewarded for generating repeat customers. In retailing, a commission structure can reinforce sales efforts, and in technical areas such as computer repair services, labor income can be shared with technicians who do quality work. These are monetary rewards, but nonmonetary rewards can be just as important. For example, entrepreneurs can create employee-of-the-month awards, issue certificates to those who attain certain skills, hold company dinners or picnics to recognize achievements, and do many little things on a daily basis to enrich an employee's self-image. In a California Kinko's copy center store, for instance, the manager had a birthday cake delivered to a cheerful young sales clerk on a day that was not her birthday. The icing read, "Happy Unbirthday to a Fun Employee with a Great Smile." At a Virginia Toyota service center, a bulletin board is loaded with cards and letters from customers. It is prominently placed for employees and customers to see, and the service manager writes boldly on these notes the names of employees who did the good work. Near Philadelphia, a Pepsi distributor staged a three-piece band to intercept a route driver at a customer location that marked his one-year record of 100 percent on-time deliveries.

Rewarding performance is important to reinforce positive behavior, and it can take the form of a simple but sincere "thank you." It can also take the form of a monetary reward, but all monetary rewards are sensitive and require careful thought. For example, a discount golf and tennis outlet near Atlanta that went out of business in 1986 had commissions for sales clerks with premiums for those who exceeded quotas. This approach created keen competition but eventually led to almost cutthroat behavior as sales personnel pressed customers into quick purchases of high-priced goods. The result was not higher sales volume but declining sales because customers seldom returned. Many products were returned (nearly 16 percent) because once purchased, the products were not really what customers wanted. New management took over the store, changed incentives to storewide bonuses, and established a policy of quality service. Customers were assured of full refund policies, and return-visit discounts were given on golf and tennis equipment. Sales personnel were urged to cooperate for higher overall sales levels based on repeat customers.

Gain Sharing and Employee Equity Plans. One form of bonus that can be tied directly to performance is gain sharing. **Gain-sharing programs** assure employees a percentage of increased profits, income, or cost savings. *Profit sharing* is another common term, but gain sharing implies a splitting of benefits with employees for good performance. In profit sharing, the assumption is that bonuses are paid much like dividends on earnings. In gain sharing, profits may not increase immediately, but cost savings or projected benefits from new technology or service innovations may be shared with employees through bonuses.

Closely associated with gain sharing are recent initiatives to establish employee stock ownership plans, or **ESOPs**. The ESOP is a method of systematically selling shares of stock to all employees. There is no need to base stock shares on net profits or periodic performance indicators, although it is common practice to do so, and in many firms employees buy into the firm through an allocation of wages. The shares of an ESOP are literally treated as stock "placed in trust" for the employee's benefit. When employees leave the firm or retire, their ESOP shares are either converted to a form of retirement income or cashed out. Because ESOPs are complicated (and subject to IRS regulation), careful planning is necessary to establish an ESOP program. Nevertheless, employees are given a way of becoming directly involved with the venture's success through equity ownership.

Working with a Vision. Returning to an earlier point, the entrepreneur is limited in what can be offered to employees, yet if the firm has growth potential, emphasizing a *vision* for growth can pay dividends. Employees must be able to share this vision of success and, most important, be able to share in its success. Apple Computer Corporation has become the neoclassic example of a firm that "sold" the concept of its future to an initially small band of employees. These employees not only had stock options and prospered as the firm grew, but they were also assured of internal promotions with growth. Apple's employees grasped the opportunity to fashion their own careers. They *anticipated success* and made it happen. They shared the prestige and fame of Apple, which more than made up for giving up careers at big-name corporations.

Although most ventures remain small or experience limited growth, their founders should attempt to create a vision of success and establish a way in which employees can share in that success. A firm that grows to have 20, 50, or 100 employees will need dedicated and competent managers. Someone will have to lead the parade, and even if the owner remains at the helm, there is no reason why other executive positions cannot be filled from employee ranks. To repeat an important point made in Chapter 1, every one of the *Fortune* 500 firms began very small with an entrepreneur and a vision. Quite often employees who were part of the initial entrepreneurial team rose to prominence, eclipsing the careers and wealth of their corporate counterparts.

Epilogue on Human Resources

Small firms face more difficulties in hiring and training than large ones do because, first, they lack the resources to pay well or to provide good benefits, and second, they offer limited career advancement opportunities. Consequently, smaller enterprises have fewer traditional motivational tools to insp   performance. Motivation comes down to individual incentives, personal attention, and unique opportunities for self-actualization. These are particularly important in service companies. When those ventures have potential for growth, employees may find that they can share in wealth creation through gain-sharing programs, profit sharing, equity ownership options (such as ESOPs), and other types of equity sharing programs that encourage quality performance.

For entrepreneurs aspiring to wealth, those wanting to create ventures of some magnitude, the challenge is to create in employees a sense of excitement. Employees must be able to *anticipate success* and to want to share in it. This advice is perhaps the essence of entrepreneurial leadership.

▶ CHECKPOINT

Explain what is meant by "creating a vision" for an enterprise.

Describe an entrepreneur's responsibility for attracting and retaining good employees.

Identify and discuss methods of training employees, and explain how an entrepreneur can develop human resources.

Briefly describe the nature of, and limitations to, techniques of motivating employees in small service organizations.

▲▲▲▲▲▲ SYNOPSIS FOR LEARNING

1. *Explain the nature of professional and personal services.*

Professional services are based on the expertise of individuals who usually have attained a significant level of education, internship, and experience. They usually hold credentials from national associations that maintain standards of practice and expertise. These include physicians, certified public accountants, and attorneys. Personal services are based on performance by individuals who may be trained vocationally, such as real estate agents, and although their careers may have less rigorous educational requirements, they often are licensed through an association or government agency. However, these are oversimplified descriptions because personal services also extend to computer consultants, therapists, and engineers who may be well educated and professional experts in their fields.

2. *Describe merchandising and the factors that are critical for retailing success.*

Merchandising is concerned with retailing products or combinations of products and services to final consumers. As a general description, merchandisers buy inventory in bulk, break it down into stocked components, and resell to customers. Thus the critical success elements center on purchasing the right types of inventory, managing stocks in a cost-effective manner, and providing a personalized service to consumers who pay for the value added through quality retailing and assistance.

3. *Explain distributive services as an industry.*

Distributive services focus on moving physical products, information, or people from one point to another. The best distribution enterprises accomplish their tasks in efficient, safe, and cost-effective ways. Airlines move people, mail, and cargoes. Trucks, ships, railroads, and couriers do the same, but more often focus on merchandise transported between manufacturers, growers, government agencies, warehouses, suppliers, and retailers. Viewed as a global business, a distributive service such as containerized shipping is important to a nation's manufacturing economy. Also, distribution services are concerned with the facilitation of contracts, such as wholesaling, brokerage, or foreign sales through export-import transactions.

4. *Discuss information services and recent innovations.*

Information services are usually viewed as applications of computers and telecommunications technology, and although this view is correct, it is not complete. Information services can also include traditional publishing, newspapers, desk-top newsletters, advertising media, conference management, and graphic art. Electronic technology has inspired a broad spectrum of new information services and has changed traditional ways of accomplishing work. These changes extend to new media in video entertainment and training, data-base management, network marketing, computer-linked shopping networks, facsimile communications, and portable (go-anywhere) laptop workstations, among others.

5. *Describe success factors for service enterprises.*

Service enterprises face the same management challenges as manufacturers with the exception of actual production. Because service enterprises deal directly with customers, they place far greater emphasis on human resources. Most services have close contact with customers; therefore, having good employees is crucial. Consequently, success in services is highly correlated with human-resource management. This begins with finding good employees through effective recruiting. It also includes training employees, motivating them to perform well, and rewarding them equitably for good work. This process can be quite different from personnel practices in established corporations where most employees follow well-defined career paths. In entrepreneurial companies, careers are difficult to establish, and promotions are limited.

NOTES

1. John Naisbitt, *Megatrends: Ten New Directions Transforming Our Lives* (New York: Warner Books, 1982), pp. 35–36.

2. John Elkins, "Megatrends Update," unpublished presentation through the Rocco Forum on the Future, Harrisonburg, VA, March 17, 1988.

3. Jay O. Krasner, Michael S. Krasner, and Scott A. Krasner, "M.D.'s Who Have Given Up Clinical Practice to Become Entrepreneurs: Circumstances, Experience-to-Date, and Risk Propensity Profiles," in Neil C. Churchill et al., eds., *Frontiers of Entrepreneurship Research, 1987*, pp. 184–186.

4. Reginald S. Gynther, "Accounting Concepts and Behavioral Hypotheses," in Michael Schiff and Arie Y. Lewin, eds., *Behavioral Aspects of Accounting* (Englewood Cliffs, NJ: Prentice-Hall, 1974), pp. 353–372.

5. *The Price Waterhouse Guide to the New Tax Law* (New York: Bantam Books, 1986), pp. 211–213.

6. John Naisbitt and Patricia Aburdene, *Re-inventing the Corporation* (New York: Warner Books, 1985), p. 27.

7. J. M. Juran and Frank M. Gryna, Jr., *Quality Planning and Analysis*, 2nd ed. (New York: McGraw-Hill, 1980), pp. 227–242.

8. "Can U.S. Postal Service Lick Its Troubles?" *U.S. News and World Report*, December 16, 1985, p. 54. Also see "Federal Express Ads Ask 'Spare a Quarter?'" *Advertising Age*, September 9, 1985, p. 6.

9. Brett Kingstone, *The Dynamos: Who Are They, Anyway?* (New York: John Wiley & Sons, 1987), pp. 217–223.

10. "The Top 100, 1989," *Association of Collegiate Entrepreneurs* (Wichita, KS: ACE, 1989), p. 1.

11. "Home Shopping: Is It a Revolution in Retailing—or Just a Fad?" *Business Week*, December 15, 1986, pp. 62–69.

12. Steven L. Alter, "How Effective Managers Use Information Systems," in *Winning the Race against Time: How Successful Executives Get More Done in a Day*, a compilation by the *Harvard Business Review*, 1986, pp. 78–85.

13. Select Committee on Innovation, "Science and Technology in Innovative Processes," *Technovation*, Vol. 9 (1989), pp. 137–142.

14. Brett Kingstone, "Money Is a Result of Good Business— Good Business Is a Result of Creating Value for Your Customers," unpublished invited lecture at the Association of Collegiate Entrepreneurs annual conference, Washington, DC, March 5, 1988.

15. Jimmy Calano and Jeff Salzman, *CareerTracking* (New York: Simon and Schuster, 1988), p. 96.

16. John J. Kao, *Entrepreneurship, Creativity, and Organization* (Englewood Cliffs, NJ: Prentice-Hall, 1989), p. 102. Also see "The Business Week Corporate Elite," *Business Week*, October 20, 1989, p. 280.

17. Sue Birley, "New Ventures and Employment Growth," *Journal of Business Venturing*, Vol. 2, No. 2 (1987), pp. 155–165.

18. W. M. Greenfield, *Calculated Risk: A Guide to Entrepreneurship* (Lexington, MA: D.C. Heath, 1986), pp. 217–219. Also see "Employees: To Hire or Contract," *Venture*, August 1984, p. 33.

19. Greenfield, *Calculated Risk*, pp. 214–216.

20. Elkins, "Megatrends Update."

21. "Company Builders," *Inc.*, October 1989, pp. 158–165.

22. Office of Advocacy, *Small Business Administration, Titles* (Washington, DC: Small Business Administration, 1989).

23. Patricia A. Galagan, "IBM Gets Its Arms around Education," *Training and Development Journal*, January 1989, pp. 35–41.

24. Greenfield, *Calculated Risk*, pp. 215–216.

25. Calano and Salzman, *CareerTracking*, p. 96.

26. "Pinehurst Wins Prestigious Grounds Award," *The Putter Boy*, Vol. 1, No. 4 (Winter 1989), p. 4.

27. "The Entrepreneurs," *PBS Film Series with Transcript* (Boston: WGN, 1986).

CASE 7-1

Services Make Human Resources Productive

Steve Ettridge founded Temps & Co. with the idea of making a lot of money. Temps & Co. is a Washington, DC, area employment agency supplying temporary office help, and as the 1980s came to an end, Ettridge was on a roll. Annual sales were on track: about $25 million for 1989, up from $21 million in 1988, $20 million in 1987, and $12 million in 1986. This was an enviable record for a small company with only a few years in business, but after salaries and overhead expenses, Temps & Co. barely inked a profit.

Ettridge had been working on the assumption that higher sales had to generate profits eventually, but as he looked forward to the 1990s, he reasoned that prices for temps had to go up or expenses had to come down. Higher prices would neither serve his clientele nor fit with Ettridge's philosophy of maintaining value for money. Friends and advisers told him to "cut and slash . . . get mean and be tough on expenses." He studied competitors' practices, listened to experts, sought assistance from professional accountants and consultants, then rejected them all. In Ettridge's view, their recommendations would mean hurting his people, and people were his business, but he did take several interesting steps that were highly successful.

One of those steps was to make this company a more pleasant place to work for his temporary help. "Temps," as they are called, normally come to work every day by 8:00 A.M., then sit around until an assignment comes up. Assignments come from clients who typically call in for help between 9:00 and 10:00 when office help are absent or something has occurred to require more people. Most assignments last less than two weeks, half of those for only a day or two when regular employees are sick. For the temps waiting on call, the morning routine is boring, and when no assignments emerge, they can sit idle for hours, perhaps even days. Consequently, the temporary help industry has a huge turnover as people quit; they always have one foot out the door looking for something better.

Ettridge also had to pay temps for their idle time, and he found that his cost for replacing an employee who quit was at least $250, plus staff time for recruiting and interviewing new workers. His monthly out-of-pocket costs for keeping a good team of temporaries was slightly more than $10,000, in addition to staff salaries. In 1989, Ettridge decided to pay temps to come in to work, then provide free soft drinks, morning coffee, and snacks in a nice lounge area. In addition, he set up training areas and developed self-improvement programs for skills updating, word processing, foreign languages, and data management. Company turnover dropped rapidly, employees were better skilled and motivated, and Ettridge saved money. Personnel staffing costs were halved, and he estimated that the total program cost him less than $20 a person each month. Savings were on the order of $250 a person each month.

Knowing that he was on to something good, Ettridge decided to do much more for his employees and for his clients. A client who needed a $5-an-hour receptionist, for example, would get a $10-an-hour temp skilled at office filing, word processing, and reception duties; the client was billed $5, but the temp was paid the full rate. Moreover, Temps & Co. rates were set higher than the competitors. The result was a much higher demand for business from clients who were more than satisfied and often voluntarily paid higher rates to have better skilled temporary help. This outcome helped solve two problems. First, highly skilled employees who had been less in demand than employees with basic skills were now being requested, thus reducing idle time. Second, marketing efforts to line up and retain clients were reduced because the temps were generating business on their own, not waiting for assignments to come in. Ettridge extended this idea and began assigning idle employees to potential clients for a day of free services. The temps' salary and expenses were less than a small newspaper ad, and Ettridge reduced commercial marketing efforts, reducing costs while increasing business. Temps also began earning cash bonuses for their marketing results, and they were paid bonuses for recruiting qualified employees. Within months of implementing these measures, profits more than doubled.

Enriching the company's atmosphere, as well as its employees, is not a new concept, but many service businesses behave in just the opposite manner. Instead of paying or spending to improve services, they try to keep employee costs to a minimum, hold down benefits, and squeeze overheads. Good cost control is essential, but there are other considerations. Often small investments in human resources pay huge returns. For example, Earl Hess, founder of Lancaster Laboratories in Pennsylvania, solved the problem of high employee turnover by providing child care. Many of Hess's employees were working parents who were absent or late, or who quit, to be closer to their children. Hess set up a child-care program with recreational facilities for after-school activities for older children. Parents and their children can lunch together, visit, and enjoy compatible schedules. General Business Services of Germantown, Maryland, simply believes in a policy of fair treatment that extends to all decisions. The policy includes noncash incentives such as more holidays and flexible working hours, tuition assistance, and greater employee participation in decisions.

CASE QUESTIONS

1. Contrast "success factors" described in the chapter with incidents in the case. In your answer explain how service companies could address problems noted in the case.
2. Describe the service philosophy and how it relates to clients. In your answer, examine policies that could improve a service business in "temps."
3. It makes sense that if a service business is based on human effort, the effort will be the highest cost, and a company should logically try to keep the cost to a minimum. Explore this rationale, and explain how costs can be addressed without exploiting human resources or clients.

Sources: Tom Richman, "How to Build a Profit Margin," *Inc.*, February 1989, pp. 91–92. Also Joan C. Szabo, "Small-Business Update," *Nation's Business*, August 1988, pp. 10–12.

CASE 7-2

Putting Service on the Line

Steven and Valerie Bursten operate their Indianapolis business, Decorating Den Systems, Inc., as a family business. Steven founded the company and set up a franchise system with a very clear idea of high-quality interior decorating services. He requires skilled and enthusiastic franchise owners capable of individualized service to clients, providing decorating consulting, a wide selection of materials, and access to name-brand furnishings. Valerie, a former TWA cabin attendant, is on the road selling franchises when she is not involved in purchasing and training. The key to the business, she insists, is training franchise owners to create a marketing focus on distinct client groups, then helping them to develop the skills to complement their talents. Most franchise owners are women, and being a role model is important to Valerie.

In contrast to the Burstens, Nancy and Norman Peters entered business very cautiously. They opened an independent photo-processing lab to print high-quality photos for people who needed special services not usually provided by the one-hour minilabs. The whole point of the business, Nancy says, was to supplement her husband's pension. They worked out of their home in Hendersonville, North Carolina, and set out to find customers. Expecting a good return on advertising, they placed ads in newspapers and magazines but had disappointing responses. Business trickled in, but after some months, they realized that most orders were from repeat customers and almost always for single prints that clients wanted for their own businesses or promotions. It took several months of heavy losses to realize that their potential for profitable business rested on large-account photos for commercial uses, not film and photo processing. Most orders today are for high-quality catalog sheets, postcards, brochures, and promotional materials.

The concept of David Hall and Pat Gallup, PC Connection sells an extraordinary range of accessories and equipment for all types of personal computers. Started in 1982, PC Connection initially targeted IBM PC markets, then launched the MacConnection division to handle Apple products. After seven years, the company topped $100 million in sales. The service provided by PC Connection has made it one of the most respected firms in the business. They were the first to provide a toll-free customer service hotline with a full range of technical support. Employees who handle calls are intensively trained not only in technical details but also in customer service. You won't hear "computerese" spoken by PC Connection employees. Instead, the emphasis is on clarity of explanations and patience with customers who are, for the most part, not well versed in computer jargon. Elsewhere, a client may be told to "expect delivery in three to four weeks," a common practice of mail-order companies that do not stock inventory, only take orders, and transship products. In contrast, PC Connection will deliver overnight, guaranteed, and for a fixed price that most recently was $3 an order.

CASE QUESTIONS

1. Identify and contrast the types of businesses and their markets described in the case.
2. What are the critical success factors in each business? Describe their distinctive competencies, and express your opinion about what sets them apart.
3. Identify a service-related business in your area and describe the services, customers, and characteristics that made it successful.

Sources: "Insider," *Inc.*, March 1989, p. 21; Nancy A. Peters, "Sharpen Your Focus and Aim High," *Nation's Business*, August 1988, p. 9; and Sylvia Helm, "Perfect Partners," *Venture*, July 1986, pp. 38–39.

PART THREE

▲ ▲
▲ ▲ **Marketing and**
▲ ▲ **New Venture Development**
▲ ▲

Marketing is a critical dimension of all new ventures that is addressed in Part Three. Chapter 8 is a composite presentation on market research as it relates to starting new ventures. Market research is a complicated process that cannot be addressed thoroughly in one chapter; however, our intention is to alert readers to the responsibilities of conducting research and indicate how entepreneurs must set about to accomplish it. Chapter 9 identifies the fundamental marketing strategies of new ventures during their start-up and early growth stages. Consequently, the chapter describes the key elements of a marketing plan that are necessary to launch a new venture. Chapter 10 is a special chapter that addresses global marketing opportunities and unique strategies needed to "go international" with a new venture. With so many changes taking place in Europe, Asia, and the Soviet Union, there are tremendous opportunities for entrepreneurs in foreign markets.

Chapter 8

Marketing Research for New Ventures

OBJECTIVES

1. Describe the marketing concept and its relevance to new ventures.
2. Explain marketing research in terms of pre-start-up planning.
3. Describe primary sources of market research information.
4. Describe the five forces of a competitive analysis.
5. Discuss the major implications of market research for entrepreneurs.

Satisfying customers is the fundamental objective of successful marketing in every organization. Achieving this objective involves far more than simply providing good service, and as we shall see, success often rests with effective market planning. Consequently, entrepreneurs must do a great deal of serious market research to understand who their customers are and how best to serve them. Research activities should take place before opening the new venture, and they should continue throughout the venture's existence.

The chapter begins by defining the *marketing concept*. This philosophical approach to business should prevail in every enterprise, although it is often ignored. We follow this topic with a descriptive presentation on *marketing research*. This is not an attempt to be comprehensive but an effort to stimulate an appreciation of how market research is generated and used. Consequently, we examine research questions that entrepreneurs ask, the types of research employed, and the ways in which those answers are used for effective planning.

Success often rests with a quality business plan that provides a clear marketing strategy. Therefore, entrepreneurs should seek out the best market research information available. Later in the chapter, we introduce several sources of marketing information and tell how to find help when researching. The importance of market research cannot be overemphasized, and that is the focal message in this chapter.

THE MARKETING CONCEPT

The **marketing concept** is a consciously articulated philosophy of business that says, in essence, "The consumer is king." Specifically, the consumer is seen as "the fulcrum, the pivot point about which the business moves in operating for the balanced best interests of all concerned."[1] This concept translates into three considerations for a successful business:

1. Entrepreneurs must make a concerted effort to establish customers and, in doing so, satisfy those customers by giving them value in products and services that they want and need.
2. Entrepreneurs must focus on long-term profitability by creating a reputation for service and quality, not by focusing myopically on short-term sales.
3. Entrepreneurs must integrate marketing with other facets of doing business so that a coordinated management effort is achieved without disproportionate emphasis on any one function.

A Commitment to Customers

Satisfying customers means giving value in exchange for patronage. Sales come from both parties agreeing to a fair exchange, but more specifically, customers buy products and services that they believe are worthwhile, not what sellers feel are important.[2] To emphasize the point, consider that airlines sell "seats" on flights, but passengers buy "destinations." Advertising agencies recognize this fact and compose exotic ads for flights to Hawaii or to the Florida Keys to play to travelers' desires. The exotic image is the message to customers, but success is measured by a high proportion of filled seats on each flight.

Entrepreneurs who take the time to empathize with prospective customers learn a great deal of useful information. Putting oneself in customers' shoes helps to understand what motivates them to make purchases. For example, the owner of a 7-Eleven franchise store near Baltimore recently visited 23 other nearby convenience stores, and in each instance he bought a few items to update his knowledge of the competition. He came away with an interesting perspective, however, because in only three stores did sales clerks attempt more than a hollow "thanks," and he felt that only one clerk was cheerful. In fact, he was stunned at the dreariness and aloofness of clerks who just stuck their hands out to collect money. He also became aware that his own employees behaved the same way, and he resolved to change this behavior. He used role-playing techniques to convince employees that they could make their jobs less dreary by consciously being nice to customers. He worked the cash register, for example, and imitated both cheerful and aloof behavior. His employees took turns acting out customer roles, and within a few days, everyone was encouraging conversation with customers, smiling, and having a better time. During these friendly exchanges, customers offered suggestions for merchandise, and the store began to stock many of these products. Within two months, sales volume was noticeably higher and employees began to recognize a pattern of more repeat customers. Another example is illustrated in the profile on Sports-Town, Inc.

Empathy for consumer perceptions often encourages new products or design innovations. Consider, for example, the form and function of most consumer electronic products such as stereos. They can be remarkably similar and boring, partly because of microchip technology that has eliminated all the complex but interesting attributes of mechanical record players. Older stereo systems had conspicuous turntables, tone arms, and record changers. Similarly, clocks used to have moving parts and were audible, and there is still something special about the soft ticktock of a grandfather clock's pendulum. Today, CD players, stereos, digital clocks, LED watches, and most other consumer electronics are monotonously quiet and immobile. They function well, but the "form" and "feeling" of time and music have disappeared. These

PROFILE △

How to Grow in a Saturated Industry

Sports-Town, Inc., is the brainchild of entrepreneur Thomas K. Haas, whose 1987 experiment with one store in Atlanta, Georgia, was so successful that he attracted $20 million in capital for expansion. In 1989 the expansion paid off in $80 million in sales. Sports-Town is the Toys 'R' Us of sporting goods, with huge almost stadium-sized warehouses loaded with inventory ranging from dollar-discount gadgets to expensive, high-quality equipment. Everything is sold at the lowest margin possible, and volume determines success. At the same time, the company ensures highly trained sales staff who are enthusiastic and attentive to every customer.

How Sports-Town can compete in a saturated industry dominated by several huge corporations is a mystery to some, but not to Haas. Market research revealed three vital pieces of information to him. First, consumers wanted a broad selection of products to choose from, and many sporting-goods stores featured a narrow selection of particular brand items. Second, although the industry is saturated, there were several important geographical areas with few competitors, including Atlanta, the site of his first store. Third, and not least important, the economics of sporting-goods sales showed that sports equipment had very high elasticities of demand. Consequently, customers were extremely sensitive to prices. Haas reacted to these findings and created an extraordinary venture.

Source: Mark Henricks, "Big Enough to Fill a Stadium," *Venture*, April 1989, pp. 22–23.

perceptions may be changing, however, as product designers are starting to create fashion timepieces and radios formed in the shape of an ocean wave or a music stanza. Several companies are also conducting market tests on "designer CRTs" for computers. These innovations are in response to consumers who prefer more "form" with "function."[3]

Responding to customer preferences is enhanced by understanding their *perceptions*. The marketing concept encourages entrepreneurs to tune in those perceptions, to do marketing research necessary to understand customers' needs, and to make decisions based on those needs rather than rely on preconceived notions or the owner's intuition.

A Long View toward Profitability

Too often, customer service is misinterpreted in the short term as an overt effort to satisfy all customers (thereby maximizing sales) through tactical price discounts, sales, and enthusiastic advertising. Customer service does not mean acquiescence to consumer whims; it is not that simple. Every organization must first provide for a profitable long-term existence; service has no meaning if the firm cannot survive to provide it. Therefore, implicit in the marketing concept is the need to ensure the long-term continuity of predictable quality, sales, and service, and, in turn, viability of the enterprise.[4]

The marketing concept is interwoven with an explicit assumption that every organization has a responsibility to its constituent **stakeholders**. These include a corporation's stockholders, private investors, lenders, and key executives who have a vested interest in the venture. Stakeholders also include the company's employees, its customers, and the community at large. In the extreme, society is a stakeholder that benefits from the introduction of new value-added products or necessary services by entrepreneurs. Exhibit 8-1 summarizes stakeholder interests, which include, but are not limited to, profits.

Exhibit 8-1 Stakeholders and Their Interests

Equity stockholders	Profitable return on investments, wealth accumulation
Employees	Income and job stability, pride of successful venture
Customers	Reliable source for products and services, value-added enterprise
Suppliers and vendors	Stable customer for products and services, competent distributor
Managers and owners	Career positions, higher-valued enterprise, wealth accumulation, and psychological satisfaction
Local citizens	Contributor to community economy, job source, tax source to community
Society and humankind	Value-added products and services, social improvement through new enterprise, innovation, creativity

Profits provide the financial strength to support human-resource programs, wages, and appropriate benefits for employees. From a customer viewpoint, profits are just as essential, although most would be perfectly happy with wide-screen color televisions priced at $100 or microcomputers at $101. A firm might be able to offer these prices to a few lucky customers at its going-out-of-business sale, but the relationship would end there. Customers really want an enterprise to be successful because that is the only way to be assured of service-after-sale warranties and predictable distributors. Also, communities are stakeholders interested in profitable businesses that sustain tax revenues and employment.

From an entrepreneurial perspective, it makes sense to fashion a marketing strategy that will improve sales volume, but it is nonsense to risk long-term profits solely to generate sales volume. What is needed is a strategic approach to marketing so that sales reinforce a *composite* set of objectives, including customer satisfaction, profitability, and long-term continuity of the firm.

Integrated Objectives

Marketing is not an isolated activity; neither is production, finance, staffing, or any other organizational activity. However, this message too often falls on deaf ears. Entrepreneurs who create their ventures based on technical experience (e.g., an engineer who goes into private consulting) often forget or ignore marketing. On the other hand, marketers who start new ventures often forget other aspects of the business. It is not unusual to find inventors who, preoccupied with their creations, expect customers to beat a path to the cash register automatically. For the inventor, marketing can be like an unwanted trip to the dentist. Yet the same individual will not hesitate to spend money on the best production equipment. Unfortunately, marketers can be equally myopic, pouring money into sales promotions while equipment rusts or accounting ledgers go untouched. It is easy to focus intensely on gaining sales volume yet lose control of costs and go bankrupt.

A classic example of this was the demise of W. T. Grant, a giant chain retailer that established aggressive sales quotas during the 1970s. Marketing objectives dominated decisions, and credit policies were so lax that nearly anyone who could sign a charge card could get Grant's credit. In the end, most stores had extraordinary sales but could not collect on their credit accounts. The firm made record sales but spent itself into bankruptcy.[5] Entrepreneurs in smaller firms make similar mistakes. A recent example is the experience of Bill Rodgers, winner of many marathon races, who focused carefully on designing running apparel but neglected other aspects of his business, subsequently risking everything.[6] (See the accompanying profile.)

Marketing must be integrated with other functions, but such integration is seldom easy to achieve because there are natural barriers that divide specializations. Engineers tend to work too intensely on product designs, whereas marketers tend to overemphasize sales efforts. Consequently, salespersons prefer exciting designs and fancy packaging, but those in manufacturing prefer simplicity and function over form. Individuals keen on finance will create tight budgets and encourage prices that provide optimal profit margins; salespersons prefer low prices to stimulate sales, and they tend to be impatient with budget constraints. If entrepreneurs plan well, however,

PROFILE △

Running a Different Kind of Race

Bill Rodgers was a four-time winner of both the Boston Marathon and the New York City Marathon, and perhaps the premiere runner in the world during the late 1970s when running was beginning to be popular. He launched his own apparel enterprise in 1978, registering $3.5 million in first-year sales, and envisioned a nationwide network of multimillion-dollar sports apparel stores. All his energy went into designing apparel, winning races, and filling orders. Rodgers had an early monopoly.

Not being interested in other business activities, Rodgers farmed out financial management, left banking to his lenders, and ignored the likelihood of competition. Competition did occur, finances became tight, and Rodgers' optimism led to overexpansion. When prices began to drop, his firm cut costs with cheaper products. Quality began to erode, and, in turn, sales eroded. By early 1987 the firm was on the verge of bankruptcy, and Rodgers was slated to lose everything. Fortunately, his firm was purchased by an experienced person with diversified business skills in finance, retail marketing, purchasing, and employee relations. The new owner revived the firm, and Rodgers emerged with his personal assets intact and stock in the rejuvenated enterprise.

Source: Joseph P. Kahn, "Heartbreak Hill," *Inc.*, April 1988, pp. 68–78.

---

they can minimize these conflicts by using marketing research to illustrate the best points from everyone's perspective. By then integrating these perspectives, entrepreneurs can implement plans based on quality products and reasonable marketing strategies.

> ▶ **CHECKPOINT**
>
> Explain the market concept in terms of a commitment to customers.
>
> Describe the meaning of long-term commitments to profitability and integration of responsibilities.

△ △
△ △ **PERSPECTIVE ON MARKETING RESEARCH**
△ △

Marketing research is defined as "the systematic and objective process of gathering, recording, and analyzing data for aid in making marketing decisions."[7] The essence of marketing research is to provide information used in decision making, and for the entrepreneur, there are fundamental differences between market information needed prior to start-up and after a firm is established.

Prior to opening for business, the entrepreneur wants to know whether a market exists for a new product or service, who is likely to be a primary customer, how to position the enterprise in a market, and how the product or service will be priced, promoted, and distributed. Addressing these issues becomes part of the *pre-start-up planning* process. Once a firm has become established, much of this information is authenticated through actual experience, and market research expands to include a continuous *competitive analysis*.

> ▶ **CHECKPOINT**
>
> Describe the essence of marketing research for planning and decision making.

MARKET RESEARCH IN THE PRE-START-UP PHASE

Before entrepreneurs actually commit themselves to opening a business, the most important question to answer is "Will it sell?" A mistake that many entrepreneurs make is to merely *assume* that their product or service will sell. Inventors become infatuated with their products and assume that everyone else should be equally infatuated. Professionals assume that their credentials will assure them of clients, and retailers assume that shoppers will flock to their stores, if only out of curiosity. Only rarely will entrepreneurs find themselves in such favorable situations. Consequently, they should question whether it will sell, and good market research will help provide the answer.

Who Is the Customer?

Developing a clear profile of potential customers is a basic element of market research. In marketing language, a customer profile is called a **customer scenario**. Customers may be young or old, married or single, teachers or students, homeowners or renters, poor or wealthy, or some combination of these or a thousand other characteristics. For example, with the increasing number of women in the U.S. labor force, there will be a continued emphasis on new services for working wives and mothers. This trend is indicated in Figure 8-1. By narrowing the focus on local working women with preschool children, an entrepreneur considering a new day-care center can establish a profile of potential customers.

A customer scenario also can reflect categories of companies or businesses, such as general construction contractors in the Cleveland metropolitan area or incorporated public accounting firms in the state of Louisiana. Classifications of consumers and organizations help entrepreneurs define their market *segments*, a topic we will address later in the chapter.[8]

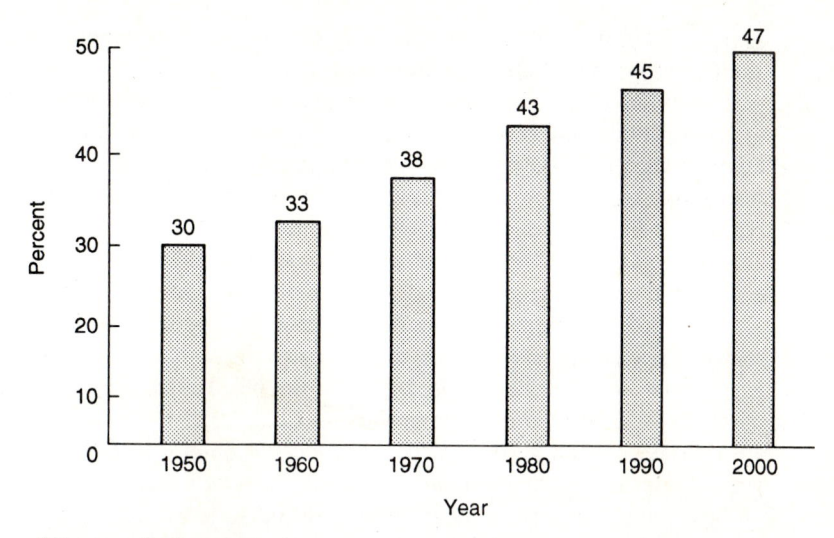

Figure 8-1 **Women as a Share of the U.S. Labor Force.** (*Source*: U.S. Small Business Administration, *Small Business in the American Economy* (Washington, DC: U.S. Government Printing Office, 1988), p. 13.)

Without having a clearly defined customer scenario, entrepreneurs often make terrible decisions. For example, a Virginia university student devised an unusual new golf putting trainer that was used effectively on the university men's golf team. The product was a small strip of mirrored steel with etched guidelines for lining up a golf ball and the putter head. Backed by a university club, the student sunk money into limited manufacturing, packaging, and advertisement. The putting device, called Tru-Putt, was introduced just prior to Christmas 1986. Everything about the effort was geared toward selling the product to male golfers. The product was placed in pro shops and demonstrated in sporting-goods stores at a price of $12.99. Nothing happened. In fact, on one of the busiest shopping days, only a few products sold in the best mall location. The shocked student began studying results in all locations and found that almost all sales had been to women. The next day he set up a department store display with signs advertising "The one gift you need for the man in your life." Nearly a thousand were sold to women, and just four to men. The appropriate *customer scenario* in this instance included teenage girls, wives, and retired women who wanted a unique gift priced under $20 for their fathers, husbands, or grandfathers.

Identifying customers in this example could have been accomplished through an inexpensive test market, a survey, a panel round-table discussion, or one of many other market research methods. Several of these methods will be described as we look at customer characteristics that contribute to scenarios of individual buyers.

Sex and Age. These are two essential characteristics to identify in the customer scenario. From the example of the Tru-Putt, it should be clear that sex is an important factor in marketing. Age is more difficult to classify, but if an entrepreneur has a specific interest, such as merchandising aerobic workout clothes, then he or she can study demographic trends, find out who takes aerobic classes, talk to manufacturers of clothes, and study magazines on health and fitness to compile data on sex and age of potential consumers. For example, if a new aerobic clothing store is proposed for an expensive resort area, then the demographic data on who lives there, visits the resort, and uses aerobic facilities will reveal a pattern with specific information on sex and age categories of potential customers.

Once data have been accumulated, they should be organized for decision making. For example, assume a high-priced resort where adult couples vacation. Shoppers are likely to be women between the age of 21 and 65, but those data need to be refined. The entrepreneur will want to know how many sales are made to women aged 21 to 30, 30 to 45, 45 to 60, and over 60. These categories are arbitrary, but the point is to break down age groups for better decisions. If 50 percent of the sales are to those between 21 and 30, then the *focal customer* is probably a fashion-conscious young woman. The entrepreneur will want to stock sizes, colors, and fashions for this age group. Clearly, if most resort customers are women between 45 and 60, then a different inventory and store image is needed.

Income Status. Consumers must have the ability to buy, and the amount of money will influence the product or service concept, price, nature of promotions, and method of distribution. In the aerobic clothing example, assume that 50 percent of the sales are to women between 21 and 30 years of age, and further assume that these are wives of professionals or are themselves young professional women with family incomes greater than $100,000 a year. Price is *not* going to be an object. In fact, a higher price may be essential to reinforce a fashionable image. If research shows that only a few women are in that income group, and that a majority fall into a $50,000 to $100,000 annual bracket, the shop may still sell expensive items but have a wider selection of moderately priced items. If income is between $30,000 and $50,000, money *is* an object, and vacationers might avoid a high-priced fashion boutique. Under $30,000? Set up bargain racks.

Occupation and Education. Both of these factors can significantly influence an entrepreneur's decisions. A travel agency positioned to serve the diplomatic community in Washington, DC, for instance, will specialize in major foreign cities and capitals, upmarket accommodations, and individual flight bookings. The agency will have multilingual staff who are skilled in services such as visa regulations, foreign health certificate requirements, and currency exchange. An office supply store located near a metropolitan courthouse can expect a high percentage of clients to be attorneys, and consequently, the store might stock legal office supplies and special legal forms. Positioning a bookstore in a university community will require a book inventory distinctly different from that of a bookstore located in a rural town. Occupations and education levels will directly influence microcomputer sales and related products such as SAT software. Occupations and education levels also influence sales of foreign language training tapes, clothing, magazine subscriptions, decorative art, investments, bank services, health care, entertainment, and insurance programs.

PROFILE △

Coming of the "Green Consumer"

Market experts predict the 1990s will be the Earth Decade. Consumers will replace their 1980s emphasis on health products with environmentally safe products. The "green consumers" will intensify their preoccupation as the year 2000 draws nearer. The result will be major changes in every business and in services supporting commercial endeavor. For example, advertising will focus on environmentally friendly product attributes, manufacturers will focus design efforts on biodegradable products, and travel agents will offer "ecotours" to untouched areas. Entrepreneurs will have to avoid products of questionable environmental safety, yet they will have before them new opportunities.

Source: Anne B. Fisher, "What Consumers Want in the 1990s," *Fortune*, January 29, 1990, pp. 48–52.

Other Customer Characteristics. These include family profiles, such as being married, single, or divorced; having preschool toddlers, teenage children, or children away at college; and having one or both parents working. Customers also can be identified by *ethnic group*, *religion*, and *domicile*. For example, Campbell Soup developed a canned nacho cheese sauce with three different flavors to match consumer tastes. Nacho cheese sauce made for American consumers on the East Coast is bland, sauce made in California for western consumers is zesty, and sauce sold in southwest Texas is laced with chili peppers for a predominantly Hispanic community.[9]

Demographic and economic information provide insights about consumers on age, sex, occupations, education, ethnicity, religion, and domicile, but there are many other personal and behavioral characteristics to consider. Marketing research is used to discover consumer buying habits to determine, among other things, whether they own homes, rent apartments, have two cars, play golf, belong to aerobic clubs, watch television news, use credit cards, take trips, have cats, belong to unions, subscribe to environmental news, own guns, or buy mutual funds. There are all sorts of things to consider, and although only a few of these will have value to any one venture, entrepreneurs often discover new ideas by remaining alert to changes. For example, with political changes in Eastern Europe, there could be millions of new emigrants heading toward America and the West, opening new opportunities for life-style products and services.[10]

Where Is the Market?

Part of the customer scenario will involve locating the potential customer base. There are obvious categories, such as large metropolitan areas, suburban communities, small

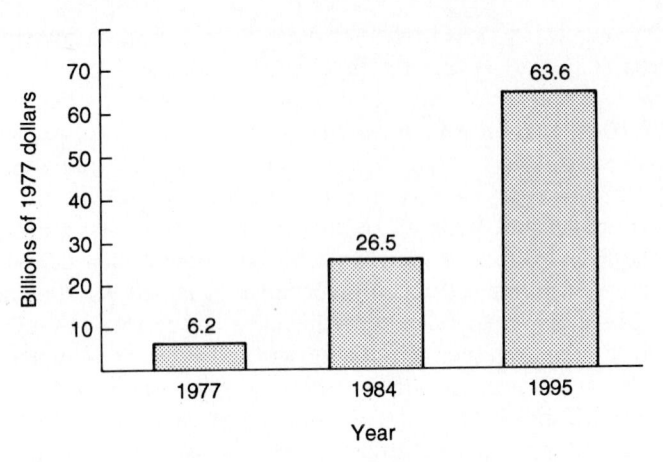

Figure 8-2 **Business Investment in Computers.**
(*Source*: U.S. Small Business Administration, *Small Business in the American Economy* (Washington, DC: U.S. Government Printing Office, 1988), p. 23.)

cities, and rural towns. Other categories include regional areas of New England, the Gulf Coast, and Southern California. These broad classifications do not reveal enough about markets, but they are useful for researching demographic trends and for using U.S. Census data to start developing a customer profile.

Market Size and Changes. It is important to determine the potential for current and future sales. Macroeconomic data, if appropriate to the venture, may be the easiest to obtain through census studies, federal sources such as the Bureau of Labor Statistics, state and local economic development agencies, Chambers of Commerce, and industry reports. Market size and potential for new sales can be studied through special reports prepared for small businesses and particular industries. For example, Figure 8-2 illustrates results from a report on investments in computers, showing that sales are expected to reach $63.6 billion by 1995. That figure represents a 140 percent increase over a ten-year period, and although growth is strong, it suggests a more competitive industry in the future than in the past with commensurate risks to emerging computer enterprises.

U.S. Census data are a primary source of information on market size and location, and they can provide more than 40 types of demographic information broken down by every zip code and county in the United States. These data are upgraded in most instances every two years, and they are supplemented by state and local demographic studies. Census reports and most other government data are public information available in most libraries, but wading through these sources requires dedication and patience. Entrepreneurs can reduce this burden by searching through a compilation of private and public information sources published and regularly updated by the Center for Entrepreneurship at Wichita State University.[11]

Local Market Characteristics. Local markets differ significantly because of population size, economic development, industrial profile, ethnic groups, weather, legislation, and culture. A product that sells well in one area may sell poorly elsewhere; therefore entrepreneurs must assess local markets. For example, car dealers in rural counties of Wyoming know intuitively that they will sell a high proportion of pickup trucks, but they would benefit from studying changes in birth rates, family sizes, and economic growth rates to be alert to changing consumer profiles. In a town with a declining teenage population, fewer sports cars will be sold. If the same town is experiencing a decline in farming or ranching, the number of pickups and farm vehicles will drop.

In another example, the growth of two-career couples has resulted in smaller families, more condominiums and town houses, fewer single-family homes, and growing satellite communities around metropolitan areas. What this trend has meant for building contractors is a major shift away from home building to multiple-unit construction. Near urban satellite areas, more shopping malls have sprung up, sales of microwave ovens have expanded, cable television has become a common amenity, and new "convenience" industries have evolved. Home-cleaning operations, for example, have become one of the fastest-growing services in the United States. Specifically, Jani-King and Rainbow International are two cleaning and maintenance companies consistently ranked among the nation's top-performing franchisors. Both focus on home and office markets in suburban areas.[12] Other convenience industries reinforce this demographic trend, with Domino's Pizza, Jazzercise, and Jiffy Lube expanding rapidly into multi-unit housing areas in suburban markets.

Segmenting the Market: What Niche to Fill

A **market segment** is one distinct customer group on which a business will concentrate its efforts. A market segment, also called a **market niche**, keenly focuses an entrepreneur's efforts on product characteristics, pricing, promotions, and channels of distribution related to a specific customer group. Retailers like Neiman-Marcus and Saks Fifth Avenue clearly understand their market niches, and they have traditionally segmented their customers according to those in select locations who want prestige products and luxury services.

Companies of every size try to establish segmentation strategies so that efficient use of resources can be achieved without ambiguity. For example, Apple Computer Corporation began selling to computer enthusiasts who demanded unique software and innovative applications. The company has expanded the sheer size of its markets, but it has not tried to be everything to everyone. Instead, Apple established niches in education, desk-top publishing, and graphic design systems. As noted in earlier chapters, Digital, Hewlett-Packard, and Xerox zeroed in on technical and scientific markets. Although IBM is pervasive in its product line, it has distinct product groups that focus on niches ranging from superconductor research to stand-alone office systems. Many other computer firms have entered the computer market without a clear market segment and failed. For example, Texas Instruments was among the early entrants to make and sell microcomputers, but TI mass-marketed a low-end system at discount prices. Trying to reach everyone, TI's shotgun approach failed, and the company lost millions of dollars.[13]

Niche Characteristics. Every niche will have characteristics defined partially by the customer scenario and partially by location. By studying market trends, entrepreneurs often discover untapped markets or, just as important, discover that competition is already intense in their market niche. One way or the other, the information is valuable to encourage a marketing strategy aimed at one *niche*, or to steer away from potential disaster. Recall that a good idea is only good if it will "sell." It follows that a glistening new fast-food restaurant in a town that already has fast-food franchises every two blocks is a risky enterprise, but the same restaurant elsewhere may be a gold mine.

Market niches can be defined for most products and services in nearly any location. As described by the customer scenario, niche characteristics mirror a specific group profile, such as foreign diplomats in Washington or working mothers with toddlers in Pittsburgh. A location can define the niche, such as the borough of Queens in New York City or the city of Las Vegas. An economic segment can provide a niche, such as steel manufacturers or wheat farmers. And products or services can describe a niche, such as Rolex watches or weight-loss clinics.

Usually, products and services must be tailored to a market niche selected by the entrepreneur. For example, aerobic workout clothes can be marketed wholesale to health clubs with particular colors and styles, monogrammed for corporate accounts (i.e., with IBM or CitiCorp logos), customized for the Olympic games, or designed with psychedelic colors for teen boutiques.

Growth Characteristics. For nearly any market segment, there will be ebbs and flows. Changes reflect economic conditions, evolving competition, or possibly a stage in the product life cycle. Entrepreneurs must have their facts straight concerning these changes and be able to identify a growing market. Few markets remain stable, and there are always opportunities arising from social changes. During the past decade, for instance, women's sporting events have become more popular, and this trend has awakened women's interests in recreational sports. As a result, new opportunities have emerged in recreational clothing and accessories. One company that has taken advantage of this change is Reebok International, a little-known manufacturer of men's gym shoes prior to 1986. Since then, however, Reebok has become the market leader in sports shoes by introducing four different lines of shoes each year, and most recently, ten models just for women.[14]

Investors and lenders will want to see hard data on growth trends, and they will take a dim view of weakly supported market information. Guesstimation is deadly, and emotional ploys are suicide. Even well-documented data will be discounted by experienced investors. Arthur Lipper, a seasoned venture capitalist and publisher, says that he only gives credence to business plans that are well supported by factual studies. Even then, he cuts in half all sales projections and doubles the time projected by entrepreneurs to break even.[15]

Growth statistics should be documented by data related to the market niche

PROFILE △

Niche Marketing in Women's Golf Attire

Less than a decade ago, women's sporting events were novel, and only a few sports stars such as the LPGA's Nancy Lopez were recognized. Winning a major golf event for women sport professionals barely provided earnings to cover travel expenses. Today, women's sports comprise one of the fastest growing sectors of the entertainment industry. Nancy Lopez is one of the pioneers who crashed through the barriers, winning her 40th major LPGA title to launch the 1990s. What she has done for golf is paralleled in sports fashions.

In golf franchise outlets, such as Pro Golf America and Nevada Bob's, half the total inventory is directed to women's fashions, equipment, and shoes. Men's and women's fashions have equal advertising space in *Golf Illustrated*, and nearly 40 percent of golf clothing sales is to women. Clothing designers have created highly profitable marketing niches in women's golf clothing, among them Hickey Freeman, Bogner Company, Bench, and the Wall Street Cotton Club. None of these companies actively marketed to women until the mid-1980s, and, incidentally, all made their names in exclusive men's wear prior to that time. Thanks to Nancy Lopez and her touring colleagues, times have changed.

Source: "Women's Majors '89," *Golf Illustrated*, December 1989, p. 41; also "For the Fun of It," *Fashion Review*, January 1990, p. 1.

---

described by a consumer scenario. Statistics should be discussed in terms of existing and potential competition, effects of economic changes, market share that accounts for substitutes, and business cycles. Economic changes include the effects of inflation, interest rates, consumer credit, and tax legislation, among other considerations. Business cycles are subject to many forces, including political influences like import quotas (or lack of them), the psychology of an active stock market, patterns of unemployment, and unusual phenomena (e.g., hijackings that affect travel). Growth also is linked to complementary products, and sales may be contingent on sales of other goods and services. For example, when major computer manufacturers configured their personal computers using $3\frac{1}{2}$-inch disk drives, they created a boom market for producers of $3\frac{1}{2}$-inch diskettes. For companies in the 8-mm home-movie industry, the technological breakthrough of VCRs devastated their markets.[16]

Sales Forecast. The result of good market research will be a well-defined sales forecast. A **sales forecast** is the quantified volume and value of projected sales within a market niche for a specific time period. When we study financial projections in later chapters, the sales forecast will be used to accurately estimate revenues, costs,

Figure 8-3 Preliminary Sales Forecast for a New Benetton Store

First-Year Sales, Opening August 1 (× $1,000)

Aug	Sep	Oct	Nov	Dec	Jan	Feb	Mar	Apr	May	Jun	Jul	YTD
2.5	14.3	19.1	28.4	43.0	10.4	9.1	4.0	4.0	7.5	18.6	23.7	184.6

Second-Year Sales (by quarter, 7/1–6/30)

1st	2nd	3rd	4th	YTD
48.6	102.9	25.8	50.5	222.8

Third-Year Sales (by quarter, 7/1–6/30)

1st	2nd	3rd	4th	YTD
42.4	117.2	26.7	52.6	242.9

profits, cash requirements, and investment needs. In addition, a sales forecast helps determine human resource, production, and management-systems requirements. A good sales forecast will specify sales volume and convert that information into monetary terms. Dollar sales value is necessary because in order to estimate sales, a price has to be estimated, which in turn influences expected sales. Figure 8-3 illustrates a sales forecast for a small Benetton retailer in a North Carolina mall. The Benetton shop has two major lines of clothing—a winter and summer line—consisting mainly of sweaters, sports tops, designer sweat suits, and accessories.

Market research will also reveal *seasonality*, the pattern of variation in sales

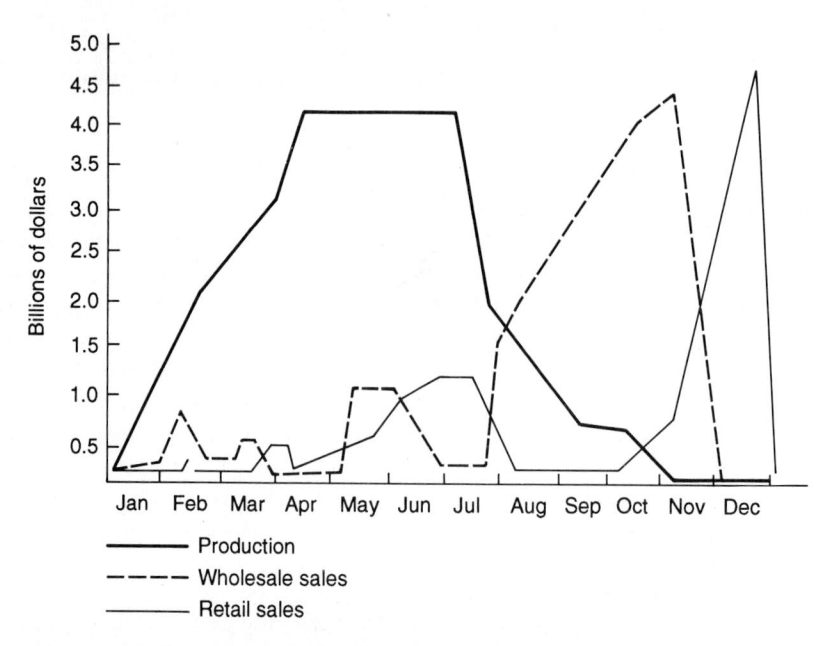

Figure 8-4 **Seasonal Patterns in Plastic Fabricated Toys.** (*Source*: Compliments of Perfecta Toy Manufacturing Company, United States and Macao, January 1990.)

over a calendar year. For example, toys sell extremely well during the two-month period preceding Christmas. Some toys also enjoy a late spring and early summer surge if they relate to warm-weather recreation. During other months, toy sales are very slow. Seasonal sales data will be important to project cash-flow needs. For example, a retail toy store may have to gross enough in November and December to cover expenses in low-sale months. Meanwhile, toys are sold wholesale in advance of retail peaks, and toy makers must produce inventory in anticipation of future demand periods. These patterns are shown in Figure 8-4.

Investors and lenders will want to see seasonal data expressed on a month-to-month basis for the first year of operations. They also like to see a three-year projection broken down into quarterly increments. Some lenders expect five- to ten-year projections, but that expectation borders on fantasy. Excellent corporations with expert planning systems rarely understand what will take place beyond a few years into the future. For example, IBM did not envision a viable microcomputer market in 1980, yet three years later IBM had captured nearly 30 percent of the microcomputer market with its introductory PC. Any firm, large or small, should be able to grasp market conditions during the coming year, and most should be able to articulate a forecast for one or two additional years. Even if conditions change, the point is to use the best information currently available so that when changes do occur, the firm is better prepared for them.

Competition: Who Are the Market Players?

Competition is always on an entrepreneur's mind. At the moment a new idea is conceived, one asks, "I wonder if anyone else is doing this?" And that question continues to be asked as long as the business exists. Rather than guess at an answer, savvy entrepreneurs will set about to answer specific questions about competition within their venture's market niche.

Existing Competitors. In most instances, existing competitors can be accurately identified. For example, almost anyone in business will be listed in commercial telephone books. If the new venture is in retailing, a tremendous amount of advertising will be done by competitors; getting answers about them requires the entrepreneur to become an avid window shopper. Professional firms often have local and regional societies with membership listings that can be obtained. These include dental associations, accounting societies, legal referral services, and data-processing societies. Many personal service firms are licensed and listed in state and local directories. For instance, guidance counselors, cosmetologists, building contractors, architects, appraisers, and real estate brokers are registered with state licensing agencies. Most enterprises will be identified, cataloged, and cross-referenced in several official data bases as well as in associations and social clubs. Accessing most of this information is a matter of spending a few difficult hours in libraries.

Researching products is usually more difficult because inventors are unlikely to disclose their ideas until they are ready to go to market. Still, a preliminary patent search will reveal products or processes that have reached a formal filing stage. To identify manufacturers who may already be making a similar product, commercial telephone books are once again very helpful. Calling firms and inquiring about their products is not difficult, and in most instances, public relations employees will be anxious to tell you about their products; that's how they get customers. Most manufacturers have brochures explaining their products, and in many instances, they have customer hotlines or toll-free numbers for inquiries. Also, the National Association of Manufacturers and the International Management Council have nationwide networks for information. Both organizations track manufacturing (and service) firms, create annually updated data bases, publish surveys, and, in general, provide a broad range of vital information to members on wages, legislation, technology, employment, trends in markets, suppliers, and so on. In addition, each year the *Thomas Register* updates a massive list of nearly 60,000 firms with brief explanations of products and services complete with contact names, addresses, and telephone numbers.

There are many sources of information. The task is to identify the best sources rather than meandering aimlessly in a library. For example, there are at least 11,000 "in-house" specialty publications that focus on particular industries. These take the form of magazines or newsletters. Even janitors have specialty publications, and the growth of home and office cleaning franchises has led to the creation of *Building Contractor Services* magazine. By studying these magazines, an entrepreneur will become well informed on specific products or markets. Read what potential competitors read.

Products or Substitutes. The question of what products or substitutes exist now is an adjunct to finding out what competitors exist. Research can also reveal lucrative market niches untouched by even the most sophisticated corporations. For example, IBM does not own the microcomputer market, and even with Apple, Hewlett-Packard, Digital, and many others in the field, Michael Dell was able to rapidly fill a $200 million niche with his PC Limited personal computer.[17] Find out what is available, and classify that information according to customer scenarios and location-specific potential. Determine what is offered in cities and suburbs, and whether a certain area of growth is untapped. For instance, Atlanta, Georgia, has many fine restaurants in the urban area, but most new housing exists in satellite communities away from the city. It can be a nightmare to drive into Atlanta (like many other cities), so the essential question is whether sufficient restaurants exist in the high-growth surrounding communities.

The crucial question is one of *availability*. Are products or services available to the target customer group? An associated question is whether these customers buy *substitutes*. If research shows that people in a certain region prefer good beef but often cannot get it, ask what they eat instead of beef. Is it chicken? Turkey? Perhaps it is seafood. If seafood is a viable substitute for beef and no one is addressing that market, then a seafood outlet could succeed.

Distribution: How Will Customers Be Reached?

A **distribution system** is the physical process of getting products to market or providing services, and although distribution questions seem "mechanical" in the sense of transporting physical goods (or locating services), they often are concerned with the basic nature of a business. Many companies have been built around strong distribution systems rather than unusual products or services.

Sears, Roebuck & Company began humbly as an entrepreneurial catalog enterprise selling farm supplies by mail order in the rural Midwest. Sears did not open its first retail store for several decades, and today its catalog remains a major part of its marketing strategy. Frito-Lay captured a large share of convenience snack foods through rapid, on-time deliveries of potato chips. The company's strategy, even when very small, was to develop the most efficient route-van system in the United States. McDonald's transformed hamburgers into an international phenomenon through a franchise distribution system. Amway relies on multilevel marketing organizations of small groups of salespersons. The Banana Republic created a "retailing event" through high-fashion stores selling military surplus clothes and safari garb.[18]

A distribution channel can *be* the business. Avon Corporation, for example, markets an enormous selection of products on a global basis, but product selection is less important than the image of "Avon Calling," the familiar jingle that identifies its distinct competency as a home distributor. Federal Express, as noted in Chapter 7, is a distribution service. Also, Domino's Pizza is defined by its distribution process, not necessarily its products.[19]

Entire industries rely on distribution channels, including telemarketing, cataloging, franchising, multilevel marketing, mail-order direct marketing, rack jobbing route systems, and many other forms of customer contact. Aside from the choice of wholesaling or retailing, new products may be licensed to firms with established market channels, joint-ventured with manufacturers, brokered through distributors, and consigned for sale. New technologies extend these options to include computer-based advertising, catalogs on disks, CD books and newspapers, and videotape retailing. Recent adopters of videotape marketing include real estate agents, personnel agencies, sports recruiters, and education consultants. Consequently, there may be obvious distribution channels for some businesses, but entrepreneurs are limited in their choices only by their imagination.

> ▶ **CHECKPOINT**
>
> Identify the major questions and categories of market research.
>
> Describe potential characteristics to be considered in a customer scenario.
>
> Define marketing research in terms of market segments, competitors, sales forecasts, and choices among distribution systems.

MARKETS FOCUSED ON ORGANIZATIONS

We have already identified a number of natural splits in markets when addressing customer scenarios. These were described by personal characteristics of potential consumers, but in reality most marketing occurs between companies. **Organizational markets** comprise the entire manufacturing sector, government at all levels, hospitals, educational institutions, all retailers, and virtually any other organization that must purchase inventory, supplies, or services. A common term used to describe marketing focused on organizations is **institutional marketing**, and although we will devote only a few paragraphs to the topic, it is a field of study equal in magnitude to consumer marketing.

Fortunately, we can abbreviate the discussion with respect to marketing research because the activities described for consumer markets parallel those for institutional markets. We can simply make a mental substitution of organizations for human beings and review the preceding part of this chapter. Instead of individual customers, the market consists of other companies. The extent of the institutional market also is much larger than imagined once we begin to question how products are distributed. General Motors, for example, makes cars for individual consumers, yet GM rarely sells cars to individuals. The company sells to new-car dealers, other corporations (fleet sales), government agencies, rental-car companies, leasing companies, police departments, and overseas export agents. Moreover, many of these organizational clients buy through authorized GM dealers, not directly from GM.

Now consider who sells to General Motors. Like most other automotive manufacturers, GM "assembles" cars from thousands of parts and materials bought from hundreds of other companies. A partial list of those items includes steel, engine parts, paint, tires, fabrics, windows, electrical ignition assemblies, ball bearings, brakes, shock absorbers, and millions of nuts and bolts. Some suppliers are large corporations, such as steel mills, and others are small enterprises, such as glass fabricators that make rearview mirrors. In addition, GM also buys services, such as advertising, public relations, health care, legal services, auditing, and economic forecasting. The company buys equipment, instrumentation, and engineering; hires transportation, shipping, and warehousing; and contracts for management development, training, and telecommunications. The story is the same for other major companies.

Developing customer scenarios for institutional markets is a matter of identifying products and services needed by organizations. Demographics play a lesser role than other considerations. Material costs, inflation, cost of capital, technological changes, and competition are more important. For the entrepreneur, location decisions are just as important as in consumer markets, and new enterprises must consider more carefully issues such as economic infrastructure, transportation systems, and industry trends. Industry trends can include new manufacturing processes, employment profiles, markets for these products and services that prospective buyers will sell, and competition within the buyer's industry. Infrastructure issues also extend to the institutional buyer's location, and they include community support systems, economic development programs, and state and local tax policies.

Corporate purchasing managers are the organizational contacts for sales, and they continuously evaluate vendors to find new sources for materials and services. The single most important responsibility for purchasing managers is to improve their organizations' performance through effective procurement. They search for improved products, better services, more reliable equipment, less-costly materials, and innovative technologies. They buy to keep their firm supplied with state-of-the-art products, to ensure that their firms get the best *quality* products for their money, to improve their own products, to reduce costs, to ensure *on-time* delivery of materials, and to

PROFILE △

Austin–San Antonio

Market forecasting is directly related to location, and one location expected to be among the best through the end of this century is the Austin–San Antonio corridor. This 90-mile stretch of Texas landscape may become a technological metroplex to rival or exceed the California Silicon Valley. Population in the corridor is approaching 3 million, but the majority of the territory is undeveloped, with a "small city" ambience. It is not a sleeping giant, however, because growth in technology and high-tech manufacturing has been tremendous. During the 1980s the corridor experienced a sevenfold increase in research and development, currently topping $1.4 billion among companies that include IBM, General Electric, Rohr Industries, Dana Corporation, Motorola, and MCC (the largest electronics consortium in the United States), among others.

Success in the corridor rests on important characteristics of its regional infrastructure. It has excellent universities and technical colleges, superb air transport systems with easy access to major hubs in Dallas and Houston, rail and highway transport systems, and a doorway to shipping through the Gulf of Mexico. Banking and insurance industries are strong, illustrated by USAA, a $15 billion insurer headquartered in San Antonio. Corridor businesses also have established global linkage with Japan, Korea, Hong Kong, and Mexico through international joint ventures and domestically situated subsidiaries of major multinational corporations.

Source: Adapted from brochures from the San Antonio Convention and Visitors Bureau, January 1990.

---

stay ahead of their competitors when possible. If entrepreneurs can create products or services with advantages that fit one of these criteria, there are opportunities in institutional markets.

> ▶ **CHECKPOINT**
>
> Explain what is meant by institutional marketing.
>
> Describe how organizational consumers differ from personal consumers.

SOURCES OF MARKET INTELLIGENCE

Issues about research, for both consumer and institutional markets, have been briefly introduced in the previous sections, and they are far from complete. Entrepreneurs will become deeply involved in more intense research questions after they have identified a particular commercial opportunity. Consequently, they will not rely on a textbook, such as this, but will immerse themselves in information related to their proposed enterprise. We can suggest categories of information sources, but we cannot provide an encyclopedia for research.[20]

Existing Competitors

As noted earlier, existing competitors can be identified through telephone directories, associations, licensing agencies, advertisements, and public documents. Gathering data from manufacturers' brochures, public relations press releases, service catalogs, and other media is largely a matter of stepping into the role of a potential consumer. Start by saying, "Okay, I want this product, now how do I find it? Who will sell it to me?" Then go to the sources to find out whether it exists, what it costs, who will deliver it, how it is marketed, what warranties exist, and so on. Become an interested consumer.

Determine the availability and potential for substitutes. Shop potential competitors. Use their products when you can. Try out substitutes. Evaluate their distribution systems. Question how your approach to business can be better than that of your competitors by trying to understand why they are successful.

Trade Publications

There are hundreds of specialized publications, magazines, newsletters, catalogs, and brochures available in nearly every product line and service that exists. We mentioned earlier that even janitorial services have a trade publication. By reading popular articles, a great deal can be learned about trends, and there is nothing wrong with calling an editor to find out how to contact a source on a story. Among national publications to consider are *Inc.*, *The Entrepreneur*, *Business Week*, *Newsweek*, the *Wall Street Journal*, and *Fortune*. There are regional magazines and many that focus on specific cities. In most daily newspapers there are sections that enthusiastically publish stories on new products or interesting entrepreneurs. Call the editors and follow up leads on those articles. If you do not know what is available, call someone who works for a trade publication and find out.

Securities Analysts' Reports

Do not overlook investment firms. Reports compiled by investment analysts can provide extraordinary information. Securities brokers, investment bankers, private investment companies, and experienced private investors make it their business to know about other businesses. Most analysts have excellent market and financial research departments, and their reports are first-rate. Since many entrepreneurs will need equity financing, analysts might not only help with market data but provide access to investors.

Government Sources

The volumes of government reports and documents in the public sector would fill several dozen large rooms. One paragraph here will hardly suggest the possibilities. However, entrepreneurs should not overlook the expertise that is available to the public. For example, when we introduced the topic of patents and trademarks, we identified toll-free numbers to call, addresses, and the *Gazette*, a publication that provides a periodic list of all new patents. By calling information numbers at the Department of Commerce, one can find out how to contact appropriate agencies, small business offices, DOC libraries, and other government sources. The Small Business Administration stocks pamphlets, provides assistance, and guides entrepreneurs toward research reports. At state and local levels, economic development agencies and Chambers of Commerce are anxious to help new businesses. Also, most of these services are free.

Potential Customers

Perhaps the most important source of market information is developed by contacting potential customers. In fact, entrepreneurs *must* find a way to communicate with potential customers. Communication can take the form of informal discussions with selected end-users or sophisticated research efforts to reach significant numbers of potential customers.

Informal chats are easy to arrange, and in some instances they result in very good information. Recall that we profiled Stew Leonard in Chapter 2, as the world's largest independent grocer. One important dimension noted in his success was a weekly round-table discussion with customers selected at random in the store. Another example that comes to mind is a student who, as a senior doing research on desktop publishing, called editors at 20 textbook publishers to discuss the concept of subcontracting work at home. She had not intended to sell anything, but landed three contract offers and subsequently decided to start a business from her dormitory room.

Formal market research implies spending time and money to set up a model of investigation. One typical approach is to use a consumer survey based on a short questionnaire. The questionnaire can be mailed to sample groups, and the survey can be done inexpensively by purchasing mailing lists of potential customers. If there is a prototype product, it can be test-marketed. Most of us have been approached by someone offering samples of new products at supermarkets or trade shows, and we have all heard of "introductory offers" on consumer products. These are forms of professional market research that can be conducted by entrepreneurs, but if budgets permit, entrepreneurs should seek advice from professional market research firms rather than attempt such programs themselves.

Other Sources and Methods of Research

Many new products and services are introduced at trade shows. For example, computer trade shows, boat shows, home and garden shows, county fairs, and conventions

Exhibit 8-2 Small Business Networks: A Sample of Sources for Help

Association of Collegiate Entrepreneurs	Wichita, Kansas
Community Economic Development Clearinghouse	Columbia, Missouri
National Cooperative Business Assn.	Washington, D.C.
American Women's Economic Development Corporation	New York, New York
The Small Business Foundation of America	Boston, Massachusetts
Inventors Workshop International Education Foundation	Camarillo, California
Center for Neighborhood Technology	Chicago, Illinois
The National Direct Marketing Assn.	Washington, D.C.
The Small Business Service Bureau	Worcester, Massachusetts
American Entrepreneurs Association	Los Angeles, California
International Council for Small Business	Milwaukee, Wisconsin

offer opportunities for entrepreneurs to set up booths. Entrepreneurs also can set up panel studies by experts, arrange "phone-a-thons," set up test markets in shopping malls, and conduct interviews by hiring part-time people to do surveys. These research methods, however, require planning and expertise to assure valid results. One additional option is to seek help from university centers that have small-business-assistance programs. Often, these universities will assign student teams to conduct market research under the supervision of a knowledgeable professor. Finally, there are dozens of organizations called networks that publish market research or have access to experts to advise entrepreneurs. Some of these are listed in Exhibit 8-2.

> ▶ **CHECKPOINT**
>
> Describe how an entrepreneur might gather research from potential customers.
>
> Identify six sources of published information on consumers, markets, products, services, locations, and competitors.

COMPETITIVE ANALYSIS: RESEARCH AFTER START-UP

Assuming that an entrepreneur has successfully launched a new venture and satisfied the initial marketing questions, a natural tendency is to just "get on with it." Start selling and don't look back. That may work for a while—at least until a competitor suddenly passes by in high gear. Smart business means staying on top of the market, and this means continuous market research. However, there are several important differences between the pre-start-up planning analysis and the post-start-up competitive analysis. Ongoing market research is called *competitive analysis* because success often rests with relative strength of the enterprise compared with competitors.

Michael E. Porter of Harvard wrote a definitive book on competitive analysis

Chapter 8 *Marketing Research for New Ventures*   259

that many corporations rely on today.[21] A **competitive analysis** is essentially a structured method of examining an organization or industry in order to provide a clear understanding of the factors that affect a business. Porter's model is shown in Figure 8-5. He created the model, calling it the *five forces model of competition*, as a strategic management technique for established profit-seeking companies. It applies equally to entrepreneurial enterprises, not-for-profit organizations, and major corporations.

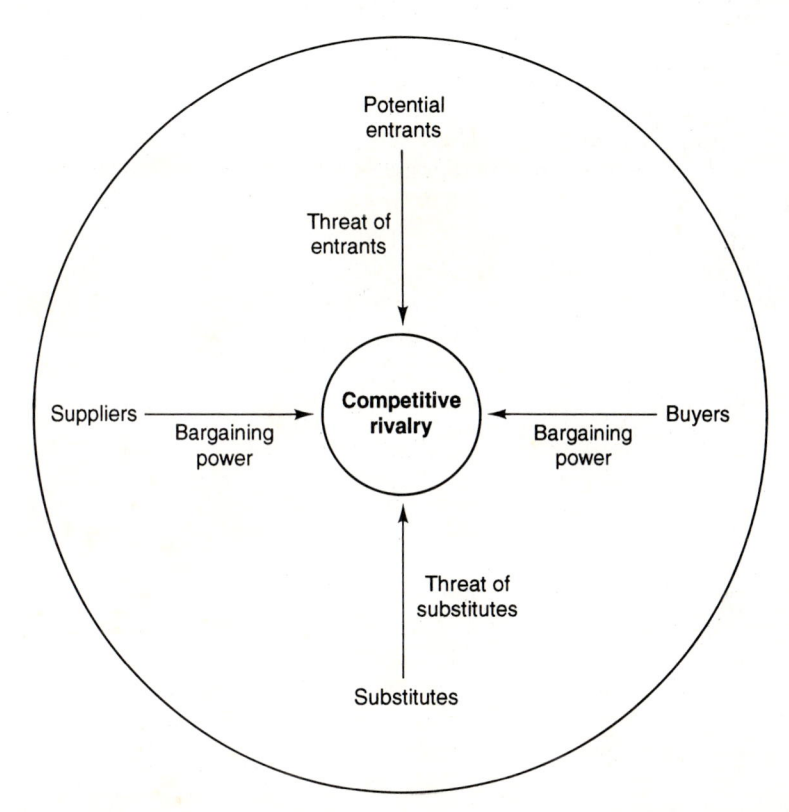

Potential entrants: Will competitors be able to enter the industry easily? Are there barriers to entry? How is the venture protected?

Power of suppliers: Will the venture be able to acquire supplies? Will large suppliers dictate prices and terms? How will the venture compete if supplies or materials are interrupted? Too costly?

Power of buyers: Will the venture be selling to several large and powerful buyers? If so, will they dictate prices and terms? How can the venture compete as a relatively smaller enterprise?

Threat of substitutes: Is the proposed product or service unique? If not, what substitutes exist? What substitute could arise? How can the venture protect its markets and customers?

Figure 8-5 **Factors to Consider in a Competitive Analysis.** (*Source*: Adapted with permission of The Free Press, a Division of Macmillan, Inc. from *Competitive Strategy: Techniques for Analyzing Industries and Competitors* by Michael E. Porter. Copyright © 1980 by The Free Press.)

The five forces are described with an emphasis on the new company in a start-up or early growth stage.

The Threat of Entry

A recently opened venture with an innovative product or service may enjoy a singular position in an industry; it may *be* the industry, as McDonald's was when first conceived. If the enterprise attracts customers, it will become well known and usually profitable. When such success is achieved by one company, others will be quick to follow. If those who follow are powerful, the new venture may collapse under the weight of competition. Therefore, the essential question is "What is the threat of other companies entering the industry?" There are several points to consider:

Capital Requirements. If the type of business requires a large initial capital investment, fewer entrepreneurs are likely to enter the industry. For example, manufacturing computers requires millions of dollars in technology, facilities, and skilled people, so although demand for computers may continue to be strong, few new companies are likely to emerge as successful competitors. Meanwhile, restaurants, dry cleaners, beauty salons, and desk-top publishers require little capital and minimum financing to enter business.

Economies of Scale. Closely related to capital requirements is the nature of a business that requires a large sales volume to offer a product or service at a competitive price. A good mechanic, for example, can build an automobile from commercially available parts, but to replicate a production sedan by Ford or Chrysler would cost four times the sticker price of a similar new car. The break-even volume on automobile manufacturing runs into the millions. In order to produce chewing gum, table salt, fertilizer, light bulbs, or newspapers, the sheer volume required is a barrier to entry. On the other hand, almost anyone can produce color-printed T-shirts that sell at competitive prices.

Experience. Cost advantages often are enjoyed by those who were first into a business or who have experience in the technology required. The first companies into biotechnology, such as Genentech and Biogen, established early leads in scientific knowledge, attracted important researchers, and stayed well ahead of new entrants.[22] Companies already experienced in electronics and the technology of business machinery—such as IBM, Hewlett-Packard, NCR, and Xerox—found it easier to enter the computer industry than others without similar experience.

Distribution Systems. Lacking established distribution systems or access to them is a major barrier to new entrants. There may be better potato chips than Frito-Lay, but no potato chip company has the same distribution capability or market network as Frito-Lay. Often, small retailers and personal service firms have tremendous potential but cannot secure a good location to compete. Location is the key to merchandising, and without access to customers, a store may simply never have a chance.

Differentiation. The extent to which an enterprise can establish a brand image, service, product innovation, or reputation describes its *differentiation* or *distinct competency*. By being distinct, an enterprise can command its market niche, discouraging new entrants. Mercedes-Benz, for example, has a distinct image and a small but secure market niche. Porsche AG has a similar profile but with an entirely different product and market niche. Neither make of car enjoys the same sales volume as American-made cars, but few companies can compete against Mercedes-Benz or Porsche in their particular markets. If entrepreneurs can establish unusual niches through differentiation, they may successfully barricade themselves against new competitors.

The Power of Buyers

Entrepreneurs may think in terms of retail customers, but often they are in the position of selling to organizations much larger than their own enterprises. Recall our discussion earlier about institutional markets. Many new ventures are positioned as suppliers, selling parts to larger companies for their manufacture or distribution. For example, Wal-Mart and K-Mart buy thousands of items every month, and in almost every instance, their vendors are smaller in sales and asset strength than either of the giant retailers. As a result, Wal-Mart and K-Mart have the power to dictate prices, terms of sales, and their preferences for packaging, product quality, and delivery.

When buyers are relatively large and command a high percentage of the smaller company's sales, the buyers wield negotiating power; entrepreneurs become price-takers and often rely for their very existence on one or two buyers. In this situation—assuming there are few major obstacles to entry—competitors can mount significant challenges by outbidding the entrepreneur for prime buyers. In addition, buyers may arbitrarily choose to create their own capability to supply the entrepreneur's products or services.

The Power of Suppliers

When entrepreneurs are buyers, they must be concerned with the market power of their suppliers. Most new ventures start small and consequently buy materials and supplies from larger companies. Therefore, suppliers control prices and terms of sale. This situation usually results in high costs to the new enterprise, and if the entrepreneur is in a low-margin business—such as fast-food retailing—the market leverage created by a powerful supplier can dictate success or failure.

Supplier power is likely to be high when there are only a few suppliers giving an entrepreneur few options to shop for inventory. In some instances, an entrepreneur may rely on specific brand items supplied by larger firms, putting the entrepreneur at the mercy of its supplier. Every microcomputer manufacturer, for example, relies on particular operating systems and branded software, and to switch to new systems or software could be difficult. On the other hand, a few successful entrepreneurs have put themselves in the position of powerful suppliers by creating proprietary systems and software. Microsoft created MS-DOS operating systems (and an extensive line of software) used by a majority of the largest computer manufacturers. Even as a small enterprise, Microsoft commanded the market among huge corporations.[23]

The Threat of Substitutes

A competitive analysis conducted after a company is established poses the same questions as in the pre-start-up planning stage. Recall that we discussed the importance of evaluating *direct* and *indirect* substitutes. A direct substitute is one that performs the same service or has exchangeable attributes with respect to the entrepreneur's business. Seafood can be substituted for beef; noodles can be substituted for potatoes; and aluminum and steel can be exchanged in a variety of manufactured products. Indirect substitutes exist as choices between unlike products or services when buyers make allocation decisions. For example, if a company is weighing its choices between buying new equipment and investing in real estate, then an entrepreneur trying to make an equipment sale is actually competing against a real estate opportunity.

Entrepreneurs with special-use products, such as medical equipment, have few direct or indirect substitutes to consider. Those in commodity goods, such as soft drinks, must consider many direct substitutes but few indirect ones because the consumer rarely makes a rational choice among dissimilar expenditures. Entrepreneurs in higher-priced durable goods, such as VCRs or furniture, have tremendous competition from direct and indirect substitutes. An interesting trade-off has begun to occur along with social changes in dual-career families. With increasing need for two incomes, and with the increase of women established in careers, *time* has become an exchangeable commodity. Working couples simply put greater value on their limited time, and they are willing to buy back some of it by paying for services they would normally perform. The accompanying profile suggests the growing importance of time.

Competitive Rivalry

The extent to which an enterprise faces competitive rivalry is partially the result of a combined effect of the other four forces. Rivalry also depends on the nature of the industry, such as trends toward new technology, industry growth potential, and intensity of competition among major market players. If all competitors are roughly the same size (either small or large), then the industry will be sensitive to prices and advertising, but relatively insensitive to outsiders. If an industry has companies of various sizes with differentiated products, then product attributes, prices, promotions, and distribution methods will result in market confusion and instability; both manufacturers and their customers will face a chaotic industry. The PC industry, for example, consists of large domestic manufacturers, smaller specialized firms, and a wide range of foreign producers who import clones.

PROFILE △

Time—Currency of the Future

As the last decade of the 20th century passes, American consumers want more *time*. Most have adequate money, and most have careers, but what they lack is adequate time to spend money or pursue interests beyond their careers. Consumers are willing to trade hard cash for time through conveniences, better services, and ready-to-eat, ready-to-use products. This demand is partially the result of an affluent, mobile society and partially the result of dual-career families with fewer children who live in condominiums, town houses, and urban apartments. Few spouses have time to shop for groceries, run errands, linger in mall stores, service their cars, do laundry, or clean their houses.

Time pressure represents a major shift in consumer buying habits and perceptions of the value of shopping. The time crunch became serious toward the end of the 1980s, and entrepreneurs rose to the challenge with house-cleaning services, rapid car service franchises, freezer-to-microwave foods, and a variety of other time-saving devices and services. Demographic forecasts and market research indicate that the time crunch will reach a crisis stage before the year 2000. Entrepreneurial opportunities likely will grow in direct proportion.

Source: Anne B. Fisher, "What Consumers Want in the 1990s," *Fortune*, January 29, 1990, pp. 48–52.

> ▶ **CHECKPOINT**
>
> Identify the five forces and explain how they can affect an entrepreneurial venture.
>
> Discuss how a competitive analysis can be adapted for a pre-start-up planning process and market research after the venture exists.

IMPLICATIONS OF MARKET RESEARCH AND COMPETITIVE ANALYSES

Once an enterprise has become established, the question is no longer whether the product or service is feasible, but whether the enterprise can reach its growth potential and compete effectively. Entrepreneurs will have made a number of pre-start-up assumptions about their businesses, and these will be evaluated in light of feedback during actual operations. The framework of a competitive analysis can be useful at any stage of a new venture, but clearly its value will be greatest shortly after the venture opens for business. That is the critical period when pre-start-up assumptions may be found faulty through the stark reality of actually competing for business.

During the competitive analysis, the fundamental market research questions should be reviewed. Specifically, entrepreneurs will want to know if the assumed customer scenario is accurate. Given early assumptions about who would buy, it is essential to evaluate actual sales to validate those assumptions, and there may be surprises. A women's fashion store geared to single adults might attract a significant number of young teenagers. A bicycle shop positioned to sell to college students might find that adult "yuppies" comprise a majority of customers. A frozen yogurt shop situated to sell to youthful customers might find that it attracts long lines of middle-aged, weight-conscious women.

Other assumptions about pricing, quality image, product utilization, warranties, promotions, styles, packaging, and delivery systems will also be questioned. Entrepreneurs often do not articulate these questions consciously, but they certainly consider them intuitively. It is better to raise the issues to a conscious level and use results from early sales efforts to analyze company strategies. For example, tracking sales from cash register receipts and examining sales patterns will reveal good days, bad days, busy hours, slow hours, and effects of special promotions. Tracking service calls and investigating returns will tell entrepreneurs a lot about perceived product quality and reliability. Conducting informal surveys among customers will often help to fine-tune marketing efforts. Some firms offer discounts to customers who volunteer to fill out brief questionnaires, providing consumer insights.

Competitors will not be idle bystanders when a new firm opens with lower prices or more aggressive promotions. If existing firms recognize the threat of a new enterprise, they tend to become price-aggressive, and unless the entrepreneur has staying power, the competition will win this battle.[24] There are two reasons for this advantage. First, established firms are more likely than new ventures to have resources necessary to stay in low-margin markets during a price war. Second, established firms already have clients and can use "hold and maintain" tactics while the entrepreneur must strive to gain initial customers.

Competitors may also react by promoting their image. If an established firm has had a good relationship with customers and reasonable quality, the new enterprise is forced to prove that its products or services are superior. Of course, these points assume that competitors exist and that all competitors are after a part of the same market. That is a fair assumption in most instances. For those innovative enterprises without competitors, the challenge is to be alert to new firms that are likely to follow with similar products or services. When these competitors emerge, it is important to evaluate them. Entrepreneurs will ask the *same questions* about competitors as they ask about their own businesses. Who are their customers? What are their products? How do they price? What is their quality image? How do they distribute? How effective is their promotion? What are their distinctive competencies? How strong are their resources?

If entrepreneurs are selling to major firms, it means that their customers have purchasing power to buy in global markets. Aside from local competitors, then, the entrepreneur must stay abreast of national trends in technology, imported products, and threats from other entrepreneurs. This is the essence of the free-enterprise system, and it is the pattern of American commerce. Being part of that picture requires players to understand how it works and accept the responsibility of continuous attention to innovation.[25]

Competitive analysis also includes evaluating management. Competitors often have *good managers* and adaptable organizations. Well-managed companies are more likely to attract the best salespersons, more-innovative engineers, and more-motivated workers. If entrepreneurs cannot compete effectively for human resources, they are unlikely to establish long-term markets. The previous chapter introduced these considerations, and they cannot be overemphasized as part of a thorough competitive analysis.

In conclusion, if entrepreneurs set about doing marketing research with a strong interest in getting answers to their questions, they will reduce the risk of early failure. If they go about this task frivolously, they are leaving their future to fate and they might as well roll dice with their resources.

▶ **CHECKPOINT**

Describe major assumptions that are made in pre-start-up plans and explain how they may found faulty after a venture becomes operative.

Explain the logic for continuous research into competitors' potential reactions and their management characteristics.

SYNOPSIS FOR LEARNING

1. *Describe the marketing concept and its relevance to new ventures.*

In essence, the marketing concept places the consumer at the focus of business activity so that decisions are made to provide the best value to consumers consistent with the overall interests of the company and its constituents. The entrepreneur makes a firm commitment to satisfy customers with useful and safe products, sold at good value, and supported through effective service. This strategy also involves developing consumers for the long-term success of the organization, not merely striving for maximum short-term sales or profits. From this viewpoint, marketing becomes only one of many essential functions to integrate with other responsibilities without disproportionate emphasis on any one activity.

2. *Explain marketing research in terms of pre-start-up planning.*

Questions to answer through marketing research before a new venture is begun form the basis for planning resources, operations, sales activities, human-resource staffing, leadership requirements, and finances. Entrepreneurs must understand who their customers are and develop a customer scenario together with demand characteristics of their markets. A customer scenario will include personal and demographic characteristics of consumers now and in the future. Entrepreneurs must also be able to describe their market size, expected changes in markets, and their particular niches (i.e., market segments). They also must be able to identify market and industry characteristics, who their competitors are likely to be, what substitutes are available, and threats (or opportunities) arising from their competitive position. In addition, they must be able to describe their supply sources and distribution systems and, using this vast array of information, produce a sales forecast that makes sense.

3. *Describe primary sources of market research information.*

Marketing intelligence can come from any person or event that influences sales or customers. There are, however, primary sources that all entrepreneurs should study. Existing competitors must be researched, yielding comparable data that help answer questions about costs of getting into business and the structure of the industry. Trade publications provide valuable insights into markets, technology, customers, changes in the industry, and management. Other printed information includes government documents, securities analysts' reports, financial news, economic forecasts, and SBA publications. Potential customers also can be surveyed or interviewed, introduced to the venture through market tests, and queried through awareness groups. Among other sources are industry and trade seminars, conventions, meetings, networks, and university centers. Potential investors often have excellent sources of information, and if they are attracted to the venture, they can provide a great deal of market intelligence.

4. *Describe the five forces of a competitive analysis.*

Porter's model of competitive analysis includes four primary forces that, together with other considerations, comprise the fifth force. The first is *threat of entry*, which is influenced by capital needed to enter business, required economies of scale, degree of product or service differentiation, expertise or experience of competitors, and proprietary position, if any, of an enterprise. The second force is *buyers' power*, which relates to the size and market leverage a buyer has to dictate prices or control terms of sales. Entrepreneurs usually find themselves selling to larger enterprises, and until they have developed a sizeable clientele, they are relatively weak in their ability to negotiate prices or terms. The third force is *suppliers' power*, which relates to vendors who provide goods and services. Because new ventures start small and must buy inventory, materials, and services from established companies, they will be at a disadvantage until they have become important to their vendors. The fourth force is *threat of substitutes*. There are direct substitutes, such as different sources of food, and indirect substitutes, such as choosing between an investment or buying an automobile. The fifth force, affected by the previous four, is the *extent of competitive rivalry*. This relates to the nature of an industry, such as one stabilized with a few close competitors or one that is dynamic with rapid changes in technology. Competitive rivalry also relates to the intensity between competitors, such as sensitivity to prices that could trigger price wars.

5. *Discuss the major implications of market research for entrepreneurs.*

Market research is a fundamental responsibility for planning a new venture, and having good information during the pre-start-up planning stage cannot be overemphasized. Entrepreneurs must establish how they will compete in clearly defined markets. The major implication of doing market research is to establish that demand exists for a product or service, and part of this task is to articulate the assumptions related to demand such as pricing, quality, distribution, and the distinct competency of a venture. A thorough competitive analysis will result in an understanding of the venture, its strengths and weaknesses, and both the threats it may face and opportunities that may arise. As long as entrepreneurs are in business, market research is a pervasive and important responsibility.

NOTES

1. Fred J. Borch, "The Marketing Philosophy as a Way of Business Life," in *The Marketing Concept: Its Meaning to Management* (New York: American Management Association, 1957), p. 41.

2. Kenneth W. Olm and George G. Eddy, *Entrepreneurship and Venture Management: Text and Cases*, (Columbus, OH: Charles E. Merrill, 1985), p. 191.

3. Stephen MacDonald, "When Product Design Carries a Message," *Wall Street Journal*, Wednesday, March 23, 1988, p. 29.

4. William G. Zikmund, *Exploring Marketing Research*, 2nd ed. (New York: Dryden Press, 1986), pp. 10–11.

5. "Investigating the Collapse of W. T. Grant," *Business Week*, July 19, 1976, p. 61.

6. Joseph P. Kahn, "Heartbreak Hill," *Inc.*, April 1988, pp. 68–78.

7. Zikmund, *Exploring Marketing Research*, p. 8.

8. William M. Pride and O. C. Ferrell, *Marketing: Basic Concepts and Decisions*, 5th ed. (Boston: Houghton Mifflin, 1987), pp. 77–83, 116–117.

9. "Marketing's New Look," *Business Week*, November 2, 1987, pp. 64–69.

10. "Let's Change the Immigration Law—Now," *Fortune*, January 29, 1990. Also see Anne B. Fisher, "What Consumers Want in the 1990s," *Fortune*, January 29, 1990, pp. 48–52.

11. Ron Christy and Billy M. Jones, *The Complete Information Bank for Entrepreneurs and Small Business Management* (New York: American Management Association, 1988).

12. "The Franchisor 100," *Venture*, November 1987, pp. 42–48. Also see "The Franchise Fast-Track," *Venture*, March 1988, pp. 44–47.

13. Al Ries and Jack Trout, *Marketing Warfare* (New York: McGraw-Hill, 1986), pp. 184–185.

14. "Sneakers That Don't Specialize," *Business Week*, June 6, 1988, p. 146.

15. Arthur Lipper III, *Venture's Guide to Investing in Private Companies* (Homewood, IL: Dow Jones–Irwin, 1984), pp. 115–117.

16. Ann Hughey, "Sales of Home Movie Equipment Falling as Firms Abandon Market, Video Grows," *Wall Street Journal*, March 17, 1982, p. 25.

17. Brett Kingstone, *The Dynamos: Who Are They, Anyway?* (New York: John Wiley & Sons, 1987), pp. 129–134. Also see "The ACE 100—1989," *ACE News*, Wichita State University, March 1989, p. 1.

18. Kenneth G. Hardy and Allan J. Magrath, *Marketing Channel Management: Strategic Planning and Tactics* (Glenview, IL: Scott, Foresman, 1988), pp. 3–11. Also see Eric N. Berkowitz, Roger A. Kerin, and William Rudelius, *Marketing*, 2nd ed. (Homewood, IL: Richard D. Irwin, 1989), pp. 171–174.

19. Donald D. Boroian and Patrick J. Boroian, *The Franchise Advantage: Make It Work for You!* (Schaumburg, IL: National BestSeller, 1987), pp. 28–34.

20. William G. Zikmund, *Exploring Marketing Research*, particularly Chapters 4 and 5 on exploratory research and secondary research. Also see Christy and Jones, *The Complete Information Bank*, particularly Chapter 3 on periodicals and Chapter 8 on government information.

21. Michael E. Porter, *Competitive Strategy: Techniques for Analyzing Industries and Competitors* (New York: Free Press, 1980).

22. "Clouds Gather over the Biotech Industry," *Wall Street Journal*, January 30, 1989, p. B1.

23. Julianne Slovak, "The Billionaires," *Fortune*, September 11, 1989, p. 66.

24. George McKinney and Marie McKinney, "Forget the Corporate Umbrella—Entrepreneurs Shine in the Rain," *Sloan Management Review*, Vol. 30, No. 4 (Summer 1989), pp. 77–82.

25. Arvind V. Phatak, *International Dimensions of Management*, 2nd ed. (Boston: PWS-Kent, 1989), pp. 83–84.

CASE 8-1

The Book Nook

Joyce Haines and Susan Pierce, co-owners of the Book Nook, had just finished stocking shelves with textbooks for the next school term at James Madison University. It was the middle of August, and as they looked at their jam-packed little store, Haines turned to Pierce and made a halfhearted prediction: "Susan, in 30 days we'll be celebrating, but by Christmas we'll be broke again."

"That's a cheery outlook," Pierce replied, "but I know what you mean. We have to get more students in here during the semester . . . just making the big bucks when classes start won't work."

Haines and Pierce had opened the Book Nook one year earlier on the well-founded premise that students would buy their textbooks off campus if prices were lower than the campus bookstore's. As recent graduates, the founders had a good idea of prices charged on campus, and students were forever complaining of "rip-off" prices on textbooks. The campus store was similar to other campus stores, charging nearly 40 percent premiums on new textbooks and 50 percent or more on used books.

When the Book Nook first opened, Haines and Pierce had stocked $25,000 in used textbooks, most of them purchased through an end-of-semester advertising blitz in the student newspaper. They set prices several dollars below campus prices, and when the new semester opened, they had students lined up for a block to buy texts. That was the previous September, and the new owners had been exuberant, but then October and November were what Joyce called "cobweb months" when the two partners had little else to do than dust shelves. In December they used their profits to restock for the spring semester and also had a good Christmas season by selling gift items. Then, in spring, they added sorority and fraternity items ranging from embossed stationery to gag gifts. Several student clubs came to them in February and March with fund-raising ideas, and through consignments, the store made enough to pay bills. Summer school sales had been a disaster, and in order to stock for the current year, Haines had gotten a loan from her father.

Thinking about the situation, the two partners sat staring at their stacks of books and wondered how to survive this year. The preceding April, Haines had considered putting in several photocopy machines to attract more students, but Pierce had argued against it because close to campus there was a Kinko's, and in town there was a Kwik Kopy, both stores very popular. Instead, Pierce wanted to stock a broad range of books to target the local community rather than just students. Haines had argued that the locals would not mix with students, and the two merchandise lines would be different.

The physical location of the business was also an issue. The store was about a half mile from the JMU campus in the nearest shopping center. They had good access from the main road to campus and ample parking. The store was about 1,200 square feet and nicely appointed. McDonald's, Wendy's, Burger King, and Pizza Hut were on the road facing the shopping center, so the store had high visibility for students and community residents. Kinko's was on the other side of campus, and although Kwik Kopy was nearby, it had a less prominent location.

The JMU student population was slightly over 10,000, and most students came from higher-income families in Northern Virginia. The local population was about 80,000, including county residents who shopped in the city, and there was another private college nearby and a community college ten miles away. Haines felt these markets had potential for expanding into the photocopy business.

"Why," she asked, "won't the copy center idea work? Susan, I just know we could do a good business in photocopies. We could set up binding, term paper assistance, lettering, and maybe even color copying if the equipment's not too expensive. Nobody around here does color work."

"What will that get us?" Pierce asked. "If equipment costs us $1,000 a month, we'd have to make 100,000 copies a month to break even. Every student at JMU would have to make 10 copies a month. But if you're serious, let's do a survey, you know, hire a student to do a questionnaire to check it out."

"You don't sound excited," Haines said frowning. "Have you got a better idea?"

"Actually, I've been thinking about local schools," Pierce said. "We have eight high schools in the area and about 20 elementary schools. My sister-in-law who teaches fourth grade told me that throughout the year all teachers buy tests, exercises, quizzes, and so on. They have to order all these things through catalogs, and they never have the chance to look at them firsthand before they order. It's all mail order with no service, and teachers have budgets to spend several hundred dollars each year. Now the game is classroom software, and no one is addressing that market. We could stock samples and catalogs here, and maybe even go out to schools to help teachers select materials."

CASE QUESTIONS

1. If Haines and Pierce decide to investigate the photocopy option, what questions will they have to answer to determine whether it is worthwhile?
2. If they decide to research the market for teaching materials, what data on markets and merchandise will they need to have?
3. Based on serving university students, what merchandise mix might be appropriate to compete successfully? Explore other options for the store and customer groups they might address.

CASE 8-2

Get a "Jolt" out of Life

Just as Coca-Cola and Pepsi were launching their new low-caffeine cola drinks to fire yet another salvo at each other, "Jolt" came along and grabbed nearly 5 percent of the giants' markets. These events took place in 1986, when a health-conscious America was clamoring for low everything in their refreshments, yet Jolt cola was advertised as having "all the sugar and twice the caffeine" needed to give you a blast with every sip. Johnny Carson and David Letterman put Jolt into their punchlines, and health-conscious consumer groups boycotted the new drink, asking for a federal investigation to see whether caffeine levels were legal.

Jolt was founded in Rochester, New York, by Joseph Rapp and his 27-year-old son as an alternative to the "wimpy-tasting colas" on the market. They used natural cane sugar and loaded their cola drink with caffeine at a level twice as high as either Coke or Pepsi (5.9 mg per ounce, just under the federal limits of 6 mg per ounce). The following year, Rapp and son introduced a low-calorie alternative with NutraSweet, but with the same caffeine level as the original formula.

Although most people believed Jolt would be a short-lived fad, it has flourished. Reaching supermarket shelves and deli coolers, Jolt has national distribution, and the upstart entrepreneurs are laughing all the way to the bank. Jolt has less caffeine than regular coffee, yet it has the eye-opening zing to be a substitute. Non-coffee-drinking students find Jolt an easy way to get rolling in the morning or to energize for late-night studying.

Whether a fad or the real thing, Jolt has made it to the big time, competing with the giants. Meanwhile, Coke and Pepsi slug it out for market share, each controlling significant resources in distribution markets, vying for preferential contracts among the leading makers of synthetic sweeteners, and flexing their marketing muscle to gain shelf-space advantages. Both companies have the leverage to negotiate with retailers for prime shelf space, and both have the purchasing power to control their supply costs. Both also have huge financial reserves capable of sustaining a cola marketing war. Jolt is viewed like a mosquito that might get swatted if it continues to buzz around the big guys. On the other hand, Jolt's entrepreneurs are not unusually concerned—a little bite here and there in a $20 billion market adds up.

CASE QUESTIONS

1. Analyze the case in terms of Porter's model of competitive strategy, specifically addressing the threats of new entrants and substitutes.
2. Describe Jolt's position with respect to its suppliers. Is the company vulnerable to its buyers?
3. How would you describe Jolt's competitive position with respect to the major cola companies? How could Jolt compete for customers?

Sources: "New Markets Give Share to Jolt," *Beverage Industry*, January 1987, p. 12. Also "Coke vs. Pepsi: Cola War Marches On," *Wall Street Journal*, June 3, 1987, p. 23.

Chapter 9

Marketing: Functions and Strategies

OBJECTIVES

1. Identify and describe the marketing functions that must be addressed by all new ventures.
2. Describe an expanded view of a company's "product."
3. Explain how distribution is part of marketing infrastructure.
4. Identify and discuss the categories of promotions.
5. Address the concept of pricing with respect to new ventures.
6. Describe the primary growth strategies employed by entrepreneurs.
7. Explain the major elements of a marketing plan.

Although market research often points the way toward new opportunities, it is a strong marketing strategy that leads to success. Obviously, there are many other things to do in a new venture, such as setting up the business, acquiring inventory, staffing the enterprise, and obtaining financial resources. Marketing activities, however, mobilize an enterprise, changing it from an elegant idea to a viable business.

This change takes place through a conscious effort to solidify an entrepreneur's ideas into a marketing plan with a clear marketing strategy. The plan must be in place prior to start-up, but it is subject to change as competition occurs and the company grows. If market research is accomplished with care, information will be at hand for making good marketing decisions. This chapter builds on marketing research, described in the previous chapter, to introduce marketing responsibilities and marketing strategies specific to new ventures.

FUNDAMENTALS OF MARKETING

Marketing consists of a multitude of activities that include decisions about the company's products or services, pricing policies, promotions, and methods of distribution. The ultimate goal is to facilitate exchanges between an enterprise and its customers. This exchange relationship exists as one party becomes willing to "give something of value" to "receive something of value" from the other party. Marketing is the process of conceiving that exchange, and then accomplishing the tasks necessary to deliver the goods or services in a manner that satisfies customers and meets business objectives.[1]

Marketing Functions

Marketing is explained in terms of four general activities, and although most business students have studied these before, they are important to emphasize because they capture the essence of marketing. The four activities concern decisions about the firm's *product*, its *price*, methods of *promotion*, and how products are *distributed*.[2] Brief definitions of these activities are as follows:

> *Product*: Used as a catchall term, **product** includes physical objects or services being sold, together with packaging, image, brand name, and warranty. In addition, a product includes physical attributes that influence consumers' perceptions, such as colors, shapes, sizes, and materials. A product can also relate to the "business concept," such as fast-food franchising.
>
> *Price*: From a consumer's viewpoint, **price** is the monetary unit required for a purchase, and from an entrepreneur's viewpoint, it is the unit of income. Prices communicate information about value, image, and competition, and they influence decisions about distribution, market segmentation, product characteristics, and related services. Pricing policies are key factors in forecasting. In turn, all these factors influence pricing decisions. For example, prices convey something about image, but the image a store has will convey something about its prices.
>
> *Promotion*: The act of communication that provides consumers with information about a company's products, its services, or the venture itself is **promotion**, and it is through promotional activities that the venture attracts consumers. They include advertising, personal selling, direct marketing, public relations, and other creative methods of bringing buyers and sellers together.
>
> *Distribution*: Often referred to as the *placement* function, **distribution** is concerned with how products or services are made available to customers. Distribution can mean the physical channels of transporting products from manufacturers to end users, warehousing, wholesaling, and retailing. It can also relate to marketing systems such as catalogs, telemarketing, franchising, and computer-based network markets.

Marketing Strategy

A **marketing strategy** is a consciously formulated plan that describes how the new venture will compete. It focuses the enterprise on a target market to fill a gap or create a niche. A well-articulated marketing strategy provides guidelines for the entrepreneur concerning *expected results*, *allocation of resources*, *responsibilities for marketing*, and *ways in which the enterprise will be controlled*.[3] "Expected results" are expressed in sales forecasts and operating budgets, but more important, they constitute the entrepreneur's *strategic marketing objectives*. An "allocation of resources" reflects what a firm has to use and the tactics employed to achieve results. "Responsibilities" are those activities required to implement a marketing plan. "Control" issues concern methods of feedback necessary to track performance. Feedback provides planning information for future decisions. The strategic marketing process is shown in Figure 9-1 as it relates to the entrepreneur's overall strategic objectives.

The Marketing Plan

A **marketing plan** solidifies the marketing strategy by defining customers, sales forecasts, and marketing objectives. Consequently, the marketing plan synthesizes market research and the entrepreneur's strategy into a blueprint for action. The plan is implemented through a **marketing program**, which addresses the marketing activities summarized earlier—decisions regarding product or service characteristics, pricing, promotional activities, and methods of distribution.[4]

The following passages will describe individual marketing activities with particular attention to new ventures. They are introduced to pave the way for describing marketing strategies and the marketing plan. We will address the four activities in

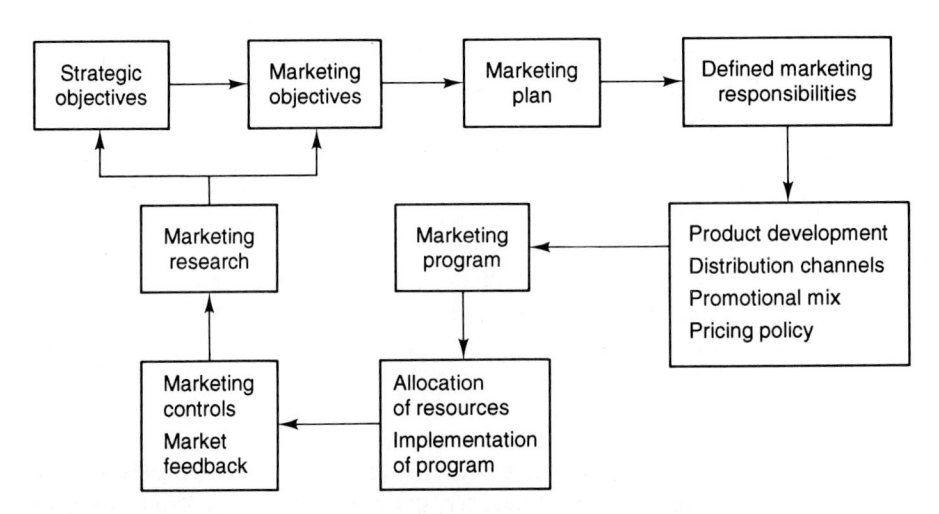

Figure 9-1 **Elements in Marketing Strategy**

the sequence of *product*, *distribution*, *promotion*, and *price* as a logical way in which entrepreneurs address market planning decisions.

> ▶ **CHECKPOINT**
>
> Describe the primary functions of marketing and responsibilities for marketing decisions.
>
> Define marketing strategy and the elements of the strategic process.
>
> Explain how marketing plans and strategies are interrelated.

PRODUCT CONCEPTS

A product is anything tangible or intangible, favorable or unfavorable, that a consumer attributes to a purchase.[5] This includes the form, function, psychological utility, and benefits, real or perceived, in products and services. Marketing niches are developed around these "packages" of attributes. It is important to recognize these attributes and the ways in which consumers perceive them within two broad classifications: *consumer goods* and *industrial goods*.[6]

Consumer Goods

Consumer goods are bought by individuals for personal use, and often consumers will be encouraged by distribution methods that make purchasing convenient and enjoyable. They will want products packaged, formed, colored, and priced to reinforce their individual perceptions of value. Consumer behavior is predicated primarily on the type of product being sold, but the total package of product attributes determines consumer perceptions. This point is illustrated in the profile on Singapore Airlines, an organization that sells passengers on the idea of luxury services, not merely air travel. It is useful to further differentiate of products as *convenience*, *shopping*, or *specialty* goods. We address each of these separately.

Convenience Products. Well-understood items that most buyers need little information about are known as *convenience products*. They are *commodities* in the sense that there are many substitutes, prices are usually undifferentiated, and little time is spent by consumers to do comparison shopping. Examples include soft drinks, gasoline, potato chips, toothpaste, chewing gum, and cereals. *Brand* recognition is often the only way to differentiate commodities from one another, so manufacturers such as Procter & Gamble will spend a great deal of money on national advertising, hammering home the brand image. Yet at the retail level, very little promotional effort will be exerted, and prices among competing brands will be similar.

PROFILE △

The Product Is an Experience

A good product includes a lot more than its function. Even the best port wine can be enhanced by its package and served in a way to make it an experience, not just another refreshment. That is the message conveyed by Singapore Airlines when it advertises "The Art of Decanting a Fine Old Port," describing a 20-year-old premium port wine presented to first-class passengers in a hand-cut crystal decanter, poured into a crystal glass, and served on an elegant tray. Passengers may consume a fine port, but they are buying an experience.

Source: Singapore Airlines advertising.

Entrepreneurs probably have few opportunities to introduce products in commodity markets. Convenience goods have low margins and are distributed by major competitors in well-established markets. Nevertheless, there are many aspiring entrepreneurs who try to enter convenience markets with new products. Generally they have no idea of the competition and fail quickly. Those few who succeed usually have a specialized niche—a segment of consumers who look for something different in their soaps, toothpastes, and soft drinks.

For example, Soho all-natural sodas and New York Seltzer soft drinks were established through carefully selected health food stores and delicatessens. They do not compete with Coca-Cola or Pepsi, but by being unusual soft drinks, they have attracted a select clientele. Both soft drinks occasionally can be found in stores alongside commodity drinks, but they are more often found in specialty stores and delis. Other similar products occasionally make a dent in commodity markets, such as a new beer line called Chic and Chic Lite. These two brews were launched in 1985, and by early 1988 they accounted for more than $1.1 million in sales for Locon, Inc., a Massachusetts venture that also markets wine coolers. Soho soft drinks and New York Seltzer are sold to health-conscious consumers, and the beer and wine products are marketed to women through selected liquor stores and restaurants.[7]

Shopping Products. Items that engage a consumer's mind in active planning are called *shopping products*. Consumers will consciously think about their purchases. They will make comparisons, consult consumer buying guides, and be significantly influenced by promotions. Shopping products include VCRs, home appliances, microcomputers, furniture, clothing, and sports equipment. Major purchases such as automobiles and houses also fall into this category. Product features become extremely important to consumers, but quite often prices are not directly comparable to those of substitutes. Although there may be many choices, (e.g., many brands of VCRs),

PROFILE △

Selling Causes and Cosmetics

The London-based Body Shop, with 420 stores in 38 countries, has opened 14 stores in the United States, becoming one of the most promising enterprises for the 1990s. The Body Shop, born as a dream of a dedicated group of environmental activists less than 13 years ago, struggled for recognition during its early years. That struggle took place before consumers became sensitive to environmental issues. Now, commodities that seldom got a second glance from consumers—toothpaste, soap, cosmetics, laundry detergents, hair sprays, and deodorants—are under close scrutiny. Consumers read labels before they buy, and what they want is clear: products that are environmentally safe. The Body Shop provides these commodities, perhaps better than anyone else. Products are even packed in degradable bags. Commodities therefore may be finding new lives as "specialty items" in the coming decade, and if the Body Shop is a sign of our times, new marketing opportunities are transforming consumer merchandising.

Source: "Leading the Crusade into Consumer Marketing," *Fortune International*, February 12, 1990, p. 29.

---

most consumers do not view shopping goods as having undifferentiated substitutes. Product quality, reliability, service after sale, warranties, access to repair facilities, reputation of retailers, credit availability, packaging, and many other factors augment the product's image in addition to its function.

Shopping products tend to have larger margins and are sold through fewer outlets than convenience goods. Larger margins help offset lower sales volumes and heavier expenses for promotions, and it is in this category of products that entrepreneurs have been most successful because consumers react to unusual products or those distributed and promoted in unusual ways. When the microcomputer market began to "shake out," for example, it was because consumers became interested in clones, PCs with unusual attributes or software, and computers with price advantages.

Specialty Products. Items with unique characteristics that few consumers consider buying—or that consumers consider buying only rarely—are considered *specialty products*. A luxury car, an expensive fur coat, or a private airplane will be beyond most of our means, but when consumers decide to buy one of these items, they will search intensely to locate a satisfactory seller. Consumers do not typically engage in comparative shopping or scan advertisements for good prices. They are concerned with quality. Substitutes will not do, and consumers expect exquisite service. From the entrepreneur's viewpoint, inventory is expensive and sold with very high margins, and those who can establish specialty niches do extremely well. Top-notch restaurants, world-class vacation resorts, Madison Avenue advertising firms, prominent art and antique dealers, luxury condominium developers, and investment jewelers are among those in specialty markets. Donald Trump built his real estate empire on the concept of creating a quality image with exquisite services for a narrow range of wealthy buyers, and although he has had trouble managing his personal aspirations, his concept of renovating exclusive New York properties has proved to be a sound business.[8]

A specialty product, however, is often a matter of perception; it is viewed relative to consumer incomes and their patterns of purchasing. A world-class vacation, for instance, may be a once-in-a-lifetime event for most of us, but for the "rich and famous," it is a seasonal getaway. Therefore, one's target market only partially defines the product. If an entrepreneur establishes a women's clothing boutique in an upper-middle-income neighborhood, it may not attract those who shop Georgio's in Beverly Hills, but wage earners who splurge on fashionable attire will want to savor the experience.

Other Consumer Products. Products not easily classified into one of the three categories include those things that are often essential but do not constitute a motivated purchasing effort by consumers. For example, eventually most of us will need the services of mortuaries. We will buy caskets, urns, cemetery plots, or perhaps some unusual program, such as a burial at sea. We try to avoid these purchases, just as we avoid purchasing insurance, emergency road repair services, and estate planning services. There are other products that may not be essential, depending on one's viewpoint, yet fall into a similar "avoidance" pattern for purchasing. These include, for example, encyclopedias, investment seminars, and preventive dentistry.

Some of these products or services are not marketed; there is little price competition; and their enterprises exist with little or no advertising. Mortuary services are examples. At the other extreme, some require aggressive promotion and are price-sensitive. Life insurance policies are examples. Differences between all types of consumer goods are summarized in Figure 9-2.

Convenience	Shopping	Speciality	Other
Commodities or common services; low margins and many competitors: toothpaste, soap, cereals, soups	Major items or services with higher margins and competitors; differentiated products and services: furniture, VCRs, microcomputers	Expensive items with unique characteristics; few competitors or substitutes: fashion clothes, antiques, luxury vacations, jewels	Essential services having intangible value; consumers may avoid: life insurance, legal services, funeral services, family and estate planning

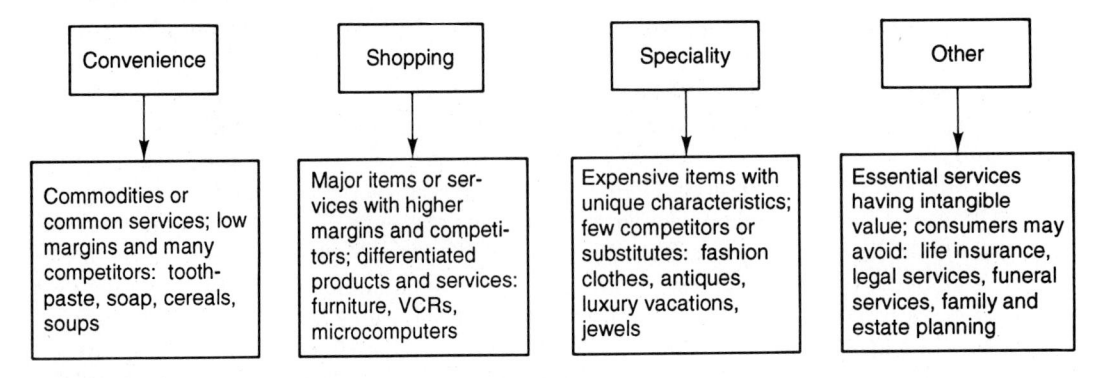

Figure 9-2 **Classifications of Consumer Goods**

Industrial Products

Industrial products are sold to other organizations as raw materials, equipment, component parts, process materials, supplies, and services. Marketing of industrial products is called *institutional sales*, as noted in Chapter 8, and there are five categories of industrial products: *direct materials*, *indirect materials*, *capital equipment*, *contracted services*, and *MRO supplies*. (MRO stands for maintenance, repair, and operating.) Figure 9-3 summarizes these products, which are described in the following paragraphs.[9]

Direct Materials. Between 30 and 50 percent of a manufacturer's total overhead consists of *direct materials*, including raw materials, subassemblies, and component parts used in production. When we think of raw materials, we think of steel for cars, plastic resins for toys, aluminum alloys for aircraft, and grains for cereals. These materials offer few opportunities for entrepreneurs, yet there are thousands of subassemblies and components essential for manufacturing that *do* offer opportunities.

Consider a product with very simple materials, such as this textbook. The printing company that actually creates the book must have huge rolls of paper, cover materials, special inks, materials for printing plates, and various art materials used directly in the production of the text and cover. Over the years there have been hundreds of innovations in papers, treatments, inks and coloring agents, photographic processes, binding materials, glues, and art materials.

When technologies are in rapid change—whether in printing or space robotics—opportunities rise exponentially. For example, after the *Challenger* disaster, NASA decided that space work would eventually have to be done with robots. Bids went out for designs, and one of the winners was an entrepreneurial venture with four creative partners in their early 30s. The company, called Honeybee, developed a Flight Telerobotic Servicer (FTS) that looks like the *Star Wars* C-3PO. It works much the same way, without the movie fantasy features, and is designed for construction work on the space station *Freedom*, a NASA project slated for the late 1990s. The Honeybee FTS project will require more than 400 new parts and assemblies, and only half of these have been developed since the FTS was designed. A majority of those have come from other entrepreneurs and small research companies.[10]

Selling to industrial markets is at once an art form and a technical specialty. Sales representatives cannot approach a purchasing manager armed only with enthusiasm. They have to be extremely well informed about the technical attributes of their materials, their competitors' materials, and state-of-the-art technology. Many sales representatives come from engineering disciplines and train for marketing roles. Promotional activities are more attuned to technical specifications than to emotional ploys. Attractive brochures and technical manuals are common sales tools, and advertising is positioned in trade magazines, such as *Industry Week* or *Quality Progress*. Entrepreneurs must have excellent distribution systems to assure on-time deliveries of high-quality materials.

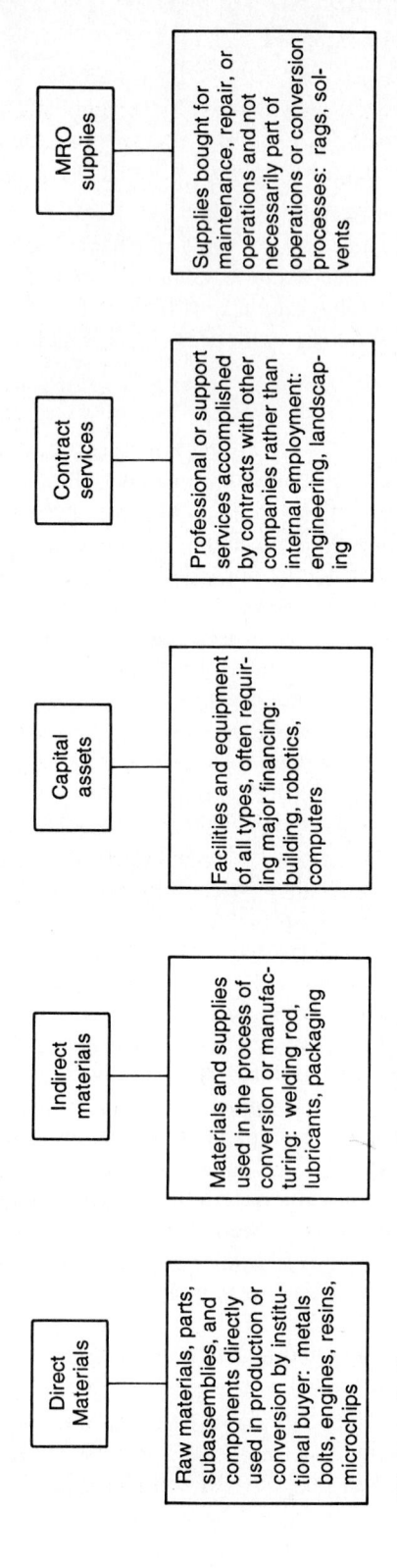

Direct Materials	Indirect materials	Capital assets	Contract services	MRO supplies
Raw materials, parts, subassemblies, and components directly used in production or conversion by institutional buyer: metals bolts, engines, resins, microchips	Materials and supplies used in the process of conversion or manufacturing: welding rod, lubricants, packaging	Facilities and equipment of all types, often requiring major financing: building, robotics, computers	Professional or support services accomplished by contracts with other companies rather than internal employment: engineering, landscaping	Supplies bought for maintenance, repair, or operations and not necessarily part of operations or conversion processes: rags, solvents

Figure 9-3 **Classifications of Industrial Goods**

Indirect Materials. Supplies used in manufacturing and "process" materials used in conversion methods to create products constitute *indirect materials*. Book publishers, for example, need editing pencils, art pens, camera film, ink filters, imprinting materials, and similar supplies. Since these are consumed in actual production processes, they are classified as "materials" rather than "overhead," and purchasing managers make decisions about indirect materials similar to those for direct materials. Vendors also follow similar guidelines in selling these items.

Entrepreneurs are less likely to have opportunities in indirect materials because, like consumer commodities, indirect materials have many substitutes, low margins, and well-established vendors. Entrepreneurs make significant strides in institutional markets when they can address growth markets. As printing technology advanced, for example, Quill Corporation grew from a small catalog company to a nationwide distributor of office and printing supplies focused on computer-based systems.[11]

Capital Assets. Usually, *capital assets* are not procured in the same manner as materials. Equipment purchases typically require capital budgeting, executive involvement, and intricate contracts between vendors and buyers. Major equipment includes production machinery, inventory-handling equipment, telecommunications equipment, computers, and similar assets. Industrial marketing requires extensive technical capabilities, often team efforts by vendors, and months of negotiation. Major equipment purchases seldom end with the consummation of a sale. Instead, they include an ongoing commitment for installation, technical assistance, warranty programs, and equipment updates and modifications.

Although major equipment is seldom offered by start-up ventures, there are outstanding examples of enterprises that succeeded because they fought to establish industrial markets. Digital Equipment Corporation, MCI, Sun Systems, AST Research, Lotus Development Corporation, and Microsoft Corporation are just a few that began small but grew rapidly by concentrating on institutional sales.

There is a more lucrative niche for entrepreneurial firms in *accessory equipment*. Accessories are capital assets, but this category includes smaller-ticket items such as small electrical tools, drafting tables, engineering instruments, computer peripheral equipment, and so on. This list can be quite extensive, and there are always new products coming to market that enhance productivity. Training officers, for example, have progressed from school-type blackboards to graphic displays to video training aids to interactive simulation systems. Someone had to create these innovations and then convince institutional buyers of their benefits. Institutional marketing involves well-placed advertisements in publications that are frequently read by managers and purchasing officers, presentations and demonstrations by technical experts, and a strong service-support profile by the venture.

Contracted Services. A broad range of professional consulting activities are *contracted services*, including engineering design work, marketing research, advertising, management systems consulting, legal services, accounting, and labor relations services. There are many opportunities to carve out niches through service contracts, and industrial firms often make use of contracted services rather than full-time departments. Janitorial services, as described in Chapter 8, constitute one of the fastest growing service industries in the United States, with significant growth in corporate accounts. Industrial facilities and commercial buildings are also maintained through contracted landscape and lawn service firms. Software development is an enormous field, and corporations spend an estimated $60 billion annually on educational programs and training.[12]

The marketing effort required for services is substantially the same as for direct materials or capital assets. Purchasing managers may be involved in buying these services, but usually corporate executives will make a collective decision. Entrepreneurs must have solid promotional programs to supplement personal presentations. The reputation of the entrepreneur and his or her firm will often weigh more than the perceived intrinsic value of the service because the entrepreneur is selling "intangibles." Executives will be sensitive to service prices because it is difficult to measure the value of results or to compare the exchange value of money for services. Most corporate buyers, however, will have a good idea of market prices. Consequently, there are major players in service fields who can demand "luxury prices," and corporate executives who want those services do not question price. Major public accounting firms, for instance, have differentiated their services to the extent that price is a minor issue. Well-known advertising agencies, media specialists, safety experts, quality-control firms, and labor relations interventionists have become the "BMWs" of institutional contract services.

MRO Products. Maintenance, repair, and operating (MRO) supplies constitute a significant market. These products include light bulbs, paper towels, toilet paper, computerized billing forms, and hundreds of similar items. These are *vital* supplies that no company can do without. A temporary shortage of pencils might not stop work, but the firm that runs out of toilet paper is asking for a riot. Production can stop when a company lacks essential supplies. For example, a company that manufactures wooden desks requires a significant amount of sandpaper, cleaning solvents, and rags. If the firm runs out of any of these items, the entire assembly process can shut down.

Most MRO products are commodities in the sense of having many substitutes, and there are usually many suppliers competing for limited sales. Purchasing managers will spend little time selecting items or negotiating prices, but instead, they will put a premium on convenience and hassle-free purchasing. They do not want to be bothered by purchasing decisions, but they also do not want to risk running out of toilet paper. Frequently, MRO purchases are based on standing orders, such as monthly supplies of rags and uniforms, delivered at regular intervals. Landing these contracts can be lucrative, especially if a venture can establish a reputation for reliable service.

Other Product Considerations

Classification and market niche of products will determine *packaging* and *labeling* requirements. Often packaging is more critical and expensive than the product itself, and depending on the intended customer, product labeling can be extremely detailed.

PROFILE △

Caterpillar—A Demanding Customer

Caterpillar, Inc., makes half-million-dollar giant earth-moving equipment but relies on a worldwide system of plants and suppliers that provide everything from washers costing ten cents each to automatic robot welders costing as much as the company's finished products. The company has undergone a metamorphosis, changing from a snaillike bureaucracy to a responsive integrated manufacturer. With more than $1.5 billion committed to plant modernization, Caterpillar has chosen the best suppliers from 30 countries to provide state-of-the-art manufacturing technology as well as simple office supplies. A common requirement for all suppliers, however, is the highest quality and rapid, on-time delivery. Major vendors, such as Cincinnati Milicron, which provides robotic technology, and entrepreneurial companies, such as CoverAll, which supplies maintenance uniforms and rags, get Caterpillar's contracts because they deliver quality goods and services.

Source: "Can Caterpillar Inch Its Way Back to Heftier Profits?" *Business Week*, September 25, 1989, p. 104. Also, personal communication with Dr. Sam Black, Director of Quality, Caterpillar, Inc.

Packaging consumer goods, for instance, establishes brand awareness and product image. Laundry detergents are differentiated visually by their packages and canned soups by their color schemes. Consumer labels provide distinctive names and brand identification. Packaging and labeling must also comply with FDA regulations, safety codes established by the Consumer Product Safety Commission, and specific packaging methods and information disclosure for hazardous materials, foods, medications, and protection against tampering.[13]

Methods of distribution will also affect packaging and labeling. Individual light bulbs packaged for retail sales will have brightly colored protective containers with one to four bulbs to a pack, and packaging is often more costly than the products. The same light bulbs sold as MRO products may be bulk packed in dozens and boxed by the gross. These containers will have minimum product information, simple labels, and protective but colorless boxes. Usually bulk packaging is relatively inexpensive compared with retail packaging requirements.

▶ CHECKPOINT

Describe an "expanded" concept of a product and its attributes.

Identify and discuss different types of consumer and industrial products.

DISTRIBUTION

If entrepreneurs have defined their products and services clearly, and if they have identified their target customers well, their methods of distribution should be equally clear. A luxury consumer item intended for specialty markets and high-income consumers will not be offered through a discount channel; Cartier jewelry does not go on sale. Shopping products that compete on price will have to be placed in stores or catalogs that can attract appropriate customers. Commodities vie for high visualization, such as retail shelf space or low-cost mass markets. Consequently, entrepreneurs must select *channels* of distribution that reflect the appropriate quality and image of their products or services.

Matching Markets with Products and Services

Effective distribution strategies will define channels that complement product and service characteristics. Entrepreneurs, therefore, must consciously select ways to position their ventures through market channels that match expectations of consumers with characteristics of products and services. There are three strategic categories for distribution called *intensive*, *selective*, and *exclusive* distribution systems.[14]

Intensive Distribution Systems. Channels with wide coverage of many different consumers in multiple outlets, such as positioning convenience goods (e.g., candy and soft drinks) in fast-turnover locations (7–Eleven stores, chain groceries, and sports arenas) are *intensive distribution systems*. These systems are usually complex and will include at least one intermediary who speeds products to market through wholesaling. In this instance, "intensive" means that there is rapid replenishment of multiple retail outlets. Wholesale distributors, for example, fill racks in stores along a regional route, regularly restocking dozens of different products from as many manufacturers under distribution contracts.

Most entrepreneurs will not have products in this category, and services are seldom channeled through systems of intermediaries, yet if a new venture has an item capable of high-volume sales, the entrepreneur has to be prepared to shift into an intensive channel effort. Early versions of "flying rings" (e.g., Frisbees) were marketed in a selected number of West Coast stores that sold beachwear, but to generate volume, the rings were licensed to toy manufacturers who had wholesale distribution connections to penetrate mass markets.

Selective Distribution Systems. For *shopping* goods and most consumer services, *selective distribution systems* are appropriate. Selective systems are those that "differentiate" among competing dealerships so that brands can be established. For instance, GE washers and dryers are sold under license agreements by a few selected appliance stores in a given area. Dealers expect to have markets protected by manufacturers who guarantee limited (or no) competitors with similar branded products. In turn, manufacturers expect a high level of service and promotion by their dealers. Office equipment dealers are selective distribution stores with contractual agreements with hundreds of manufacturers that make furniture, office machines, copiers, office supplies, and other similar products.

Entrepreneurs with distinct services prefer selective channels to establish their service image and the perception of product attributes they want to convey. Employment agencies, travel agents, real estate firms, insurance agencies, advertising agencies, and other similar firms will establish channels by positioning services in niches that reinforce appropriate consumer expectations.

Exclusive Distribution Systems. An exclusive channel implies a direct link between manufacturer and dealer. Manufacturers maintain substantial control over quality and consumer service levels through strict contracts called *exclusive agency agreements*. Products are custom ordered, and only rarely are there intermediaries such as wholesalers. Bertram yacht and Rolls-Royce automobiles are examples of products handled through exclusive channels. In most instances, exclusivity means *specialty* products in luxury markets, but in some instances, these are not luxuries in the normal sense; they are simply "seldom-purchased" items. For example, most individuals never encounter patent attorneys, but when one needs patent help, a specialty market exists. Patent attorneys must have an established way of being accessible to their potential clients. This statement holds true for tax accountants, surgeons, counselors, management consultants, architects, and many other services that clients seek only infrequently.

Channels of Distribution

Within the three strategic distribution systems, there are two types of channels: *consumer* and *industrial*. Each of these has several alternatives to consider. Figure 9-4 describes four options for consumer channels.

Consumer Channels. The first of four alternative consumer channels is a direct link between manufacturers and end customers; there are no intermediaries or retailers. Farmer's markets are examples in which food is grown, trucked to market, and sold directly to customers. Traditionally, IBM has maintained a network of company sales offices that sell IBM products directly to end users.

A second alternative is a two-tier system of dealers. Manufacturers sell exclusively to authorized dealers as independent business enterprises, which in turn serve retail customers. This distribution channel is employed by IBM mainly for products targeted to retail markets such as stand-alone personal computers and software. Direct marketing through catalogs relies on this two-tier system, and although catalogs have traditionally suggested a "discount image," that assumption is no longer true today. Many companies with luxury product lines use catalogs, such as *The Sharper Image*. The mail-order business, once dominated by throwaway cheap advertisements, has become the fastest growing marketing system in the country with a significant number of high-quality, high-priced product lines. For example, *Patagonia, Inc.*, called by some the best mail-order catalog in America, sells unusual and expensive specialty

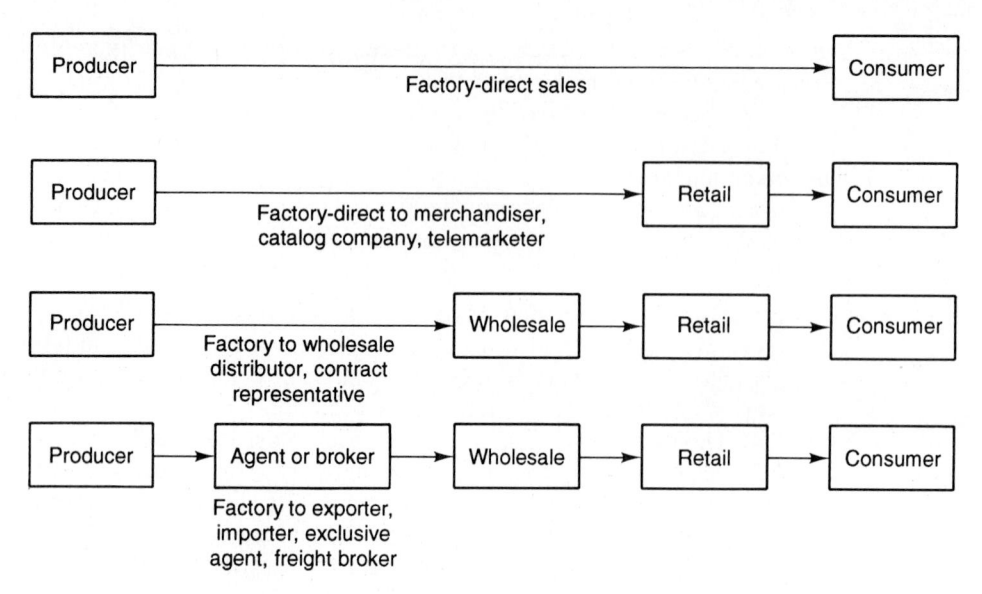

```
Producer ──Factory-direct sales──▶ Consumer

Producer ──Factory-direct to merchandiser, catalog company, telemarketer──▶ Retail ──▶ Consumer

Producer ──Factory to wholesale distributor, contract representative──▶ Wholesale ──▶ Retail ──▶ Consumer

Producer ──▶ Agent or broker ──▶ Wholesale ──▶ Retail ──▶ Consumer
           Factory to exporter, importer, exclusive agent, freight broker
```

Figure 9-4 **Consumer Distribution Channels**

items for outdoor adventurers interested in everything from mountaineering to kayak white-water boating.[15]

A third option involves wholesalers positioned in the chain between manufacturers and retailers. This is a three-tier model, and as noted earlier, it is common for commodity products. A fourth channel adds an intermediary positioned between the manufacturer and wholesaler. This intermediary is an agent or broker who negotiates vendor contracts for regional store chains. Such a contract might involve an agent who negotiates with Wal-Mart on behalf of Wilson Sporting Goods. Once the contract is signed, wholesalers are given the contract to service their regional customers. Agents are crucial for exporting and importing because few manufacturers or retailers have the expertise to deal with the complexities of international markets. Large companies like Toys R Us send company executives to Hong Kong to buy toys, but they deal with Hong Kong toy agents, not directly with manufacturers who may be scattered throughout Southeast Asia. Far East agents set up annual trade shows to attract other overseas agents and company representatives.[16]

Industrial Channels. Industrial marketing channels exist between two or more institutions or companies. Alternative channels are illustrated in Figure 9-5. The least complicated is between producer and consumer, but unlike the consumer market, the buyer usually is another manufacturer that may be much larger and far more sophisticated than the seller. As explained in Chapter 8 on marketing research, automobile manufacturers are primarily "assemblers" of cars who purchase materials, subassemblies, and parts to fabricate a finished product.

A second option is for *industrial distributors* who operate similar to wholesalers

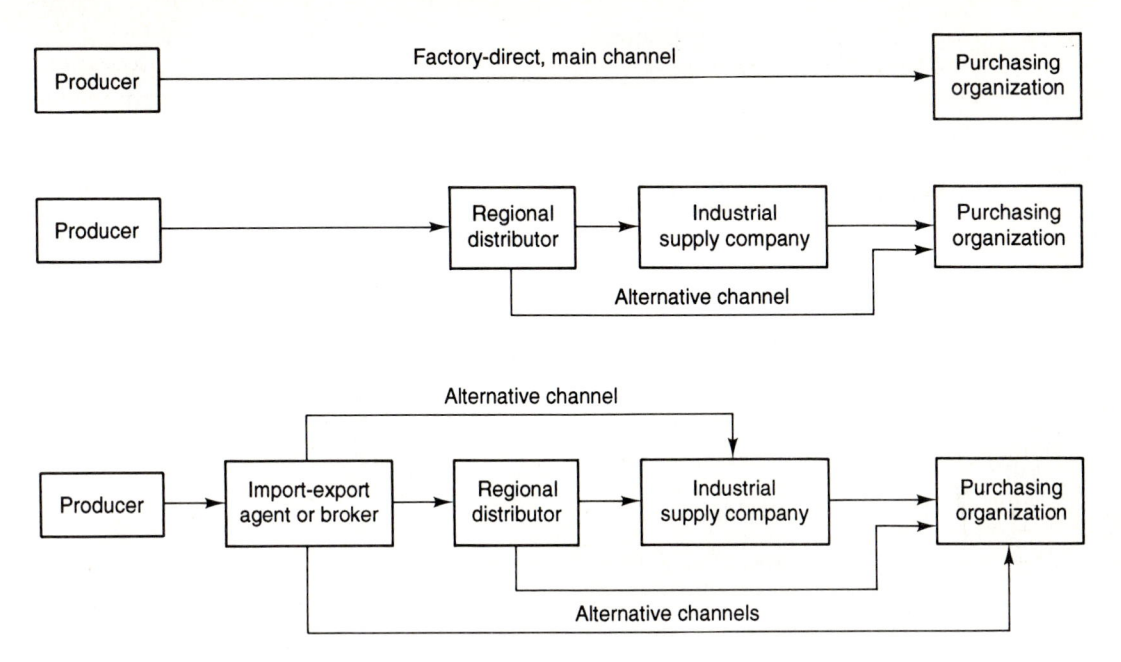

Figure 9-5 **Industrial Distribution Channels**

in consumer markets. Industrial distributors—commonly called industrial supply companies—provide "supermarkets" of parts, components, supplies, and tools to a variety of manufacturers in a service area. Most industrial supply companies will have several thousand items ranging from machine screws to large electric motor assemblies, and their customers are equally diverse, ranging from huge manufacturers to small machine shops.

A third option has an agent or broker between the industrial distributor and the manufacturer. The role of an agent here is to negotiate contracts between industries, or between parties in export-import markets. Depending on the nature of the product and the parties involved, the industrial agent may do little more than negotiate the deal while buyers and sellers arrange physical distribution between themselves. For example, Poly-Chem Associates, Inc., a Virginia company, acts as agent for several chemical companies, negotiates on behalf of those companies with wholesalers in such places as Korea, Taiwan, and Nigeria, and then transmits orders to the chemical companies that ship direct to overseas destinations.[17]

Service Channels. Professional services are positioned in predictable ways so that clients know where to go for help. For example, doctors who are general practitioners typically have neighborhood offices with easy access for patients, and surgeons typically establish themselves with hospitals where they not only perform their work but often initiate patient contacts. New channels have emerged in recent years, however, and doctors, for example, have begun to open their own medical centers and outpatient clinics. Others have organized into associations such as health maintenance organizations (HMOs) to provide a full range of medical services, including insurance and billing systems for patients under group medical plans. In effect, this is a form of institutional marketing by one association to others such as corporations, school systems, and government agencies.

Franchise systems also provide new service channels. Examples include fast-growing 1st Optometry and Ryan's Hygienist Centers. Personal service franchise services are exemplified by Red Carpet Realty and the Money Mart.[18] Traditional offices for services are being replaced by systems of business enterprises, but most professional and personal service enterprises remain independent. Those that do create group practices or enter into franchises are attempting to position their services in new markets.

> ▶ **CHECKPOINT**
>
> Describe both consumer and industrial distribution channels and various options for selecting channels.
>
> Identify alternative service channels and new methods of professional services using distinct marketing channels.

PROMOTION

The role of **promotion** is to facilitate exchanges between organizations and their customers. Commercial enterprises are concerned with attracting customers; professional services are concerned with informing clients about their services; and not-for-profit organizations must let their constituents know what they do. Different types of enterprises will have distinct promotional mixes utilizing a variety of promotional methods. We will describe these methods and address the concept of an effective promotional mix.

Advertising

Advertising is a form of impersonal broadcasting through commercial mass media. The pervasive type of promotion is advertising because it is the one form that punctuates our daily lives. Advertising is like a shotgun blast aimed at a flock of geese; there is no guarantee you will hit anything, but if you fire enough shots, you will certainly get their attention.

There are two approaches to advertising. First, a company will try to *pull* products through a distribution system by firing information salvos through mass media. Automotive companies spend millions on nationwide television spots. These are designed to solidify consumer preferences for their cars. When Lee Iacocca appears on television for Chrysler, he is trying to establish a preferential image over competition and to implant in our minds that we ought to seek out retail dealers. He is trying to "pull" us into Chrysler's channel of distribution.

The second approach is a *push* system where advertising is directed toward one channel member. Advertising is supplemented by other promotional activities such as personal selling efforts. Chrysler may put together factory rebate offers coupled with low-interest incentive buying plans to "push" dealers into an intense sales effort. Wholesalers and retailers rely on advertising to attract consumers to inquire into specific purchases. These advertising efforts can occur at every point in the distribution channel. Consequently, manufacturers offer incentives to wholesalers; wholesalers offer quantity discounts to retailers; and retailers target ads for end consumers. The promotional mix showing advertising and other forms of promotion in both pull and push systems is shown in Figure 9-6.

Entrepreneurs use advertisements that range from commercial listings in telephone books to national television spots, but for most new ventures, mass television advertising (such as 30-second spots during the Superbowl) are too expensive and have little effect. Smaller companies prefer local media or special publications that reach select customer groups. For example, a new type of garden tool may be telemarketed over cable television channels. It may also be positioned in garden stores with a promotional program aimed at retailers. A new computer program may be advertised through direct advertising brochures or slick advertising packages mailed to computer owners. A travel agency may place ads in a few well-defined travel and

Pull System

Advertising	Sales promotions	Personal selling	Publicity
Emphasis on producer who "pulls" consumers through national ads; support of advertising for retailer to attract local buyers	Producer initiates sales promotions for retailer, incentives for distributors	Retailer initiates personal selling as customers are pulled into stores and dealers	Producers seek major publicity to enhance product and company images; local stores and dealers seek community publicity

Push System

Advertising	Sales promotions	Personal selling	Publicity
Producer allocates advertising budget to emphasize retail efforts; retailers emphasize ads to attract customers	Producer supports retailers but does not directly offer sales promotions; retailer initiates main sales efforts	Retailer emphasizes personal contact with customers to anchor sales promotions; no involvement by producer	Producer may seek publicity for image and support of brand, but retailer initiates active publicity effort

Figure 9-6 **Promotion Mix for Pull and Push Strategies**

leisure magazines. The options for advertising are enormous, and entrepreneurs should study how others do it by reading journals such as *Advertising Age*.

Sales Promotion

Sales promotion is a term used to imply an activity that is specifically designed to induce sales by *enhancing value* for the consumer. This value may be created through volume discounts to wholesalers or retailers who can realize greater profits. Sales promotions provide direct inducements for specific purchases. If entrepreneurs want to "push" their products through wholesalers, then wholesalers must be induced to push products deeper into the distribution channel. This effort may take the form of no-interest vendor credit or extended credit, allowing distributors to stock inventory without immediate cash outlays. Subsequently, some retailers can sell inventory before they have to pay for it.

Many sales promotions are geared to events such as Mother's Day or Easter, and entrepreneurs can offer incentives such as special gift boxes, eye-catching point-of-purchase display cases, discount coupons, and so on. Some sales promotions are staged events such as promotional contests and trade fair demonstrations. Introductory sales promotions can be devised through direct mail campaigns that offer samples, two-for-one sales, free catalogs, gifts with purchases, and many more. This form of marketing has become so popular that new sales promotion ventures have been established to help other entrepreneurs. Telemarketing, contest companies, and mail-list merchandisers, among others, form a "facilitating" group of intermediaries that have become part of the distribution channel.[19]

Publicity

Publicity is the result of public service announcements or news generated through media. Newspaper articles, magazine stories, talk show interviews, human interest radio spots, recognition in public affairs, and many other avenues for publicity are open to entrepreneurs. Ostensibly, publicity is free, but most companies allocate rather large budgets to *public relations*, the function responsible for creating a favorable organizational profile. Because public relations requires initiative and may cost time and money, entrepreneurs do little to attract media attention, yet their corporate counterparts are quick to write press releases or to do things that are newsworthy.

Entrepreneurs have many publicity opportunities. For example, sponsorship of civic events and nonprofit fund-raising events usually carry an incentive for businesses. This incentive can be sponsorship signs, newspaper stories, public awards, or having the firm's name conspicuously displayed as a sponsor. Sponsoring a 10-mile charity running event might be an excellent way for a sporting-goods store to make the enterprise visible to several hundred runners and spectators. By sponsoring a cross-country bike race, a bicycle shop could do the same. The options for the bicycle shop owner might include giving a racing outfit to a contestant, providing the winner's trophy, or setting up comfort stations. Charity golf tournaments offer excellent op-

PROFILE △

Marketing Success at Subway Sandwiches

Steve Lauer opened his first Subway Sandwich franchise, a small shop in northern Colorado, at the age of 21, expanded to three units by 1988, and welcomed the 1990s with 11 highly successful locations. He succeeded with a unique marketing plan based on becoming a recognized supporter of community events.

Keeping conventional advertising to a minimum, Lauer allocated a majority of his promotional budget to support charities. These included the annual March of Dimes Walkathon, Red Cross Blood Drive, Great American Smokeout, and more than a dozen youth-oriented sports programs. Today Lauer helps youth baseball leagues by printing coupon books worth $20 in merchandise that kids sell for $1, keeping all net proceeds. Lauer sponsors awards and banquets for youth sports contests, and he promotes a Player-of-the-Game award for adults through the community softball league. Lauer also provides coupon books free to elementary school teachers as awards they can give to students in reading and literacy programs.

His public relations campaign is coupled with point-of-purchase posters, circulars promoting sports and charity events, and personal visits to schools. Lauer reaches more than 16,000 potential customers through direct involvement with youth programs, and he enjoys enthusiastic coverage by public media in recognition of his community endeavors. The result has been a steady stream of new customers, raising the gross revenue of his stores by 30 percent more than the franchise average. More important, Steve Lauer enjoys what he is doing and finds satisfaction in making customers feel good about coming into his shops.

Source: "Nice Guys Finish First: Subway Sandwiches, Fort Collins, Colo.," *Inc.*, October 1989, p. 79.

---

portunities to sponsor entrants, create special awards, provide trophies, or underwrite refreshments.

Human interest news stories are attention grabbers. The "local kid who makes good" story is always a favorite of editors because it sells newspapers. Talk show hosts search for entrepreneurs with unusual products or services. The "Pet Rock" fad several years ago gave Johnny Carson joke material for months, and needless to say, it prompted heavy sales. When Robert Lewis Dean topped $2 million in sales in his Washington, DC, limousine company at the age of 19, he made the cover of *Nation's Business*. That was 1985. When he lost it all in 1987, Geraldo Rivera put him on national television. The good news helped sales, but oddly enough, the bad (or sympathetic) publicity on *Geraldo* helped Dean launch a new nationwide network of limousine services.[20] Publicity also is well utilized by the founder of Subway Sandwiches (see profile).

Personal Selling

Advertising is like a shotgun blast, but *personal selling* is like a rifle shot. It is the personal effort of an entrepreneur to convince a consumer that a purchase has fair exchange value for both parties. Unlike publicity, which can often be beyond the control of an entrepreneur, personal selling is an intensely controlled process. Unlike sales promotions that can be impersonal, selling is a human endeavor. Personal selling can also be far more expensive than other methods of promotion, but it is often the most effective.

Merchandising relies on personal sales to a significant degree because sales clerks conclude actual purchases. In many instances, consumers need little persuasion; sales clerks are "order takers" who simply consummate sales. Grocery store cashiers fit this scenario; however, customers may not return if cashiers are rude. They are *salespersons*, and even if the customer has already selected groceries, it is important to reinforce the store's image of service to bring customers back again.

At the other end of the spectrum are outside salespersons who are "order getters." These individuals work in fields where customers resist shopping, such as in life insurance. Institutional sales are based largely on "order getting," and sales calls can be even more expensive than comparable advertising.[21] Between the two extremes, there is every shade and degree of sales effort ranging from a pleasant smile by a clerk to a "cold call" pitch by a door-to-door salesperson. Entrepreneurs control the personal sales process, the behavior of their people, and, consequently, the image their consumers have of them. As discussed in Chapter 7, hiring and training the right people is crucial.

The Promotional Mix

A **promotional mix** is the result of a conscious effort to select promotional methods that reinforce a marketing strategy. Advertising alone will not attract long lines of customers. Sales promotions alone will not communicate to customers who you are and what you have to sell. Publicity can be important but irregular, and it will not sufficiently inform the public about your enterprise, your products, or your services. Personal selling clearly focuses on the intensity of human effort and links buyers and sellers, but salespersons cannot fashion sales from thin air; they need support systems or other promotional means to prospect for customers and to reinforce the image of the firm they represent.

The entrepreneur's task is to make sound decisions about allocations of time and money to each facet of promotion consistent with a grand marketing strategy. There are no prescribed mixes one can use because there are too many considerations that change rapidly in dynamic markets, yet there are logical patterns to consider. For example, the "pull" system discussed earlier implies heavier advertising in mass markets coupled with sales promotions to support dealer incentives. In addition, manufacturers' sales representatives can play significant roles as technical experts who link dealers with manufacturers. Publicity in major firms is accomplished through public relations offices, but small enterprises, such as personal service firms, tend to maintain low publicity profiles. This limitation should not prevent, say, a public accounting firm from offering free public service tax seminars or from contributing to charities.

> ▶ **CHECKPOINT**
>
> Identify and describe the major types of promotional activities available to entrepreneurs.
>
> Explain the concept of a promotional mix and different approaches to allocating resources to promotional activities.

PRICING

The fourth marketing factor is *pricing*. The price one pays for a product is the exchange value, and the price one asks is the composite value of a product or service coupled with a "premium" to reward risk taking. Prices are known by other names, including fares, fees, interest, tips, tuition, and taxes. All are prices for different types of products or services. Prices also impart a sense of quality, and they reflect the image of a store, service, location, or product; they communicate perceptual messages to consumers. Therefore, prices must coincide with strategies that reinforce the entrepreneur's business and reputation.

Pricing Objectives

Entrepreneurs tend to think of prices and profits together, and it is certainly important to have pricing strategies that yield profits; however, prices can be set arbitrarily low, perhaps sacrificing profits, to build up a customer base. If the enterprise is in a decreasing-cost industry, increased volume will result in lower costs and higher profits. The *pricing objective* is always to *make profits*, but often building a high sales volume has priority. A long-term growth strategy that requires increased market share will have comparable pricing objectives whereby profit maximization is not a preemptive consideration. In any event, customers must believe they are getting greater value for their money compared with competitors.

Most entrepreneurs must be concerned with *survival*. In the short run, this means meeting or beating competitors' prices to stay in the game. In the long run, it means having a price configuration that provides *at least* a break-even income plus sufficient profits to keep the entrepreneur in business. If the enterprise has investors, pricing must be sufficient to recover costs, reward the entrepreneur, and provide a sufficient *return on investment* to investors. If investors are interested in long-term growth, they may ignore short-term survival tactics of setting low prices, but eventually pricing objectives must clearly indicate how investors will benefit.

Prices can also be set to attract (or dissuade) certain customers. High prices in an elegant antique store will most likely attract those persons with sufficient income to make purchases without worrying about the family budget. High prices may also dissuade "shoppers" who, at best, might buy small items. Those high prices will discourage the window-shoppers and bargain hunters. In contrast, discount stores and most direct-mail catalogs have low prices. This is a strategy of low price, low cost, high volume, and high inventory turnover.

Perhaps the most important pricing objective is to *provide positive cash flow*. No one can stay in business when cash evaporates. When you are out of cash, you are out of the game. Prices can be set to recover cash outlays as quickly as possible *if* there are no other considerations. For products that have proprietary patent protection and little competition, high prices may be established early to recover heavy start-up costs rapidly. As soon as competition intensifies, this strategy is no longer an option; survival will dictate more competitive prices. Protecting cash flow, however, should not result in exploitation; customers should receive what they perceive as a fair exchange. Prices set too high or too low may undermine sales or fail to cover costs, and in either event the enterprise risks early failure.

Price Considerations

A number of factors will influence prices beyond an entrepreneur's objectives. There will be a price range that is acceptable to consumers, and good market research will reveal this price range. The promotional mix will also influence prices so that most sales events imply low-price incentives (e.g., year-end closeout sales). As mentioned earlier, competition will influence pricing decisions, and entrepreneurs will want to stay abreast of market prices to meet threats of aggressive competitors.

Competition and personal sales efforts also imply some flexibility in pricing decisions to allow field representatives negotiating room with clients. This flexibility does not mean that a salesperson can set prices, but it does mean that logical pricing policies should exist. These will provide quantity discounts, adjustments for differential cost factors (such as variances in shipping or special handling costs), and seasonal discounts.

Pricing must also meet expectations of those who buy and resell products in the distribution channel. Wholesalers, for example, must have low enough prices to profit from selling to retailers, and in turn, retailers must have sufficient margins to make reasonable profits. It follows that an entrepreneur with a product planned to list at $9.95 and produced at a cost of $5.00 may believe he or she has a winner only to fail in the marketplace. For example, assume that an entrepreneur needs a 30 percent gross margin (incidentally, 30 percent is low, considering overhead and tax expenses). Then assume the product will be wholesaled. The entrepreneur marks up the $5.00, charging wholesalers $6.50. At the same margin, wholesalers must price at $8.45. This leaves only $1.50 for retailing (17.8 percent). Street-smart wholesalers will avoid this product, realizing that retailers will be reluctant to buy a low-margin product. Worse yet, the entrepreneur may manufacture 10,000 items on the strength of what appeared to be a profitable idea, only to end up with $50,000 in unsalable junk. Pricing under four options for distribution is shown in Figure 9-7.

Pricing for industrial markets is much like pricing consumer goods, but decisions will almost always involve quantity price discounting. Margins will be lower than in consumer markets, but sales will usually be in large volumes negotiated through standing sales contracts. These contracts are cost-effective because they reduce promotional expenses, simplify orders, and allow for bulk transportation. Contracts often include seasonal discounts for industrial buyers who can purchase in advance, stock up, and therefore offset potential losses in slow months for their vendors. It makes sense that buyers who follow this practice expect a discount for purchases made in the off season.

Legal Considerations in Pricing

Marketing is becoming more regulated to protect consumers against fraudulent advertising, misleading labels, unsafe packaging, and predatory pricing. There are several dozen major federal laws that influence marketing decisions, and the aspiring entrepreneur would be wise to study federal regulations as well as state and municipal regulations. The most carefully regulated area is in consumer prices, reviewed briefly here.

The *Sherman Act*, known for its antitrust mandates, was enacted nearly a century ago, but it still affects pricing decisions. The Sherman Act prohibits conspiracies to control prices, and this provision restrains managers from fixing prices or discussing pricing decisions in a way that could be interpreted as collusive price setting. Entrepreneurs must set prices independently, but this law does not prevent them from doing marketing research on competitors' pricing.

Estimated cost of $4.00 each, planned retail list of $9.95. Entrepreneur must price to ensure that intermediaries and retail stores have sufficient gross profit margins to want to sell the product. Depending on necessary distribution channels, a good product may not have sufficient margins to succeed.

Factory-direct:	$9.95 − 4.00 = 5.95; $5.95/4.00 = 149% margin	Excellent gross
Factory to retail	$4.00 x 1.5 = $6.00 to retailer ($2.00 = 50% margin); $9.95 − 6.00 = 3.95; $3.95/6.00 = 66% margin	Reasonable gross for all
Factory to wholesale and then to retail:	$4.00 x 1.33 = $5.32 to wholesaler ($1.32 = 33% margin); $5.32 x 1.33 = $7.08 to retailer ($1.76 = 33% margin); $9.95 − 7.08 = $2.87; $2.87/7.08 = 41% margin	Marginal gross for all
Factory to import agent, wholesale, then retail:	$4.00 x 1.25 = $5.00 to agent ($1.00 = 25% margin); $5.00 x 1.25 = $6.25 to wholesaler ($1.25 = 25% margin); $6.25 x 1.25 = $7.81 to retailer ($1.56 = 25% margin); $9.95 − 7.81 = 2.14; $2.14/7.81 = 27% margin	Poor gross and probably not sufficient to market products

Figure 9-7 **Pricing to Maintain Margins**

The *Federal Trade Commission Act* prohibits deceptive pricing. Deceptive prices can arise in many ways, such as stating a price and then adding on conditions and strings so complicated that consumers no longer understand how much they are paying. Some insurance policies used to be stated in such a way that policyholders understood the price but had no idea what they were buying. The Truth in Lending Act is a variation on this theme whereby interest rates and finance charges must be clearly explained and documented.

The *Robinson-Patman Act* may influence pricing decisions more than any other law. The Robinson-Patman Act was passed before World War II, and coupled with the later Clayton Act, it prohibits discriminatory prices. For example, a store cannot sell two identical items to different customers under similar circumstances at different prices. These laws were enhanced in 1975 with the passage of the *Consumer Goods Pricing Act*, which prohibits "fair trade" pricing. Manufacturers can no longer require retailers to maintain a particular price on goods, a practice that used to be common.

What is "discriminatory" is subject to a library full of litigation. We do know that prices cannot be different for different social, ethnic, or religious groups. One cannot discriminate on socioeconomic factors, income status, sex, age, or personal characteristics. However, prices *can* be differentiated for customers when sales result in different costs to sellers, when lower prices are offered in good faith to meet competition, and when differentiated prices do not damage competition.[22]

Differential prices are offered to many different customers. Quantity discounts, trade discounts, discounts for "standing contracts," and other forms of lower prices reflect lower costs of high-volume orders. Individual home buyers can qualify for different interest rates based on a risk profile that implies cost differences for lenders who can establish patterns of higher (or lower) loan defaults for borrowers. Children get reduced prices on movie tickets, haircuts, transportation, and other services based on competitive practices. Senior citizens enjoy discounts, again in response to competitive practices. Both children and senior citizen differentials are socially acceptable as long as they do not threaten competition or restrain trade. Group rates on travel, off-season discounts, and group insurance premiums are justified in part on lower costs and in part on competition.

Entrepreneurs need to understand that these federal regulations exist, together with many state and local ones, and that it is relatively easy to violate laws if they go about setting prices in capricious ways. Having good intentions is a plea that will fall on deaf ears with authorities.

▶ CHECKPOINT

Identify the major considerations in pricing decisions, and show how those decisions relate to profits, growth, and competition.

Describe pricing responsibilities for establishing policies related to markups, discounting, and retail lists.

Identify and discuss primary regulations that influence price decisions.

MARKETING STRATEGIES

As defined earlier, a **marketing strategy** is a consciously formulated plan that describes how a new venture will compete. It focuses the enterprise on activities related to competing in its market niche, subsequently providing guidelines for decisions about strategic objectives, allocation of resources, and responsibilities required to implement a marketing plan. Having described the marketing concept and the fundamental activities of marketing that comprise a *marketing plan*, we can tie those things together and discuss marketing strategies relevant to an entrepreneurial enterprise.

Strategic Objectives

Objectives vary tremendously. Some are simple, such as to survive, but others can be quite complex. For example, when the newspaper *USA Today* was launched, management set a strategic objective to achieve a circulation of 1 million papers among readers in professional and managerial positions. The newspaper positioned itself to sell in 15 major metropolitan areas representing 54 percent of the national target market. The marketing plan defined to fulfill this objective included a unique product with superior graphics and articles focused on current events, sports, weather, and contemporary features. Pricing was competitive, with a newsstand price lower than other daily papers. Distribution was extremely important for rapid penetration, and *USA Today* created eye-catching vending machines, direct mail subscriptions, and point-of-purchase displays. Company promotions included television advertising to "pull" the product through the system, unusual and very colorful outdoor signs, and aggressive sales promotions for potential subscribers.[23] For *USA Today*, this was an aggressive growth strategy concentrated on a unique product.

Most entrepreneurs do not have the resources to consider such aggressive growth plans, but then again, most entrepreneurs are not in business simply to make enormous amounts of money. Recall from Chapter 2 that many entrepreneurs are in business to achieve personal objectives, or because circumstances forced them to seek independent livelihoods; others are motivated by autonomous life-styles. It follows that most entrepreneurs will avoid aggressive or risky marketing objectives. In contrast to *USA Today*'s strategic objectives, most personal service entrepreneurs (e.g., beauticians, management consultants, and interior designers) simply want to establish single-location businesses with comfortable profits. Between these extremes are entrepreneurs like Jimmy Calano of CareerTrack, introduced in Chapter 1, who wanted a challenge, but not a pressure-packed situation; $40 million in income was a result, not an objective.[24]

Marketing strategies for single-location businesses will reflect less aggressive objectives, such as attaining solvency through sustained sales. Subsequently advertising will be budgeted narrowly, a few appropriate sales promotions will be used during special events, prices often approximate those of competitors, and distribution will be a matter of choosing a decent location. For Calano's early growth stage, he established a single approach to sales through direct mail. Calano relied on personal sales efforts by calling on interested clients, and he priced well below competition to attract a growing market segment. Distribution was carefully defined by offering seminars in several major cities that had also been targeted in direct mail promotions.[25]

Entrepreneurs should be able to establish objectives that can be easily measured. Calano expressed his early objectives as a desire to establish 100 seminars by the end of his first year in business, 240 by the end of year 2, and 360 by the end of year 3. He eclipsed these targets and reached more than a thousand seminars before his third year. *USA Today* sought 1 million readers within three years; it met that objective six months before the target date. Several types of objectives can be considered with similar measurable criteria.

Growth. Growth is measured through sales activities and should be expressed in terms of sales dollars or units sold. A retail clothing store will have too many different items to set up unit sales objectives, but the store should have dollar-volume targets that reflect an accurate sales forecast. These should be expressed monthly for the first year, and quarterly for at least two additional years. Unit sales would be an appropriate measure for a computer hardware store, and a tax accountant might set a target for number of customers served.

Profitability. Every commercial enterprise will have profit objectives, but these can be expressed several ways. For example, in a business where prices and costs are sensitive, an entrepreneur will want to track "return on sales" to monitor the gap between income and expenses, and calculate a targeted "rate of return" on assets, equity, and investments. Most companies can use these criteria to indicate how well they are utilizing assets to generate sales.

Customer Service. An essential objective is to define how the enterprise will serve customers. This definition can be expressed in terms of product quality, diversification, or innovation. Spalding Sports Worldwide, a company that makes hundreds of sporting-goods items, has marketing objectives for each of its major product divisions. For its Top-Flite golf balls, the objective is to have a diversified line of recreational golf balls (see adjacent profile). Apple Computer has an objective of making the Macintosh customer a "literate user" through innovative software. Tandem Corporation, maker of the NonStop Computer, sought to develop the highest-quality software for technical design and production systems, and the company's strategy was to license software through a network of independent software alliances. Tandem fulfilled its objectives by hiring specialists with the sole task of creating this network alliance and coordinating software development with 100 developers.[26]

Human Resources. In addition to the personal aspirations of founders, most excellent companies have human resource objectives such as helping employees improve their career opportunities, or improving performance through job skill training. Entrepreneurs can learn from larger firms that have well-articulated objectives for human resources. Hewlett-Packard, for example, addresses strategic objectives in the essential areas of growth, profitability, customer service, quality, and innovation, but in addition, HP has equally important objectives for corporate citizenry

PROFILE △

Top-Flite "Pulls Through" Sales

Spalding Sports Worldwide, the corporation that makes Top-Flite golf balls, attracts buyers through a three-tier marketing system designed to "pull" customers into pro shops and stores. National advertising drives home product characteristics and brand names, making it easy for buyers to recognize and ask for Spalding products. Top-Flite marketers display at national events, major golf tournaments, and international sports conventions. Sporting-goods wholesalers and golf-equipment distributors are given sales support materials such as point-of-purchase displays and eye-catching posters. Golf professionals enjoy discounts, tournament sponsorship, and well-devised sales campaigns that ensure golfers see the Top-Flite brand. Most golfers may not know that Spalding makes Top-Flite balls, but they know the Top-Flite label and often ask for it by name when making purchases.

Source: Advertising by Top-Flite.

---

and maintaining effective human resources.[27] A new venture may not have the resources to be this ambitious, yet even small companies can provide a safe working environment, health benefits to employees, and perhaps the opportunity to share in success through profit-sharing plans.

Other Objectives. All entrepreneurs want something from their enterprises, and as noted earlier, their preferences may include autonomy, opportunity to be innovative, or the challenge of a new life-style. Perhaps an entrepreneur may want a family enterprise that can be taken over by a son or daughter. Another individual may want to create a salable business that can provide a retirement nest egg. Yet another person may want the recognition that comes from having a glitzy business to pay for equally glitzy possessions. Many entrepreneurs have objectives inspired by their hobbies or social interests. Sharon Citrin created her pet food line of Good Nature treats from a personal desire to find nutritious food for her pets[28] (see the profile "Puppy Love"). Personal objectives will be accounted for in a well-articulated marketing strategy that guides decisions.

General Approaches to Strategy

Unlike managers of major corporations who may consider strategies such as global diversification or conglomerate acquisitions, entrepreneurs have fewer choices. Most new ventures *concentrate* on a product or service in a select market, and although entrepreneurs may think about diversification, they must first establish the fundamental

PROFILE △

Puppy Love

As a health-conscious individual, Sharon Citrin preferred natural foods, and as a pet lover, she became concerned about Timmy, her pet terrier. "There was nothing being sold in the supermarkets that I considered good enough for my pet," she explained. After carefully reading labels on pet foods, she was determined to create an all-natural diet for Timmy, and it was not long before she was preparing several doggy snacks for her friends' pets. "What I started as a hobby just became more interesting and intriguing than my job," she said.

Citrin, a former art teacher, decided to turn her passion for healthy pet food into a business. In 1979 she created CherAmi Natural Pet Foods, and began selling to nearby pet stores and veterinarians' offices. Business was slow, and Citrin was not anxious to advertise or create fancy promotions. Instead, she made personal sales calls for five years. High demand for her pet food convinced Citrin to try mass-marketing with Florida's Publix supermarket chain with a product called Doggie Biscuits. It sold so well that by 1985 every major grocery chain was interested. She added several products to her Good Nature brand line, and soon found herself competing with Purina Bonz, Milk Bones, and Alpo Snaps.

Supermarkets, however, expected fully integrated marketing efforts, sales promotions, displays, price incentives, and efficient inventory distribution. As a result, the company went public in 1986 to underwrite a professional marketing program, but, more important, Sharon Citrin realized her dream of creating healthy pet foods.

Source: Susan Ochshorn, "I Am My Own Boss: Sharon Citrin," *Venture*, July 1986, pp. 48–49.

business endeavor. Once established, a venture may be positioned to diversify into new products or markets. These strategies are called *product* or *market diversification*, and another latter-stage strategic option is *vertical integration*.[29] This is a strategy of expanding backward into the vendor chain to secure resources, or of reaching forward into distribution channels to consolidate intermediaries. As with diversification strategies, integration is an option seldom considered at a firm's inception. Primary strategies for new ventures are shown in Figure 9-8, and described in the following paragraphs.

Concentration. Entrepreneurs will want to consider how to grow, and at what pace to establish that growth. An intense growth can be achieved through "market penetration" tactics that include low prices, pervasive advertising, and sales promotions. Growth can also be achieved by concentrating on a specific market with, for example, high-priced goods for select clients in upmarket locations.

Concentration

```
┌─────────────────────┐      ┌─────────────────────┐
│ Focal product,      │      │ Directed to a       │
│ service, or line    │ ───> │ distinct market     │
│ of merchandise      │      │ segment or niche    │
└─────────────────────┘      └─────────────────────┘
```

Concentric diversification of products or services

```
┌─────────────────┐    ┌──────────────────┐    ┌──────────────────┐
│ Focal product,  │    │ New products or  │    │ Directed to same │
│ service or line │ ─> │ services closely │ ─> │ market segment   │
│ of merchandise  │    │ related to those │    │ or niche as those│
│                 │    │ initially offered│    │ initially offered│
└─────────────────┘    └──────────────────┘    └──────────────────┘
```

Concentric diversification of markets or customers

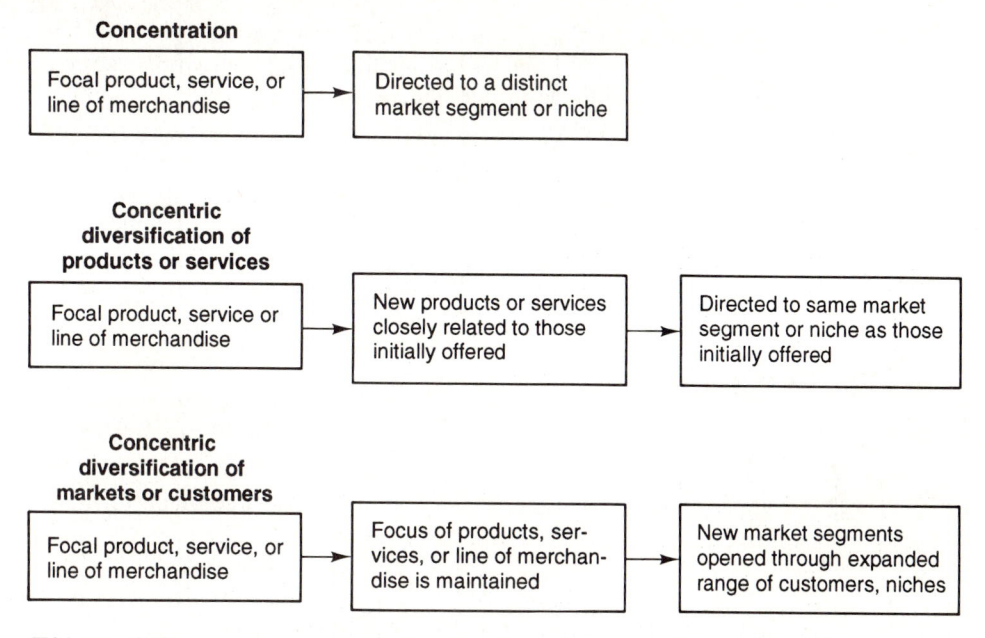

```
┌─────────────────┐    ┌──────────────────┐    ┌──────────────────┐
│ Focal product,  │    │ Focus of products│    │ New market       │
│ service, or line│ ─> │ services, or line│ ─> │ segments opened  │
│ of merchandise  │    │ of merchandise   │    │ through expanded │
│                 │    │ is maintained    │    │ range of         │
│                 │    │                  │    │ customers, niches│
└─────────────────┘    └──────────────────┘    └──────────────────┘
```

Figure 9-8 **Common Start-up Strategies**

New Market Development. Another method of intense growth is to develop several closely associated markets. This is called *concentric diversification* in which the entrepreneur emphasizes finding new customer niches. In this instance, a computer sales and service firm may want to specialize in small office systems but also reach out for sales in education systems. To do so, the firm needs not only to compete on price, but also to create a marketing plan to enhance the product image and the firm's reputation among select consumer groups.

New Product Development. A third alternative is *product diversification*, which means to develop new products or services that are closely associated with existing products and services. This also is called *concentric diversification*, and in some instances, *related diversification*. Entrepreneurs consciously choose to add to their product lines, yet they stick close to their initial products or services, building on their distinct competencies. A computer sales firm, for example, may concentrate on office systems but offer microcomputer systems, software, repair services, training, electronic networking, custom programing, or office supplies that coincide with mainstream hardware sales.

Other Strategy Considerations

Students of strategic management will quickly recognize that these options are far from inclusive, yet for entrepreneurial ventures, they represent the most common options. Business plans that are successful in attracting investors and lenders will have a market strategy that portrays a vision of accelerated growth. A proposed new product, for instance, might be acceptable to investors only if the entrepreneur intends to set up a wholesale distribution system or establish a plant for manufacturing. These options for "integration" imply an early plan to *stage the enterprise*—that is to time the sequence of events to make it successful. For example, the delivery-only concept of Domino's Pizza for a single store would not have been exciting, but the plan to have a small chain of stores in several years with potentially hundreds of stores sold through a franchise format was a superb strategy communicated to investors.

▶ **CHECKPOINT**

Describe marketing objectives and how they relate to strategic plans for a new venture.

Identify and explain the primary strategies most common for new ventures.

THE MARKETING PLAN

A **marketing plan** defines customers, sales forecasts, and market positioning to support strategic objectives. It is the entrepreneur's framework for making decisions within the selected marketing strategy. The marketing plan comprises a major section of the formal business plan, and in addition to providing guidelines for the entrepreneur, it communicates to investors, lenders, and employees expectations and a program of activities.

The marketing plan was outlined in Chapter 4 when we addressed how to write a business plan. The outline was followed in Chapter 8 as we described marketing research activities. As a concluding comment to this chapter, the marketing plan is a synopsis of the strategy and an entrepreneur's statement of how he or she will fulfill marketing responsibilities.

Specifically, the plan will define the marketing objectives, strategies, customer scenario, market segments, products or services to be offered, a sales forecast, and stages of development required to fulfill marketing objectives. The plan will describe distribution systems, promotional activities, and pricing decisions, explaining how they are part of the infrastructure of the venture's marketing activities.

The final element of the marketing plan is to address a *marketing program*. Introduced earlier in the chapter, a marketing program is the "action plan" that defines responsibilities for implementing decisions about *product*, *distribution*, *promotion*, and *pricing*. Business plans seldom have a marketing program spelled out in detail, but the functional decisions will be delineated in the planning section, and a complete business plan will describe who is going to implement those decisions. Consequently, the marketing program will identify founders or employees responsible for product development, sales management, promotions, and distribution. Whether spelled out or not, a marketing program should exist to coordinate those activities that must be done to launch the enterprise.

> ▶ **CHECKPOINT**
>
> Describe the elements of a marketing plan and how they relate to the marketing strategy and to marketing functions.

▲▲▲▲▲▲ SYNOPSIS FOR LEARNING

1. Identify and describe the marketing functions that must be addressed by all new ventures.

Within the framework of a marketing strategy, entrepreneurs must devise a marketing plan as a way of attracting customers, effecting sales, and ensuring continuous patronage by a satisfied clientele. The four most common marketing functions emphasize *product*, *distribution*, *promotion*, and *price*. These labels identify decisions that must be made to conduct business. Product development, design, packaging, labeling, and service combine as an "expanded" concept of a product. A product is more than its physical attributes and includes its function, form, image, and perceived benefits. Distribution is concerned with methods of getting products to market, selecting channels through which they will be marketed, and providing services essential to transfer "value" to consumers. The promotion function involves a conscious effort to formulate a *promotion mix* that can include advertising, personal selling, sales promotions, and publicity. Pricing responsibilities relate to setting prices that reinforce marketing objectives. Prices must reflect the value and image of a product or service, and related decisions will concern discounts, policies for marking up products, and meeting competitors' pricing challenges.

2. Describe an expanded view of a company's "product."

Every product will have a function, even if it is psychological, such as satisfaction from owning a piece of art. Besides function, however, products have form, design, and packaging characteristics. Perceived safety, utility, and image also are important so that, for example, environmentally safe commodities such as laundry detergents will attract certain consumers willing to pay a premium for the value they perceive. Labels that convey safety and use information are also important, and the service-after-sale support (such as warranty service) becomes part of the product purchase. Anything that is perceived as a product attribute can influence sales and is therefore part of the product concept.

3. Explain how distribution is part of marketing infrastructure.

The infrastructure of a marketing plan is often built solely on a firm's distribution system. For example, Frito-Lay potato chips and Domino's Pizza are successful in large part because of their unique distribution techniques. Some products have obvious marketing channels, such as common brands of toothpaste sold retail and supplied through commodity wholesalers. However, even simple products can often be more successfully marketed through other channels that may include specialty stores, catalogs, telemarketing, video programs, direct-mail ordering, agents, brokers, export companies, telethons, sales displays, or trade shows. Entrepreneurs must consciously plan distribution and develop the most effective channels for reaching customers.

4. *Identify and discuss the categories of promotions.*

Advertising is a method of mass communication to target markets through paid media. Selection of media is important to reach the correct consumer groups in cost-effective ways. Local media, such as newspapers or billboards, are more effective than national television for services that have a predominantly local appeal. Radio may be preferred over newspapers for announcing sales or reaching commuters. Magazines may be more effective to display artistic pictures of such products as furniture or sports equipment. Entrepreneurs have many choices for advertising mixes. Personal sales promotions include sale events, point-of-purchase displays, promotions at conventions, booths at fairs, special discounts and introductory offers, among others. Personal selling is the one-to-one encounter of salesperson with customer, and, of course, it can range from door-to-door sales campaigns to impersonal telephone solicitation. Publicity is the result of doing things that are newsworthy. It is a form of nonfee promotion that can stem indirectly from company activities or directly from company sponsorship of community events, programs, and charities.

5. *Address the concept of pricing with respect to new ventures.*

Pricing is always done with clear objectives in mind. If the entrepreneur seeks to penetrate a given market, prices will be set low to gain rapid sales. If profitability is more important—or if the entrepreneur wants to create an exclusive market—then pricing may be high. Entrepreneurs must also consider discount policies, quantity cost-price relationships, markup policies for distributors and wholesalers, competition, and the image communicated through prices. It is also important to be aware of legal pricing behavior, and there are many laws that regulate price-setting.

6. *Describe the primary growth strategies employed by entrepreneurs.*

An established corporation will have many strategic alternatives, but a new venture typically begins with a *concentration* strategy that focuses on one product or service in one distinct market segment. The business can grow within this concentrated arena or choose to become diversified. The primary form of diversification is called *concentric diversification*, meaning that new products or services will be added that are closely associated with the original ones and that build on the entrepreneur's distinct competency. The business can also diversify into new markets, thereby maintaining its distinctive product or service, but targeting new customer groups.

7. *Explain the major elements of a marketing plan.*

The marketing plan will define the marketing objectives, strategies, the customer scenario, market segments, products or services to be offered, a sales forecast, and stages of development. The plan will describe distribution systems, promotional activities, and pricing decisions, explaining how they are integrated to support the business's purpose. These elements constitute a *marketing program*, which is an action plan for implementing the planned decisions. The program will also define responsibilities for those decisions.

NOTES

1. Philip Kotler, *Marketing Management: Analysis, Planning, and Control*, 6th ed. (Englewood Cliffs, NJ: Prentice-Hall, 1984), p. 8.
2. William M. Pride and O. C. Ferrell, *Marketing: Basic Concepts and Decisions*, 5th ed. (Boston: Houghton Mifflin, 1987), p. 8.
3. Ibid., pp. 548–549.
4. Eric N. Berkowitz, Roger A. Kerin, and William Rudelius, *Marketing*, 2nd ed. (Homewood, IL: Richard D. Irwin, 1989), pp. 44–46.
5. Theodore Levitt, "Marketing Intangible Products and Product Intangibles," *Harvard Business Review*, Vol. 81, No. 3 (1981), pp. 94–102.
6. Pride and Ferrell, *Marketing*, pp. 204–206.
7. "Suds for Lady Chuggers," *Venture*, November 1986, pp. 18–19.
8. Alan Farnham, "The Billionaires: Do They Pay Their Way?" *Fortune International*, September 11, 1989, pp. 30–34.
9. Richard M. Hill, Ralph S. Alexander, and James S. Cross, *Industrial Marketing*, 2nd ed. (Homewood, IL: Richard D. Irwin, 1975), pp. 37–38.
10. Jeff Goldberg, "Desperately Seeking Cyborg," *Omni*, July 1989, pp. 12, 64.
11. "How to Save Money on Office Supplies" (Lincolnshire, IL: Quill Corporation, 1990), p. 1.
12. John Naisbitt and Patricia Aburdene, *Re-inventing the Corporation* (New York: Warner Books, 1985), p. 166.
13. Pride and Ferrell, *Marketing*, p. 225. Also see Felix Kessler, "Tremors from the Tylenol Scare Hit Food Companies," *Fortune*, March 31, 1986, pp. 59–62.
14. Kenneth G. Hardy and Allan J. Magrath, *Marketing Channel Management: Strategic Planning and Tactics* (Glenview, IL: Scott, Foresman, 1988), pp. 18–22.
15. Paul B. Brown, "The Anti-Marketers," *Inc.*, March 1988, pp. 62–65, 68, 70, 72.
16. "Toy Show Sets New Contract Records," *South China Morning Post*, Business Post Section, January 23, 1990, p. 1.
17. Interview with Charles Conrad, CEO, Poly-Chem Associates, Inc., February 2, 1990.
18. Donald D. Boroian and Patrick J. Boroian, *The Franchise Advantage: Make It Work for You!* (Schaumburg, IL: National BestSeller, 1987), pp. 34, 58.
19. "Info & Insights for Direct Mailers," *PS*, a quarterly newsletter published by ACS Direct Mail Services, Hutchinson, KS, fall 1987.
20. Robert Lewis Dean III, "On Entrepreneurship and Personal Imagery," keynote speech to the Association of Collegiate Entrepreneurs, Washington, DC, March 5, 1988.
21. Pride and Ferrell, *Marketing*, p. 443.
22. Ibid., p. 490.
23. Kevin Higgins, "*USA Today* Nears Million Reader Mark," *Marketing News*, April 15, 1983, p. 1.
24. James Calano and Jeff Salzman, *Real World 101: How to Find a Job, Get Ahead, Do It Now, and Love It!* (New York: Warner Books, 1984), p. 50.
25. Gail Ignacio, "Preaching What They Practice," *Venture*, May 1988, pp. 31–33.
26. "SIA Alliance Report," *Systems Integration Age*, February 1988, pp. 6–19.

27. Rowland T. Moriarty and Thomas J. Kosnik, "High-Tech Marketing: Concepts, Continuity, and Change," *Sloan Management Review*, Vol. 30, No. 4 (1989), pp. 7–17.

28. Susan Ochshorn, "I Am My Own Boss: Sharon Citrin," *Venture*, July 1986, pp. 48–49.

29. Arthur A. Thompson, Jr. and A. J. Strickland III, *Strategic Management: Concepts and Cases*, 4th ed. (Plano, TX: Business Publications, 1987), pp. 20–22, 161–163.

CASE 9-1

Selling in a Nontraditional Market

Jan Bell Marketing, Inc., a Fort Lauderdale manufacturer of fine jewelry, is one of the fastest-growing public companies in the United States. Annual sales exceed $200 million, up from $7.3 million in 1983, its founding year. Few new ventures realize any first-year profits, so Jan Bell's launch was like a rocket blast. More astounding was that the company achieved success by selling its custom-designed jewelry through discount and wholesale clubs. From the viewpoint of classic marketing theory, Jan Bell violated a fundamental rule of positioning a good product in the wrong market, but facts prove otherwise.

Jan Bell's founders, Alan and Janice Lipton and partner Isaac Arguetty, purposely set out to create exquisite designs in jewelry, but to establish a marketing system for mass-market discounting. Instead of selling luxury items through elegant jewelry stores in prime locations, the company positioned its products for bargain hunters.

Using mainly gold and diamonds, their designs are subcontracted for manufacture, resulting in hundreds of identical items. Each retail location, however, will have only one (or a limited number) of any particular item. Jan Bell's markets are specifically selected for their high sales turnover and low pricing policies. Nearly 80 percent of the company's sales are to the wholesale price club industry, and the remainder are to department stores. Jan Bell sells to six of the eight major wholesale club chains, and its jewelry sales represent about 1 percent of their combined sales. This figure may seem small, but the $20 billion industry is a phenomenon that is itself expected to increase threefold before the end of the decade, and Jan Bell's products are sold in 260 of the 300 largest warehouse club stores.

This strategy may represent a major shift in retailing, and Jan Bell is riding the wave to success. The founders had to minimize the costs of jewelry manufacturing to implement their marketing plan. They buy gold and diamonds on the commodity exchanges of international markets, and inventory control and distribution expediting is closely monitored for both materials. Bulk purchasing and subcontracted manufacturing assure the lowest-cost scenario, eliminating operational overhead. By paying well for exquisite designs, they create quality merchandise with the look and feel of custom jewelry, but mass production brings the per-item cost down dramatically. Distribution is simplified by direct shipment to wholesale club warehouses. Jan Bell has no retail space or overhead, no location expenses beyond their design and administration facilities, and a parsimonious promotion budget limited to presentation materials for sales representatives.

The company also enjoys rapid turnaround in cash flow because the discount clubs replace inventory rapidly. Unlike department stores and retail jewelers, there are few problems with credit collection or slow-moving inventory. Jan Bell also leverages its market research data to generate demand beyond its ability to supply jewelry. For example, the company can demonstrate how its low-price formula of less than 20 percent margin results in a whopping $17,000 per square foot sales volume. Sales volumes for department stores and fashion retailers generate between $150 and $200 in the same space. Wholesale price clubs determine their inventory on a turnover of $400 to $600 per square foot. The arithmetic is simple, and Jan Bell's products are getting all the floor space they need. Their buyers are highly sensitive to merchandise that maximizes floor-space profits, and contracting is largely a matter of selecting Jan Bell's designs for future deliveries.

CASE QUESTIONS

1. Describe Jan Bell's marketing plan, and explain why it is working so well.
2. Discuss from a consumer's viewpoint the image of Jan Bell's products, and in your answer, explain how other jewelers might market similar items.
3. Examine the concept of wholesale price clubs, their customers, and how they might devise their marketing plans.

Source: Jeffrey L. Seglin, "All That Glitters," *Venture*, April 1989, p. 27.

CASE 9-2

A Minimum Effort Pays Off

Professional Training Systems, Inc. (PTS), produces educational software on interactive videodiscs for the health care industry. Founded in 1988 by John Hayes, PTS expected sales to break the $10 million mark in 1989 and, with new product development, to triple by 1992. Hayes is one of the new "miminalists" who has no aspirations of creating or managing a large organization. With fewer than 30 employees, PTS relies on strategic alliances to achieve its objectives.

Staff at PTS have two responsibilities: They conceive of and plan new products, and they establish the marketing plans to succeed. John Hayes is responsible for orchestrating the strategic alliances. For example, the company's most recent product is an interactive video series of training programs for nurses. The courseware was developed for nurses lacking formal degrees who must meet new federal regulations requiring certain demonstrated skills and education mandates. Hayes and his staff had the ability to produce the programs, but not to develop program content or to market to nurses.

To accomplish the task, Hayes formed an alliance with the American Health Care Association (AHCA), the Educational Testing Service (ETS) of Princeton, New Jersey, and a Washington federation of state nursing home groups. Course content and program development were guided by AHCA, bringing to the alliance expertise on most aspects of health care as well as years as the premiere organization concerned with health care policies on Capitol Hill. In addition, ETS is a nationwide testing service famous for administering college entrance exams, SATs, and a variety of highly reputable public and private qualifications-testing systems. The role of ETS in the alliance was to administer coursework, monitoring and recording nationwide testing results from nurse study programs. The ETS stamp of approval would prove to be an exceptionally important endorsement.

With AHCA creating the program and ETS administering it, the Washington federation of nursing homes provided the initial test markets and the launchpad for mass circulation of the courseware. It remained for Hayes's organization to produce the program, manufacture the products, and implement a marketing plan. Hayes and PTS accomplished all this with a handful of staff. Production planning and control was entirely the work of PTS, but experts were hired for video graphics, hard-copy publications, and student materials. Production, packaging, and distribution were accomplished through subcontracting.

The PTS marketing effort was coordinated by Hayes and company; AHCA was given responsibility for advertising through its monthly journals and magazines; and, in turn, the company was influential in attracting nurse organizations and nonprofit organizations to adopt the software. The Washington alliance and AHCA were also extremely well networked with health care organizations where they could encourage institutional adoptions. Thousands of organizations were reached when ETS included the program in its nationwide lists of educational services.

CASE QUESTIONS

1. Describe the marketing objectives and the marketing plan for PTS, Inc.
2. What advantages and disadvantages do you envision for the "minimalist" approach? How does it change the role for an entrepreneur?
3. Identify a familiar product or service, and explain how a marketing effort might be established for it using strategic alliances.

Source: Edmund L. Andrews, "The New Minimalists," *Venture*, January 1989, pp. 37–39.

Chapter **10**

International Markets: New Venture Opportunities

OBJECTIVES

1. Describe changes in Europe that provide opportunities for global trade.
2. Explain why the Pacific Rim is important to American business.
3. Examine how entrepreneurs can become involved in exports and imports.
4. Identify ways entrepreneurs can "go international" with investments.
5. Describe how entrepreneurs can find information and help on overseas opportunities and exporting.

An unfortunate misconception about small businesses—and about most new ventures—is that they are anchored to local domestic markets. International business is viewed, inappropriately, as the sacred domain of large enterprises, and until recently, even large American enterprises viewed international business with little interest. During the 1980s, however, America became firmly rooted in global business, and by 1990 nearly every *Fortune* 500 company had international interests; half of those companies earned nearly one-third of their gross income from foreign markets.[1] There also has been tremendous growth in small business exporting, and U.S. exports are expected to double by the year 2000 with 38 percent of a $1.87 trillion market going to small enterprises.[2]

A majority of small enterprises will continue to operate domestically because the nature of their businesses is geared to personal service and local clientele; community physicians, store owners, beauticians, and attorneys are unlikely to "go global." For those with products and services that can be exported, however, there are many exciting overseas opportunities.

There are insufficient superlatives to explain what has happened to reshape world economies, and with each remarkable change, new megamarkets have opened. In early sections of this chapter, we examine these markets and major changes taking place internationally. In later sections, we describe different ways to do business internationally and problems entrepreneurs might encounter.

THE CHANGING INTERNATIONAL ENVIRONMENT

Winds of change swept through Europe and Asia as the world slipped into the 1990s. The Berlin Wall came down, East and West Germany reunified, Poland put its first Solidarity government into office, Czechoslovakia and Hungary turned out Communist Party leaders in favor of prodemocracy forces, and Romanian dictator Nicolae Ceauşescu was disposed and executed.

Dramatic changes have also taken place in the Soviet Union since Mikhail Gorbachev unleashed reforms under *perestroika* to try to reposition the U.S.S.R. for global business. As this is being written, changes within the Soviet Union reflect political movements toward independence by Soviet republics and economic reforms for less-restrictive trade, but there is much uncertainty in Soviet politics. In Asia, the People's Republic of China capped ten years of "open-door policy" by repressing democratic idealists, yet the PRC has expanded trade with the West. Equally important, member nations of the European Economic Community (EEC) will reshape their economic boundaries after 1992, creating a European trading block. As you can see in Figure 10-1, trade is vital to major countries, and trade is becoming more extensive. Consequently, we want to examine changes that are occurring and the implications of these changes.

Eastern Europe

Events in Eastern bloc countries not only have changed the economic map of Europe, but also have made free-world markets accessible to an additional 140 million people. It is estimated that pent-up demand, if turned into effective buying power for Western goods and services, could exceed $300 billion annually by the turn of the century.[3] Commercial opportunities, however, will not materialize overnight, nor will they be uniform among Eastern European nations.

The most promising changes are likely to occur as East and West Germany unify with a strong common currency.[4] Hungary is also a promising market because it has benefited from U.S. and International Monetary Fund (IMF) loans. Hungary has been a cooperative member of international trade organizations, thereby opening its doors to EEC and American business.[5] Poland may emerge during the next few years as a trading economy; however, Poland suffers from instability and soaring inflation to complicate its situation.[6]

Czechoslovakia and Yugoslavia both have tenuous trade links with the West, but even if they opened their doors widely, their economies are viewed as "mildly developing" with little to offer for export in exchange for goods they sorely need from the West. Consequently, their trade potential is limited in the near future, and

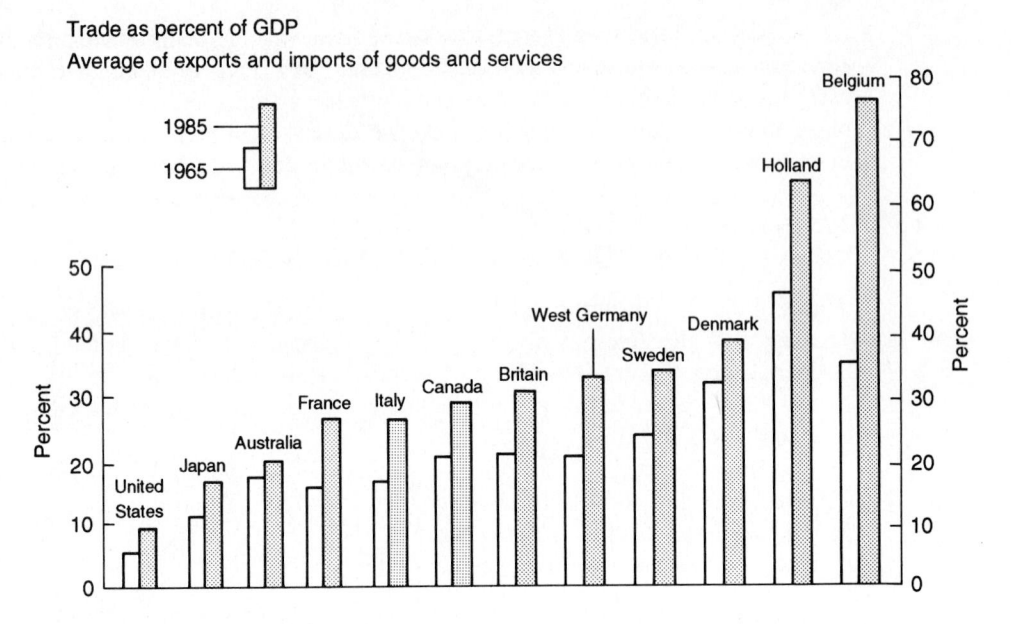

Figure 10-1 **The Importance of Trade.** (*Source*: *The Economist*, November 1, 1986, p. 98. Reprinted with permission.)

Yugoslavia suffers from internal unrest. The three remaining countries of Bulgaria, Albania, and Romania are in political and economic disarray; they are not promising places to do business.

All Eastern bloc countries entered the 1990s in turmoil, but they also brought with them the shambles of centrally controlled economies. None have organized securities markets, currencies convertible for foreign exchange, or infrastructures to support foreign trade and investment. These criteria are crucial for global business, yet trade opportunities will improve as each country stabilizes and develops financial and legal mechanisms to support foreign trade.[7]

The Soviet Union

The Soviet Union is facing extraordinary changes. The pace of change will quickly date anything presented here, but understanding the structure of the U.S.S.R. and its economy will provide a framework for future events.

Political and National Profiles. Americans seldom appreciate that the U.S.S.R. comprises 14 diverse peoples, each with national identities, languages, and customs. Much of the recent turmoil has occurred between these national groups. For example, Armenia, Azerbaijan, and Georgia remain locked into ancient religious and ethnic conflict. Disputes have been going on since the fourth century between

Armenians and Azerbaijanis, and between Christians and Shiite Muslims in these regions.[8] Similar clashes persist over national rights and boundaries among several other Soviet states.

The heart of the Soviet Union is *Russia* (145 million people) which is essentially the country created by Cossack conquests of the 17th and 18th centuries. It extends from Siberia to the Eastern Baltic enclave. The Baltic republics bordering Scandinavia include *Estonia* (1.5 million people), *Latvia* (2.6 million), and *Lithuania* (3.6 million). Each republic clings to its own sense of national identity and resents Russian rule, imposed by Stalin in 1940.

The *Ukraine* (51 million) and *Byelorussia* (10 million) are Slavic peoples whose major industrial and commercial cities are Kiev and Minsk. These are situated between Eastern Europe and the heart of Russia. During World War II, the Ukraine bore the main thrust of the German invasion, and when the Germans retreated, Stalin regained control of both regions with military power. *Moldavia* (4.2 million), also a border country, is adjacent to Romania and the Ukraine. Stalin annexed Moldavia in 1940.

The mixing bowl of the Transcaucasia region, between the Black and Caspian seas, includes *Armenia* (3.4 million), *Azerbaijan* (7 million), and *Georgia* (5 million). Georgia and Armenia reject Soviet economic doctrine, and free trade is pervasive in black markets. The majority of Central Asia constitutes five Muslim republics. *Kazakhstan* (16 million) is about half Russian and half Kazakhs and Ukrainians. *Kirgizia* (4 million) is mainly populated by one-time nomadic Kirgiz tribes. *Tajikistan* (5 million) also has its predominately Tajik population rooted in tribes that anchored the ancient silk trade. *Turkmenistan* (3.4 million), the southernmost border country, was annexed from the British in the 18th century. Finally, *Uzbekistan* (19 million), inhabited mainly by Uzbeks, is a citadel of Islam.[9]

Economic Trends. Among the 14 republics of the U.S.S.R., 13 are bidding for national independence. They are being discouraged by Soviet intervention, yet under Gorbachev's leadership, they were being encouraged to establish for-profit enterprises and to "pay their own way." Under *perestroika*, individual companies and cooperatives have been making reforms to become accountable for revenues and expenses. Prior to these changes, companies and cooperatives could operate at huge losses and be given infusions of money to continue, but the money to cover losses came from diverted resources, creating an impoverished nation. Gorbachev said, "All bets are off . . . pay your way or go under . . . no more handouts." This policy implied a move toward a market economy and increased global trade.[10]

Essentially *perestroika* is an effort to make far-reaching economic reforms that require not only fundamental industrial restructuring, but also globalization of Soviet trade relationships. Without these changes, the Soviet economy may crumble. Why this situation exists is beyond this text, but in general, the U.S.S.R. has severe shortages of consumer goods and a defunct industrial system that cannot fulfill shortages or convert resources for trade (despite having an abundance of exportable natural resources such as oil and gold). Specifically, the U.S.S.R. must establish an internal market system to stabilize supply and demand while nurturing external trade to underwrite its capital resource expansion.[11]

Implications for Entrepreneurs. Entering the Soviet market may sound like a formidable task reserved for only the largest companies, but smaller companies have distinct advantages, and they are being vigorously courted by the Soviets. Large companies such as PepsiCo and McDonald's entered joint ventures with Soviet partners, and more than 300 major trade agreements were concluded between Western and Soviet firms by 1989; however, another 320 contracts were concluded between firms that had less than $10 million of capitalization. In effect, more than half of all international business involved small enterprises, and 90 percent of those were "entrepreneurial" (i.e., owned and operated by enterprise founders).[12]

There are five important reasons that small companies do better in the Soviet market, either as joint-venture companies operating in the U.S.S.R. or as trade partners:[13]

1. *Financing*. Larger companies need complex financing, international loans, and equal or heavier commitments from their Soviet counterparts. Smaller ventures can be financed independently, and their Soviet partners have adequate capital to be involved. Soviet companies lack sufficient capital for huge projects.
2. *Human resources*. Setting up a factory that requires several thousand employees in the Soviet Union is a major problem because often the skilled personnel are not available. A smaller enterprise requiring few employees can be started in almost any region with local skills and local authority.
3. *Economies of scale*. Larger companies tend to produce in quantity, and large service enterprises usually are structured for major accounts. Both types of enterprises are interested in high-volume turnover. They enjoy economies of scale but also have high-threshold break-even points. Smaller firms operate at low volumes, and although they face higher costs, they are accustomed to smaller, localized sales. This pattern fits easily into Soviet markets, which are smaller and are more efficiently served by small enterprises.
4. *Resources*. Soviet resources are limited, and everything from office supplies to raw materials is allocated under quota systems. Even when purchases can be made in open competition, few resources are plentiful. Therefore, large enterprises often cannot obtain sufficient materials to operate efficiently. Smaller companies with lower-volume sales can take advantage of limited resources to compete effectively for materials.
5. *Infrastructure*. The Soviet economy may be decades away from having an infrastructure to support major transactions. For example, shipping 200 hogs to market by train requires one livestock rail car; shipping 2,000 requires an entire train. One rail car can be easily located, but a train will take months to arrange through a complicated bureaucracy. There are few Soviet banks, and they are accustomed to handling local cash transactions. Foreign exchange transactions require central banking authority and can take months to conclude. Commercial long-distance trucking is rare, highways are poor, and warehouse facilities are embryonic. Consequently, small companies with low-volume sales find the existing infrastructure adequate, but large firms have difficulty.

> **Exhibit 10-1 Essential Provisions of Soviet Joint Venture Regulations**
>
> - JVs have the status of legal entities under Soviet law and will operate independently on the basis of their own operating budgets and financing.
> - JVs must be approved and registered with the state on the basis of a negotiated agreement between the partners.
> - Land, mineral rights, and water and forest resources are leased to the JV by the State.
> - The JV statutes are by partner agreement and determine the aims of the venture, its location, the participants' shares, the assets, the administrative structure, and priority in liquidation.
> - Share of assets is determined in rubles based on agreed prices related to world markets with currency converted at official exchange rates.
> - Equipment and materials contributed by the Western partner are duty-free.
> - JVs may conduct import and export operations and participate in domestic markets.
> - All foreign currency expenditures by the JV must be based on internally generated currency from foreign sales or other such means.
> - JVs may apply for financing on commercial terms from Soviet banks in both hard currency and rubles.
> - Tax on profits is set at 30 percent, with an initial two years' exemption and other incentive rates, and a further 20 percent tax on profits transferred abroad.
> - Labor is on the basis of negotiated collective agreements that must conform to various aspects of Soviet laws.
> - Profit after tax shall be distributed in accordance with the partners' share of the assets.
>
> *Source*: Basial Kalymon, "East-West Joint Ventures: Changing Opportunities in the USSR," *International Business Scene*, Vol. 1, No. 2 (Summer 1990), p. 10. Copyright, Ontario Centre for International Business.

Recognizing these limitations on large enterprises, William Norris, chairman of Control Data Corporation, proposed a network of joint ventures between Soviet and small U.S. companies. The network would break down large projects into dozens (or hundreds) of small operations, each one focused on projects that would not overwhelm Soviet systems. For example, the conversion of computer technology into marketable microcomputer products might require 200 individual ventures located in various cities, some dedicated to production, others to research, and still others to systems development.[14] Although this program sounds simple, doing business in the U.S.S.R. can be complicated. This is shown in Exhibit 10-1 by the complexity of joint venture regulations.

The People's Republic of China

Before the most dramatic changes in Eastern Europe and the U.S.S.R., the People's Republic of China reached a crisis when more than 400,000 people demonstrated in Beijing for democratic reforms. Confronted with demands, Chinese officials used troops to crush demonstrators in Tiananmen Square. The June 4 incident, however, may have been the turning point for change, inscribing 1989 in history as the year when the political and economic systems of the Chinese Proletariat were challenged.[15]

Economic Outlook. At the time of the Tiananmen Square disaster, China's supreme leader Deng Xiao-ping was in his tenth year of the "four modernizations," an economic program aimed at opening China to Western technology. Although no one expected the ferocity of repression, there was a general feeling that China had made changes too quickly, yet despite the crackdown, trade and foreign investment in China continued to increase. Western powers simply could not ignore a nation of nearly 1.2 billion people with nearly $90 billion of direct foreign investment by early 1990. The pendulum had perhaps swung too far for a hard-line retrenchment by Chinese leaders, but any conclusion about China's future is dangerous because, historically, its leaders have barricaded themselves against international political pressure.[16]

Nevertheless, China's exports to the United States in 1989 were estimated at $17.5 billion, and imports of U.S. goods and services were nearly $20 billion. It has a commercial banking system capable of rapid and efficient transactions through 24,000 branches, and the PRC is second only to Hong Kong in containerized sea van shipping; Hong Kong reverts to China as a "Special Administrative Region" in 1997. Economic growth in China has exceeded 9 percent per year since 1979, and demand has outraced supply, opening more opportunities for foreign trade.[17]

Implications for Entrepreneurs. Although China does not have convertible currency and is socialist, the PRC embraces trade and international investment. By 1990, China had more than 5,000 joint ventures with Western companies. Most of these were located among five "special economic zones" (SEZs) where there are special tax concessions, reduced property costs, and cooperative labor markets making foreign investment attractive. Many Chinese companies have American partners that include, for example, Jeep, GE, Motorola, Procter & Gamble, NCR, and Boeing, but the majority are small ventures without distinguished names that account for nearly 90 percent of foreign investment.[18]

Smaller enterprises benefit through Chinese subsidiaries or joint ventures by reducing their manufacturing costs. Thus toy manufacturers with small plants in one of the SEZs can hire factory workers at less than $50 a month, procure state-allocated materials at controlled prices about 60 percent cheaper than elsewhere, and enjoy tax relief if finished products are exported. Currently, nearly 40 percent of all toys exported to the West come through Hong Kong, and are fabricated in China. Fashion garments, watches, hand tools, plastic wares, shoes, handbags, CD players, electric motors, television sets, radios, and power sources for microcomputers are among more than 800 products made in China destined for Western markets. In the Guangdong Province (the mainland territory adjacent to Hong Kong), there are nearly 10,000 factories contracted with foreign firms.[19]

The Pacific Rim

In capsule form, the Pacific Rim comprises about 20 countries ranging from the oil-rich tiny kingdom of Brunei to superpower Japan. Together the PacRim nations represent approximately 300 million people in market-driven economies. Most of these countries also are anxious to attract American trade and foreign investment. They include Taiwan, South Korea, Indonesia, Malaysia, Australia, New Zealand,

PROFILE △

Manufacturing Opportunities in a Global Environment

The demand for products has continued to be strong in Western nations, but many domestic companies find that foreign manufacturing is cost-effective. Workers in China, Thailand, Malaysia, Mexico, India, and many other developing nations are no longer barefoot and uneducated. Overseas companies are anxious to expand manufacturing, and many U.S. companies are obliging with foreign investments and joint agreements for products that, made overseas, are destined for Western markets. However, just as this demand has influenced foreign workers to embrace manufacturing, the workers have created a reciprocal demand for new products ranging from machinery to household goods. Consequently, there is a pent-up demand for U.S. exports with tremendous opportunities worldwide. In 1970, American manufacturers exported less than 10 percent of production, but by the end of the 1980s, manufactured exports had more than doubled to exceed 20 percent of U.S. production.

Source: Isaiah Frank, "Financing Third World Economic Growth," *Economic Impact* (Washington, DC: U.S. Information Agency, 1988), pp. 6–10.

Thailand, Singapore, Hong Kong, and Japan. Other PacRim countries include the Philippines, Sri Lanka, Burma, and Vietnam.

PacRim Markets. Exempting Japan and China, the six smaller nations of Taiwan, South Korea, Malaysia, Singapore, Hong Kong, and Thailand account for nearly three-quarters of all microelectronic consumer products imported to the United States. These include VCRs, microwaves, radios, CD players, televisions, telephones, small appliances, and microcomputer "clones." Many products with Japanese or European brand names (e.g., Sony, Panasonic, Philips, National, NEC) are manufactured through subsidiaries in these countries. None are backward or depressed. To the contrary, they enjoy high growth and have high-tech industries with exceptional banking systems, skilled workers, excellent university systems, and thriving stock markets. Combined, they export to the West the equivalent of Japanese trade to the United States, and they import nearly an equal amount.[20]

Japanese Markets. In Japan, there is a continuing saga of negotiations between the United States and Japan to "open" trade. However, many American firms have operations in Japan, and many more export products to Japan that range from office software to space technology. The issue is not that Japan is "closed," but that a prevailing U.S. trade deficit with Japan means the Japanese consistently export more than they import.[21] News headlines focus on macro data and industries such as autos and electronics, but Japan is complex, and in many instances, it depends heavily on U.S. imports. For example, Lotus, Microsoft, Genentech, and Mead Imaging have established major markets in Japan, and the Japanese rely heavily on U.S. products such as medical equipment, agricultural chemicals, instrumentation, pharmaceuticals, processed meat, and poultry.[22]

Implications for Entrepreneurs. The combined strength of the Pacific Rim is comparable to the combined European markets. The PacRim region also has the infrastructure to support new enterprises. Political philosophy notwithstanding, most PacRim nations also have the resources to underwrite industrial expansion. Most PacRim nations have free markets, and their people thrive on entrepreneurship. Taxes are generally low, costs are reasonable, capital is plentiful, and their governments aggressively court foreign enterprises of every size.

Europe after 1992

Western nations that comprise the European Economic Community (EEC), also called the Common Market, will become a confederation of "open-border" nations after 1992. This arrangement is the result of a treaty called the Single Market Initiative in which EEC nations will form a marketplace with nearly 320 million consumers. Fulfilling the potential benefits of the European market will depend on this federation's reduced trade barriers. Common Market studies indicate that the federation could experience more than a 7 percent increase in GNP and create 5 million new jobs through enhanced trade of competitive goods positioned in global markets.[23]

There is no comparable federation in North America or the Far East, but the United States and Japan set the cadence for economic activity in their hemispheres. Japan and other Pacific Rim nations comprise a geographic region that constitutes a competitive market, and North America is aligned with Canada through the U.S.-Canada Trade Agreement. Although neither region has a legal premise similar to Europe, there will emerge a tripartite trade environment with Europe, Japan, and the United States. This global view was first noted by Kenichi Ohmae as a *triad of power* that could dominate international trade. More important, global trade *within* these regions is expected to increase, and trade between regions will complicate international relations.[24]

Global Opportunities in Perspective

These earthshaking events—ranging from *perestroika* to the Single Market Initiative—promise to reshape the business world as we know it. Headlines will focus on giant companies doing extraordinary deals and on politicians who are made larger than life through their media presence; however, it will be an age ripe with entrepreneurial endeavor.

It will be the 10,000 small companies that contribute to China's reforms, each carving out market niches in global trade to effect an "open door" with the West.

It will be thousands of small ventures in border regions of the U.S.S.R., each encouraged to be responsible for profits and losses, that will compete for Western goods and technology. It will be the Pacific Rim economies that embrace adventurers. It will be consumers in Eastern Europe that will soon want commodity imports, services, and technology. And it will be individual entrepreneurs from industrialized countries in the West that will meet these global challenges.

Theoretically, there are enormous opportunities for entrepreneurs in global business, but realistically global trade requires astute planning and knowledge of how to "go international." These issues will be addressed in the next three sections on exporting, importing, and methods of establishing global ventures.

> ▶ **CHECKPOINT**
>
> Describe changes that have taken place in Europe, the Soviet Union, and Asia to create opportunities for international trade.
>
> Explain the interdependence of Japan and the United States.
>
> Discuss how entrepreneurs can benefit from foreign trade.

EXPORTING

Exporting is the process of selling domestic goods or manufactured products to foreign consumers. For example, the American company Weyerhauser, Inc., can sell lumber to a Japanese contractor for use in housing, or Compaq can ship fully assembled microcomputers from the United States to its export agent for resale in Nigeria. Exporting is the easiest way to enter global markets with little cost or risk to the domestic company, and exporting can be relatively simple.[25] Consequently, exporting is particularly attractive to entrepreneurs who seldom have capital for foreign investment or the expertise to set up international ventures.

Entrepreneurs can choose to become *direct exporters* or *indirect exporters*. Direct exporters bypass intermediaries to sell directly to overseas buyers. Direct exporting requires taking responsibility for selecting overseas markets, making contacts with foreign customers, arranging shipments and payments, and handling necessary documentation required to export. These tasks can be demanding; therefore, most companies choose to export by indirect means, using intermediaries.[26]

Direct Exporting

Direct exporting has the advantage of personal control by entrepreneurs, but they must understand foreign markets and have experience negotiating with foreign customers. Assuming that a product needs no special modifications, the major task is to select a *distribution channel* to reach the target customer. Consequently, an entre-

```
┌─────────────────┐                          ┌──────────┐
│ Domestic        │      ╱────────╲     ┌───▶│ Foreign  │
│ manufacturer    │     │ Directly │    │    │ retailers│
│ or marketing    │────▶│ contracts│────┤    └──────────┘
│ company         │     │   with   │    │    ┌──────────┐
│ seeking export  │      ╲────────╱     ├───▶│ Foreign  │
│ markets         │                     │    │wholesalers│
└─────────────────┘                     │    └──────────┘
                                        │    ┌──────────┐
                                        └───▶│ Overseas │
                                             │distributors│
                                             └──────────┘
```

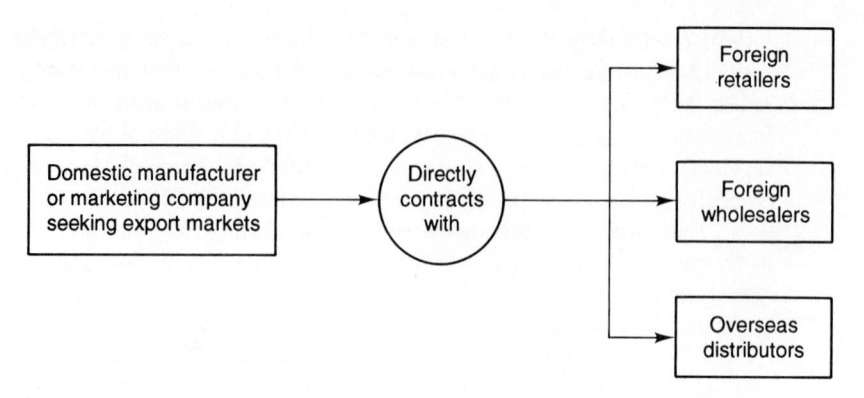

Figure 10-2 **Direct Exporting as a Form of Going International**

preneur's primary responsibility is to identify the best channel and then negotiate sales to foreign customers within that channel. There are three standard channels for direct exports, as shown in Figure 10-2. In addition, companies sell directly to end users. These are described below.

Foreign Agents. A foreign agent is any person or company legally entitled to import goods to an overseas location. Most foreign agents are foreign in the sense that they are citizens or legally registered companies of the nation to which goods will be exported. This sounds obvious, yet some foreign agents are not "foreign"— they are American enterprises that represent overseas interests. For example, a company called Gilman Office Supplies has offices in California that contract directly with Apple Computer Corporation and Hewlett-Packard to export Apple microcomputers and HP laser printers to Hong Kong. Gilman is a division of Inchcape (a British corporation) that has worldwide distribution of several hundred products constituting $11 billion in annual sales.[27] Gilman (Hong Kong) sells Apple and Hewlett-Packard equipment, but in California, Gilman is a registered foreign agent of Inchcape. The arrangement is for Gilman as the registered agent in California to buy directly from the manufacturers, Apple Computers or Hewlett-Packard.

Distributors. A foreign distributor is a merchant or wholesaler who buys directly from the domestic exporter and resells products while providing all necessary support services overseas. Unlike an agent, the distributor is not representing someone else—the distributor is the customer. Sales are made through direct contracts, and the distributor is usually carefully selected by the exporter to handle sales exclusively in a distinct market. For example, Toyota maximizes its world distribution of automobiles through a system of contract distributors. Inchcape, the British trading company with its hands in Apple, Hewlett-Packard, and Jaguar, also is the exclusive distributor for Toyota in five Pacific Rim countries and three European countries. Toyota has separate distributor contracts in Canada, the United States, South America, and the Middle East.[28]

Foreign Retailers. An exporter can also sell directly to foreign retailers who resell through stores, catalogs, direct-marketing promotions, trade shows, or telemarketing. This approach can be attractive to entrepreneurs with unusual products. Some Rolex watches, for example, are retailed by licensed dealers (a method discussed later), but nearly half of all Rolex watches are sold directly to jewelry stores in 47 countries under contracts tightly controlled by Rolex. Ralph Lauren's sports accessories are sold through airline catalogs, duty-free airport shops, major department stores, and specialty retailers. In order to sell directly to foreign retailers, exporters must assume the burden of negotiating contracts, transporting products, and arranging financial transactions.

Direct Sales to End Users. A sizable export business exists between domestic companies and overseas customers that are end users. For example, major companies such as Boeing sell aircraft directly to foreign-owned airlines, and Cincinnati Milicron sells industrial robots directly to foreign manufacturers. In the medical field, there are nearly 200 U.S. and Canadian companies that sell medical instruments and pharmaceuticals directly to independent foreign clinics, doctors, dentists, hospitals, and government agencies. Nearly half of these medical equipment companies are privately held and have less than $10 million in sales, and approximately a quarter of those are ventures started since 1980.[29]

Indirect Exporting

Entrepreneurs can simplify the export process by indirect marketing through an expert intermediary. Having someone else handle foreign negotiations and legal transactions minimizes an entrepreneur's responsibility. Perhaps more important, intermediaries usually have excellent market connections to arrange sales efficiently. Several types of intermediaries are summarized in Figure 10-3 and described in the following sections.[30]

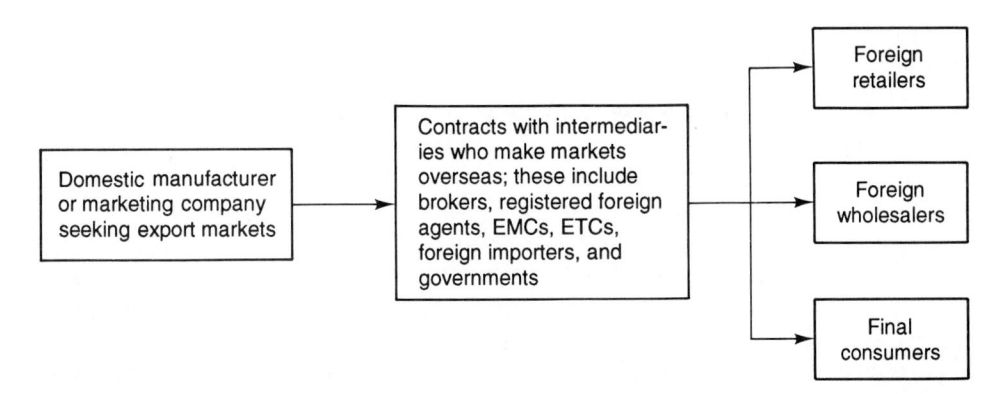

Figure 10-3 **Indirect Exporting as a Form of Going International**

Commission Agents. Foreign traders are commission agents who act simply as middlemen to find outlets for exporters' products or to find products to meet import demands for their clients. They may receive "finder's fees" or commissions from one or both parties to the transaction, but they do not become involved beyond a brokerage role. In most Western countries, commission agents must be registered traders licensed to transact business, and once licensed, they act as wholesale brokers. They find buyers and sellers, negotiate terms, handle transactions, and clear products through customs. In some countries, agents must be government branches. For example, in the Soviet Union, agents appointed through the Ministry of Foreign Trade monitor trade activity, handle monetary transactions through a special bank (the U.S.S.R. Bank of Foreign Trade), and negotiate with foreign companies as representatives of Soviet enterprises.[31]

Export Management Companies (EMCs). An export management company is a private business that contracts as manufacturers' representatives for exporting. Most EMCs develop a reputation in a specific industry, such as chemicals or electronics, and do business in many different markets. Unlike a commission agent that focuses on one country, the EMC will market wherever there are profitable sales. They seldom handle more than a few product lines in an industry; however, they often represent many companies at once. This practice is potentially dangerous to the exporter because the EMC could represent several competitors at the same time. Consequently, entrepreneurs must carefully select an EMC that adequately handles similar products, but that does not play competitors against one another.

For example, USKO Investments, an EMC positioned to transact business in Seoul, Korea, represents 23 chemical manufacturers from the United States, Great Britain, Canada, and Japan. Although USKO sells to clients in Asia, the Soviet Union, the United States, and Canada, the company is careful to maintain confidentiality among clients and does not "cross sell" similar products in the same markets.[32]

Usually, EMCs represent exporters directly, selling their brand-name items without modifications, but they can also be licensed to buy in bulk and sell under local brand names. Most of the 2,000 registered EMCs in the United States also provide support services, advertising, warranty services, foreign exchange transactions, and physical distribution for their clients.

Export Trading Companies (ETCs). Prior to 1982 export trading companies were trade intermediaries similar to EMCs. They were private companies organized to facilitate trade and represent clients within a specialized field. Then, in 1982, the United States passed the Export Trading Company Act, substantially broadening the power of ETCs. The act was meant to encourage American exports by supporting ETCs through government-funded programs, loan guarantees, and direct support by government agencies to pursue and negotiate foreign buyers.[33] Therefore, ETCs can trade in exports for direct sales; EMCs only manage exports for a commission. In addition ETCs customarily take title of goods either through a direct purchase from the manufacturer or a guarantee that, in effect, insures the exporter of proceeds from a specific foreign sale. Exporters can also create their own ETCs and obtain independent financing without risk to the parent company.

Export trading companies are the primary marketing channels for nearly 60 percent of all Japanese goods, and the 1982 act basically allows U.S. firms to emulate Japanese export systems. Virtually every major Japanese and European company maintains ETCs. For example, JETRO (Japan Trading Organization), Itoh, Mitsui, and Mitsubishi are trading companies. Since 1982 more than 300 American companies have registered ETC subsidiaries that include BankAmerica Corporation, Citicorp, Security Pacific Corporation, Sears, and First Chicago Corporation. These are monolithic organizations with access to capital, services, shipping, and insurance, but the majority of American ETCs are smaller companies that handle limited product lines in specific geographic regions.[34]

Export Merchants or Remarketers. Although they call themselves "brokers," export merchants are *remarketers* of exportable products. They buy directly from U.S. manufacturers, take full title to goods, and then resell them overseas. The exporter's customers are domestic merchants, not foreign end users, yet the products are exported. The essence of this business is expert negotiations. The manufacturer is negotiating for sales to broaden its global markets, and the merchant is negotiating as a purchasing agent. This is a convenient channel of indirect exporting because the manufacturer is relieved of overseas marketing.

Merchants typically cluster in port cities and near to points of export control because many of their activities include physical warehousing, packaging, loading, and shipping products. They also maintain foreign offices to facilitate distribution, foreign exchange transactions, and marketing.

Piggyback Marketing. Piggyback marketing is a contractual arrangement between a foreign company and a domestic exporter to market noncompeting products. For example, Sony Corporation markets Whirlpool appliances in Japan. Sony has a wide range of electronic appliances that are concentrated in audiovisual markets (television sets, radios, recorders, and VCRs), but it has never developed its own household appliances. Meanwhile, Whirlpool concentrates on stoves, dishwashers, clothes washers, dryers, and disposals. By marketing Whirlpool products, Sony enhances its product line, and Whirlpool benefits from the distribution by Sony. For small manufacturers, piggyback marketing is an excellent option with minimum risk.[35]

The Export Decision

Deciding to become an exporter can be a giant leap in thinking; however, it is remarkably similar to the *pre-start-up planning process* described in Chapter 4. The elements of business planning are the same. Aspiring exporters must take due diligence to determine the commercial feasibility of the product or service, do thorough market research, structure responsibilities, and obtain the necessary resources. Planning is more complicated for exports than for domestic sales in the sense that entrepreneurs are unfamiliar with foreign markets, culture, foreign exchange, and host-country legal issues. In addition, the U.S. government imposes legal restrictions on exporting to certain nations and requires licenses for all transactions.

Clearly, there are too many issues to be described in detail. Later in the chapter, however, we will return to these issues as they relate not only to exporting but to foreign investments and overseas services.

> ▶ **CHECKPOINT**
>
> Identify various methods of direct exporting.
>
> Describe options available for indirect exporting.
>
> Discuss EMCs and ETCs, and explain how they differ as export intermediaries.

IMPORTING

Entrepreneurs seeking to expand their businesses may not need to look further than their home markets, but rather than provide domestic goods to customers, they can import goods. The United States is still the most affluent marketplace in the world, and the rising trade deficit attests to increasing opportunities for foreign-made products. Faced with a trade deficit, the U.S. government is not anxious to encourage imports, yet they are an inevitable fact of economic life. No country has all the resources, products, or technology it needs.

Importing is conceptually the reverse of exporting with similar choices for distribution. Consequently, entrepreneurs can import directly from foreign companies, buy from agents or brokers, contract through trade commissions, or become piggyback marketers for foreign products. Similar planning considerations also exist, such as market research and organizing for the import market. Also, there are legal restrictions, quotas, licensing requirements, and foreign exchange regulations that mirror those for exporting.

One activity of importing that differs substantially from exporting is sourcing products. **Sourcing** is the process of finding products and contracting for their importation. This can be accomplished in several ways, as described in the following paragraphs.

Direct Sourcing. Entrepreneurs can travel overseas, attend foreign trade shows, or negotiate with foreign representatives who call on U.S. customers. Direct sourcing is a purchasing process in which entrepreneurs contract directly with foreign manufacturers. There are no intermediaries, and often goods are transported directly from the foreign company to the domestic point of sale. For example, American toy retailers such as Toys R Us travel to Hong Kong and Taiwan twice yearly on buying trips (January and June) to conclude toy contracts. Often top executives are involved. The Toys R Us buying trip to Hong Kong in January 1990 included the company president, two vice-presidents, and four regional managers. In two days at the Hong Kong Annual Toy Fair, they contracted for nearly $20 million in toys destined for sale during the 1990 Christmas season. A month later, Toys R Us signed similar contracts, mainly with foreign manufacturers, at the Annual New York Toy Fair. In addition, Toys R Us stocks year-round toys through foreign representatives that come to the U.S. to negotiate contracts.[36]

Subcontracting. Many domestic importers contract overseas production, specifying the products to be made. The Franklin Mint, for example, designs its collector chess sets, coins, and model cars, then subcontracts manufacturing to foreign companies who produce, package, and deliver the final goods directly to U.S. Franklin Mint distribution points. The Franklin Mint collector car series is contracted to Perfekta Toys, Ltd., Macao, with manufacturing facilities in the People's Republic of China.[37] Franklin Mint is strictly an importer without investment overseas; it pays for products when they are shipped.

Indirect Sourcing. Using intermediaries to source products or arrange for manufacturing is the most common practice. Indirect sourcing is accomplished through the same channels as indirect exporting; however, agents or brokers work on behalf of their import clients. Consequently, they are commissioned to locate products, arrange contracts, and handle details necessary for importation. For their efforts, they receive a commission based on a percentage of the contract value, and in some instances, they receive a retainer fee as an import representative.

Other Methods of Sourcing. The most reliable way to source products is directly, and the easiest method is to contract through a broker. However, there are other methods. One method is to attend trade shows. Most industry and professional associations hold regular trade shows that range from industrial machinery to office supplies. The computer industry has monthly trade shows in regional U.S. locations, annual conferences, and seminars that focus on themes such as software development or computer-aided design systems. These are huge conventions intended to facilitate contracts. Another option is to advertise in trade journals and foreign newspapers. Sourcing importers simply let potential sellers know how to contact them for specific products.

The safest way to identify potential import sources is through government-sponsored programs. There are hundreds of programs at federal and state government levels to help businesses in trade. The United States and Foreign Commercial Service (US&FCS), for example, maintains trade lists, puts out publications on products and services, and has a vast array of commercial intelligence. A part of the Department of Commerce, US&FCS maintains posts in 63 nations representing the most active U.S. trading partners.[38]

▶ **CHECKPOINT**

Describe the process of importing and why it is important.

Explain what is meant by "sourcing" overseas products.

Identify several methods of direct and indirect import contracting.

ESTABLISHING INTERNATIONAL VENTURES

Importing and exporting activities do not require overseas investments; both activities can be conducted domestically. However, most companies involved in global business have some international presence. This may take the simple form of having an overseas branch office, or it may be a major investment such as creating a wholly owned foreign subsidiary (see Figure 10-4). In any event, the decision to "go international" represents a major transformation in business.

The transformation involves working with people from another society with unfamiliar cultural values, laws, monetary systems, and political structures. These will be discussed later in this chapter, but before we look into them, it is important to understand how entrepreneurs establish international ventures.

Licensing

Licensing is the process of contracting with foreign firms, granting to them proprietary rights to use technology, copyrights, trademarks, or specific products or services

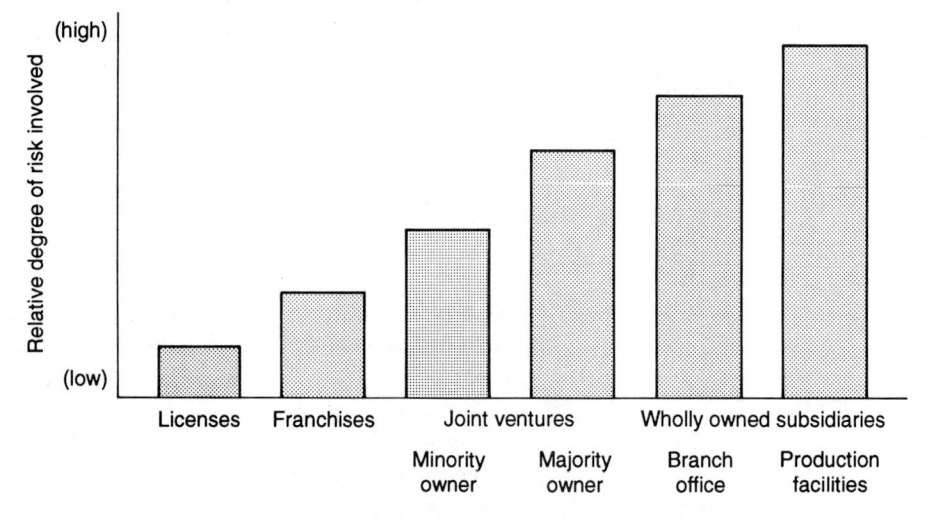

Figure 10-4 **Progressive Stages of International Involvement**

PROFILE △

John Johnson, Ebony *Magazine*

Starting with only an idea and a loan from his mother, who put her furniture in hock, John Johnson founded the largest black-owned corporation in America. His first enterprise, the *Negro Digest*, was launched during World War II to provide news about their own life and culture to the black population. The digest was the forerunner of *Ebony* magazine, now the cornerstone of a publishing empire that includes several major publications, hair products, perfumes, fashions, and personal care products.

Success was not easy for Johnson. He had to persist in a society that was unaccustomed to black business owners, fight an uphill battle for distribution of his products, and sell to a population that, at the time, had little money to spend. However, Johnson never once doubted that he would succeed, and for every problem he faced, he was determined to find a solution. Today, Johnson's enterprises stretch across the globe through international licensing for overseas publications and black personal care products. The next step may be expansion into overseas subsidiaries for fashion merchandising.

Sources: *The Entrepreneurs: An American Adventure* (Boston: Enterprise Media, 1987); personal communication with Johnson Enterprises and *Ebony* magazine.

---

owned by domestic companies. Licensing is a simple way to expand business overseas because the foreign licensee assumes the risk and investment of doing business; the domestic licensor grants access to proprietary knowledge or technology in exchange for royalties.[39] Disney Corporation licenses the right to manufacture Mickey Mouse electric toothbrushes to Hasbro Toys (with manufacturing in Europe and the Far East), and in turn, Hasbro sells children's toothbrushes with a singing image of Mickey Mouse in 16 countries. For each toothbrush shipped, Hasbro pays Disney a small royalty.

Licensing arrangements include contracts to manufacture and market products, to conduct research, and to provide services. Manufacturing used to be the most common form of licensing whereby an established product or technology gained a foothold overseas through a foreign company with the necessary production and marketing capabilities. Today, however, licensing extends to thousands of products and services including fashion designs, watches, kitchen appliances, sporting goods, software, public relations, advertising media, and merchandise retailing. Any company that has a successful trademark, patent, copyright, design, business concept, or technological process can, in effect, "rent" to a foreign business. In some instances, this is simply a matter of contracting with retailers to distribute a product such as

Estée Lauder perfume or Liz Claiborne clothes. This type of licensing requires no foreign investment, and it shifts the burden of international trade to the licensee.

More complex international licensing can involve capital investment and a commitment to help the licensee become established. Specifically, if a company such as Interplak (the maker of the jet-streamed patented dental hygiene plak remover) wants to license the manufacture and sale of the instrument to a French company, Interplak will spend the time and money necessary to register its patent in France, legally register its trademark, train local personnel, and provide the licensee with technical and service support (research, quality control, promotion, technical maintenance, marketing research, and distribution). Because both parties want the product to succeed, extensive investment and a commitment of time and effort are not unusual. Often they are part of the license contract.

Quite often the value of a license is not merely in obtaining the right to use a product, but in the support provided by the licensing company. Disney is unlikely to provide design assistance for a Mickey Mouse toothbrush; however, Interplak's licensing strength rests with its ability to provide expertise to support its overseas licensees. Consequently, entrepreneurs who contemplate licensing must be ready to provide technical, legal, and personal assistance.

Franchising

Franchising is a method of doing business by which a franchisee is granted the right to offer, sell, or distribute goods or services under a system created by the franchisor.[40] Specifically, franchising is a special form of licensing that involves rights to a *business concept*. The business concept is a "system," such as McDonald's, Precision Tune, or 7–Eleven, and it is an effective way to expand internationally. (Chapter 12 addresses franchising more thoroughly.)

The first major Soviet venture to grab headlines in 1990 was the giant McDonald's restaurant in Moscow. It was by no means the first Western investment in the U.S.S.R., but the McDonald's grand opening seemed to be a turning point in East-West relations. It also represented the mainstream of free-enterprise capitalism—fast-food franchising. Visitors to Beijing (and the infamous Tiananmen Square) are often stunned to see the Kentucky Fried Chicken sign above one of the busiest franchises in China. Tourists in Tokyo, Hong Kong, and Singapore can shop at neighborhood 7–Eleven markets, rent Hertz cars, and, of course, eat at McDonald's.

Most of the high-volume, high-profit American franchise locations are overseas. Of the top ten McDonald's restaurants, nine are overseas, and the top four in sales and profitability are in Hong Kong.[41] Virtually any successful business concept can be replicated in hundreds of foreign markets, and franchises can range from large Coca-Cola bottling plants to small-shop Mail America outlets.

Joint Ventures

Moving up the scale of international involvement, entrepreneurs can pursue joint ventures with foreign companies. A **joint venture** is a shared ownership by two or more organizations in which the investors have an equity investment in a separate enterprise.[42] The crucial point here is that unlike a license or franchise that seldom requires *direct* investments, the joint venture requires specific equity investments by all parties. Consequently, the organizations are responsible for operational control and for profits and losses. By definition, they are separate legal entities of at least two organizations; some foreign joint ventures, run as consortia, have more than a dozen "investing companies." Joint ventures may be created between private companies, between companies and state-owned firms, or between companies and agencies from several consortium countries.

Joint ventures have become the primary vehicle for foreign investment in developing countries, the Soviet Union, and the People's Republic of China. In most instances, the foreign government mandates a joint venture (as opposed to franchising or exporting) with at least 51 percent ownership held by one of its own private or state-owned organizations. This requirement gives the foreign power control and a majority voice in any dispute. They also control foreign exchange transactions, capital decisions, and market strategies. The majority control is rationalized to protect national interests, such as political ideologies. These restrictions can become perplexing distractions to the minority investor; however, they can also assure tremendous benefits because "official" partners can cut through red tape and open doors normally closed to foreigners.

Setting up an international joint venture in China, for example, is a bewildering process of negotiating with a private Chinese company and with a state political agency. All Chinese joint ventures are at least approved through a complex bureaucracy, and most operations are dependent on state-owned or state-controlled organizations (see Figure 10-5 for an example). Specifically, resources (materials and supplies) are allowed to be purchased only through a government-controlled quota system; a Chinese joint venture does not "procure" materials through a purchasing system as in the West. Prices are fixed by government, supply quantities are dictated, and delivery schedules depend on priorities assigned by centrally controlled agencies. Most labor is hired through a government agency assigned to recruit and select personnel, and the joint venture pays a state employment agency that, in turn, pays employees. Consequently, joint venture managers have limited opportunities to secure independent supplies or hire (and fire) personnel.

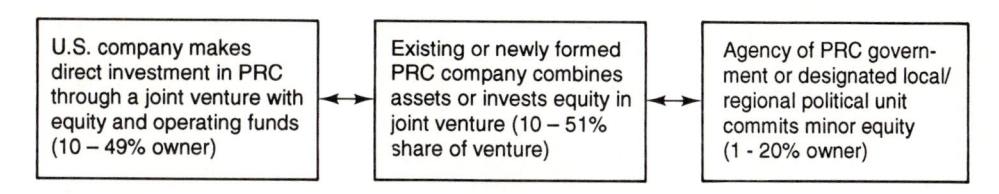

U.S. company makes direct investment in PRC through a joint venture with equity and operating funds (10 – 49% owner)	Existing or newly formed PRC company combines assets or invests equity in joint venture (10 – 51% share of venture)	Agency of PRC government or designated local/regional political unit commits minor equity (1 - 20% owner)

An example of a new enterprise, joint venture in PRC with three owners (example share: U.S. firm = 45%, PRC firm = 45%, and government agency or political unit = 10%)

Figure 10-5 **Pattern of Joint Venturing in the People's Republic of China**

This picture of Chinese joint ventures seems bleak, yet there is a great deal of slippage in the system, and resources and personnel can often be secured legally through an economic system that is undergoing change from a dogmatically controlled economy to a somewhat accommodating market system. Also, because China is anxious to increase exports, joint ventures are given ample resources, financing, personnel, and support to expand rapidly and to export to their full capacity. The legal structure of joint ventures is similar the world over, but in reality they operate in many ways, limited only by idiosyncrasies of people in power.

There are several important advantages of joint ventures. For example, labor costs in developing countries are extremely low, and a joint venture with an existing foreign operation can take advantage of these low costs. Domestic material prices controlled by a state may be far lower than those in competitive markets. Shipping is often subsidized by state agencies, reducing transport costs. Joint ventures may also enjoy "tax holidays" (three to ten years of operations without domestic taxation). Also, they may be provided low-cost real estate leases, low-interest loans or government-backed bonds, and government contracts that ensure a profitable market. In addition, joint ventures that bring with them Western technology may be given favored trade status, access to export distribution channels, and legal protection against competitors.

The combination of these factors can result in very low-cost products, sold through subsidized markets, and protected against competition. This is precisely the formula that helped Korea and Taiwan to expand their economies by more than 300 percent in less than two decades, accumulate huge foreign exchange trade balances, and become cash-rich exporting nations. It is the same formula that China and the Soviet Union are attempting to endorse, and it is the mechanism of U.S. diplomacy to help underdeveloped nations create stable and growing economies. The last point is particularly important for entrepreneurs because the U.S. Department of Commerce actively encourages international joint ventures and works closely with quasi-public organizations such as the Export-Import Bank (EximBank) and the Overseas Private Investment Corporation (OPIC) to help new businesses go international.[43]

Wholly Owned Foreign Operations

Unlike joint ventures that limit ownership and operational control, a wholly owned foreign operation is entirely owned and controlled by the parent company, in one of two ways: An American company can set up an overseas branch, or it can acquire an existing overseas company as a subsidiary. Each type of foreign operation has advantages and disadvantages.[44]

Overseas Branch. An **overseas branch** is part of the parent corporation and simply an extension of domestic operations. A branch of a Boston-owned company located in London is essentially the same as a branch located in New York City. Branch assets and liabilities are part of the domestic corporation. Profits or losses are part of the parent's finances, and taxes are paid in the parent's country on total company profits. This arrangement can be advantageous if home-country taxes are lower than those overseas. A branch is established by registering the parent company in the host country and obtaining necessary permits to conduct business. In addition, branch profits can be transferred home with few complications.

Branch operations, however, start from scratch. They must be staffed, financed, organized, and managed like most new ventures. They also must establish markets and often face competitive environments without a local track record. Consequently, unless the parent has an established reputation—like Citicorp or IBM—a branch will have to fight for a competitive position alongside other local companies. These can be major disadvantages.

Foreign Subsidiary. A **foreign subsidiary** is a separate company organized under a foreign nation's legal code with accountability distinct from the parent company. Specifically, the subsidiary has independent assets and liabilities, and it is taxed by the host nation. This can be an advantage if the foreign tax rate is less than at home. Also, because the subsidiary is a separate legal entity, liability usually extends only to its operations, not to the parent. This factor can be important if the subsidiary is in a politically sensitive environment.

A subsidiary's earnings, however, cannot be repatriated (transferred home) without paying home-country taxes and having currency converted through foreign exchange. Establishing a subsidiary can also be expensive and complicated because a parent company either creates a subsidiary from scratch or acquires an existing overseas company. In either instance, the parent must comply with all existing host-country laws and often establish overseas financing. These requirements can prove advantageous in a country where the host government is anxious to help new ventures, subsequently offering tax and financial incentives. However, there can be disadvantages in well-developed economies where other domestic companies compete for funding and governments discourage foreign investment.

These considerations notwithstanding, the most important advantage to acquiring a subsidiary is rapid access to established foreign markets. By acquiring an existing overseas company, the parent immediately penetrates trade barriers, avoids start-up complications, and has a functional organization in place. Furthermore, if the subsidiary is not successful, the parent can sell it (or write it off) without imposing direct liabilities on the parent corporation.

Entrepreneurs should not feel exempt from acquiring subsidiaries or operating overseas branches. Many small companies—as small as one-person trading companies—are candidates for acquisition, and a small business can often open a successful small branch.

For example, Dickson Poon was a sole proprietor of a small watch-retailing store in 1980, but through a combination of acquisitions and branch expansion, he owned 96 retail outlets in 17 countries by 1990.[45] Now called the Dickson Group, the company has exclusive fashion and jewelry shops representing such brands as Rolex, Chopard, La Montre Hermes, Polo/Ralph Lauren, Guy Laroche of Paris, Carrera, and Charles Jourdan. Dickson Poon built his company one location at a time, initially reinvesting meager earnings, then leveraging his group assets for loans. In 1986, Dickson Poon registered his company as a public stock corporation, and he now operates by establishing corporate overseas branches. Whether the new location is a branch or subsidiary depends on the country of operations, tax rates, and foreign exchange restrictions. Consequently, the Dickson Group has branches in West Germany, France, Switzerland, and the United Kingdom, but it has subsidiaries in Hong Kong and other Asian countries.

Transnational Services

Services are less tangible than products, but most services can be taken overseas through similar methods as product-based companies. The problem is how to define international services. For lack of a better term, they are called *transnational services*, indicating a borderless business concept.[46] This category includes commercial banks, which are similar in most Western nations, insurance companies that provide fundamentally similar services, and accounting services that have similar professional responsibilities. Domestic banks do not export services in the sense of transporting tangible products, but they do set up branches or wholly owned operations. Professional service companies avoid the term "subsidiary," however, preferring instead the term "affiliates."

With due regard for legal considerations (such as host-country banking regulations), services can go international through similar methods open to manufacturers or merchandisers. The essential difference is that service enterprises must rely on skilled employees who are knowledgeable about local conditions. Also, service marketing requires customized client assistance because clients have unique requirements influenced by culture, social values, economics, and political and legal systems in each country. Consequently, an American bank cannot take its domestic roster of services to Brazil or Thailand and expect the same success it may have enjoyed at home; few Brazilians need auto loans or mortgages, and few Thais use checking accounts, preferring cash. Life insurance policies are rare in socialist countries, and health care services in many countries are provided through government programs.

What these differences mean for the entrepreneur is that overseas services must be tailor-made for specific foreign markets. In addition, although executives may be expatriates, operational staff must be hired locally; they must be able to deal directly with local clients as equals, not as foreign visitors. Companies that are staffed predominantly by expatriates will essentially serve other foreign companies. For example, an American company staffed by Americans will serve American or other Western clients.

These limitations aside, there are many opportunities for entrepreneurial services in foreign markets. Specifically, independent teaching services are needed in developing countries; management consulting firms also do well in both developed and underdeveloped countries; and accountants skilled in international trade provide services to multinational corporations as well as small businesses everywhere. With the rapid rise in information technology, there are strong markets for IT engineers, software specialists, and telecommunications experts. Attorneys skilled in international law are also in high demand. Shortages exist everywhere in medical services. Some, like nursing services, are equally critical in North America, Eastern Europe, and underdeveloped nations of West Africa. Counseling for family planning is needed in Asia and Africa. Construction opportunities exist nearly everywhere. And not least among needed services are import-export agents, insurers, sourcing companies, and shipping companies.

▶ **CHECKPOINT**

Describe licensing and franchising and how they differ.

Discuss advantages and disadvantages of joint ventures.

Explain the critical issues for establishing foreign services.

THE FOREIGN ENVIRONMENT OF BUSINESS

Services and their counterparts in manufacturing and merchandising have several things in common. They must take into consideration cultural, legal, political, and economic characteristics that exist overseas. No one can simply transplant a domestic business into a foreign environment without adjustments.

Major Environmental Issues

A comprehensive study of environmental issues would be an encyclopedic effort; however, there are four major environmental considerations to address. These are summarized in Figure 10-6, and each affects decisions about going international and managing a foreign venture.[47]

Culture consists of values, beliefs, and attitudes shared by members of a society that collectively influence their behavior. For example, in Japan, women seldom achieve promotions to important managerial posts, and although this situation is changing, entrepreneurs in Japan will find that "doing business" is generally reserved for men. Consequently, an American woman may find it difficult to do business in Japan. In Nigeria, payoffs are normal in business transactions, but such practices are illegal for U.S. citizens (regardless of where they are in the world), and entrepreneurs who adapt to "normal" Nigerian customs may find themselves indicted at home under the Foreign Corrupt Practices Act.[48]

Political systems clearly differ between countries. Recall that early in the chapter we saw how Soviet trade is controlled through official government trade agencies, and later we saw how China mandates guidelines for joint venture involvement. Most countries have trade quotas for both imports and exports, and these are controlled politically through agreements and treaties. More important, changes in government leadership can dramatically alter these agreements.

Legal systems affect taxation, licensing, bank lending, hiring practices, and safety regulations, among many other factors. From a practical viewpoint, something

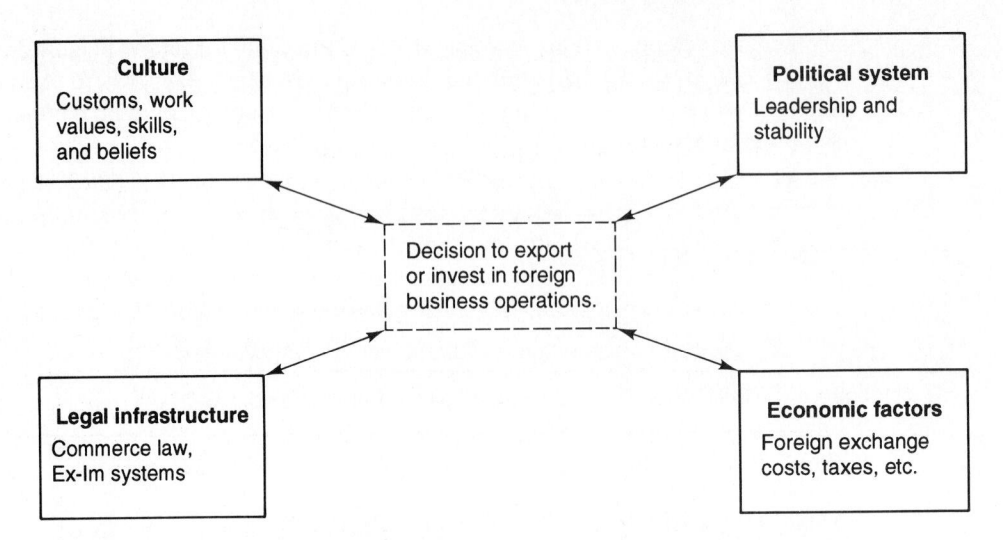

```
        Culture                              Political system
     Customs, work                          Leadership and
     values, skills,                        stability
     and beliefs
              ↘                              ↗
                 Decision to export
                 or invest in foreign
                 business operations.
              ↗                              ↘
     Legal infrastructure                   Economic factors
     Commerce law,                          Foreign exchange
     Ex-Im systems                          costs, taxes, etc.
```

Figure 10-6 **Environmental Factors Influencing Decisions to Go International**

quite simple such as safety codes for children's toys may require entrepreneurs to redesign their products. Contracting for sales, resources, distribution, or investments is unique in every country. As noted earlier, foreign subsidiaries must be set up under domestic laws of foreign host nations, and unlike the United States where it is easy to go into business, in other countries business owners may have to be local citizens, post bonds, have government sponsorship, or be screened for licenses.

Economic differences influence all overseas decisions. Because foreign customers may be more (or less) affluent than domestic ones, product quality, packaging, promotion, and methods of distribution will differ. Also because most foreign countries have more pronounced differences in incomes among various groups of consumers than in the United States, prices can drastically affect consumers' buying decisions. In Marxist systems where resources are centrally allocated, cost and availability of raw materials are not "market driven." Consequently, controlled resources may be scarce or plentiful, depending on host-country political priorities; they may also be low in price or expensive.

These insights on environmental issues are equivalent to the light given off by a firefly at night; they provide only a brief flicker of reality. The entrepreneur contemplating going international will want to invest time in a reasonable study of laws, foreign trade requirements, economics, cultural issues, and political systems related to overseas markets.

Implications for Entrepreneurs

Although it is beyond our purpose here to explore these implications in detail, we can describe categories of questions to be answered before launching international ventures. Before entering a trade agreement, exporting, importing, establishing an overseas distribution office, or creating a subsidiary or joint venture, six critical questions must be answered.[49]

What Legal Requirements Must Be Satisfied? Entrepreneurs must determine license requirements in the United States and for the host foreign country. For example, U.S. export regulations are quite specific that anyone involved in trade must have one of two types of licenses: a general license or a validated license (see Figure 10-7). A **general license** is a broad grant of authority to all exporters for certain categories of products. Therefore, entrepreneurs can register for a general license if their products fall under one of the government's approved categories. For example, textiles, lumber, hand tools, cereals, food grains, and soft drinks can be exported under a general license. However, semiconductors, aerospace technology, and communications equipment are not subject to general licensing. These products (and most new items not previously exported) require a **validated license** which is a specific grant to export issued on a case-by-case basis.

In addition to meeting U.S. regulations, entrepreneurs must also obtain permits at the destination, and these are often difficult to obtain. For example, the U.S. automotive industry is generally licensed to export cars almost anywhere in the world, but some countries have import quotas that block American trade. Similarly, U.S. cars, although they are exportable to the United Kingdom, are not importable because they have left-hand steering wheels. Ivory and most animal furs were, until recently, exportable with few restrictions from African nations, but they have been rigorously denied import licenses by the United States.

There are many other legal considerations that entrepreneurs must satisfy before they decide to go international. These include meeting safety regulations for packing and shipping, registering customs, meeting tariff restrictions, complying with foreign exchange rules, registering with trade associations, and bonding. When the venture is a simple export business, these legalities may be minimized, yet everyone involved overseas must also take care not to violate government sanctions—such as boycotts imposed against South Africa and Cuba. When the venture involves foreign investment, such as setting up a subsidiary, then commercial laws for the country involved come into play.

General license	Validated license
A "general" export grant for a broad range of products such as textiles, chemicals, lumber, prepared foods, grains, and cereals	A "specific" grant related to one type of product that must be reviewed, such as aerospace technology and semiconductor instrumentation

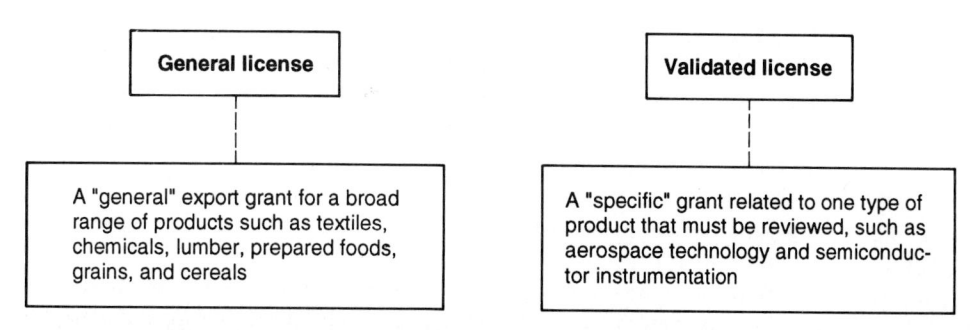

Figure 10-7 **General and Validated Licenses for Exporting**

What Are the Costs of Doing Business Overseas? Entrepreneurs will want to do the same careful market research for overseas markets as for domestic markets to ensure they can deliver cost-effective products or services. In most instances, there will be additional costs to exporting. These can include export documentation, contracting, packing and shipping, insurance, warehousing, and customs fees. They can also include the cost of product modification, registering foreign patents, trademarks, or copyrights, travel for contract negotiations, and technical support services. Initially, export prices are pushed up by higher costs; however, when markets are opened in new high-volume areas, costs can be spread over more items, thereby reducing individual prices.

Overseas costs are often hidden from the entrepreneur doing research from home. As described earlier, a venture could look very good on paper, but because of weak infrastructure in the host country, a new venture can face unexpected problems. For example, inadequate trucking in Mexico might require a business to set up its own transport system, or inadequate electricity supply in China might force a joint venture to install its own power-generating system.

What Human-Resource Issues Must Be Resolved? In underdeveloped countries, there are many people willing to work quite inexpensively, yet because they lack education or skills, "qualified" labor may be nonexistent. Even if workers are plentiful, they may have to be trained extensively. Even then, they may be unable to cope with complicated technology. When investing overseas, foreign governments often control personnel, constraining the company's management of its human resources. In addition, local managers may be needed, yet they usually lack organizational leadership skills; transferring managers overseas is seldom a long-term solution. Also, joint ventures may be required to have government liaisons (e.g., political officers) that further complicate operations.

What Technical and Organizational Changes Are Needed? Products may have to be redesigned, but more often, changes are made in color schemes, packaging, trade names, and logos to coincide with foreign customers' expectations. For example, the number 4 connotes bad luck in the Chinese culture, and the number 8 means good fortune; as a result, a product like Formula 409 has a label displeasing to Chinese, but a cleanser named Power 88 is very popular.

Technical changes are usually necessary to conform to skill levels of local employees. Sophisticated computers are difficult to use in developing countries where local language is not adaptable to standard software. Also, many societies are unfamiliar with production systems, common accounting methods, and standard purchasing practices. In terms of organizational authority, many foreign cultures expect autocratic decision making or a caste-type management system, so that making assignments or promotions becomes extremely sensitive.

Other technical considerations can include complications such as material sensitivity to unusual climatic conditions or electric power systems that are incompatible with equipment. Other organizing problems can include reporting procedures that are unfamiliar, language barriers, local prejudices among employees with different ethnic or religious backgrounds, and work habits that contradict Western notions of motivation and productivity.

How Will Marketing Be Accomplished Overseas? As discussed earlier, there are many different channels of distribution, ranging from direct exporting to overseas brokerage. In addition to different channels, promotion methods (advertising, personal selling, public relations) must agree with local customs. Pricing will be controlled by law in some countries, and in others, pricing will be unpredictable. In places like Brazil where inflation is a serious problem, prices can change every few hours, complicating plans and market forecasts.

Marketing is often accomplished overseas through informal networks of business contacts and friends. Such habits can be frustrating to entrepreneurs who enter new markets expecting to compete as they have at home only to find that sales do not occur until the business is "networked" through social affiliations. In countries where payoffs and bribes are common, a new venture may be boycotted until its managers "ante up" to petty politicians. In most instances, however, marketing challenges can be overcome by developing local marketing staff, licensing with established firms, or forming joint ventures.

How Will the Venture Be Financed? Domestic lenders are unlikely to finance overseas assets or to risk money on foreign operations beyond their control. Consequently, overseas financing is essential. Fortunately, many U.S. banks and financial intermediaries have overseas offices specifically positioned to serve compatriot organizations. Investors look at overseas ventures in the same way they look at domestic operations. They assess market strength, management, profitability, and the risk of the proposed venture.

In addition, many foreign governments have strict financing requirements, such as mandating that a high percentage of assets be secured by outside means; this requirement brings capital into the country. In other instances, foreign governments may require a majority of financing to be from internal sources, thereby giving control to host-country investors or lenders. Financial requirements are specific to each country, but, in general, financing is accomplished in much the same way as for domestic ventures, subject to variations in legal requirements for stock corporations, loans, and private-placement investments. Because regulations vary widely, the U.S. government has several assistance programs designed to help entrepreneurs understand foreign markets and finances.

> ▶ **CHECKPOINT**
>
> Identify and discuss the four major considerations affecting decisions to go international.
>
> Define and explain the differences between a general and a validated export license.
>
> Discuss the major issues to be addressed before going international.

GETTING HELP—SOURCES OF INFORMATION

There is an extraordinary amount of information available from agencies of the U.S. government, state agencies, and foreign embassies. The first place to go for help is a district office of the United States and Foreign Commercial Service (US&FCS). There are district offices in every state and overseas. Local Chambers of Commerce will provide telephone numbers and contacts, and a reference to services is published annually in a manual called *A Basic Guide to Exporting*, published by the U.S. Department of Commerce.[50] The purpose of this section of the chapter is not to provide details of these services, but to alert readers to the types of assistance available and describe examples of services.

U.S. Department of Commerce

In addition to publications like the *Basic Guide to Exporting*, the Department of Commerce has five major divisions with more than 600 programs and assistance services focused on international business. Under the U.S. and Foreign Commercial Service, there are offices for export counseling, marketing assistance, product development, trade show information, trade mission coordination, and publications, among others. The US&FCS regularly publishes its *Commercial News USA*, which describes sales opportunities overseas, marketing news, services, listings of foreign trade legations, and incentive programs for exporters. Under its Export Promotion Services, the US&FCS actually provides foreign sales leads, and export officers provide counseling for businesses.

The Trade Development Office provides assistance on specific industries, such as aerospace, and counselors specialize in more than 400 products and services, including construction, textiles, clothing, banking, advertising, electronics, and shipping, to name a few. The Trade Administration Office handles export licensing, compliance counseling, and legal affairs. The International Economic Policy Office provides specific country information relating to international trade. And the DOC's Minority Business Development Agency was created to encourage minority-owned ventures to go international. This agency provides comprehensive planning assistance to American minority enterprises, including direct sales leads and foreign liaison support services.

Small Business Administration

The U.S. Small Business Administration administers export programs through every SBA field office located in every state. Referral services exist through offices of the U.S. Chamber of Commerce, and the SBA has established a special branch called the Office of International Trade in Washington, DC, for direct counseling assistance. The breadth of assistance provided through the SBA, or coordinated through state trade development services, is vast. For example, they sponsor nearly 400 seminars each year focused on exporting and international trade, provide one-on-one counseling in 42 states, distribute market studies, make referrals for export services, disseminate sales leads, and publish information on trade shows, foreign inquiries, financial programs, and market opportunities. In addition, the SBA has financing programs for operational support or federally sponsored loan guarantees. These programs vary with federal budgets and are coordinated with state-sponsored programs, but in essence, funding assistance is available through the SBA and state agencies.[51]

The Export-Import Bank

Known as the EximBank, the Export-Import Bank is structured to assist directly with trade financing. It has international services and counseling for Export Trading Companies (ETCs) and a special office for small business assistance. The EximBank focuses on financial support programs and can provide export credit insurance, working capital guarantees, commercial bank guarantees, direct loans, and liaison services with domestic and foreign financial institutions. The agency's Small Business Credit Program is specifically designed to help entrepreneurs and small enterprises underwrite international trade. Assistance is available for working capital, equipment purchases, plant construction, raw material procurement, and development of feasibility studies. Exhibit 10-2 summarizes EximBank programs.

Overseas Private Investment Corporation (OPIC)

The Overseas Private Investment Corporation, or OPIC, is a unique organization because it operates as an independent and self-supporting corporation, yet it is fully owned by the U.S. government. It is structured much like an insurance company to protect American investors against losses in international trade. Also, OPIC is mandated to work only with companies trading with (or investing in) developing countries. For example, OPIC does not become involved in trade with the EEC, Japan, or Canada, yet it has extensive involvement in the Caribbean, South America, and Africa. The corporation writes insurance to protect exports, underwrite shipments against loss, guarantee foreign exchange payments, pay for overseas contracts, and protect against political risk (such as having a business taken over by fiat or to avoid losses due to insurrection or war). In addition, OPIC will intervene on behalf of the insured to negotiate disputes and to arbitrate foreign exchange issues.

Other Assistance

Although the agencies that we have described are important, they are only a few of those who provide direct assistance for international trade. The U.S. Department of the Treasury, for example, is the definitive source for customs information regarding exports and imports. The U.S. Agency for International Development (USAID) provides direct funding for international development programs such as constructing irrigation systems in Ethiopia or underwriting reforestation in Pakistan. The Private Export Funding Corporation (PEFCO) is an investor-owned company with government support to underwrite export of U.S. goods and services. The Department of Agriculture has nearly a hundred programs to support international trade or foreign aid.

Exhibit 10-2 **Selected Programs of the Export-Import Bank and Cooperating Banks**

Exports	Related Programs
Short-term (up to 180 days): Consumables Small manufactured items Spare parts and accessories Raw materials	Export credit insurance and working capital guarantees available for short-term exports with 180-day terms
Medium-term (181 days to 5 years): Mining and refining equipment Construction equipment Agricultural equipment General aviation aircraft Planning and feasibility studies	Export credit insurance, commercial bank guarantees, small business credit, medium-term credit, and working capital guarantees available for medium-term operations and exports
Long-term (5 years and longer): Power plants LPG and gas producing plants Commercial aircraft and locomotives Heavy capital goods Selected major overseas projects	Direct EximBank loans and financial guarantees with participating financial institutions.

Source: *A Basic Guide to Exporting* (Washington, DC: U.S. Department of Commerce, 1986), p. 48.

Some of these are well known, such as the Food for Peace program, but others, such as the Commodity Credit Corporation (CCC) and Export Credit Guarantee Program (ECGP) get little attention in the popular press. Nevertheless, they can be important sources for export funding in the agricultural sector. The Department of Agriculture also has the a Minority and Small Business Coordinator, which is an agency that helps minority-owned businesses and small enterprises find overseas markets and fund exports. Finally, there is the Office of the U.S. Trade Representative, which provides comprehensive counseling and referral services. Entrepreneurs will often find that toll-free numbers are available at local Chambers of Commerce, and libraries have details of services and addresses to write to for help.

▶ CHECKPOINT

Identify four primary government sources of export assistance.

Discuss how an aspiring entrepreneur would go about getting help locally and through state agencies.

Explain financial assistance available through agencies such as OPIC.

Chapter 10   International Markets: New Venture Opportunities   **341**

▲ ▲
▲ ▲   SYNOPSIS FOR LEARNING
▲ ▲

1. *Describe changes in Europe that provide opportunities for global trade.*

The most important changes have taken place in Eastern bloc countries where former Communist regimes have been replaced by popular governments intent on creating market-driven economies. Germany, now unified, promises to be an even greater force in European politics and in global trade. Closely associated with these changes are those taking place in the Soviet Union, where individual republics of the U.S.S.R. are anxiously encouraging economic changes. Although many of these republics and a majority of Eastern bloc nations are economically depressed, several are on the brink of industrial development. Consequently, they represent potential new markets for EEC and American technology. The 1992 Single Market Initiative also promises a realignment of economic relations that will include more than 340 million people engaged in trade with few restrictions.

2. *Explain why the Pacific Rim is important to American business.*

The Pacific Rim constitutes about 20 countries and 300 million people that, currently, have more dollar volume trade with the United States than all of Europe combined. Several PacRim countries also represent the fastest-growing economies in the world. These include Hong Kong, Singapore, South Korea, and Taiwan. Others are Thailand, Malaysia, Indonesia, Australia, and New Zealand, each providing open markets for Western goods and services, and they are in need of new technology. Many industrialized nations are already involved in PacRim business, and entrepreneurial ventures are among the leading companies spearheading global trade in the Pacific. If China and Japan are considered in this Asian profile, Pacific markets are genuinely the largest in the world.

3. *Examine how entrepreneurs can become involved in exports and imports.*

Exporting is the process of selling domestic goods to foreign consumers, and importing is the procurement of overseas goods for domestic consumption. Entrepreneurs can engage in either activity *directly* by generating overseas markets and distribution systems or "sourcing" foreign products for domestic markets. They can also engage in trade by contracting with foreign agents or overseas distributors. More often, entrepreneurs resort to *indirect* methods, such as contracting with commission agents and export management companies (EMCs) to handle trade. In addition to these intermediaries, export trading companies (ETCs) provide comprehensive export services and liaisons with overseas buyers. There are also brokers and remarketers that buy directly from U.S. manufacturers for resale overseas. Finally, entrepreneurs can "piggyback" by licensing or contracting with companies that have established overseas distribution systems.

4. *Identify ways entrepreneurs can "go international" with investments.*

Most small enterprises develop overseas investments through an incremental process that begins with licensing. Licensing is the process of contracting with foreign companies, giving them the right to use, sell, or manufacture products or technology.

Some services are also licensed, such as express parcel delivery services. Franchising also is an option, under which an entrepreneur sells the rights to a "business system" such as McDonald's. A more complicated investment involves joint venturing where equity investments by two or more companies create separate enterprises. Beyond joint ventures, entrepreneurs can invest in wholly owned foreign operations. These can range from branch offices to comprehensive production facilities. Service companies prefer wholly owned subsidiaries or affiliated offices.

5. *Describe how entrepreneurs would find more information and help on overseas opportunities and exporting.*

The most direct source for locating assistance is the U.S. Department of Commerce through its U.S. and Foreign Commercial Service agency. Every state also has development agencies, trade development offices, and a network of Small Business Administration offices. Perhaps the easiest place to start is the local Chamber of Commerce, where government resources are listed together with state and regional services. Special minority business programs also exist to assist minority-owned small businesses; and for entrepreneurs interested in developing countries, the Agency for International Development is an important resource. Financial assistance is provided through the SBA, USAID, Department of Commerce, Department of Agriculture, the Export-Import Bank, and the Overseas Private Investment Corporation.

NOTES

1. Joseph Duffey, "U.S. Competitiveness: Looking Back and Looking Ahead," in Martin K. Starr, ed., *Global Competitiveness: Getting the U.S. Back on Track* (New York: Norton, 1988), pp. 72–94. Also George Anders, "Going Global: Vision vs. Reality," *Asian Wall Street Journal*, September 29, 1989, pp. 1–2, 5–6.
2. *Economic Report of the President* (Washington, DC: U.S. Government Printing Office, 1988), p. 251. In addition, Office of Advocacy, Small Business Administration, *Small Business in the American Economy* (Washington, DC: U.S. Government Printing Office, 1989), pp. 23–25.
3. Mark Alpert, "Wary Hope on Eastern Europe," *Fortune International*, January 29, 1990, pp. 75–76. Also Murray Hedgecock, "Capitalists Cast Eyes East," *South China Morning Post*, February 11, 1990, p. 11.
4. Timothy Aeppel, "German Unity Could Cost Bonn Status as Capital," *Asian Wall Street Journal*, February 15, 1990, pp. 1, 5.
5. Jackson Diehl, "Kremlin Decides It Can Learn from Its Allies," *Washington Post*, October 13, 1987, p. A1.
6. Organization for Economic Cooperation and Development, *Financial Market Trends* (Paris: OECD, 1988), pp. 32–33. Also see Mark Alpert, "Wary Hope on Eastern Europe," *Fortune International*, January 29, 1990, pp. 75–76.
7. Terrence Roth, "Kohl Urges Talks on a Monetary Union with East Germany Based on the Mark," *Asian Wall Street Journal*, February 7, 1990, pp. 9, 14.
8. Peter Millar and Peter Godwin, "Diverse Peoples Who Make Up the Fragmented Soviet Empire," *South China Morning Post*, January 29, 1990, p. 17.
9. *Peoples of The U.S.S.R.*, an information report by the USSR Trade Representative, Washington, DC, July 1989. Also "Ethnic Populations within the Soviet Union," *East-West Committee Bulletin* (Paris: International Chamber of Commerce, 1988), pp. 3–4.

10. "Gorbachev's Vision of Reforms," *The Economist*, January 14, 1989, p. 44. Also see Mikhail Gorbachev, *Perestroika: New Thinking for Our Country and the World* (New York: Harper & Row, 1987), pp. 17, 23, 100.

11. Judy Shelton, *The Coming Soviet Crash* (New York: Free Press, 1989), pp. 3–5, 56–60, 201–205. Also see Michael R. Sesit, "World Markets Ponder 'Gorbachev Factor,'" *Asian Wall Street Journal*, February 7, 1990, pp. 9, 13.

12. Charalambos Vlachoutsikos, "How Small- to Mid-Sized U.S. Firms Can Profit from *Perestroika*," *California Management Review*, Vol. 31, No. 3 (1989), pp. 91–112.

13. Ibid., pp. 93–98. Also *Time*, April 10, 1988, p. 81.

14. "Data Control Seeks to Unlock Soviet Market," *Los Angeles Times*, June 16, 1988, Section 4, p. 1.

15. Chris Donnolley, "Winds of Change," *Asia Magazine*, December 17, 1989, pp. 10–11.

16. Ministry of Foreign Economic Relations and Trade, *Economic Record of Trade and Development*, January 25, 1990, Tables 2 and 7, pp. 27–32. Also John Frankenstein, "Trends in Chinese Business Practice: Changes in the Beijing Wind," *California Management Review*, Vol. 29, No. 1 (1986), pp. 148–160.

17. "Thorny Issues Will Hamper New Economic Plans," *Standard China Trade*, August 1989, pp. 20–22.

18. William H. Davidson, "Creating and Managing Joint Ventures in China," *California Management Review*, Vol. 29, No. 4 (1987), pp. 77–94. Also James B. Stepanek, "Getting Ready for Post-Deng China," *Asian Wall Street Journal*, February 15, 1990, p. 10.

19. Shen Peng, "Across China: Promising Future for Guangdong–Hong Kong–Macao Trade," *International Business*, Vol. 9 (1988), pp. 14–17. Also "Hong Kong Trade—Past, Present and Future," *The Hongkong Manager* (May/June, 1989), pp. 13–16.

20. "Regional Affairs," *Far Eastern Economic Review*, September 28, 1989, pp. 13–19, 26, 31–38, 138–151.

21. Charles W. Joiner, "Harvesting American Technology—Lessons from the Japanese Garden," *Sloan Management Review*, Vol. 30, No. 4 (1989), pp. 61–70.

22. Susumu Awanohara, "Tokyo Touches Base," *Far Eastern Economic Review*, September 14, 1989, pp. 14–15. Also Susan Bartlett Foote and Will Mitchell, "Selling American Medical Equipment in Japan," *California Management Review*, Vol. 31, No. 4 (1989), pp. 146–161.

23. Michael Bartholomew, "Profit Now from Europe's 1992 Opening," *Wall Street Journal*, July 25, 1988, p. 16.

24. Kenichi Ohmae, *Triad Power: The Coming Shape of Global Competition* (New York: Free Press, 1985), pp. 1–6, 28–30, 210. Also Walter S. Mossberg, "U.S.-Japan Trade Pact May Make Sense," *Wall Street Journal*, September 19, 1988, p. 1; and Kenichi Ohmae, "The Global Logic of Strategic Alliances," *Harvard Business Review*, Vol. 89, No. 2 (March–April 1989), pp. 143–154.

25. Alan C. Shapiro, *Multinational Financial Management*, 3rd ed. (Boston: Allyn and Bacon, 1989), pp. 9–10.

26. U.S. Department of Commerce, *A Basic Guide to Exporting* (Washington, DC: U.S. Government printing Office, 1986), pp. 17–21.

27. Personal interview with John Zinkin, Managing Director of Gilman Office Supplies, November 10, 1989, Hong Kong.

28. *Inchcape: Organisation and Global Developments*, Inchcape Ltd., 1989, p. 3. Also see Ohmae, "The Global Logic of Strategic Alliances."

29. Boeing Company, *Annual Report, 1988*, Seattle, Washington, published 1989, pp. 2–3. Also "Industrial Robots: An International Market," *Cincinnati Milicron*, 1987, p. 4; and Foote and Mitchell, "Selling American Medical Equipment in Japan."

30. U.S. Department of Commerce, *A Basic Guide to Exporting*, pp. 17–19.

31. "Foreign Trade Rights?" *Soviet Business and Trade* (Washington, DC: Welt, 1987), pp. 2–3.

32. Personal interview with H. K. Kwon, Managing Director of USKO Investments, Ltd., Seoul, Republic of Korea, February 16, 1990.

33. U.S. Department of Commerce, *Export Trading Company Guidebook* (Washington, DC: U.S. Government Printing Office, 1988), p. 2.

34. Deloitte, Haskins & Sells, *Expanding Your Business Overseas: An Entrepreneur's Guidebook* (New York: Deloitte, Haskins & Sells, 1985), pp. 47–48.

35. Ibid., p. 48.

36. "Toys R Us Make Record Deals at Annual Toy Fair," *South China Morning Post*, January 24, 1990, Business pp. 1, 3. Also "Toy Buyers Hint at What Kids Will Be Getting Next Christmas: Heavy Sales in 'Gory Toys' and 'Realistic Dolls' in New York," *South China Morning Post*, February 19, 1990, Business p. 1.

37. Personal interview with Eric Yeung, Managing Director, Perfekta Toys, Macao, November 11, 1990.

38. Office of the United States Trade Representative, *U.S. Department of Commerce: Commercial Attaches* (Washington, DC: U.S. Government Printing Office, 1988).

39. Donald Weinrauch and Arthur Langlois, "Guidelines for Starting and Operating an International Licensing Program for Small Business," *Journal of Small Business Management*, 1983, pp. 25–29.

40. *Franchising Today* (Chicago: FranCorp, 1989), pp. 6–7.

41. "McDonald's Record—The Big Mac Index," a panel presentation at the Third Annual International Management Conference, Managing in a Global Economy III, Hong Kong, June 1989.

42. U.S. Department of Commerce, *A Basic Guide to Exporting*, p. 82.

43. U.S. Department of Commerce, *Information Resources and Trade Assistance*, various data sheets and pamphlets (Washington, DC: Foreign Commercial Services, 1989).

44. Deloitte, Haskins & Sells, *Expanding Your Business Overseas*, pp. 63–67.

45. "Dickson's 10th Anniversary," *Dickson Group Report*, February 27, 1990, pp. 1–4.

46. U.S. Department of Commerce, *A Basic Guide to Exporting*, pp. 25–26.

47. David H. Holt, *Management Principles and Practices*, 2nd ed. (Englewood Cliffs, NJ: Prentice-Hall, 1990), pp. 666–672.

48. U.S. Department of Justice, *The Foreign Corrupt Practices Act of 1977* (Washington, DC: U.S. Government Printing Office, 1988).

49. U.S. Department of Commerce, *Understanding the Export Decision* (Washington, DC: International Trade Administration, 1989), pp. 1–4.

50. U.S. Department of Commerce, *A Basic Guide to Exporting* (Washington, DC: International Trade Administration and US&FCS, 1990).

51. National Association of State Development Agencies, *State Export Program Database* (Washington, DC: Small Business Administration, 1989).

CASE 10-1

Coming Together: The U.S.-Canada Trade Agreement

Canadian and U.S. interests are quickly melding together, and by 1999 economic barriers to trade will be nearly nonexistent. The U.S.-Canada Free Trade Agreement (CFTA) systematically removes trade restrictions and quotas, and by 1999, Canadian tariffs, which average 10 percent, will be lifted. As this relationship evolves, economists predict that U.S. gross national product will increase by $45 billion, creating 750,000 new jobs. Canada expects a 5 percent increase in GNP, and a tremendous boost in development and technology. Already, Canada is the largest trading partner of the United States, well above second-ranked Japan, and Canada enjoys a healthy $12 billion trade balance on more than $156 billion in annual transactions.

The CFTA also represents the first international agreement that guarantees unimpeded service transactions. More than 150 categories of services are covered in the CFTA, ranging from tourism and telecommunications to insurance and management consulting. Canadians and U.S. citizens working in one another's countries would be treated equally for contracts, and this equal treatment will also open the door for most engineering firms and research companies to pursue business on both sides of the border.

Along the St. Lawrence Seaway, U.S. power companies are exploring joint agreements to generate electricity. Shipping companies are exploring mutual investments for port development and transoceanic trade. In the Great Lakes region, automotive companies that have traded in parts and materials under a 1965 agreement are combining forces. Rather than being either U.S. or Canadian, many of these companies will lose their national identities. "Corporate America" will have true meaning after two of the three major North American countries erase economic borders.

Large corporations may not, however, become the chief beneficiaries of the new North American alliance. The fleet of foot are expected to make the greatest economic strides, and trade economics experts expect entrepreneurs to touch off a small-business export boom. Already, hundreds of American ventures have appeared along the British Columbian coastline, tripling the U.S. presence in Canadian aquaculture. Fishing, logging, canning, food processing, and related businesses in commercial boat building, marine repairs, and industrial construction have attracted expansion through northwestern U.S. enterprises.

In California and Washington state, independent vintners are going north in a hurry. Prior to the CFTA, for example, California wine products had 66 percent markups in Canada, a result of tariffs and quota restrictions. Stimson Lane Wine & Spirits, Ltd., a U.S. vintner, had to charge $12 in Canada for a blush wine from California that sold domestically for $6.49. Now that CFTA has relaxed restrictions on international investments and trade quotas, Stimson can ship wines without recourse, selling them in Canada at prices comparable to U.S. prices. At the same time, Canadian wines have become popular in the Midwest states.

The most significant change for small businesses will be the elimination of costly import-export licenses and elimination of similar legal entanglements that previously discouraged entrepreneurs from venturing north or south. Large corporations always had the means to overcome these barriers through their legal and export staff offices, but entrepreneurs were effectively stopped at borders by nightmarish regulations. With regulations simplified and import-export licenses soon to be completely eliminated, small business owners are free to explore new horizons. Many restrictions will remain on sensitive materials and products such as military weapons and strategic chemicals, but for the vast majority of products, services, and technologies, the border will become little more than a political convention.

CASE QUESTIONS

1. Explain why significant trade barriers between the United States and Canada existed prior to CFTA. In your opinion, why did either country have trade restrictions?
2. After CFTA is fully implemented, what advantages and disadvantages might develop for both the United States and Canada? Explore how these influence new venture creation and small business exporting.
3. Identify opportunities that might evolve from CFTA for U.S. and Canadian entrepreneurs.

Sources: Albert G. Holzinger, "Whipping Up Trading Fervor," *Nation's Business*, August 1988, pp. 13–14; Jay Finegan, "Northward, Ho!" *Inc.*, July 1988, pp. 37–38; and William Annett, "Farming's New Frontier," *Venture*, March 1989, pp. 35–40.

CASE 10-2

Going Global with a View toward China

In 1960, America's trade with Asia was barely half of its trade with Western Europe. By 1986, trade with Asia eclipsed that with Europe, and the outlook for the 1990s is for double-digit growth. Japan, Hong Kong, Taiwan, and South Korea account for most of this growth, but the future may rest with trade inside the People's Republic of China. Large multinational corporations represent a majority of foreign investments, but entrepreneurs on both sides of the Pacific represent a majority of export and import transactions.

One American entrepreneur who is benefiting from trade relations is Joseph Meringola, founder of Medical Action Industries, Inc. (MAI). Meringola started his venture in 1977 to supply a disposable gauze surgical pad to hospitals. The gauze pad is called a laparotomy sponge ("lap"), and it is a common supply item. With hospital costs increasing dramatically, small-ticket items like laps came under close scrutiny. The laps sold at about $60 for a case of 100 items when Meringola opened for business. He intended to beat competitive prices by a few pennies, establish a market, and then expand into similar low-cost items. Meringola, together with other suppliers in hospital supplies, was more successful than he had imagined, and a decade of price wars ensued. Today, a case of laps sells for half the price, about $30, and dozens of other similar items have had precipitous price reductions.

The chief reason for price reductions is that nearly all these common supplies are imported. Meringola had succeeded because he was one of the first to seek out overseas sources for lower-cost items. He began in 1980 by working through a Chinese agent in New Jersey who had personal connections in China. The agent made all the arrangements, and MAI simply wrote a check or gave the agent a letter of credit for imported supplies. That system trimmed costs to MAI by 50 percent, and the company enjoyed an explosive growth in sales. He signed orders in New York for 100,000 units a month, and word got around. Purchasing offices started calling him, and it looked as if he could have signed for a million units a month. Unfortunately, a high percentage of lap sponges coming from China through his broker were defective. Meringola was reluctant to take orders for fear of destroying his reputation. Poor quality was draining all the profit from sales, and he had to resolve the problem.

Meringola started going to China himself in 1984. He eventually found local agents in China that helped him contract with manufacturers, and MAI began receiving higher-quality merchandise. That approach worked for a while, but as orders mounted, quality declined. The problem, it seemed, was that his China agents had several excellent sources, but their manufacturing capacity was limited. When orders swelled, they relied on smaller, less dependable sources, and quality control was impossible. Gauze pads were often stained, some were unsterilized, many were not sewn properly, and most shipments were erratic. As Meringola saw it, he had several choices. He could send his own people to China periodically to control quality; he could move everything to Hong Kong and control quality through Hong Kong agents who have excellent reputations and connections; or he could invest in a joint venture in China to co-manufacture his products. All three options would be very expensive, and profit margins would not justify them without an enormous increase in business.

Meringola elected to go through Hong Kong export brokers who bought products from China, then transshipped them to the United States. Meringola was pleasantly surprised to find that quality improved significantly while costs actually decreased. This worked well until 1989 when political events in China seriously disrupted normal export channels. China, however, continued to be interested in foreign investments, and Meringola found that he was welcomed by the Chinese, who helped set up "cooperative manufacturing" contracts for his medical supplies. This arrangement is short of being a joint venture, and MAI has no direct investment in China; however, several MAI executives travel to China regularly to supervise production. The company has also helped the Chinese to purchase American technology to improve the quality of production.

Currently MAI buys from eight Chinese companies, supplying more than 5 million lap sponges and nearly 3 million operating room towels to American hospitals each month. Meringola's business is expected to double before 1995, and he is considering what to do next. Arrangements are satisfactory now, but they would not be adequate for continued growth. Consequently, Meringola is considering a joint venture in China, perhaps through an alliance that includes Hong Kong traders who have freight and warehousing capabilities. Recently MAI contributed $750,000 worth of equipment to his "cooperative" Chinese companies, but a direct investment or joint venture would mean much more.

CASE QUESTIONS

1. Explain the advantages and disadvantages of "going international," and specifically explore the risks shared by MAI in its China ventures.
2. Describe the progression of going international, and describe how small business ventures can export or import without heavy investments or risks.
3. Discuss the concept of "sourcing" and how MAI approached it. What other options would MAI have?

Sources: Joel Kotkin and Yoriko Kishimoto, "Winning in the Asian Era," *Inc.*, September 1988, pp. 71–76. Also John Birmingham, "One Founder's Far Eastern Foray," *Venture*, June/July 1989, pp. 79–80.

PART FOUR

Organizing and Financing the New Venture

In this final part of the text, several important topics are introduced concerning organizing, financing, and managing new ventures. Chapter 11 introduces the concept of an entrepreneurial team and addresses the human-resource issues related to organizing a new venture. This chapter also identifies legal structures for companies and contrasts how the various types of business formations can help or hinder entrepreneurs. Chapter 12 explains how entrepreneurs buy existing businesses and how, today, many new ventures are created through franchising. This chapter bridges the topics of organization and financing. Chapter 13 focuses on methods of financing new ventures, and it includes debt and equity sources, with a special section on venture capital. Chapter 14 is the summary chapter for the text, but it is no less important than earlier ones. It addresses management responsibilities for new and growing ventures, and it describes challenges for entrepreneurs as their ventures go through several transitions from start-up to mature enterprise. The chapter concludes with a brief look at entrepreneurial careers.

Chapter 11

The Entrepreneurial Team and Business Formation

OBJECTIVES

1. Describe the concept of an entrepreneurial team and the roles of founders and team members.
2. Examine the nature of a board of directors and the roles of directors.
3. Explain the importance of personal and social networking in new ventures.
4. Define a sole proprietorship and identify its major advantages and disadvantages.
5. Contrast the various types of partnerships and their characteristics.
6. Describe a corporation and its general advantages and disadvantages.

The success of an enterprise is more often determined by the individuals who lead it forward than by its products or services. The entrepreneurial team transforms creative ideas into commercial realities through their hard work and determination. A well-used phrase by venture capitalists is that they prefer a grade A entrepreneurial team with a grade B idea rather than the other way around. The implication is clear: Entrepreneurs must provide inspiration and direction, and they must be able to create organizations to sustain growth.

For the independent small business, the owner must wear several hats at once—leading, managing, and administering the new enterprise. For the corporate venture, a company "champion" must assemble a team of like-minded people capable of breathing life into an innovation. For the high-growth new venture, an entrepreneur must have the foresight to find partners or hire people with complementary skills needed to guide the enterprise toward success.

Just as important, a business venture must be legally structured in such a way as to reflect a logical organization consistent with the firm's purpose. A small tailor shop, for example, is unlikely to establish a corporation with a complex board of directors, and an aerospace manufacturer is unlikely to have a sole proprietorship with unlimited accountability vested in one person.

As we shall see, the choice of a legal form of business, its organizational structure, and the entrepreneurial team all rely on a complex set of conditions. The chapter is separated into two general parts: one dealing with the human element of creating an entrepreneurial team, and the other addressing legal formation of new ventures.

MATCHING HUMAN RESOURCE NEEDS AND SKILLS

New ventures succeed or fail on the performance of founding entrepreneurs. An exceptional new product positioned in the best possible market has no life of its own without a skilled founder. It is the capability of a determined entrepreneur or the strength of an entrepreneurial team that breathes life into an enterprise. Consequently, investors and bankers carefully evaluate the founder or the initiating team to determine the venture's chances for success. Financial backers almost always prefer seeing a skilled team in place rather than an individual effort, yet they put tremendous weight on the leadership role of the focal person who instigated the venture.

Consider the experience of ShenVenture, Inc., a venture capital firm in Virginia. The firm invested in only three projects out of 43 that were given serious consideration during 1990.[1] Nearly every project that was rejected had questionable leadership, and the three that were funded had sound entrepreneurial teams. One of those rejected, for example, was a plan by a reputable dentist for a new dental instrument. The dentist had developed an impressive new diagnostic probe with good market potential, but he had no intention of becoming actively involved with the venture. He wanted someone else to create a team for him, either to manufacture and sell the instrument or to sell the entire concept to an established company. From ShenVenture's viewpoint, there was neither a "team" nor a "champion" to make this desire a reality. Another rejected proposal was for a franchise chain of sporting goods stores. The entrepreneur already had one successful store with an excellent sales record. The concept was good and his merchandise was in high demand. Franchising, however, is a corporate enterprise requiring skills in site location, legal contracting, procurement, financing, marketing, and corporate leadership. The sporting goods entrepreneur was an excellent retailer but lacked the organizational skills and experience to establish a corporate endeavor. A successfully funded project, similar to the plan for a sporting goods franchise, was for a retail bicycle business chain. The entrepreneur had two successful locations and demonstrated his ability to create a management team at each store with knowledge of biking and sales experience. The business had cost-effective procurement, accounting systems, and a capable staff. The proposal included options for his staff to buy into the new venture, and they were genuinely interested in being part of the new venture.

These examples illustrate three important criteria for establishing a successful entrepreneurial team. First, the founder must have the personal skill and commitment to head the venture. Second, the founder must either have a team or be able to identify

PROFILE △

Donald Bonham

Fiesta Mart, Inc., located in Houston, Texas, is a storybook success with 12 supermarkets and nearly 2,500 employees, a "small business" became "large" through the personal touch of founder Donald Bonham. After 39 years in the grocery business, starting with the purchase of a neighborhood store when he was 21 years old, Bonham commands an enterprise with sales in excess of $350 million. He competes with industry giants such as Kroger and Safeway but holds a strong market share in selected market niches.

The story of Fiesta Mart is a story of understanding customer needs. In Bonham's view, even a small neighborhood grocer can be tremendously successful by identifying special needs of customers, then giving those customers the best he can offer. Bonham emphasizes marketing to Hispanic, African, Oriental, and Indian customers, and inside his stores, everything has an international theme. Greetings are written in English, Spanish, French, Vietnamese, Chinese, Korean, and Arabic. Food products from around the world are stocked. More important, his stores reflect a comfortable, welcoming environment for non-American-born consumers. However, Bonham's success is based on more than "niche marketing." He makes an extraordinary effort to understand the demographic changes taking place in society, the ebb and flow of immigration, the cultural needs of potential consumers, and the economic reality that most non-American-born consumers constitute a low-income segment of society. This effort is at the heart of his business decisions.

Most of Fiesta Mart employees come from the same populations that their stores serve. Employees are encouraged to be creative and to enrich the culture of their stores This leads, for example, to unusual color schemes, suggestions for products, and special promotions that bring a touch of "homeland" to their customers. Don Bonham has personally established scholarships at Rice University for minority groups that comprise his business market, and he and his wife are active community supporters who have a genuine interest in helping others fashion successful life-styles through minority enterprise programs.

Fiesta Mart, Inc., began as a family-operated business, and it remains a family enterprise, with Don Bonham and his wife active in its daily affairs. But it is far from being a "mom and pop" operation. Although the enterprise could grow to rival national chains, in Bonham's view that would destroy the nature of his reasons for being in business. He enjoys the rewards of being independent and has a tremendous sense of accomplishment in being part of the community he serves.

Source: Gail Rickey, "Success with a Social Conscience," *Successful American Entrepreneurs*, Summer 1987, pp. 12–15. Copyright Kwik-Kopy Corporation. Adapted with permission.

who is needed on a team to launch the venture. And third, the team must be able to share in the success of the new venture. The last point is crucial. If an entrepreneur intends only to "hire in" nine-to-fivers, success will rest solely on the resilience of the founder; employee contributions may be limited to their willingness to work for wages. What an entrepreneur needs is enthusiastic people who can share in the vision, complement one another's skills, and emotionally "buy into" the venture concept.[2]

The Founder's Role

Founding entrepreneurs are responsible for defining their businesses and identifying human resource requirements. Consequently, founders must first understand their own skills and limitations, then have the ability to attract others to the venture. A dentist who has a knack for inventing new instruments may one day revolutionize the industry, yet if he lacks marketing acumen, his inventions will probably never be commercially developed. Similarly, an enthusiastic entrepreneur skilled in sales who rushes to market without a solid business concept may do little more than waste energy running in circles. The inventor and the marketer may form a good team, but they will also need to demonstrate their conceptual ability to lead an enterprise and to be financially responsible. Occasionally an individual comes along who has capabilities in all these areas, but more often, entrepreneurs must face the reality of needing help. Consequently, an entrepreneurial team is needed, and the lead entrepreneur must have the human resource skills to organize this team and to focus its efforts on fulfilling the venture's objectives.

In the pre-start-up stage, entrepreneurs should be able to define in the business plan the skills needed and the roles of team members. When possible, these team members or partners should be specifically identified. Founding entrepreneurs are expected to fulfill leadership roles, but often they may be more effective in the background. For example, an inventor-dentist might be more valuable in the role of a technical adviser than in a management position. Instead of trying to start his own venture, the dentist could therefore bring in an experienced person with marketing and leadership skills (preferably gained in the dental instrument industry). A computer hardware specialist who lacks merchandising skills would be well advised to bring in someone with strong retailing experience to open a microcomputer franchise dealership. An expert interior designer might realize far better success with a partner who enjoys direct customer sales; the designer might be more comfortable doing back-room design work.

When the new venture is intrapreneurial (developed through the innovation of corporate employees), then the founder's role is that of a champion who brings together a corporate team. In this sense, the intrapreneur must provide the motivation to encourage team efforts that succeed in convincing management that a new product or service deserves attention. The corporate team often works after hours, uncompensated, and in the shadows of the organization to transform an idea to commercial reality. If a new product is involved, then designers, market researchers, design engineers, and other support staff will be essential.[3]

When the new venture is an independent small business, the founder may have

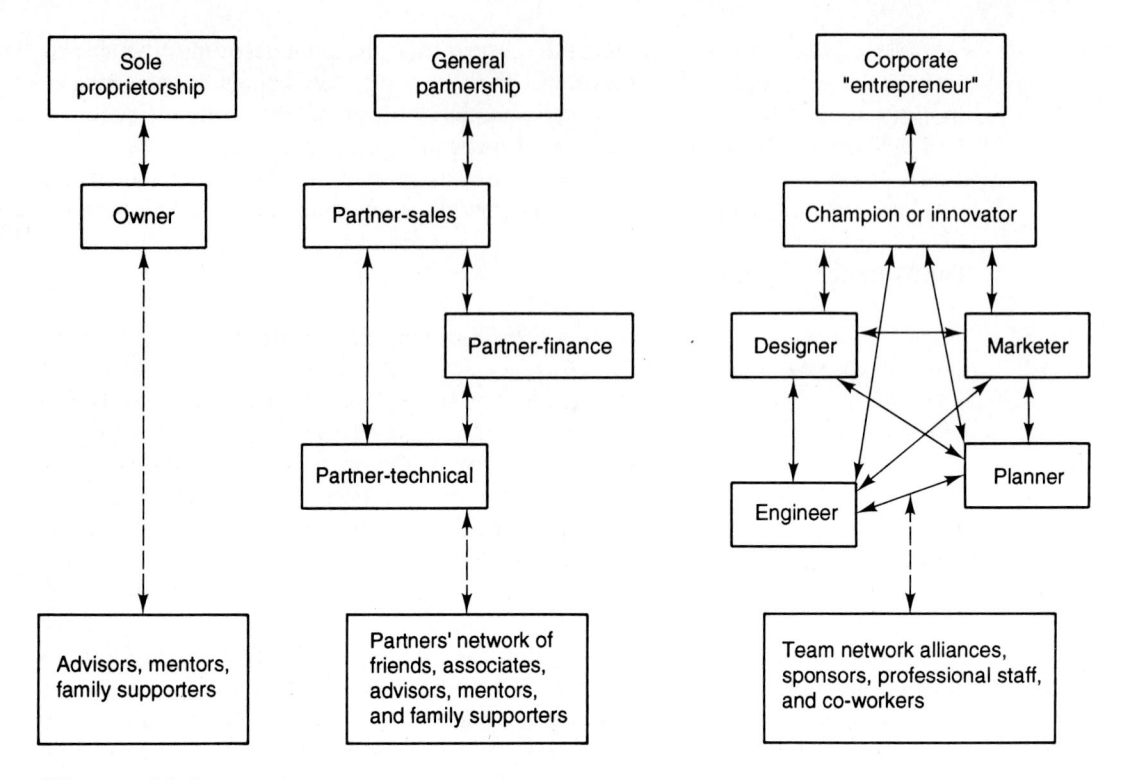

Figure 11-1 **Composition of Entrepreneurial Teams**

to assume responsibility for all roles. Perhaps more than any other reason, what causes so many small businesses to fail is the fact that few independent entrepreneurs are competent in the many skills needed in business. Nevertheless, investors and bankers want the small business founder to assess his or her particular skills honestly, then to identify ways in which help can be obtained. Retailers, dentists, computer specialists, and interior designers can bring technical or marketing skills to their ventures through outside assistance. Accounting or bookkeeping help, for example, can be contracted through local agencies. Entrepreneurs also can hire office managers if money permits. They also can find help through local SBA offices. In many instances, marketing can be contracted, but independent business owners can rarely find substitutes for their leadership responsibilities. With few exceptions, bankers identify an entrepreneur's leadership profile as the most important criterion when considering a loan application.[4]

Team Member Roles

Team members are partners in the emotional sense that they have joined together to pursue a dream; they are adventurers bound together by a common purpose. In most instances, team members have a stake in the venture as partners, stockholders, or employees who expect to share in success through stock options or bonuses. Venture capitalists often become active team players through board positions and operational consulting. In a corporate environment, employee teams often gather through casual friendships, yet they become united through their mutual commitment to see a project succeed.

All team members embrace their functional specialization, such as being responsible for marketing, customer service, or product development, but they must also be part of the "general management" process of planning and problem solving. As noted earlier, they cannot be nine-to-fivers, but must be able to contribute to the venture with enthusiasm. They are associates who, together, will create a business infrastructure and establish a sense of "culture" that gives the venture its unique image. They will also face crises together, and share in the wealth of success or the agony of failure.

Once an enterprise is established and begins to grow, team-member roles change. Their individuality as founders is less important than their ability to build an organization. As founders, all team members have to be entrepreneurs in the sense of accepting risk and being innovative. As members of an expanding enterprise, they must be managers capable of building and leading an efficient staff. They must transform themselves from mavericks who launched the venture to professional managers who can make it grow. Research has shown that decision-making behavior in small entrepreneurial firms is significantly different from that of large rapidly growing enterprises. Specifically, founding entrepreneurs and their team members tend to focus on operational issues and immediate problems, whereas managers in larger companies tend to focus on long-range strategic issues.[5] This difference implies that entrepreneurs and their founding team members may not be capable of leading ventures during later stages of development. Therefore, roles of entrepreneurs and their team members must be described in terms of the stage of venture development as well as their functional skills.

The founding entrepreneur ultimately has the responsibility for identifying roles and for guiding the venture through changes, yet they can find assistance in these matters. In the next section, we explore how assistance is obtained through boards of directors, and later we look into networks and mentors.

▶ CHECKPOINT

Identify three criteria for forming the entrepreneurial team.

Describe the entrepreneur's leadership role as a general manager.

Explore the roles of founding team members in a small new venture.

THE BOARD OF DIRECTORS

A formal board of directors is required by law for incorporated companies, but each state regulates corporations and therefore has specific guidelines for directors' responsibilities. When a corporation is publicly traded, the Securities and Exchange

Commission (SEC) regulates board activities and generally holds a company's directors responsible for corporate conduct. Privately held unincorporated companies do not have to have boards, yet in practice many do.

Board Composition

Smaller companies with boards usually limit the number of directors to between five and seven persons. Entrepreneurs are notoriously reluctant to share decision-making authority, and small boards are often dominated by the founder or the founder's family. It is not unusual to find a new venture board with the founder, his or her spouse, a son or daughter, and parents in director positions. In addition to naming family members to board positions, entrepreneurs commonly hand out directorships to powerful investors, or simply "load" boards with friends. None of these combinations are particularly beneficial, and they are often ineffective. Researchers who have looked closely at small-company boards suggest that most are poorly conceived and "passive" decision-making bodies.[6]

More enlightened entrepreneurs will select board members who can help the venture succeed. Selected members will include those with experience in the venture's line of business. Ideally, they will have executive decision-making skills, contacts outside the enterprise, and perhaps specialized knowledge in fields such as finance or law. Several of these directors may include operating team members and investors, but they will be selected for their potential contributions to strategic decisions. Outside directors (those having no internal position or investment) also can make important contributions. For example, outside directors might provide access to customers, professional associations, government agencies, or financial institutions. Those with related experience often know the industry's competitors and suppliers, and they usually are familiar with industry processes and marketing strategies. Regardless of their connections, however, it is crucial that they be *active* decision makers.

There is no ideal composition for a board of directors, but there are two important observations. First, boards comprising mainly insiders (the founder, family members, friends, and active investors) tend to focus on short-term budgets and operational problems. Second, boards comprising mainly outside directors tend to focus on external relations that can augment social and professional networks to attract capital, clientele, and management talent.[7] Consequently, lopsided boards—either too internally or too externally focused—may be less effective than those with members who can address operational problems and strengthen external relations.

Director Roles

Directors are legally responsible for the general conduct of business. Ultimately, board members are accountable for the performance and professional behavior of board-appointed officers. Exactly how this accountability is translated into board-level decisions varies with company circumstances and is left to the courts to interpret; however, it is clear that board members must often face the prospect of removing the CEO and key officers. Such an action can be traumatic because a founding

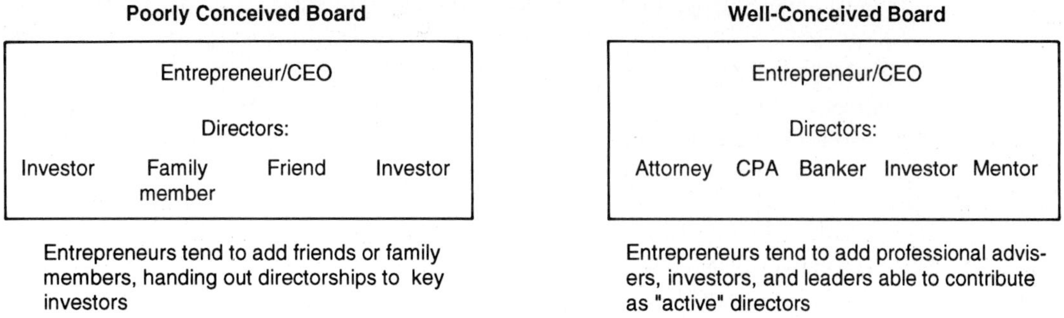

Figure 11-2 Composition of Boards of Directors

Poorly Conceived Board

Entrepreneur/CEO

Directors: Investor, Family member, Friend, Investor

Entrepreneurs tend to add friends or family members, handing out directorships to key investors

Well-Conceived Board

Entrepreneur/CEO

Directors: Attorney, CPA, Banker, Investor, Mentor

Entrepreneurs tend to add professional advisers, investors, and leaders able to contribute as "active" directors

---

entrepreneur who was instrumental in appointing board members can be fired by them. The founder's equity interest may not be at risk, but his or her operating authority can be stripped. Unfortunately such removals happen with some regularity when entrepreneurs cannot adapt to new roles in growing companies.

Although legal responsibilities are important, board-level assistance is of greater interest to entrepreneurs. Board members are supposed to assist in determining objectives, formulating strategies, unraveling complex problems, arbitrating executive conflicts, monitoring budgets, and providing expertise in legal, financial, and ethical decisions.[8] From an entrepreneur's viewpoint, board members are "mentors" and consultants who can not only perform their legal duties but also provide valuable insights about business operations. In this sense, directors are members of the entrepreneurial team who do not rubber-stamp decisions but *actively* participate in directing the company.

Behavior by board members is a matter of how the personalities of founders, team members, and directors mesh. If an entrepreneur is reluctant to share decision-making authority, the board may behave as a consultative body. At the other extreme, a strong board may behave as if it is in partnership with company founders. When new ventures are unincorporated proprietorships or partnerships, boards do not have legal status and are consequently limited to advisory roles.[9] Nevertheless, they can be influential in helping entrepreneurs solve problems and build social and professional networks. As we shall see in the next section, networking is an important part of creating an effective organization.

> ▶ **CHECKPOINT**
>
> Describe how venture management can benefit from careful selection of corporate board members.
>
> Identify primary roles of board members and responsibilities of a corporate board of directors.

NETWORKING—EXTENDING HUMAN RELATIONS

Networking is a process of creating alliances with people and organizations beyond the immediate boundaries of the venture. It is a process of linking up with the right people to get things done, and the difference between a successful and an unsuccessful venture often rests on "knowing people in the right places."[10] As noted earlier, outside directors may be able to provide this linkage through their personal contacts. Regardless of board activities, however, entrepreneurs must find ways to develop effective networks that open channels to resources, markets, and expertise. In simple terms, they must establish connections.

Personal Networks

A **personal network** consists of individuals within someone's immediate circle of daily relationships. These include family members, friends, and co-workers with whom a person has close ties. Personal networks result from *roles* in life, such as being part of a family.[11] As roles change, personal networks change. Students, for example, meet other students and become acquainted with faculty members, often forming lifelong relationships. In career positions, they find friends among colleagues, and in their leisure time they extend these contacts to club members and social friends. Of course, marriage bonds together another person's network of family and friends.

Entrepreneurs create new roles for themselves by pursuing their ventures, and in doing so, they begin to expand this circle of personal affiliations. If entrepreneurs

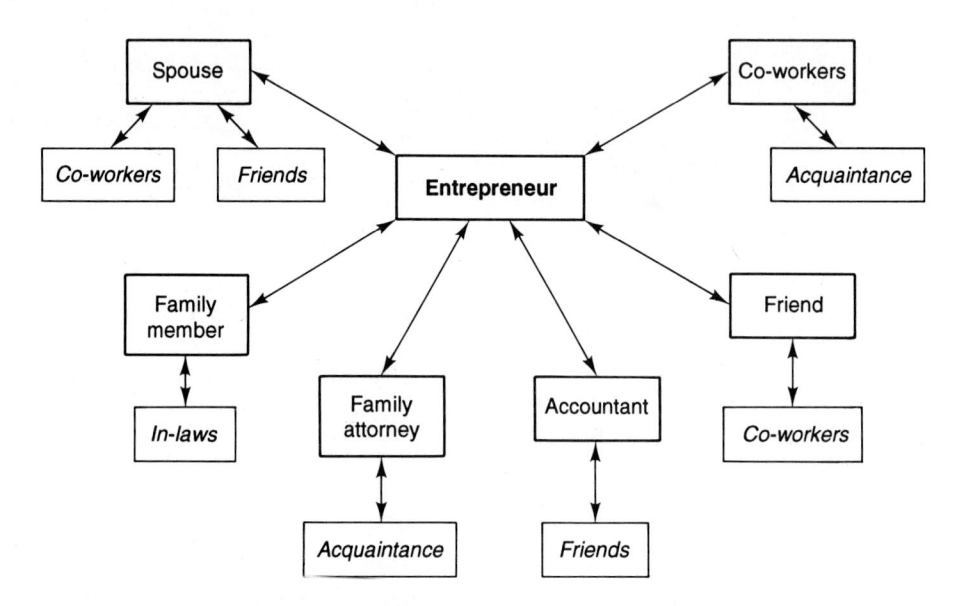

Figure 11-3 **Personal Networks**

are good at forming friendships, they may develop personal networks that include business partners, investors, customers, suppliers, and lenders. Many of these individuals may be counted simply as friends, not persons to whom entrepreneurs turn for specific help. In this sense, network members consist of *weak ties*, or "casual acquaintances," who provide little in terms of direct help for the new venture. Other network members will be *strong ties*, meaning that they can be expected to help when called upon, and in most instances their personal relationships with entrepreneurs are very close.[12] A father-in-law, for example, may be a strong tie who can personally assist the entrepreneur, but a banking acquaintance may be a weak tie who does not become involved in the venture more than by being helpful in nudging forward a loan application.

Having a very close personal network with strong ties is important, but these groups tend to be small and have a high density; that is, people know one another but are not necessarily well networked outside their own circles. Strong networks consist of individuals who can roll up their sleeves and contribute to the venture. Personal networks with weak ties may be more beneficial in the sense that entrepreneurs can call on these acquaintances to introduce them to customers, suppliers, investors, and lenders. Most entrepreneurs have a few close associations (strong ties) that provide personal support, but much more frequently it is casual acquaintances (weak ties) that provide useful information and access to resources.[13]

Social Networks

Distinct from personal networks, **social networks** are described as loosely connected affiliations within the community or industry.[14] This distinction does not exclude the strong-tie linkage of a personal network, but only shifts the emphasis away from personal toward professional associations. Perhaps more important, personal networks evolve through casual relationships, whereas social networks are construed as purposely developed. Researchers have found that successful entrepreneurs spend nearly 20 percent of their time developing contacts that constitute social networks.[15]

Social networks provide access to resources and expertise, and research has shown that a majority of successful entrepreneurs use networks advantageously. For example, founders use network contacts to gain access to bankers for start-up capital, operating loans, and introductions to private investors. They also find networks useful in choosing attorneys, obtaining accounting help, finding suppliers, attracting skilled employees, locating facilities, uncovering market research data, and opening doors to specific customers such as government agencies. Network contacts also lead to beneficial arrangements such as venture planning assistance, access to venture capital, and intelligence on new technology and competitors.[16]

Special Network Considerations

Personal and social networks are crucial extensions of the entrepreneurial team. Although network members are not directly involved in the new venture, they help mold the venture, influence the entrepreneur, and have a substantial effect on enterprise

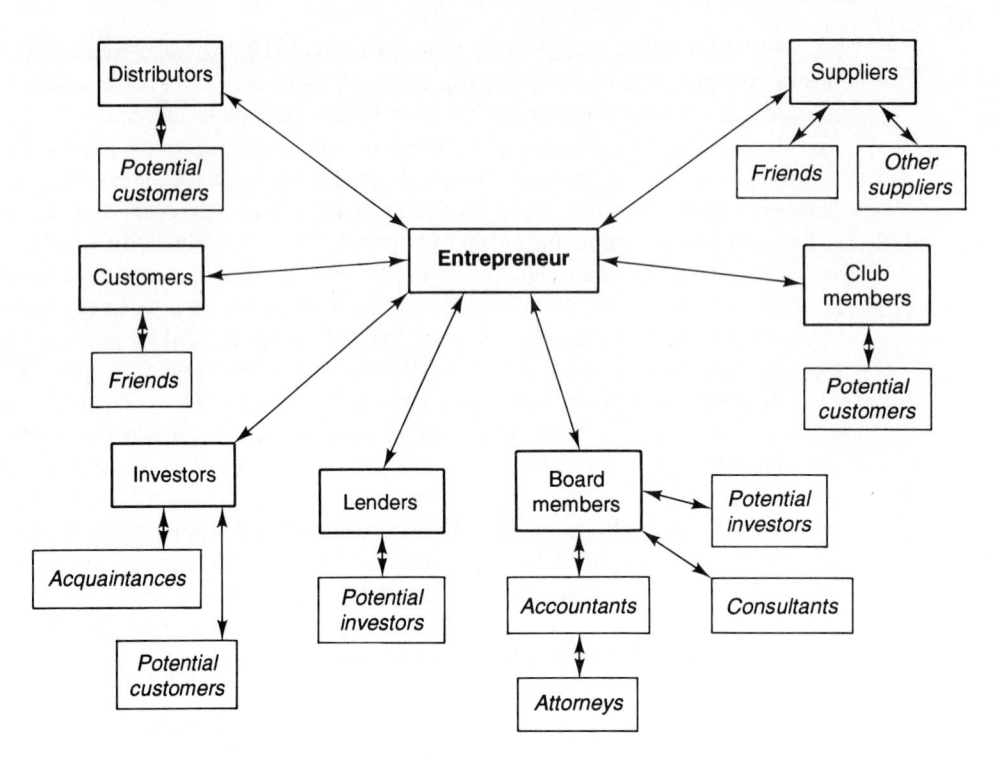

Figure 11-4 **Social Networks**

growth. However, many entrepreneurs lack effective networks and, more important, are thwarted in their attempts to create networks.

Specifically, women tend to have fewer contacts in the business world than men do, and although they may have many personal friends, these friends are not necessarily in positions to help them with their ventures. This situation may be a result of gender divisions in business, but it is also a function of how formal and informal networks in American society have evolved. Rotary Clubs, CEO groups, Young Presidents Organizations, venture capital clubs, and regional management groups have predominantly male memberships, creating a sex-segregated society. This pattern is no less apparent among organizations where networking occurs informally, such as golf and fitness clubs.[17] Consequently, women entrepreneurs tend to have a more difficult time than men gaining access to resources and information.[18]

Networking also can be more difficult for minority business owners who must find corridors into established business circles. Although minorities can be frustrated in their efforts to make contacts, they often find extremely strong support within their minority ranks.[19] Black, Asian, and Hispanic entrepreneurs tend to find mutual support *within* their community or among businesspeople with similar personal characteristics. To the extent that these contacts are established and well networked, minority entrepreneurs can often find rather substantial assistance. The immigrant population in the United States has historically found ways to band together, supporting aspiring entrepreneurs who have similar ethnic, racial, or religious characteristics.[20]

Without regard for personal characteristics, entrepreneurs with work experience related to their new ventures develop networks more quickly than those who enter unfamiliar fields. For this reason, corporate entrepreneurs may be more successful in finding rapid access to resources and markets. An engineer with several years experience in microelectronics, for example, will have knowledge and experience that is easily transferred to a new venture for developing microcircuit devices. Transferability is particularly important in technical fields because aspiring entrepreneurs can accumulate a tremendous amount of product and market information that is advantageous in their new ventures. This topic can be quite controversial because these entrepreneurs often take with them information gained while working on proprietary projects, yet it is a fact of life; employees cannot be expected to erase their accumulated knowledge, only to behave ethically. More important, corporate employees who become independent entrepreneurs benefit from established networks of industry contacts including customers, distributors, and suppliers.[21]

Networking is one of the many responsibilities facing founders who must attract human and material resources necessary to make a venture successful. Developing personal and social networks also requires conscientious efforts by founders and their team members. As we shall see, networks are also influenced by the legal formation and organization of a business enterprise.

▶ **CHECKPOINT**

Define personal and social networking, and, from your own experience, describe your personal network affiliations.

Examine how an entrepreneur can benefit from "loose ties" in a social network. What expertise might be important to secure by networking?

LEGAL FORMS OF BUSINESS IN PERSPECTIVE

There are three general categories of legal business formations in the United States: sole proprietorships, partnerships, and corporations. Federal laws, state laws, and regulatory agencies (such as the SEC) create several dozen options for various forms of partnerships and corporations, and with the exception of sole proprietorships, each of these has subtle differences. Sole proprietorships must also follow some regulations, but conceptually they are simply "individuals" doing business in the best tradition of free enterprise. Most partnerships and corporations are defined by law and regulated under state commercial codes. Selecting an appropriate form of business is one of the first decisions by a founder, and each form of business has its own special attributes.

Exhibit 11-1 Three Common Forms of Ownership

Sole proprietorship	Owner is only investor and is solely responsible. Business earnings are taxed as owner's personal income. Owner is personally liable for all business affairs.
General partnership	Two or more owners have joint responsibilities. Partners are taxed on prorated share of earnings. Partners are jointly and severally liable for business affairs.
Incorporation	Stock ownership defines separate legal entity. Corporate income is taxed; stockholder dividends are taxed. Stockholders have limited liability for business affairs.

Selecting a Legal Formation

Selecting a legal form of business involves a decision with at least three important criteria: preferences of the entrepreneur, profile of the enterprise, and advantages and disadvantages of the legal business entity.[22] These criteria are described here and in the sections on each legal formation.

Preferences of the Entrepreneur. Recall from Chapter 1 that entrepreneurs often go into business to escape a nine-to-five world. Many are motivated by the opportunity to be self-sufficient, autonomous, and in control of their own destinies. Consequently, they tend to avoid the complex organizations implied by incorporation and the entanglements envisioned with partnerships. Among entrepreneurs who do incorporate or attract partners, there is seldom a strong urge to share decision-making authority. Entrepreneurs tend to want to "go it alone," and this desire influences their decisions about choosing a legal structure.[23]

Profile of the Enterprise. When a new venture is launched, it is almost always small. Therefore, it makes sense to adopt a small structure that is easy to administer. As we shall see, partnerships and corporations can be kept simple, but usually they require shared authority, some complexity in accounting and tax reporting, and responsibilities under regulatory guidelines. As a venture begins to grow, more resources and people are needed, and the basic structure of a "one-person" organization is no longer possible. The complex responsibilities of growing enterprises create an evolutionary process that typically leads to revised legal formations. A restaurant owner who began as a sole proprietor, for example, may need partners as the business grows, and if the restaurant expands into a chain or franchise, incorporation may be a logical choice.

Advantages and Disadvantages of a Business Entity. Business law books are filled with issues that relate to advantages and disadvantages of various forms of business. These are too numerous to describe in detail, yet some advantages and disadvantages should be emphasized.[24] Tax regulations differ for each type of enterprise, and for some statutory forms of business (e.g., limited partnerships and "S Corporations"), owners benefit from preferential tax rules. Legal liability also differs among business formations; corporate stockholders benefit from limited liability, whereas proprietors are fully accountable for all business activities. Also, there are tremendous differences in how each type of business can be financed. Publicly traded corporations registered with the SEC can sell stock, for example, but partnerships and proprietorships cannot.

Other Practical Considerations

Entrepreneurs select a legal formation on the basis of emotional issues (personal preferences), management issues (e.g., size of the enterprise), and rational issues (e.g., legal liability), but in practical terms, new ventures need access to resources. As explained earlier, resources can be acquired through effective networking. Sole proprietorships are, by definition, one-person businesses where networks depend on the owner's personal circle of friends and acquaintances. Partnerships bring together two or more network groups, and corporations open multiple networks through their directors and investors. Resource networks, therefore, are important to consider and may take precedence over other criteria.

The Internal Revenue Service indirectly influences how businesses are formed through reporting requirements, registration procedures, and tax treatment for assets and liabilities. Also, other regulatory agencies, such as the Food and Drug Administration (FDA) and the Federal Trade Commission (FTC) influence selection decisions. As a business expands, it will add employees and face different benefit requirements that influence entrepreneurs to change their legal structures. In addition, state and local authorities control licensing regulations that affect formation decisions. Businesses that expand internationally will have more complex issues to consider, amplified by both domestic and foreign regulations.

> ▶ **CHECKPOINT**
>
> Describe the three categories of considerations for selecting a specific legal form of business.
>
> Explain several practical considerations that influence a founder's choice for a legal business formation.

SOLE PROPRIETORSHIP

A **sole proprietorship** is the business of one person, independently owned and without partners. The person "is the business" with full accountability for taxes, finances, and legal liability. In the strictest sense of the word, the business does not exist apart from the proprietor. A sole proprietorship is easy to establish by registering the business with city or county authorities. Aside from paying a small fee for a business license (often no more than $20), there is little formality or cost.[25] Depending on the type of business, of course, there may be other costs involved before being able to open legally for business. Restaurants, for example, must obtain health permits; discos have to obtain appropriate liquor licenses; and courier services have to obtain a variety of road-use and vehicle permits. Most owners find that they have other regulations to satisfy, such as zoning, EPA waste disposal, and insurance, and these considerations often influence the choice of business formation.

Consider the example of a single-chair beauty salon owned and operated by one person. Because it is an unincorporated proprietorship, once the owner has a location and is ready to open, she would go to the appropriate city or county office, register the business name (e.g., Style Shoppe), and pay her fees. Registration forms usually require the owner's name, address, and a statement that she will be legally responsible for debts and liabilities of her business. If authorities require the shop operator to have a cosmetology license and health permit, then these must be filed with the business application. Also, in most municipalities licensing clerks will advise business owners about special requirements, such as restrictions concerning noise, business hours, and posted signs.

The name "Style Shoppe" in this example is the business trade name, alternatively called a DBA (doing business as) or a fictitious name. If a business exists in the registration area with a DBA of "Style Shoppe," the owner will not be granted a business license. Consequently, owners usually check on existing names and select at least one alternative name before registering. If the owner has aspirations of expanding to other areas, it will be wise to make a thorough check of state-registered trade names that are reserved or protected. Beyond these considerations, there are few obstacles to opening a locally owned sole proprietorship.

From a legal and tax standpoint, the sole proprietorship and owner are synonymous. At the end of a tax year, business earnings are reported to the IRS on a tax schedule attached to the owner's individual return. If the business accumulates debts, the owner is legally liable for them regardless of how well the business is

Exhibit 11-2 **Primary Advantages and Disadvantages of Sole Proprietorships**

Advantages	Disadvantages
Autonomy and self-direction	Unlimited legal liability for business
Business income reported as owner's personal income	Unlimited liability for financial debts
Fringe benefits supported by business	Credit an extension of owner's personal collateral and financial strength
Simple to start and administer	Access to external resources limited
Inexpensive as a form of business	Assistance and support limited to owner's personal network
	Business ends with owner's death

doing. Even if the business closes, bills will accrue to the owner. If the business is sued (perhaps a customer slips on a wet floor and is injured), the owner is fully liable. Liabilities can be a substantial burden for owners; however, if an entrepreneur has no intention of expanding, the sole proprietorship can be a reasonable choice.

Advantages of the Sole Proprietorship

Compared with other legal forms of business, the sole proprietorship has the singular advantage of simplicity. Decisions are made by one person without meetings or committees, investments (and therefore profits or losses) are vested in one person, and administrative requirements are minimal.[26] Advantages derived from this scenario are as follows:

- Autonomy of control and decision making.
- Self-direction without sharing authority or requiring coordination with partners or stockholders.
- Direct taxation as an extension of the owner's personal income tax return.
- Favorable tax rates for small businesses. In many instances, businesses that are moderately profitable will have a lower effective tax rate as income reported under an owner's individual rate schedule than under a corporate schedule. Also, there is no double taxation as there is in corporations, where profits are taxed, then dividends to shareholders are taxed again.
- Many expenses and business losses can be deducted, thereby reducing personal income tax liability.
- Few regulations, little compliance reporting, and minimal administration for proprietorships keep business administration simple.
- Special benefits can be realized. Self-employed individuals often benefit from special types of insurance and retirement funds not available to wage earners.

The federal tax code is notoriously complicated, and as it changes, tax advantages realized one year are often lost the next. Much of the tax code is also subject to interpretation (such as when a part of one's home can be used as a business expense). Nevertheless, a proprietor usually can benefit from legitimate business expenses, such as having the owner's health insurance paid through a business insurance plan. Also, because a proprietorship's income is not distinguished from the owner's personal income, cash from the business can be used to pay personal bills. From an accounting standpoint, this is not a good practice, yet proceeds from the business are the owner's without restriction.

Disadvantages of the Sole Proprietorship

Because sole proprietorships are "one-person" businesses, there are severe constraints for raising investment capital and securing resources.[27] As noted earlier, the owner is fully liable for debts, legal actions, and disposition of profits and losses. Important disadvantages to consider are these:

- The proprietor is personally liable for any and all debts; thus all an owner's personal assets are collateral subject to loss.
- As a legal entity, the business exists only in the persona of the owner, and legal claims, lawsuits, or regulatory obligations rest with the owner who is personally accountable.
- Because a sole proprietorship "is" the person and the business assets belong entirely to the owner, the business and its assets are subject to inheritance laws. Consequently, there is no legal continuity; the business legally ends with the owner's death, and its assets are treated as private property.
- Without legal continuity, there is no automatic succession, and a proprietor's ability to secure loans, contract for resources, and attract investors is constrained by the owner's health and longevity.
- A sole owner is limited to a network of family and personal acquaintances that seriously constrains his or her ability to garner resources and vital market information.
- Potential employees recognize the succession problem and are often reluctant to consider working for a sole proprietorship which, by definition, will end with the owner's death. Moreover, the business can be terminated at will. An employee's career is never secure.
- Although most sole proprietorships enjoy a lower relative tax rate than corporations under current IRS guidelines, rules and procedures for tax accounting are too complicated to assume this to be a consistent advantage. Quite often, statutory partnerships and corporations can realize special tax advantages for fringe benefits, expenses, and capital gains not available to sole proprietors.
- A proprietorship cannot pay a salary to the owner; consequently, there is no tax-deductible salary expense to reduce business income. Although favorable individual tax rates may apply, many other legal forms of business can pay salaries and offer extensive fringe benefits, thereby reducing taxable income.

Many of these advantages and disadvantages depend on changeable variables such as gross business income and the entrepreneur's outside income, wealth, and expenses. Also, the relative difference in objective benefits, such as low tax rates, may be small when compared with offsetting emotional considerations, such as an autonomous life-style. In addition, an entrepreneur can often find good legal and accounting advice to structure business assets in such a way that disadvantages are minimized. For example, an owner's home may be transferred to a spouse, eliminating it as an "asset at risk" in the event of a business lawsuit. To summarize, advantages and disadvantages are no more than general considerations that vary greatly with individual circumstances.

▶ **CHECKPOINT**

Define the concept of a sole proprietorship.

Describe key advantages and disadvantages of a sole proprietorship.

PARTNERSHIPS

A **partnership** is an association of two or more persons as co-owners to conduct a business jointly. There are several types of partnerships, each with specific requirements for investment and tax accountability, but the purpose of any partnership is to combine forces to pursue a specific business.[28] By joining together, partners can create a synergistic team complementing one another's talents. In addition, partners represent a strong business profile for obtaining loans or attracting investors because they have combined assets and an expanded operational team. Partnerships are most likely to be created to strengthen the entrepreneurial team, not merely to take advantage of financial leverage, yet they also benefit from expanded social and professional networking.

As a general rule, partnerships must *file* partnership tax returns, but partnerships are not taxed; income is allocated to individual partners who are subsequently held accountable for taxes. But business losses are also passed on to individual partners, who often realize an advantage by being able to reduce their personal income tax liability. Certain types of partnerships have been criticized as "tax-shelter vehicles" because of the potential for write-offs; however, the fundamental reason for creating partnerships should not be blurred. That purpose is to bring individuals with unique and complementary talents together in a mutually beneficial endeavor.

General Partnerships

A **general partnership** is a formal or informal association in which the co-owners share unlimited liability for the business.[29] Each partner is fully responsible for operating the business regardless of his or her percentage share of investment. Each partner is also legally liable for business conduct and cannot avoid liabilities created by other partners. Therefore, creditors can sue the partnership, and sue the individual

Exhibit 11-3 **Primary Advantages and Disadvantages of General Partnerships**

Advantages	Disadvantages
Partners provide synergy of action, expertise, and interest	Unlimited legal liability for business by all partners, jointly and severally
Business income reported as partners' personal income	Unlimited liability for financial debts by all partners, jointly and severally
Partners have strong profile for obtaining debt financing	Entrepreneurs must share authority and cooperate in making decisions
Fringe benefits supported by business	Business ends with death or withdrawal of any partner
Partners have expanded network of contacts for accessing resources	Infusions of equity difficult without adding more partners
Simple and inexpensive to start	Partners accountable to one another, often resulting in conflict

partners, for any debt; courts can pursue liability claims against the combined partnership and the individual partners. If partners have not protected their personal assets in some way, they risk unlimited liability just as if they were sole proprietors.

A general partnership can be created informally without express written agreement. If two or more people invest in a new venture and there is no formal agreement clarifying the situation, courts will interpret the enterprise as a general partnership. Although there is no partnership without investment, partners can join forces on the strength of a handshake. Obviously, it is better to have a formal, written agreement to avoid misunderstandings. A formal agreement is particularly important in the event a partnership is terminated by the death or withdrawal of a partner. Without a written agreement there can be substantial legal battles over distribution of partnership assets and debt settlements.

Advantages of General Partnerships. The greatest advantage of a general partnership is the opportunity to have a rich mixture of talented partners. One partner may be a brilliant innovator, another an excellent salesperson, and yet another an excellent administrator. By combining their efforts, partners can often be far more successful than they could individually. As noted earlier, partners often can leverage their combined credit and financial strength to secure favorable business loans. Through their expanded networking, they also realize broader exposure to customers, suppliers, and professional experts. Compared with sole proprietorships, partnerships seem to be more stable (less apt to go out of business and not based entirely on one person's longevity). Consequently, attracting competent employees can be easier.

General partnerships are not complicated, and with the exception of filing an annual partnership form with the IRS, a general partnership enjoys the same flexibility and simplicity as a sole proprietorship. Unlike sole proprietorships, however, partnership investments are considered capital assets and subject to special accounting conventions. Unlike proprietorships, for example, partnerships must document and keep separate personal and business investments. Although complicated, this particular convention can simplify partnership dissolution or probate of partnership assets.

Disadvantages of General Partnerships. Partnerships, like sole proprietorships, suffer from lack of continuity because a partnership terminates on the death or withdrawal of any one of the partners. Many partnership agreements resolve this problem with provisions for buying out partnership interests or insuring individual partners so that business can continue uninterrupted. Perhaps the greatest disadvantage is unlimited legal liability. Because any partner can sign contracts or obligate the venture, and because in small ventures equal partners often have equal access to business funds, one partner can bind all partners to debts, contracts, and obligations arising from his or her behavior. Unless the partnership agreement restricts unilateral action by one partner, this can be a significant problem; it is not unusual to hear about a partner stripping a firm's assets and disappearing. Finally, entrepreneurs value autonomy, but partnerships, by definition, require joint decisions and shared responsibilities. Consequently, conflicts can arise from this basic contradiction; partnerships can be very fragile in terms of owner relationships.

Limited Partnerships

To overcome personal liability in general partnerships, a statutory form of partnership was created. *Limited partnerships* were created by federal law under the Uniform Limited Partnership Act, and most states have passed similar legislation.[30] A **limited partnership** requires one or more "general" partners who are responsible for managing the venture with unlimited legal liability. Unlike general partnerships, however, limited partnerships must also have one or more "limited" partners who cannot become involved in management, and subsequently their liability is limited to their investments. Limited partners behave somewhat like corporate stockholders, but profits and losses pass through to all partners, who are individually accountable for taxes. Limited partnerships are therefore legal entities positioned midway between general partnerships and corporations.

The general partner is not protected from legal liability, and in addition, the general partner is accountable to limited partners for properly conducting business on their behalf. Limited partners can sue general partners, but general partners are usually well compensated for management responsibilities. This unusual relationship can result in complicated partnership agreements, and agreements must also comply with federal and state regulations that can be perplexing. To create a limited partnership, a *certificate of limited partnership* must be filed with the state and recorded as a public record. Like general partnerships, limited partnerships must file annual tax returns as "information" even though profits and losses pass through to investors.

Advantages of Limited Partnerships. The provision for limited liability is the principal advantage of a limited partnership, but most investors also enjoy tax advantages from expenses that can reduce personal income tax liability. Prior to 1986 revisions in the tax code, these advantages led to a proliferation of limited partnerships in real estate development, oil and gas exploration, cattle ranching, and other front-end-loaded investments with "sheltered" features such as accelerated depreciation and resource depletion allowances. Many liberal tax allowances have been rescinded,

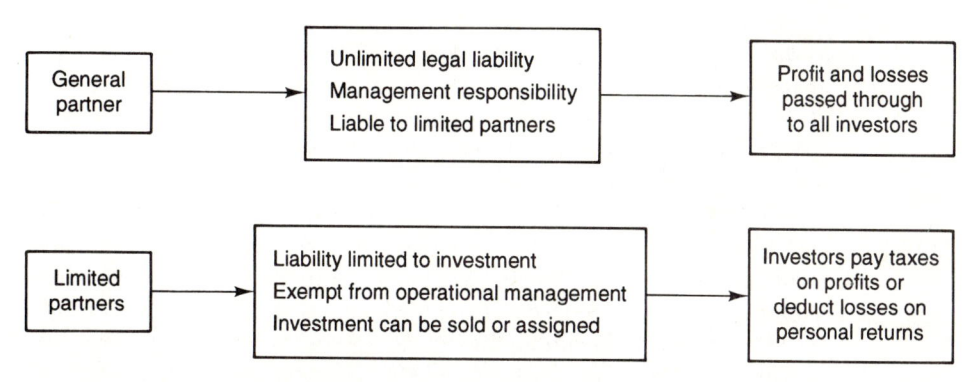

Figure 11-5 **Structure of Limited Partnerships**

General partner → Unlimited legal liability / Management responsibility / Liable to limited partners → Profit and losses passed through to all investors

Limited partners → Liability limited to investment / Exempt from operational management / Investment can be sold or assigned → Investors pay taxes on profits or deduct losses on personal returns

yet ventures that are economically sound will provide legitimate tax benefits and long-term profit potential to investors.

A distinct advantage is that limited partners can sell or assign their investment interests, and because they are capital assets, investments can be willed without dissolving the partnership. Limited partnership agreements usually have a provision for buying back a limited partner's interest, which can be sold or reallocated without disrupting business operations.

Disadvantages of Limited Partnerships. The complexity of formal limited partnership agreements coupled with intricate compliance requirements results in a sensitive business structure. Limited partnerships must have clearly stated purposes, carefully detailed operational guidelines, and unambiguous means of terminating the venture. Because the partnership is subscribed at the outset, there is little flexibility for obtaining new equity or assuming debt. Unlike other forms of business, limited partnerships cannot pursue business activities, obtain debt, or expand beyond the tenets of the original agreement.

R&D Limited Partnerships

Entrepreneurs with high-tech innovations or complicated research ideas can benefit from **research and development limited partnerships**. Called an **RDLP**, this limited partnership evolved from tax-incentive legislation and the Economic Recovery Tax Act (ERTA) of 1981. The U.S. Department of Commerce encourages entrepreneurs to use RDLPs for developing technological research.[31]

An RDLP comprises a general partner and limited partners, much like the standard limited partnership. Unlike the standard limited partnership, RDLP partners can include any "legal entity" recognized in the United States. Consequently, partners can include individuals, partnerships, joint ventures, corporations, not-for-profit organizations, universities, trusts, or government agencies. Also, RDLPs can be established with a variety of unusual partners allowing combinations of capital and expertise far beyond any single organization's independent capabilities.

The RDLP also has a tax-shelter advantage that allows huge incentives for research and development. These incentives are quite important because research expenses under other forms of enterprise are often difficult to justify and are seldom given special treatment by the IRS, but the fundamental purpose of an RDLP is to allow the broadest latitude through unorthodox combinations of organizations. When RDLPs are successful, their technological innovations are shared equally by all partners. When those partners include government agencies, universities, and private corporations, the result is a wide dispersion of technology with rapid commercial application. For example, the 14-member Microelectronics and Computer Technology Corporation (MCC) was established to pursue supercomputer applications in artificial intelligence. Involving more than 250 scientists, MCC has annual research budgets approaching a quarter-billion dollars. It employs research facilities of several dozen corporations and universities. Also, MCC partners are companies that, under normal circumstances, are fierce competitors, including IBM, Honeywell, Xerox, Motorola,

Semiconductors, and Hewlett-Packard. When the RDLP research project is completed, the partnership will terminate, but meanwhile, MCC has extraordinary access to expertise and resources, and the partners will mutually benefit in the end.[32]

An RDLP does not have to include megacorporations, universities, and government agencies, nor does it have to pursue glamorous technical research, but it does have to qualify under rigorous criteria to be registered. For those entrepreneurs with interesting technological ideas but few resources, the RDLP may be an ideal vehicle. It is encouraged by federal authorities, and the Office of Productivity, Technology, and Innovation of the U.S. Department of Commerce will provide free assistance to entrepreneurs interested in establishing an RDLP.

▶ **CHECKPOINT**

Define and contrast general and limited partnerships.

Describe advantages and disadvantages of both types of partnership.

CORPORATIONS

A **corporation** is a legal business entity, created by law and managed through a board of directors who are responsible to stockholders for appointing and directing operating officers.[33] A corporation has an indefinite life unhampered by succession issues that plague sole proprietors or termination clauses required in most partnership agreements. A corporation is also a taxable entity subject to state and federal regulations, and it has legal liability for business conduct apart from its stockholders. As a legal entity, a corporation can do most things that a private businessperson can do, such as acquiring property, accumulating wealth, selling assets, entering into contracts with other companies, making investments, and bringing legal actions.

Incorporating a business is neither complicated nor expensive, and most states have incorporation packets that provide filing forms, instructions, and schedules of fees to help entrepreneurs. The usual procedure is for a corporate name to be selected, founding directors to be named, a principal officer to be identified with a legal address, and "articles of incorporation" to be drawn up with specific information about the number and classification of shares to be issued. The articles are filed with state authorities (with nominal filing fees), and within a few weeks the entrepreneur is sent a "certificate of incorporation" verifying that the business has been registered. This is the simplest scenario, but corporate filings can be far more complex when they involve several types of stock shares and intricate business arrangements.

The rationale for incorporating a business is not simple and requires careful thought. Recall from earlier descriptions of sole proprietorships and partnerships that entrepreneurs select a legal form of business to enhance their access to resources, to obtain capital, and to attract expertise. These are equally important criteria for incorporation with similar advantages and disadvantages.[34]

Exhibit 11-4 Primary Advantages and Disadvantages of Incorporation

Advantages	Disadvantages
Limited liability for investors	Complicated form of administration
Access to external resources enhanced through broad networks	Entrepreneur must share authority and decision making with board
Assistance and support enhanced through board of directors	Double taxation as corporate income is taxed and investors' dividends are taxed as personal income after distribution
Unlimited life as legal entity assures succession and control	Regulated at federal and state levels and subject to substantial compliance
Stock and other securities issues provide financial expansion	Entrepreneur may lose control of venture he or she founded
Salaries, benefits, other expenses can be effective income allocations	

Advantages of Corporations

There are several types of corporations, and because they are regulated under laws of the states in which they are domiciled, advantages differ somewhat in each locale. Generally, all corporations have the following advantages:

- Limited liability for individual stockholders usually protects investors from legal actions and debt liabilities. They may risk their stock investment, but not personal assets. There are instances, however, when stockholders are held accountable for corporate obligations, such as when a company has incorporated to defraud creditors or circumvent previous legal obligations.
- Access to expanded equity capital is achieved through incorporation by issuing stock. When they create a successful track record and attain a certain size, corporations can issue other financial instruments such as bonds and debentures, and ultimately they can register with the SEC to sell equities through established exchanges. This process is called going public.
- Broad social and professional networks are established by having diversified investors, an active board of directors, and responsible team managers.
- Continuity of ownership distinguishes corporations from all other forms of business. Corporations are not required to terminate at a predetermined time or to dissolve with a founder's death; the corporation continues. Stock is a private asset that does not affect a corporation's legal status when sold, assigned, or inherited.
- Because the corporation is empowered to do most things a private citizen can do (e.g., borrow money or purchase assets), but also because it has an indefinite life, creditors face less risk with a corporation than with an unincorporated business. In addition, a corporation is not as vulnerable to personal ownership disputes as partnerships or family businesses.
- A corporation can create separate corporate subsidiaries, joint ventures, and trusts that stand apart from other operations. This ability provides autonomy in ownership

and separation of legal and financial liability. Sole proprietors and partners cannot assure autonomy for multiple business interests because their assets are totally at risk in each venture.
- Tax advantages exist, but they cannot be generalized to all corporations. Tax rates for small corporations are seldom lower than for individuals who have similar net income from proprietorships and partnerships; however, corporate tax advantages can be *created* through effective use of accounting options unavailable to sole proprietors and partners. For example, a corporation can pay salaries, thereby reducing taxable income (salaries are deductible), and if these matters are handled correctly, founders will pay taxes on their salaries at favorable rates. Also, a corporation can rent equipment or facilities from founding entrepreneurs, thereby transferring money out of the company, avoiding taxes on some proceeds. Paying health-care benefits, contributing to retirement funds, and providing other fringe benefits are opportunities for corporations not readily available to proprietors. These are a few of many legal and ethical ways to reallocate corporate income, but corporations are closely regulated in an attempt to minimize abuses.

Disadvantages of Corporations

Although advantages of incorporation sound impressive on the surface, there can be major disadvantages. Most of these arise from complications of federal and state regulations, but owners' preferences are also important. Some of the disadvantages follow:

- From an entrepreneur's viewpoint, incorporation requires a major shift of authority; sole proprietors have autonomy and self-direction, but corporations are subject to direction by a board of directors. Also, when shares are sold, ownership becomes diluted, and entrepreneurs often find themselves in minority ownership positions with little influence in the ventures they created.
- Although incorporating is not necessarily expensive or complicated, the costs and filing regulations can become a significant burden. A corporation must also carefully document stockholders' meetings, transactions, board minutes, management initiatives, and so on. Corporations must keep rather comprehensive records for federal and state agencies, the IRS, and stockholders.
- Corporations distribute income to stockholders through dividends, and dividends are declared after corporate taxes are paid. Consequently, corporate income (in the form of dividends) is taxed again as investors' personal income. This "double tax" burden is a significant disadvantage for small profitable firms.

Electing to Be an "S Corporation"

Many of the administrative and tax complications of incorporation can be put to rest by electing to incorporate as an *S Corporation*. Originally called a **Subchapter S Corporation**, this option was created in 1958 under the Small Business Tax Reform Act.[35] After several changes in the tax code, this election is now officially called **S**

PROFILE △

Dave Bing—NBA Star Turns to Steel Business

Former Detroit Pistons star Dave Bing made a good living and saved a small fortune in his 12-year NBA career, but after retiring in 1978, he turned to manufacturing as a way to establish a business career that would also help the rust-belt community near Detroit's Big Three automakers. After spending two years learning the steel business at a small Detroit mill, Bing sank his NBA savings into his own company, Bing Steel, and began processing high-quality rolled steel for automotive production. Ten years later, Bing had not only survived the rust-belt economy but also cracked the $50 million sales barrier.

In Bing's view, his corporation provides a vehicle for income that he can use in his ultimate goal of helping his community, yet he keeps close control of the company and his aspirations. In 1989 he sponsored a charity NBA all-star game headed by Magic Johnson that kicked off a $1.8 million campaign to help public schools restore programs cut from school budgets because of reduced tax revenues. He sees the 1990s as a decade of educational revitalization in one of the most turbulent manufacturing regions in the United States. Building and expanding his company is secondary to his personal commitments.

Source: "Charity Slam Dunk," *Fortune*, September 11, 1989, p. 106.

Corporation Status, but its original reason for existing has not changed. The purpose of S Corporations is to help small businesses attract equity capital through incorporation while retaining the organization and control enjoyed in a general partnership.[36]

Entrepreneurs who are interested in the S Corporation election should consult with a knowledgeable attorney to clarify their options, but there are several advantages to consider. Stockholders benefit from all net income (before taxes), which is passed through to individual investors. This provision avoids the double-taxation problem, and just as important, corporate losses are passed through to investors who can use them to offset personal income. Operating on a calendar-year basis, S Corporations have less complicated reporting requirements than other corporations. Also, S Corporations enjoy more relaxed guidelines concerning specific tax issues such as capital gains, passive income, rents, royalties, and tax credits. Administration of an S Corporation tends to mirror that of a partnership with the exception of directors' reports and stockholders' meetings. Consequently, S Corporations can remain relatively uncomplicated.

An S Corporation is limited to 35 stockholders, regardless of the amount of their individual or total capital investment. This limit can be a serious constraint on attracting capital, but for the small business enterprise, it is not a major obstacle. When an S Corporation exceeds 35 investors, it automatically becomes a regular corporation in the eyes of the IRS. Also, some states do not recognize S Corporation status, and several others simply treat S Corporations like regular corporations. In addition, S Corporation status is not necessarily an advantage if the company is growing rapidly and earning significant profits because individual investors may suddenly find themselves paying taxes on huge corporate profits. Moreover, corporate profits do not have to be distributed to be taxable.

Other Corporate Considerations

Selecting a form of business often comes down to IRS considerations, and as U.S. tax codes change, relative advantages and disadvantages seem to become magnified. Between 1972 and 1986 (14 years), there were four comprehensive tax reforms that significantly affected tax accountability, and during that same period there were more than 200 modifications in federal tax guidelines. Considering the importance of choosing a business formation, which is a long-term decision, the instability of tax regulation suggests careful evaluation of all alternatives. Clearly, tax benefits accrue through various incentives such as S Corporation Status, guidelines on deductible expenses, and special sections of the tax code that are enacted periodically. For example, Section 1244 of the Internal Revenue Code allows a corporation to deduct certain investment losses as ordinary losses (as distinct from capital losses, which are restricted).[37] In addition, many states have several additional categories of incorporation for businesses domiciled and operating exclusively within those states.

Tax considerations are vital, but the most important criterion for incorporation rests with stockholder liability and access to financial resources. From an operational perspective, essential considerations involve leadership and human relations among the entrepreneurial team. In conclusion, it is vital to make the choice of legal formation from a strategic viewpoint. If the new venture is unlikely to become large or need professional management, there is little reason to adopt a complicated legal structure. If, however, the venture is expected to grow and to need infusions of capital, a corporate formation that initially seems complicated may be essential as the enterprise expands.

> ▶ **CHECKPOINT**
>
> Describe the nature and benefits of incorporation.
>
> Explain the advantages of S Corporation status.
>
> Explore the personal and strategic considerations of incorporation.

SYNOPSIS FOR LEARNING

1. *Describe the concept of an entrepreneurial team and the roles of founders and team members.*

The entrepreneurial team is more than the official founder(s) and close staff members. It comprises those who have the enthusiasm and commitment to help, and to be part of, the new venture. The team is the heart of the enterprise. It sets the pace of development, instills a philosophy of leadership, and provides the inspiration to transform entrepreneurial dreams into commercial realities. The founder's role is to define the enterprise and the team needed to make it a successful venture. Team members have functional roles, management duties, or director's responsibilities, but they are also adventurers bound to the new enterprise, not nine-to-fivers.

2. *Examine the nature of a board of directors and the roles of directors.*

A board of directors is required by law for corporations and is the chief decision maker. The board is accountable to stockholders for performance and for appointing executives, and it is therefore liable for business conduct. Directors fulfill important roles beyond their decision-making duties. These include roles as mentors, professional advisers, and members of an expanded social network. Directors often provide important access to resources, investors, professionals, and industry groups that are crucial to a venture's success.

3. *Explain the importance of personal and social networking in new ventures.*

Personal networks consist of family, close friends, and acquaintances within a person's immediate circle of daily relationships. These networks may consist of "strong ties," such as family members who will provide direct help to the entrepreneur, or "weak ties," such as people affiliated with a church who will not provide direct help yet may be able to introduce entrepreneurs to their friends for assistance. Social networks are described in terms of community and industry contacts that can open channels for entrepreneurs to necessary resources, suppliers, customers, and investors. Networking is crucial because it opens channels that entrepreneurs need in their industries and markets to succeed.

4. *Define a sole proprietorship and identify its major advantages and disadvantages.*

A sole proprietorship is an unincorporated one-person business, and the founder has unlimited legal and financial liability as an owner-operator. The proprietorship income is undifferentiated from other income an owner might have, and the business assets are his or her personal assets. The most distinct advantage is the ability of a founder to find autonomy of ownership, but a small business proprietor may also benefit from favorable tax rates (or business deductions that reduce taxable personal income). Self-employed individuals also have opportunities to purchase business insurance, invest for retirement income, and make personal expense items deductible under the business. The major disadvantage is the unlimited liability of an owner. In the event of a lawsuit, the owner's personal assets are at risk equally with business assets. The owner's wealth also stands at risk for all business debts. In addition, a proprietorship ends with the owner's death so that succession is not assured. This limitation further reduces an owner's ability to obtain significant financial underwriting.

5. *Contrast the various types of partnerships and their characteristics.*

A general partnership is an association of two or more individuals for the purpose of pursuing a joint enterprise. General partners have unlimited legal liability and are mutually responsible for individual partners' business conduct, debts, and contracts. Partnerships provide synergistic results as they combine resources and talents to accomplish results beyond partners' individual abilities. They also provide added strength for obtaining financial backing. Limited partnerships were created by law, and they comprise general and limited partners. General partners have unlimited liability and are responsible for managing the venture. Limited partners are exempt from operations, and their liability is limited to the extent of their investments. Empowered to have unrestricted partners, R&D limited partnerships can include individuals, public and private organizations, trusts, and government agencies. Legislation aimed at encouraging scientific research and development created RDLPs.

6. *Describe a corporation and its general advantages and disadvantages.*

A corporation is a legal entity, created by law and managed through a board of directors. A corporation has an indefinite life; consequently, it is unhampered by succession problems and is able to secure long-term credit. In addition, a corporation can issue stock and securities to obtain equity financing. The most important advantage is limited liability for stockholders; personal and corporate assets are separate, and stock can be sold or assigned without disrupting business. Unfortunately, corporations pay taxes on income before profits are distributed. Once distributed as dividends, they are taxed again as stockholders' income creating a form of double taxation. From an entrepreneur's perspective, incorporation may be beneficial in terms of investors, networking, and protection of personal assets.

NOTES

1. Investment Committee Notes of ShenVenture, Inc., Harrisonburg, Virginia, as reviewed with CEO Jackson Ramsey, September 4, 1990.

2. James W. Henderson, *Obtaining Venture Financing: Principles and Practices* (Lexington, MA: D. C. Heath, 1988), pp. 262–263, 266. Also T. T. Tyebjee and A. V. Bruno, "A Model of Venture Capital Investment Activity," *Management Science*, Vol. 30, No. 9 (1984), pp. 1051–1066. In addition, Donald M. Dibble, ed., *Winning the Money Game* (Santa Clara, CA: Entrepreneur Press, 1975), pp. 44–46, 59–62.

3. Gifford Pinchot III, *Intrapreneuring* (New York: Harper & Row, 1985), pp. 166–169.

4. John W. Nelson III, "Ask Your Banker: What Does a Loan Officer Consider," *The Savant*, Vol. 7, No. 1 (October 1990), p. 7.

5. Ken G. Smith, Martin J. Gannon, Curtis Grimm, and Terence R. Mitchell, "Decision Making Behavior in Smaller Entrepreneurial and Larger Professionally Managed Firms," *Journal of Business Venturing*, Vol. 3, No. 3 (1988), pp. 223–232.

6. R. Chaganti, V. Mahajan, and S. Sharma, "Corporate Board Size, Composition and Corporate Failure in the Retailing Industry," *Journal of Management Studies*, Vol. 22, No.

4 (1985), pp. 400–417. Also F. Bucy and S. Seaman, "Relationship between Role, Composition and Perceived Benefits of Boards of Directors for Privately Owned Firms," *Frontiers of Entrepreneurship Research,* 1988, pp. 499–500.

7. Roger H. Ford, "Outside Directors and the Privately Owned Firm: Are They Necessary?" *Entrepreneurship Theory and Practice*, Vol. 13, No. 1 (1988), pp. 49–57.

8. Ibid., p. 49.

9. H. W. Fox, "Quasi-Boards—Guidance without Governance," *American Journal of Small Business*, Vol. 9, No. 1 (1984), pp. 12–19.

10. Howard Aldrich and Catherine Zimmer, "Entrepreneurship through Social Networks," in Donald L. Sexton and Raymond W. Smilor, eds., *The Art and Science of Entrepreneurship* (Cambridge, MA: Ballinger, 1986), pp. 3–23.

11. Robert Merton, "The Role-Set: Problems in Sociological Theory," *British Journal of Sociology*, Vol. 8 (1957), pp. 106–120.

12. Mark Granovetter, "The Strength of Weak Ties: A Network Theory Revisited," in Peter V. Marsden and Nan Lin, eds., *Social Structure and Network Analysis* (Beverly Hills, CA: Sage, 1982), pp. 105–130.

13. Ibid., p. 112. Also Aldrich and Zimmer, "Entrepreneurship through Social Networks," pp. 12–13.

14. Alan L. Carsrud, Connie M. Gaglio, and Kenneth W. Olm, "Entrepreneurs—Mentors, Networks, and Successful New Venture Development: An Exploratory Study," *Frontiers of Entrepreneurship Research*, 1986, pp. 229–238.

15. Howard Aldrich, Ben Rosen, and William Woodward, "Social Behavior and Entrepreneurial Networks," *Frontiers of Entrepreneurship Research*, 1986, pp. 239–240.

16. Howard Aldrich, Ben Rosen, and William Woodward, "The Impact of Social Networks on Business Foundings and Profit: A Longitudinal Study," *Frontiers of Entrepreneurship Research*, 1987, pp. 154–168. Also David H. Holt, "Network Support Systems: How Communities Can Encourage Entrepreneurship," *Frontiers of Entrepreneurship Research*, 1987, pp. 44–56.

17. Barbara J. Bird, *Entrepreneurial Behavior* (Glenview, IL: Scott, Foresman, 1989), pp. 294–295.

18. Donald L. Sexton and Nancy B. Bowman-Upton, *Entrepreneurship Creativity and Growth* (New York: Macmillan, 1991), pp. 209–210.

19. Peter J. Bearse, "An Econometric Analysis of Black Entrepreneurship," *Frontiers of Entrepreneurship Research*, 1984, pp. 212–214. Also Robert D. Hisrich and Candida G. Bush, "Women Entrepreneurs: A Longitudinal Study," *Frontiers of Entrepreneurship Research*, 1987, pp. 187–199.

20. Albert Shapero and Lisa Sokol, "The Social Dimensions of Entrepreneurship," in Calvin A. Kent, Donald L. Sexton, and Karl H. Vesper, *Encyclopedia of Entrepreneurship* (Englewood Cliffs, NJ: Prentice-Hall, 1982), pp. 72–90.

21. Barbara J. Bird, *Entrepreneurial Behavior*, pp. 294–298. Also Gianni Lorenzoni and Oscar A. Ornati, "Constellations of Firms and New Ventures," *Journal of Business Venturing*, Vol. 3, No. 1 (1988), pp. 41–57

22. John D. Donnell, A. James Barnes, and Michael B. Metzger, *Law for Business* (Homewood, IL: Richard D. Irwin, 1983), pp. 484–492.

23. Manfred F. R. Kets de Vries, "The Dark Side of Entrepreneurship," *Harvard Business Review*, November-December 1985, pp. 160–167.

24. Kenneth W. Clarkson, Roger L. Miller, and Gaylord A. Jentz, *West's Business Law*, 3rd ed. (St. Paul, MN: West, 1986), pp. 588–601.

25. David E. Brody, *Business and Its Legal Environment* (Lexington, MA: D. C. Heath, 1986), pp. 292–293.

26. James W. Henderson, *Obtaining Venture Financing* (Lexington, MA: D. C. Heath, 1988), pp. 211–212.

27. Ibid., pp. 212–213.

28. Robert C. Ronstadt, *Entrepreneurship: Text, Cases and Notes* (Dover, MA: Lord, 1985), pp. 598–599.

29. Ibid., p. 598.

30. Clarkson, Miller, and Jentz, *West's Business Law*, pp. 1078–1092.

31. D. Bruce Merrifield, "Industrial Survival via Management Technology," *Journal of Business Venturing*, Vol. 3, No. 3 (1988), pp. 171–185.

32. Dwight B. Davis, "R&D Consortia: Pooling Industries' Resources," *High Technology*, October 1985, pp. 42–47.

33. Clarkson, Miller, and Jentz, *West's Business Law*, pp. 600–601.

34. Ibid., p. 601. Also Henderson, *Obtaining Venture Financing*, pp. 214–218; and Judith H. McQuown, *Inc. Yourself: How to Profit by Setting Up Your Own Corporation* (New York: Warner Books, 1984), pp. 2–7, 13–27.

35. Clarkson, Miller, and Jentz, *West's Business Law*, pp. 651–652.

36. *Arthur Young 1988–1989 Federal Tax Highlights* (New York: Arthur Young, 1989), pp. 166–169.

37. Henderson, *Obtaining Venture Financing*, pp. 222–223.

CASE 11-1

Defining a Start-up: Who Is in Charge?

Artemis Capital Group, Inc., named after the Greek goddess of hunting, operates as a six-member partnership founded by five women who left Goldman, Sachs & Company and one woman from Citibank. The company is legally registered as a corporation, but its founders are adamant that it is a partnership in spirit. Titles are "paper only" to meet registration requirements, and there are no operating titles. The women share open office areas, have identical investment interests, and have a unified mission: to become the single most dynamic woman-owned investment company on Wall Street.

The partners include Deborah Buresh, 37, Aimee S. Brown, 37, Phylis Esposito, 39, Sandra Alworth, 42, Robin Wiessmann, 37, and Roberta Connolly, 40. Each of the founders brought to the partnership at least seven years in specialized roles in underwriting investments, and being similar in age, they have compatible career interests. The venture was carefully thought out prior to its founding, and each person has a particular niche to fill. Brown, for example, specializes in airport finance, and Esposito is an underwriting specialist. Alworth concentrates on municipal investments, and Connolly manages Artemis's marketing services. Wiessmann and Buresh are traders experienced in bonds and capital markets. Who is in charge? No one . . . and everyone. Company decisions are made in a "bullpen," and management responsibilities rotate.

In contrast to Artemis, Illinois Computer Cable, Inc. (ICC), was founded by Jim Eme, who at age 36 had been disillusioned in a corporate sales position, left that position to set up ICC, and soon after attracted three other men from his old company to join him. Three of the four men remain with ICC after four years in business, but the company has gone through a bloodbath to survive.

Eme, the original founder, set up ICC to manufacture cable assemblies for computer systems and office equipment such as network and printer connections. As an engineer who grew up with the computer industry, Eme knew the technology and the market. Not being oriented to sales, Eme enticed Ralph Dote, aged 31, to join him because Dote was a million-dollar salesperson with their old company. Dote did not have a degree, but he was an enthusiastic salesman who knew how to pump up customers. Within a few months, both men realized that neither had enough executive talent to run a company, and they turned to another man, 20 years Eme's senior, who had been a mentor at the old company. Bob Ohlson came on board as the third member of the team, and John Berst quickly followed from his position in financial administration at the partners' old company.

Ohlson was an "ideas man" who seemed to have what Eme called "a golden tongue" and exceptional skills at organizing the company. Berst seemed to be the workhorse administrator who could run both production and finance, making sure all the i's were dotted and the t's crossed. Ohlson was the consensus choice for CEO, and ICC's board of directors comprised the four men.

Structured as a corporation, ICC was envisioned by Eme as a partnership where there would be no management hierarchy. The others were uncomfortable without a structure, and their first battle was over management. Ohlson prevailed with his definition of corporate authority, starting with him at the top receiving a $90,000 salary. Berst, Eme, and Dote each had lower salaries and vice-president positions that they agreed upon reluctantly. Soon this system began to unravel. Eme was soon isolated as a "thinker" who did not seem to pull his weight by being involved in either sales or management. At the other extreme, Ohlson exerted himself, often rudely ridiculing Eme or Dote as SOBs who were weak links in the enterprise. Berst was always in the middle walking a tightrope.

Board meetings were small wars over internal issues, and salaries and positions were shuffled several times. Ohlson set up daily responsibilities for each of the men, often dictating what had to be done. When sales fell off, Ohlson hired an outside salesman to replace Dote as sales manager, demoting Dote in the process. For several years, innuendo and backstabbing plagued ICC. Employees who were hired rarely stayed, and the one-time friends became reclusive at work. Eventually, legal entanglements ensued, Ohlson was either fired or quit (no one knows exactly), and the remaining three men tried to sell out to one another.

On the verge of bankruptcy, the partners decided they had no choice other than to revive the company and put personal problems on hold. Berst was put in charge, and Eme assumed the role of head of R&D. Dote controlled sales. After several months, all three settled into these roles comfortably, and ICC enjoyed tremendous success. After two years, the trio decided they could make the company work, and today sales top $6 million with a product line of 21 products, including the Ethernet cable hoods and network cable connectors.

CASE QUESTIONS

1. Discuss why both companies were incorporated yet described as partnerships, and describe the advantages and disadvantages that result from their legal formations.
2. What are the possible pitfalls for each company that might arise from its structure of management authority?
3. What alternative legal structures were available to each company? Describe the advantages and disadvantages of each.

Sources: Michele Morris, "Three on the Money," *Your Company*, fall 1990, pp. 18–22. Also Edward O. Welles, "Blowup," *Inc.*, May 1989, pp. 63–78.

CASE 11-2

Serendipity Enterprises, Inc.

Founder Ken Blake incorporated Serendipity Enterprises, Inc. (SEI), in 1986 to take advantage of changes in the tax code. Prior to that time, SEI had been a sole proprietorship, owned and operated by Blake, a skilled printer. The enterprise evolved from a printing business in the late 1970s to become a fast-growing desktop publishing company when it was incorporated. Blake's personal skills in printing, typesetting, and graphics were enhanced by several key employees with computer skills. Examples of recent SEI contracts include the graphic illustration and typesetting of a complicated chemistry book for a major publisher and creating an integrated algebra course using software and student manuals for high schools.

By incorporating, Blake found he could properly write off expenses for business use no longer allowed for a proprietorship under the 1986 tax revision. Personal health insurance, business travel expenses, and certain interest charges, for example, were treated as corporate expenses and deductions. He also established a modest salary for himself, taxable as personal income, and allowed business profits to be appropriately allocated to corporate earnings.

The major reason for incorporating, however, was to protect his family. A dispute over property in 1985 when Serendipity was still a sole proprietorship had resulted in a serious lawsuit, and although he won the suit, he realized that had the decision gone the other way, his family assets would have been at risk. With the business growing, there was a higher risk of litigation, and Blake decided to separate business and personal assets.

Shortly after incorporating, Blake also found that he had cancer. The cancer was caught early and its spread arrested, but it gave him pause to think of how the business would be controlled in his absence. He was still a young man in his early 40s, and he had three sons. His oldest son, a junior in college, had worked in the business for several years and was skilled at desk-top work as well as graphics development. Blake's staff included an office manager and several excellent employees, but no one who could take over as the head of a corporation. Aside from management issues, Blake wondered how he could protect his family's interests. His wife and sons were minority stockholders, having acquired stock at incorporation from assets that were transferred to the company. Nevertheless, Blake realized that if he died suddenly, there would be a succession problem, and he wondered what would happen to his stock.

CASE QUESTIONS

1. Describe the possible advantages and disadvantages for Blake by incorporating. Could a proprietorship have been more advantageous?
2. Explain the problems faced by entrepreneurs for succession. In Blake's situation, what are his options?
3. What other forms of business could Blake have chosen? Explain the possible advantages and disadvantages of each.

Chapter 12

Business Acquisitions and Franchising

OBJECTIVES

1. Describe the advantages and disadvantages of acquiring established businesses.
2. Identify and explain considerations for evaluating a business opportunity.
3. Explain the three most commonly used methods of valuing a business.
4. Describe major considerations for structuring an acquisition.
5. Define franchising and the role of franchisors.
6. Explain franchising from the franchisee's perspective.

Entrepreneurship is most often described in terms of starting a new venture, not buying an existing one. Nevertheless, buying into business is probably just as common today as starting from scratch. Buying usually involves finding a suitable ongoing business to purchase, but it also can occur through a transfer of ownership, such as when a retiring business owner sells the firm to a son or daughter. It also occurs as growing ventures are reorganized under new forms of ownership with new investors. Not least of all, buying into business through *franchise contracts* has become quite common.

Franchising is the fastest growing segment of American commerce, and it has two roles for entrepreneurs. First, becoming a *franchisor* is the process of creating a business concept that can be replicated and sold. In this role, the entrepreneur establishes a venture based on selling businesses. Second, becoming a *franchisee* is a method of acquiring a business within a network or chain of similar enterprises. Because franchises have become prominent in American society, we will explore how entrepreneurs become involved in these acquisitions.

The focus of this chapter is on criteria for buying and selling businesses. Because there are somewhat different concerns for buying an independent venture and acquiring a franchise, we will describe each separately; however, we will concentrate on entrepreneurial decisions, not corporate mergers and acquisitions. Consequently, we want to emphasize the role of the entrepreneur and tools that can be useful in making the purchase decision.

RATIONALE FOR ACQUIRING A BUSINESS

The decision to buy a business begins with a personal examination of *why* a person would want to buy any business. Occasionally someone will receive an inheritance, quit work, and buy the first small business that "looks good." Too often, this is an emotional decision without justification; buying a business is not like buying a used car, nor is it justified because a person has a little spare cash. There are, however, sound reasons for buying into business, and there are sensible ways to go about making an acquisition. Figure 12-1 describes the usual ways to buy into business.

Considerations for Making an Acquisition

Aspiring entrepreneurs must decide whether to buy a business or to start one, and the decision must encompass both personal and commercial considerations.[1] Although these can be quite extensive, there are five major categories of issues: the entrepreneur's experience, nature of the business, location, personal and business risks, and enterprise costs.

Experience. Having experience relevant to the proposed venture is often essential, such as when the entrepreneur needs to demonstrate particular skills. Examples include construction contracting, medical technology, microelectronics engineering, and specialty services such as advertising. Skilled entrepreneurs may still be inexperienced in business. An experienced computer technician, for instance, may have no background in merchandising, and rather than start a retail computer store from the ground up, a wiser choice might be to acquire a ComputerLand franchise or an existing retail store. If the technician obtains a franchise, it will be a complete "system" with assistance, training, and inventory. If the technician acquires an ongoing enterprise, it will be in place together with experienced staff and established clients. An aspiring entrepreneur who has had no experience in starting a new venture may benefit from buying an existing one, thereby avoiding the pitfalls of creating a new enterprise.

Nature of the Business. The type of business proposed often leaves an entrepreneur with no choice other than to start from scratch. During the early years of microcomputer development, for example, there were no franchise chains and very few existing retail stores. The would-be computer retailer had to acquire a license from one of the manufacturers, such as Apple or IBM, and build the enterprise. Every

Chapter 12 Business Acquisitions and Financing

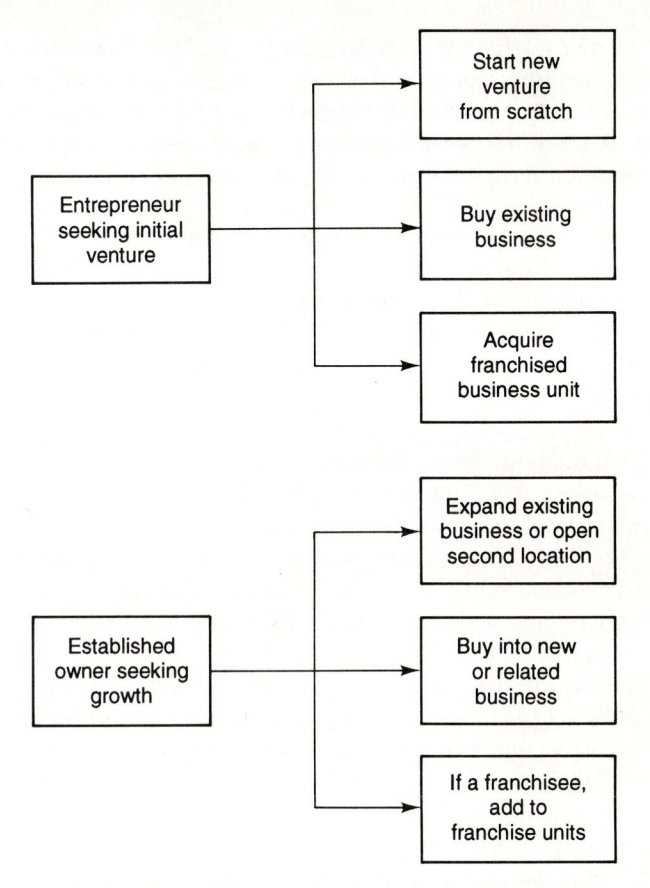

Figure 12-1 **Primary Alternatives in Acquisition Decisions**

business concept, product, or service has had a similar embryonic period, including fast-food restaurants like McDonald's, convenience markets like 7–Eleven, fashion enterprises like Liz Claiborne, landscape contractors like Lawn Doctor, and so on. During the years of formation, there are exciting opportunities and risks for new ventures, yet there are few opportunities for acquisitions until an industry becomes established. Entrepreneurs involved in each industry's early formative years were the innovators who had to transform new concepts into commercial realities.

On the other hand, if the nature of the business has a parallel among existing enterprises, an acquisition with some modifications may result in healthy profits. An office supply store, for example, might be purchased to provide a foundation enterprise for a new concept in office systems that includes telecommunication workstations. Many small manufacturers are acquired by entrepreneurs who have innovative products but need production and distribution systems. For example, Bush Industries, a New

York manufacturer of "electronic-age furniture" began in 1978 by purchasing a small manufacturing company that made composition-board television stands and bookcases.[2] These inexpensive products were sold through chain stores, including Sears and K-Mart. The new owners acquired the business because it had reasonably good production machinery and strong ties with established customers. They continued to produce television stands and bookcases, thereby securing cash flow; however, Bush quickly expanded its product line to include unique designs for microwave cabinets, VCR and stereo entertainment centers, microcomputer desks, printer stands, and a variety of accessories to complement home and office "electronic" equipment. Bush began with a marginally profitable business, 42 employees, and an obsolete product line, and within ten years he fashioned a $50 million business on a growing product line.

Location. Most entrepreneurs start or acquire businesses near their homes rather than pursue unfamiliar markets. Thus their choices are often limited. In some instances there may be no businesses to buy, and in others there may be major obstacles to starting new ones. In Williamsburg, Virginia, for example, the majority of commercial activity centers on Colonial Williamsburg, one of the oldest established towns in the United States, which is bordered by William and Mary College. A huge number of tourists and students shop within a one-square-mile area that is historically preserved. Entrepreneurs wanting to locate in this market have few opportunities to build new facilities. Instead, they scramble for vacant leases or bid for licenses to operate in or near the colonial townsite. Over a period of nearly 300 years, Colonial Williamsburg has hosted 15 generations of entrepreneurs representing nearly 6,000 successful enterprises ranging from apothecaries to zoological societies. New enterprises have evolved from established ones, a few have been passed down through the generations, and some have replaced obsolete businesses.[3] Similar patterns of evolution exist in every community.

Business Risks. Entrepreneurs try to account for risks that can influence the valuation and price of an acquisition.[4] These include economic conditions, financial arrangements, market potential, and management. Some risks can be analyzed objectively, including costs of capital and physical facilities, but evaluating profit potential requires market research and accurate sales forecasts, which can be complicated. Unless the buyer intends to operate the business in exactly the same way as the seller, previous records provide little insight into future potential, and the buyout is riskier. Most buyers also make modifications, changing inventory, services, facilities, and personnel. These are meant to improve the business, but they also introduce greater risk for the acquisition.

Personal Risks. Perhaps the greatest risk is associated with changes in management. New owners almost always assume that they can succeed where others failed (or at least improve a successful business), but untested entrepreneurs have no assurance of success. They bring to the business new ideas, personalities, and leadership styles that cannot be objectively assessed. Also, experienced and skilled personnel are important, and those who remain with the venture can improve the business's likelihood of success. (Recall from Chapter 11 the importance of having a solid entrepreneurial team.) From a personal perspective, entrepreneurs take psychological risks associated with the potential for failure, and they often involve family and friends who share in this risk.

Enterprise Costs. Cost factors include all potential operating expenses and capital expenses of the acquisition. These are described in this chapter under "Methods of Valuation," but as an introduction, consider the costs of physical assets for a new venture. If a person opens a new restaurant, the start-up costs of new equipment and furnishings can be quite high. By purchasing an existing business, these costs may be reduced considerably; used restaurant equipment and furnishings would bring a seller very little money on the open market compared with their value as assets of an ongoing business. Consequently, a seller can often benefit substantially even when the price of the business is a bargain for the buyer. Costs of purchasing new assets rather than buying them as part of a business are almost always higher, but the buyer must be careful to buy serviceable assets; obsolete or unnecessary equipment has little value.

Acquisitions by Established Entrepreneurs

Nearly a third of all small business acquisitions are made by owners of established enterprises. Although we are not concerned with the "corporate" merger and acquisition strategies that are typical of *Fortune* 500 companies, we are concerned with entrepreneurial growth, and growth is often achieved through direct acquisition of existing businesses. Most franchisees, for example, own multiple store locations, and start-up entrepreneurs often expand through acquisitions to create chain networks.[5]

There are several fundamental reasons why established businesses expand through acquisition. The main reason is to expand sales, thereby increasing the company's customer base. With expanded sales, an enterprise strengthens its financial leverage, opening new opportunities for bulk purchasing, improved distribution, and economies of scale. These advantages can be further leveraged through *vertical integration*. A retailer, for example, may "buy back" into the company's distribution channel (called the value chain) to acquire a regional wholesaler or a manufacturer. A wholesaler can "buy forward," acquiring retail outlets. Vertical integration eliminates one or more profit-taking points in the value chain, thereby reducing overall costs (or increasing profits). This process is illustrated in Figure 12-2.

Another major reason for expansion is to acquire products or services that complement the existing enterprise. For example, the Green Spot, a North Carolina retail nursery, bought a Pennsylvania Christmas tree farm that not only provided seasonal trees to the nursery but also sells trees to many other retailers. During the following three years, the nursery also purchased a commercial landscaping service, a lawn care franchise, and a hydroponic greenhouse operation.[6]

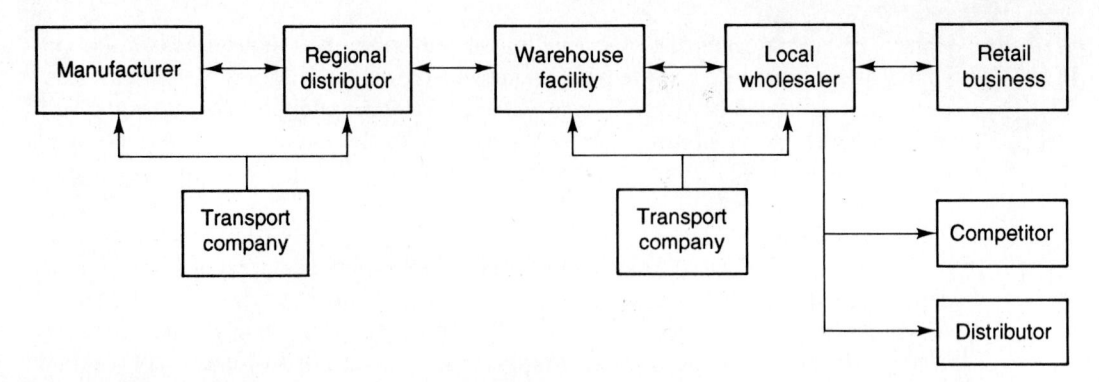

```
Manufacturer ↔ Regional distributor ↔ Warehouse facility ↔ Local wholesaler ↔ Retail business
                    ↑                        ↑
              Transport                 Transport                    → Competitor
              company                   company
                                                                     → Distributor
```

Logical acquisitions can be made by consolidating any adjacent pair in the "value chain." A retailer may buy "backward" by acquiring a local wholesaler, or the wholesaler may buy either the transport company or warehouse facility.

To consolidate the market by reducing competition, a retailer could buy one of the competitors. Also, businesses buy "forward"; thus a manufacturer may buy the regional distributor or the transport company.

Figure 12-2 **Buying into the Value Chain**

Expanding vertically within the distribution channel or horizontally with complementary businesses also has human-resource benefits. With slightly larger operations, professional staff can be retained in procurement, accounting, and sales. A family-owned nursery, for example, can still operate under the founder's leadership, even with three or four small subsidiary businesses, yet also be large enough to justify full-time employees in purchasing, sales, landscape engineering, and accounting. Additional benefits can be realized by having sufficient employees to qualify for group medical insurance, retirement plans, vacation benefits, and incentive programs such as profit-sharing plans.

The rationale for buying into an initial venture differs from that for expanding an existing business, but many advantages are similar, and business evaluation methods are the same. In the following pages, we will examine several useful techniques for evaluating smaller enterprises.

▶ **CHECKPOINT**

Describe five considerations for buying an ongoing business.

Explain how entrepreneurs with established businesses view the acquisition process.

PROFILE △

"Selling Up" into Success

Most acquisitions by established companies are made to expand control over new markets or resources. In the process, "sellers" usually lose control or are absorbed, yet some sellers go in search of buyers who need their enterprises. Ken Meyers of Smartfoods, Inc., decided to "sell up" into success rather than sell out. Smartfoods had a very successful business processing and distributing an all-natural popcorn product in the northeast. In 1988, Smartfoods posted $10 million in revenues. Meyers, however, could not break into the national supermarket industry, which in 1989 represented 400,000 stores. Lacking national distribution and unable to gain a significant share in the $8 billion salty snack market, Meyers took Smartfoods to Frito-Lay, Inc., as a buyout candidate. He sold the company for $14.5 million, and became president of a wholly owned subsidiary of Frito-Lay, Inc., backed with a $4 billion international distribution network.

Source: "A Smart Deal for Smartfoods," *Venture*, May 1989, p. 91.

EVALUATING ACQUISITION OPPORTUNITIES

Buying an existing business has several potential advantages over starting from scratch. An existing business has a track record of performance that can be verified, and there are objective data for making an informed decision. Assets are known and can be evaluated; profits and cash flow are documented; and patterns of sales activity can be determined. An ongoing business will also have an organization with appropriate systems for supply, personnel, and distribution. In addition, thorny issues such as patent rights, copyrights, and trademarks will have been resolved by the exiting owner. Also, the business's reputation can be ascertained. Most important, because there is a performance history, investors and lenders are less apprehensive about providing financial support.

These advantages depend, of course, on the relative success enjoyed by the owner and on the potential for a new owner to enjoy the same (or better) success. Answering these questions requires *due diligence*, which is a common phrase used by investors, attorneys, and accountants to mean that a thorough evaluation is made of the prospective enterprise. Aspiring entrepreneurs who are not skilled in due-diligence evaluations should find professional assistance.

Evaluating the Business Venture

Complete and accurate information about the enterprise is beneficial in negotiating a fair purchase agreement. Consequently, both sellers and buyers must have a clear idea of the venture's value. Evaluating a business involves three categories of information: *business assets*, *operational performance*, and the *business environment*.[7]

Business Assets. Tangible assets include accounts receivable, inventory, facilities, equipment, vehicles, patents, copyrights, and trademarks. Intangible assets include goodwill (reputation), proprietary information (e.g., mailing lists or trade secrets), and experienced, productive employees.

Evaluating tangible assets often is straightforward. Accounts receivable, for example, are verified for their book value, collection history, and age. Book values will be adjusted through accounting methods that take into consideration time value of money for "aged" (long outstanding) receivables, percentage of bad accounts, and cost of collecting overdue accounts. Inventory is valued according to its age, quality, and salability. If inventory has been returned by customers as faulty, the book value of inventory will be reduced by replacement costs of projected future returns. Also, inventory that has been difficult to sell or is obsolete may be written off as valueless.

Professional assessments can be obtained on facilities and vehicles to establish market values, and equipment can be valued using standard accounting procedures such as replacement cost or market value. Book value of physical assets is seldom relevant to a prospective buyer because depreciation practices can result in differences between book and market values. Moreover, an asset can be depreciated to its salvage value yet still have a useful service life that must be considered in the purchase price. The relationship between book, market, and useful value is illustrated in Figure 12-3. Professional assessments can also be obtained for patents, copyrights, and trademarks. Royalty income received from, or attributed to, patent licenses and copyrights can be established, although these figures may be somewhat subjective.

Intangible assets are far more difficult to evaluate. *Goodwill* is by far the most subjective asset to consider because it is the intangible value of a business's ability

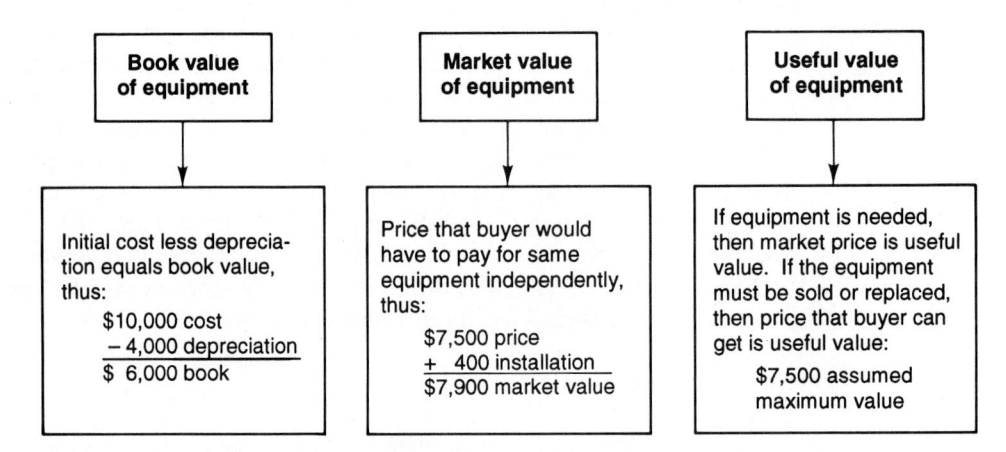

Book value of equipment	Market value of equipment	Useful value of equipment
Initial cost less depreciation equals book value, thus: $10,000 cost − 4,000 depreciation $ 6,000 book	Price that buyer would have to pay for same equipment independently, thus: $7,500 price + 400 installation $7,900 market value	If equipment is needed, then market price is useful value. If the equipment must be sold or replaced, then price that buyer can get is useful value: $7,500 assumed maximum value

Figure 12-3 Book Value, Market Value, and Useful Value

to produce excess earnings.[8] Accountants usually assign a premium value based on the ability of the business to generate income in excess of the average generated by comparable enterprises. It is assumed, of course, that comparable businesses can be found and their earnings verified, and in the end, goodwill usually creates a discrepancy between the seller's and buyer's visions of business value. Goodwill should take into account a realistic assessment of the enterprise's reputation, image, customer base, credit rating, pattern of sales growth, and potential for the new owner to enjoy similar success.

Operational Performance. Buyers analyze sales from several perspectives. First, sales volume and growth (rate of change in sales) are determined. This determinatiion involves evaluating marketing factors that influence sales, including market strategies, merchandise quality, competition, pricing tactics, promotional programs, and distribution decisions. Second, sales patterns are determined in order to understand seasonal variations, turnover rates for merchandise, and consumer profiles. Having a clear idea of who buys a firm's products and when customers make purchases often sheds light on why they buy. Also, a business that has impressive sales data may rely on only a few customers who may not remain with the new owners. Third, sales trends are reviewed in terms of credit policies that can impede or encourage sales volume. Other considerations are after-sales service, installation and delivery practices, and individual skills of the seller and his or her staff. The important point is that a buyer must feel confident that sales can be maintained or improved after acquisition. Consequently, the buyer must question every possible issue that might influence sales performance.

If the venture to be acquired is involved in manufacturing, operational issues include product design, process engineering, production systems, plant utilization, inventory control, raw material supply, and product distribution. In addition, the buyer will want to know about factory operations, safety records, environmental regulations, quality control, and compliance requirements such as waste disposal. Minor oversights in any of these areas could prove to be disastrous. For example, the seller may be unaware of (or choose not to reveal) pending legislation requiring huge capital costs to overhaul waste disposal facilities. The buyer could easily make the purchase and face impossible costs for plant modifications.

Other operational considerations include accounting and financial reports that could be misleading, facility costs (maintenance, insurance, utilities requirements, warehousing, etc.), and human resources. Although many of these will come to light through due-diligence research, human resources must be evaluated to establish capabilities of employees, compensation trends, employee turnover, labor relations, fringe benefits, training requirements, and employee expectations for leadership. Moreover, the buyer will want to evaluate local labor market conditions, risks of losing key people after acquisition, and the influence of the seller's personal involvement on employee behavior.

Most operational performance criteria can be objectively appraised (e.g., sales can be traced or compliance requirements can be determined), but the entrepreneur must be extremely diligent in asking the correct questions. Merely tracking sales performance, for example, does not reveal the possibility of strong sales volume due to the owner's liberal credit terms; relying on similar credit policies after acquisition could prove to be unprofitable. Also, the seller may have artificially boosted sales to make the purchase look attractive when, in reality, many customers will subsequently default on their payments. Other considerations may require judgments, such as how the seller personally influenced performance. An admired owner who has earned the loyalty and respect of company employees may be an irreplaceable person; the new owner may not enjoy the same loyalty or respect, and employees may perform poorly.

Business Environment. Entrepreneurs must ask the same marketing research questions whether buying a business or starting a new venture. When starting ventures, entrepreneurs conduct market research about potential consumers, competitors, and sales based on projected marketing strategies. When conducting due-diligence evaluations for existing businesses, the same ground is covered but questions vary slightly. For example, rather than asking if a market can be established for a product, the buyer asks whether the existing market can be improved. Instead of analyzing potential competition, buyers gather information on actual competition and the means by which previous owners were able to position their ventures in the industry successfully.

This process involves using statistical market data for comparative research on industry and local market characteristics. It includes a competitive analysis to understand the strengths and weaknesses of the acquisition. In addition, due diligence requires investigation of external threats and opportunities that may not be apparent in purchase negotiations. (A review of Chapters 8 and 9 will provide detailed descriptions of marketing research, environmental analyses, and competitive strategies.) The major difference between new venture planning and acquisition evaluation is that while founders may have well-conceived ideas of market potential, buyers have useful evidence from historical records.

The business environment extends well beyond market considerations. For example, federal regulations and changes in tax legislation affect business operations and profits. Also, product safety requirements, merchandising restrictions (e.g., "truth in advertising" rules), and fair labor practices will influence business activities. Some of these regulations are summarized in Exhibit 12-1. In addition, technological changes may signal potential threats or new opportunities. For example, several years ago the proliferation of VCR sales led to an extraordinary growth in home video rentals, but the market has become relatively saturated, and laser disc technology threatens this industry.[9] Similarly, desk-top publishing has forced many local printers out of business, and facsimile machines have changed office communications.

Screening Acquisition Candidates

A majority of acquisition candidates never get past a screening review. The screening process is a preliminary study of the most critical factors for success or failure. If irreconcilable issues do not surface, then a more comprehensive evaluation may be

Exhibit 12-1   Selected Major Legislation Related to Business

Pure Food and Drug Act, 1906	Natural Environmental Policy Act, 1969
Federal Trade Commission Act, 1914	Environmental Quality Improvement Act, 1970
Water Power Act, 1920	Occupational Safety and Health Act, 1972
Food, Drug, and Cosmetics Act, 1938	Equal Employment Act, 1972
Federal Water Pollution Control Act, Amendments, 1961	Consumer Product Safety Act, 1972
	Noise Control Act, 1972
Oil Pollution Act Amendments, 1961	Rehabilitation Act, 1973
Air Pollution Control Act, 1962	Fair Labor Standards Amendments, 1974
Drug Amendments, 1962	Employee Retirement Income Security Act, 1974
Clean Air Act, 1963	Magnuson-Moss Warranty Act, 1975
Equal Pay Act, 1963	Resource Conservation and Recovery Act, 1976
Civil Rights Act, 1963	Foreign Corrupt Practices Act, 1977
Automotive Products Trade Act, 1965	Pregnancy Discrimination Act, 1978
Water Quality Act, 1965	Fair Debt Collection Practices Act, 1978
Fair Packaging and Labeling Act, 1966	Trade Agreements Act, 1979
National Traffic and Motor Safety Act, 1966	Comprehensive Environmental Response, Compensation, and Liability Act, 1980
Child Protection Act, 1966	
Age Discrimination in Employment Act, 1967	Economic Recovery Tax Act (ERTA), 1980
Air Quality Act, 1967	Tax Equity and Fiscal Responsibility Act (TEFRA), 1982
Consumer Credit Protection Act, 1968	
Radiation Control for Health and Safety Act, 1968	Deficit Reduction Tax Act, 1984
Child Protection and Toy Safety Act, 1969	Tax Reform Act of 1986

pursued. More often, however, irreconcilable issues do surface, and potential buyers walk away. Problems may become obvious from preliminary investigation of price, terms of sale, location, operational costs, or the nature of the business. Many successful businesses are simply not suitable for buyers; few entrepreneurs, for example, could become morticians.

Asking critical questions early can help avoid spending time and money on due-diligence studies. Assuming an acquisition candidate is suitable, there are several "go or no-go" situations.[10] If the business owes more than its assets are worth, or if it is having severe cash-flow problems, there is no reason to give it serious consideration. If the company has obsolete inventory or steeply declining sales, it might be better to walk away. Business value depends on its profits, as shown in Exhibit 12-2. Also, if the owner has lawsuits pending, hostile employees, or a poor reputation with suppliers or customers, it is a risky endeavor. These weaknesses can drain a new owner's resources, and although there may be logical reasons behind troubled businesses, these firms are best left to "turnaround specialists" or bankruptcy courts. A turnaround specialist is a person or team backed with high-risk capital to take enterprises from the brink of failure to success. They expect to fail most of the time, but they profit from bringing in the long shot. Most entrepreneurs cannot play this game.

Exhibit 12-2 Business Value Depends on Profits

Many advantages of owning a small business are found in the owner's ability to legally and ethically utilize business expenses for personal benefits. Employing children is common, and providing medical insurance for family members is typical, but other items show up on business expenses that provide cash flow or benefits to owners and their families, yet reduce profits and minimize taxes. These include rent proceeds on equipment and facilities, club dues, travel expenses for business meetings, personal reimbursements for services, and so on.

Tax advisers are often quick to help small business owners find these legitimate expenses and tax deductions, and each item usually translates to increased cash flow to the owner. However, expenses combine to reduce profits—a smart move if the owner never intends to sell the enterprise.

A business that minimized profits and taxes for any length of time will also have minimized the value of that business. Buyers look to "cash flow" and "continued profitability" to establish a company's value. "Hidden income" becomes unrecognized profits, and the result will be a low business valuation.

If business expenses are carefully documented, and if they can be explained to potential buyers, a higher value may be achieved, but the buyer must feel assured of having the same opportunities. In many instances, this is not the case. The logical approach is to manage well to record cash flow and profits as they occur, taking appropriate benefits without subordinating decisions to tax rules.

Finding Acceptable Candidates

Acceptable ventures often can be found through management consulting firms, accountants, and attorneys who have already made preliminary screening studies of selected acquisition candidates. Because these professionals earn their fees by putting together successful deals, they rarely spend much time on marginal businesses; there is no percentage in chasing a bad deal. These professionals tend to have mutual social contacts, and they learn about opportunities through their networks. Most opportunities are not publicized because owners tend to avoid letting either customers or employees know that the business is up for sale. Employees and customers could become alarmed, assuming correctly or incorrectly that it is time to "leave the sinking ship." The result could be disastrous for sales (and the subsequent business value), but in addition, lenders and suppliers who get wind of a sale often close down credit.[11]

Nevertheless, a few businesses are advertised in local newspapers, and others are listed with business and real estate brokers. A few more appear in professional publications and industry magazines under classified "business opportunity" ads. A variety of business opportunities surface through personal contacts. For example, distributors, suppliers, and consultants often get wind of an opportunity and pass this information along. Bankers are particularly important sources because they become acutely aware of their clients' business problems. When a business begins to have problems, bankers have problems, and by getting buyers and sellers together, bankers can often avert disasters.

Regardless of how the business opportunity is identified, once it has passed preliminary screening, the difficult evaluation work begins. This evaluation is carried

Chapter 12 Business Acquisitions and Financing

out before serious negotiation takes place, and using the guidelines described earlier, a *business valuation* is conducted.

> ▶ **CHECKPOINT**
>
> Describe three categories of information for evaluating a business.
>
> Explain the screening process and how entrepreneurs find acceptable acquisition candidates.

METHODS OF VALUATION

The single most important consideration for placing a value on a business is *cash*; an entrepreneur needs to have positive cash flow, not tax write-offs or "book value" wealth based on creative accounting. Sellers will price their business on the strength of net cash flow, and buyers will establish their offers based on expectations for future cash flows. For most small business enterprises, there are three methods of valuation commonly used: *book value*, *multiple of earnings*, and *discounted future earnings*. These are summarized in Figure 12-4.

Book Value Method

The **book value method** of valuation uses a company's financial statements to establish the net worth of the firm. It is also called the "balance sheet method" and the "net

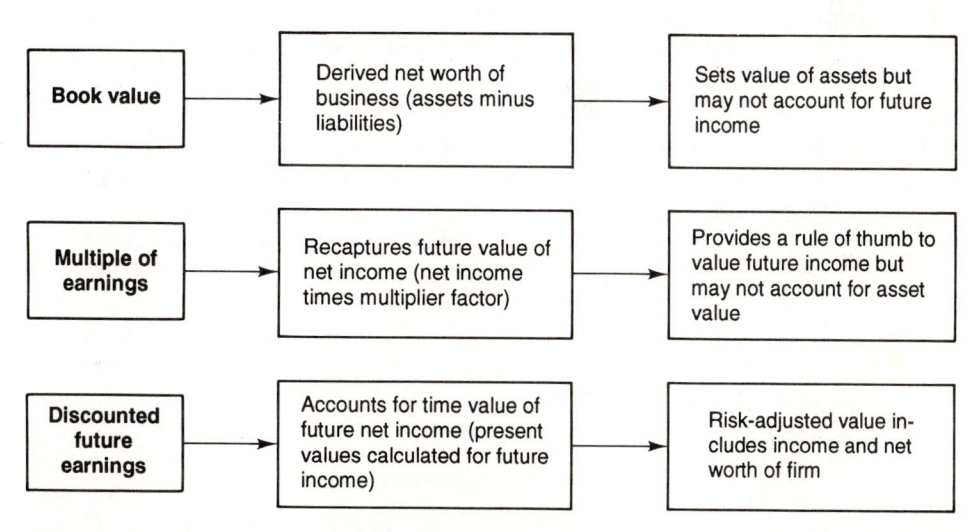

Method	Description	Result
Book value	Derived net worth of business (assets minus liabilities)	Sets value of assets but may not account for future income
Multiple of earnings	Recaptures future value of net income (net income times multiplier factor)	Provides a rule of thumb to value future income but may not account for asset value
Discounted future earnings	Accounts for time value of future net income (present values calculated for future income)	Risk-adjusted value includes income and net worth of firm

Figure 12-4   **Primary Methods of Valuation**

worth approach." Using balance sheet data, liabilities are subtracted from the value of tangible assets to derive a value for owner's equity. This is the value of the business without considering goodwill.[12] For example, if a company's balance sheet showed $100,000 in current assets (cash, receivables, and inventory), $200,000 in equipment (at cost), and accumulated depreciation of $50,000, then its tangible assets would be worth $250,000. Deducting current liabilities of $20,000 (payables) and long-term liabilities of $80,000 (equipment and operating loans), the book value of the business would be $150,000. This balance sheet is shown in Exhibit 12-3.

The book value shown in Exhibit 12-3 is not necessarily the market value or a fair value for buying or selling the business. As noted earlier, all tangible assets must be evaluated in order to correct inaccuracies that result from accelerated depreciation, bad debts, obsolescence, and usefulness. Specifically, accounts receivable will seldom be worth their face value because of overdue payments, uncollectibles (i.e., bad debt write-offs), and customer returns. Inventory is valued at full cost only when it is entirely salable; more often, inventory is devalued to account for slow-moving items, potentially obsolete stock, and allowances for breakage, poor quality, and warranty replacements. Book value for equipment and facilities will be adjusted to reflect market or *useful* value. For example, a fully depreciated machine carried on the books at zero (or perhaps at a low salvage value) may actually have years of useful life remaining and therefore be an understated asset. Facilities that have been depreciated often *appreciate* in value. At the other extreme, some assets carry high book values, yet because of obsolescence or poor care, they may be worthless. Using the data in the same example, Exhibit 12-4 illustrates a more realistic "adjusted book value."

Using the book valuation method also requires a subjective evaluation of intangible assets. If the company has been making money, a premium for *goodwill* is appropriate. The goodwill premium is a one-time multiple of net profits to compensate the seller for the company's "image" and "market potential." This premium can be zero for an unprofitable or very-low-profit business, and it can be several hundred percent if profits are strong and future profit potential is exceptionally good. Profits, however, can also be misleading. Recall that we emphasized "cash flow" as the essential consideration for pricing a business, and also recall that profits seldom reflect cash flow. Consequently, when evaluating goodwill, it may be better to add a multiple of net cash flow. If annual net cash flow is expected to be $20,000, for example, a

---

Exhibit 12-3 Book Value of Business

Current assets (cash, receivables, and inventory)	$100,000
Long-term or fixed assets (equipment)	200,000
Less accumulated depreciation	− 50,000
Total assets	$250,000
Less:	
Current liabilities (payables)	− 20,000
Long-term liabilities (equipment and bank loans)	− 80,000
Net value (or book value)	$150,000

Exhibit 12-4 Adjusted Book Value to Establish a Purchase Price

Unadjusted book value	$150,000
Less:	
Allowance for doubtful receivables	−10,000
Allowance for unsalable inventory	−15,000
Allowance for warranty replacements	5,000
Subtotal after deductions	$120,000
Plus:	
Increase for market value of equipment	5,000
Adjusted book value	$125,000

multiple of 1 for a nongrowing, low-profit business would result in goodwill of $20,000. If the business is expected to grow and has strong profit potential, a multiple of 2 or 3 may be appropriate, yielding goodwill valued at $40,000 or $60,000.

The book value method can be complex, and it presents many problems for adjusting asset values to reflect their useful value to a buyer accurately. If the company has good bookkeeping, it is a useful method, because everyone involved can understand how values were decided; it is all recorded in the accounting ledgers. When a buyer is acquiring a firm *for its assets*, this is an important method to use. To illustrate, a person might buy a restaurant with no intention of continuing with the same menu or dining atmosphere, but the location, kitchen equipment, and furnishings are the acquisition targets.

Multiple of Earnings Method

When the buyer intends to continue an existing business, the **multiple of earnings method** is used to capitalize net income.[13] A value is established by multiplying net annual income by a factor that accounts for risk, future income potential, and the buyer's expectations for investment payback. A risky business, one with low growth potential, may have a multiplier of only 2. Consequently, a business that has generated on average $20,000 net income during the past several years will be valued at $40,000. If the buyer puts forward a $40,000 bid, he or she is saying, in effect, that the business is either too risky or has too little potential, and the buyer wants a "payback" in two years.

For a rapidly growing business with potential for high net income, a multiplier of 10 might be used. Thus an extremely attractive business with $20,000 average net income will be valued at $200,000. In this case, the buyer is sending a message that he or she expects to bring about an acceleration in growth and to benefit from what the prior owner has already accomplished. To achieve a two-year payback period in this instance, the $20,000 earnings must nearly triple for each of the following two years. Although this expectation may seem unrealistic, it is not uncommon, nor is it uncommon to see multiples as high as 20 times earnings for businesses well-positioned for explosive growth. The purchase price of a business dramatically changes with the assigned multiplier as shown in Figure 12-5.

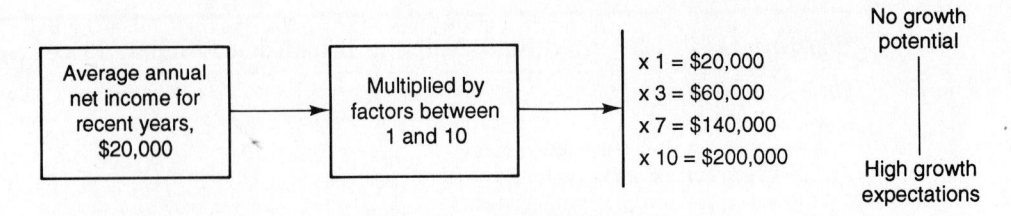

```
Average annual          Multiplied by          x 1 = $20,000       No growth
net income for          factors between        x 3 = $60,000       potential
recent years,     -->   1 and 10         -->   x 7 = $140,000
$20,000                                        x 10 = $200,000     High growth
                                                                   expectations
```

Figure 12-5 **Effect of Multipliers on Business Value**

An equivalent valuation technique is used for corporations and expressed in terms of a **price/earnings ratio** for outstanding shares. Securities analysts use the P/E ratio as a translation of a "capitalization rate" applied to business earnings. For example, a capitalization rate of 20 percent is a P/E ratio of 5.0 (1.00 divided by 0.20), suggesting a risky deal with a low share value. Capitalization rates account for alternative investments plus a risk-adjusted premium. If alternative investments yield 12 percent, then a 20 percent capitalization rate implies an 8 percent risk premium. Stable businesses have capitalization rates between 8 and 12 percent with stock valued through P/E ratios of between 12.5 and 8.3. High-growth businesses have lower capitalization rates that result in higher P/E ratios. For example, a profitable, high-growth enterprise may have a 5 percent capitalization rate (P/E = 20.0).

Slight changes in multipliers and P/E ratios can result in tremendous differences in valuations. Consequently, expert analysts use rather sophisticated evaluation models to establish prices. Addressing these techniques is beyond our intentions in this book, but some insight can be gained by studying Robert Morris and Dun and Bradstreet reports. These report P/E ratios and often identify share prices and multiples paid in corporate acquisitions; however, published data will seldom help small business entrepreneurs because few small business transactions are published, and those that are seldom provide comparable acquisition data.

Discounted Future Earnings

The **discounted future earnings method** is also called the "present value" model because it uses net present value (NPV) techniques to derive a value based on future earnings.[14] Specifically, expectations for future net cash receipts are "discounted" to reflect present values. These discounted future net cash receipts are added to a projected future cash value of the enterprise to provide an offering price.

These NPV techniques are used to estimate "present" value of "future" receipts, and in order to do so, a *discount rate* must be established. The discount rate is a risk-adjusted return expected from a comparable investment. If, for example, a person could earn 7 percent interest on a risk-free government security, and a relatively low-risk business opportunity seems to justify a small 2 percent premium, then the discount rate for valuing that business would be 9 percent. If the business seems to be risky, a large risk premium of 10 percent could be assigned, resulting in an 17 percent discount rate. Most small businesses are assigned risk premiums between 5 and 10 percent, and risk-free base interest rates tend to vary between 7 and 12 percent. As a result, discount rates for most small business valuations range between 12 and 22 percent, but it is not unusual to find assigned discount rates as high as 35 percent.[15] To illustrate this valuation method, a 15 percent rate is used to discount a five-year income projection in Exhibit 12-5.

There are additional considerations that can raise or lower the purchase price. The present value assumes, for example, a cash equity investment. In many instances, the buyer will have to borrow most of the purchase price, and if the loan interest is substantial, the discount rate will rise, thereby reducing the purchase price, or, alternatively, interest costs will be deducted from net cash flow. If the buyer will also operate the new business, then allowance must be made for an equitable salary or draw against business profits. This will further reduce net annual cash flow and the purchase price.

On the other hand, the seller may self-finance a significant portion of the purchase price through a note or a profit-sharing contract. Payments to the seller may reduce cash flow, but risk sharing by the seller can also reduce the discount rate. The lower discount rate results in a higher net present value and higher purchase price. Therefore, how the acquisition is structured and financed will influence decisions by both buyers and sellers.

Exhibit 12-5 Example of the Discounted Future Earnings Method

To illustrate the discount technique, assume that a buyer wants an annual return of 15 percent on the investment. Accordingly, a 15 percent rate will be used to discount annual net cash receipts. Also assume that the business will provide a stable net cash stream of $20,000 for five years. In addition, assume that the business will have a net worth at the end of five years of $200,000 (projected assets less liabilities). A table is created for annual data with the net worth in year 5 added to annual cash flow. Using present value factors from a handbook (or NPV formula), today's value is calculated:

Year	Net Cash Flow	PV Factor	Today's Value
1	$ 20,000	0.8695	$ 17,390
2	20,000	0.7561	15,122
3	20,000	0.6575	13,150
4	20,000	0.5717	11,434
5	220,000	0.4972	109,384
Totals	$300,000		$166,480

The total value of the projected cash flow stream in today's dollars is $166,480. This includes the estimated net worth of $200,000 at the end of five years. If the 15 percent discount rate is appropriate, then a buyer should pay $166,480 for the business.

> **CHECKPOINT**
>
> Describe the "book value" method of valuation and its benefits.
>
> Explain how a "multiple of earnings" method is used in valuation.
>
> Describe the "discounted earnings" method and risk-adjusted rates.

STRUCTURING THE ACQUISITION

Ultimately, the purchase price depends on negotiations and compromises between sellers and buyers, but it is not always a matter of cash. Sellers usually want to receive substantial money, and buyers usually want to pay as little as possible, but there are many ways to *structure* a purchase, and there are considerations other than money that influence the final price.

Perspectives of Sellers and Buyers

From the seller's perspective, the business may represent a lifetime of effort; giving it up—particularly at a bargain price—may be emotionally depressing. Successful entrepreneurs are proud of their accomplishments and want psychologically rewarding prices. In this situation, some sellers also want to stay partially involved with the business, and they may accept as part of the purchase price an equity share. Sellers, in effect, help finance the purchase, but in return they expect a more favorable purchase price. Rather than invest, sellers may extend personal loans or take back notes, and in some instances, they remain with the business under salary agreements. On the other hand, if a seller is disgusted with the business, feels little pride, and simply wants to get away quickly, a buyer may get a bargain price, but only with hard cash in hand.

Sellers also must consider tax effects of the purchase, and rather than sell for cash (which is usually fully taxed when sold), they may prefer to have payments over several years. Retiring owners find payment terms beneficial and are willing to negotiate loans, royalties, consulting fees, lease payments on assets, and rental terms for facilities. It is also common to barter, trading assets for part of the deal, such as taking back a car or vacation home from the buyer for inventory or equipment. Sellers also participate by helping buyers obtain bank loans through guarantees, co-maker notes, and mortgage agreements.

From a buyer's perspective, the ideal situation is a low price, little or nothing down, and low-interest payments on loans leveraged through acquired assets. This is the fundamental logic of a *leveraged buyout* (LBO). Unfortunately, all those conditions seldom come together in one package, and if they did, the buyer should be skeptical about the business; it might be on the verge of collapse or have hidden liabilities. Nevertheless, there is merit in trying to leverage the business using future cash flow, and a buyer may indeed be able to structure an acquisition without a major initial cash investment.

Leveraged Buyouts (LBOs)

In the uncomplicated form of a leveraged buyout (LBO), the buyer uses company assets as collateral for loans and future cash flow from collectible accounts to service those loans. In effect, the purchase is financed with future earnings.[16] During the 1980s, as major corporations changed hands through extraordinary leverage gambits, LBO financing became the so-called sweetheart of corporate acquisition strategies. Coupled with "junk bond" manipulations and billion-dollar deals on Wall Street, LBOs shot to prominence and subsequently became obscure when the junk bond market crashed. It is unfortunate that LBOs have been so closely linked to junk bonds and other financial manipulations because, realistically, almost every business purchase has substantial leveraged buyout terms; few deals are made with hard cash and equity transactions. For small and medium-sized businesses, the LBO is a fact of life, not a recent innovation in financing or a manipulative investment.[17]

Buyers evaluate businesses on their potential to generate cash flow, and purchase prices are predicated on the ability of a business to collateralize, and subsequently to pay down, the purchase price. How the business is leveraged and who is involved constitute the negotiated terms of sale, and although LBOs have been treated as part of the faddish "takeover" mentality of the 1980s, they remain important financial tools in all business acquisitions.

Leverage is created by buyers who rely on their ability to borrow against assets, then structure loan payments in such a way that additional equity is unnecessary to maintain a profitable cash flow. For a stable business with an established product line and dependable cash flow, this is a comfortable way to finance the business. If a company falters, however, the debt service may become unbearable. More important, if the company grows rapidly, proceeds from the LBO may be insufficient to fund expansion; money is essential for growth, and a fully leveraged business may have no further debt capacity. Many problems with LBOs stem from very high leverage ratios that restrict future growth, not merely from languishing business operations. In either instance, optimistic forecasts can lead to cash-flow problems, and if the business is heavily leveraged, the buyer will become entangled in debt service.

One solution to this dilemma is to leverage only cash-producing assets, in effect pledging future cash flow, but not other assets. This approach leaves equipment and facilities free to underwrite expansion, but it also means a lower leverage ratio and probably higher interest rates because the lender has less tangible collateral to support the loan. Another option is to borrow on fixed assets with specific, collateralized loans. This leaves cash-producing assets free for expansion but limits leverage to the loan value of assets used for collateral. In either instance, the buyer will have to meet higher equity requirements for the initial purchase. Exhibit 12-6 illustrates an LBO based on assets.

The relative advantages of LBO financing also depend on who is involved, and it is not unusual to find employees buying into a purchased venture. This possibility

Exhibit 12-6 A Leveraged Buyout Scenario

Assume that a business was being purchased on its book value without "goodwill." The purchase price was net of assets minus liabilities, adjusted in some instances for market values of equipment or doubtful receivables. Bank financing reflected "loan values" to account for the asset risk and collateral value. After all liabilities were cleared, loan proceeds were used to satisfy the purchase price.

Asset	Book Value	Loan Value	Liabilities	Net Proceeds
Cash	$ 22,000	$ 10,000	$ 0	$ 10,000
Receivables	61,000	30,500	0	30,500
Inventory	87,000	65,250	62,800	2,450
Plant facility	296,000	312,800	236,800	76,000
Equipment	102,000	76,500	78,000	– 1,500
Totals	$568,000	$495,050	$377,600	$117,450

Loan value on cash was only $10,000, reflecting a restriction by the bank on $10,000 maintained as compensating balances. This released $12,000 cash for operations. The bank loaned 50 percent on receivables and 75 percent on inventory. The plant facility was appraised separately by the bank, and a collateral loan of 80 percent of its appraised value was allowed. Incidentally, the plant appraisal was higher than the depreciated book value at $391,000 ($\times$ 0.8 = $312,800), yielding buyers a substantial asset for leverage. At the same time, the 75 percent loan on equipment would not cover equipment liabilities.

The purchase price was the "net book value" of assets minus liabilities, or $568,000 – $377,600 = $190,400. By leveraging assets only (not future income), the buyer was able to obtain $117,450 after paying all debts. The buyers had to come up with $72,950 cash to complete the deal.

---

can be quite important from a lender's viewpoint because existing employees have inside knowledge about business operations, and if they are willing to share in ownership, the credibility of the business is enhanced. Lenders and other investors will be favorably attracted to the employee-based leveraged buyout. In many instances, businesses are offered to key employees with support and participation by owners.

Other Considerations

Although leveraged buyouts are normal in small business acquisitions, there are advantages for a cash sale. If the buyer has access to money or low-interest loans, it may be better to negotiate for a low cash purchase price and underwrite the business with private assets. For example, a buyer with sufficient home equity may be able to obtain a home-equity loan at favorable rates. In addition, interest for a home-equity loan under current tax rules is deductible against personal income. The combination of low interest and tax advantages will almost certainly provide capital at a lower cost than bank-financed business loans would.

When a business is purchased for its assets, not its operational income, structuring the purchase by collateralizing each asset may be better, particularly if the buyer intends to change the business by dropping product lines or replacing technology. If the assets are isolated from operations, they can be sold without disrupting the business. New assets can also be purchased with few complications. A similar option is to purchase assets and specific liabilities, thereby avoiding hidden obligations and unrecorded liabilities. For example, a buyer may arrange financing for tangible assets (isolating equipment for resale or replacement), then assume liabilities for leased facilities, employee pension plans, insurance, and vendor credit.

Also, LBOs or private side deals may involve suppliers and customers. If suppliers have a significant interest in maintaining the business account, they may provide inventory and services with favorable terms or long-term financing. Some suppliers may buy into the new venture. This practice is not uncommon for regional distributors who must maintain inventory volume and a strong turnover to protect their own businesses. Less common but also possible is customer involvement. If the existing business has provided an important service for a customer (such as a regional distributor supplying a retailer), the upstream customer may be interested in helping the buyer (in this case, the new distributor). Customers may become parties to an LBO as private investors or lenders, stockholders in a buyout company, or partners with the entrepreneur.

Structuring the acquisition is an art that relies on negotiating skills. It is also an act of creative financing that benefits both parties. Structuring tools include asset barter, bank loans, private loans, leveraging of assets or future income (or both), contract arrangements for participation in future income, equity investments (with a broad range of options), and cash payments. The importance of these options depends on sellers' and buyers' intentions, business performance, industry trends, competition, supplier and customer relationships, economic trends, loan availability, and interest rates.

As we conclude this section and turn to the topic of franchising, remember that franchising is a form of business acquisition. Most of the preceding points apply to buying and selling franchises with some particular adaptations.

> ▶ **CHECKPOINT**
>
> Contrast seller's and buyer's perspectives for purchase terms.
>
> Describe an LBO and the advantages and disadvantages of leveraging.

FRANCHISING

A **franchise** is a form of business ownership created by contract whereby a company grants to a buyer the rights to engage in selling or distributing its products or services under a prescribed business format in exchange for royalties or shares of profits.[18] The buyer is called the *franchisee*, and the company that sells rights to its business

PROFILE △

Fred DeLuca, Founder of Subway Sandwiches

Starting with $1,000 and a business plan to create a chain of "sub" sandwich stores in 1965, Fred DeLuca spent nine years struggling with his idea of making "submarines" as popular as hamburgers. He began franchising in 1974 with a business system based on small stores, low overhead, and a simple menu. With established training programs, procurement channels, and excellent shop management systems, DeLuca launched Subway Sandwiches. By 1988, Subway had become the number-one U.S. franchisor in sales growth with 2,650 units operating and 3,000 slated to open by 1990. DeLuca's projections are for 5,000 units by 1994.

Subway's success is due in part to a low initial franchise fee of $7,500 and an option for existing franchisees to buy additional units for $1,000. Subway generates 8 percent royalties, and with strong advertising resources, the company name has become firmly established in 30 states. DeLuca provides franchise consulting through field coordinators, maintains a national procurement system that assures shop owners high-quality food products at low prices, and rolls out new units through a company site selection and leasing program that is adding 22 new locations a week.

Source: Gail Ignacio, "Great Expectations," *Venture*, December 1988, p. 48. Also International Franchise Association, "Subway Sandwiches of Milford, Conn.," fact sheet (Washington, DC: International Franchise Association, 1989).

---

concept is called the *franchisor*. The contract between them is called the franchise agreement, and it is a regulated form of business under state and federal commercial laws. Entrepreneurs interested in franchises can obtain specific information on a franchisor from government offices in the state where the franchisor is registered.

Franchising must be considered from two distinct viewpoints. First, the small business entrepreneur can consider buying into business as a franchisee. Second, the successful entrepreneur with an innovative business concept can consider becoming a franchisor. Franchising is a system of business acquisitions, and we will describe this system and address both entrepreneurial viewpoints.

Franchising as a Business System

A franchisor expands through a network of income-producing enterprises that share a common name, use common materials, sell similar products, and benefit from integrated distribution systems and national brand-name advertising. The franchisee usually receives a protected market, guaranteed supplies, training, and technical assistance for site selection, purchasing, accounting, and operations management.

Also, franchise owners occasionally receive financial support from franchisors in the form of credit for inventory and supplies.

We recognize franchises such as McDonald's and Wendy's, but franchising encompasses many industries besides fast foods. Most mall-type stores that sell clothing, toys, photographic supplies, records, shoes, and computers are franchises. Also, printers, furniture stores, auto rental companies, convenience stores, sporting-goods outlets, video-rental stores, and day-care centers are frequently franchises. Today, franchising extends to nearly every category of business, and the U.S. Department of Commerce has identified franchising as the fastest-growing business sector in the country with the potential for $100 billion in sales by the end of the century.[19]

Stunning changes have occurred in many industries. For example, Red Carpet Realty began franchising in 1977, and within ten years nearly a third of the home real estate market was in franchising. Nationally known realty franchisors include Century 21, ERA Realty, Better Homes and Gardens, Coldwell Banker, and the industry innovator, Red Carpet Realty. Franchise barbers include Hair Performers, the Hair Cuttery, UniSex, Image 21, and other recently opened chains. Additional franchising examples that may be familiar include 1st Optometry, Ace Hardware, Omni Hotels, Budget Rent-a-Car, Merle Harmon's Fan Fair, Money Mart, Jiffy Lube, and Mail America. All together, more than 45 categories of franchise industries with more than 2,000 business options exist in the United States.[20]

Many franchisors are now subsidiaries of major corporations. For example, John Deere and ARCO changed to franchise formats for retailing, and PepsiCo bought into franchising with its purchases of Kentucky Fried Chicken, Taco Bell, and Pizza Hut. Still, most franchises start with a simple idea by an entrepreneur who develops a business format that can be replicated successfully.

A franchise is a *business system* in the sense that it is capable of being replicated with consistent success.[21] The franchise provides owner-operators with a predictable method of doing business. It is a "turnkey" purchase with complete planning and operations management defined. Facilities are duplicated. Equipment is purchased in bulk and installed. Inventory is provided through established procurement systems. Administration and management control systems are set in place with support service and training for franchisees. Employment systems and personnel benefits often are included in the franchise, but national marketing programs are the essential focus of the system. Franchisors will usually help buyers plan their capital funding and cash-flow requirements, leaving as little as possible to chance. The franchise system is represented in Figure 12-6.

The Franchisor's Viewpoint

Most franchise chains were created by a founding entrepreneur in a single location. They seldom had unique products or services, but they created unusual business systems that could be easily managed. Consequently, the business of franchising is selling business systems, *not* selling hamburgers, real estate, or computers. Entrepreneurs become franchisors either by converting their existing businesses into chains or by creating new business concepts intended as franchises. Red Carpet Realty was

```
┌──────────┐      ┌─────────────────────────┐      ┌──────────┐
│Franchisor│─────▶│Franchisor provides:     │─────▶│Franchisee│
└──────────┘      │  Business concept       │      └──────────┘
      ▲           │  Marketing plan         │            │
      │           │  Site selection         │            ▼
      │           │  Operations plan        │      ┌─────────────────┐
      │           │  Staffing plan          │      │Franchisee pays: │
      │           │  Owner training         │      │  Initial fee    │
      │           │  Administrative system  │      │  Royalties      │
      │           │  Consulting             │      │  Inventory price│
      │           │  Merchandise            │      │  Leases and rentals│
      │           │  National brand advertising│   │  Advertising fees│
      │           └─────────────────────────┘      └─────────────────┘
      │                                                   │
      └───────────────────────────────────────────────────┘
```

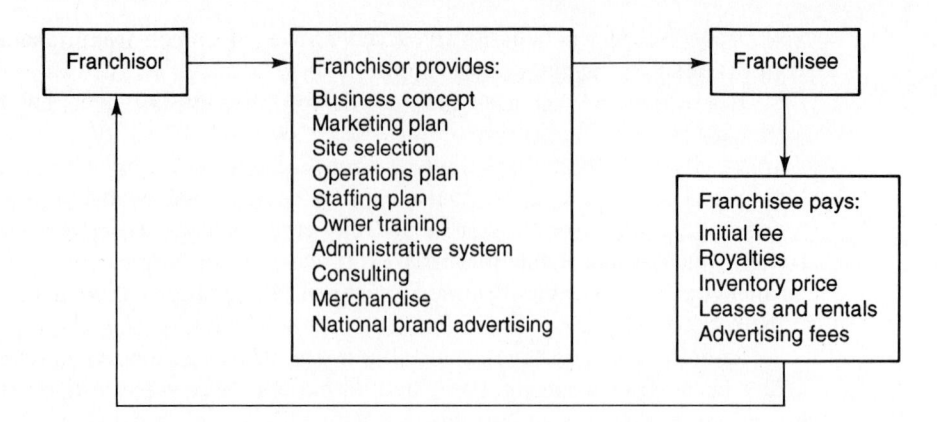

Figure 12-6   **Franchise System and Support Services**

a *conversion* by independent real estate brokers who formed a network of services unified under one name. They expanded rapidly through referral systems, regional advertising, and cost-effective human-resource systems.[22] ComputerLand was among the first chain of franchise outlets created specifically to sell microcomputer systems. The concept of ComputerLand was innovative in the sense of providing one-stop sources for licensed national-brand equipment, supplies, and repair services. Instead of buying computer hardware from one place, software from another, and supplies from yet another, consumers were able to purchase complete systems from ComputerLand.

Critical success factors for franchising Red Carpet Realty and ComputerLand were similar. They offered customers comprehensive service, quality performance, and consistency. As a result, their consumer bases expanded, and in turn, demand for franchise locations increased. As the number of locations grew, franchisors enjoyed greater economies of scale and broader consumer acceptance achieved through national brand advertising. This succession of events resulted in economic power that transformed fledgling enterprises into corporate giants.

The strength of franchising rests with having successful franchises that provide a consistent stream of income. Poorly managed locations, overextended owners, or inconsistent performance damages the entire network. Consequently, franchisors are not just interested in selling or licensing locations, but in developing the most successful network of high-performing franchises possible. Franchisors can generate revenue from the following sources:[23]

1. *Initial franchise fees*: The initial franchise fee is a single payment by the buyer to acquire the franchise rights. At minimum, a low initial franchise fee provides ownership rights, and the franchisor provides a prepackaged business plan complete with start-up procedures, vendor contracts, and guidelines for operations. This low-end fee is often less than $10,000. A more extensive contract will require a hefty fee, perhaps as much as $200,000,

but in addition to the minimum benefits, the fee will cover a start-up program including management training, site selection assistance, accounting and control systems, and on-site consulting by company personnel who act as mentors to "jump start" the new business.
2. *Royalties*: The heart of a franchise program is the ongoing income derived from sales. There are several ways to structure royalties, but the most common is a percentage of gross sales. This percentage can range from 4 percent for low-margin businesses such as donut shops to 20 percent for high-margin businesses such as computer service centers. Some franchise agreements replace royalties with percentage splits in gross profits, and others specify fixed payments based on sales volume. These agreements are negotiated to account for differences in location and extent of support services provided. In rare instances, franchisors collect a flat monthly fee.
3. *Products and supplies provided to franchisees*: Franchisors become vendors for their franchise owners, and although individual owners are not always required to buy materials and supplies from the mother company, it is usually beneficial to do so. One of the strengths of a franchisor is the ability to buy in bulk, distribute efficiently, and guarantee quality. For stores with patented or copyrighted products, the franchisee may have no choice of vendors. For computer stores or sporting-goods shops, the benefit of the franchise is national-brand licensing rights, and the franchisor will have established procurement systems.
4. *Services to franchisees*: Franchise agreements can specify certain basic services provided by the company for which franchisees pay a retainer or periodic fee. These services can include bookkeeping services, purchasing contracts, legal assistance, marketing research, benefit planning, maintenance, payroll accounting, and technical advising. In some instances, franchisors arrange leases on equipment or fixtures and assist with credit, collections, and security. Most services are prearranged in the basic agreement, but they are almost all subject to negotiation.
5. *Promotional fees*: Although not a profit center for franchisors, national promotion and advertising fees are specified in the franchise agreement. These will be part of the franchisor's marketing program, and, typically, a franchisee will pay the company a monthly "advertising" fee based on gross sales volume. This can be a small percentage of sales, seldom no more than 1 percent, or a flat monthly fee. Periodically, additional fees are collected for joint promotional campaigns, and franchisees usually can participate in special marketing efforts on a voluntary basis.
6. *Real estate income*: New franchise outlets that require unique physical facilities are usually built by franchisors and leased to franchisees. Examples include stand-alone 7-Eleven markets, Jiffy Lube garages, and McDonald's restaurants. Others that make use of existing store fronts or mall locations are usually independently leased by the franchisee. Examples include the Foot Locker stores, Merle Norman Cosmetics shops, and Mail America service centers. Although franchisors are seldom directly involved in mall

leases, they control (and occasionally help finance) renovations and store fixtures. Income from property rental agreements and site leases often exceeds income from royalties, and the exact terms depend on local costs, property locations, and property financing.

Successful franchisors protect their business income by protecting their franchisees; a good franchise benefits both parties, but a poor one only weakens the entire chain. Consequently, franchisors are not interested in creating marginal franchises, but in forming cooperative endeavors where both parties are committed to long-term success. This point is important because franchising, like any industry, has had its share of flimflam artists selling "dreams" through pyramid organizations. These hucksters come and go, but in general franchise performance has been stable and profitable. In contrast to independently owned businesses with failure rates that often exceed 50 percent during the first two years, franchises have enjoyed a 90 percent success rate for the same period.[24]

The Franchisee's Viewpoint

Franchising provides a systematic way to pursue the American dream, but with a safety net. For the individual owner buying into a business, the franchise offers a comprehensive business system based on a record of proven success. This past success does not guarantee that the new owner will enjoy equal success, but it does ensure that the franchisee will have a workable marketing program developed through verifiable market research that reduces the risk of starting a new venture.

Because franchising requires uniformity and consistency, the entrepreneur gives up autonomy over many business decisions in purchasing and merchandising. Also, the owner must conform to the franchise agreement, which can restrict growth and limit potential to the capacity of the location. Franchisees often overcome these limitations by buying additional outlets or expanding into a master franchise.

A **master franchise** is a contract that allows an entrepreneur to establish multiple locations within a defined geographic area.[25] In effect, the parent company grants to an entrepreneur the right to become a regional franchisor who can contract independently. This practice opens a third tier of owner-operated locations controlled through the master franchise as shown in Figure 12-7. Most franchisors provide master franchise options for selected regions, and by doing so, they create a form of regional management that diffuses distribution and decision-making control. Companies involved in global expansion prefer master franchising agreements to corporate-directed activities. For example, McDonald's has master franchise agreements in more than 20 U.S. metropolitan areas and in more than 30 foreign countries. In Hong Kong, the McDonald's franchise includes 43 locations, including four of the five largest-volume McDonald's outlets in the world.[26]

Master franchises are complicated arrangements between franchisors and other well-established businesspersons who have the resources to expand rapidly and manage growth. Individual franchises are not necessarily expensive or complicated, and the entrepreneur does not have to be experienced to become involved. However, buying into a franchise requires careful consideration.

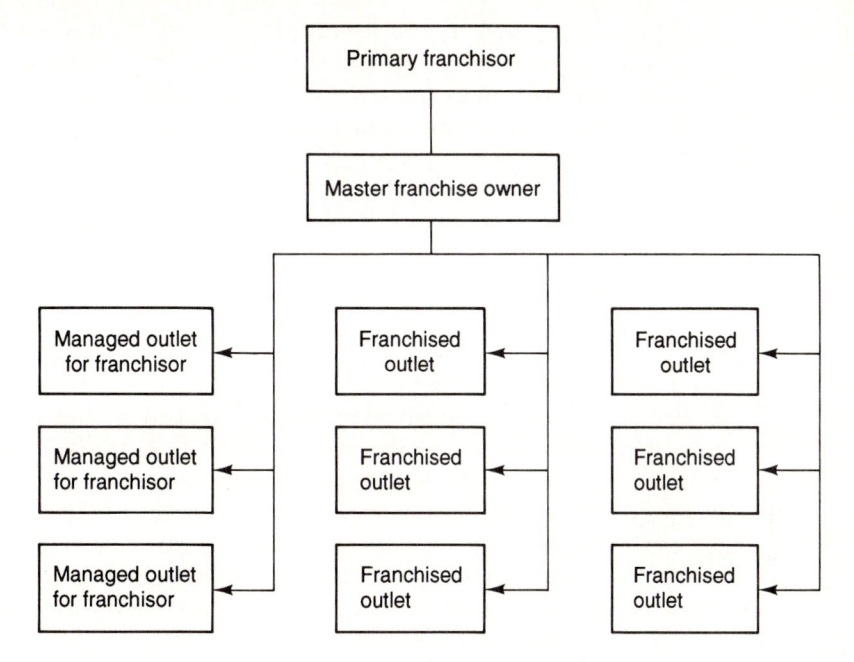

Figure 12-7 **A Master Franchise Relationship**

The Franchise Process

Almost all franchise opportunities are registered with the International Franchise Association in Washington, DC. Aspiring franchisees, however, usually discover opportunities as customers or through advertisements. Franchisors tend to promote their businesses through publications that relate to their business fields. Golf shop franchises, for example, are regularly advertised in *Golf Digest* and *Golf Illustrated*. Advertisements for others such as the Hair Affair and Mail America, appear in *Inc.* magazine and *The Entrepreneur* magazine. An individual interested in a franchise can use these sources or contact an existing franchise owner. Because franchise territories are protected, most franchise owners are not threatened by the prospect of competitors, and usually they will be quite informative about the business and about people to contact.

Once in contact, a franchisor will "prequalify" a prospective franchisee before handing out sensitive business information. The prequalification may require a conference between the parties or a background credit check on the prospect, but occasionally an entrepreneur can prequalify with a telephone call. The Federal Trade Commission regulates all franchisors, and under federal law, they are required to provide *disclosure statements* to prospective owners who demonstrate within reason their genuine interest in the business. Consequently, entrepreneurs who are serious can obtain a thorough evaluation of the business.

Disclosure statements include detailed copies of all agreements that the parties must sign, schedules of initial franchise fees, royalties, profit-sharing arrangements, distribution terms, and purchasing contracts. In addition, the franchisor must specify support services that can include training, on-site consulting, merchandise, equipment purchase or lease options, and advertising programs. Included in all disclosure statements are mandatory *audited* performance data covering sales volume, costs, and profits. Also, franchisors must include proprietary information on their corporation, including owners' and managers' qualifications, patents, copyrights, and trademarks.

Although disclosure statements provide information necessary to make a sound evaluation of the business opportunity, they are seldom sufficient for actually deciding to contract for a franchise. Disclosure information provides a foundation for negotiations. Recall that we described earlier many of the services available and the types of assistance provided. These are all subject to negotiation, and experienced entrepreneurs often prefer to handle most of their own activities such as accounting, leasing, purchasing, employee training, and maintenance. Location decisions are usually made jointly by a franchisor site-selection team and the franchisee, but there may be little latitude for decisions about facilities or unique designs. Some obligations are not negotiable (or have a narrow range of options), including franchise fees, royalty schedules, brand management, inventory, use of proprietary patents, copyrights, and trademarks, and legal rights of both parties.

Few franchise contracts are signed by the prospective franchisee without due diligence (as described earlier) and legal assistance. Subsequent to initial meetings with the franchisor, prospective franchisees will take the negotiated proposal to a professional accountant or attorney experienced in due-diligence research for thorough review. This is not an act of mistrust by the franchisee, but only sensible behavior, and most reputable franchisors will insist on a legal review of the proposal. We emphasized earlier that franchisors protect themselves by protecting their franchisees; therefore, enlightened franchisors want to establish a cooperative relationship from the outset. Consequently, if neither party has anything to hide, due diligence will be welcomed, and in most instances, professional help during negotiations will be expected.

A Concluding Comment

Although franchising appears to be very attractive, it is not necessarily less expensive or more profitable than opening an independent business. It is certainly less risky because the franchisor provides an established business concept and a proven marketing program, but independent entrepreneurs and their franchise counterparts have similar operating requirements. They both face the same long hours, personal commitment, and management challenges; success will always rest with the personal skills of the owner-operator. In terms of buying into business, there are several differences between independent ventures and franchises. Everything is negotiable when purchasing an independent business, and the seller usually helps with some form of financing or equity assistance. There are fewer negotiable issues in the franchise contract, and only rarely will a franchisor become involved in financial assistance beyond credit.

Chapter 12 Business Acquisitions and Financing   411

Perhaps most important, the independent entrepreneur is autonomous and can sell or assign the business and its assets. The franchise is a contractual arrangement with restrictions against selling or assigning the business, yet franchises regularly change hands with the blessing of the franchisor and a new contract.

▶ **CHECKPOINT**

Define the concept of a business franchise.

Describe how a franchisor profits from a good franchise concept.

Explain what a franchisee can expect from buying into a franchise.

▲▲ SYNOPSIS FOR LEARNING
▲▲
▲▲

1. *Describe the advantages and disadvantages of acquiring established businesses.*

The chief advantage of buying an ongoing business is that its track record can be verified, thus reducing the risk of starting a new venture. If the company has had a reasonable performance record, then data on sales, cash flow, profits, merchandise, customers, and markets can be ascertained. Owners often help to obtain financing, or they extend personal credit, to facilitate the purchase. From an operational viewpoint, a good acquisition that remains intact will have the benefits of established suppliers, bank connections, established clients, and capable employees. Disadvantages result from the potential of buying a business that may have hidden liabilities, a declining market, or an unprofitable business concept. Also, buyers often find good businesses, but in an effort to improve them, make changes that undermine success.

2. *Identify and explain considerations for evaluating a business opportunity.*

There are three categories of evaluations to consider. The first concerns business assets that can be evaluated in terms of book value or their market value. The second involves business operations to examine sales trends, credit policies, pricing, promotional activities, and distribution systems. These require careful due-diligence analysis and market research. Also, the buyer will want to understand human-resource issues, including how the owner's personal skills and abilities influence operations and whether capable employees will stay after acquisition. The third category involves an evaluation of the business environment. This encompasses external market trends, competition, industry characteristics, consumer profiles and buying patterns, economic conditions, financial trends, and costs related to operating the business.

3. *Explain the three most commonly used methods of valuing a business.*

The book value method uses company financial statements to establish the net worth of a firm. This method compiles asset values, subtracts liabilities, and makes adjustments as necessary for doubtful accounts, marginal inventory, or market value of assets. The result is a "book" value without consideration of goodwill or earnings. It is useful for providing an objective value of a firm's tangible assets. A second method is more a "rule of thumb," but it is often used to account for future income. This is called the multiple of earnings method because average annual net income is multiplied by a factor of between 2 and 10 to produce an estimate of value. For public corporations, a P/E ratio is used to compare the business with similar companies to capitalize earnings. Low multiples (or P/E ratios) suggest a low valuation and a riskier business; higher multiples suggest a high-potential business with expectations for strong future earnings. A third method is the discounted future earnings method (or present value approach). Future earnings are discounted using a risk-adjusted discount rate to derive a current value that accounts for the time value of money.

4. *Describe major considerations for structuring an acquisition.*

Because acquisitions are negotiated between buyers and sellers, there are many ways to structure deals. From a seller's perspective, a high price and all cash is the ideal; buyers would like to pay a low price, put nothing down, and have favorable financing. Between these extremes, sellers often help with financing through personal investments, notes for part of the purchase price, help with bank loans, or contractual arrangements for personal assistance. Buyers can consider low-cost loans on personal assets, such as their homes, partial leveraging of fixed or liquid assets through bank loans, or LBOs. The primary consideration is to structure a purchase in such a way that the new owner has a positive cash flow, potential for growth, and flexibility for added debt.

5. *Define franchising and the role of franchisors.*

Franchising is the process of creating networks of business systems with consistent and repeatable operations. Franchisors sell business concepts and the collective support of operational systems necessary to succeed. They offer brand merchandise, image, inventory and distribution systems, training, and various options for administrative, personnel, and consulting services. Most important, they provide a marketing plan complete with verifiable performance on comparable outlets. Combined, these support systems reduce the risk associated with a new venture and the likelihood of start-up mistakes. In return, the franchisor collects franchise fees, royalties, and profits from merchandise and services provided to the buyer. Many franchisors also derive income from property and equipment leases.

6. *Explain franchising from the franchisee's perspective.*

Franchisees become contractual owners of proprietary business systems with rights to national brand products, patents, copyrighted materials, and valuable trademarks. Coupled with a strong marketing plan provided by the franchisor, the franchisee can start a business with few complications. The franchisee, however, must comply with the terms of a franchise agreement that often limits one's decision-making control. A franchisee has little to say about merchandising, business format, inventory purchasing, and operational systems, but success is still determined by the capabilities of the owner-operator.

NOTES

1. Deloitte Haskins & Sells, *The Buy/Sell Decision: Small and Growing Businesses* (New York: Deloitte Haskins & Sells, 1987), Sec. 1. Also "Acquisition Strategies," *Small Business Report*, Vol. 12, No. 1 (January 1987), pp. 32–34.

2. "Message from the President," *Stockholder's Report*, Bush Industries, Inc. (1988), p. 1. Personal communication with Paul Bush, President and CEO, Bush Industries, Inc.

3. *A Guide to Colonial Williamsburg* (Williamsburg, VA: Williamsburg Historical Society, 1988), Foreword and pp. 2–3. Also John D. Hunt, "Evolution of the Township: A Spirit of Determination," unpublished working paper on entrepreneurship in Virginia, James Madison University, May 1989.

4. Lawrence K. Finley and Charles T. Hays, "Small Business Valuation for the Potential Buyer," *Entrepreneurship: New Direction for a Global Economy—ICSB/USASBE* (1988), pp. 104–108.

5. Arnold S. Goldstein, *How to Get Started in Buying and Selling a Business* (New York: John Wiley & Sons, 1983), pp. 77–78.

6. Personal interview with Joyce Connor, co-owner of the Green Spot Nursery, October 1990, Southern Pines, North Carolina.

7. Donald F. Kuratko and Richard M. Hodgetts, *Entrepreneurship: A Contemporary Approach* (New York: Dryden Press, 1989), pp. 193–194.

8. James Howard, "Defuse the Hostility Factor in Acquisition Talks," *Harvard Business Review*, Vol. 82, No. 4 (1982), pp. 54–57.

9. Hugh Aldersey-Williams, "Upgrading the Main-Street Cinema," *High Technology*, June 1987, pp. 23–26.

10. Lawrence Finley, *Entrepreneurial Strategies: Text and Cases* (Boston: PWS-Kent, 1990), pp. 178–179.

11. John B. Clarke, "Due Diligence and Doing the Deal," *Ernst & Young Acquisition Notes* (Richmond, VA: Ernst & Young, 1990).

12. James W. Henderson, *Obtaining Venture Financing* (Lexington, MA: D. C. Heath, 1988), pp. 329–333.

13. Thomas J. Martin, *Valuation Reference Manual* (Hicksville, NY: Thomar Publications, 1987), pp. 7–8.

14. Joel K. Worley and Fess B. Green, "Determinants of Risk Adjustment for Small Business Valuation in a Growth Industry," *Journal of Small Business Management*, Vol. 27, No. 4 (1989), pp. 26–33.

15. Arthur Lipper III, *Guide to Investing in Private Companies* (Homewood, IL: Dow Jones-Irwin, 1984), pp. 263–264.

16. John Kitching, "Early Returns on LBOs," *Harvard Business Review*, Vol. 89, No. 6 (1989), pp. 74–79. Also "Small Leveraged Buyouts Are Big Business Now," *Business Week*, December 10, 1984, pp. 138–140.

17. Lee P. Hackett and Scott E. Fredrick, "You Can Be Your Own White Knight," *Financial Executive*, September/October 1989, pp. 48–52. For some insights on junk bonds and LBO controversy, see James Kaplan, "Thy Brother's Keeper," *Investment Vision*, November/December 1990, pp. 28–31.

18. David D. Seltz, *How to Get Started in Your Own Franchised Business* (Rockville Centre, NY: Farnsworth, 1980), pp. 6–8.

19. A. Kostecka, *Franchising in the Economy, 1986–1988* (Washington, DC: U.S. Department of Commerce, 1988), pp. 8–10.

20. Donald D. Boroian and Patrick J. Boroian, *The Franchise Advantage* (Schaumburg, IL: National BestSeller, 1987), pp. 32–36.

21. Ibid., pp. 16–17.

22. Ibid., pp. 34–36.

23. Russell M. Knight, "The Independence of the Franchisee Entrepreneur," *Journal of Small Business Management*, Vol. 23, No. 2 (1984), pp. 53–61.

24. Boroian and Boroian, *The Franchise Advantage*, pp. 66–67.

25. *Franchise Opportunities Handbook* (Washington, DC: U.S. Department of Commerce, 1988), pp. 1–2, 6.

26. Peng S. Chan and Robert T. Justis, "Franchise Management in East Asia," *Academy of Management Executive*, Vol. 4, No. 2 (1990), pp. 75–85.

CASE 12-1

Sage Renovations: Buyout Valuation

Jim Forrest had just experienced one of the most exciting and most frustrating weeks of his life. The excitement began the previous Sunday when his boss offered to sell the business to Jim. During the week, Jim had talked to three bankers, an attorney, and an accountant, and they had all advised him differently. Frustrated, Jim asked for and received help in evaluating the business offer from the regional SBA office.

The background information is interesting and typical of many similar small business buyouts. Jim had worked seven years at Sage Renovations, Inc., starting as an hourly paid worker, rising to project supervisor, and being promoted to general manager early in 1990. His boss, Fred Stimpson, had made an initial offer to sell Sage Renovations for $360,000, and he agreed to help Jim with financing. Fred, who was 58 years old, had started Sage Renovations 16 years earlier as a home contracting business. When Fred started, it was just himself and his son who worked part-time while attending college. His son became an aerospace engineer and moved to Los Angeles. Consequently, Fred had no family member to succeed him, and he was worn down by the business. Fred and his wife had invested wisely, incorporated the business two years earlier, and now wanted to sell the business and pursue other interests. Jim was an excellent employee, smart even though poorly educated, and he had helped Fred build up a strong client base.

Sage Renovations had been reasonably profitable every year. The company employed five full-time workers and an office manager in addition to Fred and Jim. On big jobs during the high season, they hired part-time help. The business consisted of exterior home and building renovation using stucco sealant and a variety of special processes for painting, weatherproofing, and sealing concrete and stucco walls. Several years ago, the company expanded into preformed siding materials, and most Sage contracts included window and door repairs.

Fred provided Jim with information on past earnings with projections for five years. He also provided an income statement and balance sheet for the year 1990. He expressed to Jim that he felt "goodwill" was worth $100,000 based on the strength of their contracts. In 1988 net sales were $512,140, before-tax profits $46,100, and after-tax profits $32,760. In 1989 net sales were $564,600, before-tax profits $47,290, and after-tax profits $38,950.

CASE QUESTIONS

1. Make an evaluation of the buyout opportunity using discounted cash flow and multiple of earnings methods. (Assume 20 percent required rate of return with PV factors for five years of 0.833, 0.694, 0.579, 0.482, and 0.402.)
2. Assume that you are a bank loan officer evaluating the business for a loan. What method of valuation would you use and what approximate value would you assign to the business?
3. Analyze the goodwill in Sage Renovations. Describe other information you would need to provide an accurate valuation for this business.

Summary of Projected Sales and Earnings

	1991	1992	1993	1994	1995
Net sales	$680,000	$740,000	$780,000	$820,000	$850,000
Profit before taxes	54,000	60,000	66,000	74,000	78,000
Profit after taxes	44,000	49,000	54,000	58,000	61,000

Sage Renovations, Inc.
Income Statement, Year Ending 12/31/90

Net sales		$622,800
Cost of sales:		
Direct wages	$192,400	
Contract materials	117,700	
Supplies	14,800	
Other job costs	26,500	
	$351,400	
Gross profit from operations		$271,400
Operating expenses		164,700
Total depreciation		23,517
Net income before interest and taxes		$ 83,183
Interest expense		31,090
Profit before taxes		$ 52,093
Income taxes		9,890
Net profit after taxes		$ 42,203

Sage Renovations, Inc.
Balance Sheet, as of 12/31/90

Assets	
Current assets	
Cash on hand	$ 56,900
Accounts receivable	83,200
Materials and inventory	41,600
Total current assets	$181,700
Fixed assets	
Building and land	$240,000
Operating equipment and vans	164,000
Office equipment	12,000
Less accumulated depreciation	−88,920
Total fixed assets	$327,080
Total assets	$508,780
Liabilities	
Current liabilities	
Accounts payable	$ 33,100
Wage expense and tax/FICA payable	17,800
Total current liabilities	$ 50,900
Long-term liabilities	
Real estate mortgage	$168,700
Note payable to bank	76,000
Total long-term liabilities	$244,700
Total liabilities	$295,600
Shareholders' equity	
Common stock	$100,000
Retained earnings	113,180
Total shareholders' equity	$213,180
Total liabilities and shareholders' equity	$508,780

Notes: Depreciation: building, $38,500; operating equipment and vans, $45,920; office equipment, $4,500.

CASE 12-2

The Franchise Option

Founded in 1980, Travel Agents International, Inc., began as a regional travel agent in the heart of Florida. The company targeted a "youthful" retired market of affluent people. Most of these retirees had relocated to Florida from northern states with ample retirement incomes and the urge to travel. Looking for unusual tours and recreation opportunities, they represented a huge market of anxious travel customers. Most also visited their previous homes or went north to see family members each year.

Travel Agents International found a profitable niche among retired residents, and within two years, the company had opened several offices in resort retirement communities. With the growth in franchising, TAI reorganized in 1982 and began offering franchise offices, each networked together for an integrated travel system. The company has retained its headquarters business in Seminole, Florida, but now has nearly 300 franchise locations.

Potential franchise owners are screened on application to ensure they have sufficient resources and a career interest in developing a personal service business in travel. The parent company earned $67,000 net profit on approximately $5 million in gross sales in 1988 and expected a similar financial profile into the 1990s. This sales figure represented income from franchisees, not travel sales or services. The company assures potential franchise owners that this income is adequate to provide franchise services, yet represents a low profit because money is reinvested in services for new franchise owners.

The company offers franchises at a flat fee of $39,500 for a complete business package that includes training and help with initial licensing. Depending on the location of the business, the owner will have to spend between $40,200 and $87,600 to furnish an office and acquire reservations linkage through travel networks. The owner must arrange his or her own lease, or buy a location, and if the franchise is successful, the company offers "area" or master franchise options. Franchise royalty fees are expressed in a fixed monthly charge of $785 with a fixed advertising charge of $335 per month.

Prospective franchise owners are interviewed at their own expense, usually in Florida, and the company reserves the right to decline an offer to anyone they feel unsuitable for the travel business. Applicants must also provide a full disclosure of their financial position and demonstrate the ability to meet franchise costs plus projected operating costs for the first year. Franchisees buy travel supplies and subscribe to catalogs from the parent company.

CASE QUESTIONS

1. Make a list of questions you would ask as a prospective franchise owner, and briefly explain why these questions are important.
2. Assume that a typical travel franchise office can expect a net profit after taxes of 8 percent on sales. Based on case information, what scenario can you describe for sales and profits if you bought into this franchise? Would it be a good investment? Why or why not?
3. Visit a local franchise service business with a predefined list of questions about the requirements for owning a similar franchise. These will be used for discussion and comparison in class.

Source: "The Franchise 100," *Venture*, December 1988, pp. 42–43. Information courtesy of Travel Agents International, Inc., Seminole, Florida.

Chapter *13*

Financial Resources for New Ventures

OBJECTIVES

1. Explain how financing is influenced by effective asset management.
2. Describe alternative methods of financing ventures with equity.
3. Explore the role of venture capital in new venture financing.
4. Describe sources of debt financing for new and expanding ventures.
5. Explain how the SBA and other government agencies assist in financing.

Financial resources are essential for business, but particular requirements change as an enterprise grows. Obtaining those resources in the amount needed and at the time when they are needed can be difficult for entrepreneurial ventures because they are generally considered more risky than established enterprises. As we shall see, financing means more than merely obtaining money; it is very much a process of managing assets wisely to use capital efficiently.

The critical issue is to assure sufficient cash flow for operations, as well as to plan financing that coincides with changes in the enterprise. Businesses obtain cash through two general sources, *equity* or *debt*, and both can be obtained from literally hundreds of different sources. Our intention in this chapter is to introduce ways of acquiring financial resources for ventures in the start-up and early development stages. In addition, we will address the private equity market known as venture capital and describe government assistance for small businesses. Sections of the chapter focus on asset management, equity funding, venture capital, debt financing, and government programs.

ASSET MANAGEMENT

Managing assets effectively is crucial because underwriting assets creates liabilities that, if uncontrolled, can devastate a business. Cash is the most important asset to manage, and to generate cash, businesses must generate sales. In order to generate sales, most businesses must have inventory and facilities, service enterprises need offices and staff, and manufacturers face more extensive requirements, including plant and equipment.[1] There are instances when few assets are needed. Management consultants, for example, might require only the means of personal survival, a telephone, and a mail drop box to get started, but they are exceptions. For the vast majority of entrepreneurs, finding assets required to cultivate sales is an urgent task.

Asset management for the start-up entrepreneur is a matter of determining what is needed to support sales, and then *gaining access to* those assets at the optimum cost. The term "gaining access" is used because there are alternatives other than a cash purchase of assets. Equipment can be leased, for example, and office furniture can be rented; even pictures and plants can be obtained through office rental centers. Manufactured products initially can be subcontracted rather than made, thereby avoiding the expense of procuring materials, equipment, and plant facilities. Entrepreneurs, therefore, have choices about what assets to obtain, when they must be obtained, and how to gain access to them.

Inventory Decisions

Most retailers and wholesalers must have inventory in their possession before they can generate sales, and for start-up enterprises, suppliers normally require cash on delivery (COD) until entrepreneurs establish themselves as reliable customers. In many instances, entrepreneurs also have no choice among suppliers, particularly if the merchandise is brand-name inventory such as Reebok shoes or Compaq computers sold through distributors with protected territories. Consequently, new ventures are faced with cash outlays in exchange for salable merchandise. Through careful planning, however, it is possible to plan inventory purchasing so that stock is acquired and replenished as cash becomes available. For example, a women's aerobic clothing store can begin with essential inventory needed for a complete merchandise line, but instead of stocking four or five items in each size and color required for a one-month inventory, two or three items can be stocked for a half month's inventory. This procedure may give the business time to generate income needed to supplement merchandise.

Planning is the key to inventory procurement decisions. If aerobic clothing can be acquired on short notice, then a lower stocking level can be maintained. Normally the store owner will pay premium prices for merchandise under these circumstances, but if price premiums are less than the cost of borrowing money, then an incremental stocking strategy may be beneficial. This problem becomes less crucial when suppliers extend credit or when entrepreneurs can negotiate among competing suppliers.

When suppliers extend credit, there is time to generate sales that can be used to pay for inventory. If substantial sales are made for cash or on credit cards that can be quickly converted to cash, then a good part of inventory will be self-liquidating. Such a situation is not uncommon in retailing where "small-ticket" cash sales occur, but it is rare when a store must extend installment credit or is selling "large-ticket" items such as appliances. Wholesaling to other businesses tends to create credit lags; wholesalers may be allowed 30-day credit by their sources, but they usually have to extend 30-day credit to retailers. Thus a repeating pattern of delayed payments affects everyone's cash flow. Figure 13-1 illustrates a cash conversion scenario.

Periodically, suppliers offer favorable terms to their customers, allowing several months before payments must be made for inventory.[2] In effect, suppliers lend inventory to their customers, and these favorable terms can be granted for several reasons. First, suppliers may have such keen competition that they use favorable credit to secure orders. Second, they may have inventory stockpiled, and by signing orders, they can reduce stock while using sales orders as collateral for loans. This situation is common for wholesalers of seasonal products such as Christmas toys, winter clothes, school supplies, and swim wear. Third, wholesalers who deal in imported products must purchase overseas in foreign currencies, and they tend to buy in bulk when exchange rates are favorable. By signing advanced orders with customers, they obtain collateral in the form of receivables to finance imports, but to obtain these orders, they must offer incentives such as extended credit.

Once a business has been established, inventory can become collateral for operating loans. A music store, for example, may have an expensive merchandise line that includes pianos, organs, guitars, drums, and brass and woodwind instruments. The line, called a "floor plan," is never depleted, only sold and replenished. As a result, the store may perpetually have $100,000 invested in merchandise that can be leveraged with a bank. Bankers rarely offer more than 70 percent of the inventory value, and the loans they provide are short-term notes or personal credit lines.[3] As we shall see later, these loans must be repaid quickly, so they are useful for underwriting operating expenses such as payroll, but not for capital requirements such as new equipment. Nevertheless, if inventory is used as collateral for replenishing stock

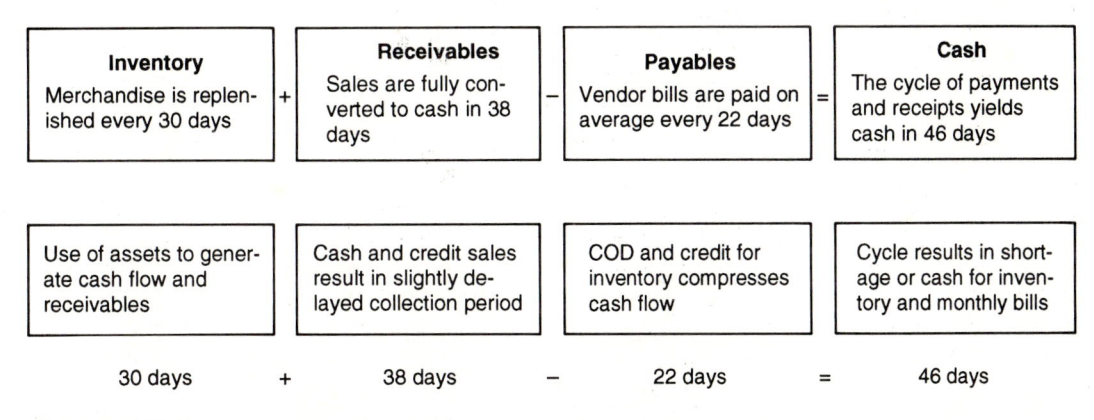

Inventory		Receivables		Payables		Cash
Merchandise is replenished every 30 days	+	Sales are fully converted to cash in 38 days	−	Vendor bills are paid on average every 22 days	=	The cycle of payments and receipts yields cash in 46 days
Use of assets to generate cash flow and receivables		Cash and credit sales result in slightly delayed collection period		COD and credit for inventory compresses cash flow		Cycle results in shortage or cash for inventory and monthly bills
30 days	+	38 days	−	22 days	=	46 days

Figure 13-1 **Cash-Flow Gap Created by Pattern of Sales**

(i.e., matching sources and uses), and if 70 percent loan values can be obtained, then the store owner has to be concerned only with paying for the remaining inventory from operations.

One additional planning consideration is also important. When inventory and sales are "booked," they are reconciled at the end of each month. This procedure can be misleading in terms of cash-flow requirements. Assume, for example, that an entrepreneur makes an initial purchase of one month's inventory and is given 30 days' credit. At the end of the month, accounts are reconciled, and the income statement appears to show that sales paid for inventory. If all sales were cash transactions, this conclusion might be true. If sales occurred regularly during the month or involved consumer credit, however, it could be false; the entrepreneur will be in a cash-flow trap, unable to replace inventory. On the other hand, if sales occur in clusters during brief periods each month (or seasonally), then carefully timed inventory purchasing might result in a positive cash flow by stocking inventory "just in time" to meet sales demand, thereby generating revenue before bills come due. This situation occurs several times a year in seasonal retailing during Christmas shopping months, spring sales, and late summer back-to-school sales.[4] The coordination of purchasing and sales is illustrated in Figure 13-2.

Accounts Receivable Decisions

An **account receivable** is a consumer's promise to pay later, and it is an asset owned by the entrepreneur that can be sold or used as collateral. The value of a receivable, however, is no greater than its probability of being paid. New ventures without track

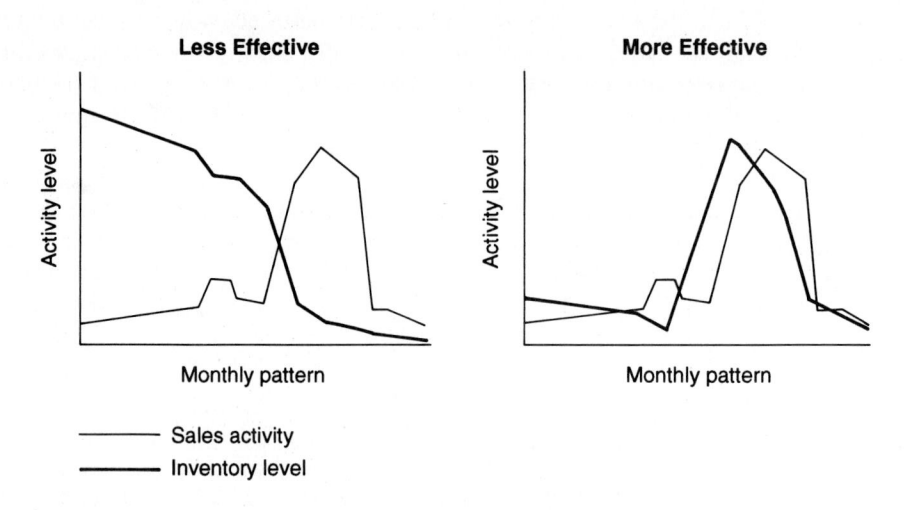

Selling from stock purchased at beginning of month is less effective; business holds and pays for idle inventory. Buying stock to complement sales cycle is more effective.

Figure 13-2 **Coordinating Purchases with Sales Activity**

records for collecting their receivables subsequently find it difficult to sell or borrow against these assets; therefore, careful asset management practices are important.

In most instances, managing receivables is similar to managing inventory; decisions about either directly affect cash flow. Receivables and inventories also affect one another. Poor purchasing will affect sales and reduce the value of receivables in two ways: Sales can suffer because of weak merchandise, or the entrepreneur may resort to lax credit terms to induce sales, thereby generating doubtful accounts. The logical answer to both problems is to pursue a plan whereby inventory is purchased in a timely manner and consumer credit is coordinated with supplier credit terms.

Consumer credit policies can be made to correspond with credit extended by suppliers. For example, 30-day supplier credit allows an entrepreneur to extend 30-day consumer credit or to offer credit card financing, which is normally processed during each calendar month. By orchestrating consumer receivables with inventory procurement, gaps in cash flow requirements can be minimized. Retailers can also take advantage of unusual supplier credit, such as extended credit terms created through foreign exchange advance orders, to offer consumer incentives. These incentives can dramatically improve sales, and they include layaway options, installment financing, and cash rebates. In each instance, receivables are generated before inventory accounts must be satisfied, and the receivables can be used as collateral for operating loans.

Banks follow similar guidelines when establishing loan limits for accounts receivable. They may allow up to 70 percent of the asset value for financing but expect payment when receivables are collected. In some instances, this limit will be as high as 80 percent for businesses with excellent collection records, but on the other hand, new ventures without collection histories may be turned down for loans.[5] As an alternative to borrowing against receivables, a business can sell them. This practice is called *factoring*, and it results in an entrepreneur giving up income by discounting receivables to a factor company.

Managing receivables involves marketing decisions, and although these decisions seem to have little to do with financing, they influence financing requirements. A decision to emphasize cash sales, for example, reduces accounts receivable and provides immediate cash flow for purchasing. This policy may reduce finance required for merchandise, but it will restrict sales and subsequently reduce the net worth of the business. Extensive consumer credit may have the opposite effect, but too much latitude results in bad accounts and lengthy collection periods, thereby defeating the benefits gained from increased sales. Excessive credit selling also defeats financing of receivables and puts greater cash flow pressure on the entrepreneur to replace inventory.

Equipment Decisions

Equipment is important to a business because it can help earn profits, not because it has residual asset value.[6] A computer system, for example, is a depreciating asset, and its residual value declines every day whether it is being used or not. Vehicles, office machines, furniture, store fixtures, production machinery, handling equipment, and tools depreciate systematically. They also become obsolete, often quite rapidly.

Therefore, an equipment asset standing idle is simply an unjustified expense, not an investment. An efficiently utilized asset contributes to business earnings.

Entrepreneurs, therefore, must make sound decisions about how to equip and furnish their enterprises, but they must also understand the costs associated with purchasing assets. The cost of buying equipment includes the purchase price as well as delivery, installation, and financing costs. It also includes operating costs such as maintenance and repairs, and the costs associated with depreciating value. As an alternative, some equipment can be leased. However, a leasable asset must have certain characteristics. It must be tangible, have numerous other possible users, be easily transferred between users, have independent value apart from the business, and require little effort to reacquire or repossess.[7] Vehicles, data processing equipment, common production machinery, construction equipment, office machines, and furniture meet these requirements and can be leased. Proprietary equipment, special-purpose machines, nonstandard fixtures, unique furniture, and modified vehicles are rarely leased.

Leasing is not alternative financing. It *eliminates* financing because the asset is owned by the lease company, not the entrepreneur. By leasing, however, the entrepreneur "gains access to" equipment, thereby satisfying the primary requirement of good asset management. Whether leasing is a cost-effective option depends on the equipment, its utilization, and lease terms. If costs of buying and leasing are comparable, and if equipment is in danger of becoming obsolete, then leasing may be the better choice. It can reduce the risk of owning an obsolete asset with little residual value. Leasing companies usually recognize the danger of obsolescence and charge a premium to cover their replacement costs. New car leases, for example, take into account reduced market value for outdated models, and monthly lease payments typically are higher than purchase loan payments. Nevertheless, an entrepreneur can write lease payments off as expenses, thereby reducing tax liabilities, and if the leasing company requires little or no down payment, the net cash flow of a lease may be less than a direct purchase. A lease-buy example is shown in Exhibit 13-1.

If equipment is used sparingly, then a short-term lease/rental agreement may be beneficial. For example, retailers with seasonal sales can lease display stands, temporary locations, cash registers, furnishings, and delivery vans, thereby maximizing asset utilization without making loan payments for assets that remain idle most of the year. Hickory Farms of Ohio has year-round retail stores, but because they sell a majority of their gift food items during the November-December holiday season, they concentrate on short-term leasing arrangements for a majority of facilities and equipment. Hickory Farms pays premium lease prices, but they avoid paying for idle assets during the remainder of the year.[8]

A corollary to leasing is *subleasing*. A specialized business such as a perfume boutique can arrange with a large department store to sublease a counter area rather than set up an independent business location. This practice is becoming quite common as major stores encourage specialty merchandisers to contract for counter space or in-store boutiques. Stores benefit by improving space utilization and cash flow from leases, and lessees benefit by having significant exposure to customers without capital expense for facilities. Store subleasing usually takes the form of a "participation

Exhibit 13-1 Buy or Lease: An Illustration

A delivery van purchased for $20,000 can be financed for five years with a 10 percent down payment. Interest is 12 percent, and depreciation assumes ACRS five-year property. The entrepreneur is in a 28 percent tax bracket. Assume the van can be sold in five years for $4,000.

Cash Required to Purchase Van		Offsetting Benefits to Own Van	
Down payment	$ 2,000	Cash from sale	$ 4,000
Taxes and charges	600	Tax savings: interest and costs	2,451
Loan payments	24,967	Tax savings: depreciation	4,749
Five-year maintenance	2,500	Less tax gain from sale	− 266
Total cash out	$30,067	Total cash in	$10,934

Net total cash flow out for purchase: $30,067 − 10,934 = $19,133

The same delivery van can be leased with a security payment equal to two monthly payments. Leasing closing includes taxes normally paid by the dealer. Lease payments are determined on the dealer's estimate of the van cost less residual value after five years plus costs for periodic maintenance (by dealer) and implicit interest expense. The entrepreneur's tax bracket is 28 percent.

Cash Required to Lease Van		Offsetting Benefits of Leasing	
Security payment	$ 934	Tax savings: security	$ 261
Lease closing cost	200	Tax savings: all costs	280
Lease payments	27,086	Tax savings: payments	7,584
Five-year maintenace	800		
Total cash out	$29,020	Total cash in	$8,125

Net total cash flow out for lease: $29,020 − 8,125 = $20,895

On the surface, purchasing the van seems better at a lower total cost; however, if the "time value" of money for the down payment and closing costs ($2,600) is considered versus the lease ($1,134), the gap is closed. Changes in assumptions about down payment, cash from sale of van, tax rate, or loan interest rate affect calculations.

---

contract" if the specialty item has an established brand name. For example, Estée Lauder sells cosmetics in more than 30 countries and 7,000 retail locations through counter leases in which Estée Lauder pays a percentage on cosmetic sales to the department store.[9] Ralph Lauren, Liz Claiborne, and Pierre Cardin follow similar strategies, but more important, when these businesses were struggling to get started, the option of merchandising through in-store boutiques assured them of low-risk market penetration without financing long-term equipment and facilities.

Another corollary is *subcontracting*. Because most manufacturers have excess production capacity (idle machinery and labor), they are willing to perform contract work for an entrepreneur. As long as the product being made is not in direct competition with the manufacturer's product line, compatible contracts can be drawn up minimizing the entrepreneur's need to capitalize production facilities. These arrangements quite often turn into long-term supplier relationships in which entrepreneurs completely forgo the cost of manufacturing in favor of merchandising products made elsewhere. Redgate Communications Corporation, for example, was an entrepreneurial venture started by Georgetown University graduate Ted Leonsis who, in 1982, had an idea for a personal computer software magazine. He published *LIST* as his first venture, but it was typeset, printed, bound, boxed, and distributed through a dozen different companies; Leonsis had little more than a rented office and a telephone. Today, Redgate publishes magazines for Apple, Commodore, Compaq, Hewlett-Packard, Wang, and Lotus, among others, yet by subcontracting production and distribution, the company can focus almost exclusively on editorial and marketing activities.[10]

Facilities Decisions

Gaining access to physical facilities involves decisions about real estate and property management. Options available to entrepreneurs are numerous, but most decisions depend on location requirements. A fashion retailer may have no alternative to leasing a high-cost mall location, but for most entrepreneurs there are choices among types of malls, storefronts, renovated offices, and stand-alone buildings. In some instances, the entrepreneur must decide between buying property and leasing space. A landscape nursery business, for example, does not always have a clear-cut decision. If a highly visible location is required to sell plants, then a nursery might buy or build the facility together with land or a greenhouse for plant stock. On the other hand, the nursery might lease a retail location and buy or lease low-cost rural land for growing plants.

Real estate does not depreciate like equipment, and this fact complicates the decision to buy or lease. Because land is finite, market forces tend to drive up land values, particularly in expanding areas with high demand. Buildings and plant facilities affixed to the land deteriorate and eventually lose their value, yet market forces tend to drive up prices resulting in real estate appreciation. Although buildings and plant facilities are *depreciated*, entrepreneurs realize capital gains through market *appreciation*. Clearly, an entrepreneur could buy a real estate asset, enjoy tax benefits from depreciation, yet realize capital gains from appreciation. On the other hand, buying real estate usually requires a substantial down payment and initial costs for legal services and closing. Owning property also requires cash outlays for maintenance, repairs, insurance, and taxes. Acquiring a property that results in net gains depends on real estate financing, the entrepreneur's negotiating skills, and economic conditions. Exhibit 13-2 illustrates lease and purchase options and assumptions of financing.

Leasing real estate reduces front-end cash outlays associated with buying property. Lease payments are usually higher than amortized mortgage payments, but many of the additional expenses of ownership can be avoided. For example, maintenance, repairs, insurance, property taxes, and improvement costs can be assumed by the owner or negotiated in the lease. A lease is a contract, and consequently almost everything is negotiable. A periodic lease for real estate is an expense, and although it can reduce the need for start-up capital, it has no asset appreciation value for the business.

Exhibit 13-2 Real Estate Lease or Purchase

Assume that an 1,800-square-foot location can be leased for $10 a square foot, $18,000 a year on a five-year lease. Also assume that it can be purchased for $140,000 with 20 percent down payment and mortgage payments of $15,048 a year. This example assumes 11.25 percent interest and that property appreciates at 2 percent annually. The situation after five years is as follows:

Cash Required for the Purchase		Cash Required for Five-Year Lease	
Down payment	$ 28,000	Security payment	$ 3,000
Closing costs	4,000	Lease payments	90,000
Loan payments	75,240	Insurance/legal	1,200
Insurance/legal	2,450	Maintenance	2,400
Maintenance	7,600	Total cash out	$96,600
Property taxes	3,750		
Total cash out	$121,040		

Offsetting Benefits of Purchase		Offsetting Benefits of Leasing	
Tax savings from:		Tax savings from:	
Closing costs	$ 1,120	Lease payments	$25,200
Other expenses	3,864	Other expenses	1,008
Depreciation	7,056	Total benefits	$26,208
Interest expense	16,547		
Appreciation if sold	14,571		
Less tax/costs of sale	− 8,080		
Total benefits	$35,078		

Net Cash Position in Five Years		Net Cash Position in Five Years	
Total cash outlay	$121,040	Total cash outlay	$96,600
Cash benefits	− 35,078	Cash benefits	− 26,208
Recovery of equity	− 28,000	Net cash out	$70,392
Net cash out	$ 57,962		

On the surface, purchasing is a better choice, provided that the location can realize 2 percent appreciation and be sold after five years. These calculations do not take account of the time value of money for the very heavy initial cost of purchasing ($32,000 in cash). If the business faces cash flow problems by making the purchase, the initial outlay may cause the business to borrow for operating funds. However, the net appreciation represents at least a 9 percent return on the investment.

An interesting twist to leasing is the possibility of establishing a *leasehold interest in property*.[11] A leasehold interest is treated as an asset because it can appreciate in concert with local property values. Consider the situation in which an entrepreneur signs a ten-year lease for a 2,400-square-foot building at a rate of $5.00 per square foot. That is an annual lease for $12,000, or $1,000 per month (2,400 × 5.00 divided by 12 months). If the contract does not prevent subleasing or assigning lease rights, then the lessee can negotiate with others interested in the building. Now suppose that

PROFILE △

Glen Jackson—Minimizing Business Costs

Glen Jackson describes his business as "liquidity." In fact, he controls several large plots of farmland, enjoys a chauffeured limousine when he spends an evening out, has four expensive delivery trucks on the road each week, employs more than 400 workers, and has both wholesaling and retailing businesses in fresh foods. Jackson, however, owns little and owes less.

He started in business at the age of 19 in San Diego County selling fresh avocados to small stores. He picked the avocados himself at a "you pick 'em" farm. Later, Jackson hired friends to pick, and he made 200-mile trips back and forth from remote county farms to the city selling fruits and vegetables. Demand for fresh foods was so good that Glen decided to grow his own. Having no money to purchase land, he leased acreage from the federal government in San Bernardino County. He had to drill water wells for irrigation and then cultivated 2 acres with varieties of plants.

Today, he has more than 160 acres leased at a cost of about $11 per acre. Jackson transports 8 tons of produce each week during three peak growing seasons. He hires part-time workers to plant and harvest, thereby minimizing labor costs and avoiding full-time employees. Jackson also rents delivery vehicles during peak seasons and contracts delivery services. He subleases space in six supermarket produce sections, and wholesales to stores and farm markets in three counties. Jackson owns a few tools and a 1983 pickup truck. Although tight-lipped about how much he earns, Jackson says it is close to six figures, but more important, it is almost all cash. What does he owe? Nothing beyond his leases.

Source: Interview with Glen Jackson, September 1990.

---

property values increase after several years so that comparable leases are $8.00 a square foot. The entrepreneur has a lease liability for $5.00 ($1,000 a month) but a leasehold at "market value" at $8.00 ($1,600 a month) which can be subleased, sold, or assigned for the remaining years. In effect, the leasehold interest is worth $600 a month, and if five years remain on the original lease, it is worth $36,000.

Leaseholds are not uncommon, but owners usually protect themselves with "acceleration clauses" that increase lease payments periodically. These increases can be negotiated every few years by a formula in the original lease agreement. In the absence of acceleration clauses (or when payments increase less than market values), the lessee benefits. This situation can be particularly attractive in long-term leases for land and buildings. For example, 99-year leases on agricultural and commercial land were common after World War II, and many of these leaseholds today still have a half century of life remaining. Astute owners today realize the potential of underestimated long-term lease values, and they are more discerning, yet ten- and twenty-year renewable leases at favorable rates are not unusual.

Evaluating any asset decision is accomplished by "discounting" future cash requirements for various alternatives, then comparing the "present value" under each scenario. (This technique was illustrated in Chapter 12.) Having carried out this procedure, the entrepreneur may lack the financial resources to choose the best option. The acid test is whether the entrepreneur can meet operational cash-flow requirements without jeopardizing the business; when a venture is out of cash, it is out of the game. All decisions concerning assets are therefore subordinated to maintaining a positive cash flow. Few new ventures can do so without capital underwriting in the form of equity infusions and debt financing.

▶ **CHECKPOINT**

Describe how inventory and accounts receivable can be managed to minimize requirements for financing and to improve cash flow.

Explain alternative means for "gaining access" to facilities and equipment, and describe how subleasing and subcontracting are useful.

EQUITY FINANCING

Equity is capital invested in a business by its owners, and it is "at risk" on a permanent basis.[12] Because it is permanent, equity capital creates no obligation by an entrepreneur to repay investors, but raising equity requires sharing ownership. New ventures often have difficulty attracting equity investors until they survive the initial start-up stage, but as they become more firmly established, equity sources become more accessible. Figure 13-3 illustrates how equity requirements and sources change with growth.

Personal Sources

Entrepreneurs must look first to individual resources for start-up capital. These include cash and personal assets that can be converted to cash. A personal car, for example, may provide cash through refinancing, and second mortgages can be obtained for home equity. Life insurance policies may also have accumulated equity, and other assets such as stamp and coin collections have capital value. These are not unusual sources, but some assets also can be converted to business use, including personal trucks or vans, computers, telephone answering systems, furniture, and tools, among others.

Family members and close friends also may become involved as informal investors, but having them invest can lead to controversy if their participation is not

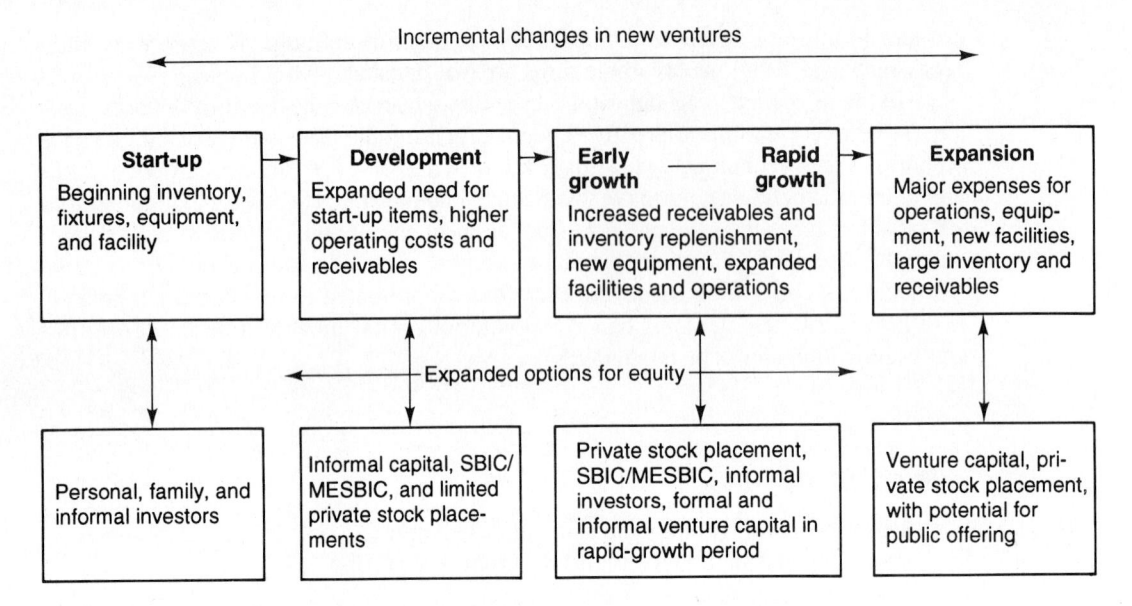

```
                    Incremental changes in new ventures
    ←─────────────────────────────────────────────────────────→

  ┌─────────────┐    ┌──────────────┐    ┌──────────────────┐    ┌──────────────┐
  │  Start-up   │    │ Development  │    │ Early    Rapid   │    │  Expansion   │
  │ Beginning   │    │ Expanded need│    │ growth   growth  │    │ Major expen- │
  │ inventory,  │ →  │ for start-up │ →  │ Increased recei- │ →  │ ses for ope- │
  │ fixtures,   │    │ items, higher│    │ vables and inven-│    │ rations,     │
  │ equipment,  │    │ operating    │    │ tory replenish-  │    │ equipment,   │
  │ and facility│    │ costs and    │    │ ment, new equip- │    │ new facili-  │
  │             │    │ receivables  │    │ ment, expanded   │    │ ties, large  │
  │             │    │              │    │ facilities and   │    │ inventory and│
  │             │    │              │    │ operations       │    │ receivables  │
  └─────────────┘    └──────────────┘    └──────────────────┘    └──────────────┘
```

─── Expanded options for equity ───

Figure 13-3 **Financial Needs and Equity Sources with Growth**

clear to everyone. Recall from Chapter 11 that a sole proprietorship has no investors other than the entrepreneur, and, by definition, when more than one person invests, a business becomes a partnership. Consequently, when parents or friends provide cash to "help out," they can become legally liable for the business. Formal agreements with family and friends may seem unnecessary, but they will help avoid misunderstandings, and as described in Chapter 11, there are ways to bring in silent or limited partners without confusion. Entrepreneurs, however, give up part of their ownership in return for these investments.

Informal Risk Capital

Beyond family and friends, there are many wealthy individuals who enjoy investing in new ventures. There are more than 500,000 individuals in the United States whose individual net worth exceeds $1 million; the 400 richest represent more than $125 billion. From this vast pool of resources, nearly $5 billion is invested each year in new ventures. Wealthy investors typically invest between $10,000 and $50,000 in risky ventures to broaden their portfolios. This equity pool is called *informal risk capital* because investors find entrepreneurs through personal contacts, and they often invest on hunches or recommendations; they seldom engage in complex investment analyses.[13]

Although private investors do not make complicated investment decisions, they are not naive. Research shows that most are extremely well-informed about business, and they are usually self-made entrepreneurs in their own right. Also, they are well-networked with other professionals who are not easily deceived in business deals. In addition, many of these so-called angels have been involved in dozens of equity deals and in the venture capital industry, giving them exceptional intuition for judging entrepreneurs and their ventures.[14]

Private Placement Securities

By forming a corporation, an entrepreneur can raise equity through stock equity. A **private placement** is the limited sale of stock to private parties within Securities and Exchange Commission (SEC) guidelines, but it does not constitute a registered security offered to the public through an organized exchange. Private placements are defined under the 1982 SEC *Regulation D*, and they provide the means for selling stock to relatives, friends, employees, and other private parties. Regulation D specifies investors' qualifications for three categories of private placements, described in the following paragraphs.[15]

Rule 504 Placements. A total stock placement of less than $500,000 can be offered to private parties without providing disclosure statements of security registration information normally required in a public stock offering. Under Rule 504, there are no limits on the number of investors or their qualifications.

Rule 505 Placements. A total stock placement of no more than $5 million is allowed, but the business is required to disclose certain information to investors. The SEC reviews applications for 505 status and specifies information required to sell securities, but the process is less complicated than registering public securities. Stock can be privately sold to an unlimited number of "accredited purchasers," but to no more than 35 "nonaccredited purchasers." *Accredited purchasers* fall into one of six categories:

1. Institutional investors including banks, registered investment companies, small business investment companies (SBICs), insurance companies, and venture capital companies.
2. Tax-exempt organizations approved by the SEC with more than $500,000 in verifiable assets.
3. Directors, executives, or general partners of the corporation or partnership offering the private placement securities.
4. Any individual whose income is expected to exceed $200,000 in the current year and who had income in excess of $200,000 for each of the previous two years.
5. A person who buys at least $150,000 of the privately placed security and who can demonstrate a combined family (self and spouse) income that is at least five times the security purchase price.
6. Any individual with a combined family (self and spouse) net worth that exceeds $1 million at the time of purchase.

Rule 506 Private Placements. A total stock sale in excess of $5 million is allowed, but disclosure information must provide details of the business in a prospectus approved by the SEC. Information requirements are far less rigorous than those for public securities, and compliance reporting is simplified, but to qualify for 506 status, a business must carefully document its placement proposal. Under Rule 506, a company can sell securities to an unlimited number of accredited purchasers but no more than 35 nonaccredited purchasers. This is similar to limitations under Rule 505 except that nonaccredited purchasers must also be *sophisticated* investors. To meet the test of ''sophistication,'' investors must be knowledgeable about investments. Although no specific guidelines exist, sophisticated investors are those who regularly invest in similar enterprises, and they must have knowledge of the type of business or industry.

Small Business Investment Corporations

A **Small Business Investment Corporation (SBIC)** is a company chartered under the auspices of the federal government specifically to help underwrite small businesses; SBICs provide equity and debt financing to small corporations with less than $6 million in net worth and less than $2 million in after-tax earnings averaged over the previous two years. These restrictions are defined by federal regulations under the Small Business Administration to limit SBIC investments to small companies with growth potential. Investors are given a strong incentive to focus on these higher-risk ventures. For each dollar of paid-in capital from private sources, SBICs are eligible for up to three dollars in government-guaranteed loans. This program provides SBICs with capital for underwriting new ventures, yet their risks are moderated by SBA guarantees.[16]

A **Minority Enterprise Small Business Investment Company (MESBIC)** is similar to an SBIC, but it is chartered specifically to underwrite a special category of business. To qualify for MESBIC financing, a company must demonstrate majority ownership by those considered socially or economically *disadvantaged*. The term ''minority enterprise'' is misleading, although entrepreneurs who qualify as members of racial or ethnic minorities are given special consideration under several programs including the MESBIC. These investments are considered a higher risk than those made by SBICs, and the SBA allows higher leverage for loan guarantees; rather than a 3-to-1 ratio, MESBICs qualify for a 4-to-1 ratio, subsequently reducing investors' risk and providing more capital for disadvantaged businesses.[17]

Public Offerings

Publicly listed corporations sell stock through SEC-regulated exchanges, and *going public* is a major step for any business. An entrepreneur who decides to do so is making an *initial public offering (IPO)*. Generally, an IPO should not be attempted for less than $3 million of underwriting, and most brokers will not consider an IPO with fewer than 250,000 shares. Also, shares offered under an IPO represent considerably less than 50 percent of the net worth of a company because existing owners will want to maintain control.[18] It follows that an IPO of $3 million representing 30 percent public ownership means that a company's net worth should be at least $10 million. Consequently, an IPO is not a common alternative for most small ventures.

Nevertheless, if a business grows to the point of requiring significant capital and is prepared to go through the trouble of filing, an IPO can be beneficial. Selling securities rapidly provides needed capital, but there are other reasons for going public. Public companies enjoy credibility with bankers and major customers not afforded to closely held companies. Also, the value of a company is established through marketable securities. Publicly traded stock also provides liquidity for estate planning; shares can be sold or assigned with little difficulty and without disrupting business continuity.

Disadvantages of going public are often overshadowed by expectations of a huge cash infusion and the "glitter" of an IPO. When the costs are tallied and the glitter wears off, IPOs do not always look attractive. The cost of an IPO can easily exceed 20 percent of the issue.[19] Consequently, a business must be able to replace this cost through net earnings to maintain its stock value. For a company with potential for at least 30 percent growth in net earnings, the cost of an IPO presents no problem, but for others, the IPO may result in a general devaluation of shares. The glitter rapidly fades with the burden of registering a new security. Under the Securities Act of 1933, public offerings are registered with the SEC, and companies must comply with federal and state regulations.

Registration normally requires that a company's balance sheets be audited for the previous two years; other financial statements must be audited for three years. Accounting fees will be substantial because in addition to audit expenses over several years, accountants are involved in preparation of the registration statement, documenting the investment prospectus, and assisting underwriters with federal and state inquiries. Other costs include legal fees, document printing costs, federal and state filing fees, and taxes. The SEC and securities dealers who underwrite the IPO also levy fees, and there are substantial hidden costs in terms of time and expenses by the company to pursue registration. Even for simple IPOs, the process can take up to ten months after initial filing.

After a company has gone public, the SEC requires regular and frequent reporting by the company to its shareholders and the public. This involves management of a company under public scrutiny coupled with formal stockholder meetings, detailed information and financial controls, and continuous attention to shareholders' interests. Entrepreneurs seldom have a role in this process unless they can make the transition to a professionally managed company. As a result, founders who had control before the IPO often find themselves on the fringes of their creation.

Gaining a Perspective on Equity Financing

In addition to the sources of equity described, there are several alternatives for IPO registration, a variety of government programs that provide grants, equity support, and direct financial assistance, and alternative legal structures (e.g., limited partner-

PROFILE △

IPOs—Not for Everyone

In 1984, Gemini Pacific Corporation, a resort developer in Los Angeles, decided to "go public." With net earnings that approached $1 million on slightly over $12 million in sales, GPC operated in a growth market with potential for rapid expansion. The company began thinking of an initial public offering (IPO) when it found it could not attract equity capital or secure loans large enough to underwrite expansion. During 1984 and 1985, GPC put together a strong IPO prospectus based on solid marketing research, improved sales, and slightly improved net earnings.

The company filed for a $4 million public offering in 1986 and began the rigorous process of auditing, meeting with underwriters, and preparing several hundred pounds of documentation. Seventeen months later, in early 1988, a "final meeting" with underwriters occurred, and GPC was told it would have to revise the IPO and wait a few more months because the IPO market was not favorable. The board reviewed the process and found it had spent slightly more than $200,000 in accounting and legal fees, and underwriter fees would require nearly $400,000 more. Coupled with marketing research costs and other heavy expenses, the board expected the IPO to net no more than 72 percent of the placement. Also, management had been so busy with the offering that business was neglected; profits were dropping and debts were mounting so that further delays could be a serious problem.

Faced with another huge bill for current-year auditing and yet another delay, the company called off the IPO, consolidated its operations, and began planning for 1989. Through a private merger, GPC found alternative funding that repositioned the company for rapid growth in several new markets.

---

ships) that entrepreneurs can consider. State economic development programs and federal agencies also provide various kinds of financial assistance.

For the entrepreneur in a start-up venture, access to equity capital is restrictive; considering an IPO, for example, is impossible until the business has been successfully established for several years. Also, a new venture will not be able to qualify for SBIC or MESBIC assistance until it has attained a reasonable degree of success. At inception, new venture founders must rely primarily on personal equity, family, friends, and "angels." Recall from earlier chapters that an enterprise progresses through several development stages, and at each stage, there will be different capital requirements; different financing methods also exist at each stage. Entrepreneurs, however, often attract financing through *venture capitalists* who are apt to invest at any stage of development.

Chapter 13 Financial Resources for New Ventures

> ▶ **CHECKPOINT**
> Describe personal and informal risk capital as equity sources.
> Identify and explain three forms of making private placements.
> Explore the advantages and disadvantages of "initial public offerings."

VENTURE CAPITAL

Venture capital is an alternative form of equity financing for small businesses, and a *venture capitalist* is similar to a mutual fund manager who finds equity investments for a pool of investors. Unlike mutual fund managers and most other security specialists, venture capitalists focus on high-risk entrepreneurial businesses. They provide start-up (seed money) capital to new ventures, development funds to businesses in their early growth stages, and expansion funds to rapidly growing ventures that have the potential to "go public" or that need capital for acquisitions.[20]

The Venture Capital Industry

There are approximately 450 venture capital firms in the United States (excluding SBICs), and they invest nearly $3 billion annually through equity placements. The venture capital industry consists of wealthy individuals, foreign investors, private investment funds, and limited partnerships or closely held corporations funded through insurance companies, pension funds, and endowments. Also, venture capital units funded by major corporations such as General Electric and Xerox have begun to appear. Consequently, the venture capital industry is not a well-defined economic sector like banking or public securities.[21]

The venture capital industry evolved from the government's efforts to establish the SBIC program. During the early 1960s, nearly 400 SBICs were in operation, and private investment capital was attracted to SBICs, which in turn invested in small businesses. As described earlier, SBICs are still attractive sources for acquiring capital; however, during the late 1960s, private investors decided they could do just as well on their own without government involvement. Those investors pioneered the industry which, today, has more than 300 known venture capitalists. Individually, they represent investment pools that average $92 million, and they have more than 90 percent of their money placed in small enterprises with less than $5 million in sales or assets.[22]

Venture capitalists provide equity to small firms that find themselves in a vacuum for financing. Specifically, very small companies and family enterprises can attract private equity between $10,000 and $50,000 with little difficulty, and by forming partnerships or small corporations, they can usually find four or five times that amount of capital. At the other end of the scale, "larger" small businesses valued in excess of $5 million have access to traditional forms of corporate securities, development bonds, and public offerings. Between these extremes, there is a gap in financial underwriting. Entrepreneurial firms are caught in a vacuum of funds, and this is the market that venture capitalists serve. During the late 1980s, the average venture capital investment was $865,000, ranging between $350,000 and $1.4 million.[23]

The trend, however, is for investments to be larger, and there is a growing number of institutional venture capital funds actively pursuing new venture financing.[24] These include, for example, General Electric, Xerox, Merrill Lynch, and Prudential-Bache. Each has created venture capital limited partnerships or venture capital units to fund entrepreneurs. Institutional underwriting is on the order of $2 million for each deal, and most investments are "packages" in which several venture capitalists participate. Corporate or large private venture capitalists become *lead investors* in these packaged investments, then three or four others buy into the enterprise. Lead investors tend to take substantial equity positions while followers tend to make smaller investments, but combined, they represent deals that often exceed $10 million.[25]

Criteria for Investments

Although the venture capital industry is evolving toward larger and more complicated financing, there will always be a need for incrementally smaller deals funded through individual capitalists who are attracted to high-risk new ventures. Consequently, entrepreneurs will always have access to—or create a demand for—venture capital. However, money is a finite resource, and venture capitalists carefully analyze potential investments. They receive, on average, about 650 proposals each year from entrepreneurs, and they fund about 15 ventures (roughly 2 percent of all proposals).[26]

Successfully funded proposals are those with successful (or potentially successful) entrepreneurs. The single most important criterion is the *capability of the entrepreneur to sustain an intense effort to make the business work*. The second most important criterion is the entrepreneur's *demonstrated knowledge of his or her markets*.[27] Research on how venture capitalists evaluate proposals show that five of the most important criteria relate to characteristics or abilities of entrepreneurs. In addition to these two most important criteria, venture capitalists evaluate how well an entrepreneur manages risks, the entrepreneur's leadership characteristics, and how effectively the entrepreneur articulates his or her proposal. The evaluation includes assessments of a formal proposal or business plan, "due-diligence" investigations through background reports and references, and personal interviews with individuals who are on the "short list" of promising proposals.[28] Criteria most often used in venture capital decisions are shown in Exhibit 13-3.

Objective criteria used by venture capitalists are similar to criteria for most other investments and include potential growth and profitability. Unlike other investors and lenders, venture capitalists must achieve very high returns on their investments because they are underwriting risky businesses. Their rule of thumb for profit potential is *at least ten times return in a period between five and ten years*.[29] This rate of return may seem exorbitant, and venture capitalists are often criticized as financial barons who exploit small business owners. High returns are necessary, however, because

Exhibit 13-3 Criteria Most Frequently Used by Venture Capitalists as Investment Decision Guidelines

Criterion	Ranking[1]
Entrepreneur capable of sustained effort	1
Entrepreneur familiar with market	2
Entrepreneur able to evaluate and react well to risk	3
Market or industry attractive to venture capitalist	4
Product fits well with investor's long-term strategy	5
Target market enjoys significant growth rate	6
Product or innovation can be legally protected	7
Entrepreneur has demonstrated leadership ability	8
Potential to return 10 times investment in 5–10 years	9

[1] Research through several different organizations and by independent investigators between 1985 and 1988 has shown consistent responses by corporate and independent venture capitalists for the top three criteria. Several studies have higher ratings on leadership and market potential, and some include criteria such as management's track record and the entrepreneur's ability to articulate the business concept.

Sources: Ian C. MacMillan, Robin Siegel, and P. N. Subbanarasimha, "Criteria Used by Venture Capitalists to Evaluate New Venture Proposals," *Journal of Business Venturing*, Vol. 1, No. 1 (1986), pp. 119–128. Also Robin Siegel, Eric Siegel, and Ian C. MacMillan, "Corporate Venture Capitalists: Autonomy, Obstacles, and Performance," *Journal of Business Venturing*, Vol. 3, No. 3 (1988), pp. 233–247.

---

venture capitalists have a track record of succeeding with new ventures in only about one of every three investments. Their subsequent net profits range between 20 and 35 percent, which reasonably account for risk-adjusted expectations.

Relationships with Venture Capitalists

Entrepreneurs seek out venture capitalists for their money, and although venture capitalists seek out new ventures with high risk-return potential, they envision long-term business relationships with entrepreneurs. This kind of relationship is illustrated by the services provided by venture capitalists and the potential advantages to entrepreneurs of having venture capitalists as equity shareholders.

Capital is only the obvious benefit. Venture capitalists are extremely well informed about the industries in which they invest, and most have experienced market research departments that provide information vital to the enterprise. As stockholders, venture capitalists are anxious to help businesses succeed, and they provide consultation to assist entrepreneurs in every way possible. Most venture capitalists maintain frequent contact with their entrepreneurs, and through their contacts, they provide access to prospective customers, suppliers, and professional services. In many instances, they also become "mentors." These relationships are described in Exhibit 13-4.

Venture capitalists are involved, but they do not try to take over the business. They are primarily investors and are not interested in managing the businesses in

Exhibit 13-4   Assistance and Involvement by Venture Capitalists

Providing advice on management and board decisions
Introducing entrepreneurs to suppliers and distributors
Linking relationships between entrepreneurs and lenders
Introducing entrepreneurs to management consultants
Developing relationships with securities firms and brokers
Facilitating expansion financing or IPO underwriting
Monitoring all investors' interests through involvement
Providing technical assistance on products and innovations
Acting as guarantors on loans or leases
Developing new customers or new markets through networking
Finding key resources, locations, or facilities
Motivating entrepreneurs through personal assistance
Developing leadership through personal "mentoring"

Source: Adapted from Arthur Lipper III, *Investing in Private Companies* (Homewood, IL: Dow Jones–Irwin, 1984), pp. 66–75, 92–94, 137–139. Reprinted with permission.

which they invest. To do so would mean that venture capitalists would have to personally assume management responsibilities for a dozen or more new businesses every year. Consequently, entrepreneurs are not likely to lose control of their businesses. To the contrary, venture capitalists invest because they are reasonably convinced that entrepreneurs are capable. Occasionally they seize control when an enterprise is threatened with failure, but such an action is not unlike board decisions to replace executives of other corporations.[30]

Finding Venture Capitalists

Most venture capitalists do not advertise in the Yellow Pages. They remain private, and although they are located throughout the country, they are clustered in major cities like New York, Chicago, Boston, San Francisco, Washington, DC, and Dallas. In addition, major accounting firms and securities brokers are involved as venture capitalists or have access to them. Companies such as Ernst & Young, Arthur Andersen, Price Waterhouse, and Deloitte & Touche have consulting divisions specifically created to assist entrepreneurs, and they are well networked with venture capitalists.[31]

Entrepreneurs can find venture capitalists through such trade associations as the National Venture Capital Association and the National Association of Small Business Investment Companies. Formal venture capital networks exist with ties in every state, and these are listed in *Pratt's Guide to Venture Capital Sources*, which is updated regularly.[32] State offices of the U.S. Small Business Administration keep track of well-known venture capitalists in their regions, and in many states, there are state-operated venture capital funds that are not only sources of funds themselves but also members of venture capital networks.

> **CHECKPOINT**
>
> Describe the venture capital industry and its investment criteria.
>
> Explain relationships between entrepreneurs and venture capitalists.

DEBT FINANCING

Small enterprises have fewer choices than large firms for obtaining debt financing. They are excluded from financial sources such as money raised through the sale of bonds, debentures, and commercial paper. Also, many small businesses are limited by their size; they are local enterprises with small inventories or markets that provide few assets for collateralizing loans. Small entrepreneurial ventures created with the intent to grow are still in their development stages and are risky; they have not yet established their performance or asset strength to underwrite substantial debt.[33]

Nevertheless, there are several important ways to obtain debt financing. Recall from our earlier descriptions of "managing assets" and "equity financing" that a variety of methods were explored for obtaining capital through loans or direct support from vendors, wholesalers, customers, and informal investors. We also described methods of using personal and business assets as leverage for financing start-up inventory, accounts receivable, equipment, and facilities. These are important, but they are predominately noninstitutional sources. In this section, we focus on *institutional* debt sources.

Commercial Banks

Most commercial loans are made to small businesses. This fact may be surprising, but nearly 90 percent of all commercial loans are made to businesses with less than $1 million in total assets. The remaining loans which are made to large enterprises, actually represent slightly more than half of the dollar value of all loans placed.[34] Although large firms get the lion's share of dollars, small businesses represent the vast majority of bankers' clients. Consequently, entrepreneurs have no reason to be shy about applying for bank loans.

Commercial banks provide *unsecured* and *secured* loans. An unsecured loan is a *personal* or *signature* loan that requires no collateral; the entrepreneur is granted the loan on the strength of his or her reputation.[35] Unsecured loans are usually small loans for several thousand dollars, but they can be quite useful for meeting emergency cash flow requirements such as paying wages or bills. Unsecured signature loans usually must be paid back within a year, and they will have high interest charges. Entrepreneurs also establish personal "lines of credit" through their banks, and these are treated in the same way as credit card accounts that must be paid down or cleared each month.

Secured loans are those with *security* pledged to the bank as assurance that the loan will be paid. There are many types of security a bank will consider, such as a *guarantor*—another credit-worthy person or company that agrees to pay the loan in the event the borrower defaults—but most security is in the form of tangible assets pledged as collateral. (Types of security for loans are shown in Exhibit 13-5.) Collateral is forfeited to satisfy debts when borrowers default, and most commercial loans fall into this category of so-called *asset-based lending*. Many loans can be secured through agreements that specifically tie debt to certain assets. We have mentioned a few of these earlier, such as inventory loans, accounts receivable loans, and equipment loans. When debt is collateralized by specific assets, only those assets can be attached or repossessed to satisfy the loan. Consequently, entrepreneurs prefer asset-based loans with specific security; car loans are usually written in this manner. On the other hand, bankers prefer to have a general lien against as many assets as possible, thus giving them greater protection against default and more assets to choose from in the event of default.

Most new ventures in the start-up phase lack performance records or assets to secure substantial loans, and lenders will require general liens against all tangible assets before writing a loan. In addition, they tend to write *short-term* loans with repayment periods of less than one year. Current assets such as inventory and receivables are seldom used to secure loans for longer than several months. The length of time depends, of course, on why the money is being borrowed and the collateral being offered. *Intermediate-term* loans are common for equipment, renovations, and furniture that have a limited useful life and are expected to depreciate rapidly. For example, intermediate-term loans are characteristically used to purchase computer systems, and the repayment period seldom exceeds three years. *Long-term* loans are those that can be repaid in more than one year, but the upper time limit varies according to the type of asset being collateralized. Most people and businesses can

Exhibit 13-5   **Types of Security and Collateral Used in Commercial Loans**

Type of Security	Description
Comaker	Individual who signs as secondary principal
Endorser	Individual who pledges to back loan
Guarantor	Individual who personally guarantees loan
Real property	Real estate, leaseholds, and land
Personal property	Items that have mortgage value such as stamp collections, coins, and antiques
Securities	Stock and bonds that can be pledged
Equipment	Capital assets that include machinery, computers, and instrumentation
Merchandise	Retail and wholesale products with market values as saleable items
Inventory	Other than merchandise: raw materials, partial assemblies, and finished goods
Accounts receivable	Items receipted as sold with verifiable credit outstanding
Vehicles	Equity in cars, vans, trucks, and moving transport equipment
Insurance policies	Cash surrender value of policies in effect

secure car loans for a period of three years; loans for recreational vehicles and commercial trucks can be secured for five years or longer. Real estate can be secured for a period between 10 and 25 years, although commercial bankers prefer real estate loans not to exceed 15 years.

Not all commercial banks are willing to loan to small businesses, even if the businesses have strong collateral. Large banks including Chase Manhattan, CitiCorp, and Chemical Bank of New York have historically avoided new ventures and small loans, yet many large institutions have recently created small-business lending divisions. In most instances, entrepreneurs must seek loans through community banks that make it their business to serve the small business sector. Community banks are independently chartered and serve local clients; consequently, they thrive on small businesses. There are more than 13,600 banks in the Federal Reserve system, and nearly 13,000 of them are community banks with deposits of less than $100 million. In addition, private banks with lower deposits represent 4,000 more local lenders that focus on small enterprise loans.

Finance Companies

There are three types of finance companies, and although all are asset-based lenders, each serves a different clientele. These are sales finance companies, consumer finance companies, and commercial finance companies. Figure 13-4 summarizes these companies.

Sales finance companies focus on loans for specific purchases like automobiles and farm machinery. On the surface, most of their customers are "end users," such as individuals who have their new cars financed through finance companies like General Motors Acceptance Corporation (GMAC).[36] In reality, most customers are the businesses through which the finance companies offer credit. This is a matter of perspective. For example, GMAC has agreements with GM dealers to provide automobile financing for dealers' customers. The individual car buyer only sees, or cares about, the ease of securing a GMAC loan, but GMAC is really financing the dealer, because GMAC takes loans thereby converting inventory (cars) into receivables (dealer receivables from GMAC), and these are converted rapidly to cash. Consequently, GMAC assumes the risk of financing sales, and the dealer enjoys liquidity. Sales finance companies also provide direct loans for their business clients. For example, GMAC will extend loans to dealers to replace inventory.

Consumer finance companies focus on short-term loans secured by personal assets, and most consumer loans are for small amounts at high rates of interest. These loans are typically negotiated directly between finance companies and consumers for purchases such as furniture, appliances, vacation trips, and home repairs. Consumer finance companies occasionally contract with retailers to finance their consumer purchases, and in doing so, emulate sales finance company operations. Because interest rates are high and terms of repayment short, entrepreneurs consider consumer finance companies as lenders of last resort.

Commercial finance companies are focused predominantly on small business and agricultural lending. Their primary business is making loans on commercial,

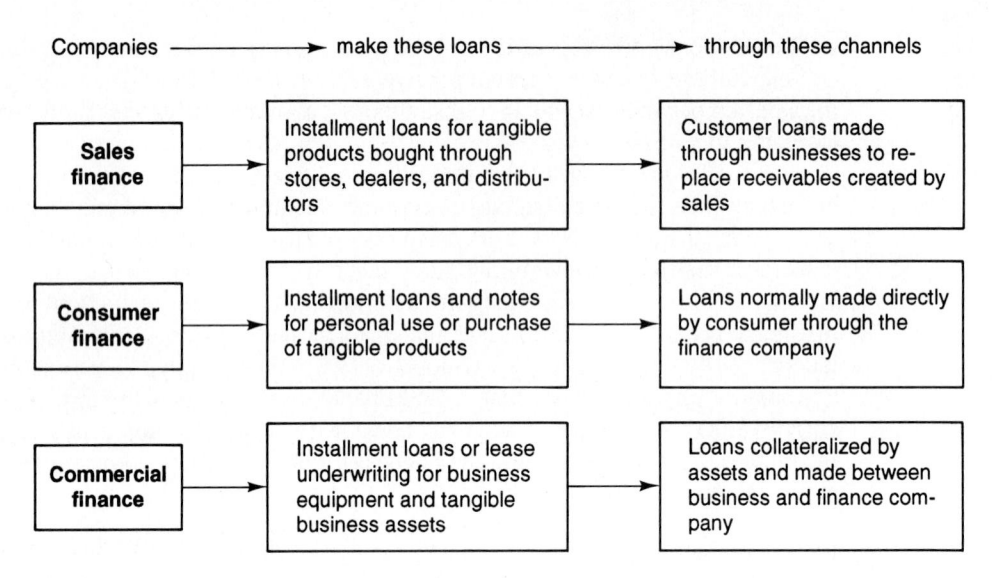

Companies	make these loans	through these channels
Sales finance	Installment loans for tangible products bought through stores, dealers, and distributors	Customer loans made through businesses to replace receivables created by sales
Consumer finance	Installment loans and notes for personal use or purchase of tangible products	Loans normally made directly by consumer through the finance company
Commercial finance	Installment loans or lease underwriting for business equipment and tangible business assets	Loans collateralized by assets and made between business and finance company

Figure 13-4 **Focus of Finance Company Activities**

industrial, and agricultural equipment. They also make loans under the SBA loan guarantee program, underwrite leasing companies, and provide factoring for inventory and accounts receivable. As a result, commercial finance companies play an important role in new venture financing. Most loans are written for intermediate terms of one to three years, and interest rates are low compared with other finance company rates. Loans are written according to the value of the asset being offered as collateral, and therefore most are low-risk loans.

Other Financial Sources

Insurance companies loan a portion of their funds to corporations for real estate development, mortgage underwriting, and building construction. They are seldom interested in small business loans under $1 million, yet some life insurance companies make smaller loans if the business venture fits into their overall investment portfolio. Savings and loan associations, originally chartered for loans restricted to real estate and certain consumer goods, now have wider latitude to compete with banks. Mutual savings banks, credit unions, franchise lenders such as the Money Store, and thrift institutions provide asset-based loans, second mortgages, and personal, unsecured loans for limited amounts.

▶ **CHECKPOINT**

Describe types of loans and their uses made by commercial banks.

Explain alternatives offered by different finance companies.

GOVERNMENT PROGRAMS

There are more than 300 federal government programs that annually provide a total of nearly $3.2 billion in direct loans, grants, subsidies, and loan guarantees to small businesses.[37] Clearly, we can only describe a few of these here, and our focus will be on the government agencies that account for a majority of small business assistance.

The Small Business Administration (SBA)

The SBA has provided approximately $2.7 billion in annual loan guarantees during the late 1980s. Congress curtailed SBA allocations for the early 1990s, and direct loans that previously accounted for more than $200 million in small business financing have been minimized. Nevertheless, SBA direct loans and loan guarantees remain important support programs for small business.[38]

Direct Loan Assistance. Direct loans are extremely restricted, yet there are loan participation programs in which the SBA works together with banks or through local agencies to provide financial support to several dozen categories of qualified borrowers. These include handicapped persons, disabled veterans, and small business owners who have suffered from natural disasters such as floods or hurricanes. Loans are also made to help small businesses comply with federal air-and-water pollution regulations, occupational safety and health requirements, and relocation in compliance with federal actions such as highway construction or closing of military bases. These participation loans are called *Economic Opportunity Loans (EOL)*, and they are handled through commercial banks or qualified lenders. Entrepreneurs cannot approach the SBA directly for loan assistance; however, lenders certified by the SBA have special divisions with loan officers experienced in small business applications.

SBA-Guaranteed Loans. Loans guaranteed by the SBA are the prominent means of financial assistance from the federal government. Entrepreneurs apply for commercial loans through banks or qualified lending institutions in the usual manner, and only after their applications are turned down can they ask for SBA assistance. Normally, this process is handled by the lending institutions that rejected the loan applications. The purpose is to help those small businesses that cannot obtain loans through the usual methods. The SBA application is processed by the bank, and if it is successful, the SBA informs the bank that it will guarantee the loan, specifying the amount to be guaranteed and the rate of interest the bank can charge. The SBA can guarantee up to 90 percent of a loan amount or $750,000, whichever is less. Consequently, the SBA does not make the loan but only reduces the bank's risk of making the loan. As a concession, the bank must agree to a slightly lower interest rate than it might normally charge.

Qualifying for an SBA-guaranteed loan requires that the borrower meet the criteria for being classified as a small business. These criteria are usually not difficult to meet for young ventures with few employees and limited sales. As a general rule, any business will qualify if it has fewer than 25 employees and if its sales do not exceed $1 million; manufacturers and health service enterprises can qualify as long as they have fewer than 500 employees. However, SBA guidelines include numerous exemptions. Construction companies, for example, can qualify without an employment ceiling as long as annual sales do not exceed $6 million.

Borrowers also must have appropriate collateral as security; the SBA does not accept unsecured applications. Collateral includes assets normally considered as security by lenders, including real estate, machinery, inventory, equipment, personal property, and receivables. The SBA will also consider as security cosigned endorsements by guarantors. These are evaluated by the SBA in the same manner as they are evaluated by commercial lenders. The application must be accompanied by cash-flow projections and several other documents together with a description of how the business will use loan proceeds. A summary of SBA application requirements is shown in Exhibit 13-6.

If the loan is approved, the SBA will restrict the use of the money. For example, SBA loans cannot be used to purchase real estate, repay past-due executive salaries, consolidate personal liabilities, or satisfy shareholder claims; they are meant to underwrite operations or business expansion. As a result, the ability of the business to generate cash flow to repay the loan is the single most important consideration in the loan application.

Exhibit 13-6   Items That Must Be Addressed in an SBA Loan Application

1. Applicant information	Names of owners, background, addresses, business name, date started, legal ID, and other relevant personal history
2. Management of business	Names, personal data on managers
3. Use of loan proceeds	Description of how loan will be used in business operations
4. Collateral pledged	Itemized list of all business and personal assets to secure the loan
5. Disclosures	Descriptions of existing or previous government financing, personal and business debts, family members with SBA, police records, bankruptcies, insolvencies, and lawsuits
6. Personal history	Statement to support disclosure
7. Personal balance sheet	Balance sheet on borrower(s)
8. Financial statements	Cash flow, income, and sources-and-uses-of-funds statements
9. Business description	Brief executive summary or statement of business venture
10. Résumés and cosigners	Résumés of owners, managers, and all cosigners
11. Equipment and assets	List of business equipment and assets whether pledged or not
12. Investors' interests	Statement of financial interests by any customer, vendor, or contractor with whom business is conducted
13. Other interests	Franchise or subsidiary intentions
14. Declination letters	Refusal letters by lenders on formal loan applications

The Small Business Innovation Research Program (SBIR)

Perhaps one of the most exciting opportunities for small businesses is participation in the federally funded Small Business Innovation Research Program (SBIR).[39] Originally funded by the National Science Foundation in 1979 as a limited experiment, the SBIR Program gained congressional backing in 1982 under the Small Business Innovation Development Act. Today, the SBIR Program allocates in excess of $50 million annually to businesses with proposals for developing scientific innovations. Total funding for SBIRs now exceeds $1 billion to nearly 8,000 small businesses.

The SBIR Program has three phases. Phase I is a grant award of up to $50,000 for the purpose of investigating the feasibility of an innovation. An award recipient has six months to create a feasibility plan that can include conducting laboratory tests, building prototypes, doing market research, and developing a feasibility report. At the end of six months, the report is reviewed, and if it seems feasible, a Phase II award of up to $500,000 can be awarded for operating expenses. Entrepreneurs have two years to complete Phase II development operations, which can include further testing, market research, limited production, and other essential developmental activities. At the end of this period, a complete report must enumerate how the business spent its money and what results were achieved. Phase III is not a funded stage of the program; however, federal agencies who have supported SBIR grants usually support successful projects by helping entrepreneurs to find private financing and by providing assistance to commercialize their innovations.

Qualifying for SBIR grants is a competitive process.[40] More than 8,000 proposals are received each year with fewer than 1,000 grants approved. Under the Small Business Innovation Development Act, applicants must be independently owned companies with 500 or fewer employees and be able to demonstrate capability for scientific or technological research. Through the first eight years of SBIR grants, award recipients have had, on average, fewer than 35 employees with nearly half of all initial Phase I awards going to companies with fewer than 10 employees. Unlike most other government programs, the SBIR is a *grant program*. Entrepreneurs are given operating money, not loans or loan guarantees, and there is no assumption of repayment. On the other hand, SBIR funds are carefully monitored, and recipients are thoroughly screened.

Industrial Development Bonds (IDBs)

Industrial development bonds are tax-exempt bonds issued through a local municipality or nonprofit corporation that serves as an intermediary for funding economic expansion.[41] Businesses can apply for IDBs to purchase plant, production equipment, or commercial facilities such as hotels, recreation centers, and industrial parks. There are few restrictions on the types of projects that can qualify for IDBs except that state and municipal agencies that allocate funds are strongly interested in ventures that enhance economic activity.

Used for long-term financing, IDBs are awarded to businesses through local authorities. The bonds are, in effect, low-interest direct loans, and applicants have to demonstrate how their projects will enhance employment, improve local business development, or increase economic activity. The money for IDBs comes from a complicated reallocation process that involves federal, state, and local authorities, and although there are more applicants than can be funded, the IDB program has underwritten more than $6 billion in projects.

Other Government Programs

Entrepreneurs can find financial assistance through many programs other than those designated for small businesses.[42] The Farmers Home Administration (FmHA), for example, provides guaranteed long-term loans for rural development. These loans are limited to applicants who reside in cities or rural areas with less than 50,000 population, and although FmHA is viewed as a "farmer's program," it exists to help any rural enterprise with start-up working capital, equipment purchases, and expansion. The Department of Housing and Urban Development (HUD) provides loans and grants for rehabilitation of blighted city areas. Unlike FmHA, HUD operates predominantly in metropolitan areas, and HUD funds are administered through local authorities. Entrepreneurs have used HUD funds for remodeling downtown stores, refurbishing historic sites, and converting older buildings for residential and commercial uses.

The Department of the Interior offers "preservation grants" for historic building restoration. Consequently, entrepreneurs who want to open antique stores or similar businesses that would complement historic sites may find enthusiastic support from the Department of the Interior. Another grant-based program, offered through the Department of Energy, provides direct funding for innovations in energy conservation. These grants do not have to be repaid, and the DOE is eager to support new developments in water conservation techniques, cogeneration for electric power, geothermal exploration, pollution control innovations, building techniques for solar power utilization, and so on.

At state and local levels, program funding is available through economic development agencies, municipal development projects, and private development companies. For example, State Business and Industrial Development Corporations (SBIDCs), funded through state governments, make long-term loans for capital equipment and small business expansion. These SBIDC loans are arranged through lenders, and regulations vary from state to state, but, in general, they are targeted to small enterprises capable of enhancing economic growth within the state.

For entrepreneurs involved in foreign trade, there are several federal programs and agencies that actively support international expansion by small businesses. The Export-Import Bank (Eximbank) provides several types of insurance for underwriting exports, thereby reducing the risk by domestic firms selling goods to developing countries.[43] The Eximbank also provides working capital for small ventures to finance operations or to procure materials and equipment needed for manufacturing products. The State Department has export-support programs, grants for overseas economic

PROFILE △

The Small Business Credit Program of Eximbank

The Small Business Credit Program covers loans made to finance capital goods and services of U.S. small business exporters. The Eximbank enables U.S. banks to offer medium-term fixed-rate export loans through Eximbank guarantees that effectively eliminate the loan risks. Banks are assured of repayment, and the small business exporter is provided low-interest, fixed-rate capital to pursue foreign markets.

Commercial banks that provide export financing face several risks that are removed by the Small Business Credit Program. First, bankers cannot make sufficient loans for medium or long terms without risking the possibility that costs of money (rates they pay) will accelerate before the loans are repaid. Second, with few exceptions, foreign exchange rates fluctuate, thereby increasing the risk to the borrower, and subsequently to the lender. Third, many foreign buyers simply default on payments.

Entrepreneurs benefit from having insured loans and immediate cash flow without risks of buyer default or foreign exchange fluctuation. Loans can be written for as long as five years, and the interest rate is determined by an Eximbank classification system. Borrowers must qualify as small businesses under SBA guidelines, and guarantees cover up to 85 percent of the export contract value.

Source: U.S. Department of Commerce, *A Basic Guide to Exporting* (Washington, DC: U.S. Government Printing Office, 1986), pp. 46–47.

---

development, and special departments for helping establish foreign markets. Also, the United States Agency for International Development (USAID) directly sponsors companies involved in overseas projects, but USAID is concentrated in high-priority development regions such as the Caribbean and less-developed African countries where they encourage enterprise development.[44]

> ▶ **CHECKPOINT**
>
> Describe the SBA loan guarantee program and how entrepreneurs can qualify for SBA assistance.
>
> Explain how the SBIR program can benefit entrepreneurs.
>
> Describe other assistance such as IDBs, FmHA loans, and Eximbank aid.

SYNOPSIS FOR LEARNING

1. *Explain how financing is influenced by effective asset management.*

Underwriting assets creates liabilities; consequently, with the exception of cash, having too many unproductive assets creates burdensome liabilities that require financing. Stocking large inventories or allowing accounts receivable to accumulate threatens cash flow. Idle facilities or equipment create unnecessary costs. Prior to start-up, entrepreneurs can reduce financial burdens by planning assets carefully. In many instances, inventory can be "staged," receivables can be controlled through credit policies, and equipment can be leased rather than purchased. Real estate can also be leased or purchased, but merchandisers might consider creative ways to gain access to customers such as subleasing space in large stores. The key is to "gain access" to assets while minimizing financing.

2. *Describe alternative methods of financing ventures with equity.*

Personal sources of equity capital include individual cash and near-cash assets, family investments, and equity from close friends. Informal risk capital is obtained from wealthy individuals who seek high-risk ventures for small investments. These personal and informal equity sources can be enhanced through various forms of partnerships and small corporate formations. Privately placed securities are those sold to outside investors, but not through public channels regulated by the SEC. Private placements have several definitions that limit stockholders and their qualifications. Equity can also be obtained through SBA-backed Small Business Investment Corporations (SBICs) and Minority Enterprise SBICs. Venture capital is an important source of investment that is provided by private organizations, corporate venture units, and institutional capital groups. Going public through an initial public offering (IPO) is a major change for entrepreneurs as they seek public securities underwriting

3. *Explore the role of venture capital in new venture financing.*

Venture capitalists provide equity capital to high-risk ventures caught in a financing gap during their early development periods. This gap exists because small businesses usually can find debt and equity to finance their start-up and early growth periods, and when they accumulate substantial sales or assets, they can attract large-scale financing or go public. Between these extremes, financing is difficult to obtain. Venture capitalists invest in young ventures caught in this gap with average placements of about $865,000. Venture capitalists also provide personal support, access to new markets, technical and research assistance, and channels to needed resources. They expect high returns on investments, but these are justified by the high risk in new ventures.

4. *Describe sources of debt financing for new and expanding ventures.*

Commercial banks provide the most common form of debt financing through small business loans. These are usually asset-based loans requiring collateral; however, banks often make personal "unsecured" loans to help entrepreneurs meet short-term cash flow requirements. Finance companies also make direct loans, but in most instances, finance companies are lenders of last resort. A major exception is the "commercial" finance company that make loans on specific assets such as machinery and equipment. A variety of lenders help small businesses, including mutual savings banks, credit unions, franchise lenders, and thrift institutions.

5. *Explain how the SBA and other government agencies assist in financing.*

The Small Business Administration is the most active federal agency in assisting small businesses. Loans guaranteed by the SBA are the prevalent means of obtaining government support, but direct loan assistance is available under certain programs. The Small Business Innovation Research Program (SBIR) provides direct grants to businesses engaged in scientific development. With an SBIR Phase I grant, entrepreneurs are provided up to $50,000 for development feasibility plans; Phase II grants can be as much as $500,000 for commercialization of their innovations. Industrial Development Bonds provide low-interest loans for projects that result in economic progress in a specific area. Other government programs exist under the Farmers Home Administration, Department of Housing and Urban Development, Department of the Interior, and Department of Energy. State and local economic development programs and federally sponsored international programs such as the Eximbank are also important sources of financial assistance.

NOTES

1. Glenn A. Welsch, Ronald W. Hilton, and Paul N. Gordon, *Budgeting: Profit Planning and Control*, 5th ed. (Englewood Cliffs, NJ: Prentice-Hall, 1988), pp. 394–400.
2. David F. Groebner and C. Mike Merz, "Solving the Inventory Problem for the Sale of Seasonal Merchandise," *Journal of Small Business Management*, Vol. 28, No. 3 (1990), pp. 19–26.
3. "Guidelines for Small Business Loans," *Bank Line*, policy notice from Dominion Bank Services, Inc., Richmond, Virginia (1990), p. 2.
4. Lowell E. Stockstill, Sharon L. Dietz, and Wayne O. Maurer, "A Cash Flow Focus for Small Business," *Journal of Business and Entrepreneurship*, Vol. 1, No. 2 (1989), pp. 45–55.
5. Leo R. Cheatham, J. Paul Dunn, and Carole B. Cheatham, "Working Capital Financing and Cash Flow in the Small Business," *Journal of Business and Entrepreneurship*, Vol. 1, No. 2 (1989), pp. 1–12.
6. Lawrence Finley, *Entrepreneurial Strategies: Text and Cases* (Boston: PWS-Kent, 1990), pp. 202–203.
7. *Financing Your Business: Guide for Smaller Businesses and Entrepreneurs* (New York: Price Waterhouse, 1984), p. 24.
8. Charles O. Conrad, President, Cloverleaf Shopping Center and Conrad Investment Corporation, Harrisonburg, VA, personal communication, January 1991.
9. Kathleen Deveny, "Can Ms. Fashion Bounce Back?" *Business Week*, January 16, 1989, pp. 64–70.
10. Brett Kingstone, *The Dynamos: Who Are They Anyway?* (New York: John Wiley & Sons, 1987), pp. 217–223.
11. James W. Henderson, *Obtaining Venture Financing: Principles and Practices* (Lexington, MA: D. C. Heath, 1988), p. 242.
12. *Financing Your Business: Guide for Smaller Businesses and Entrepreneurs* (New York: Price Waterhouse, 1984), p. 11.

13. William E. Wetzel, Jr., "Informal Risk Capital: Knowns and Unknowns," in Donald L. Sexton and Raymond W. Smilor, eds., *The Art and Science of Entrepreneurship* (Cambridge, MA: Ballinger, 1986), pp. 85–108.

14. Robert D. Hisrich and A. D. Jankowicz, "Intuition in Venture Capital Decisions: An Exploratory Study Using a New Technique," *Journal of Business Venturing*, Vol. 5, No. 1 (1990), pp. 49–62.

15. Securities and Exchange Commission, Director of Economic and Policy Analysis, *Analysis of Regulation D* (Washington, DC: U.S. Government Printing Office, 1988).

16. Entrepreneur, Inc., American Entrepreneurs Association, *Entrepreneur's Guide to Business Start-ups* (Irvine, CA: Entrepreneur, Inc., 1990), pp. 148–149.

17. *The Small Business Investment Act*, Section 301(d) (Washington, DC: U.S. Government Printing Office, 1989). Also U.S. Department of Commerce, *A Directory of Federal Government Assistance Programs for Women Business Owners* (Washington, DC: U.S. Small Business Administration, 1988), pp. 16–19.

18. Joel Corman, Ben Perles, Andrew Catalan, and Shawmut Bank, "The Initial Public Offering: A Financing Option for Small Business," *Journal of Business and Entrepreneurship*, Vol. 1, No. 2 (1989), pp. 81–93.

19. Ibid., p. 82.

20. Richard B. Robinson, Jr., "Emerging Strategies in the Venture Capital Industry," *Journal of Business Venturing*, Vol. 2, No. 1 (1987), pp. 53–77.

21. David J. Brophy and Mark W. Guthner, "Publicly Traded Venture Capital Funds: Implications for Institutional 'Fund of Funds' Investors," *Journal of Business Venturing*, Vol. 3, No. 3 (1988), pp. 187–206. Also Robin Siegel, Eric Siegel, and Ian C. MacMillan, "Corporate Venture Capitalists: Autonomy, Obstacles, and Performance," *Journal of Business Venturing*, Vol. 3, No. 3 (1988), pp. 233–247.

22. John B. Maier II and David A. Walker, "The Role of Venture Capital in Financing Small Business," *Journal of Business Venturing*, Vol. 2, No. 3 (1987), pp. 207–214.

23. *Raising Venture Capital: An Entrepreneur's Guidebook* (New York: Deloitte Haskins & Sells, 1989), pp. 3–5.

24. Siegel, Siegel, and MacMillan, "Corporate Venture Capitalists," pp. 233–247.

25. Hollister B. Sykes, "Corporate Venture Capital: Strategies for Success," *Journal of Business Venturing*, Vol. 5, No. 1 (1990), pp. 37–47.

26. Maier and Walker, "The Role of Venture Capital," pp. 207–214.

27. Henderson, *Obtaining Venture Financing*, pp. 264–266.

28. Hisrich and Jankowicz, "Intuition in Venture Capital Decisions," pp. 49–62.

29. Arthur Lipper III, *Investing in Private Companies* (Homewood, IL: Dow Jones–Irwin, 1984), pp. 155–158.

30. Ibid., pp. 140–141. Also *Financing Your Business*, pp. 13–14.

31. David J. Brophy, "Venture Capital Research," in Sexton and Smilor, eds., *The Art and Science of Entrepreneurship*, pp. 119–143.

32. Stanley E. Pratt and Jane K. Morris, *Pratt's Guide to Venture Capital Sources*, 11th ed. (Washington, DC: Unipub, 1989).

33. Henderson, *Obtaining Venture Financing*, p. 275.

34. Ibid., p. 276.

35. Finley, *Entrepreneurial Strategies*, pp. 204–205.

36. General Motors Corporation, "Consolidated Report to Stockholders," *Annual Report*, 1988, pp. 1, 16.

37. U.S. Department of Commerce, Economic Development Administration, *Guide to Federal Assistance Programs* (Washington, DC: U.S. Government Printing Office, 1989), pp. 1–4, 17, 22–35.

38. U.S. Small Business Administration, *Fact Sheet* (Washington, DC: SBA Office of Advocacy, 1990), pp. 1–2.

39. Henderson, *Obtaining Venture Financing*, pp. 287–288.

40. Ibid., p. 287. Also *The States and Small Business: Programs and Activities* (Washington, DC: SBA Office of Advocacy, 1986), pp. 1–3, 12.

41. Office of Economy Development, State of Virginia, Richmond, personal communication, January 1990.

42. U.S. Department of Commerce, Economic Development Administration, *Guide to Federal Assistance Programs* (Washington, DC: U.S. Government Printing Office, 1989). Also *The States and Small Business: Programs and Activities* (Washington, DC: SBA Office of Advocacy, 1986).

43. Alfred C. Holden, "The Eximbank State/City Pilot Initiative for Small Business Exporters: Goals, Achievements and the Path Ahead for Export-Finance Support at the Local Level," *Journal of Small Business Strategy*, Vol. 1, No. 1 (1990), pp. 25–36.

44. Export-Import Bank of the United States, *Financing and Insuring Exports: A User's Guide to Eximbank and FCIA Programs* (Washington, DC: Eximbank, 1988).

CASE 13-1

To Lease or Not: A Cash Flow Question

Goudreau Corporation of Danvers, Massachusetts, specializes in marine projects such as bridge and pier construction. Most of the company's projects are contracted with government agencies. These range from small municipal bridges to state and federal pier and dockage facilities. The company's founder, Henry Goudreau, faced a severe financing problem several years ago when government contracts began requiring 90 percent surety bonding by contractors. In effect, a contractor had to show $90 in liquid assets for every $100 in a contract bid. Bidders that could not demonstrate this liquidity were disqualified from government contracts. The majority of small businesses could not meet this requirement, and at the time, Goudreau, with only $2 million in sales, faced elimination from his primary market.

The company was profitable and had a very good line of credit used to buy operating equipment. When the crisis occurred in 1987, Goudreau had about $200,000 tied up in trucks, machinery, and office computers. Also, his sales forecast indicated a strong likelihood for $5 million in sales by 1990, perhaps doubling by 1995, and such a level of activity would require more than a million dollars in new equipment for engineering design work, trucks, and construction machinery.

The question was how to underwrite new equipment while also increasing the liquid assets required to be a qualified bidder for government contracts. Several options came to mind for Goudreau.

First, he could sell all his existing equipment to someone looking for a capital investment, then lease it back at a monthly payment that would make a profit for the investor. This plan would erase his fixed assets and his long-term liabilities from company records. He estimated that this type of deal would cost him a premium of about 15 percent payable through the leases to attract investors.

Second, he could sell off the equipment and lease new equipment from an equipment leasing company. This approach would have the same effect as finding a private buy-leaseback arrangement, but it would open a channel for more equipment needed in the future, and the premium would be an interest payment of perhaps 14 percent. On the other hand, he would lose the tax advantage of depreciation on all equipment because he would not own it.

A third option suggested by a commercial finance company was to create a "capital lease" with them. A capital lease is a contract lease in which the lessee takes title to the equipment at the end of the lease. Consequently, the equipment is carried on the company books, is depreciated, and is an expense for tax purposes. The commercial finance company would charge higher interest rates than the implied premium in a straight "operating lease," but the interest would be deductible. The capital lease would require no down payment, and it would be treated as a loan, thereby preserving cash liquidity.

A fourth option was to rely on conventional loans, as the company had done in the past, thereby keeping its tax advantages on equipment and a relatively low interest rate of about 11 percent. Loan payments would also be lower than lease payments spread out over a slightly longer period. Unfortunately, this choice would not solve the liquidity problem, but with the larger asset base, perhaps the company could attract equity investors through private stock placements.

To resolve the immediate crisis, Goudreau elected to sell a majority of his equipment and replace it with operating leases. He arranged the leases with equipment leasing companies rather than commercial finance companies or bank lenders, at premiums that approached 14 percent. This move increased his immediate liquidity and allowed the company to win nearly $5 million in contracts during the following three years. Profits, however, were squeezed by the added cash flow, and Goudreau was still faced with finding ways to finance expansion while maintaining the delicate balance of liquidity required in his business.

CASE QUESTIONS

1. Describe the advantages and disadvantages of obtaining leases on equipment identified in the case. What should be considered in lease decisions?
2. If the company elected to use equipment loans, what sources are available, and what are the advantages and disadvantages of asset-based loans?
3. Describe the options available for attracting private equity to solve the liquidity problem.

Sources: Don Nichols, "For Sale or Rent, No Money Down," *Venture*, April 1989, pp. 54–55. Also Howard E. Van Auken and Richard B. Carter, "Acquisition of Capital by Small Business," *Journal of Small Business Management*, Vol. 27, No. 2 (1989), pp. 1–9.

CASE 13-2

Public-Sector Programs Address Seed Capital

Seed capital is always difficult to arrange, and it is particularly difficult for entrepreneurs who market unusual products or who have no track record to justify conventional underwriting. Recognizing this problem, public funds are being made available through several states to help new ventures. As we entered the 1990s, at least 11 states had substantial investment funds earmarked for seeding new ventures, and 14 others were considering tax-based funds or legislated control of state pension funds for this purpose.

Jack Keester is one entrepreneur who benefitted from Nebraska's seed capital fund. Keester had developed a new power transmission process for making electrical energy more efficient. The complex technology was not understandable to conventional lenders, and investors felt the company would be too risky.

The state, however, invested $500,000 in Keester's plan in exchange for a 35 percent equity position. That was in 1987, and Keester's company, Addax, Inc., posted $700,000 in sales by 1989, proving his system effective and salable. Consequently, Addax was positioned for growth well into the 1990s, and investors put several million dollars into the company.

Similar seed capital risks have occurred elsewhere, and in Iowa, the state has poured $4.2 million into 36 new ventures since 1983. Connecticut uses a state-supported limited-partnership fund to invest in new ventures. Michigan takes a different approach by underwriting bank loans through tax-supported insurance, and West Virginia provides a 50 percent tax credit on qualified ventures. State officials who administer funds are not reluctant to help small ventures, but they tend to be more enthusiastic about entrepreneurs who have been able to attract support from other conventional or government programs.

Cheryl Mann, for example, was able to obtain an economic development grant from Virginia to establish her mushroom food-processing company in a southern rural area of the state. Mann had previously qualified for an SBA loan through the Minority Enterprise program to fund her first-year operations. When the money ran low, Mann demonstrated that her idea was still feasible, and although she had no collateral assets for extended credit, she convinced state authorities that the business would be economically viable and provide additional employment in her area.

Consider the situation of Maury Brown of Tallahassee, Florida. Brown developed an unusual method of refrigerating a small "icehouse" that could be used for storing up to 4 tons of fish. His idea was to have stand-alone small refrigerated units that served as icehouses for rural fishing villages. Brown had come to Florida from his home in the Virgin Islands, where commercial fishermen often could not get their catches iced down soon enough to prevent spoilage. The small icehouses could be located in villages or on outer islands where electricity was nonexistent or unreliable. Brown's "iceboxes" had very little actual ice, but consisted of cooling elements that could create a frost on fresh fish. The system was operated through solar cells and storage batteries. When Brown applied for an SBIR grant in 1989, he was initially turned down, but a Florida business assistance councillor suggested that he should apply for a development grant from the state and also look into federal programs that could help Brown introduce his product in developing Caribbean economies.

CASE QUESTIONS

1. Identify and describe government-sponsored finance programs that Brown could consider to develop his icebox.
2. Brown and Mann are both minorities. Identify their options for state or federal support that could be beneficial. Aside from minority issues, Mann also has an unusual business. What federal assistance is available to help her with loans or business development?
3. Research your state programs and describe assistance available for new ventures or small business beyond those identified in the text.

Sources: Abby Livingston, "State Capital," *Venture*, May 1989, pp. 57–62; case scenario on Cheryl Mann courtesy of Cheryl Mann and the Augusta County Department of Economic Development, Augusta County, Virginia; SBIR review on Maury Brown courtesy of Maury Brown, January 1991.

Chapter 14

Managing Growth and Transition

OBJECTIVES

1. Describe the organizational life cycle for an entrepreneurial venture.
2. Contrast entrepreneurial roles during various transition stages.
3. Explain growth and diversification as strategic issues for new ventures.
4. Explore the concept of an entrepreneurial career.

New ventures pass through transitional stages that present new challenges to their founders. These transitional stages are represented by an organizational life cycle. Our attention throughout this book has been focused on establishing a new venture, which is the first stage of the organizational life cycle. We have also addressed later stages of growth when an enterprise goes public or begins to diversify globally. In this chapter, we are concerned with changes that occur between these extremes, when established ventures grow, mature, and, in many cases, decline. As we shall see, there are several important challenges facing entrepreneurs during these transition stages.

The organizational life cycle requires changes in entrepreneurial behavior, and because many entrepreneurs cannot adapt to new role responsibilities, their ventures can fail or be terminated. In some instances, the venture survives but the entrepreneur is ousted. Consequently, there are many issues to consider for successfully managing ventures during their transition from embryonic to mature organizations. This concluding chapter will also address the concept of an entrepreneurial career, building on the challenges that face entrepreneurs as they start and nourish new ventures.

THE ORGANIZATION LIFE CYCLE

The **organization life cycle** follows a well-known pattern of early growth, rapid growth, maturity, and decline. Management textbooks illustrate the cycle with a graphic curve similar to the one in Figure 14-1. During the initial development period, a company with a successful innovation can be expected to experience slow growth. This period is followed by one of rapid growth, which varies in both intensity and duration as a company expands its customer base and product line. At some point, the company's products or services meet rigorous competition that moderates growth, and as markets become saturated, maturity is reached. For many enterprises, this stage is followed by a period of decline, which, if not reversed, will result in termination. The life cycle is a general representation of what a company can experience in the long run, but more important is how entrepreneurs perceive their roles during life-cycle transitions.

The Entrepreneur's Perspective

A modified life cycle in Exhibit 14-1 describes transition stages for entrepreneurial ventures. In this model, the life cycle is identified with five stages: *start-up*, *expansion*, *consolidation*, *revival*, and *decline*. These are explained in terms of three variables: *growth*, *product/market definition*, and *organization*.[1] As the venture progresses from one stage to the next, conditions change, requiring different decisions for managing growth, developing products and markets, and organizing the company.

Start-up Stage. During the start-up stage, growth is inconsistent. Sales seldom meet a founder's expectations, and they can occur haphazardly. In extreme circum-

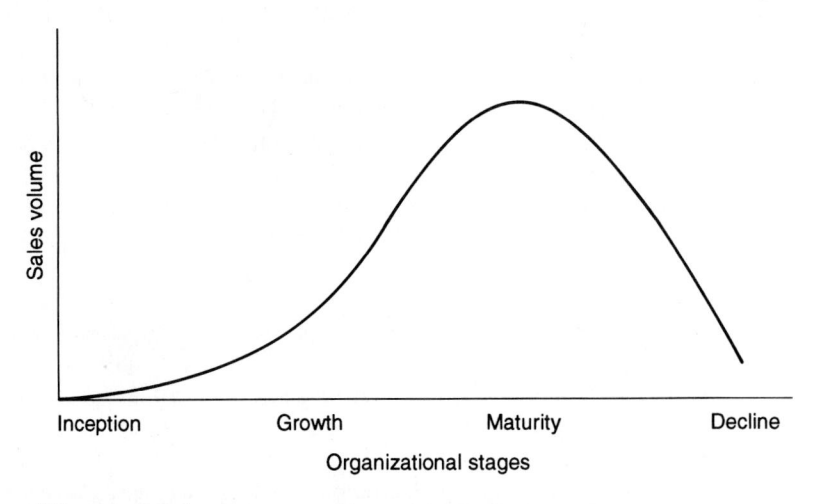

Figure 14-1 **The Organizational Life Cycle**

Exhibit 14-1 The Entrepreneur's Perspective of an Organizational Life Cycle

Stages in the Life Cycle

Variables	Start-up	Expansion	Consolidation	Revival	Decline
Growth	Slow and inconsistent	Rapid	Slow or dormant	Rapid	Negative
Product/market definition	Single product or market or both	Multiple products or markets or both	Limited new products in specific market niches	Innovative products positioned in high-potential markets	Obsolete products with little or no potential
Organization	Founder is the organization	Functional specialists with some delegation	Structured divisions with strong staff and tight control	Special divisions focused on products and markets	Inefficient or bureaucratic structure

Source: Adapted from Steven H. Hanks, "The Organization Life Cycle: Integrating Content and Process," *Journal of Small Business Strategy*, Vol. 1, No. 1 (1990), pp. 1–12.

stances, markets will be chaotic with exciting spurts and disappointing sputters. This chaos can absorb entrepreneurs in daily struggles to survive. In the worst-case scenario, markets may be dormant, leaving the entrepreneur bewildered. Inconsistent growth does not provide a pattern of sales to help guide an entrepreneur's decisions. Although products and services are usually targeted to narrow market niches, confusion persists. During this initial stage, entrepreneurs modify their products, change distribution systems, alter services, and experiment with marketing tactics in an attempt to survive; they are "fighting fires" every day.

Consequently, the organization is centralized, and authority is vested in one person or a very small team of founders. Decision making and the founders' personal preferences are undifferentiated. The venture's objectives also are undifferentiated from those of the founders. The organization is therefore a personal expression of a single entrepreneur or a few partners. It follows that the psychological characteristics of founders largely determine how the venture progresses through the start-up stage.

More than half of all new ventures do not have business plans prior to their start-up period; founders merely "press on" with their ideas, relying on intuition and personal skills to create business inertia.[2] This statistic may allow some insight into the question of why there is a high mortality rate among new ventures during the start-up stage. Unfortunately, few entrepreneurs of failed ventures can be studied; they quietly disappear or find new challenges. Successful founders, however, reinforce the characteristics profiled in Chapters 1 and 2 of determined, optimistic, and energetic entrepreneurs who have the vision and foresight to struggle through start-up difficulties.

Debbi Fields, founder of Mrs. Fields Cookies, started with one product and no plan other than to offer delicious cookies to the public through a neat little mall store.[3] The only thing on her mind at start-up was to have a little fun while surviving the test of "doing her own thing." At times, she had to stroll through the mall with a tray of cookies, hawking her wares like a street vendor. Her charm and marketing wit saved the venture, yet it was not until she and her husband Randy Fields developed a long-term strategy for expansion and manging the venture that growth ensued. Debbi Fields began with a simple objective to have an interesting little business; she made the transition to managing a corporate network of stores with more than $100 million in sales (see the accompanying profile).

Domino's Pizza founder Thomas S. Monaghan started with a family restaurant in a Michigan suburb.[4] During the 1960s, Domino's remained a family business with little growth. Family members were interested in a small business that provided income and the autonomy of ownership apart from traditional jobs in local automotive factories. They did not envision generating millions of dollars or creating a nationwide enterprise. Monaghan, however, had other ideas, and Domino's pizza-delivery system was launched. That event occurred after a decade in the family business, yet it signaled a major transition fostered by the vision and somewhat controversial objectives of its founder.

Domino's experience is characteristic of family-owned businesses where family objectives clash with the aspirations of a particular member. If family priorities override those of the lead entrepreneur, the business may survive start-up problems but never grow beyond the stage of early expansion. If family continuity is important,

PROFILE △

Debbi Fields

Holding control over a global chain of retail stores, manufacturing, distribution systems, and a corporate business exceeding $100 million with several divisions might take a scaled-down version of General Motors to operate—if it were run by traditional managers. This is not the case for Debbi Fields, the fashionable founder of Mrs. Fields Cookies. With codirector and husband Randy, Debbi Fields orchestrates a 120-member staff through information systems, hands-on site visits, personal motivation, and effective delegation to retail managers. Having heard that entrepreneurs "lose control" and lose their businesses, the Fields resolved to build a personal enterprise that retained that close-touch service and spirit of independence without losing control or losing the business. With a net 18 percent profit margin and a 15 percent growth rate in sales, there seems to be more than a secret recipe in Mrs. Fields' success.

Source: Tom Richman, "Mrs. Fields' Secret Ingredient," *Inc.*, October 1987, pp. 65–72.

---

family members often adapt to organizational roles. If a growth orientation prevails, however, then the family business is dissolved. Family members usually lack the skills to accept functional responsibilities required in a more complex organization. Business continuity is disrupted as the small venture is transformed into an expanded organization.[5]

Expansion Stage. During the expansion stage, rapid growth results in a pattern of success that is useful for evaluating market position and new-product potential. The venture is transformed from a single-line enterprise operating in a limited market to a multiline company penetrating new markets, as shown in Figure 14-2. Product and service lines are broadened through innovation and development, and the organization expands through functional authority. Decision making may be centralized during early growth, but departmentalization ensues, leading to a dispersion of authority. To meet these challenges, entrepreneurs must enlarge the enterprise and delegate authority for functional coordination.

Entering the expansion stage marks a critical turning point, and as the examples of Debbi Fields and Thomas Monaghan suggest, entrepreneurs must be able to accept leadership roles quite different from their founding roles. One such role requires leadership vision evidenced through a higher level of effort or aggressiveness. The entrepreneur must set this pace through strategic implementation of well-defined plans, and consequently one of the transition requirements is to become a competent planner. As noted earlier, although more than half of all start-up enterprises have no formal business plans, nearly 85 percent of expanding ventures have well-articulated business

Start-up Stage

| Single product or restricted line of merchandise and services | → | Positioned to compete in one market or to serve limited clientele |

Expansion Stage

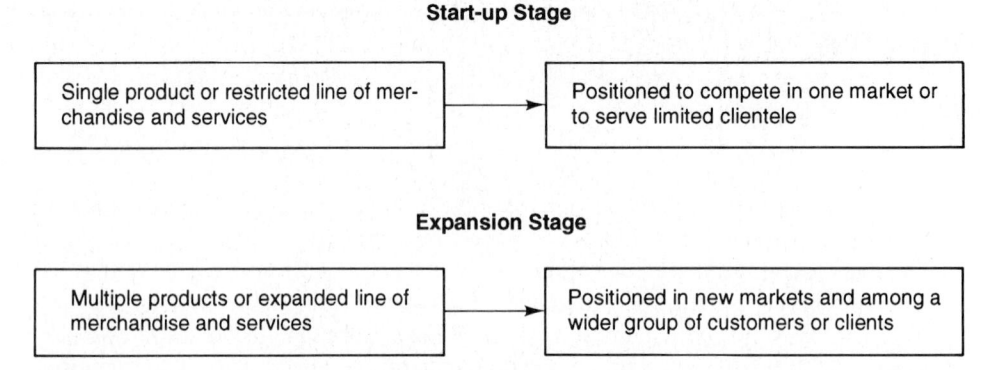

| Multiple products or expanded line of merchandise and services | → | Positioned in new markets and among a wider group of customers or clients |

Figure 14-2 **Expansion of Products and Markets**

plans.[6] This kind of planning represents a major reversal of behavior, and successful entrepreneurs of rapid-growth firms do not just "push on" with their ideas hoping for success.

Changes in leadership behavior tend to create the strategic turning points that result in successful expansion, or else expansion thrusts entrepreneurs into new leadership roles which, if handled well, result in success.[7] The causal relationship is less important than the fact that entrepreneurs make the transition. Tom Monaghan, for example, specifically created a system of management and led Domino's Pizza toward rapid expansion through a unique approach for pizza home delivery. Mrs. Fields Cookies became so popular that Debbi Fields was forced to take charge of a growing business, and by transforming herself into a capable manager, she led the company to success.

External impetus more often creates opportunities for a given industry, but it is the internal leadership that generates the momentum required to take advantage of those opportunities. The microelectronics industry, for example, has kindled the imagination of several thousand entrepreneurs during the past decade. Hundreds of microcomputer firms, software companies, consultants, and hardware manufacturers have rushed to the market with their ideas. One of these, ASK Computers, was the brainchild of Sandra Kurtzig, who began with a start-up niche in engineering applications for small computers, then broadened her line into scientific instrumentation and integrated information systems.[8] Kurtzig drove her company through the expansion stage but also built an organization with the best managers she could find. Within two years of founding, she created departments, delegated responsibilities, and positioned the company for a public offering. By going public, ASK Computers further diversified and hurtled toward $200 million in sales. When growth in the computer industry began to stabilize and company sales slowed in the late 1980s, Sandra Kurtzig began to consolidate. Recognizing that her company was on the verge of another transition, Kurtzig questioned her personal desire to head a public corporation in a competitive industry. Rather than trying to make the transition, she chose to leave

PROFILE △

Domino's Pizza—An Inspired Marketing Strategy

Thomas S. Monaghan, founder of Domino's Pizza, Inc., entered the 1970s with one pizza parlor, a pile of debts, and a great idea—to take the fast-food concept right to the consumer's door. More than just home delivery, Domino's was going to become the most efficient system going, without restaurant facilities or in-house services. In Monaghan's view, achieving that goal required a motivated army of enthusiastic employees, and part of the marketing strategy was to give every Domino's employee the opportunity to move up the ladder, manage, and eventually own and operate a Domino's outlet. The strategy rested on the traditional merits of good advertising, a strong brand image, and a good product concept, but the foundation of success was personal selling through Domino's people committed to superb customer service.

Source: "Presto! The Convenience Industry: Making Life a Little Simpler," *Business Week*, April 27, 1987, pp. 86–94. Also Wendy Zellner, "Why the Pizza King May Abdicate the Throne: Domino's Monaghan Is Thinking of Selling Out and Focusing on Charities," *Fortune*, September 25, 1989, p. 32.

---

her venture, explaining that she felt her talents were better suited for the challenge of a new venture with rapid-growth opportunities. Subsequently, Sandra Kurtzig left her highly successful ASK Computers at the pinnacle of her career to begin a new publishing venture, *Entrepreneurial Woman* magazine.[9]

Consolidation Stage. As competition intensifies within a growing industry, businesses are faced with marginally smaller incremental shares of markets. The result is a competitive struggle at a slower rate of growth during what is often called an industry shakeout period. Weaker companies fail, some are sold or merged with others, and many *consolidate* to remain profitable.

Consolidation occurs differently for every organization. Manufacturers may trim back operations, reduce product lines, or retreat from marginally profitable markets. Service companies reduce staff, streamline distribution systems, and withdraw from high-risk markets. In all cases, organizations tend to shift authority downward as middle- and higher-level staff are reduced to improve efficiency. The result is a flatter organization that is euphemistically described as "leaner and meaner."

A consolidated company can successfully maintain this downsized posture for a prolonged period of time; growth is not essential, as we shall see later. The consolidated company, however, must rationalize having a smaller market segment with commensurate profits. For example, Dave Bing, former NBA Detroit Pistons star, founded a steel company in 1978 to provide high-quality rolled steel to the Detroit auto industry. (Bing was profiled in Chapter 11.) The company grew rapidly to more than $50 million a year in sales, then leveled off during the mid-1980s. Facing stiff competition, Bing focused on specialty steel supplies, subsequently settling into a pattern of "constrained growth." This meant less-enthusiastic expansion, yet sales and profits have been stable in an otherwise turbulent industry.[10]

Revival Stage. The revival stage is one of "rekindling" organizational growth.[11] Rapid growth can be achieved by clever repositioning of product lines and services through purposeful market segmentation. Repositioning sets the stage for a strategy of product or service diversification. In order to achieve rapid growth, innovation is essential, and because the company needs to incubate new ideas, greater responsibility is given to division managers for independent development. In effect, company executives attempt to revive a spirit of entrepreneurship in their operational managers by empowering them with authority for self-direction. As a result, organizations are restructured through product, geographic, or customer divisions, and the functional hierarchy is subordinated to divisional leadership.

To the extent that innovative products and services emerge, the company can experience a revival in growth. If repeated consistently, innovation results in a pattern of upward growth as illustrated in Figure 14-3. Corporations with strong performance records recognize this cycling of innovations and therefore commit significant resources to research and development. Although small ventures cannot emulate corporations like 3M or Du Pont, there is much to be learned from firms that have a constant flow of innovative products to replace obsolete lines or to revive languishing markets.[12]

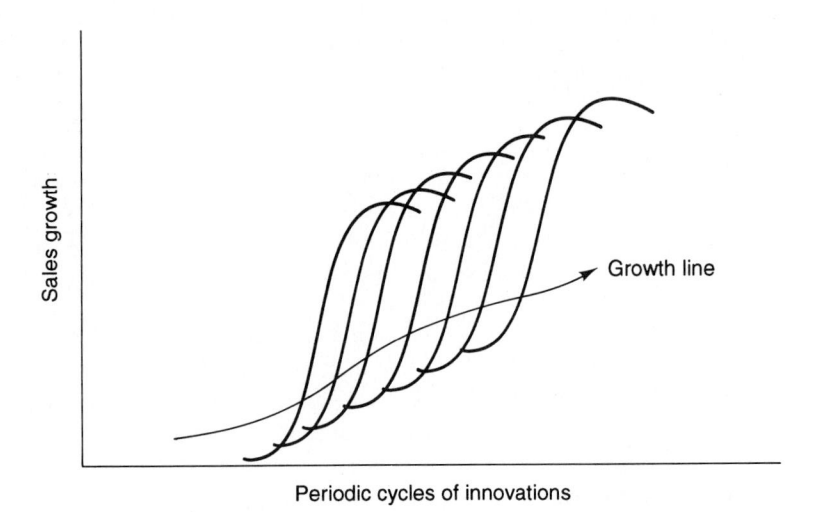

Figure 14-3 **Growth Based on Cycles of Innovation**

Decline Stage. Growth declines once again if revival strategies are short-lived or ineffective. Companies in decline often are those that have diversified too widely or created excessively bureaucratic organizations. Consequently, it is not unusual to find that a declining venture has lost sight of its distinct competency in products or services that initially proved successful. Founding entrepreneurs—if they are still with their ventures—will have failed to adapt to leadership challenges in previous stages and subsequently pushed their companies to the brink of disaster.

Successful ventures will not complete the life cycle; by definition, they avoid decline. They will have enjoyed growth through product or market expansion, consolidated when necessary, and experienced a revival of growth consistent with their capabilities and the industry in which they compete. The last stage implies perpetuation of innovations through the *intrapreneurial* process described in Chapter 3. In each of these stages, successful entrepreneurs will have adapted to new roles in concert with organizational changes.

> ▶ **CHECKPOINT**
>
> Describe each stage in the life cycle in terms of growth.
>
> Explain how an organization changes during each life-cycle stage.

CHANGING ENTREPRENEURIAL ROLES

Between the initial start-up and revival stages, entrepreneurs experience a metamorphosis. They change from a persona of the founding entrepreneur to that of an organizational executive. At the venture's inception, the entrepreneur and the new venture are bound as one entity, and as the business grows, it follows a biological pattern of evolution that reflects the founder's skills and aspirations.[13] As the company continues to expand, it requires business-related skills often beyond those of the founder; functional expertise is needed, marketing and operation skills are required, and decision-making tasks are beyond the scope of one person. Consequently, the biological growth cycle is superseded by an organizational life cycle.

The entrepreneur who adapts to this environment, in effect, embraces the necessary metamorphosis; the entrepreneur who resists constrains the organization to the narrow limitations of his or her personal abilities. How adaptation occurs is unclear, but research provides insights into the prevalent role characteristics of successful leaders at each stage in a venture's life cycle.

Founding the Venture

Throughout this book, a composite role has been emphasized for founding entrepreneurs that encompasses all the functions of a start-up business. The founder must wear many hats. From a psychological viewpoint, the founder's personal life is not distinguishable from the venture; entrepreneurs embody the inspiration, objectives, emotion, and creativity of their enterprises. They identify with every problem and decision. Unfortunately, this intense involvement does not mean entrepreneurs are effective leaders or managers, and if they are good in one role, there is no guarantee they are good in another.

There is a difference between leaders and managers.[14] Leaders are involved emotionally in a venture, think strategically to create opportunities and resolve conceptual, long-term problems, and provide the inspiration necessary for sustained momentum. Managers, in contrast, have a "transactional orientation" that permits them to maintain psychological distance between their personal lives and business decisions. Consequently, they tend to focus on operational tasks and on solving organizational problems. This distinction does not mean that managers are not good leaders or vice versa, only that it is difficult to integrate these roles consistently. During the start-up stage, leadership probably outweighs the importance of management because the new venture is in a chaotic state. Success depends on shaping expectations, developing creative ideas into marketable commodities, and adjusting to idiosyncratic phenomena.

It would be extremely helpful to have a "theory of entrepreneurship" to help guide founders, but there is no consensus among researchers on such a theory. There is, however, a strong movement to redefine entrepreneurship within the context of *disequilibrium* and *chaos*.[15] Specifically, classic economic theory explains business in terms of an equilibrium in which small changes in economic and social variables have little effect on the overall system. Consequently, an entrepreneur may introduce a highly successful innovation, but as profits accrue, competitors are attracted to the industry, eventually absorbing demand and "equalizing" economic effects. A theory based on disequilibrium rejects this sequence, suggesting instead that new ventures create chaos with profound implications for society, such as the birth of entirely new industries. Over the years, we have seen this pattern in automobiles, electricity, entertainment, and microelectronics, to name a few. These two concepts are contrasted in Figure 14-4.

If a chaotic theory is valid, then individual entrepreneurs exist in a world where disequilibrium is normal. Consequently, idiosyncratic behavior is the rule, not the exception, and entrepreneurs are the antiequilibrium force in society. This profile of behavior suggests emotion, inspiration, intuition, dedication, persistence, contrariness, and vision—characteristics more commonly attributed to those in leadership roles than those in management roles. Still, business failures are largely attributed to poor management, such as the inability to control resources, resolve problems, or achieve task-related results. Management responsibilities, therefore, cannot be set aside.[16]

Guiding the Venture through Expansion

Chaos may persist into the early stages of expansion, but if a company has progressed this far, then a great many problems have already been resolved. The primary focus of operations will have shifted away from survival in uncertain markets to managing

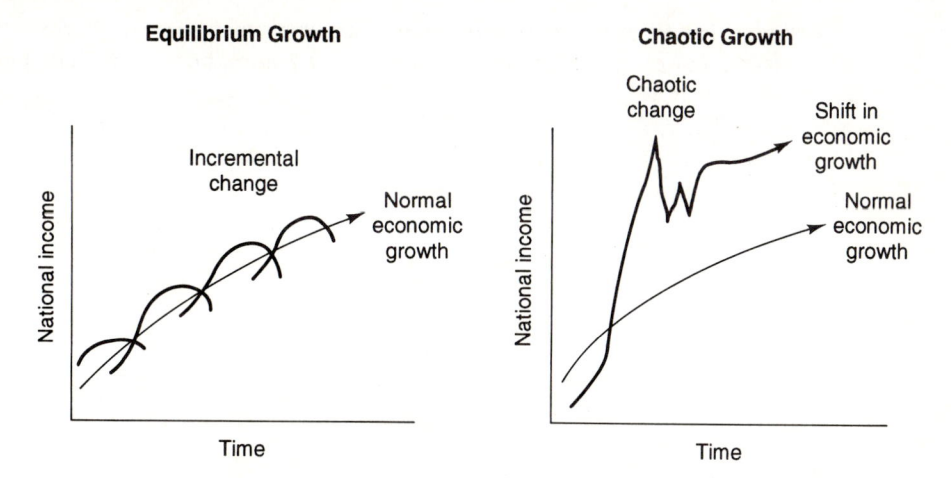

Figure 14-4 Contrast of Equilibrium Growth and Chaos

growth in well-defined markets. As the rate of expansion increases, more emphasis is placed on planning and controlling activities. Therefore, an entrepreneur begins to experience the metamorphic effect of transforming behavior from intuitive leadership to coherent management. As emphasized earlier, being oriented either to a leadership or a management role does not mean one can ignore the other; they are not mutually exclusive roles.

Management responsibilities surface rapidly as a venture expands. An entrepreneur is seldom capable of doing all that must be done with respect to functional management activities. These activities include marketing, cash-flow management, inventory control, purchasing, credit management, and human resource development. Depending on the type and complexity of the organization, many other functional activities are possible, such as research and development, production control, logistics and distribution, and management accounting.

During expansion, the entrepreneur's focal role is that of an executive general manager who plans these activities, defines human resource requirements, and guides subordinates toward fulfillment of organizational objectives. Fred Smith, founder of Federal Express, identified his role during the rapid-growth stage as a "transitional state of mind" when he had to develop the ability to assimilate information from many different disciplines, synthesize his vision into workable plans, and learn to trust his people to execute activities that achieve success.[17]

It may be impossible to overemphasize the entrepreneur's role as one of strategically organizing the venture with the best people that can be hired. Researchers have found that one notorious error made by entrepreneurs is believing, mistakenly, that they cannot afford to hire top-quality people.[18] With this attitude, they reluctantly hire staff and perceive each new person as an expense, not an asset. As a result, their ventures are poorly staffed, and entrepreneurs suffer from several types of growing pains. The four most common growing pains are summarized in Exhibit 14-2. They

---

Exhibit 14-2 **Growing Pains That Result from a Poorly Staffed Organization**

The entrepreneur is overwhelmed with work; there are not enough hours in the day to manage activities, plan, and lead the venture.

The entrepreneur and other managers spend their time "putting out fires," not attending to strategic growth and development.

The entrepreneur is too busy to be aware of what others are doing, and employees are no longer aware of what must be done.

The entrepreneur, subordinate managers, and employees lose track of where the firm is going and what they are trying to accomplish.

Source: Adapted from Steven H. Hanks, "The Organization Life Cycle: Integrating Content and Process," *Journal of Small Business Strategy*, Vol. 1, No. 1 (1990), pp. 1–12.

---

translate to an overworked entrepreneur with a frustrated and ineffective staff that lacks direction.[19]

These problems can be reversed through effective human-resource planning and management. Hiring the best people is a form of asset management, not cost control, and first-rate people tend to pull their companies through, succeeding because of their own impatience to achieve.[20] Entrepreneurs become team builders, and, ideally, they will encourage subordinates to use their skills without undue restriction.

The entrepreneur's role as a strategist is also crucial. Recall from earlier remarks that although few start-up ventures have formal plans, nearly 85 percent of those in the expansion stage do have formal plans. It follows that entrepreneurs must transform their behavior from making strategic decisions based entirely on intuition to making strategic decisions based on a formal strategic planning process. This transformation may sound simple, but it requires an extremely difficult adaptation from relying on personal judgment to making systematic evaluations of the competitive environment. This transition is shown conceptually in Figure 14-5. The entrepreneur becomes a strategist to carefully plan long-term market and product development and to obtain the human, material, and financial resources necessary to implement plans.

Planning for, and finding, financial resources is arguably as important as planning for, and finding, human resources. A growing venture certainly needs both, but a venture cannot grow without capital. Consequently, one vital aspect of the entrepreneur's transformation is to become a competent financial manager. Financial concepts taught in business schools rarely apply to embryonic ventures, but they become increasingly more useful as the venture expands. Recall from Chapter 13 that financial requirements change with each stage of venture development. Small businesses rely on personal resources and debt. During expansion, entrepreneurs must acquire financing in ever-increasing amounts to underwrite growth, and in most instances, their ventures are too small to attract sufficient capital or to go public. Therefore, they find themselves intensely occupied with managing capital assets and finding financial resources.[21]

Entrepreneurs find themselves adapting to many more management activities

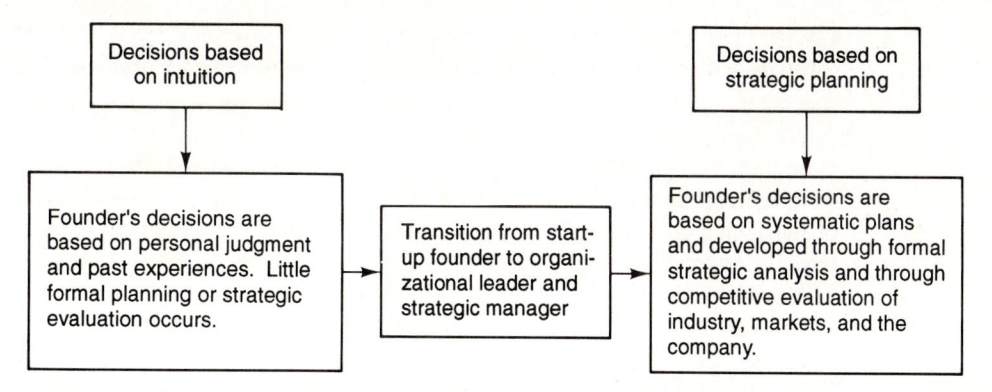

```
[Decisions based on intuition]
        ↓
[Founder's decisions are based on personal judgment and past experiences. Little formal planning or strategic evaluation occurs.] → [Transition from start-up founder to organizational leader and strategic manager] → [Founder's decisions are based on systematic plans and developed through formal strategic analysis and through competitive evaluation of industry, markets, and the company.]
                                                                                                                                            ↑
                                                                                                                            [Decisions based on strategic planning]
```

Figure 14-5 **The Transition from Intuitive Decision Making to Strategic Management**

during the expansion stage, but in general, entrepreneurs spend less time on operational activities and more time on strategic management of resources during expansion. In addition, they spend more time on coordination and communication activities with their staff, delegating incrementally more authority consistent with the growth of their ventures.

Managing Consolidation

Rapid growth cannot continue indefinitely, and at some point industries go though "shakeout periods." Managing an enterprise in this environment is substantially different from managing a growing venture. During rapid growth, management is concerned with gaining new resources, finding expansion capital, adding employees, and developing new products or services. When things slow down, these tasks are reversed. New resources may be needed but in lesser quantities; capital becomes scarce; and the organization may have to be trimmed down in size. Leader and manager roles are no less important during consolidation than in other stages, but decisions are seldom pleasant.

Managing during consolidation is not a "gatekeeping" function to maintain the status quo. To the contrary, it is a fight for survival. Intuition and inspiration play lesser roles, and *rationalization* becomes a preeminent concern as managers grasp for marginal improvements. Lee Iacocca became a folk hero when he rationalized Chrysler Corporation by closing factories, downsizing operations, and retrenching the automaker's technology. To employees and their families who lost their jobs during the downsizing, Iacocca was far from a folk hero, yet he succeeded in consolidating the company, thus buying time to rejuvenate Chrysler.[22] Donald Burr failed to consolidate People Express and subsequently was held to account for the airline's collapse. Between these extremes, there are entrepreneurs who make the transition seem painless. William C. Norris, one of the founders of Control Data Corporation, spearheaded the venture's early growth, but he also carefully positioned CDC to compete effectively when the computer industry stabilized after several years of spectacular growth. Norris has been called a management wizard for being able to sustain innovative growth without wholesale layoffs or downsizing.[23]

People Express and Control Data Corporation provide interesting contrasts. Both were entrepreneurial ventures only a few years ago, and their founders either failed or succeeded during the consolidation stage. Donald Burr continued to expand People Express aggressively, buying assets and adding routes to his company's line, until the company literally ran out of money; expectations for growth never materialized. William Norris concentrated on specific research and development in scientific and engineering computing for particular markets; his company remains one of the most successful in the computer industry.

Entrepreneurs are more likely to leave their ventures during consolidation. For example, Ronald D. Roberts, cofounder of Peachtree Software, Inc., began like most other software developers in the early 1980s with a single product targeted for a single market.[24] He developed the Peachtree accounting package for accounting firms and small offices that used MS-DOS systems. Peachtree enjoyed exceptional growth, and by 1986 it controlled 30 percent of the accounting systems software market. With IBM as a proprietary customer, Peachtree added dozens of innovative software applications to its commercial line. But in 1987 the software shakeout began, as hundreds of new companies entered the field. Prices came down, marketing costs went up, and profit margins were squeezed. Peachtree had to abandon unprofitable products, reduce operations, and find additional financing to support research and development. Roberts decided that his skills were not suitable for managing a consolidation effort, and to his credit, he left the company, which was subsequently sold. Roberts started a new venture called Clockwork Systems, developing software for legal services, where he felt his creative entrepreneurial skills were more useful.

Turning the Venture Around

Reversing a company's pattern of poor performance is called turning it around, and for those ventures suffering from reduced sales and profits, the turnaround begins during the consolidation stage. More to the point, decisions made to achieve consolidation help reposition the company so that it can be "turned around." It is during the revival stage, however, that turnaround efforts are realized. This is the time when market segmentation becomes more keenly focused through customer-oriented activities. It is also when research and development begin to pay off in high-yield products and services. And it is the time when a streamlined organization can regain the offensive for competing effectively.[25]

For those entrepreneurs who survive earlier stages and who are also capable of turning their ventures around, the metamorphosis is complete. They will have grown with, and been transformed by, the responsibilities of managing their ventures. Although their roles are significantly different by the time they reach a revival stage, their responsibilities are no less challenging. As founders, entrepreneurs have to be visionaries and aggressive competitors. As turnaround managers, they have to inspire

Chapter 14   Managing Growth and Transition   469

PROFILE △

Barry Gibbons—Turnaround at Burger King

Barry Gibbons took the reins at Burger King after the ailing company had gone through the hands of Pillsbury and the British firm Grand Metropolitan during the mid-1980s as a victim of buyout mania. In 1988, Gibbons took over a Burger King organization of 6,000 outlets and 36,000 employees that had neither grown nor made more than nominal paper profits for three years. In Gibbons' mind, Burger King's image was tarnished, and there was no enthusiasm among employees to do more than sling hamburgers and collect paychecks; the organization was "numb" and without direction. Gibbons saw an organization and its employees caught in a vacuum. Into the void, Gibbons poured creative ideas, incentives for performance, and a spirit for quality aimed at giving customers total satisfaction. There were no wholesale closures or layoffs, but instead, incentives for people to stay and grow. Administrative and distribution costs were cut, but customer service and marketing budgets were increased. By 1990, Burger King had increased operating earnings by 25 percent and posted its best annual sales growth in a decade.

Source: Brian Dumaine, "The New Turnaround Champs," *Fortune*, July 16, 1990, pp. 36–44. Also Burger King, Inc., Annual Report 1990.

---

their employees to be visionaries and aggressive competitors. Therefore, they can neither lose their entrepreneurial zeal nor suffocate their organizations with controls. As this stage, the entrepreneur is a professional manager who leads but does not dominate, delegates but does not abdicate, and controls but does not stifle the organization.

Another way to explain the turnaround process is that during consolidation managers must "stop the bleeding" of a wounded company. Farsighted managers can, of course, consolidate early to prevent problems. After the company is reasonably stabilized, it is management's responsibility to transform the organization into a growing force. For example, Barry Gibbons turned Burger King around through tough cost-control measures and a personal philosophy of service that revived the company from several years of dormancy. Today, the company has regained a competitive position in the fast-food industry. Instead of using cut-and-slash tactics, however, Gibbons restructured outlets and rekindled a spirit of quality service.[26]

Turning around smaller companies is not substantially different from rejuvenating larger organizations such as Burger King. The critical point is that managers must identify the focal activity (service, product, or distinct competency) on which the company's future can be built, then make the difficult decisions to channel resources into that activity. Because a small venture is likely to have very limited resources, the channeling process also requires sacrifices.

This process is particularly difficult for family-owned businesses and partnerships where a few people are personally and emotionally involved in the business. A turnaround under these circumstances often means bringing in outside managers who can make difficult decisions while remaining psychologically detached. At the extreme, these outsiders are "hired guns" who oust managers and employees who do not fit into future plans. Then they refocus the organization on high-potential activities. At the minimum, outsiders bring new values to the venture, and they provide the talent necessary to manage assets efficiently. In every situation, they must provide the leadership necessary to "fill a vacuum."[27]

At the beginning of this section, we emphasized that entrepreneurs go through a series of changes that transform them from intensely involved individual founders of new ventures to executives of complex organizations. We also emphasized that if the transformation does not occur, either the venture suffocates or the entrepreneur does not survive organizational evolution. Perhaps the essential requirement for entrepreneurs to survive this transformation is to have, or to develop, strategic management capabilities.

▶ **CHECKPOINT**

Describe an entrepreneur's role during start-up and expansion.

Explain role responsibilities during consolidation and revival.

PERSPECTIVE ON STRATEGIC MANAGEMENT

Making effective strategic decisions is a theme that occurs throughout the organizational life cycle, and as described earlier, the nature of these decisions changes as a company evolves. Entrepreneurs are preoccupied with survival during the start-up period; consequently, their strategies are limited to making a single product or service successful. With rapid growth, their strategic emphasis shifts to intense market development. As growth slows and the industry begins to shake out, entrepreneurs must adopt competitive strategies that can require severe retrenchment decisions. As entrepreneurs struggle to revive their ventures, they must focus their companies on distinct competencies that, in the long run, will stimulate growth and profitability.

Most strategic alternatives available to small, nonpublic ventures are concerned with internal changes that can be made through reallocation of limited resources; few small ventures can consider acquisitions, mergers, or complicated strategic alliances with other companies. These internal alternatives emerge from strategic planning to realign a venture's markets, refocus its research and development on high-potential products, or redefine its image. In contrast, large diversified corporations are more concerned with leveraging their financial strength to alter their portfolios. Smaller firms seldom have financial strength or portfolios with which to be concerned. Consequently, there is a fundamental difference in the nature of strategic planning for small and large businesses; small-business planning is not large-company planning on a smaller scale.[28]

Although limited by their resources, entrepreneurs are concerned with ways to pursue *growth* and *diversification*. Both depend on the founder's objectives and, of course, on many external limitations and industry characteristics beyond our interests here. A fundamental relationship between growth objectives and diversification strategies is shown in Figure 14-6. Growth tends to preoccupy entrepreneurs, and diversification tends to be the strategy of choice to achieve it. As we shall see, however, neither is essential for success.

Growth

The term *growth* permeates strategic planning, and it is consistently used to explain changes in the organization life cycle. Growth, however, in and of itself is not a strategic objective; it is only the means to an end. A venture grows for many different reasons. Higher sales volume may be necessary to establish an image, increase the firm's asset base, meet competition, improve profits, or satisfy an entrepreneur's dream of heading a large organization. Growth may, in some instances, be essential to survival. Real strategic objectives exist apart from growth, yet depending on an entrepreneur's personal preferences and competitive circumstances, growth may be unnecessary.

For a majority of small businesses, growth is not a major consideration beyond the point of gaining stability. An independent retailer, for example, may have no desire to expand beyond his or her capacity to own and manage a store personally. A beautician may find personal satisfaction with a single location and the autonomy of ownership. Management consultants can do quite well operating as proprietorships

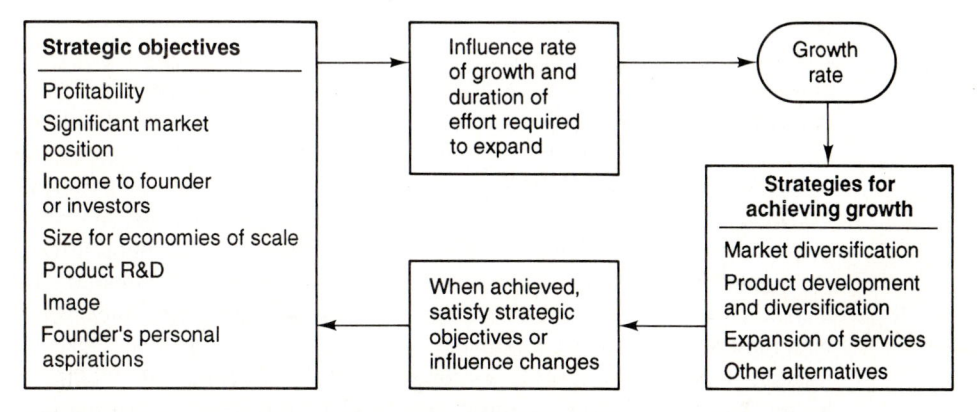

Figure 14-6 **Objectives and New Venture Growth**

or small partnerships without creating bureaucratic organizations. Tax accountants can individually handle a finite number of clients and may be satisfied with this limitation. The list goes on, but the point is that growth may be valid for these businesses only as an initial effort to position their ventures for profitable operations. Their founders may not be interested in the burden of expansion and may subsequently pass up opportunities, but lost opportunities will be less important than peace of mind.

Growth may also be dictated by external circumstances such as industry changes, and there is a long continuum of growth rates. At the minimum, a slow-growth industry may prevent a venture from rapid expansion, and expansion efforts are limited to small incremental changes. At the maximum, an industry may be growing so rapidly that the hackneyed expression "grow or die" is very much a reality. Home construction contractors often face a minimum-growth scenario. In this instance, local population trends vary widely, and in most communities, demand for housing is cyclical—at times very high and at other times very slow. Contractors try to forecast demand to take advantage of high demand, then fall back and retrench during lean times. Contractors who do not expand during peak demand periods, however, do not necessarily lose money or become overwhelmed by competition, they simply do not build as many houses. It is possible to have a small contracting business and avoid the roller coaster changes typical in the housing industry.

At the other extreme, an industry may be expanding so rapidly that strong high-volume businesses will preempt the competition. This has certainly been the case for software developers and computer companies, and it is generally true for most industries that rely on scientific innovations. During the past decade, the proliferation of computer companies created a mirror image of the classic life-cycle curve, and as more and more competitors flocked to the industry, battles for market share ensued. Prices and profit margins plunged, product lines expanded rapidly, and there was a huge turnover in companies. Each competitor, ranging from IBM to hundreds of long-forgotten start-ups, scrambled to preempt the others with innovative products, and being large did not assure success. In fact IBM suffered several disasters, including the introduction and demise of the IBM PCjr, and Exxon Corporation lost more than $10 billion on its Exxon Information Systems division, which was dissolved. Although many more smaller ventures crashed, a few of these—Compaq, Apple, Tandem, EDS, Digital, and Control Data Corporation—are now among the leading names in computing. They did grow, and few had any choice in the matter. The industry and competition required increased sales to finance research and development, cost-effective manufacturing, and spiraling marketing expenses.

Growth for growth's sake was not essential for all computer companies. Analog Devices, Inc., for example, grew at a rate of nearly 40 percent annually during the period 1984 to 1988; however, this was the heyday of exponential growth in microelectronics, and it occurred while the industry was expanding at more than 300 percent annually. Analog seemed doomed because it was losing market share, yet it succeeded with modest growth by providing extremely high-quality products. Analog's founders also positioned the company in a strong market niche that helped redefine the company as an innovator in scientific instrumentation.[29] Sun Microsystems was started in a rented apartment by three young entrepreneurs in 1982, went public in 1986, and approached $2 billion in sales by 1988, but the venture never competed directly with major firms in the retail limelight. Instead, Sun Microsystems focused on scientific workstations and computer-aided design systems. Growth was never an objective—only a result—of creating computer systems that could solve engineering problems.[30]

Apple Computer may be the classic example of the "grow or die" issue. In 1976 the first Apple Computer was assembled by hand in a garage by the company's founders. Steven Jobs and Stephen Wozniak had no idea they were laying the foundations of a multibillion-dollar industry, and when they were faced with actually manufacturing Apple machines in 1978, they were simply being swept along by their own inertia. There was no concern for growth, no concept of market share, and no sense of competition; the entrepreneurs simply wanted to create fun machines that could do remarkable things. When IBM exploded onto the market in 1981 with its PC, industry analysts predicted Apple would collapse. It almost did because it had no marketing strategy, and the founders had few specific objectives other than to enjoy the fun of invention.[31]

In the business and office markets, IBM rolled over Apple; Apple lost its momentum; both Jobs and Wozniak lost their company. They never made the transition in management required to keep the company afloat. The new CEO, John Sculley, consolidated product lines (e.g., retired the Apple III and the Lisa, among others), closed major retail distribution projects, and repositioned Apple in several well-defined market segments. The Apple II remains targeted to home users and schools, the Macintosh and Macintosh SE lines are directed toward college and small-business markets, and the high-end Macintosh II with network enhancements and laser printing technology is positioned mainly for businesses requiring desk-top publishing. Apple regained momentum in these market segments, reviving the image and reputation of the company as a technology leader with innovative products.[32]

Growth was, and remains, essential in the computer industry, but a high rate of growth is not a panacea for success. The crucial point is that growth must be achieved for a reason, and too much growth can be just as devastating as stagnation; this point was illustrated earlier when we described how People Express expanded beyond its capabilities. Unfortunately, entrepreneurs are often dreamers, and like Steven Jobs and Stephen Wozniak, who propelled us into the information age, they are champions of change but not necessarily strategists capable of managing growth.

Diversification

Diversification is the process of expanding into new markets or developing new lines of products or services. Consequently, it is a particular form of growth achieved either by finding new customer groups or by expanding lines offered to existing customers. This definition is oversimplified because both forms of diversification can occur at once and in numerous combinations. Several options are illustrated in Figure 14-7. Diversification problems are similar to those described for growth. Too little diversification in a rapidly changing industry can result in preemption by competitors

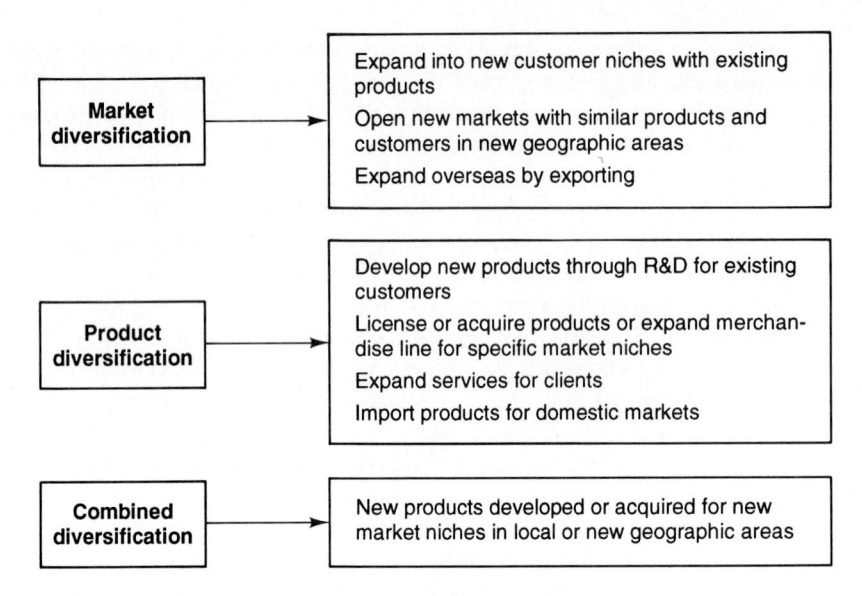

```
Market             →   Expand into new customer niches with existing
diversification         products
                        Open new markets with similar products and
                        customers in new geographic areas
                        Expand overseas by exporting

Product            →   Develop new products through R&D for existing
diversification         customers
                        License or acquire products or expand merchan-
                        dise line for specific market niches
                        Expand services for clients
                        Import products for domestic markets

Combined           →   New products developed or acquired for new
diversification         market niches in local or new geographic areas
```

Figure 14-7 **Diversification Options for New Ventures**

or stagnation as older products become obsolete. Too much diversification can result in a quagmire of misdirection; entrepreneurs simply lose track of what they do best by trying to do too much, and they do nothing well.[33]

Nevertheless, diversification is an important strategy that can be highly successful. Recall that Analog Devices, Inc., succeeded in the computer field by creating a strong position in microelectronic instrumentation. Analog's distinct competency rests with scientific applications of microcircuitry. How the venture got there is often referred to as the corridor principle, a concept discussed briefly in Chapters 2 and 5. The *corridor principle* explains how a venture can start with one product, and through the struggle to make it commercially successful, make modifications that result in an entirely new product. Alternatively, a business initially positioned in one market can find itself competing in a new market segment far removed from the entrepreneur's original intentions.[34]

By experimenting with microprocessing equipment, Analog found itself with new designs for laboratory instruments. Years ago, the Caterpillar Company put treads on its tractors to stop them from sinking into mud, and the company found that it had created a new industry in off-road equipment. College students know the name Eastpak, the company that created the knapsack revolution. Eastpak succeeded during the 1960s by providing canvas duffle bags and backpacks to the U.S. military. The company was prosperous during the Vietnam war years, then became stagnant when military contracts subsided. Eastpak redesigned its backpacks, added vivid colors, and began selling to college bookstores. Within a few years, college sales completely eclipsed military contracts, and Eastpak was in a new line of business with global markets.[35]

The Eastpak example illustrates how a small modification can dramatically change the strategic direction of a business firm. In this instance, diversification was intentional as a way to survive. By following a few hunches, product designers led the company "down a corridor" into new markets. Diversification can therefore be extremely productive, but diversification without reason can be disastrous. As noted earlier, Apple Computer Company was so successful with its Apple II that founders Jobs and Wozniak fell into the trap of believing they could sell almost anything they created. They sank millions into the Apple III and Lisa computers, and neither system survived. Similarly, IBM failed with the PCjr, among other products, and the champion of electronic gadgetry, Sony Corporation, brought out Betamax VCR systems only to have it rejected by customers.

> ▶ **CHECKPOINT**
>
> Explain why growth is important but can also be nonessential.
>
> Describe diversification and how it is a strategic alternative in expansion, consolidation, and revival stages.

IMPLICATIONS FOR ENTREPRENEURIAL CAREERS

If there is such a thing as an entrepreneurial *career*, it is captured in the image of an individual obsessed with the challenge of starting new ventures. Nearly 60 percent of those who succeed with new ventures sell or leave their creations before they mature, then start over again. Of those who fail, about the same percentage start again—and fail again—and start once more.[36] Entrepreneurs seldom stay with their ventures through the entire organization life cycle. Even in very successful ventures, entrepreneurs tend to become bored and leave when there is no longer a significant challenge. This lack of challenge may well have been what prompted Sandra Kurtzig, founder of ASK Computers, to leave her company at the height of success.

One of the more interesting examples is Mitch Kapor, who founded Lotus Development Corporation, drove the company to become the market leader in spreadsheet software with nearly $300 million in sales, then quietly said goodbye to his employees and left the corporate reins in his staff's hands.[37] Kapor was only 36 years old when he departed, but he started the transition two years earlier by grooming managers to assume corporate control. After leaving, Kapor launched a development fund to invest in other new ventures, thereby maintaining his entrepreneurial interests but without corporate management responsibilities.

Career Patterns

The concept of a career suggests a "job" or "profession" based on certain skills or occupational qualifications. An entrepreneurial career cannot be described in these

PROFILE △

Opportunities for Black Entrepreneurs

Ronald O. Thompson, president and CEO of General Railroad Equipment and Services, Inc., is a successful black entrepreneur who propelled his venture to $25 million in revenues while he was still in his 30s. Thompson's business in St. Louis is manufacturing railroad cars and shipping containers for industrial use. His entrepreneurial education began at the age of six waiting on customers at his parents' dry cleaning store in Detroit. By the age of 15, he was active in managing the store, handling money, and dealing with customer relations.

Today, Thompson not only heads his corporation but also has joined with several other black entrepreneurs to establish the Minority Youth Entrepreneurship Program in St. Louis. The purpose of MYEP is to show blacks that entrepreneurship is a viable career alternative. The program takes high school students through courses at Washington University, helps arrange field trips and seminars, and introduces them to entrepreneurial opportunities. Thompson and his MYEP partners also finance scholarships and awards for new venture plans.

Thompson was motivated to set up MYEP by the appalling statistics of low income and high unemployment among blacks. "We just participate as consumers and workers," Thompson explains. That, in his mind, is an economic trap, and too few blacks own businesses where they have the opportunity to accumulate wealth or at least to control their own destinies. He hopes to turn this situation around through community-based educational programs that help competitive black youth realize that they have alternatives to dead-end jobs.

Source: Joan Delaney, "Making a Difference: Black Youths Learn to Be Boss," *Venture*, December 1988, pp. 67–70.

---

terms, yet there is a pattern of behavior that implies a strong commitment to the "adventure" of starting new ventures. More accurately, there may be three patterns of entrepreneurial behavior. One relates to small business owners, another to entrepreneurs who embrace the challenge of growth-oriented ventures, and the third to intra-corporate entrepreneurs (intrapreneurs) who find ways to satisfy their ambitions within established companies.

The small-business career emerges from personal aspirations of business owners who prefer the autonomy of ownership rather than a job. Put another way, the small-business entrepreneur satisfies career goals through local ownership of an enterprise not destined to grow substantially. Some consciously choose this alternative, but others are forced into it by circumstances. In either situation, the small business owner who has the entrepreneurial spirit remains in small business, starting new ventures, selling, buying, and restarting. Failure for these individuals is having to reenter the job market, not in having an unsuccessful business. Success is having a self-determined life-style that may be little more than "income substitution" of ownership rather than a wage-based job.[38] Success may also mean having a prestigious community-based enterprise together with an attractive net income and country club membership.

Growth-oriented entrepreneurs, such as Sandra Kurtzig or Mitch Kapor, often purposely choose to start new ventures, but they seldom plan to be entrepreneurs. That statement may sound confusing, but there is a difference between starting a venture and consciously setting out to make a career of starting ventures. Those who start new ventures are often driven by their dreams or by the challenges of their innovations. Many are swept along by the inertia of their ideas, but for those whom we think of as being in entrepreneurial careers, there is a pattern of continued effort to transform ideas into commercial ventures; they are addicted to the idea of "growing a business." Win or lose, the majority try again and again, but their intention is to do well, score well, and do it all again.[39]

Behavior of corporate entrepreneurs is less clear, but if 3M's Art Fry is a good example, then once their creations become successful, entrepreneurs lose interest in them and anxiously search for new projects. Art Fry invented the Post-it notepad, became its corporate champion until it was successful, then moved quickly to pursue new ideas for 3M adhesives and industrial products.[40] Behavior of intra-corporate entrepreneurs is unclear because they tend to be primarily identified as company employees with corporate careers; it is difficult to analyze their behavior apart from the corporate environment. Nevertheless, their behavior is not unlike that of growth-oriented entrepreneurs who thrive on new adventures. In those instances when corporate managers and employees are formed into a "spinoff" or new venture unit (i.e., a subsidiary or autonomous division with corporate backing), the leadership team has been found to behave similarly to founders of independent businesses. More important, they tend to remain in these new roles, embracing the challenge of creating new ventures rather than returning to salaried occupations.[41]

The Influence of Entrepreneurial Education

As we bring this book to a close, the question that remains unanswered is whether formal coursework in entrepreneurship helps prepare students to pursue entrepreneurial careers. Some of the best minds in the field have researched the question and answered with an unqualified *yes*. Exactly what to teach and how to teach it are unresolved questions, but there is a consensus that formal education provides a better understanding of the entrepreneurial process, the challenges facing founders of new ventures, the skills needed in managing new ventures, and the problems that must be solved to succeed.[42] These objectives were introduced at the beginning of this book, and although merely reading a text in entrepreneurship will not help "create" entrepreneurs, it may help students become more aware of entrepreneurial opportunities.

The concept of entrepreneurship has been around for a very long time, but its popularity today is evidence of resurgent faith in the spirit of individual initiative.

Entrepreneurs are inspired people and adventurers who can at once disrupt society and instigate progress, and as we have seen, starting independent ventures often provides career opportunities to those disadvantaged through social or economic circumstances. Entrepreneurship education seeks to provide constructive direction for those who choose, or who are forced into, a career path apart from traditional roles in established organizations. To those ends, we hope this book has been useful.

> ▶ **CHECKPOINT**
>
> Describe each of three career patterns for entrepreneurs.
>
> Expand upon each of the major objectives for entrepreneurship education in terms of topics presented in this book.

SYNOPSIS FOR LEARNING

1. *Describe the organizational life cycle for an entrepreneurial venture.*

Interpreted for new ventures, the organizational life cycle has five stages: *start-up*, *expansion*, *consolidation*, *revival*, and *decline*. Successful ventures will not complete the cycle, avoiding the stage of decline through appropriate consolidation and revival strategies. All new ventures must survive the crises of start-up, and once established, they will experience some degree of growth during the expansion stage. This growth can be slow and steady or rapid and chaotic, depending on the nature of the business and founders' aspirations. Although the rate of growth will vary in both intensity and duration, all ventures will eventually experience a slowdown as competitors enter the field and markets become saturated. This stage is called the industry shakeout period, and astute entrepreneurs will implement strategies to meet the competitive challenge. One major strategic alternative occurs as the venture (and perhaps the industry) enters a consolidation stage. Consolidation is concerned with repositioning the venture in particular markets. It buys time for the enterprise to recuperate from the shakeout, regaining its growth in new products or new markets. The revival stage assumes innovation as a renewal process to take advantage of new opportunities. Decline occurs when these strategies fail, products become obsolete, or management fails to reposition the firm as a competitive business.

2. *Contrast entrepreneurial roles during various transition stages.*

During start-up, entrepreneurs wear multiple hats. They must provide the creative drive and zealous leadership necessary to establish a new venture. They are less concerned with managing assets or strategic planning than with survival. As the venture grows, entrepreneurs must make a transition away from the persona of a creative founder toward that of a responsible manager capable of planning, organizing, and controlling an expanding business. In effect, they fashion an established business from the chaos of an initial start-up. As competitive forces increase and the industry evolves toward maturity, entrepreneurs must become effective managers capable of consolidating their assets and repositioning their ventures. The transition between managing during expansion and consolidation is often impossible for entrepreneurs, but even more difficult is "turning the company around" to achieve a revival. It is during this stage that the venture is substantially redefined as a competitive enterprise, and entrepreneurial zest is less important than effective strategic management. During decline, decisions are less pleasant as entrepreneurs—those who remain with their ventures this long—must find a systematic way to terminate their ventures.

3. *Explain growth and diversification as strategic issues for new ventures.*

Growth is not in itself a strategic objective—only a means to an end. Ventures grow to satisfy image, increase a firm's asset base, meet competition, improve profits, or satisfy an entrepreneur's personal objectives. Growth may be essential to survive in rapidly expanding industries, but it is not essential to all ventures. Community-based enterprises and personal service firms tend to have limited potential, and many entrepreneurs in high-potential industries simply choose to constrain growth within narrow market niches. Diversification is the process of expanding into new markets, developing new products, or adding new services. All forms of diversification can occur at once and in numerous combinations, but the key point is that diversification is a strategic means to achieve growth. Consequently, it can be the vehicle of expansion or the means to revive a struggling company. Too much diversification, however, can end in a quagmire of misdirection.

4. *Explore the concept of an entrepreneurial career.*

An entrepreneurial career is a concept that is not well-defined like the idea of a job or a professional occupation. There are three general entrepreneurial career patterns. The first relates to small-business ownership, the second to growth-oriented ventures, and the third to intracorporate behavior. A small-business career is concerned with owning and operating local enterprises. The small-business entrepreneur may seek only a substitute for job income or to avoid working as an employee. Most seek self-direction, and success is often measured as being able to maintain an independent life-style. The growth-oriented entrepreneur is committed to "growing new businesses," and success is measured in terms of starting ventures and achieving significant growth. Win or lose, the growth-oriented entrepreneur is not satisfied with the prestige of ownership but with the challenge of transforming ideas into commercially successful enterprises. Intracorporate entrepreneurs are those who choose to remain within established companies as employees but realize their goals through individual efforts and innovations. They may be members of innovation teams who create "spinoff" divisions or subsidiaries for their companies, or they may simply be mavericks who enjoy the challenge of transforming new ideas into realities. Success is measured in terms of personal achievement within the bounds of their organizational careers.

NOTES

1. Steven H. Hanks, "The Organization Life Cycle: Integrating Content and Process," *Journal of Small Business Strategy*, Vol. 1, No. 1 (1990), pp. 1–12.
2. Jeffrey C. Schuman and John A. Seeger, "The Theory and Practice of Strategic Management in Smaller Rapid Growth Firms," *American Journal of Small Business*, Vol. 2, No. 1 (1986), pp. 7–18.
3. Tom Richman, "Mrs. Fields' Secret Ingredient," *Inc.*, October 1987, pp. 65–72.
4. Wendy Zellner, "Why the Pizza King May Abdicate the Throne," *Business Week*, September 25, 1989, p. 32.
5. Bernard Barry, "The Development of Organization Structure in the Family Firm," *Family Business Review*, Vol. 2, No. 3 (1989), pp. 293–315.
6. Schuman and Seeger, "The Theory and Practice of Strategic Management," pp. 7–18.
7. Mathew C. Sonfield and Russell M. Moore, "Innovative Turning Points in the Path to Entrepreneurial Success," *Journal of Small Business Strategy*, Vol. 1, No. 1 (1990), pp. 60–64.
8. Sandra Kurtzig, "Meeting the Entrepreneurial Challenge," keynote address to the 1989 International Conference of the Association of Collegiate Entrepreneurs, San Francisco, March 12, 1989.
9. *Learn from the $131 Million Woman*, an editorial brochure from *Entrepreneurial Woman*, Irvine, California, November 1989, p. 1.
10. "Charity Slam Dunk," *Fortune*, September 11, 1989, p. 106.
11. Hanks, "The Organization Life Cycle," pp. 1–12.
12. Christopher Knowlton, "What America Makes Best," *Fortune*, March 28, 1988, pp. 40–45.
13. Donald L. Sexton and Nancy B. Bowman-Upton, *Entrepreneurship: Creativity and Growth* (New York: Macmillan, 1991), p. 246.
14. Barbara J. Bird, *Entrepreneurial Behavior* (Glenview, IL: Scott, Foresman, 1989), pp. 325–327.
15. Harold Stevenson and Susan Harmeling, "Entrepreneurial Management's Need for a More 'Chaotic' Theory," *Journal of Business Venturing*, Vol. 5, No. 1 (1990), pp. 1–14.
16. Albert V. Bruno and Joel K. Leidecker, "Causes of New Venture Failure: 1960s vs. 1980s," *Business Horizons*, Vol. 31, No. 6 (1988), pp. 51–56.
17. "Fred Smith," *Inc.*, October 1986, pp. 35–38, 42–46, 49.
18. Jeffrey C. Susbauer and Robert J. Baker, Jr., "Strategies for Successful Entrepreneurial Ventures," *Journal of Business and Entrepreneurship*, Vol. 1, No. 2 (1989), pp. 56–66.
19. Hanks, "The Organization Life Cycle," pp. 1–12.
20. Susbauer and Baker, "Strategies for Successful Entrepreneurial Ventures," pp. 56–66.
21. Richard B. Carter and Howard E. VanAuken, "A Comparison of Small Businesses and Large Corporations: Interrelationships among Position Statement Accounts," *Journal of Business and Entrepreneurship*, Vol. 2, No. 1 (1990), pp. 73–80.
22. Maynard M. Gordon, *The Iacocca Management Technique* (New York: Ballantine Books, 1985), pp. 153–166.
23. "The Chief's Personality Can Have a Big Impact—For Better or Worse," *Wall Street Journal*, September 11, 1984, pp. 1, 12. Also C. G. Burck, "A Group Profile of the Fortune 500 Chief Executives," *Fortune*, May 14, 1986, pp. 173–177.
24. "Once Is Not Enough," *Inc.*, July 1987, p. 12.
25. Hanks, "The Organization Life Cycle: Integrating Content and Process," pp. 1–12. Also Sexton and Bowman-Upton, *Entrepreneurship: Creativity and Growth*, pp. 253–255.

26. Brian Dumaine, "The New Turnaround Champs," *Fortune*, July 16, 1990, pp. 36–44.

27. W. Gibb Dyer, Jr., "Integrating Professional Management into a Family Owned Business," *Family Business Review*, Vol. 2, No. 3 (1989), pp. 221–235.

28. Sandra J. Hartman, Olof Lundberg, and Michael White, "Planning in Small vs. Large Businesses: Do Managers Prefer Different Tools?" *Journal of Small Business Strategy*, Vol. 1, No. 1 (1990), pp. 12–24.

29. Nathaniel Gilbert, "How Middle-Sized Corporations Manage Global Operations," *Management Review*, October 1988, pp. 46–50.

30. Eileen Davis, " 'Small Caps' Tough it Out," *Venture*, April 1988, pp. 34–35. Also Brett Kingstone, *The Dynamos: Who Are They Anyway?* (New York: John Wiley & Sons, 1987), pp. 45–60.

31. Brian O'Reilly, "Growing Apple Anew for the Business Market," *Fortune*, January 4, 1988, pp. 36–37. Also Bro Uttal, "Behind the Fall of Steve Jobs," *Fortune*, August 5, 1985, pp. 20–24.

32. "How Two Pioneers Brought Publishing to the Desktop," *Business Week*, October 1, 1987, p. 61.

33. W. M. Greenfield, *Calculated Risk: A Guide to Entrepreneurship* (Lexington, MA: D. C. Heath, 1986), pp. 446–447.

34. Robert Ronstadt, "The Corridor Principle," *Journal of Business Venturing*, Vol. 3, No. 1 (1988), pp. 31–40.

35. Johnnie Roberts, "Pentagon Supplier Finds Niche Selling Knapsacks to Students," *Wall Street Journal*, September 17, 1984, p. 31.

36. Robert Ronstadt, "Ex-entrepreneurs and the Decision to Start an Entrepreneurial Career," *Frontiers of Entrepreneurship Research* (Wellesley, MA: Center for Entrepreneurial Studies, 1984), pp. 437–460.

37. "1–2–3 Creator Mitch Kapor: The Young Founder of One of the World's Leading Software Companies Gives Some Provocative Reasons for Walking Away from It All," *Inc.*, January 1987, pp. 31–38.

38. David L. Birch, "Matters of Fact," *Inc.*, April 1985, pp. 31–36, 39–42.

39. Bird, *Entrepreneurial Behavior*, p. 174.

40. Gifford Pinchot III, *Intrapreneuring* (New York: Harper & Row, 1985), pp. 282–284. Also Kenneth Labich, "The Innovators," *Fortune*, June 6, 1988, pp. 50–53, 56, 60.

41. Eric Flamholtz, *How to Make the Transition from an Entrepreneurship to a Professionally Managed Firm* (San Francisco: Jossey-Bass, 1986), pp. 3–16.

42. Karl H. Vesper, "New Developments in Entrepreneurship Education," in Donald L. Sexton and Raymond W. Smilor, eds., *The Art and Science of Entrepreneurship* (Cambridge, MA: Ballinger, 1986), pp. 379–387.

CASE 14-1

Forever Young

Ben & Jerry's Homemade, Inc., ranked third in the premium ice cream business behind corporate giants Pillsbury (Häagen-Dazs) and Kraft (Frusen Gladje), refuses to grow old while it grows up. Marking its tenth year in 1988, Ben & Jerry's Homemade, Inc., began in a renovated Burlington, Vermont, gas station. Today it grosses more than $32 million, and forecasts for the 1990s indicate an industry ready to double in size. Founders Ben Cohen and Jerry Greenfield refer to themselves as "weird" and "funky," and in fact they look more like middle-aged dropouts in shaggy jeans and T-shirts than successful businessmen. They don't want to be any different from what they are, and they don't want to grow up. Yet they are astute managers with a genuine sensitivity to the needs of their employees and a commitment to innovation.

Jerry Greenfield prefers the title "Undersecretary of Joy," and his employees do not laugh at this self-description. To the contrary, when addressing a plant meeting of 150 workers, he recently proposed a "Joy Committee" to bring more fun and humor to the workplace, and employees applauded. Jerry Greenfield's ultimate goal is to have an organization of happy people, not merely satisfied with their jobs but anxious to work because they can be creative.

Naturally, Ben & Jerry's Homemade has its share of crises, but they are greeted by unusual responses. For example, when production fell short of peak orders, the alarm sounded, and everyone came together to get the product out. Even Ben and Jerry did a stint, wiping containers and emptying garbage. Jerry recognized that the pressure fatigued workers, and he hired a masseuse to give them massages during breaks. When a problem occurs, Ben & Jerry's managers have responsibility for solving it, but they include employees in decisions. Meetings are informal, with an attitude of "Hey, gang, what do we do about this?"

Innovation extends to the monthly staff meetings, held in a plant receiving bay. During these meetings, production stops so that all employees and managers can attend. The events resemble town meetings rather than corporate staff meetings. Coffee, cider, and doughnuts are served, communication is open, suggestions are taken seriously by managers, and recognition awards are announced. These awards include a "Fred-of-the-Month" award, given to employees who come up with money-saving ideas. Recipients also get a "Fred's Famous T-shirt" to wear. Who is Fred? Fred Lager, hired in 1982, is an experienced businessperson with an MBA, and as chief operating officer, he has been influential in bringing the firm from an entrepreneurial venture to a multimillion-dollar growth corporation. Being cost-conscious at Ben & Jerry's is known as being "Fredlike," but that's not why Lager was hired. Lager was brought in during a pivotal growth period when the founders realized they needed experienced management at the helm.

Ben & Jerry's Homemade, Inc., is again at a crossroad in growth. Having survived its early growth, the company is positioned for rapid growth where professional reorganization may be necessary. Ben Cohen and Jerry Greenfield realize that the transition must occur, but they reject the notion that their company has to become "old" or stifling in the process. They would prefer not to grow if it means taking the fun out of work or reducing the creativity of any employee. Their employees evidently agree. On the job, they still wear the an emblem of commitment. It is a T-shirt created by employees during a tribute to the firm's tenth anniversary and to their founders' philosophy: "Be 10 again!"

CASE QUESTIONS

1. Identify the probable life-cycle stage in which the company finds itself, and describe the problems management is most likely to have to face.
2. What responsibilities might Fred Lager have had when he was brought into the company as the chief operating officer?
3. How might Ben and Jerry's roles have changed during the first transition, and what adaptations might they face in the most recent transition?

Source: Adapted from "Forever Young," by Erik Larson. Copyright 1988 by Erik Larson. First published in *Inc.* magazine. Reprinted by permission of Georges Borchardt, Inc., for the author.

CASE 14-2

Is Entrepreneurship Education Useful?

For five dollars, you can own a "weather stone," one of several products being offered by a fifth-grade class at the Hunt School in Hunt, Texas. The stone is no more than a rock mounted on a small shingle that you put outside and watch. If the rock is wet, it's raining; if it's white on top, it may be snowing . . . and so on. The weather stone may be a tongue-in-cheek product, but the entrepreneurship class for fifth graders is not. Fifth and sixth graders run concession stands, organize car parks for school events, and have created several innovative board games. The class has been engaged in free enterprise education since 1983, earning as much as $40,000 a year from projects. Profits not only help underwrite new projects but also purchase new school equipment such as video machines and computers.

Entrepreneurship programs for youngsters, while applauded by many, are questioned by some educators who insist that they create mercenary instincts at the expense of fundamental education. Many children find that the stress of trying to run their own businesses is too much. Others find the reality of hard work to research, develop, and sell something too much; they prefer to study in traditional ways. Still others find they are simply not cut out to pursue entrepreneurial careers. Those who support the programs point out, however, that these results are also important to give students a broader perspective on their own career aspirations.

Similar programs for grade school youth exist in dozens of cities across the United States, and more are being introduced. At the high school level, activity is often more pronounced. More than a hundred thousand high school students are involved in special programs and courses funded through state and local economic education agencies and foundations such as the Hugh O'Brien Youth Leadership Program. One program in the South Bronx area of New York focuses on disadvantaged youth. Founded by Steve Mariotti, the South Bronx project is designed to give inner-city youth an alternative to life on the streets. Mariotti's program brings students into seminars, takes them on tours through businesses, and introduces them to local entrepreneurs who have succeeded. Students also brainstorm a project, set up the business, and actively market a product or service. They are responsible for developing their own business plans and for succeeding or failing with their projects.

All youth programs have several things in common. They require students to develop their own ideas, plan ventures, develop their products or services for commercialization, and then go to market. They do their own market research, product design, licensing, venture administration, selling, and accounting. In many instances, they also must find financial backing. Advocates point out that students learn a wide variety of new skills through applications. They are introduced to bookkeeping systems, market research methods, planning systems, and economic processes. Mariotti claims that the most important aspect of his program is the "psyche" value of becoming mentally stronger through personal involvement and self-directed activities.

Critics of these programs say that students may benefit from learning the mechanics of business, but the psychological redirection of effort toward making money is inappropriate. Young students, they say, should be out playing games and learning humanistic values; older students should be preparing themselves for careers. The controversy also involves the question whether entrepreneurship can be taught in the sense that most students simply do not have entrepreneurial personalities.

CASE QUESTIONS

1. Discuss the concept of an entrepreneurial career and whether students can be taught to be entrepreneurs.
2. Based on what you have covered in this course, describe what you might envision as beneficial for grade school or high school students in courses similar to those in the case.
3. Take a position with respect to the controversy of whether to offer youth programs in entrepreneurship. Why would you support or oppose them?

Sources: Jeffrey O. Krasner and Jeffrey L. Seglin, "Dick and Jane Write a Business Plan," *Venture*, March 1989, pp. 50–52. Also Steve Mariotti, "Inc., Coming of Age," *Inc.*, April 1989, p. 66.

Appendixes

Two appendixes are provided as guidelines for creating a formal new venture "feasibility plan." The term *feasibility plan* is used instead of *business plan* because a comprehensive business plan can be extremely complicated and detailed, requiring far more attention than space allows. Nevertheless, the feasibility plan contains all the elements of a complete business plan without unnecessary details. Feasibility plans are realistic *initial* efforts by aspiring entrepreneurs to document their ventures and to describe how they intend to get them off the ground. Consequently, Appendix A provides an outline of a plan based on the model described in Part One of the text. Appendix B is an example with real-world data and projections of an actual company. Names of the company's founders and their investors have been disguised to protect their privacy, but the company and its products and markets are accurately presented.

Appendix A

Guidelines for a Feasibility Plan (Simplified Business Plan)

The following guidelines are provided to assist in preparing a feasibility plan. Depending on the type of business, some topics may be omitted or presented in a different order. The topics do not have to use the titles suggested, but the fundamental elements outlined should be included in a written plan. Appendix B provides an actual plan for reference that is similar to this outline.

Feasibility plans will have a "cover" that identifies the name of the business, date of preparation, and a business address. Most entrepreneurs also include a "confidentiality clause" together with a control number, and some require a signature line for those who receive the plan.

I. EXECUTIVE SUMMARY

The opening section is called the **executive summary**. It is a synopsis of the proposed enterprise that is intended to capture a reader's interest. Usually no longer than three pages, it includes the following:

Definition of the Business Venture. The company must be identified to include when it was formed, by whom, and for what purpose. The most important requirement is to explain the *purpose* of the new venture.

Product or Service. The entrepreneur must describe clearly what will be sold. If there is a proprietary interest (patent, trademark, or copyright), it should be stated. The executive summary should briefly describe how far the entrepreneur has gone to develop the product or service.

Market Characteristics. Existing and potential markets must be briefly described in terms of size and geographic characteristics. The plan must provide a summary of data to validate projections.

The Entrepreneurial Team. An entrepreneurial team may include only the founding entrepreneur, but other key personnel are usually essential for the firm's success. These individuals should be identified.

Financial Summary. Critical financial considerations should be summarized to include start-up estimates, cash-flow requirements, and profits or losses. These should be extended in annual increments for at least three years. The plan will establish what is needed and is being sought from investors and lenders.

II. BUSINESS DESCRIPTION

Following the executive summary, the plan will provide detailed sections on each major topic. Essentially the same points covered in the executive summary are covered here, but they are covered in far greater detail. In some instances, the business is so obvious that no description is needed. In other instances, entrepreneurs cannot adequately describe the business before explaining their products or services. Consequently, information in this section may occur later.

III. PRODUCTS OR SERVICES

Explain the **product or service concept**. The explanation should include an adequate description of the product, its purpose, distinct attributes, and how it is used. Include, when necessary, technical data on its manufacture, operation, and ownership. Identify legal protection (patents, trademarks, copyrights). If the business has multiple products (e.g., retail merchandise), explain the nature of the inventory and identify, when possible, the primary lines of business. A women's boutique, for instance, may specialize in sportswear. For services, describe how the service is performed and any special qualifications required such as professional licenses or credentials.

IV. MARKET RESEARCH AND ANALYSIS

The objective of **market research and analysis** is to establish that a market exists for the proposed venture. This may be the most difficult part of the plan, but it also may be the most important. Entrepreneurs must provide a credible summary of potential customers, markets, competitors, and assumptions about pricing, promotion, and distribution.

Potential Customers. Research should describe a **customer profile** that includes demographic information such as age, sex, family income, occupation, and location of potential customers.

Markets. A market exists only when there are qualified buyers, but the entrepreneur must remember that the feasibility plan is a forecast of *future* markets, not merely those that exist. Therefore, *market trends* are important to identify, including unusual opportunities for the new business.

Competitors. It is essential to identify competitors and to analyze how competition is likely to change when the new venture becomes established. The minimum requirement is to identify existing competitors and to explain their strengths and weaknesses.

Assumptions about the New Venture. A formal marketing plan comprises the next major section of the feasibility plan, yet it is important to describe in the marketing research section assumptions that support market projections for the new venture. Specifically, the preparer of the plan needs to identify the market niche, prices, promotional efforts, and distribution methods to justify market research contentions.

Market Niche. A **market niche** is a carefully defined segment of a broader market. It defines the *positioning* of a product or service to create a distinct marketing focus. A brief statement in the plan should explain this focus.

Pricing Systems. Market research is predicated on a price system that helps describe the venture's market. Normal prices and pricing policies, means of discounting, credit policies, and price strategies should be defined. This statement does not have to elaborate, but it has to be sufficient to justify sales forecasts.

Methods of Distribution. A **method of distribution** is the manner in which products or services are brought to market. The choice of a *distribution system* often defines the market niche, pricing system, and promotional activities.

The Sales Forecast. Ultimately, marketing research must conclude with solid data on projected sales. A **sales forecast** is the culmination of research to indicate the quantity of sales and expected gross sales revenue during the planning period. The forecast is the single most important piece of information in the plan. A good plan will describe projected sales in the executive summary, but it will present well-documented information here on specific market data and how sales are expected to occur during the first three to five years of business.

V. THE MARKET PLAN

The **market plan** describes an entrepreneur's intended strategy. It builds on market research and distinctive characteristics of the business to explain how the venture will succeed. Some issues addressed in the research section may be reserved for the market plan, such as describing a market niche, but, generally, this section focuses on specific marketing activities.

Prices. Well-defined prices are required. Pricing policies should be identified here if they have not been adequately identified earlier. Bulk prices, terms of sale, wholesale prices, retail prices, and methods used to derive price schedules, such as cost-plus pricing or price-lining, should be indicated.

Promotions. Promotional strategies, including options for employing promotional tools, constitute the *promotional mix*. It is a conscious effort to select promotional tools from advertising, personal selling, public relations, point-of-purchase displays, direct-mail solicitation, and sampling, among others.

Distribution Channels. If distribution channels have not been identified earlier, they must be described here. These may include wholesaling, retailing, mail order, catalog sales, telemarketing, contracting, or working through domestic or foreign brokers and agents.

Service and Warranty Considerations. Identify any unusual warranties or guarantees that support the marketing effort. These may be standard warranties or special warranties, and they may include after-sale service, customer support, hotline consulting, or some combination of services that enhances sales.

Marketing Leadership. The market plan should explain how organizational members will be involved in the marketing effort. From a strategic perspective, investors want to know who is going to be responsible for actual marketing.

VI. MANUFACTURING OR OPERATIONS PLAN

Depending on the nature of a business, this section may not be required, but most businesses will have some form of inventory or method of operations, and most will have facility requirements. For ventures that manufacture, design, or sell products, as well as for service firms that require capital equipment, this section may be extensive.

Facilities. Nearly every business requires physical facilities. Retailers are usually involved in choosing a location and either securing a lease or purchasing a store. Manufacturers face far more complex issues in leasing or purchasing properties, assuring transportation services, and dealing with legal issues such as EPA requirements and zoning ordinances. Service enterprises will be concerned with having offices easily accessible to clients.

Inventory Management. Retailers will describe beginning inventory required to open for business and explain how merchandise will be replenished. Manufacturers will describe raw materials and supplies needed in inventory prior to production, and they will also describe projected finished-goods inventory at opening.

Human Resource Requirements. From a manufacturing viewpoint, human resource requirements should be summarized with information on the number of personnel and type of skills needed. If the business depends on unusually talented personnel, such as research scientists, these requirements should be identified. In most instances, specific personnel details can be omitted, and a later section describes the persons involved in the founding team.

Operational Rationale. If the firm will engage in R&D, the plan should spell out the extent of this effort. If operations include manufacturing, the plan should describe vendor relations, supply requirements, maintenance, and transport requirements. Manufacturers also will be expected to describe their quality-control policies, safety requirements, and other specific operations related to the enterprise.

Legal and Insurance Issues. Most businesses must consider insurance and legal protection to avoid disasters. Specifically, entrepreneurs will need business liability insurance, and when the business relies on a few talented people, the founders may want life and disability insurance on key people.

VII. LEADERSHIP—THE ENTREPRENEURIAL TEAM

Recall an earlier comment that investors put greater emphasis on the entrepreneurial team than on the business concept. Consequently, entrepreneurs must take care to profile the entrepreneurial team honestly but effectively. They should emphasize team members' strengths, past successes, and positive characteristics, and they should include brief résumés of the principals. Each person's role in the new venture should be described briefly, including board members or investors who may be influential.

VIII. MAJOR EVENTS, RISKS, AND PROGRESSIVE CHECKPOINTS

Major events, critical risk factors, and activities that constitute progressive checkpoints are important to delineate in the plan. They provide the entrepreneur with a set of controls for monitoring the new venture. Major events might include a schedule for lining up facilities, testing prototypes, hiring personnel, acquiring inventory, and staging a grand opening. Some business plans address these issues under "marketing strategies" or "operations."

IX. FINANCIAL DOCUMENTATION

Since money is the objective measure used to gauge a firm's progress, financial statements can logically be expected to come under close scrutiny. Financial statements for a new venture, called *pro formas*, are projections based on previously defined operating and marketing assumptions. The business plan should describe the assumptions that underpin financial projections and special considerations such as "development stages" when no income will be produced. It should also explain how invested money or loans will be utilized and accounted for in the financial statements. A "sources and uses" statement or a "start-up statement" can be included, along with appropriate explanations. Schedules and statements should include the following:

Start-up Projections. The plan should identify the sources and uses of funds at start-up, or alternatively, it should list and describe how invested equity or loan proceeds will be utilized.

Income Statement. Also called a *profit and loss statement*, an income statement should be provided in detail for at least three years. Common practice is to project the first year in monthly data, then project additional years in quarterly summaries. The income statement is required to show revenue, cost of goods sold, operating expenses, and net income.

Cash-Flow Statement. First-year projections (by month) and subsequent years (by quarter) should compound with income projections. These cash-flow projections reflect information from the profit and loss statement adjusted properly for credit sales (actual cash flow indicated rather than accrual income), noncash expenses (depreciation), and cash obtained and used outside of operational income (e.g., capital from investors and cash payments on loan principle).

Balance Sheet. A comparative set of balance sheets should provide the opening position of the business and projected results for three to five years. Some lenders will expect monthly data for the first year (comparable to the income statement and cash-flow statement), but annual data are standard.

Break-Even Analysis. The break-even analysis is a summary calculation of when the business will begin to turn a profit. It may not be required if the break-even data are summarized elsewhere. It is one of several supplements that can be included. Others include schedules for capital equipment, assets, debts, receivables, or graphic tables or charts on sales, income, and profits.

X. APPENDIXES

If not included elsewhere, résumés on founders and key personnel should be enclosed as appendixes. If the business has had a past history and the business plan is being developed for additional equity financing or an SBA loan application, appendixes that show past performance for up to three years may be required.

Appendix **B**

An Integrated Feasibility Plan for Poly-Chem Associates, Inc.

Appendix B   *An Integrated Feasibility Plan for Poly-Chem Associates, Inc.*   493

Poly-Chem Associates, Incorporated, Feasibility Plan for Polymer-Related Marketing and Distribution
October 1, 1990

The Poly-Chem Associates, Inc., feasibility plan is *confidential* and contains proprietary information including trade secrets of Poly-Chem Associates, Inc. Neither the feasibility plan nor any of the information contained in the plan may be reproduced or disclosed to any person under any circumstance without express written permission of Poly-Chem Associates, Inc. This is neither a public document nor a public offering.

Control Copy Number _____

Poly-Chem Associates, Inc.
48 Carlton Street
Harrisonburg, VA 22801

I. EXECUTIVE SUMMARY

Poly-Chem Associates, Incorporated, is an international trading company with a focal interest in polymer chemicals. The fundamental purpose of Poly-Chem is to establish global markets in polymer-based chemical products for agriculture, horticulture, professional landscaping, and sports turf development. Through licenses and contracts, Poly-Chem has secured marketing rights to a family of high-quality polymer products, and through field research, we have developed cost-effective methods for utilization of these products. The company has proprietary data and field methodologies crucial for effective use of synthetic polymers. Consequently, our primary objective is to provide customers with outstanding field services in conjunction with products of the highest quality.

The Company

Headquartered in the United States, Poly-Chem evolved from a partnership of its founders and was capitalized in August 1989 as a Virginia Corporation. Incorporation followed several years of research by the partners, who found that recently developed synthetic polymers could be commercialized as soil amendments. Specifically, *cross-linked polyacrylamides* were found to have the extraordinary ability to retain water and water-soluble compounds, subsequently releasing moisture, fertilizer, and pesticides efficiently to plants.

The cofounders are Dr. Vernon C. Jones and Mr. James W. Sims. Jones has had 22 years in university education and research. As a biochemist, he has demonstrated knowledge in the chemical field. Sims was president of his own chemical supply company with 30 years experience in the industry. The founders have equal shares of common stock, totaling 16 percent of authorized shares valued, July 1, 1990, at $80,000 on incorporation. The net asset value was determined by owners' equity transferred from research, facilities, equipment, and cash. Subsequently, $37,500 of shares were purchased at par of $100 by three private investors.

Product Summary

Synthetic polymers have existed for nearly six decades, and processes have evolved for hundreds of plastics, synthetic clothing, filters, packing materials, and industrial products. However, few of these items are biodegradable. Their main strength rests on resilience of material (such as polyvinyl chloride), but their major weakness is a staggering ecological threat. Cross-linked polyacrylamide, however, is a degradable and environmentally safe compound that will last for as long as ten years, yet will totally degrade into natural elements without harmful residue.

Poly-Chem realized in early 1989 that cross-linked polyacrylamide had many potential uses reconfigured as a family of commercial products. The product line is marketed under the registered trademark PolyGro, and *PolyGro* will be the term used hereafter. PolyGro has coarse-grain crystals similar in size to unrefined sugar. In their

Appendix B   An Integrated Feasibility Plan for Poly-Chem Associates, Inc.

dry crystal form, they are white and hard. In their hydrated form, they become a translucent gel, much like tiny sponges, each crystal about the size of a pencil eraser.

Market Characteristics

Polyacrylamide products evolved during the mid-1980s in the form of soft crystals of various sizes between 0.01 mm and 1.8 mm in diameter. The crystals act like tiny sponges to absorb water and water-soluble amendments. They expand rapidly and retain up to 400 times their weight in water. This unique property turns each crystal into a reservoir; an ounce of crystals can absorb nearly a gallon of water. When crystals are mixed with soil, far less water is needed to ensure healthy plant growth. Consequently, irrigation is reduced while natural rainfall—even if parsimonious—is efficiently used. Plants, trees, crops, and turf germinate better, grow faster, and produce higher yields.

Potential for such a product is obviously great in an era when water and agricultural land are rapidly becoming scarce as the world's population expands. Most people in affluent nations, however, are not yet concerned with limitations of water and land resources. Therefore, demand is embryonic in societies unaffected by resource scarcities such as water. Nevertheless, even in the most prosperous societies, these resource scarcities are beginning to be felt; water management—both urban and rural for human consumption and agriculture—will soon be among the most crucial issues in every society.

Poly-Chem has focused its energies on *bulk* and *wholesale* markets, rather than retail trade, home gardens and lawns, or other small-volume users. This represents a "niche" strategy directed toward three customer sectors: commercial agriculture, professional landscaping, and sports turf development. Each sector has several distinct customer groups that constitute an industry potential in the United States of more than $900 million annually within ten years. The global market is on the order of 83 magnitudes greater.

Poly-Chem intends to focus on its three target niches and also constrain itself realistically to the areas of Virginia, North and South Carolina, and Florida. With expansion, we expect to market in Southern California, and several overseas customers have expressed interest. Based on our primary markets, we expect significant initial growth as follows:

	1991	1992	1993	1994	1995
Sales (1,000 pounds)	534	3,875	5,148	7,651	10,950
Gross income ($1,000)	1,827	11,494	16,839	23,653	33,959
Net income ($1,000)	119	585	1,316	2,256	3,968

Investment Objectives

Poly-Chem is seeking $240,000 in equity underwriting for a three-year period. The investment will be used for field research, equipment, and market development during the start-up period. Market development requires field projects with application and technical consulting. Consequently, a significant investment will be made to contract researchers in relevant fields. Eventually, the founders intend to take the company public on the strength of sales in polymer products.

II. PRODUCT CHARACTERISTICS

The scientific characteristics of PolyGro have been established during several years of testing in both Britain and the United States. Information in this section focuses on *cross-linked polyacrylamide*. This is the technical term for synthetic polymer marketed under Poly-Chem's trademark of PolyGro. Reference will be made to PolyGro and to polyacrylamide, which are interchangeable terms.

Absorptive Capacity

While PolyGro can optimally absorb up to 430 times its weight in deionized water, it is unusual to find an ideal water source. Consequently, the following table summarizes PolyGro's water-absorptive capacities under various conditions:

Water Characteristics	Absorptive Capacity (ml/gm dry product)
General conditions:	
Deionized (0.1)[1]	410 ± 20
Soft, potable (52)[1]	199 ± 17
Hard, potable (300)[1]	162 ± 14
Brackish upper estuary[2]	97 ± 7
Deionized water circulated through different soils:	
Coastal dune sand (pH 7.9)	197 ± 22
Calcareous rendzina (pH 7.6)	174 ± 14
Brown earth (pH 6.8)	212 ± 13
Gault clay (pH 5.9)	184 ± 10
Iron-humus podzol (pH 4.7)	180 ± 13

[1] Soluble salt concentration, mg/l.
[2] Conductivity, 3.2 mS/cm.

Testing indicates that PolyGro in the soil lasts more than five years with at least 95 percent of its water-storage capacity. When hydration cycles were simulated for a ten-year period, PolyGro retained 91 percent of its capacity. Absorption was not significantly affected by fungi, bacteria, microorganisms, or fertilizers.

Water Release

Although many water-absorbing polymers have the ability to soak up huge amounts of water, only cross-linked polyacrylamide (PolyGro) has a sufficiently slow reaction time to prevent waterlogging and rapid evaporation. As a result, it is a consistent water source to plant root systems that is highly efficient.

Degradation

The useful life of PolyGro is determined by its exposure to ultraviolet rays. Exposed directly under a UV light, PolyGro degraded approximately 3 percent over a six-week period; simulated for one year, degradation was 16 percent. In contrast, starch-based polymers degraded 58 percent in six weeks and 100 percent in six months. Polyvinylalcohols degraded 26 percent in six weeks and 97 percent in one year.

Starch-based polymers, polyvinylalcohols, and polyacrylamides are all sold under various trade names as "superabsorbents"; however, polyacrylamide products stand up best and eventually break down to pose no environmental hazard. The rapid degradation of competing products seems more environmentally attractive, but their short useful life renders them uneconomical. PolyGro's reasonably long life cycle translates to huge cost savings spread over a five-year period.

When PolyGro degrades, it dissolves into water and carbon dioxide, with less than 0.1 percent inert amine residue. Repeated and extensive testing (OECD, EEC international hazard safety examinations) has proven PolyGro and its by-products following degradation to be completely harmless to human beings, animals, plants, and the environment. A "nontoxic, nonhazardous" classification has been approved by OSHA. *PolyGro is environmentally safe.*

Leaching

PolyGro, with its high molecular weight and resistance to breakdown, does not leach in its active state. Its by-products (water, carbon dioxide, and inert amine) will leach once degraded, but without harmful effects. PolyGro greatly decreases leaching of fertilizer and pesticides. Consequently, soil amendments and nutrient efficiency are greatly enhanced, and plant growth is optimized.

Evaporation

Research has found that polymers can decrease evaporation rates by as much as 75 percent. Clearly, these rates vary with differences in atmospheric humidity, temperature, soil conditions, and application techniques.

Aeration

Compaction tests on soccer fields and golf course greens indicate that polymer-treated ground remains soft and aerated. Compaction was avoided because of the constant expansion and retraction of polymer crystals during normal hydration and evaporation. Consequently, plant growth was enhanced by oxygenation of the soil, creating stronger root systems.

Grass Seed Germination and Turf Applications

PolyGro users have noted its effects on lawns under weather conditions ranging from optimal to severe drought. Lawns are lusher because of increased seed germination; turf growth is resilient to distress; and there is a dramatically decreased need for watering and lawn amendments. The result is lower-care turf, especially in high-use areas, making PolyGro excellent for use in sports fields.

Under excessive rainfall conditions, PolyGro absorbs water for future use and improves the runoff of excess water through improved aeration, resulting in a marked improvement in soil structure. Consequently, there is less waterlogging, and there are drastic decreases in the occurrence of disease.

Tests on the effects of polyacrylamide on new grass establishment were conducted along the A-4 roadway in Britain during summer when there was little rainfall and temperatures reached 80°F. Four A-4 roadside plots were chosen; two were treated with polyacrylamide to a depth of 4 inches, and two left untreated. Plots were sown with a low-maintenance amenity grass mixture at a rate of 75 kg/ha.

Each was watered to field capacity, left for 24 hours, then rewatered to field capacity. No further irrigation was carried out, and in the following 14 days only two periods of rainfall occurred: A light rain occurred 3 days after sowing, and a 40-minute thunderstorm occurred 5 days after sowing. No rainfall occurred between the 6th and 15th days. Researchers took a germination count 7 days after sowing and a count of seedling establishment after 14 days. Results are shown in the following table, indicating significant improvements:

	Germination (emergence/m^2)	Established Seedlings (g/m^2)
Untreated plots:		
1	790	174
2	865	214
Mean	827	194
PolyGro-treated plots:		
1	973	792
2	987	746
Mean	980	769

Appendix B   An Integrated Feasibility Plan for Poly-Chem Associates, Inc.

Tests on Established Grass and Golf Tee Boxes

A series of tests were undertaken in the same near-drought conditions in Great Britain on two garden lawns and side-by-side comparisons on golf tee boxes. During this test period over several weeks, established grass surrounding both sites had turned a dead-looking yellow-brown from serious lack of rainfall. The tests, therefore, were considered to be "under full-stress turf conditions."

At each site, checkerboard squares of plots were designed with alternating plots treated and untreated. Each square was 1 m^2, and turf was removed to a depth of 4 inches. Soil was then either treated with PolyGro (at 1:1,000) and returned or returned untreated. The plots were initially watered to capacity and rewatered 24 hours later. While some light rain fell during the first week, no rain fell during the following two weeks. After the two dry weeks, control plots, which had flourished following the initial watering, returned to a yellow-brown state similar to the surrounding turf. Polymer-treated plots, however, remained green and healthy. Researchers measured results, as shown:

Grass Weights in Kilograms Per Square Meter for Lawns and Golf Tees

	Garden Lawns 1 Treated	Garden Lawns 1 Untreated	Garden Lawns 2 Treated	Garden Lawns 2 Untreated	Golf Course Tee Site Treated	Golf Course Tee Site Untreated
1 week	13.2	12.1	10.3	11.0	16.1	14.0
2 weeks	14.1	10.7	10.2	8.4	15.8	12.2
3 weeks	17.5	2.1	8.2	3.7	14.9	6.4

The tests on garden lawns and golf course tee boxes indicated that PolyGro extended by at least ten days the onset of wilting and deterioration—and while ordinary grass was dying, polymer-treated grass was *flourishing*. Parallel tests in greenhouses indicated that polyacrylamide was able to maintain established grass well beyond the ten days found by drought tests in the field experiments.

Flowers and Shrubbery

The best-known and most popularly documented advantages of PolyGro all apply to flowers and shrubbery. Small and medium-sized plants all benefit from the improved water and nutrient delivery, increased aeration, and protection from drought and transplant shock offered by PolyGro.

One district council in Britain used PolyGro in raising half its 4,000 trays of bedding plants. Varieties of plants grown included lobelia, alyssum, tagetes, impatiens, salvias, rudbeckia, verbena, and *Begonia semperflorens;* the district nursery raised these from seed in standard compost. The borough applied polyacrylamide to compost in half the trays at recommended rates, and left half as a control. Seedlings in treated compost emerged on average three weeks earlier than the control plants. The borough found that plants grown in polymer-treated soil only needed one-third to one-half the water of untreated plants, and slow-growing varieties in particular could be grown more economically, with three weeks less growing time, saving heating costs and bench space.

Following the preceding tests on flower development, PolyGro was applied into beds of geraniums. Tests were made with 300 cuttings of each of three geranium types taken from stock plants; half were treated and half were not. Within 18 days all cuttings in the polymer-treated section had rooted, although those in the untreated section had not. The treated bed remained friable and well aerated throughout. A large-scale test in Britain used 8,000 potted geraniums; 2,500 were polymer-treated and 5,500 remained untreated. Treated plants required nearly one-third less water and one-sixth less plant compost, and they flowered two weeks earlier than untreated geraniums. *PolyGro reduced watering costs by more than 85 percent.*

Tree Establishment and Growth

Tree planting for urban streets, parks, or commercial orchards is subject to fundamentally different economics from turf or shrubbery planting. When a tree is planted, it is generally of extraheavy standard or is semimature in size with a substantial leaf canopy. However, transplanted trees tend to have a fragile and limited root system, and survival rates are low without expensive maintenance and watering.

Use of PolyGro reduces losses due to transplant shock (both bulb and bare-root) as it maintains water and nutrient supply to root systems. In the short term, PolyGro increases tree survival rates while reducing maintenance costs, and in the long term, it enhances growth.

Manchester, England, tested polyacrylamide for street-lined trees. One hundred trees were planted in a topsoil and peat medium treated with polymer at the standard rate, and an equal number of trees were left untreated. All trees were then watered to capacity. Subsequent maintenance watering was applied to the untreated trees every three weeks, a rate which just kept them from wilting. PolyGro-treated trees were monitored with the intention of watering only as needed. *For every dollar spent on polymer treatment, the city saved four dollars on maintenance watering.*

Polyacrylamide was also applied during planting of a commercial apple orchard. A total of 1,094 trees were planted with treated backfill (at 1:1,000) in 8-gallon pockets. Separately, 934 trees were planted in the same fashion but without polymer. Increased growth and improved foliage condition were noted throughout the polymer-treated area. Of the 1,094 trees given polymer treatment, 26 were dead at summer's end; of the 934 without polymer, 143 died. Although nearly 17 percent of untreated trees died, 97.6 percent of those treated with PolyGro survived. During the following year, 20 trees from each group were selected and analyzed. Results show an increase in growth of more than 200 percent, as follows:

	Untreated Trees	**Polymer-Treated Trees**	**Increase (percent)**
Trunk growth	283 cm	826 cm	192
Offshoot growth	606 cm	1,956 cm	223
Total	889 cm	2,782 cm	
Average extension growth	44.5 cm	139 cm	213

These results are applicable to all trees, but they have especially strong implications for fruit growers. Solid establishment and strong performance of trees in polymer-enhanced soil significantly decrease the time to yield, resulting in earlier cash harvests for an orchard. We also know that thousands of trees of more than 40 varieties are planted each year using polymer by the U.S. Forest Service. However, the USFS has not kept statistical data, and it is careful to avoid statements that would endorse products. Nevertheless, the USFS recommends implantation and transplantation using *polyacrylamide products*.

Agricultural Germination, Growth, and Yields

Use of PolyGro in agriculture results in increases in both germination and yield of up to 30 percent. Poly-Chem, Inc., conducted tests at four commercial sites and a vegetable farm in 1989. At the vegetable farm, the owners planted tomatoes, broccoli, lettuce, green beans, sweet corn, and peppers in garden plots. Plots were divided into control, 15-pounds-of-polymer-per-acre, and 30-pounds-per-acre areas, with some planted by bedding and some by in-row processes. After four weeks, total germination from seed for bedded plants was 11.4 percent greater with PolyGro than in the control. In-row germination rates were not statistically different from bedded plants, with an 11.2 percent increase for treated rows.

Sorghum, corn, and bean fields were all in-row planted at the commercial sites. Test fields planted at 30 pounds per acre showed an 11.8 percent increase in germination over the control field; at 15 pounds per acre, the germination increase was 10.6 percent. The variety of corn planted is normally harvested in 106 days; however, in the 30-pounds-per-acre field, it was ready for harvest at 87 days, 19 days early; the 15-pounds-per-acre field was ready on day 93, or 13 days early. The control field was ready for harvest on day 107. Yields increased by 24.9 percent on corn at 30 pounds per acre and by 22.2 percent on corn at 15 pounds per acre.

Sorghum was all harvested on the same day, 82 days after planting. The control field yielded 24.3 tons per acre; the 15-pound field, 27.8 tons per acre; and the 30-pound field, 31.2 tons per acre. This was an increased yield of 28.4 percent with 30 pounds per acre and 14.4 percent with 15 pounds per acre.

These tests showed that PolyGro more than paid for itself in the first test season. Owners estimated their net profit for the initial year at 18 percent, and productivity increased by about 26 percent per acre. A California commercial grower experimented with canning-tomato fields. Three half-mile rows were planted at a rate of 15 pounds of polymer per acre. The grower reported that tomatoes matured a full two weeks earlier, yielding 30 percent more tomato by weight. Another application in California consisted of using polymer for cotton. Polyacrylamide was applied to 40-acre fields at a rate of 5 pounds per acre, drilled into cotton rows with 30–35 cotton seeds per yard at planting. Treated rows had double the normal emergence rate (25–26 plants per yard compared to the usual 12–13) and emerged 36–48 hours earlier.

PolyGro and Fertilizer

Where applicable, the tests were all undertaken with standard rates of fertilizer application. Yet experiments indicate that even better results are achieved when fertilizer application to polymer-treated plants and soil is cut in half. Specifically, a 50 percent reduction in fertilizer application results in at least a 10 percent increase in plant weight over that found in polymer-treated plants to which the normal rate of fertilizer has been applied.

Soil Stabilization and Erosion Control

Experiments indicate the application of micronized polymer in a water solution of approximately 1:10 greatly decreases slope erosion, helping seedlings to resist shifting. The advantage to such a process is in the stabilization of a hillside long enough for grass and shrubbery to take root. One promising application is in grass hydroseeding. Although hydroseeding has proven itself popular and convenient, it has not always proven effective, especially in sloped or hilly areas. The use of PolyGro may greatly improve the effectiveness of hydroseeding, keeping the seed fixed in the desired location while helping it to germinate and take root more quickly.

III. MARKETS AND DEMAND EXPECTATIONS

Poly-Chem's management envisions two broad markets—domestic American customers and foreign export customers. The domestic market is further segmented into several types of customers that relate to PolyGro uses. Foreign markets are too broad to be classified; however, Poly-Chem has already opened several overseas opportunities, which will be explained momentarily.

Domestic U.S. Markets

The polymer industry is not geographically segmented within the country; competitors sell to chains (such as K-Mart), PGA member golf courses nationwide, national seed distributors, and catalog wholesalers. Key competitors may have advantages in some areas, but the industry is so new and fragmented that no one has a distinct geographic market or customer.

Poly-Chem has consciously focused initially on two regions—the southern states on the East Coast and Southern California. The southern states include Virginia, North and South Carolina, Georgia, and Florida. Southern California includes San Bernardino and San Diego counties and the Desert Center area.

Estimates of total market capacity are based on three types of users and several important assumptions. The users include agriculture, landscape, and resort development. One basic assumption is that our markets consist of *bulk* buyers. Second, the total potential in each market is extremely large, but, realistically, we envision being able to serve only a small number of customers during the next five years. Third, we have private production data from polymer manufacturers that cannot be legally related, yet we are confident that total polymer sales by all sources in the U.S. represent market penetration of less than 0.01 percent; no one has a foothold in any market.

Virginia

Agriculture. The total agricultural land under cultivation is nearly 2.1 million acres. High-yield vegetables are produced on 740,000 acres, and feed grains and silage are grown on more than 900,000 acres. The remainder is disaggregated into small dairy farms, herb farms (such as Shiitake Mushrooms), and contract planting (such as brewer's barley). In addition, approximately 220,000 acres are devoted to "subsistence" farming, largely owned by Mennonites.

To simplify the analysis, Poly-Chem views its Virginia agricultural market for the five-year projection as buyers who control more than 1 square mile of high-yield vegetables and contract growers who use crops in value-added production such as beer or institutional foods (e.g., canned vegetables).

Based on those criteria, Virginia has approximately 450,000 acres for direct bulk marketing. Assuming a nominal application rate of 15 pounds per acre and annual "halving" of application over five years, the potential market for polymer is 13 million pounds during the period 1990–1995. Of course, these major buyers are not going to rush to buy polymer, and if they did, production capacity could not meet this demand. Realistically, our objective is to reach 12 major agricultural customers each year beginning spring 1991. This would represent a target of roughly 7,680 acres per year or 38,400 acres implanted by spring 1995. The economics of this estimate follow:

12 buyers at 640 acres = 7,680 × 15 pounds rate of application
= 115,200 pounds the first year
12 at reduced rates (years 2–5 = 7.5 + 3.7 + 2.0 + 2.0) = 116,700 pounds

Five-year total potential = 231,900 pounds

Assuming 12 buyers added (linear growth) in 1992 through 1995, then the second-year customers would have the initial purchase (115,200 pounds) plus three add-on years (total of 101,000 pounds). Using the same logic for third-, fourth-, and fifth-year customers—and including the first-year base—total demand based on our marketing objectives for 1991–1995 in agriculture is as follows:

First-year customers	= 231,900 pounds
Second-year customers	= 226,200 pounds
Third-year customers	= 201,200 pounds
Fourth-year customers	= 172,800 pounds
Fifth-year customers	= 115,200 pounds
Total five-year demand	= 947,300 pounds

There are several points to note in this analysis. First, each of the 12 annual buyers has only 640 acres (the lowest quartile minimum for acreage under cultivation by corporate/contract growers). Second, they will implant polymer for high-yield vegetables or "value-added" crops using minimum rates for in-row planting. Third, 60 customers represent less than 1 percent of that current market niche in Virginia. Consequently, these estimates are conservative.

Agricultural Revenue. From a sales revenue perspective, assuming these low estimates and a bulk price of $4.00 per pound, Virginia agriculture sales would gross *$3.9 million* from delivery dates of spring 1991 through 1995. We caution, however, that initial marketing campaigns may include price incentives (discounts), and sales will not generate cash flow until product is delivered several months later. Sales will also be seasonal (not one new customer per month for 12 months a year, but nearly all contracts between October and March).

Virginia Landscaping. Although there are no accurate public estimates of the number or size of commercial landscape companies in Virginia, a sample of four county telephone listings provides some information. Rockingham, Augusta, Page, and Highland counties were used. Each of these is a low-density county representing four of the eight least commercialized in Virginia to provide conservative projections. Combined, they had 283 landscape contractors, 312 listed nurseries, and 721 listed building contractors. Personal contacts and phone calls in 1988 and 1989 revealed that about 9 percent of these maintained their own landscape equipment or sold wholesale to commercial developers. Our assumption, therefore, is that only about 9 percent of landscapers, nurseries, and building contractors statewide would be viable customers for substantial bulk orders. With 23 counties in Virginia, conservative estimates of customers follow:

Landscape firms	1,627 × 0.09 = 146
Commercial nurseries	1,794 × 0.09 = 161
Building contractors	4,145 × 0.09 = 373
Total potential customers	= 680

Based on test markets in 1990 to several customers in each of these groups, we have cautiously determined demand on contractors' estimates. Data are vague, yet they indicate a trend to reasonably expect that each potential customer engaged in landscape contracting can expect to implant a minimum of 400,000 square feet of turf, 4,800 trees, and 12,400 ornamental shrubs. If we also target only ten of the 680 customers in our niche each year, those ten should have a total potential of at least 4.0 million square feet of turf, 48,000 trees, and 124,000 shrubs for *private development contracts*.

At standard rates of polymer for each category of application, these figures equate to an annual demand for PolyGro of 24,000 pounds for turf, 18,000 pounds for trees, and 41,000 pounds for shrubs. The *total private annual demand for major contracts is 83,000 pounds of PolyGro*. Based on contractors' estimates of public-sector sales (city, county, and state agencies for roadsides, grading, parks, recreation, schools, and public works), public use of landscape products exceeds private use. Consequently, if Poly-Chem markets to an equal number of public-sector customers, annual demand doubles to 166,000 pounds of polymer.

For estimation purposes, we assume that ten commercial landscape clients can be contracted each year (linear growth) beginning in 1991 so that by 1995, Poly-Chem may represent 50 commercial customers, about 7 percent of our target market (0.5 percent of the total market).

For the five-year projection period, commercial landscape demand capable of being serviced by Poly-Chem in Virginia is 1.25 million pounds. Assuming a wholesale discounted price to contractors, a price level of $3.65 per pound is used for projected total sales of *$4.56 million*.

Virginia Golf Courses. Poly-Chem will focus on golf course development, replanting existing ones and implanting new ones. According to the Mid-Atlantic PGA, there were 63 golf courses in the Virginia Association in January 1990. This number increased rather slowly since 1980 when Virginia listed 44 courses; the annual increase was no more than two new courses each year. However, the 44 courses in 1980 had a total of 774 holes (several had more than 18 holes, and others had only a nine-hole layout). By 1990 there were 1,512 holes among the 63 courses. Therefore, the number of courses changed slowly (compared with national developments), but renovations and extended layouts represented a significant increase—nearly doubling course capacity (by number of holes) in ten years.

Assuming each golf hole averages 280,000 square feet tee-to-green (net of greens, rough, and subsidiary landscape), then Virginia has planted more than 20 million square feet of *new turf* each year since 1980. The MAPGA estimates that new golf courses in Virginia will increase during the 1990s to, perhaps, a total of 96. These include only those expected to meet MAPGA standards, and at least 25 courses will have multiple resort layouts (i.e., 27 or 36 holes).

Using those estimates, Virginia can expect to build about 891 new holes in ten years, or turf at least 250 million square feet each year. If polymer is used at applied rates of 6 pounds per thousand square feet, total potential demand is about 1.5 million pounds for fairways (net of greens and course amenities). Each new course would require about 18,000 pounds initial implantation for fairways and 6,000 pounds for greens. If total course turf acreage is implanted, a rough estimate for each course is demand for 32,000 pounds of polymer.

Poly-Chem's objective is to contract one new course and one renovation in

1991, and two in each subsequent year through 1995, for a total of ten courses under contract by the end of spring 1995. A conservative demand estimate of Poly-Chem's total projected Virginia market, 1991–1995, is 345,000 pounds for turf and 154,000 pounds for additional plants; a total of 499,000 pounds. At a price of $4.00 a pound, revenue is projected at $1.99 million over five years.

Consolidated Virginia Markets. Combining the three major customer groups and five-year marketing objectives, Poly-Chem envisions having less than 1 percent of the agricultural market, less than 0.5 percent of the landscape market, and 4 percent of the golf course market by 1995 (see the table on page 507).

These combined projections indicate sales of about 2.7 million pounds of PolyGro between 1991 and 1995. Revenue for that period would be about $10.5 million. This result assumes low market penetration and conservative demand estimates.

We present this detailed information on Virginia to provide a foundation for analyses of other states. Subsequent projections will not repeat assumptions or annual break-out data, but will summarize five-year demand. Domestic market data will then be aggregated.

North and South Carolina

Poly-Chem management has not conducted formal marketing research in these or other states; however, based on U.S. statistical data, North Carolina has more land under cultivation than Virginia does, a substantial timber industry for soft-grain and furniture-quality hardwoods, a landscape and nursery industry slightly smaller than Virginia's, and a golf course development market nearly double Virginia's. South Carolina has a larger agricultural market than either North Carolina or Virginia, less timber and landscape activity, and a golf course industry comparable to North Carolina's. With these comparisons in mind, Poly-Chem's potential in the Carolinas should mirror Virginia statistics.

Two caveats affect projections for market projections in the Carolinas. First, Poly-Chem has no presence in these states, and market development will have to be "staged" slowly over several years. Although we have proximity and some initial contacts with potential buyers, the company will face a high-cost marketing effort to establish initial markets. Second, golf course recreational development in the Carolinas has had explosive growth, but data are not well documented. These two factors combine to reduce projections for total sales substantially; however, they also indicate potential in golf course development and associated landscaping that is more than double Virginia estimates. Using the same assumptions as used for Virginia, demand estimates for these states are as shown in the tables on page 508.

Total effective demand for North Carolina, assuming extremely low market penetration and slow "staging" for 1991–1992, approaches 1.9 million pounds, more than half that total in recreational golf course development. This figure equates to about $7.5 million in polymer sales through 1995 (see the table on page 508).

Total effective demand for South Carolina will be less than North Carolina

PolyGro Virginia: Demand and Revenue (× 1,000 rounded down)

	1991 Demand (pounds)	1991 Revenue (dollars)	1992 Demand (pounds)	1992 Revenue (dollars)	1993 Demand (pounds)	1993 Revenue (dollars)	1994 Demand (pounds)	1994 Revenue (dollars)	1995 Demand (pounds)	1995 Revenue (dollars)
Agriculture	115	460	172	688	201	804	230	920	260	1,040
Landscaping	83	302	166	605	249	908	332	1,211	415	1,514
Golf courses	56	224	112	448	112	448	112	448	112	448
Totals	254	986	450	1,741	562	2,160	674	2,579	787	3,002

PolyGro North Carolina: Demand and Revenue (× 1,000 rounded down)

	1991 Demand (pounds)	1991 Revenue (dollars)	1992 Demand (pounds)	1992 Revenue (dollars)	1993 Demand (pounds)	1993 Revenue (dollars)	1994 Demand (pounds)	1994 Revenue (dollars)	1995 Demand (pounds)	1995 Revenue (dollars)
Agriculture	25	100	50	200	75	300	100	400	200	800
Landscaping	25	91	50	182	75	273	100	365	200	730
Golf courses	80	320	120	480	160	640	220	880	440	1,760
Totals	130	511	220	862	310	1,213	420	1,645	840	3,290

PolyGro South Carolina: Demand and Revenue (× 1,000 rounded down)

	1991 Demand (pounds)	1991 Revenue (dollars)	1992 Demand (pounds)	1992 Revenue (dollars)	1993 Demand (pounds)	1993 Revenue (dollars)	1994 Demand (pounds)	1994 Revenue (dollars)	1995 Demand (pounds)	1995 Revenue (dollars)
Agriculture	10	40	20	80	40	160	80	320	160	480
Landscaping	10	36	20	72	40	145	100	365	200	730
Golf courses	80	320	120	480	160	640	220	880	440	1,760
Totals	100	396	160	632	240	945	400	1,565	800	2,970

because of more distant markets, yet landscaping and recreational development may be much higher than projected. Total PolyGro demand approximates 1.7 million pounds for gross sales through 1995 of $6.5 million.

Florida

Poly-Chem has not engaged in formal market research in Florida, and the state has several disaggregated regions that make projections difficult. The South Florida area—Dade and surrounding counties—is characterized by fast-paced urban growth, major public works, and a pressing water problem. This water problem is compounded by population demand on limited water resources and rising water and irrigation costs that threaten horticultural development. The urban problem is not addressed here, yet it presents a potential market, mirrored by other urban centers with similar problems such as Atlanta, Los Angeles, and San Diego.

The second Florida region is the agricultural belt in the middle of the state. This is one of the highest value-added agricultural regions in the United States, and it is reaching a crisis stage of irrigation. According to the Indian River office of Agricultural Extension, fruit growers with nearly 800 square miles of orchards were forced to ration irrigation water each of the past three years (1987–1989). In addition, an increased number of small Indian River growers sold out or failed during the past two years, partly because of rising irrigation costs and partly because of late frost problems. This region has also seen a rapid growth of real estate development. The Florida PGA would not disclose growth data on new courses or resorts but said in 1989 alone there were 112 applications for zoned developments "in and around the Orlando area." The PGA also suggested that there are political conflicts over water rights and irrigation between resort developers and municipalities.

The third region is the North Florida and "panhandle" area. Much of this region has relatively slower growth than southern regions, is less agrarian than the Indian River region, but has greater potential for planned communities, redevelopment, and coastal resort construction. Market potential is unknown for this and other regions of Florida; however, if the *Statistical Abstract of the United States* data are reliable, then Florida as a whole almost matches total activity of Virginia, North Carolina, and South Carolina combined.

A necessarily naive market forecast is presented for Florida based on two assumptions: First, Florida has far more pressing water problems and development than Virginia, suggesting more immediate demand of greater volume in all sectors. Second, income and spending levels in Florida are far greater than in Virginia, representing more major markets. Data in the table that follows suggest potential in Florida that is in general more than four times the Virginia market, with some modifications. Because our negotiations in Florida focus on distributors who have a primary interest in resort development, marketing is most likely to favor landscape and recreational applications; agricultural markets will not evolve rapidly. Also, agriculture has less "effective" demand; golf course, recreation, and community development will prosper.

The data in the table on page 511 assume that a major distributor can be contracted to make the Florida market, and that the distributor is capable of servicing major customers in target markets. Consequently, Florida's potential for PolyGro is 9.3 million pounds through 1995. This equates to $35.5 million in gross sales.

Southern California

As in the case of Florida, no formal market research has been conducted by Poly-Chem; however, we have been approached by three major distributors in Southern California. Based on their independent assessments of market potential, California should match Florida with slight adjustments. These include a slightly reduced demand in resort development golf courses and a slight increase in agriculture. They also project a major market for home lawns, turf, public-sector landscaping, and forestry. However, we assume no data for these markets and will actively pursue them only as our distributors identify opportunities (see the table on page 511).

Projected demand for Southern California is for 8.8 million pounds of PolyGro. This figure equates to $33.3 million in sales through 1995.

Summary of Domestic U.S. Demand

These data were discussed with potential distributors in Florida, North Carolina, and California, existing customers in Virginia, and representatives of three PGA regional section heads. In each instance, the initial conclusions by Poly-Chem were taken lightly; the impression was that management's estimates far exceeded realistic market potential. A closer reading of assumptions and total market growth in our target sectors, however, led to a complete reversal of opinions. In each instance, distributors concluded that we were understating market potential and also ignoring major market opportunities.

In this analysis, we have selected those states and bulk customer markets where Poly-Chem can reasonably expect to initiate sales. As in most businesses, markets often occur serendipitously, and although we shall pursue those markets identified, we are proceeding cautiously to stage each cycle of endeavor.

Combining the total forecasts for domestic sales for the five states and their three target customer groups, Poly-Chem intends to reach conservative sales objectives. Consequently, total PolyGro estimated sales between 1991 and 1995 are *24.4 million pounds*, grossing *$93.3 million*. These figures assume allowance for materials provided at cost for tests and allowances for reasonable returns.

Foreign Markets

No attempt will be made to project foreign demand or individual markets in countries where PolyGro could have a tremendous reception. However, foreign markets could easily eclipse total domestic sales in each of several regions, and these markets may evolve far more rapidly than in the United States.

PolyGro Florida: Demand and Revenue (× 1,000 rounded down)

	1991 Demand (pounds)	1991 Revenue (dollars)	1992 Demand (pounds)	1992 Revenue (dollars)	1993 Demand (pounds)	1993 Revenue (dollars)	1994 Demand (pounds)	1994 Revenue (dollars)	1995 Demand (pounds)	1995 Revenue (dollars)
Agriculture	40	160	220	880	240	960	280	1,120	340	1,360
Landscaping	332	1,211	664	2,423	996	3,635	1,328	4,847	1,920	7,008
Golf courses	224	896	332	1,328	560	2,240	820	3,280	1,050	4,200
Totals	596	2,267	1,216	4,631	1,796	6,835	2,428	9,247	3,310	12,568

PolyGro California: Demand and Revenue (× 1,000 rounded down)

	1991 Demand (pounds)	1991 Revenue (dollars)	1992 Demand (pounds)	1992 Revenue (dollars)	1993 Demand (pounds)	1993 Revenue (dollars)	1994 Demand (pounds)	1994 Revenue (dollars)	1995 Demand (pounds)	1995 Revenue (dollars)
Agriculture	115	460	172	688	230	920	460	1,840	680	2,720
Landscaping	332	1,211	664	2,423	996	3,635	1,328	4,847	1,920	7,008
Golf courses	210	840	232	928	360	1,440	480	1,920	600	2,400
Totals	657	2,511	1,068	4,039	1,586	5,995	2,268	8,607	3,200	12,128

Hong Kong. The Hong Kong government annually replaces 42,000 ornamental plants in established beds and on roadsides. In addition, government agencies plant an estimated 143,000 trees and stabilizing shrubs. Hong Kong also sponsors the Far East International Flower Show. Turnover of potted plants and seedlings for export approaches $430 million annually. In the private sector, more than 180,000 housing units are begun each year, each with communal gardens and individual plants, and there are approximately 220 private (or estate) parks, each with complete ornamental or recreational landscaping. The Hong Kong market has also experienced water cost increases in five of the past ten years, and Hong Kong is rapidly coming to face water shortages as their PRC source and domestic mains are near 90 percent of capacity now. Consequently, the market potential in Hong Kong can quickly evolve into a multimillion-dollar distribution area. Poly-Chem has concluded a contract with Witgang Far East, Ltd., to distribute PolyGro there.

South Korea. South Korea faces critical shortages in water and has a rich market for PolyGro. Water is available, but irrigation systems and usable water resources are short; water rationing has occurred in major urban areas, and major crops have been lost during the past several years. Developers, public agencies, recreation companies, and industries cannot find (or afford) sufficient maintenance personnel for turf and horticulture care. In addition, Korean labor is moving rapidly from farms to higher-paying industry jobs, generating shortages in agriculture. Thus huge productivity increases are needed in agriculture to replace labor-intensive work. Poly-Chem has concluded a multiyear exclusive agency contract with H. K. Kwon, of Seoul, Korea, to represent PolyGro there.

Southeast Asian Markets. Major irrigation and water resource management issues exist in most Asian nations. Poly-Chem is currently in communication with representatives of the Asian Development Bank, the government of the Philippines, and golf course developers in Thailand. These markets are expected to build up slowly unless distributors come forward; however, Poly-Chem is currently in negotiations with export trading companies in Taiwan, the Philippines, and Singapore.

IV. STRATEGIC MARKETING PLAN

Poly-Chem has a very simple marketing strategy to identify primary niches for bulk sales—domestic and foreign—and to create a network of competent distributors to service those niches. Our products will be based on synthetic polymers, spearheaded by the PolyGro group of superabsorbents, and will expand with time to include potential industrial and environmental polymer compounds.

Objectives and Product Development

Our marketing objectives in terms of quantity sales and types of customers were delineated in the previous section. In the long run, we envision industrial, shipping, and public-sector markets for water absorbents, and we will add an oil-absorbent line of patented products. As a trading company, we have products from manufacturers who hold patents. They could easily become competitors, and Poly-Chem could have little protection. However, our distinctive competency of having proprietary knowledge about applications and field uses give Poly-Chem a unique strength as a marketing firm. Consequently, one of our most important objectives is to remain the industry leader in water-absorbent applications.

By working closely with an equipment manufacturer, Poly-Chem is in position to market "application systems" that include machinery and materials. Although our marketing projections do not include this family of machinery, Poly-Chem will profit from sales of these "systems applications" and equipment. A crucial thrust of our marketing plan is to help design equipment to implant polymer efficiently.

Pricing

PolyGro will follow scheduled pricing for several different markets. The base price for bulk of less than 1,000 pounds packed in 50-pound protective bags is $4.37 per pound. Variable costs of materials and shipping for inventory when purchased in similar bulk are $2.25 per pound. With greater volume, a schedule of discounts from factory storage ranges from 10 to 40 percent, and Poly-Chem expects to be able to realize scale benefits on procurement for an average cost per pound of $1.80. We will pass on to customers most of these cost savings through a similar schedule of bulk discounts.

We have signed various agreements with foreign trade associates as noted earlier, and prices to them are consistent at $3.65 per pound FOB, Virginia. As they sell at (or near) the recommended bulk price of $4.39, they realize about 20 percent per pound. We have used the 20 percent figure as a benchmark for commissions to Poly-Chem sales associates and domestic distributors.

Promotions

Poly-Chem has devised initial four-color brochures, a high-quality color video for implantation and equipment, technical specification handouts, and a research brief for presentation. We have set up sampling policies to provide individual users with one-ounce packets and instructions, distributors and commerical clients with one-pound bags and technical data.

In addition, Poly-Chem scheduled presentations at four selected U.S. trade shows in early 1991. These included flower and nursery shows and recreation and golf course management fairs. Previously, Poly-Chem was a participant at the annual Hong Kong Territorial Farm and Agriculture Show, May 1990, and in June the Korean distributor hosted a golf course and sports turf exhibition specifically for PolyGro.

The company has several lists of annual trade fairs and shows that will be budgeted each year in our market regions. Banners, display booth equipment, brochures, and video presentations will be used together with actual plants, flowers, and visual demonstrations.

The heart of promotional activity, however, is hands-on demonstrations and field testing by potential customers. PolyGro is a product that can be touched, seen, and understood by the way it hydrates and releases water. Most customers cannot appreciate its potential by looking at literature or videos. Yet by making a test risk-free to them, Poly-Chem can demonstrate the product's capabilities. Our strategy is to budget significant tests, either giving customers samples or selling to them in bulk at extremely low prices (our factory costs) with fully guaranteed performance satisfaction.

We prefer to be physically present for larger demonstrations and field tests, and in the future we intend to budget equipment and materials for this purpose. This "risk-sharing" approach to field research and demonstrations will be the largest budget category for marketing in the future. Poly-Chem intends to support research for distributors and, in so doing, rapidly expand both markets and research opportunities.

Distribution

PolyGro is sold in bulk in 50-pound sealed containers, rated safe and nonhazardous for international shipping by the EEC. We have repackaged in various plastic containers ranging from 4-ounce bottles to 10-pound containers; however, given our market strategy, we will offer only a one-pound container to supplement nursery and landscape contract sales where "self-product" is an important visual addition to those customers' businesses.

For our major customers, the standard 50-pound bag, delivered individually or palletized, will be the business mainstay. For very large orders (in excess of 1,500 pounds), a "bulk bag" of that weight can be provided factory-direct, and these can be containerized for overseas shipments.

Staging of Sales

Patterns of sales activity presented earlier illustrate four stages of market development. Poly-Chem is in the first stage now, and the company will evolve into a fourth stage of growth.

Stage One. One objective for stage one, agreed upon in August 1989, was to have four foreign distributors contracted by January 1991, each capable of 20 tons of annual sales. By May 1990 we had contracted two and were in negotiation with four others. Also during this initial stage, we intended to have contract distributors in four eastern states and California. By May 1990 we had a sales and distribution agreement in San Diego and three independent Virginia agents. We were also in negotiation with a major distributor in Central Florida, but Poly-Chem is behind schedule for distributors in the Carolinas.

During stage one, we intended to help bring to fruition equipment design with Olathe Manufacturing. This objective was accomplished, but not without early problems with prototypes and implantation techniques. However, by May 1990, two types of equipment were in production—a pressurized implantation tank using a wand for deep-root treatment of existing plants, and a tractor-pulled turf implanter for golf course and commercial landscape projects. This equipment is crucial to advancing sales because no other effective methods have been devised beyond age-old hand broadcast and use of a Rototiller. We have also tested methods for in-row agricultural applications and verified methods for existing farm equipment.

Stage Two. Beginning spring 1991, Poly-Chem will launch the second stage of marketing. Although stage-one market development efforts will continue in earnest, stage two will be the "actual" launch effort for organized sales. We call this the "start-up" period, which will extend through summer 1992 (the second complete season of cycled sales). We have definite sales objectives and budgeted expenses for activities during this stage. Sales projections were described earlier in detail, and budgeted expenses are shown under the "financial" section on a "start-up" schedule.

Stage Three. Early growth may start to occur during stage two, but we expect significant signs of growth during stage three that begins with the third year of actual sales (spring 1993). This will also be the first clear period of sustained profitability after recapturing start-up and initial research expenses. The end of stage three "early growth" is arbitrary, and for planning purposes we simply use the end of the five-year planning period (1995).

Stage Four. If the company progresses as planned, stage four will be a rapid growth period requiring second-round financing for market and product expansion. This will be a major turning point at which Poly-Chem will have to evolve professional management (as opposed to entrepreneurs) and professional underwriting with a view toward a public offering.

V. COMPETITION AND INDUSTRY CHARACTERISTICS

The industry for water-absorbent polymers consists of three different types of polymer compound, each manufactured by several major chemical companies in the United States, Great Britain, France, Japan, and Germany. The three types of compounds are *starch-based hydrophilic gels*, *polyvinylalcohols*, and *polyacrylamides*.

Starch-Based Polymers

Starch-based polymers (commonly called hydrogels) are the least expensive to produce, but they degrade rapidly and are not cost-effective for agriculture or horticulture. They are extremely fast acting with a high rate of absorption, making hydrogels ideal for disposable baby diapers and sanitary napkins. Several brands of hydrogels have been rigorously tested and found effective in limited applications (e.g., seed bedding, reducing transplant shock, reducing soluble salt build-up in soils). However, they degrade and become useless after a few months. (Contrasting characteristics were summarized in the "Product" section of this study.)

Although starch-based hydrogels are unrealistic for commercial applications in agriculture, horticulture, turf development and other uses similar to markets targeted by Poly-Chem, a number of competitors exist. These competitors sell polymers as "superabsorbents" and "miracle material" for every use ranging from household potted plants to fully developed golf course development. A majority of the companies sell without research support, application consulting, service, or validation of product quality. Several companies "hustle" customers with inaccurate advertising, high retail prices, and unsupported claims. This is unfortunate because knowledgeable customers and researchers recognize the sham and thus condemn all polymer products as "snake oil" remedies that will not perform as claimed. In fact, starch-based hydrogels do have viable uses (such as diapers) but not in the markets mentioned.

Polyvinylalcohols

The second type of polymer, polyvinylalcohol, is a slow-acting polymer with a very low rate of absorption, yet because it actually bonds chemically with moisture, it is a very effective product for specialized dehumidifying processes. It is expensive to produce, quickly degradable, and marketed primarily as an industrial product.

Polyacrylamides

The third product group consists of direct competitors of Poly-Chem with polyacrylamides processed in several different ways. These products are virtually undifferentiated from one another except to the expert researcher who can test for variable quality and manufacturing consistency. Three manufacturers—one U.S., one French, and one British—constitute the industry. Poly-Chem buys in bulk from both British and American suppliers.

Competitor Pricing

Starch-based polymers are sold in bulk (50 pounds) at prices that range between $3.33 and $5.50 per pound. Polyacrylamides are sold in bulk (50 pounds) at prices that range between $3.00 and $6.25 per pound. These are wholesale prices offered to dealers, nurseries, landscape companies, and golf courses. Because there are suspect packaging and mixing practices across the industry, Poly-Chem feels the most reliable price data are derived from several firms that license dealers at $4.15 per pound purchased in minimum 50-pound orders, but these are repackaged in one-pound cans and ten-pound tubs. The one-pound can retails at $16.99 in Southern California.

Poly-Chem's Comparable Pricing

Poly-Chem's prices are currently set at $4.39 (list at 50 pounds FOB), and we discount for increased orders with price breaks at 600 pounds (one standard pallet), 1,500 (a factory-direct "big bag" package), and 2,000 (one ton or more allows factory procurement discounts). We believe this pricing system is comparable to our most direct competitors with similar products, and it is ethical pricing that conforms to good business practices for discounts.

VI. LEADERSHIP AND ORGANIZATION

Poly-Chem Associates, Inc., is a common-stock corporation, established in the Commonwealth of Virginia, by Vernon C. Jones and James W. Sims, with an effective date of August 8, 1989. The registered office is in Harrisonburg, Virginia.

The board of directors includes James W. Sims, Vernon C. Jones, both principal stockholders, Henry Martin, and John T. Smith, registered agent without an equity position.

James W. Sims

As founder with equal equity interests with Vernon C. Jones, Mr. Sims was elected to the position of President upon incorporation. He is CEO of a wholesale chemical investment company, and has spent nearly 30 years in the industrial chemical business, starting two previous companies, one profitably sold and the other continuously profitable. Mr. Sims is also involved in commercial real estate development and has substantial holdings in Central Florida.

Vernon C. Jones

Dr. Vernon C. Jones is a private biochemical research consultant who was previously associated as a senior faculty member on two universities spanning 22 years of academic research experience. Together with Mr. Sims, Dr. Jones began active testing and product investigation of polymer compounds in 1988. Satisfied that polyacrylamide worked, he and Mr. Sims incorporated to pursue a commercial enterprise based on polymer applications.

Shortly after incorporation, Dr. Jones traveled to Hong Kong and South Korea to address interests by international companies. He also represented the polymer product in China and led the negotiations with the Asian Development Bank in Manila in 1990. Dr. Jones has numerous publications on related products and has been active in research with British colleagues.

Henry Martin

Henry Martin is a private investor who has previously invested in similar new ventures with chemical or industrial products. Martin is also a qualified accountant with more than 12 years experience in a major Washington-based accounting firm. He subsequently started his own investment business and owned and operated a specialty aircraft parts company with contracts under the U.S. Department of Defense.

John T. Smith

John T. Smith is the company's registered agent and a senior partner in a law firm bearing his name in Northern Virginia. As an active attorney, Mr. Smith is well respected in government circles and is a long-time associate of Mr. Sims.

Other Staff and Associates

Poly-Chem retains a corporate accountant, corporate legal counsel, a professional advertising executive as consultant, and an experienced office staff in Harrisonburg. In addition, we have arrangements for on-call consulting and research from professional associates in chemistry, agriculture, agronomy, horticulture, and engineering. These are university researchers and consultants.

Compensation

Office staff, consultants, and research associates have been paid through established wage scales and schedules of professional fees. Officers of Poly-Chem have not drawn on the equity account nor received compensation other than direct expenses, many of those deferred. Prior to "start-up" in stage one, and prior to securing appropriate underwriting, board members and Poly-Chem managers will receive no salary, benefits, or other direct or indirect income.

Equity Structure of Corporation

Poly-Chem was incorporated with 5,000 shares of single-class common stock with $0.00 par value. Based on prior partnership interests, research, facility utilization, inventory transfer, and cash investment, the cofounders were issued each 400 shares (total of 800 shares valued at $100 as founders' equity). Henry Martin holds 125 shares, and a private venture capital firm has recently purchased 250 shares, all at a value of $100 per share, totaling $37,500. These are all voting shares and represent 23.5 percent of authorized shares.

The company intends to offer additional shares under a Class B nonvoting category at $100 per share. The board has authorized a total of 2,400 shares for this purpose. This offering will permit control to be retained by existing stockholders; however, all shares participate equally in profits and losses.

VII. FINANCIAL SUMMARY AND REQUIREMENTS

As a trade company, Poly-Chem Associates, Inc., is not structured to garner tangible assets as much as to accumulate research, attain methodologies unique to the company, and establish distribution networks. Consequently, Poly-Chem has focused on these activities while avoiding asset build-up. Expenses have been on intangibles and activities related to positioning Poly-Chem as a new venture.

However, with the onset of stage one, an active start-up period, the firm faces substantial expenditures that include physical inventory, implantation equipment, field-testing instruments, and a formal sales support infrastructure. A majority of expenses will continue to occur through operations research, market development activities, and sales and service support endeavors.

Comments on Financial Data

Financial plans include a start-up period that must immediately recover sunk costs accumulated during 1989 and 1990 as the company set up operations and formulated initial market strategies. It should be important to bear in mind, however, that during this time, these costs did not include any form of executive compensation or fees; the principals worked entirely without financial support and in most instances spent considerable sums on their own accounts. These personal costs have not been recorded against company records except in obvious situations such as providing sample materials to potential customers and corresponding with distributors through fax and telephone calls.

Financial pro forma documents that follow in this section reflect marketing assumptions delineated earlier, and they cover the planning period from January 1991 through December 1995. The first three months of pro formas assume that sunk costs from 1989 to 1990 (unrecovered liabilities) are cleared, equipment and test instruments on the start-up sheet are purchased, and investment allocations are made as indicated.

Executive compensation remains parsimonious because both principals as operating managers will retain other professional interests, thus sharing leadership tasks to provide full-time coverage of the business, but individually having less than full-time activities during the first few months of commercial development. A professional staff, however, will remain in place.

The primary financial pro forma directed to investors' attention is the following *start-up summary,* which indicates Poly-Chem's intentions for the near term and the company's requirements for launching the commercial venture. The company's directors will be pleased to present and discuss all points in detail with qualified investors.

Notes to Start-up Requirements

Although Poly-Chem expects to generate income to offset a number of costs, cash-flow revenue will lag behind actual sales efforts by several months. In addition, potential distributors and customers expect field-tested data that often require one season of test planting before bulk orders are taken. Therefore, cash expenses will precede potential cash flow, and for the business to succeed, most of these start-up expenses must be shouldered without expectations of immediate returns.

Financial pro formas follow a "most likely" scenario for market development domestically and internationally; however, the start-up requirement summary can be viewed as a unilateral series of costs without related income generation. In this instance, a "most pessimistic" scenario would imply no revenue for the first year while active research and development occur.

First-Year Start-up Requirements

Management and directors compensation	$ 24,000
Office and staff wage expenses	37,500
Recovery of pre-start-up development costs (89–90)	33,000
Office requirements, to include:	
Overhead (rent, utilities, telephone)	27,400
Equipment (fax, photocopier, scales, and miscellaneous)	3,400
Postage, sample shipments, supplies	6,000
Equipment, to include:	
Olathe Implanter Model 71/831	4,800
Olathe Implanter Model 891 with transport kit	3,600
Penetrometers, compaction analyzers, lab testers	2,600
Research and development, to include:	
Consulting fees and field contracts	14,000
Patent and trademark fees and expenses	6,500
Laboratory testing and secondary research	6,000
Market development, to include:	
U.S. domestic travel and sales support	8,500
U.S. trade shows, fees, and promotions	18,000
Foreign (Asian) development expenses	14,000
Inventory for distributor support	12,500
Publications and promotions materials	8,000
Packaging and application assistance	10,000
Legal, accounting, and tax fees	4,000
Total first-year start-up costs	$243,800

VIII. PRO FORMA FINANCIAL STATEMENTS

There are several sets of pro forma financial statements that follow a rotation in this order: *income statements* monthly from January 1991 through December 1991, with calendar-year quarters, for 1992 and 1993; *cash-flow statements* for three years; *comparative balance sheet* for three years; and *break-even analysis*. Although market forecasts presented earlier extended to five years, three-year financial data seem realistic given the uncertainty of prices and costs.

Comments on Income Statements

Market projections were based on calendar-year demand, but monthly data are presented to capture seasonality during the first year of operations. This pattern repeats in future years. We assume that most of 1990 will be consumed with market development, resulting in some sales, but generally in heavy expenses noted in the start-up sheet. Consequently, 1990 results are not detailed in the pro forma statements.

    No income data are supplied for foreign sales, yet we feel that overseas markets may be substantial. Consequently, income may be understated by omission of foreign markets; however, domestic sales may be overstated if assumptions for securing distributorships do not materialize. Poly-Chem is a "variable cost" service industry; thus costs can be prorated with respect to total sales.

Comments on Cash-Flow Statements

We assume that bulk orders are FOB with a minimum 25 percent deposit on release for domestic sales, representing 50 percent of shipments. We also assume that distributors order FOB with 30-day payment schedules; however, we also assume half of these to be collected in 60 days. All cash flow is presumed to lag sales described on income statements by 90 days. Foreign sales are FOB with a letter of credit prior to shipment.

Comments on Balance Sheet

Poly-Chem will not amass assets such as facilities or excess inventory other than necessary equipment, testing instruments, and materials requirements for distributors. Intangible assets are not shown (no goodwill, proprietary research data, or technology). Balances therefore reflect liquidity more than asset accumulation.

Comments on Break-Even

Fixed costs and related components of variable costs assume the pattern of seasonal sales and support needed during the first two years. Break-even assumes initial funding is a sunk cost necessary to establish the company that must be fully recovered in the calculation.

Pro Forma Income Statement—First Year (January 1, 1991, through December 31, 1991), Poly-Chem Associates, Inc.

Line Items	Jan. 91	Feb. 91	Mar. 91	Apr. 91	May 91	Jun. 91	Jul. 91	Aug. 91	Sep. 91	Oct. 91	Nov. 91	Dec. 91	Total
Gross sales	$12,000	$26,000	$32,000	$116,000	$122,000	$88,000	$224,000	$354,000	$354,000	$360,000	$88,000	$88,000	$1,864,000
Returns and allowances	240	520	640	2,312	2,440	1,660	4,480	7,040	7,040	7,200	1,660	1,660	36,892
Net sales	11,760	25,480	31,360	113,688	119,560	86,340	219,520	346,960	346,960	352,800	86,340	86,340	1,827,108
Cost of goods sold:													
PolyGro bulk materials	$ 6,720	$14,560	$17,920	$ 51,040	$ 53,680	$38,720	$ 91,840	$138,060	$138,060	$140,400	$38,720	$38,720	$ 768,440
Direct: shipping and handling, insurance	1,200	2,600	3,200	8,120	8,540	6,160	15,680	24,780	24,780	25,200	8,800	8,800	137,860
Direct: packaging and expenses	1,440	3,120	3,840	9,280	9,760	7,040	17,920	28,320	28,320	28,800	10,560	10,560	158,960
Total cost of goods sold	$ 9,360	$20,280	$24,960	$ 68,440	$ 71,980	$51,920	$125,440	$191,160	$191,160	$194,400	$58,080	$58,080	$1,065,260
Gross profit	$ 2,400	$ 5,200	$ 6,400	$ 45,248	$ 47,580	$34,420	$ 94,080	$155,800	$155,800	$158,400	$28,260	$28,260	$ 761,848
Operating expenses:													
Commissions and distributor's allowance	$ 2,352	$ 5,096	$ 6,272	$ 22,738	$ 23,912	$17,268	$ 43,904	$ 69,392	$ 69,392	$ 70,560	$17,268	$17,268	$ 365,422
Salaries and wages	3,650	3,650	3,650	4,020	4,020	5,540	5,540	6,230	6,230	6,310	6,310	6,310	61,460
Office overhead	1,800	1,800	2,400	3,200	3,400	2,400	3,800	3,800	3,800	4,000	3,200	3,200	36,800
Warehousing expense	120	260	320	1,160	1,220	880	2,240	3,540	3,540	3,600	880	880	18,640
Equipment, office	620	620	620	710	710	730	850	950	950	980	830	830	9,400
Equipment, field and maintenance	1,117	1,217	1,200	1,340	1,140	1,260	1,017	980	1,480	1,820	980	980	14,531
Research and testing	200	800	2,000	3,200	3,600	4,000	2,000	2,600	3,600	2,000	2,000	1,200	27,200
Market development	1,600	1,800	3,000	4,500	4,800	1,000	6,500	6,500	4,800	4,000	1,800	1,800	40,500
Publications and promotions	100	120	1,200	880	880	240	1,600	1,400	1,000	400	100	100	8,020
Applications assistance	0	600	600	1,200	2,200	1,200	1,200	1,200	1,200	800	400	400	10,000
Interest on debt	0	585	585	585	585	585	585	585	585	762	762	762	6,966
Depreciation/equipment	17	18	18	21	21	21	21	30	30	30	30	30	287
Miscellaneous (samples, demos, fees)	1,600	1,300	2,500	900	700	800	1,300	2,500	1,200	700	100	600	14,200
Total operating expenses	$13,176	$17,266	$24,365	$ 44,454	$ 47,188	$35,924	$ 70,557	$ 99,707	$ 97,807	$ 94,362	$34,660	$33,960	$ 613,426
Operating income/loss	($10,776)	($12,066)	($17,965)	$ 794	$ 392	($ 1,504)	$ 23,523	$ 56,093	$ 57,993	$ 64,038	($ 6,400)	($ 5,700)	$ 148,422
Other income (equipment)	$ 0	0	0	7,200	7,200	0	0	9,600	9,600	0	0	0	33,600
Other expenses	0	0	0	3,600	3,600	0	0	5,400	5,400	0	0	0	18,000
Profit before taxes	($10,776)	($12,066)	($17,965)	$ 4,394	$ 3,992	($ 1,504)	$ 23,523	$ 60,293	$ 62,193	$ 64,038	($ 6,400)	($ 5,700)	$ 164,022
Taxes	0	0	0	703	639	0	3,764	9,647	14,926	15,369	0	0	45,048
Net income/loss	($10,776)	($12,066)	($17,965)	$ 3,691	$ 3,353	($ 1,504)	$ 19,759	$ 50,646	$ 47,267	$ 48,669	($ 6,400)	($ 5,700)	$ 118,974

Pro Forma Income Statement—Second and Third Years (January 1992 to December 1993), Poly-Chem Associates, Inc. (all items × $1,000)

Line Items	Year Ending Dec. 92					Year Ending Dec. 93				
	First Quarter	Second Quarter	Third Quarter	Fourth Quarter	Total	First Quarter	Second Quarter	Third Quarter	Fourth Quarter	Total
Gross sales	$3,218	$2,811	$3,443	$2,233	$11,705	$5,384	$3,614	$4,931	$3,219	$17,148
Returns and allowances	58	51	62	40	211	97	65	89	58	309
Net sales	3,160	2,760	3,381	2,193	11,494	5,287	3,549	4,842	3,161	16,839
Cost of goods sold:										
PolyGro bulk materials	$1,201	$1,049	$1,285	$ 833	$ 4,368	$2,009	$1,349	$1,840	$1,201	$ 6,399
Direct: shipping and handling, insurance	221	193	237	153	805	370	248	339	221	1,178
Direct: packaging and expenses	253	199	250	156	857	365	241	320	196	1,122
Total cost of goods sold	$1,675	$1,441	$1,772	$1,142	$ 6,030	$2,744	$1,838	$2,499	$1,618	$ 8,699
Gross profit	$1,485	$1,319	$1,609	$1,051	$ 5,464	$2,543	$1,711	$2,344	$1,543	$ 8,140
Operating expenses:										
Commissions and distributor's allowance	$ 790	$ 690	$ 845	$ 548	$ 2,874	$1,322	$ 887	$1,211	$ 790	$ 4,210
Salaries and wages	130	115	106	72	424	138	95	129	87	449
Office overhead	79	69	85	55	287	106	71	97	63	337
Warehouse expense	44	39	47	31	161	74	50	68	44	236
Equipment, office	2	1	2	1	6	3	2	2	2	8
Equipment, field and maintenance	3	3	3	2	11	5	4	5	3	17
Reseach and testing	75	66	81	53	275	111	74	92	66	343
Market development	79	69	85	55	287	95	64	73	47	279
Publications and promotions	32	28	17	11	87	26	18	24	16	84
Applications assistance	25	17	20	9	71	32	21	19	13	85
Interest on debt	16	14	18	12	60	27	18	25	15	85
Depreciation/equipment	1	1	1	2	5	2	2	2	2	8
Miscellaneous (samples, demos, fees)	37	30	32	20	119	45	28	37	22	132
Total operating expenses	$1,313	$1,141	$1,342	$ 870	$ 4,667	$1,986	$1,333	$1,784	$1,170	$ 6,273
Operating income/loss	$ 172	$ 178	$ 267	$ 181	$ 797	$ 557	$ 378	$ 560	$ 373	$ 1,867
Other income	$ 48	$ 12	$ 36	$ 0	$ 96	$ 72	$ 36	$ 54	$ 0	$ 162
Other expenses	28	9	18	0	55	36	18	40	0	94
Profit before taxes	$ 192	$ 181	$ 285	$ 181	$ 838	$ 593	$ 396	$ 574	$ 373	$ 1,935
Taxes	54	51	91	58	253	190	127	184	119	619
Net income/loss	$ 138	$ 130	$ 194	$ 123	$ 585	$ 403	$ 269	$ 390	$ 254	$ 1,316

Cash Budget—First Year (January 1, 1991, through December 31, 1991), Poly-Chem Associates, Inc.

Line Items	Jan. 91	Feb. 91	Mar. 91	Apr. 91	May 91	Jun. 91	Jul. 91	Aug. 91	Sep. 91	Oct. 91	Nov. 91	Dec. 91	Total
Cash receipts:													
Cash sales	$ 1,740	$ 8,300	$ 11,200	$ 35,840	$35,900	$ 15,360	$ 61,200	$ 88,400	$ 88,400	$ 87,300	$ 15,400	$ 16,800	$ 465,840
Credit (collected within 30 days)		6,080	12,100	16,300	52,930	56,100	44,850	76,430	147,360	147,360	181,500	44,600	785,610
Credit (collected within 60 days)			3,800	4,740	4,900	16,850	26,800	24,300	79,500	56,300	56,300	74,320	347,810
Credit (collected within 90 days)				140	340	200	240	760	1,830	2,390	54,900	54,900	115,700
Total cash receipts	$ 1,740	$ 14,380	$ 27,100	$ 57,020	$94,070	$ 88,510	$133,090	$189,890	$317,090	$293,350	$308,100	$190,620	$1,714,960
Cash disbursements:													
Commissions and distributor's allowance	$ 2,352	$ 5,096	$ 6,272	$ 22,738	$23,912	$ 17,268	$ 43,904	$ 69,392	$ 69,392	$ 70,560	$ 17,268	$ 17,268	$ 365,422
Salaries and wages	3,650	3,650	4,020	4,020	5,540	5,540	5,540	6,230	6,230	6,310	6,310	6,310	63,350
PolyGro bulk inventory	48,000	24,000	24,000	64,000	14,000	24,000	36,000	48,000	118,000	144,720	144,720	124,000	813,440
Direct: shipping and handling, insurance	3,200	3,540	6,630	9,750	14,420	18,320	21,140	18,600	16,940	8,860	8,800	8,800	139,000
Direct: packaging and expenses	1,440	3,120	3,840	9,280	9,760	7,040	17,920	28,320	28,320	28,800	10,560	10,560	158,960
Office overhead	2,800	1,800	1,400	2,000	1,400	3,400	3,400	4,400	3,800	4,000	3,200	5,200	36,800
Warehousing expense	380	400	320	500	2,400	1,840	2,400	1,800	3,600	120	4,800	80	18,640
Equipment, office	4,400	0	0	0	0	0	2,200	0	1,800	0	1,000	0	9,400
Equipment, field and maintenance	9,460	0	0	2,710	0	2,361	0	0	0	0	0	0	14,531
Research and testing	1,000	2,200	2,000	4,000	3,800	2,000	3,600	3,600	2,000	2,000	1,000	0	27,200
Market development	4,800	9,600	4,400	2,400	2,500	1,600	2,400	3,600	3,000	3,000	1,600	1,600	40,500
Publications and promotions													
	4,400	200	2,000	0	0	0	0	0	0	0	0	400	8,020
Applications assistance			600	1,200	2,200	1,200	1,200	1,200	1,200	800	400	0	10,000
Loan payments (principal and interest)			4,320	4,320	4,320	24,320	6,450	10,800	22,390	24,300	4,320	4,320	109,860
Miscellaneous (fees)	2,500	0	600	0	0	600	0	0	0	0	400	1,840	5,940
Payroll taxes/benefits	0	0	1,230	0	0	1,640	0	0	1,950	0	0	1,770	6,590
Corporate and business taxes	260	0	0	180	0	0	1,339	0	0	14,011	0	0	15,790
Total cash disbursements	$ 88,642	$ 53,606	$ 61,632	$127,098	$84,252	$111,129	$147,493	$195,942	$279,642	$307,481	$204,378	$182,148	$1,843,443
Net monthly cash flow	($ 86,902)	($ 39,226)	($ 34,532)	($ 70,078)	$ 9,818	($ 22,619)	($ 14,403)	($ 6,052)	$ 37,448	($ 14,131)	$103,722	$ 8,472	($ 128,483)
Opening cash balance	110,600	143,698	104,472	69,940	9,862	19,680	7,061	2,658	4,606	42,054	27,923	131,645	
Loans	120,000	0	0	10,000	0	10,000	10,000	8,000	0	0	0	0	$ 158,000
Closing cash balance	$143,698	$104,472	$ 69,940	$ 9,862	$19,680	$ 7,061	$ 2,658	$ 4,606	$ 42,054	$ 27,923	$131,645	$140,117	

Cash Budget—Second and Third Years (January 1, 1992, through December 31, 1993), Poly-Chem Associates, Inc. (all items × $1,000)

Line Items	Year Ending Dec. 92					Year Ending Dec. 93				
	First Quarter	Second Quarter	Third Quarter	Fourth Quarter	Total	First Quarter	Second Quarter	Third Quarter	Fourth Quarter	Total
Cash receipts:										
Cash sales	$1,956	$1,604	$1,909	$1,067	$ 6,536	$2,117	$1,797	$1,928	$1,222	$ 7,064
Credit (collected within 30 days)	469	844	812	744	2,869	498	1,424	1,561	1,611	5,094
Credit (collected within 60 days)	130	560	420	388	1,498	244	877	981	653	2,755
Credit (collected within 90 days)	10	80	120	144	354	102	88	149	201	540
Total cash receipts	$2,565	$3,088	$3,261	$2,343	$11,257	$2,961	$4,186	$4,619	$3,687	$15,453
Cash disbursements:										
Commissions and distributor's allowance	$ 790	$ 690	$ 845	$ 548	$ 2,873	$1,322	$ 877	$1,211	$ 790	$ 4,200
Salaries and wages	130	115	106	72	423	138	95	129	87	449
PolyGro bulk inventory	840	1,083	1,230	1,241	4,394	884	1,840	2,060	1,801	6,585
Direct: shipping and handling, insurance	240	210	301	73	824	380	244	221	112	957
Direct: packaging expense	253	199	250	156	858	365	241	320	196	1,122
Office overhead	79	69	85	55	288	106	71	97	63	337
Warehousing expense	44	39	47	31	161	74	50	68	44	236
Equipment, office	2	3	0	1	6	4	1	1	2	8
Equipment, field and maintenance	6	3	2	0	11	5	4	5	3	17
Research and testing	75	66	81	53	275	111	74	92	66	343
Market development	79	94	69	45	287	95	64	73	47	279
Publications and promotions	32	28	17	11	88	36	28	14	6	84
Applications assistance	25	17	20	9	71	32	21	19	13	85
Loan payments (principal and interest)	16	18	22	44	100	0	12	46	52	110
Miscellaneous (fees)	30	6	12	22	70	3	6	6	2	17
Payroll taxes/benefits	12	16	18	14	60	14	17	21	25	77
Corporate and business taxes	14	23	26	29	92	11	42	51	34	138
Total cash disbursements	$2,667	$2,679	$3,131	$2,404	$10,881	$3,580	$3,687	$4,434	$3,343	$15,044
Net quarterly cash flow	($102)	$ 409	$ 130	($61)	$ 376	($619)	$ 499	$ 185	$ 344	$ 409
Opening cash balance	140	38	467	597		536	17	516	701	
Loans	0	20	0	0		100	0	0	0	
Closing cash balance	$ 38	$ 467	$ 597	$ 536		$ 17	$ 516	$ 701	$1,045	

Pro Forma Balance Sheet—Opening and First Three Years (January 1, 1991, closing December 31, 1993), Poly-Chem Associates, Inc.

		Year Ending		
Line Items	Opening	Dec. 91	Dec. 92	Dec. 93
Current assets:				
Cash in bank	$110,600	$140,117	$536,000	$1,045,000
Accounts receivable	0	139,000	246,000	353,000
Inventory on hand	12,500	63,440	94,000	180,000
Advances to distributors	14,000	37,600	46,600	52,400
Prepaid expenses	22,000	4,400	6,800	9,600
Total current assets	$159,100	$384,557	$929,400	$1,640,000
Fixed assets:				
Equipment, office	$ 9,400	$ 18,400	$ 22,600	$ 39,600
Equipment, research	2,600	16,200	18,700	20,300
Equipment, field machinery	8,400	14,700	21,300	28,000
Less accumulated depreciation	0	(2,040)	(10,900)	(19,100)
Total fixed assets	$ 20,400	$ 47,260	$ 51,700	$ 68,800
Total assets	$179,500	$431,817	$981,100	$1,708,800
Current liabilities:				
Commissions payable	$ 0	$ 16,310	$ 48,710	$178,600
Accounts payable	26,500	17,600	222,600	486,000
Operating credit line	120,000	106,000	0	0
Corporate tax payable	0	0	32,600	47,000
Total current liabilities	$146,500	$139,910	$303,910	$711,600
Long-term debt:				
Equipment loan	$ 8,000	$ 17,100	$ 31,800	$ 34,400
Total long-term debt	$ 8,000	$ 17,100	$ 31,800	$ 34,400
Total liabilities	$154,500	$157,010	$335,710	$746,000
Owner equity:				
Common stock	$357,500	$357,500	$357,500	$357,500
Retained earnings	(332,500)	(82,693)	287,890	605,300
Total owner equity	$ 25,000	$274,807	$645,390	$962,800
Total equity and liabilities	$179,500	$431,817	$981,100	$1,708,800

Break-even Worksheet, Poly-Chem Associates, Inc.

Fixed Expenses Breakdown

First-year start-up (sunk) costs per schedule	$ 243,000
Fixed component salaries and office overhead	$ 163,000
Equipment: field and course	$ 47,260
Fixed component (allocated), market development	$ 337,500
Loan principal and interest required, annual	$ 129,000
Miscellaneous fees, demos, taxes	$ 212,000
Total fixed expenses	$1,131,760

Break-even Calculations

Fixed expenses	$1,131,760
Gross margin (from pro forma income statement)	42%
Break-even point	$2,694,667

Glossary

Accounts receivable Short-term credit extended to customers by allowing future payments, installments, or credit card charges.

Advertising One form of promotion that is aimed at mass markets through media and impersonal commercial messages. Unlike other promotions, advertising is indiscriminate, although media can be selected to target audiences.

Agents Intermediaries who act as distributors or resellers of products. Agents can be representatives of sellers or buyers, they can operate domestically or in foreign markets, and they can take title or simply transfer goods between parties.

Amortize The process of writing off expenditures for capital equipment by prorating costs over a period of time, such as an asset's depreciation period.

Assets Tangible or intangible possessions that have value to a business, including cash, accounts receivable, inventory, real estate, patents, trademarks, service marks, copyrights, and goodwill.

Asset-based lending Conventional loans made only to the extent that they can be secured with tangible assets pledged as collateral.

Balance sheet A financial statement that indicates a venture's position at a particular time (end of year) with respect to assets, liabilities, and net worth.

Bankruptcy The legal state of being insolvent, incapable of paying debts. Through bankruptcy proceedings under one of several laws, persons or corporations can obtain court-adjudicated relief from certain creditors.

Board of directors A formal body of elected individuals who represent the interests of stockholders in a corporation. Unincorporated companies can have boards as well, and directors in all ventures are responsible for governing the company and monitoring behavior of senior executives.

Glossary 529

Book value   The value of business assets determined by subtracting liabilities from the depreciated cost basis of assets.

Break-even analysis   A calculation that accounts for the contribution of income after covering variable costs that can be applied to fixed costs. When sales income is sufficient to recapture fixed costs, a break-even point is reached. Break-even analysis can be used to simulate price and cost relationships.

Brokers   Intermediaries who, like agents, expedite exchange of goods or services; however, brokers do not take title for customers' products.

Capital   Investments and possessions of a business used to generate income. In most instances capital is considered to include money, equity in equipment or facilities, or assets that can be transformed to business use.

Capitalization of earnings   A business term used to identify the process by which a business is valued on its income-earning potential. Future net income is evaluated by estimating the rate of earning power of a certain investment.

Cash-flow statement   A financial statement that accounts for actual cash received and spent in the course of doing business. Cash budgets are used to describe money received and spent.

Channel of distribution   The path taken to bring goods or services to business customers. Channels are usually traced from manufacturers to retailers for products through a value chain, but entrepreneurs will identify ''channels'' according to their methods of reaching customers. These include wholesaling, retailing, telemarketing, catalog sales, and export brokerage, among others.

Chaotic theory   A term loosely applied to the notion that entrepreneurs are agents of change, creating chaos by disrupting the status quo in constructive ways to instigate new products, processes, or knowledge.

Collateral   Items of value including assets or income that can be pledged to secure loans.

Commercial finance company   An institution that makes loans on equipment, assets, inventory, and receivables, serving mainly business and agricultural clients.

Commercial loan   A standard loan to a business to underwrite operations, usually secured by business or personal collateral.

Commission agents   Foreign traders who act as intermediaries to find outlets for exports or imports.

Commodity   A product or service that has become so common as to have no unique characteristics apart from those of competitors. It is indistinguishable in form or substance, although competitors seek ways to develop unusual brands. Examples include soaps, toothpastes, chewing gums, cereal grains, colas, and light bulbs.

Convenience goods   Products that are common and can be easily found, usually with many substitutes sold through many outlets. Consumers are unwilling to shop for convenience goods or to engage in comparative pricing.

Copyright   A form of legal protection for literary or artistic efforts, including publications, documents, music, art, and intellectual property (such as software). Copyrights must be registered with the Copyright Office in the Library of Congress to be useful as legal evidence.

Corporation   A legal form of business created through law that empowers a business as a legal entity (an artificial being). A corporation has a perpetual life unimpeded by the biological life span of investors, and through stock ownership, investors can realize limited liability.

Corridor principle   The idea that by doing one thing, or following one idea, new opportunities arise from these efforts, and subsequent opportunities may arise from continued efforts. Eventually, the process may result in an exceptional idea that would not have occurred without earlier activities.

Costs   Fixed costs are those that do not vary with production or sales; they are debts or expenses that must be met regardless of operations. Fixed costs include mortgages, lease payments, loan payments, insurance, and operational components of salary overhead. Variable costs are those that are incurred with production, services, and sales. (Also see **Sunk costs**.)

Creativity   The ability to bring something new into existence, conceiving the idea and articulating the new knowledge.

Current assets   Cash or assets that can be easily converted to cash in the short term, such as accounts receivable and inventories, and used to underwrite current liabilities.

Current liabilities   Business obligations that must be paid in the short run, usually from current assets. Standard accounting procedures count liabilities as current if they must be satisfied within one year.

Customer scenario   A profile of the "typical" customer in a market segment that describes personal characteristics, buying habits, and consumer expectations.

Demographics   The study of population characteristics such as age, sex, ethnic background, occupation, education, immigration and emigration, and changes in population statistics or behavior. Demographics are used to describe customer scenarios or market segments.

Differentiation   Distinguishing products or services from those offered by competitors by such means as quality, performance, design characteristics, prices, or means of distribution. A business can be differentiated by its image, market segment, warranty, or personal service of its personnel.

Discounted future earnings method   A method of valuation used to establish the market value of a business acquisition by using net-present-value techniques to convert future earning potential into current dollar terms.

Disequilibrium   In economic theory, either a shortage or a surplus creating an excess or a lessening in demand. Entrepreneurship is concerned with creating disequilibrium, or with taking advantage of opportunities that exist because of disequilibrium.

Distinctive competency   An unusual feature, service, product characteristic, or image enjoyed by a business venture to set it apart from its competitors.

Distribution   The physical movement of products through a system called the value chain.

Glossary

Diversification   The process of expanding product lines, services, or markets to include new customer groups or new products or services for existing customers.

Economic opportunity loans   Direct loans and loan guarantees made available through the Small Business Administration to qualified minority or disadvantaged persons for business operations.

Entrepreneur   A person who starts a new business, taking the initiative and the risk associated with the new venture, and who does so by creating something new or by using resources in unusual ways to provide value to his or her customers.

Entrepreneurial team   The combined effort by venture founders and key personnel who, together, provide the talent and inspiration to succeed.

Equity financing   A form of capital in which investors become partners or stockholders in a company. Equity instruments create ownership rights.

Export-Import Bank (Eximbank)   A U.S. government agency that offers direct financial assistance for overseas projects; it also offers loan guarantees and insurance for exports or foreign exchange transactions.

Export management company (EMC)   A company licensed to act on behalf of domestic companies for exporting products; EMCs specialize in one industry or range of products, such as chemicals, and represent many companies with similarities.

Export trading company (ETC)   Licensed by the U.S. government, ETCs can make direct purchases or facilitate overseas contracts for exporting domestic goods.

Factoring   Selling accounts receivable or inventory to obtain cash. Most factor deals result in deep discounting of the face value of assets.

Fair use doctrine   A concept applied to using material protected by copyright in which a person can replicate or copy certain protected materials as long as the use is "fair." Consequently, educators are allowed to use materials with few restrictions in the course of education or research.

Feasibility plan   An initial written plan comprising all the elements of a good business plan with the objective of determining whether a new venture can be expected to succeed.

Financing   Acquiring of debt or equity through various combinations to fund a venture.

Fixed assets   Capital assets of a permanent nature that are used in the venture, not sold or integrated into manufacturing or merchandise as components.

Foreign sales corporation (FSC)   A classification given to domestic companies selling exports overseas; FSCs enjoy certain tax-deferred benefits and incentives to export when doing so improves trade relations or foreign exchange balances.

Foreign trade zone   A domestic site, usually at an international port of call or at a government-licensed company, where imported products can be received duty-free for domestic use.

Franchise   A business system created by a contract between a parent company, called the **franchisor,** and the acquiring business owner, called the **franchisee,** giving the acquiring owner the right to sell goods or services, to use certain products, names, or brands, or to manufacture certain products.

Franchisee An owner-operator who contracts with a franchisor to obtain rights to the business system, usually with a protected market and branded products or services, and who, in return, pays the franchisor a fee and royalties.

Franchisor The person or company that originates a business system and provides a package of services, products, training, inventory, and support to individual owners in return for a fee and royalties.

Gain sharing A concept of sharing with employees monetary gains derived from operations; a form of profit sharing.

General partner Any of the individuals involved in a general partnership, or a specific individual or company designated "general partner" in a limited partnership agreement. In a limited partnership, the general partner has operational responsibilities and answers to limited partners for conduct.

Goodwill The value ascribed to a business in excess of its assets, derived through established patronage by clients and the firm's image or track record.

Growth The concept of expanding sales, operations, or assets, and usually a major strategic objective.

High tech A concept that suggests the current state-of-the-art technology or application of knowledge in new processes or products. High tech is relative, and in Edison's time, the light bulb was "high tech," just as the electric typewriter was in the 1930s. Today, high tech connotes microelectronic and biotechnological applications.

Income statement A financial statement that accounts for revenues and expenses associated with operations. The income statement will cover a specific period of time, such as a year, and is used in planning as a pro forma forecast of expected revenue and expenses.

Industrial development bonds (IDBs) Tax-exempt bonds issued by municipalities or nonprofit intermediaries to encourage local economic development or projects of social or economic interest.

Industrial products Products or services sold to, and used by, other businesses as value-added elements of their business ventures, including automobile windshields, wheels, ball bearings, hoses, pipes, and steel or industrial products. The act of selling industrial products is called institutional sales, and it can include supplies, maintenance materials, equipment, and services.

Informal risk capital Investments by wealthy people who seek equity positions in new ventures with potential for unusually high returns.

Innovation The transformation of creative ideas into useful applications by combining resources in new or unusual ways to provide value to society for new or improved products, technology, or services.

Intrapreneur A contrived word from the term "intra-corporate entrepreneur" meaning a person who pursues an innovation, becoming a champion for its development, but does so from within the security of his or her organizational position.

Invention The creation of new products, processes, and technologies not previously known to exist.

Joint venture A legal organization created through investments by two or more companies to pursue a commercial activity.

Leasing The process of contracting for equipment or facilities whereby the owner does not take title to assets.

Leverage Applied to financing, leverage means the use of more debt than equity to underwrite income-generating operations. This translates to a higher use of fixed-capital assets (machinery or new technology) in place of variable-cost assets (people) to accomplish tasks.

Leveraged buyouts (LBOs) The use of debt to purchase a company by pledging future earnings and assets to obtain cash for consideration.

Licensing A contract to gain access to the rights of a proprietary product, process, name brand, trademark, copyright, or technology for commercial purposes. A business owner can also use licensing to expand, such as licensing a foreign agent to sell his or her products overseas.

Limited partner A person or legal entity who is party to, and invests in, a limited partnership. Limited partners contract to invest, and they enjoy limited liability to the extent of their contract obligations. They are exempt from managing or actively participating in operational decisions.

Limited partnership A statutory form of business that is created through a contract among parties to pursue a specific business venture. The partnership must have at least one general partner and one or more limited partners.

Low tech Products or services that require little or no skill, no unusual combinations of resources, and uncomplicated techniques.

Market research The process of analyzing market information, gathering data on products or services, studying competitors, and evaluating sales potential.

Market segmentation The process of focusing on specific customer groups and separating business activities according to well-defined target groups.

Market value A method of business valuation based on recent sales of comparable assets or entire business ventures.

Marketing concept The philosophy of a consumer-oriented venture in which managers make decisions to assure customer satisfaction as their first priority.

Marketing plan The strategic plan that focuses on marketing activities to include product/service development, pricing policies, promotions, and means of distribution.

Marketing program The near-term plan to implement a strategic marketing plan with resource allocations and responsibilities for achieving marketing goals.

Mid tech Products or services that require some skill and combination of existing resources without unusual sophistication.

Minority Enterprise Small Business Investment Company (MESBIC) A company chartered by the federal government specifically to underwrite a special category of business for those small business owners considered socially or economically *disadvantaged*. (See **Small Business Investment Coroporation.**)

However, it is limited to certain private placement rules for types of stockholders and can have no more than 35 individual investors.

Sales forecast Perhaps the most critical element in a business plan, it is the prediction of future sales expressed by units (or measurable volume) and by dollar value of revenue.

Seed financing Money invested in a new venture prior to, or during, start-up to underwrite operations, assets, or business development.

Service marks A unique combination of symbols or words that have commercial value to a company to identify brands or services. Service marks are registered and must be in continuous commercial use to remain effective.

Shopping goods Products that consumers will take time to evaluate, making comparative shopping excursions to examine price, quality, and terms of sale.

Small Business Administration (SBA) The primary U.S. government agency established to assist small business ventures with direct loans, loan guarantees, consulting, market assistance, management advice, and a variety of other services.

Small Business Innovation Research Program (SBIR) A U.S. government program that provides grants to encourage innovation and technological development.

Small Business Investment Corporation (SBIC) A company chartered by the U.S. government specifically to help underwrite small businesses with equity and debt financing. The program is limited to companies with less than $6 million in net worth and less than $2 million in after-tax earnings averaged over the previous two years.

Sole proprietorship A form of business in which ownership resides with one person only who has unlimited liability for operations and debts.

Sourcing The act of searching out products or components needed for sale or integration into the production process.

Specialty goods Products that consumers rarely buy or buy only after very careful evaluation.

Spin-offs New ventures separated into subsidiaries, divisions, or independent businesses by corporations to pursue corporate innovations.

Stakeholder Any person or organization that has an interest in, or can be affected by, a business, including investors, creditors, suppliers, customers, employees, local businesses and citizens, and society at large.

Strategy An integrated long-range plan to attain a company's objectives through orchestration and deployment of the firm's composite resources.

Sunk costs Unavoidable costs that do not result in marketable assets, thus do not add to the net worth of a business and cannot be recaptured apart from future earnings. Store renovations, for example, are sunk costs that have no loan value or market value apart from business operations.

Telemarketing A form of distribution coupled with promotion using the telephone to make sales.

Trade credit Credit extended by suppliers and vendors on purchases of materials, inventory, and services.

Trademarks A distinguishing symbol, figure, or artistic rendering that can include a unique combination of letters to identify a company, product, service, or business concept. Trademarks are registered with the U.S. Patent and Trademark Office and must be in continuous commercial use to remain effective.

Value chain The progressive distribution channel from raw material vendor through manufacturer, wholesaler, regional or local distributor, to retailer.

Vendor A supplier of materials, inventory, or services needed in business operations. Vendors precede buyers in the distribution channel.

Venture capital Money obtained through private investments or public investment funds directed to high-risk and high-potential enterprises.

Venture capitalist A private individual or company that usually invests in ventures with higher risk-return possibilities than average. Most venture capitalists invest through equity instruments. Some states have venture capital funds for underwriting new ventures, and most security trading firms have funds set aside for high-risk portfolio investments.

Warranties Promises or guarantees to consumers, assuring certain performance or product quality, and usually specifying replacement of defectives or repairs.

Wholly owned subsidiary A domestic or foreign operation that is completely owned and operated by a parent organization.

Window of opportunity A time horizon during which opportunities exist before something occurs to eliminate them.

Index

Acceleration clauses, 428
Accessory equipment, 281
Accounts receivable, 422–423
   defined, 528
Acquisitions
   alternatives in, 384
   considerations for making, 384–387
   by established entrepreneurs, 387–389
   evaluating opportunities for, 389–395
   screening candidates for, 392–393
   structuring, 400–403
Acquisitive entrepreneurship, 85, 86
Added value, 31
Administrative entrepreneurship, 84–85
Advertising, 288–290, 528
   pull and push strategies of, 288–289, 292
Age
   of customers, 243–244
   of entrepreneurs, at start-up, 22
Agents, defined, 528
Agriculture, 141, 143–144
Alberts, Bas, 146
Allocation decisions, 262
Amortize, defined, 528
Angel, Rob, 216
Asset management, 420–429
Asset-based lending, 440, 441
   defined, 528

Assets
   defined, 528
   intangible, 391–392
   tangible, 390
Atari Corporation. *See* Bushnell, Nolan
Avoidance pattern for purchasing, 278

Babbage, Charles, 41
Balance sheets, 131
   defined, 528
Balter, Neil, 57
Bankruptcy, 51
   defined, 528
Banks, commercial, loans to small businesses, 439–441
Bell, Alexander Graham, 17–18, 32–33, 34, 35, 47
Ben & Jerry's Homemade, Inc., case study, 482–483
Bench model, 156
Berlin, Irving, 10
Bernstein, Jeff, 57
Bing, Dave, 461
   profile, 374
Black entrepreneurs, profile, 476. *See also* Minority entrepreneurs
Block, Henry, 222

539

Board of directors, 355–357
  composition of, 356–357
  defined, 528
Bonham, Donald, profile, 352
Book value, 390
  defined, 529
  method of valuation, 395–397
Bookkeeping, sloppy, 77
Borlaug, Norman, 144, 145
Boyer, Herb, 194
Brand recognition, 275
Break-even analysis, 131
  defined, 529
Brice Foods, Inc., case study, 136–137
Bricklin, Dan, 67
  profile, 68
Brokers, defined, 529
Burger King. *See* Gibbons, Barry
Burr, Donald, 467, 468
Bursten, Steven and Valerie, case study, 232–233
Bush, Paul, 150, 152
  profile, 151
Bushnell, Nolan, 33
  profile, 34
Business concept(s), 104–106, 117, 118, 273
  franchising, 328
Business concept section, of feasibility plan, 119–120
Business cycles, 249
Business description, 119–120, 486
Business entities, 362
  advantages and disadvantages of, 362–363
Business philosophy, and small business failure, 77–78
Business planning, 23
  responsibility for, 131–132
Business plans. *See also* Feasibility plans
  defined, 115
  Lipper on, 248
Business systems, franchises as, 405
Buyers, perspectives of, 400–401

Calano, Jimmy, 218, 224
  case study, 62–63
Canada–U.S. Free Trade Agreement, case study, 345–346
Cantillon, Richard, 3
Capital, defined, 529

Capital assets, 281
Capital requirements, 108, 260
Capitalization of earnings, defined, 529
Careers, entrepreneurial, 475–478
CareerTrack, case study, 62–63
Carlson, Chester F., 145
Carnegie, Andrew, 17, 47, 161
Cash flow, 110
Cash-flow budgets, 131
Cash-flow gap, 421
Cash-flow statement, defined, 529
Caterpillar, Inc., profile, 283
Century 21, profile, 15
Champion, entrepreneurial, 39, 40–41
Channel of distribution
  defined, 529
  pricing and, 295
  types of, 285–288
Chaotic growth, 464, 465
Chaotic theory, 464
  defined, 529
Characteristics, of entrepreneurs, 9–11, 21–23
China, People's Republic of, 311, 315–316, 318
  case study, 346–347
  economic outlook of, 315–316
  entrepreneurs and, 316
  joint venturing in, 329–330
Chouinard, Yvon, case study, 137–138
Citrin, Sharon, 299
  profile, 300
Collateral, defined, 529
Colt, Samuel, 17
Commercial finance company, defined, 529
Commercial loan, defined, 529
Commission agents, 529
  foreign traders as, 322
Commitment, 56
Commodities, 262, 275, 529
Common Market. *See* European Economic Community
Competition
  five forces of, 259
  identifying, 251–252
Competitive analysis, 259–263
  implications of, 263–265
Competitors, 264
  identifying, 123, 256

Index

Computers
  evolution of, 41–42, 43
  niche markets for, 80–81
Concentric diversification, 301
Conceptualization, 104–106
Consolidation stage, 461–462
  managing, 467–468
Consultants, 281–282
Consulting organizations, 132
Consumer distribution channels, 285–286
Consumer goods, 275–278
  avoided items, 278
  packaging, 283
Consumer Goods Pricing Act, 296
Consumer surveys, 257
Contracted services, 281–282
Convenience products, 275
  defined, 529
Cophen, Ben, case study, 482–483
Copyright registration, 118, 121, 172, 188–191
  accessing government information on, 195–196
  defined, 529
  fair use doctrine and, 190
  introduction to, 188–189
  material exempt from, 190
  new, on old material, 189
  obtaining, 190–191
  on software, 192–193
  validating property rights on, 196
  violation of, 195
Corporate entrepreneurship. *See* Intrapreneurship
Corporations, 361, 371–375
  defined, 530
  franchises as subsidiaries of, 405
  S Corporation status, 373–374
Corridor principle, 50
  defined, 530
Costs, 387
  defined, 530
  variable, 110
Creative process, 32–36
Creativity, 32–36, 206
  conceptualization and, 104
  defined, 530
  encouraging, in employees, 224–226
  versus innovation, 32

  model of, 33
  as prerequisite to innovation, 32–36
  right-brain hemisphere functions and, 37–38
  stages of, 32–36
Creative source, defined, 39
Credit, 420–421, 423
Culture, 48–49, 333
Cunningham, William, 216
Current assets, defined, 530
Current liabilities, defined, 530
Customer profiles, 122, 487
Customer scenarios, 242–243
  defined, 530
  for institutional markets, 254
  validation of, 264
Customer service, marketing strategies for, 298
Customers
  characteristics of, 242–245
  empathizing with, 237–239
  foreign, 334
  identifying, 242–245
  potential, 122, 257
  power of, 261
  satisfying, 237–239

Debt financing, 419, 439–447
Decline stage, 463
Dell, Michael S., 57, 102, 111, 252
Dell Computer Corporation. *See* Dell, Michael S.
Deloitte & Touche, 132
Demographic trends, 46–48
  entrepreneurial opportunities and, 48
  researching, 245–246
Demographics, defined, 530
Department of Agriculture, U.S., 339–340
Department of Commerce, U.S., 338
Department of Energy, U.S., 446
Department of Housing and Development, U.S., 446
Design patents, 176, 177
Development budget, 88
Differentiation, defined, 530
Digenova, Silvano, 57
Direct materials, 279
Disclosure statements, 410
Discount rate, 398

Discounted future earnings method of valuation, 395, 398–399
  defined, 530
Disequilibrium, defined, 530
Distinctive competency, 118, 261
  defined, 530
Distribution, defined, 273, 530
Distribution channels, 126
  types of, 285–288
Distribution methods, 488
  packaging and labeling and, 283
Distribution systems, 124, 252–253, 260–261, 284–288
  exclusive, 285
  industries relying on, 253
  intensive, 284
  selective, 284–285
Distributive services, 207, 213–215
Distributors, 320
Diversification, 473
  defined, 531
  options for, 473–475
Document disclosure statement, 178
Domino's Pizza, 458
  profile, 460, 461
Doskocil, Larry, 20–21
Drucker, Peter, 7, 11, 31–32, 36, 78, 152
Dun and Bradstreet, 398
Dunham, Larry, 120

Early growth stage, of venture, 112–113, 114
  continuum of, 112
Eckert, J. Presper, 41
Economic business cycles, 72
Economic factors, foreign, 334
Economic Opportunity Loans (EOL), 443
  defined, 531
Economic theory, entrepreneurship and, 3–7
Edison, Thomas A., 18, 43, 148
Education
  of customers, 244
  entrepreneurial, 21–22, 46, 477–478
  entrepreneurial case study, 483–489
  forecasts, 47–48
  market changes and, 45–46
Employees
  hiring, 219–221
  motivating, 224–227
  stock ownership programs for, 227
  training, 221–223
Employment, changes in (1970–1989), 12
Energy, shifts in, 43–44
Entrepreneurial role, defined, 7
Entrepreneurial team, 117, 118–119, 350–357
  criteria for establishing, 351, 353
  defined, 531
  feasibility study summary, 486
  member roles, 354–355
Entrepreneurial team section, of feasibility plan, 129
Entrepreneurial Woman, 461
Entrepreneurs. *See also* Entrepreneurship; Founding entrepreneurs
  career patterns of, 475–477
  changing roles of, 463–467
  characteristics of, 52–53
  defined, 531
  identifying, 8–9
  success of enterprise and, 350, 351
Entrepreneurship
  defined, 7
  economic factors and, 3–6
  in era of transformation, 57–58
  as process, 6–7
  socioeconomic view of, 10–11
Environmentally safe products, 245
  Body Shop, profile, 277
Equilibrium growth, 464, 465
Equipment
  asset value of, 423–424
  leasing versus buying, 424
  subleasing, 424–425
Equity, defined, 429
Equity financing, 419, 429–434
  alternatives, 433–444
  defined, 531
Ernst & Young, 132
Established enterprises, acquisitions by, 387–389
Ettridge, Steve, case study, 231–232
Europe
  after 1992, 318
  Eastern, 311–312
European Economic Community, 311, 318
Executive summary, 116–119, 486

Index

Expansion stage, 459–461
   from entrepreneur's perspective, 464–467
   growing pains of, 466
Experience, of entrepreneurs, 21, 22, 54, 74, 260, 385
Export-Import Bank (Eximbank), 339, 340, 446
   defined, 531
   Small Business Credit Program, profile, 447
Export management companies, 322
   defined, 531
Export merchants, 323
Export trading companies, 322–323, 339
   defined, 531
Export Trading Company Act, 322
Exporting, 319–324
   direct, 319–320
   indirect, 321
External conditions, and small business failure, 72–73

Facilities, physical, 127–128
Facsimile (fax) machines, 162
Factoring, 423
   defined, 531
Failure, of small businesses, 71–79
   external factors in, 72–73
   personal factors in, 73–79
   reversing, 79–80
Fair use doctrine, defined, 531
Families, dual-career, 262
Family enterprises, 13, 14
Farmers Home Administration (FmHA), 446
Feasibility plans, 88, 115–132, 486–491, 492–527. *See also* Poly-Chem Associates, Inc., feasibility plan (example)
   assistance with, 132
   business concept section, 119–120
   common elements in, 116–132
   defined, 532
   entrepreneurial team description section, 129, 517–518
   example of (Poly-Chem Associates), 492–527
   executive summary, 116–119, 486–487, 494–496
   financial documentation section, 130–131, 490, 518–527
   fundamentals of, 115–116
   guidelines for, 486–491
   manufacturing or operations plan section, 127–129, 489–490
   market plan section, 124–127, 488–489, 512–515
   market research and analysis section, 121–123, 487–488, 502–512
   product or service concept section, 117–119, 120–121, 487, 496–502
   readability of, 116
   writing, 115–116, 132
Federal Trade Commission Act, 296
Fields, Debbi, 114, 458, 461
   profile, 459
Fiesta Mart, Inc., profile, 352
Finance companies
   focus of activities, 442
   types of, 441–442
Financial and estate planning, 217
Financial control, and small business failure, 77
Financial documentation section, of feasibility plan, 117, 130–131, 490–491, 518–527
Financial markets, 72
Financial resources, for new ventures, 107–108, 419–449
   planning for, 107–108, 466
Financial summary, 119
Financing, defined, 531
Fixed assets, defined, 531
Ford, Henry, 8, 17, 18, 45
Foreign agents, 320
Foreign operations. *See also* International ventures
   environment, 333–337
   franchises, 328
   joint ventures, 328–330
   wholly owned, 330–333
Foreign sales corporation (FSC), defined, 531
Foreign subsidiaries, 331–332
Foreign trade zone, defined, 531
Formal venture units, 88–90
Founding entrepreneurs
   composite role of, 463–464, 465
   networking and, 361
   outgrowing of, 113–114
   role of, 353–354, 355
   successful, in start-up period, 458–459, 460–461

Four-stage growth model, 103, 104–114
  early growth stage, 112–113, 114
  later growth stage, 113–114
  pre-start-up stage, 104–106, 114
  start-up stage, 109–112, 114
Franchisees, 14
  defined, 532
  viewpoint of, 408
Franchises, 14–15, 67, 288, 383, 403–411
  as business system, 404–405
  case study, 136–137, 418
  defined, 328, 403, 531
  foreign locations, 328
  versus independent businesses, 410–411
  master, 408
  support systems, 406
Franchisors, 14, 404
  defined, 532
  viewpoint of, 405–408
Fry, Art, 34–35, 51, 477

Gain-sharing programs, 226–227
  defined, 532
Gallup, Pat, profile, 233
Gassier, Catherine, 146
Gates, William, III, 43, 50, 145
  profile, 44
Gemini Pacific Corporation, profile, 434
General license, for exporting, 335
General partner, defined, 532
Geographic location, 245–247, 260–261, 386
Gibbons, Barry, 469
  profile, 469
Gillette, King, 74–75
  profile, 75
Global business opportunities, 70, 318–319
Goldman, David, 57
Goodwill, 390–391
  defined, 532
Goudreau Corporation, case study, 452–453
Government information sources, 257
  accessing, 195–197
Government programs, for small business financing, 443–447
Government regulations, 72
Grace, Gary, profile, 225
Grant programs, 445
Greatbatch, Wilson, 50, 119
  profile, 120

Greenfield, Jerry, case study, 482–483
Ground services, profile, 207
Growth, of venture. *See also* Early growth stage; Later growth stage
  defined, 532
  managing, 471–473
  strategic planning and, 298, 471–473
Growth-oriented ventures, 84

Haas, Thomas K., profile, 238
Haines, Joyce, case study, 269–272
Hall, David, profile, 233
Head, Howard, 50
Hertzberg, Jack, 57
Hewlett, William, 145
Hicks, David, profile, 201–202
"High tech," 18–19, 148–149, 152
  defined, 532
High touch, 205–206
Hinman, Brian, 57
Hiring, effective, 219–221, 222–223
Historical evolution, of entrepreneurship, 17–21
Hollerith, Herman, 41
Hornaday, John, 9
Human resources, 128, 218, 227–228
  issues in international ventures, 336
  marketing strategies for, 298–299
  matching skills to needs, 351, 353

I Can't Believe It's Yogurt!, case study, 136–137
Iacocca, Lee, 168, 467
IBM, 18
  profile, 91
Idea germination stage, of creative process, 32–33
Ideology, business, 56
Illumination stage of creative process, 32, 35
Image, 264, 273, 278, 289
Imitative entrepreneurship, 85–86
Immigrants, 10–11, 47, 360–361
Implementation, pre-start-up, 108–109
Importing, 324–325
Income statement, defined, 532
Income status, of customers, 244
Income substitution, 11, 69
Incorporation, 362, 371. *See also* Corporations

Incorporation (*cont.*)
  advantages and disadvantages of, 372–373
  case study, 381–382
Incubation stage of creative process, 32, 34–35
Incubative entrepreneurship, 86
Indirect materials, 281
Industrial changes, 43–45
Industrial development bonds (IDBs), 445–446
  defined, 532
Industrial distribution channels, 286–287
Industrial markets, selling to, 279
Industrial products, 275
  categories of, 279–283
  defined, 532
Industrial revolution, 48
Inflation, 72–73
Informal risk capital, 430–431
  defined, 532
Information age, 205
Information services, 207, 215–217
Initial public offering (IPO), 432–433
  profile, 434
Innovation, 31–60, 105. *See also* Technological innovation
  case studies, 28–30
  creativity as prerequisite to, 32–36
  defined, 32
  importance of, 6
  in revival stage, 462
  types of legal protection, case study, 202–203
Innovation evaluation process (IEP), 158
Innovation process
  versus creativity, 32
  elements in, 37
  entrepreneurship and, 36–41
  versus invention, 36
  left-brain hemisphere functions and, 37–38
Innovation transfer, 88–89
Institutional marketing, 254
Insurance company loans, 442
Insurance issues, 129
Interest rates, 72
Internal Revenue Service (IRS)
  corporations and, 375
  legal forms of business and, 362
International Business Machines. *See* IBM

International environment, changes occurring in, 311–319
International markets, 310–347
International ventures. *See also* Foreign operations
  considerations before launching, 335–337
  costs of, 336
  establishing, 326–333
  financing, 337
  Foreign environment and, 333–337
Intrapreneur, defined, 532
Intrapreneuring (Pinchot), 83
Intrapreneurship, 11, 16–17, 67, 82–93, 350
  changing environment for, 91–92, 93
  classifications of, 84–86
  controversiality of concept of, 16
  growth-oriented ventures and, 84
  lack of personal risks in, 82–83
  new venture creation, case study, 98–99
  product development, 157–158
  views of, 83–84
Invention(s), defined, 532
  versus innovation, 36
  patentable, 173–175
Inventors, 106
  case study, 28–29
  David Hicks, profile, 201–202
  patent application by, 178–179
Inventory
  as collateral for operating loans, 421
  financial planning decisions, 420–422
  procurement decisions, 420–422
Inventory management, 128, 212–214
  small business failure and, 76
  Vidiots, profile, 214
Investment analysts' reports, 256
Investors
  entrepreneurial team and, 129, 351
  founding entrepreneur and, 56, 351

Jackson, Glen, profile, 428
Jaeger, Jim, 114
Japanese, 38, 318
  automobile manufacture, 123
  imitative entrepreneurship of, 85
  markets, 317–318
  women, 333
  videocassette recorder development, 131
Job descriptions, 220

Profits, 240
  business value and, 394
  defined, 535
  pricing and, 293
Promotion, 288–293
  defined, 273, 535
  role of, 288
Promotional mix
  defined, 292–293
  prices and, 294
Promotional strategies, 125–126
Proposals, 88. *See also* Feasibility plans
  writing, 156–157
Proprietary interest, 118, 121
Prototypes
  defined, 535
  development of, 158–159
Public corporations, defined, 535
Public offerings, 432–433
  defined, 535
Public relations, 290
Public-sector programs, case study, 453–454
Publications, specialized, 256, 279
Publicity, 290–291
  defined, 535
  for Subway Sandwiches, profile, 291
Puppy Love, profile, 300
Purchasers, accredited, 431–432
Purchasing, 212–214
Purchasing errors, 76
Purchasing managers, 254–255
Purchasing power, 264
Purpose, clarity of, 80–82

Quality, rewarding, 226

Rapp, Joseph, case study, 270–271
Real estate, leasing versus purchasing, 426–429
Related diversification, 301
Remarketers, 323
Repositioning, 462
Research and development, 84–85, 106, 128
Research and development limited partnership (RDLP), defined, 535
Retailers, foreign, 320
Retained earnings, defined, 535
Return on investment (ROI), defined, 535
Revival stage, 462, 468–470

Right brain hemisphere attributes, 37–38
Risk(s), 129–130, 386–387
  defined, 535
Rivalry, competitive, 262
Roberts, Ronald D., 468
Robinson-Patman Act, 296
Rockefeller, John D., 17, 43
Rodgers, Bill, 240
  profile, 241
Ronstadt, Robert, 7, 33

S corporation, 373–374
  defined, 535
Sales, 213
  direct, to end users, 320–321
  personal, 292
Sales forecast, 124, 249–250, 488
  defined, 536
Sales promotions, 290
Sales responsibility, 127
Salespersons, 292
Salzman, Jeff, 62–63
Sanders, Harland, 69–70
Say, Jean Baptiste, 3–4
Scale, economies of, 260
Schollhammer, Hans, 16, 84
Schumpeter, Joseph, 6–7, 8, 11, 36
Scientific knowledge, 41–42
Sculley, John, 473
Seasonality, 128, 250–251
Securities Act (1933), 433
Securities analysts' reports, 256
Securities and Exchange Commission (SEC), 355–356, 372
  Regulation D, 431–432
  reporting requirements, 433
Security, for commercial loans, 439–441
Seed financing, 88, 108
  defined, 536
Sellers, perspectives of, 400–401
Service
  friendly, 206
  level of, 211
  after sale, 126
Service concept. *See* Product or service concept
Service contracts, 281–282
Service distribution channels, 287–288

Service marks, 185, 186
　defined, 536
　filing to register, 186–188
Service systems, 204–205
Service ventures, 204–233
　growth of, 205
　infrastructure of, 205–206
　marketing effort for, 282
　matching with markets, 284–285
　as percentage of new businesses, 20
　success factors in, 218–228
　types of, 204, 206–217
Sex, of customers, 243–244
Shapero, Albert, 10–11
Sherman Act, 295
Shockley, William, 42
Shopping goods, 276–277
　defined, 536
Silver, A. David, 9–10
Simplot, J. R., 144
Single Market Initiative, 318
Small business, 66–67
　contributions to U.S. economy, 69
　defining, 13–15
　versus entrepreneurship, 210
　environment of, 67–72, 73
　failures of, 13, 71–79, 354
　versus growth-oriented ventures, 84
　hiring practices of, 219–221, 222–223
　international business opportunities for, 70
　opportunities in, 67–70
　perspective on, 12–15
　primary incentive for opening, 84
　success factors for, 79–82
　training practices of, 219, 221–223
　types of, 13–15
Small Business Administration (SBA), 222
　defined, 536
　loans to small business, 443–444
　Office of International Trade, 338–339
Small Business Innovation Research Program (SBIR), 445
　defined, 536
Small Business Investment Corporation (SBIC), 432
　defined, 536
Small business owners, 350
　clarity of purpose of, 80–82
　versus entrepreneurs, 11
　personal factors in failure, 73–79, 80
　role responsibilities of, 70–71
Smith, Adam, 3
Smith, Fred, 218
Snook, Gerry, 113
Social changes, 48–49
Software, copyright registration on, 193
Sole proprietorship, 361, 363–366
　defined, 536
Solheim, Karsten, 113
Sourcing, 324–325
　defined, 536
　direct, 324–325
　indirect, 325
Soviet Union, 311, 312–315
　economic trends in, 313
　entrepreneurs and, 314–315
Special-use products, 262
Specialty goods, 277–278
　defined, 536
Spin-offs, 90
　defined, 536
Sponsor, defined, 39
Spontaneous teams, development of, 87–88
Staged development plan, 121
Staging, defined, 121
Stakeholders, 239
　defined, 536
Start-up stage, 109–112, 114, 456–459
　operating objectives, 109–110
State Business and Industrial Government Corporations (SBIDC), 446
Stock equity, raising equity through, 431
Stock offerings, in later growth stage, 113
Strang, Jim, 110, 113
　profile, 111
Strategic planning, 102
　growth and, 471–473
Strategic thinkers, 41–42
Strategy, defined, 536
Subcontracting, 325, 425–426
Subjectivist perspective of economics, 4, 6
Subleasing, of equipment, 424–425
Subsidiaries, 90
Substitutes
　direct, 262
　indirect, 262
　threat of, 262

Success factors, 54–56
   entrepreneurs and, 350, 351
   for small businesses, 79–82
Sugar, Alan, 146
Sunk costs, defined, 536
Suppliers, power of, 261–262
Surveys, of consumers, 257
Survival, 293
   start-up stage and, 111
Swanson, Bob, 194
Swift, Gustavus, 144

Tarkenton, Fran, 222
Tauber, Cathy, profile, 213
Tax code, federal. *See* Internal Revenue Service
Team, entrepreneurial, 54
Technological innovation, 38–41
   environment for, 39–40
   key people in, 39
   opportunities and, 279
   seven conditions for success in, 39–40
Technological profile, 120
Technology, 18–19
Technology transfer process, 88–89
Telecommunications industry, case study, 169–170
Teleconferencing, 217
Telemarketing, defined, 536
Thompson, Ronald O., profile, 476
Threat of entry, 260
Threat of substitutes, 262
3M. *See* Fry, Art
Time, as exchangeable commodity, 262, 263
Timing, market potential and, 56
Trade credit, defined, 536
Trade secrets, 194
Trademarks, 118, 121, 172, 184–188
   accessing government information on, 195–196
   classes of, 186
   defined, 184–185, 537
   filing to register, 186–188
   preliminary search, 186
   validating property rights on, 196
   verification process for, 188
   violation of, 195
Training consultants, 223

Training practices
   Gary Grace, profile, 225
   Fran Tarkenton, profile, 223
Traits, of entrepreneurs, 9–11, 21–23
Transition stages, of new ventures, 455–475
Transnational services, 332–333
Trump, Donald, 278
Turnaround process, 468–470
Turnaround specialists, 393

United States Agency for International Development (USAID), 339, 447
United States and Foreign Commercial Service, 338
Useful value, 390
Utility patents, 176

Validated license, for exporting, 335
Valuation
   case study, 415–417
   methods of, 395–399
   profits and, 394
Value chain, defined, 537
Value-added transformation of resources, 4–5
Variable costs, 110
Vendors, defined, 537
Venture capital, 435–438
   defined, 537
Venture capitalists, 435–436
   criteria for investments, 436–437
   defined, 537
   finding, 438
   relationships with, 437–438
   rule of thumb for investments, 436–437
Venture products and services, 54–56
Verification stage of creative process, 32, 35–36
Vertical integration, 300, 387
Vesper, Karl H., 8, 101
Vision, 131–132, 468, 473
   creating, 218–219
   working with, 227
Voss, Rosemary, 222

Warranties, 126
   defined, 537
Watson, Thomas A., Sr., 18, 33, 91
Wealth creation, 31, 32

Whitney, Eli, 17
Wholesaling, and credit lags, 421
Wholly owned foreign operations, 330
Wholly owned subsidiaries, defined, 537
Windows of opportunity, 49
  corridor principle and, 50
  defined, 537
Wolf, Heidi, 216

Women
  in careers, 262
  case studies, 97–98, 380
  as entrepreneurs, 22, 23, 97–98, 380
  in Japan, 333
  networking and, 360
  as share of labor force, 243
Work experience of entrepreneurs, 21, 22, 54
Wozniak, Stephen, 18, 43, 145, 194, 473